What Continues to Make This Book a Best-Seller...

➧ **Heavy emphasis on English language learners (ELL)** throughout the text:

- A full chapter on **First- and Second-Language Development (Chapter 3)!**

- A full chapter on **Emergent Literacy and Biliteracy (Chapter 4)!**

- **Snapshots** of real teachers in real classrooms with real students, many of whom are ELL. Some are illustrated with video clips online.

SNAPSHOT

English Language Learners Make Masks and Act Like "Wild Things"

Shelly Abesa, a student in a language arts methods class I teach, decided to dramatize *Where the Wild Things Are* (Sendak, 1963) with second-grade students. She did her field experience at Lincoln Elementary School in Long

ELL

SCAFFOLDING

- **ELL and Scaffolding marginal notes** contain content-specific guidelines and resources for ELL students and others who need additional support.

- **New Supporting boxes** provide specific ideas for supporting the learning of ELL students, struggling readers and writers, students with disabilities, and students who speak a nonstandard dialect of English.

SUPPORTING

Support English Language Learners in the Writing Process

Keep these points in mind about English language learners:

1. They can begin to write in English before they have complete control over all the other aspects of language conventions (e.g., grammar, spelling, and

➧ **Strong coverage of assessment:**

- A new **Chapter 2, Assessing Language Arts!**

- New and updated **Assessment Toolboxes.**

➧ **New Video Icons** throughout the text refer students to selected video clips on the Companion Website.

C W

New and Greatly Expanded Chapters...

➧ **A new Chapter 12, Viewing and Visually Representing,** focuses on the visual arts, media, drama, and technology as they pertain to learning and teaching language arts in today's world of mass-mediated communication.

➧ **A separate Chapter 6, Reading,** offers increased coverage of phonics, phonemic awareness, and direct instruction in reading.

➧ **A heavily revised Chapter 8, Multicultural Education and Children's Books,** discusses current models of culturally sensitive teaching and how multicultural content can be integrated across the curriculum.

➧ **An expanded Chapter 14, Language across the Curriculum,** demonstrates how the language arts can be used to integrate teaching in the content areas.

fifth edition

Teaching Language Arts

A Student- and Response-Centered Classroom

Carole Cox

California State University, Long Beach

PEARSON
and

Boston • New York • San Francisco
Mexico City • Montreal • Toronto • London • Madrid • Munich • Paris
Hong Kong • Singapore • Tokyo • Cape Town • Sydney

Senior Editor: *Aurora Martínez Ramos*
Editorial Assistant: *Erin Beatty*
Executive Marketing Manager: *Amy Cronin Jordan*
Editorial-Production Administrator: *Annette Joseph*
Editorial-Production Service: *Susan Freese, Communicáto, Ltd.*
Text Design and Electronic Composition: *Denise Hoffman*
Composition Buyer: *Linda Cox*
Manufacturing Buyer: *Andrew Turso*
Cover Administrator: *Kristina Mose-Libon*
Cover Designer: *Suzanne Harbison*

For related titles and support materials, visit our online catalog at www.ablongman.com.

Between the time website information is gathered and then published, it is not unusual for some sites to have closed. Also, the transcription of URLs can result in typographical errors. The publisher would appreciate notification where these errors occur so that they may be corrected in subsequent editions.

ISBN 0-205-41038-3

Printed in the United States of America

10 9 8 7 6 5 4 3 2 1   RRD-VA   09 08 07 06 05 04

To my children,
Wyatt, Gordon, and Elizabeth,
and to the memory of my parents,
Alice and Gordon D. Shirreffs

contents

PART 1   Constructing a Classroom Foundation

chapter 1

Learning and Teaching Language Arts   1

chapter 2

Assessing Language Arts   39

chapter 4

Emergent Literacy and Biliteracy 111

c h a p t e r **5**

Listening and Talking   153

PART III Literature and Reading

c h a p t e r 6
Reading   191

chapter **7**

Teaching with Literature   227

c h a p t e r **10**

Spelling **325**

chapter **13**

Technology in the Classroom   435

special features

ASSESSMENT TOOLBOX

SNAPSHOT

LESSON PLAN

TEACHING IDEA

SUPPORTING

RIPPLE EFFECT

Teaching Language Arts, Fifth Edition, is designed for use as a main text in undergraduate and graduate language arts methods courses. Like previous editions, this new edition takes a consistent student- and response-centered approach to literature-based teaching in today's culturally and linguistically diverse classroom. It's firmly grounded in current social constructivist learning theory combined with a reader-response perspective toward teaching with literature.

I hope to bring this vision of a classroom to life not only through clear explanations of these guiding principles but also through examples of real teachers in real classrooms with real children, applying the ideas that have shaped the development of this fifth edition. Along with real-life examples, I've provided graphic organizers called Ripple Effects, which demonstrate response-themed teaching and learning across the curriculum. Above all, I hope I've created a readable, student-friendly, engaging, and practical text built on a strong theoretical and research base.

Content of the Text

This fifth edition of *Teaching Language Arts* has been substantially reorganized and updated to reflect current issues and developments in teaching language arts. It is divided into five parts.

Part I, Constructing a Classrom Foundation, contains Chapters 1 and 2. Chapter 1, Learning and Teaching Language Arts, begins by defining the language arts and identifying their role in integrating subjects across the curriculum. The *Standards for the English Language Arts,* written jointly by the International Reading Association (IRA) and the National Council of Teachers of English (NCTE), are introduced here, as well, and then referenced throughout the text. Chapter 1 also introduces the three theoretical perspectives that underlie the approach in this book: namely, that learning language arts is an active, constructive process; a social interactive process; and a transactional process. The foundational elements of teaching language arts are also presented, including the nature of a student- and response-centered classroom, the sources available for planning curriculum content, the structure of the classroom environment, and approaches to scheduling and grouping.

New to this edition, Chapter 2, Assessing Language Arts, presents assessment in the context of the social constructivist theory of learning and recommends the authentic assessment of language and literacy on a day-to-day basis. Many types of assessment are discussed, and numerous examples of forms and checklists are provided as Assessment Toolboxes; a number of these tools are intended for use with English language learners. Chapter 2 also examines the current national debate about the use of standardized tests in so-called high-stakes testing, as mandated by the No Child Left Behind Act.

Part II, Spoken Language and Emergent Literacy, includes Chapters 3 through 5. Chapters 3 and 4 have been extensively revised to consider the increasingly diverse nature of today's classroom. Chapter 3, First- and Second-Language Development, explains how learning a second language is both similar to and different from learning a first language. Strategies are offered for creating a suitable context for the instruction of students who are English language learners (ELL). Chapter 4, Emergent Literacy and Biliteracy, considers how views of children's developing literacy have changed over the years and how teachers can support the emergent literacy of both English-speaking and ELL students. Readers experience the teacher's role directly when they visit both a kindergarten and a first-grade classroom in which every child comes to school speaking only English and a bilingual kindergarten classroom in which students are learning to speak and write in both English and Spanish.

Chapter 5, Listening and Talking, looks at what can be considered the neglected and the suppressed language arts, respectively. Strategies are provided for teaching oral language, and special guidelines are provided for adapting these strategies for ELL students. Drama, a strong interest of mine since the days I was an elementary teacher, is now introduced in this chapter, as well. Dramatic activities provide countless ways to teach listening and talking and to develop literacy. The chapter ends with a discussion of the special concerns in assessing students' oral language skills.

Chapters 6 through 8 make up **Part III, Literature and Reading.** Chapter 6, Reading, identifies theoretical models that have been proposed to describe how meaning is constructed during reading and then focuses on what is called a *balanced approach* to teaching: one that includes phonemic awareness, phonics, direct instruction in reading, methods for using literature and writing, and specific suggestions for struggling readers and writers. Shared reading, guided reading, reading workshop, and writing to read are among the methods recommended in this approach. The ongoing controversy about phonics instruction is examined in a section on word study.

The use of children's literature is considered in detail in Chapter 7, Teaching with Literature. Basic theory is presented about how readers make meaning from their experiences with text and the range of responses, or *stances*, they may have. Guidelines for choosing children's book are provided along with strategies for teaching with literature. These concepts are extended in Chapter 8, Multicultural Education and Children's Books, which has been extensively revised for this edition. The chapter begins with a detailed discussion of current models of culturally sensitive teaching and how multicultural content can be integrated across the curriculum. The use of multicultural children's books is recommended for these purposes—in particular, the use of literature circles and literature focus units. Chapter 8 is rich with support materials, such as lists of quality multicultural children's literature and ideas for author, genre, and core book units.

Part IV, Written Language, includes Chapters 9 through 11. Chapter 9, The Writing Process, presents writing not as a product but as a recursive process, one that involves multiple starts. Writing workshop is discussed as both a collaborative and an individual approach to writing, in which students consult one another and the teacher to rethink, revise, and edit their work. Students write for real purposes and for real audiences, and writing conventions and skills are taught and assessed against this backdrop. The needs of students with cultural and language differences are considered in detail.

The conventions involved in written language are discussed in Chapters 10 and 11. Chapter 10, Spelling, opens with an explanation of the stages of spelling development and then uses these stages as a basis for assessing and teaching children of different developmental levels. The teaching strategies that are recommended all present spelling in the context of using language for meaningful purposes, not as an isolated skill. A similar approach is recommended in Chapter 11, Grammar, Punctuation, and Handwriting—namely, that grammar and other language conventions should be taught and assessed as part of the writing process, especially the editing and revising stages. Writing workshop is revisited and other approaches are introduced, such as minilessons, teacher conferences, peer editing, and self-editing. Children's literature is presented as an excellent resource for teaching about the style, structure, and conventions of written language.

Chapters 12 through 14 comprise **Part V, Integrated Teaching.** Also new to this edition, Chapter 12, Viewing and Visually Representing, focuses on the two newest language arts in the IRA/NCTE standards. Viewing and visually representing have always been essential to teaching language arts across the curriculum, and media literacy has never been more important than in today's world of mass-mediated communication. This chapter provides engaging strategies and examples across a range of experiences in viewing and visually representing, from film, video, and television to the visual and dramatic arts.

Chapter 13, Technology in the Classroom, begins with a discussion of the role of technology in the classroom and specifically in the language arts classroom. Technology is presented not as an end in itself but as another means by which teachers can help children learn. The writing process and writing workshop are both reconsidered in this chapter in a discussion of word processing. Other projects and activities include electronic messaging, Internet research, and hypermedia and multimedia projects.

Chapter 14, Language across the Curriculum, draws on the information provided in previous chapters to demonstrate how the language arts can be used to integrate teaching in the content areas. Thematic teaching, sometimes defined using terms such as *units* and *cycles,* has long been used for the purpose of integrating the various content areas. In fact, numerous examples of thematic teaching can be found throughout this text, particularly in the Ripple Effects mentioned earlier. Literary and informational texts are recommended not only for reading but also as models of writing. This chapter provides a wealth of support materials, including lists of literary and informational texts and numerous examples of student-created materials.

Special Features

- One or more **Assessment Toolboxes** appear in nearly every chapter, providing a wide range of contextualized, authentic assessment devices, and cross-references to Toolboxes in other chapters are noted at relevant spots in the text by the icon shown in the margin. The application of these ready-made tools is demonstrated using real examples of children's work, and suggestions are offered for adapting the tools for certain student groups.

- **Snapshots** give glimpses into real classrooms, showing the practical application of material discussed in the chapter and demonstrating how ideas can be transformed into actions. One or more Snapshots is included in every chapter, along with relevant examples of student- and teacher-created materials. Many of the Snapshots take place in classrooms that are culturally and linguistically diverse.

- **Lesson Plans** and **Teaching Ideas** offer specific suggestions for teaching language arts and can readily be put into practice in the elementary classroom. New to this edition are Lesson Plans on creating self-portraits and poetry, conducting a three-day core book unit on cultural diversity, and integrating the teaching of science and language arts. New Teaching Ideas propose ways of examining advertising language with children and conducting an Internet scavenger hunt.

- New to this edition is a boxed feature labeled **Supporting.** Found in most chapters, these boxes provide specific ideas for supporting the learning of ELL students, struggling readers and writers, students with disabilities, and students who speak a nonmainstream dialect of English. The specific content of each box is related to the discussion at hand and to a particular student group. For instance, a Supporting box in Chapter 9 on writing addresses the needs of ELL students in understanding the writing process.

- **Ripple Effects** serve as graphic organizers of response-themed learning, offering extensive teaching ideas and lists of children's books. Each is related to the chapter content and based on actual classroom experiences. A new Ripple Effect has been added to this edition on the Pinkneys, a noted family of African American authors/illustrators of children's books who are discussed in Chapter 8 in the section about literature focus units.

The set of **icons** introduced in the last edition has been expanded in this edition to give readers visual recognition of the following kinds of information:

- As mentioned earlier, the IRA/NCTE *Standards for the English Language Arts* are referenced throughout the text, as identified by the icon shown in the margin.

IRA/
NCTE

- Marginal notes highlight specific ideas for teaching ELL students, providing teachers with much needed assistance in culturally and linguistically diverse classrooms.

ELL

- A new category of marginal note, identified as **Scaffolding,** provides ideas for adapting instruction for students who are struggling readers and writers as well as students with specific disabilities.

SCAFFOLDING

Icons are also used to identify these types of useful **resources** in marginal notes:

- Websites and related links found on the World Wide Web (WWW)

WWW

- Software reviews and related ideas for teaching language arts

EXCELLENT SOFTWARE

- Lists of great children's books, identified by topic

GREAT BOOKS FOR CHILDREN

- Professional teacher resources

TEACHER RESOURCES

- New to this edition, video clips and related materials on the Companion Website for the text are integrated throughout

CW

The structure of each chapter has been maintained from the previous edition and will facilitate readers' use of the text upon initial reading and later review:

- **Chapter-opening questions** raise basic issues about the chapter topic. Following these questions, readers are asked to write a **Reflective Response,** drawing on their own experiences and ideas in this area. **Chapter-ending answers** go back to the same questions, providing summaries of chapter content.

- **Looking Further,** another end-of-chapter feature, suggests opportunities for exploring chapter content more deeply: discussion questions, group activities focused on understanding how language is used, suggestions for observing and interacting with children, and ideas for participation and teaching applications to try out in the classroom.

- The section of **Children's Books, Films, and Software** found at the end of each chapter identifies publication information for the children's literature and other resources discussed in text. These resources are all included in a special **Index of Children's Books, Films, and Software,** found at the end of the book. All professional source materials have been compiled at the end of the book in the **References** section. Both the children's and professional resources have been substantially updated for this edition.

- In addition to the purposes already mentioned, **marginal notes** provide definitions, expanded explanations, and cross-references to related sections of the book.

- **Visuals** richly illustrate the book, showing samples of children's drawing and writing and photos of teachers and children actually discussed in the text. Many are new to this fifth edition.

Supplements

The companion resource to this textbook, *Schoolyear Activities Planner*—still provided free with every student text—has been updated for this fifth edition of *Teaching Language Arts*. This popular, practical supplement includes teaching ideas, lesson plans, and lists of children's books and websites that coincide with the months of the schoolyear, September through June. This month-by-month planner is followed by lists of Caldecott and Newbery Medal–winning and honor books, which provide additional examples of good-quality children's literature.

The **Companion Website** for the text (www.ablongman.com/cox5e), as identified by the icon described earlier, provides online video case studies. Readers can go online and actually see and hear the teachers and students they are reading about in video clips. For example, Snapshots in Chapters 1 and 2 feature Louisiana Teacher of the Year for 2002, Avril Font. Marginal notes with these Snapshots will direct readers to the website, where they can see Avril in action in the classroom and listen to her views on teaching in an interview. Similarly, in Chapters 3 and 4, readers can go online and see ELL students, including the kindergartners in Alicia Campos's Spanish bilingual class in Los Angeles, and in Chapter 13, they can hear interviews with technology teachers Basia Gliddon and Dee Qualls. These are only a few of the examples of video case studies available to readers of this text to let them see and hear best practices in teaching language arts in classrooms, cities, and states across the country.

This text is also accompanied by an **Instructor's Manual** with additional resources for professors using the fifth edition of *Teaching Language Arts*. Please contact your local Allyn & Bacon sales representative for information on how to gain access to the Instructor's Manual.

A **RICA Guide** is also available to those instructors using the text in California. This new guide includes helpful information for students on how this text will help them study for the RICA exam.

Acknowledgments

I've learned so much from the children I taught as an elementary teacher in Los Angeles, California, and Madison, Wisconsin, and from the preservice university students and inservice teachers I've taught and whose classrooms I've visited as a professor at Louisiana State University, in Baton Rouge, and at California State University, Long Beach. My special thanks go to those I've written about in this book: Marjorie Abbott, Shelly Abesa, Paul Boyd-Batstone, Alicia Campos, Phyllis Crawford, Jaqui Denenberg, Audrey Eldridge, Avril Font, Phyllis Fuglaar, Basia Gliddon, Marion Harris, Jennifer Howard, Gene Hughes, Mauretta Hurst, Sheila

Kline, Kathy Lee, Ping Liu, Margaret Mattson, Nora Miller, James Orihuela, Dee Qualls, Willa Richardson, and Ken Roy.

I've also written about the language and literacy development of my own three children—Wyatt, Gordon, and Elizabeth. Watching them grow has provided me an education not available through books or university classes.

Many reviewers have made insightful comments and suggestions and have done much to shape the content of this book. My thanks go to those individuals who reviewed this fifth edition: Cecile Arquette, San Diego State University; Alice Galper, the University of Maryland; and Alicia Mendoza, Florida International University. I would also like to thanks once again those individuals who reviewed several earlier editions: Rosemary G. Cameron, College of St. Rose; Nancy Horton, University of North Texas; Ruth M. Joseph, Fitchburg State College; Jane E. Percival, Keene State College; Katherine Quinn, Holy Family College; Kathleen M. Scott, College of St. Rose; Gail Singleton Taylor, Old Dominion University. and Gwendolyn Webb-Johnson, Texas A&M University.

Reading Louise Rosenblatt's transactional theory gave me the explanatory power I needed to articulate my own classroom experiences and those of others with regard to teaching with literature, and her friendship and support for my research and writing efforts at putting theory into practice have also been much appreciated. I also acknowledge the California State University for funding my ongoing longitudinal research on the development of children's responses to literature and for honoring me as the Outstanding Professor of the Year for 2001.

Thanks also to Virginia Lanigan, Arnis Burvikovs, and Aurora Martinez of Allyn & Bacon and to Susan Freese of Communicáto, Ltd., for the personal encouragement to be myself and for expert professional advice and support throughout the development of this fifth edition of *Teaching Language Arts*.

Carole Cox and her children (left to right): *Elizabeth, Gordon, and Wyatt.*

chapter 1

Learning and Teaching Language Arts

Questions about Learning and Teaching Language Arts

- *What are the language arts?*
- *How do children learn language arts?*
- *How should we teach language arts?*

REFLECTIVE RESPONSE

Think about the questions above, and jot down your ideas. Take a chance. Write whatever comes to mind in response to the term *language arts*. When you've finished, perhaps compare your response with those of other students in small groups or in a whole-class discussion with your instructor. Keep your ideas in mind as you read this chapter.

The Language Arts

The *language arts* have traditionally been defined in elementary teaching as "listening, speaking, reading, and writing." But this definition is merely the tip of the iceberg. When I first thought about the questions you just responded to, I pictured the students I had when I was an elementary teacher, using language in the classroom. Sometimes, their use of language was audible and visible: talking in small groups or class discussions, writing in their journals or working together on

IRA/ NCTE

Six Language Arts
• Reading
• Writing
• Listening
• Speaking
• Viewing
• Visually representing

See Chapter 12, Viewing and Visually Representing, for many ideas for teaching these two newest language arts.

WWW

See www.reading.org and www.ncte.org for more on the national *Standards for the English Language Arts* (1996).

a movie script, drawing illustrations for a book they were writing, constructing costumes or props for a play, singing, dancing, dramatizing, or laughing at each other's jokes. Other times, my students' language use was silent and invisible: listening as I read aloud, reading independently, or staring off into space, thinking about what they would write next.

The language arts also include language conventions: spelling, punctuation, grammar usage, and handwriting. Newer skills, such as word processing and building a website, are part of the language arts, as well. An important goal of teaching language arts is achieving literacy for all children. *Literacy* has often been defined in elementary teaching as "reading and writing." This is another narrow definition. Today, the meaning of literacy may include a range of abilities, from biliteracy (the ability to read and write in more than one language) to computer and media literacy.

The national *Standards for the English Language Arts* (1996), written jointly by the International Reading Association (IRA) and the National Council of Teachers of English (NCTE), recognized that the traditional four language arts did not acknowledge the powerful role of nonprint media in children's lives. These standards redefined what students should know about the English language arts as *six* language arts: reading, writing, listening, speaking, viewing, and visually representing. These standards also defined texts more broadly, adding spoken language, graphics, and technological communications to print. Similarly, language has been redefined to include visual communication in addition to spoken and written forms of expression, and reading now includes listening and viewing in addition to print. A complete copy of the standards is provided inside the front cover of this book.

The IRA/NCTE *Standards for the English Language Arts* represent what students should know and be able to do in the English language arts. The model behind the standards-based education movement includes clear expectations for students and schools, accountability through assessment tools that show whether standards have been met, and support for classroom instruction that will lead to improved learning. But in fact, language arts content standards and curriculum are only words on paper, existing in a virtual world, until they come alive in the real world of the classroom through the actions of teachers and students. The best of all possible outcomes occurs when excellent language arts standards meet excellent language arts instruction and are integrated across an excellent curriculum.

As an elementary teacher, you will face this exciting task of integrating all the language arts across the curriculum. Whatever subject or grade you teach, the medium of communication used will be language, in any one of its many forms. It would be an oversimplification, however, to suggest that the importance of language arts in school is simply as a vehicle to learn other subject matter. Language is a system of communicating that offers countless possibilities for representation, expression, and construction of meaning. It's certainly much more than a tool. It permeates human thought and life.

Accordingly, language arts is more than just a subject. It's part of everything that happens in the classroom. You are a language arts teacher all day long.

A Day in Avril Font's Fourth-Grade Class

Let's take a look into one teacher's classroom to see how she teaches language arts all day long. It's an April morning, and the schoolday has just begun in Avril Font's fourth-grade class at Ryan Elementary School in Scotlandville, Louisiana, a small, semirural community just outside the state capital of Baton Rouge. Ryan is a Chapter 1 school, which means it qualifies for extra federal funds because of the low income of the average school family. Ten of Avril's students are white, and twenty are African American. All but two of Avril's students qualify for free lunch, and the Junior League of Baton Rouge provides all of her students with school supplies.

As you read this Snapshot, note *when* and *how* you think Avril is teaching language arts.

9:00–9:15 Business (Teacher) and Journals, Newspapers, and Books (Students)

While Avril takes care of business like taking attendance, taking the lunch count, and talking to a parent, the children choose to do one of three language and literacy experiences:

1. write in their journals
2. read the newspaper
3. read a book

9:15–9:45 Sharing with the Whole Class

Avril tells the class to meet her in the reading center. It's a comfortable place, surrounded with bookshelves. There's a big rug on the floor, which is covered with floor pillows for the children, and there are two old recliners—one for Avril, the other for students. After everyone settles in, Avril and the children talk about things that are important to them:

Avril: OK, let's share.

Child: Mrs. Font, my Paw Paw made things out of acorns for a craft show. I'll bring them in to show.

Avril: That's a neat idea for a story. Why don't you get your writing folder and jot down some ideas?

Child: OK.

Child: I got an idea of something to write about. I put a glass on the door to listen to my older sister talk on the phone. But I couldn't hear.

Avril: Try putting it on the wall. I bet that will work.

(One child reads from a book that's often used during sharing. It tells what's special about each day.)

Child: Hey, it says here that it's William Shakespeare's birthday today.

Avril Font was named Louisiana Teacher of the Year in 2002–2003.

See the video of sharing in Avril's class.

The words *Paw Paw* are commonly used in Southern Louisiana to mean "grandfather."

How to Make a Writing Folder
For each student, use a ready-made manila folder or create one by folding a piece of 11" × 18" construction paper in half. Staple a piece of paper inside to jot down "Ideas to Write About." Have the student decorate the cover and add a title like "My Writing." Keep all the student's works in progress in the folder.

Avril Font enjoys sharing time with her students.

Avril:	Who is he?
Child:	A famous writer.
Child:	He wrote poetry.
Child:	He wrote literature.
Avril:	Right. He wrote plays and poetry. Have you ever heard of *Romeo and Juliet?*
Child:	Yeah.
Child:	Over Easter, I watched Channel 27, and they had *Romeo and Juliet*, scene 2.

9:45–10:00   Planning the Day

During sharing time, Avril observed children's responses to topics of interest that emerged. Now, she thinks about ways to center learning experiences around those responses and to merge them with subjects suggested in the curriculum guide and by state and national content standards as well as with seasonal and special events. Note that the way in which she provides for children's responses as they plan the day together helps them organize into groups for different subjects that will become integrated through literature-based language arts activities.

Avril picks a student to be Secretary of the Day, whose job is to record ideas on the chalkboard under the regular headings "Language Arts and Reading" and "Social Studies, Science, and Math," written in colored chalk. Children will do these activities throughout the day during several group workshop times. Not everyone will do the same activities at the same time, but each will do all the subjects sometime during the day. Avril believes that this

Literature-based teaching is grounded in using quality children's tradebooks, both fiction and nonfiction, as sources of ideas and information.

approach helps students learn to take control and responsibility for their work and time.

> Avril: What are we doing in language arts?
>
> Child: I'm going to start a story about pizza.
>
> Avril: Why?
>
> Child: 'Cause my mama works in a pizza place.

(Other children also talk about what they're writing about.)

> Avril: Good. All of you keep writing on your own stories. Shane might want to start a story about his Paw Paw and the acorns. We'll get them ready to make into books. Sign up for turns on the computer. Write in your journals. What about reading?
>
> Child: I have a new library book about sharks. How they eat people.
>
> Avril: Sounds terrific. We'll have sustained silent reading (SSR) after recess, and you can get started reading it. Those of you who have finished your basal reader story can take the test. Continue to read your library books, and everyone read the newspaper. After lunch, I'll read the next chapter of *The Wind in the Willows* aloud.

Here's what Edreka, the Secretary of the Day, has written on the chalkboard:

Language Arts and Reading

Write own stories. Use computer.
Journals.
Bookmaking.
SSR after recess.
Take basal test if finished basal reader story.
Read library book.
Read newspaper.
Mrs. Font reads <u>The Wind in the Willows</u>.

Next, Avril and the class will plan social studies, science, and math together. The children will work together in small groups. Note the many ways in which literature-based language arts integrates the content and how children's literature is used.

> Avril: OK, let's plan social studies for today. Who would like to go to the library and research William Shakespeare? (Several hands go up.) When you come back, talk about what you find with each other and begin to think about how you might share your research with everybody else. What else are we doing in social studies?
>
> Child: St. George and the dragon. We're working on making a big dragon costume for our play of when St. George kills the dragon. We read about it in this book.

GREAT BOOKS FOR CHILDREN

Sharks

Chomp! A Book about Sharks (Berger, 1999)
Shark Attack! (Dubowski, 1998)
Sharks (Simon, 1995)
The Truth about Great White Sharks (Cerullo, 2000)

Avril's district used to require students to take basal tests, so she had them read the stories and take the tests. But her balanced, comprehensive reading program has always been much broader and students primarily read good-quality literature. Her students did do well on the tests. Avril was named Louisiana Reading Teacher of the Year in 1992 because of her success in teaching students who are traditionally considered at risk to read.

GREAT BOOKS FOR CHILDREN

St. George and the Dragon (Spenser, 1984), a Caldecott Medal–winning book illustrated by Trina Schart Hyman.

Avril:	You're doing a terrific job with your research and play. What else?
Child:	The maypole group. We have to practice the maypole dance. We did well yesterday.
Avril:	Yes, you really did. I brought the maypole ribbons. Aren't they great? What about your science research and reports and posters on animals?
Child:	Me and him want to do guppies. My cousin got 'em in an aquarium.
Avril:	Why don't you two see if you can find out how to make an aquarium? How big should it be? Calculate the volume.
Child:	OK! Can we go to the library?
Avril:	Yes. Take some notes, get some books, and we'll make plans to do it. How much will it cost? Figure out a budget.

Avril and her students also discuss plans for mathematics. Again, students will work in small groups, using their math books and a lot of manipulatives and games. Avril will monitor their progress and work with several small groups during the day. Here's what Edreka has written on the board for social studies, science, and math:

Social Studies, Science, and Math

New Shakespeare group to library.
St. George and dragon group work on play.
Maypole dance practice.
Animal reports and posters.
New guppy group to library to figure aquarium
   cost and volume.

Avril helps the children plan which activity they'll do in the first-hour block of group workshop after recess. Some will go to the writing center, some to the library, and some will work on social studies, science, and mathematics activities. The children will rotate to other subjects during the afternoon group workshop time.

10:00–10:15   Recess

10:15–11:15   Group Workshop

As the children work, Avril moves among the small groups, interacting with them as she guides and monitors their progress. She does many on-the-spot conferences with individual children or groups, as needed. But for the most part, she expects the children to be self-directed.

Writing Center. The writing center is a long table that has space for six children to sit and write together. (The other children write alone at their desks.) Plastic tubs hold student writing folders and supplies, including many types

Avril Font conferences with a student in the writing center.

of paper, pencils, and erasers. The writing center is located near a bulletin board, which provides space to display student writing, and a chalkboard, which comes in handy for group brainstorming and outlining of ideas. The computer center is next to the table in the center.

Several students are writing and discussing their stories with each other and Avril:

> *Child* (reading aloud, savoring the sound): "My Day at the Movies," by Lestreca.
>
> *Avril:* May I read it? (Reads story.) I like it. It seems a bit long in places, though. Read it to me and see what you think.

While Lestreca and Avril talk about the story, Mina works on her book, *My Mom the Seamstress* (see Figure 1.1, pp. 8–9). She asks Avril to help her think of other words for *seamstress*. Together, they look in the thesaurus and find the word *couturiere*. Mina chooses it because her mother was born in Japan and that's what she was called when she learned to design clothes and sew them without patterns. Her mother met and married Mina's father—an African American U.S. serviceman—in Japan. Avril encourages her students to share and write about their family histories and cultural heritages.

Social Studies Groups. Avril moves among the groups, who are working on different topics. One group is preparing to do the maypole dance and write a report on it:

> *Avril:* Where is the maypole gang? (Several children are on the floor, arranging the ribbons for the dance and reading books about countries that celebrate May Day.)

Child:	Mrs. Font, what's this word?
Avril:	Czechoslovakia. It's a country in Europe.
Child:	Yeah. I was gonna say that. (Spelling aloud.) C-z-e-c-h-o-s-l-o-v-a-k-i-a. (Snapping her fingers as she says each syllable. Czech- (snap) o- (snap) slo- (snap) vak- (snap) i- (snap) a- (snap)! Right?
Avril:	Right!
Child:	Look. It says in this book that in Czechoslovakia, boys put trees under their sweetheart's window on May Day.
Child:	Mrs. Font, there was an article about the maypole dance in the newspaper, but it didn't explain why it's danced.
Child:	They don't know much.
Child:	They could read about it in the encyclopedia or these books.
Avril:	You read a lot. I'm impressed.

Figure 1.1 Student's Book about Her Mother

Next, Avril moves to the group doing a play of the story of "St. George and the Dragon." They're reading and talking about how to make a dragon costume:

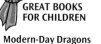

GREAT BOOKS FOR CHILDREN

Modern-Day Dragons
Komodo Dragon on Location (Darling, 1997)
Komodo Dragons (Maynard, 1997)

Child: Mrs. Font, me and him want to know, were there really dragons?
Avril: Try looking up what we call "dragons" today. I think there are some big reptiles on the Galapagos Islands. Try the atlas.
Child: I thought everything was in the dictionary.
Child: No, 'cause it's the name of a place.

The students talk some more and tell Avril what kinds of supplies they need to make the dragon costume: big pieces of cardboard, twine, colored butcher paper, and poster paint and brushes. And they figure out that talcum powder, coming out of the dragon's snout, will look like smoke. Avril tells the group that they should bring up their plans during sharing and planning tomorrow to see if anyone in the class might have some of these things.

5 | My mom sews for lots of people. She sews dresses, skirts, prom dresses, shirts, pants, shorts, and suits.

6 | One day Mrs. Font asked me to ask my mother if she could make a prom dress for Sedley.

7 | So Mrs. Font brought the stuff. My mom made the prom dress and she made three more prom dresses after that.

8 | My mother has been saving money so she could buy another machine.

The Shakespeare group has just returned from the library with books, and they're very excited. They've been reading, taking notes, and talking about Shakespeare's life. They continue talking about how to share what they find out about this author with the rest of the class:

Child: Mrs. Font, it says he served with a company of actors. (She makes a "V for victory" sign.) I want to be an actress.

Child: It says here that he wrote "Mary Had a Little Lamb."

Avril: Are you sure?

Child: Uh-hmm. It says!

Avril: Read it again.

Child (reading):   Oh. It says his plays were written as stories for children by Charles and Mary Lamb.

Avril: That's how I read Shakespeare when I was young (see Lamb & Lamb, 1957). Why don't you see if you can find that book in the library? And look for other books that tell the stories of his plays.

This group later performed scenes from Shakespeare's plays and wrote a book about his life (see Figure 1.2).

Science and Math Groups. The children tell Avril about their research on different animals and the posters they're making to share what they find with the rest of the class. The new guppy group has just returned from the library, and they're looking forward to making an aquarium:

Child: Mrs. Font, we got some books on aquariums. They tell how to make one, so we're gonna read and start working on our own. We figured out how big it has to be and how much it will cost.

Figure 1.2

Page from a Student's Book about Shakespeare

Shakespeare retired from his theater work in 1610 and returned to Stratford. His friends from London visited him. In 1613 the Globe theater burned.

Child	(reading about animals in a book): Mrs. Font, what does *droppings* mean? It says, "But their presence is revealed by their tracks and droppings."
Avril:	Try looking it up in the dictionary.
Child	(returning with dictionary): Mrs. Font, I still don't get it.
Avril:	I'll tell you what it is: It's when animals go to the bathroom, the little brown things they leave behind. *Excrement.*
Child:	You mean like dog doo?
Avril:	Yes.

GREAT BOOKS FOR CHILDREN

Read-Aloud Books for Fourth Grade

Baseball in April (Soto, 1990)
Charlotte's Web (White, 1952)
Harry Potter and the Sorcerer's Stone (Rowling, 1998)
In the Year of the Boar and Jackie Robinson (Lord, 1984)
James and the Giant Peach (Dahl, 1961)
Tales of a Fourth-Grade Nothing (Blume, 1972)

11:15–11:45   Sustained Silent Reading

Everyone reads a book of his or her choice, including Avril. They all get comfortable. Some sit at desks, and some sit in the two recliner chairs. Others are nestled in beanbag chairs or stretched out on the rug. It's absolutely quiet. Everyone's reading.

11:45–12:15   Lunch

12:15–12:30   Read Aloud

As mentioned earlier, during read-aloud time, Avril reads from Kenneth Grahame's (1980) classic book *The Wind in the Willows*. Students can respond or ask questions, and Avril does, too. It's a great time to listen to and enjoy literature, respond openly to it, and talk about words, ideas, characters, and events in the book.

12:30–1:30   Group Workshop

This afternoon group workshop is similar to the morning session except that the children rotate subjects and activities. Once again, Avril observes and has conferences with students. Today, the maypole group is practicing outside the room, getting ready for a Friday visit from the local newspaper, who will take pictures and write an article. The guppy group has gone to the office to use the phone. They're going to call a pet store to see how much aquarium supplies cost.

1:30–2:00   Physical Education

2:00–3:00   Group Workshop

In this session, the children either rotate and work in a new area or continue with a big project. The "St. George and the Dragon" group started to build the dragon costume in the last group workshop and made a big mess. (They were practicing blowing talcum powder out of the dragon's snout.) Since they already had all their materials out, the group has continued working on the costume.

The day ends at 3:00.

After school, I asked Avril, "What beliefs and knowledge guide your teaching of language arts?" Here's her answer:

I believe that teaching language arts should be student and response centered. Children should be actively engaged in using language and focused on meaning. It should stem from the ideas, interests, language, and unique talents of each child. Why write about mother's work? Because family and culture are central to each student's life, and they write best about what they know best. Why Shakespeare? Because someone noticed it was his birthday when reading *A Book of Days* (Donaldson & Donaldson, 1979), which they like. It was the same place they found out about St. George and the dragon and the maypole and decided they wanted to learn how to do the maypole dance. It was relevant to their interests, and I used their responses as a guide. Why read and write and draw and make books and build things like aquariums? The texts are boring. I love science and believe that children learn by doing. We do all hands-on science. We construct things and dramatize during social studies. We learn to read by reading and to write by writing. We use literature as texts and children's response to literature as a basis for activities. We work as a collaborative team. Students work together in groups, but their work is individual, stemming from their own ideas, interests, and responses. They just spend a lot of time sharing, planning, discussing, and helping each other. We are all a community of learners.

Avril's beliefs and knowledge about how children learn language arts reflect a *social constructivist* point of view. Her beliefs about children's experiences with literature reflect the *transactional model* of the reading process. These theories also underlie the approach to teaching recommended in this book. They are summarized in Table 1.1, including examples of classroom experiences.

Learning Language Arts

IRA/ NCTE

The three theoretical perspectives that underlie the approach in this book suggest that learning language arts is an active, constructive process; a social interactive process; and a transactional process. Each process will be explained in a following section with ideas about how it applies to language learning and teaching language arts. Marginal notes will illustrate each process with an example from Avril's class and a corresponding national standard.

An Active, Constructive Process

The constructivist theory views understanding and composing language as a building process. Children continually build new meaning on the foundation of prior knowledge they bring to the communication process. As a metaphor for

Table 1.1 Key Ideas for Learning and Teaching Language Arts: Classroom Experiences

Learning Language Arts	Student's Role	Teacher's Role	Curriculum
Active, constructive process: focused on meaning; learn by doing (listening, speaking, reading, and writing); hands-on experiences	*Choice:* books to read, writing topics, research topics, and student groups	*Observation:* listens and watches; holds conferences (on the spot, scheduled, individual, and group)	*Response themed:* based on topics of interest to students, content standards, and curriculum guides and seasonal events
Social interactive process: collaboration, sharing, planning, group workshops, and conferences	*Voice:* open discussions, personal journals, own stories, response to books, and drama	*Modeling/Initiation:* plans sharing, organizes groups, literature lessons, builds on student's responses	*Integrated:* language used across the curriculum; read and write to learn in other subjects (social studies, science, math, and arts)
Transactional process: between reader and text; open response to literature and other texts	*Control:* topics of interest, monitor progress, make decisions about what and how to learn	*Modeling/Demonstration:* reads aloud, provides direct instruction in needed skill or strategy	*Literature based:* uses high-quality children's books, both fiction and nonfiction, as texts and for independent reading
	Responsibility: to read and write daily, to manage time	*Expectations:* to stay focused, to read and write, and to work cooperatively	

language learning, constructivism means that language users are builders, meaning is what they build, and prior knowledge is the material they build with (Spivey, 1994). The constructivist view is captured by John Dewey's (1938) famous expression "learning by doing," which means that we construct knowledge by actively participating in learning events.

Swiss psychologist Jean Piaget's *cognitive theory* of learning development contributes to our understanding of constructivism. Piaget explains that all learning is an active process in which the learner continually constructs meaning (1973, 1977). Based on careful observations of his own three children over time, Piaget believed that children are able to construct a view of reality that's based on what they learn and experience as they mature. In other words, they learn throughout their lives by exploring and discovering new things. Learning is a process of adding new bits of information to what they already know. Accord-

Key Piagetian Terms
- Assimilation
- Accommodation
- Equilibration
- Schemata

ing to Piaget, young children learn to organize their experiences and adapt to their environments through the processes of assimilation, accommodation, and equilibration.

Assimilation is classifying an object into an already existing mental category or operation. Have you ever watched a baby try to put anything and everything into its mouth, including its feet? Piaget would say that the baby is assimilating new objects through the old process of eating. That is, the baby is using something it already knows how to do—eating—to try to put unknown things into an existing mental category. When my son Gordon was just learning to speak, he saw the beautiful French film *The Red Balloon* (1956); after that, he called every balloon "a red balloon." He also called every small animal "a kitty" in those early days. These are examples of assimilation.

Accommodation is adjusting a mental category or operation to include new objects and experiences in the environment. Gordon had to adjust his mental category of "balloons" one day when he was asked if he wanted a yellow, pink, or blue balloon at the grand opening of a toy store. He responded "red balloon," but the clerk said they didn't have any red ones and offered the other colors again. Gordon was temporarily in a state of disequilibrium, unable to fit this new information into what he already knew. He looked confused and longingly at the balloons, thought about them, and finally said that he wanted yellow, pink, *and* blue balloons. He had adjusted, or accommodated, his existing category of "balloons" to include not only red balloons but a new phenomenon: balloons of different colors.

Piaget's theories and stages of development will be explained further in Chapter 3, First- and Second-Language Development.

Equilibration is the self-regulatory process by which a balance is achieved between assimilation and accommodation. Through the ongoing, interacting processes of assimilation and accommodation, children construct increasingly sophisticated understandings of their environments. They continually add new information to their existing bases of ideas. For example, after Gordon visited a petting zoo and had the chance to hold and pet some rabbits, he stopped calling all small animals "kitties" and learned to call rabbits "bunnies."

Schemata are the concepts that are constructed during the ongoing processes of assimilation, accommodation, and equilibration. Schemata are already existing knowledge structures. Think of them as comprising a sort of organizational chart or map, to which new details are constantly being added. Gordon was constructing schemata for balloons and small animals as he added what he learned about each from new experiences to his prior knowledge base. After learning that bunnies weren't kitties, he continued to add new information to his existing schemata about small animals by looking at pictures and books and taking more trips to the zoo.

Piaget's contribution to learning theory, later supported by *schema theory* (Anderson, 1994; Rumelhart & Ortony, 1977), was to identify the importance of connecting new experiences to prior knowledge and organizing that new information. We make those connections through schemata. Children learn when they connect what they already know with what they discover through new experiences. This learning theory has had important implications for literacy instruction. In the highly influential national report *Becoming a Nation of Readers*, Anderson et al. (1985) maintain that literacy research shows that "reading is a constructive act" (p. 9). The current view of writing is also constructivist. Meaning exists not only in the text but in the minds of the writer and readers of the text.

Avril Font puts it this way:

> The first essential is to try to build on their ideas and language and extend all language arts experiences into all aspects of teaching and learning. I believe that oral language is the foundation for children's development of literacy. The more they use oral language, the more they can read and write. Their own language must be used, reinforced, built upon, and extended into all areas of the curriculum.

An example of constructivism in Avril's class: A student whose cousin had some guppies worked with another student to find books about fish and how to build an aquarium.

Constructivism applies to language learning in four ways:

1. Readers actively build meaning as they read, rather than passively receiving messages.
2. The text does not say it all; the reader brings information to the text.
3. A single text can have multiple meanings because of differences among readers and contexts.
4. Reading and writing are similar constructive processes, rather than separate ones.

Constructivism also applies to teaching language arts. Teachers can help students learn these four skills:

**IRA/
NCTE
Standard 1**

1. to make connections between what they already know and what they will learn
2. to use strategies for reading (e.g., make predictions) and writing (e.g., draw on prior experience)
3. to think about their own reading and writing processes
4. to discuss their responses to texts they or others read and write

A Social, Interactive Process

The learning theory of Lev Vygotsky (1962, 1978, 1986) proposes that children acquire new knowledge through meaningful interactions with other people. Whereas Piaget suggests that each child's learning is an individual, internalized cognitive process that does not depend on adult support, Vygotsky emphasizes the social, contextual nature of learning, which is a *sociohistorical* approach. He uses the *instrumental method* of studying child development. Like constructivism, it focuses on the child's active language use. The emphasis, however, is to discover

Key Vygotskian Terms
- Sociohistorical
- Instrumental method
- Zone of proximal development
- Scaffolding

how children actually use language as a psychological tool to communicate or share cultural meanings as well as how this set of cultural signs, or language, influences children's learning and cognitive development. Whereas Piaget observed individual children in isolation, Vygotsky studied how children's thinking developed in real classroom contexts. For Vygotsky, cognitive development was the result of social interaction within the environment. For example, children learn to talk by listening to their parents, siblings, and others and then talking back. Similarly, children learn to read and write by having others read to them, by participating in shared storybook readings and writing events, and by eventually reading and writing on their own. We learn about the world and ourselves through socially meaningful activity (Dixon-Kraus, 1996).

See Chapter 4, Emergent Literacy and Biliteracy, for much more on how young children learn to read and write in a first or second language.

Vygotsky's theories with reference to language development will be further explained in Chapter 3, First- and Second-Language Development.

The *zone of proximal development* is a key idea in Vygotsky's (1978) theory. He defines it as "the distance between the actual developmental level as determined by independent problem solving and the level of potential development as determined through problem solving under adult guidance or in collaboration with more capable peers" (p. 76). This means that children learn when they are supported by others who know things they do not (e.g., teachers, parents, and peers) when engaged in activities that are too difficult to do independently. Vygotsky developed the idea of the zone of proximal development in a critique of the use of IQ tests as a form of assessing students' potential (Moll, 1990). It is a key idea in understanding the relationship of child development and classroom instruction. Vygostky (1962) has written that "what the child can do in cooperation today he can do alone tomorrow" (p. 104), suggesting that good instruction is just slightly ahead of development and leads to development.

Scaffolding is a term used by cognitive psychologist Jerome Bruner (1983, 1986) to describe the support adults give children as they help them build new knowledge. This support, or scaffolding, is only temporary. It's withdrawn as children develop and move on to new levels of understanding. But then it's replaced with new scaffolding—that is, with new knowledge that's been constructed through meaningful social interaction. The teacher takes into account what the student already knows and uses that as a basis for providing support in new problem-solving situations.

A social constructivist framework also takes into account the unique cultural aspect of each classroom (Spindler, 1982) as well as the role of the family and the cultural and lingustic background of each child (Heath, 1983, 1994). Learning occurs in a particular context, which will vary from class to class and year to year (Green & Meyer, 1990). Culturally responsive literacy instruction remains sensitive to each student's ethnic culture while helping him or her gain proficiency in the mainstream culture. This is achieved by maintaining high expectations and goals for diverse students, giving consideration to their lives beyond the classroom, and making sure these expectations reflect the values and practices of their ethnic cultures. For example, a student from a culture that practices sibling caretaking would benefit from peer collaboration such as group work, whereas a student from a culture that values individual autonomy would benefit from self-selection in reading books and writing topics (Au, 1993).

Avril Font sums it up like this:

I see language as multifaceted, even tactile. A lot of people think sharing and planning together is a waste of time. It's not. The more they share and plan together, the more verbal children become. They talk to each other more, discuss more in small groups. I do not use means to correct non-standard language, but if we don't build on the ideas and language that are already there when children come to school, we are building on sand.

An example of social interactionism in Avril's class: Sharing and group workshop provide for high levels of teacher/student and student/student interaction.

According to the social interactionist view, learning language can be characterized as follows:

1. The main function of language is social communication.
2. Learning is social and requires interaction with other people.
3. Knowledge develops first through social interaction and then becomes an internalized part of the cognitive structure of the learner.
4. Learning events must take into account the sociocultural context of cognition, or daily life experiences.

It follows that teaching language arts should have these goals:

1. to provide support as the child develops new understanding through social interaction
2. to mediate learning cooperatively with support
3. to be flexible, depending on the child's response to an activity
4. to vary the amount of support, from giving direct instruction to making subtle suggestions (Dixon-Kraus, 1996)

IRA/
NCTE
Standard 7

A Transactional Process

The *transactional* process, or model, of reading, which was developed by Louise Rosenblatt (1938/1995), focuses on the active role of the reader in creating meaning from the text. Rosenblatt and other reader-response theorists (Beach, 1993) maintain that the reader and the text/author construct meaning together. According to Rosenblatt (1986), making meaning while reading is "a complex, to-and-fro, self-correcting transaction between reader and verbal signs which continues until some final organization, more or less complete and coherent, is arrived at and thought of as corresponding to the text. . . . The 'meaning'— whether, e.g., poem, novel, play, scientific report, or legal brief—comes into being during the transaction" (p. 123). She borrowed the term *transaction* from John Dewey, who defined it as a reciprocal relationship among the parts of a single situation; this is in contrast to *interaction*, which involves two separate entities acting on one another.

We can see the relationship among the transactional theory and constructivism and social interactionism with regard to teaching reading in several ways:

See Chapter 6, Reading, and Chapter 14, Language across the Curriculum, for more on Rosenblatt's transactional theory.

All three theoretical perspectives (1) emphasize the role of the reader in creating meaning from a text, (2) challenge the notion that there is one correct meaning of a text, and (3) acknowledge the influence of cultural interpretations of a text.

Rosenblatt's (1986) transactional theory gives young readers more choice and control and an opportunity to use their voices in response to literature. It also gives them more *responsibility.* Although the teacher may initiate experiences with literature, he or she will not set predetermined outcomes, such as having everyone agree on what the author meant in a story. Rather, the teacher will ask students to draw on their own prior experiences and impressions while reading to construct a meaningful interpretation of the text. The focus is on the student, rather than the teacher or even the text. In transactional teaching, teachers demonstrate this focus by asking open questions—So what did you think?—and by sharing their own personal responses. Students share responsibility for their learning by making choices when responding, by using their own voices, and by gaining control over their ideas and language (Cox, 1997).

According to the transactional theory, learning language can be characterized as follows:

An example of transactional teaching in Avril's class: Students choose fiction and nonfiction books to read for pleasure and as texts for self-selected projects based on their interests (e.g., St. George and the dragon).

IRA/
NCTE
Standard 2

1. Readers and writers play active roles in the reading and writing processes.
2. Meaning is created during reading and writing in a two-way transaction between readers or writers and the texts they read and write.
3. Readers and writers draw on their own experiences and language skills to bring texts to life.
4. There are multiple possible interpretations of a single text.

Teaching language arts should therefore be rooted in these practices:

1. Students make choices about what to read and write.
2. Teachers ask open questions and provide options for responding to literature and writing.
3. Students' voices and prior experiences are honored.
4. Instructional planning includes attention to students' ideas and experiences.

Teaching Language Arts

A Student- and Response-Centered Classroom

In a student- and response-centered classroom like Avril Font's, you'll notice that children are active and that they learn by doing. Students learn to talk by talking, to read by reading, and to write by writing. The teacher's role is to help them gain control over their own ideas and language through active engagement with learning experiences that are focused on the construction of meaning. Student- and response-centered language and literacy experiences can be defined as those that originate with the ideas, interests, and language of children. This is the alternative that John Dewey (1943) described of creating schools to fit students, rather than making all students learn the same thing, in the same way. In this type of school, teachers make time to let children share and plan together, to listen to and observe children expressing their ideas, and to make plans based on these ideas.

You may be more familiar with a more traditional teacher- and text-centered classroom. In fact, you may have spent many years in classrooms like this: sitting in rows, always raising your hand to speak, listening to the teacher give directions, doing the same worksheet as everyone else, and so on. Do you remember reading groups? Even though the groups had names like Lions, Tigers, and Bears, you and your classmates all knew that you were grouped by ability and who was in the high, medium, and low groups.

This traditional type of classroom reflects the psychological theory of *behaviorism* and a *transmission model* of teaching. Educational applications of behaviorist learning theory were made popular in the 1950s by B. F. Skinner. Early behaviorists, particularly Ivan Pavlov, conducted experiments with animals in laboratories. You may have heard of Pavlov's dogs, who salivated in response to a ringing bell that signaled meal time. Behaviorists believe that learning follows a formula of *stimulus-response conditioning,* according to which acceptable responses are reinforced.

The behaviorist view of teaching language is based on the belief that children learn through a process of environmental conditioning and by imitating adult models. Teachers condition students' learning by modeling behaviors that students are to imitate. If the students imitate those behaviors correctly, they receive *positive reinforcement,* such as praise or rewards. And if they don't, they receive *negative reinforcement,* such as criticism or even punishment.

According to this behaviorist approach, language learning is not instinctive. Moreover, language is supposedly learned in small increments, called *skills.* Mastering those skills means that an individual learns them, one by one, and builds up a repertoire until he or she can read and write. For example, children learn to read first by mastering the letters of the alphabet, then combining letters to master words, and then combining words to master sentences. Learning to read is a step-by-step, cumulative process, each step building on the previous one. The basal readers used to teach reading in this way have "scope and sequences" of these skills, prepared for each grade and building on the grade before.

This traditional view we've been discussing—based on behaviorism and transmission—is called a *bottom-up* or *part-to-whole* approach to learning to use language. It's quite different from the *top-down* or *whole-to-part* approach we'll follow in this book. According to that approach, children learn to use language by using it when they are surrounded by print and when they have many rich social interactive experiences with language that focus on meaning. This learning goes on from the time children are babies through their school years and beyond.

Longitudinal research by Walter Loban (1976, 1979) has also demonstrated that the language modes function together as children learn to use and

According to Walter Loban (1979): "The development of power and efficiency with language derives from using language for genuine purposes and not from studying about it. The path to power over language is to use it, to use it in genuinely meaningful situations, whether we are reading, listening, writing, or speaking" (p. 485).

control language. Loban found a strong positive correlation among reading, writing, listening, and speaking abilities; that is, ability in one usually indicated the presence of ability in others. But according to Loban, the most important element in learning to use language is to use it.

To help you picture the conceptual differences between a traditional teacher- and text-centered classroom and a student- and response-centered classroom (like Avril's), the following lists compare what the teacher and student do in each:

Teacher- and Text-Centered Classroom

Teacher	Student
• makes all decisions for what's to be learned	• is a passive recipient of learning
• uses textbooks and commercial materials	• imitates what the teacher has modeled
• uses teachers' guides for textbook series	• follows directions of the teacher or textbook
• emphasizes part-to-whole learning	• is evaluated on mastery of skills in a hierarchical order
• follows a sequence of skills to be mastered	• is grouped by ability
• believes the product is more important than the process	• does the same assignments as other students
• believes that motivation is	• is evaluated by comparing
• evaluates based on test questions that have single correct answers	• is competitive with other students

In Avril Font's student- and response-centered classroom, she conferences frequently with students, listening to them and honoring their voices.

Student- and Response-Centered Classroom

Teacher

- initiates hands-on, direct experiences

- provides opportunities for independent learning
- uses children's literature and student writing
- believes that learning is whole to part

- believes that the process is more important than the product
- provides options and demonstrates possibilities
- groups students based on interests, which are flexible and may change
- incorporates time for sharing and planning
- conferences frequently with students
- observes and listens to students, honoring their voices
- uses ideas and interests of students as the basis of thematic learning
- recognizes that even though all children go through a similar process and stages, not all do so at the same pace or in the same way
- encourages cooperation and collaboration among students
- uses multiple forms of authentic assessment to inform instruction

Student

- makes choices about what to read, how to respond, what to learn about

- learns by doing; active engagement
- explores and discovers things on own
- works with others in groups, which are flexible and can change
- interacts, cooperates, and collaborates

- reads self-selected literature

- writes on topics of own choosing

- has intrinsic motivation

- is responsible for and has control over learning

The following sections look at ways to create a student- and response-centered classroom, addressing curriculum content, classroom environment and learning centers, scheduling and grouping, use of literature resources and technology, and the so-called ripple effects of response-themed learning. Each section begins with an example from the Snapshot of Avril Font's class.

Curriculum Content

Avril Font uses three sources in planning curriculum content: (1) standards-based state and district curriculum guides; (2) seasonal and special events through the year; and (3) students' ideas and interests. Here's how she sums things up:

> In the morning, we come together as a class to share and plan. And of course, we have special subjects as a whole class: library, P.E., music, French, and guidance. But the rest of the day, students move through the different subjects individually and work primarily in small groups. The subjects we designate are reading, language arts, math, social studies, and science—traditional subjects. But we choose topics as a class or individually and integrate all subjects.

For example, animal study is recommended by standards-based state curriculum guides, learning the maypole dance was related to the spring season, and Shakespeare came up as a topic during sharing. All three subjects involve language and literacy experiences, however. Avril artfully blends them together, always leaving the way open for topics students are interested in:

> My favorite day or week is Do Nothing, something I reserve for when we don't have any particular topic. But something usually comes up. We had a great Hurricane Day this year. As we were wondering if the hurricane would hit us here in Louisiana, students wrote wonderful haiku and other poetry. We watched the weather change daily, tracked the hurricane on charts, and studied hurricanes in depth.

> It's easy to find out about standards-based state and district curriculum suggestions and seasonal and special events. But how do you find out about your students' ideas and interests? Here are some practical ways to do so:

● *Sharing:* Provide regular time every day for sharing at all grade levels. It's important to let children know that they can share significant experiences at school. These sharing periods will become a primary source of information for your teaching.

See Chapter 9, The Writing
Process, for more on types of
journals and books in journal
format.

● *Journals:* Provide time for students to write every day. You should write, too. Some variations on keeping individual journals are dialogue journals (teachers, aides, or other students write back and forth) and community journals (in which anyone can write observations in a journal stationed by the window, aquarium, or pet cage, for example). Or read a book in journal format, such as *Three Days on a River in a Red Canoe* (Williams, 1981).

Star of the Week items: photographs, awards, letters, books,
mementos, crafts, and so on.

● *Star of the Week:* Have one child per week be the "star," who gets to create a bulletin board and table display to share things that are important to him or her. Provide time to share these things and answer questions from other students. Record students' questions and answers on chartpaper and display or videotape them. Or turn information about the star into a short biography; prepare it on the computer and print a booklet, which other students can illustrate and give to the individual. Students can also write fan letters to the star. The first week of school, have everybody bring a picture for a Class Stars bulletin board. The second week, do a display about yourself—baby pictures and all. Let the children ask you questions to model the procedure.

- *Autobiographies:* Have students write autobiographies the first few weeks of school. Set aside a period to develop guiding questions together: Where and when were you born? Tell about your family. What are your hobbies? You should write an autobiography, too.

- *Memoirs:* Encourage students to write their personal memoirs, as writing based on students' personal experiences can be the richest kind. See, for example, Figure 1.1, pages from Mina's book *My Mom the Seamstress*, in which she writes about her mother (pp. 8–9).

- *Conferences:* Ask children about themselves during planning and writing conferences and conference with parents.

CW

See Avril conference with a student.

- *Interviews:* Pair students and have them interview each other; after that, have them share the information about their partners with the class. By having partners ask open, simple, and positive questions, all children should be able to create positive portraits of themselves. For instance: Tell me about yourself. What are your favorite things? What are you interested in?

Classroom Environment

Avril Font's classroom is an example of an environment that puts the principles of student- and response-centered teaching into practice (see Figure 1.3, p. 24). We talked about the reading center earlier as a good place for getting comfortable during sharing, planning with a friend, or curling up with a good book. Around

Avril Font has created a print-rich environment in her classroom and reads aloud to her students as often as possible throughout the day.

the reading center are seven tables, formed by pushing four student desks together. Each of these tables can be a home base for four children working
together. Two large tables are designated work centers, providing materials and
space for group work in writing, science, and mathematics.

Two other qualities of Avril Font's classroom are important:

1. The classroom is a *print-rich environment*, full of children's literature—
   fiction and nonfiction, two daily newspapers, magazines, reference books,
   textbooks, and books and reports written by the children themselves. Some

Figure 1.3

Diagram of Avril
Font's Classroom

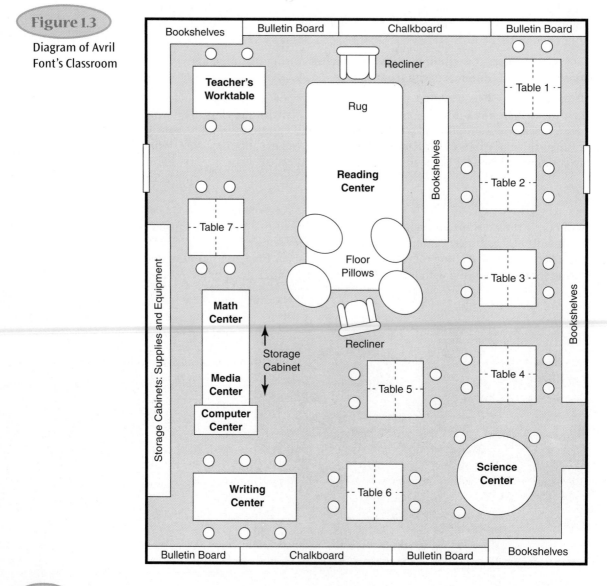

of these resources, plus many others, are available online or through various software programs. To create this kind of environment, your classroom should include a library, posters, bulletin boards, a computer with Internet access, labels, and displays of children's writing and art.

2. The classroom is organized into a variety of *centers*, or work areas that are movable and flexible. There are clear table surfaces for large art and construction projects, open floor spaces for movement and drama, tables and chairs that can be rearranged for discussion and group activities, and quiet corners for reading, talking, or planning. You should establish centers with materials for writing, art, media, and studying special topics and themes, research centers for looking into different subjects, and a computer center.

Scheduling and Grouping

Daily Schedule

Avril has developed a daily schedule that allows large blocks of time for individual and group work that emerges from students' ideas and interests:

9:00	Business (teacher) and journals, newspapers, books (students)
9:15	Sharing with the whole class
9:45	Planning the day
10:00	Recess
10:15	Group workshop
11:15	Sustained silent reading
11:45	Lunch
12:15	Read aloud
12:30	Group workshop
1:30	P.E.
2:00	Group workshop
3:00	Dismissal

Weekly Schedule

Avril Font's weekly class schedule, described in the Snapshot, is shown in Figure 1.4 on page 26.

Flexible Scheduling

The truth is, schedules always look better on paper than they work in reality. For the teacher who follows a student- and response-centered approach to teaching, it's easy to get off schedule when children are actively engaged in what they're doing and thus allowed to continue as long as they stay involved. The teacher may have to shift the schedule each day, carry over exciting activities to the next day, or even follow different schedules on different days. When I did Shakespeare with children, we needed at least a 1½-hour period to really rehearse. I scheduled rehearsals on alternating days, which increased the time spent on other days for other subjects. Many experiences like writing, drama, and art projects require

Figure 1.4 Schedule for a Week in Avril Font's Class

MONTH ____May____ WEEK ____2____ NAME _____

MONDAY	TUESDAY	WEDNESDAY	THURSDAY	FRIDAY
9:00 Student choice: Journals Newspapers Books	→ _____	(Benton's mother) → _____	→ _____	School assembly: D.A.R.E.
9:15 Sharing	→ _____	→ _____		→ _____
9:45 Planning	→ _____	→ _____	9:30 Guidance	9:45 Planning
10:00 Recess	(Talk to custodian about cardboard for dragon costume.)	(Arrange for other 4th grades to watch maypole dance.)	(Call to confirm newspaper coming.)	
10:15 Sustained Silent Reading	→ _____	→ _____	→ _____	→ _____
10:45 Group Workshops Writing conferences Math groups Minilesson: quotation marks for script-writing 11:45 Lunch	→ _____ Writing conferences Math groups Meet with Shakespeare group 11:30 French (Aquarium group— call pet shop.)	→ _____ Writing conferences Figure aquarium volume Book binding Math groups (Cut cardboard for dragon costumes.)	→ _____ Writing conferences Math groups Animal report presentations 11:30 French (Work on dragon costume.)	→ _____ Writing conferences Math groups Rehearse St. George play Maypole, Shakespeare groups work together → ( )
12:15 Read Aloud Wind in the Willows 12:30 Group Workshops Minilesson: Organizing information on animal posters 1:30 P.E. 2:00 Group Workshops Start animal posters Minilesson on budgets	→ _____ → _____ Writing conferences Aquarium budget Book binding Math groups → _____ (Practice → _____ Animal posters and reports Book binding	12:15 Library 12:45 → _____ Pet shop owner coming to talk to aquarium group Animal posters → _____ maypole dance → _____ Conference: Maypole group report Math groups	12:15 Read Aloud Wind in the Willows → _____ Minilesson: Prepare for interviews by newspaper on maypole dance → _____ all week) → _____ Minilesson: Mock interviews Math groups	→ _____ → _____ Rehearse St. George play Shakespeare group to library → Do maypole dance for other 4th grades Newspaper coming for pictures and interview Math groups

(After School) Pick up free aquarium.

larger chunks of time. You'll see the need to increase the flexibility of your schedule as your students grow in confidence and ability to take charge of their own learning experiences.

Grouping

In addition to organizing time, you must organize your students. You can do so in a variety of ways, usually in combination with one another:

- **Whole-Class Activities:** These can include sharing and planning; class discussions; initial experiences (e.g., talking about the hurricane headed your way); reading aloud by the teacher; talking about books; presenting new materials or identifying new topics or themes to investigate; getting organized to do so; and teaching initiating and demonstrating lessons. (We'll return to these types of lessons later in the chapter.)

- **Small-Group Activities:** Children work together in small groups on topics or themes of interest that are being pursued by the whole class (e.g., hurricanes) or that are of special interest just to them (e.g., Shakespeare or St. George and the dragon).

- **Individual Activities:** You should allow plenty of time for children to work alone, reading, writing, or pursuing topics of interest to them. Individual activities emerge from whole-class activities—for instance, one child writes a poem about hurricanes or studies an animal that interests him or her. Similarly, individual and group activities can be combined, such as finding out about Shakespeare's birthplace and sharing the information with another child in the group who found out about his education or one of his plays.

Literature, Resources, and Technology

Avril's room is full of books, media, paper, and art supplies, all of which are readily available to the children. But in her student- and response-centered classroom, the real raw materials for teaching language arts originate with the children themselves: their experiences, thoughts, impulses, and language. The following sections describe examples of materials you can use.

Children's Literature

Your main source of reading and reference material should be good children's books. Develop a class library to provide resources in addition to those found in the school library. Borrow materials from school and public libraries, go to garage sales, and ask parents to donate. Ask your school and public librarians for help in identifying books on special topics.

Students' Experiences

- *Shared Experiences:* Verbal, written, drawn, danced, or acted-out descriptions of objects, people, or events created in or out of class

TEACHER RESOURCES

Classic Texts on Children's Literature

Children's Literature in the Elementary School, 7th ed. (Huck, Hepler, Hickman, & Kiefer, 2000)
Through the Eyes of a Child: An Introduction to Children's Literature, 6th ed. (Norton, 2003)

www

Start with The Children's Literature Web Guide, an excellent, user-friendly, central site at **www.acs.ucalgary.ca/ ~dkbrown/index.html**.

- *Home Experiences:* Family, pets, sports, trips, movies, music, and things from home (books, pictures, awards, tapes, stories of experiences)
- *School Experiences:* Other classes (music, art, physical education), the library, assemblies, parties , fights on the schoolyard, and so on
- *Content Experiences:* Science experiments, social studies research, math applications, guest speakers, fieldtrips, and news items
- *Arts Experiences:* Art and music appreciation, creations, songs, dances, drama, and films
- *Organic Experiences:* Cooking and eating, growing things, animals and insects, and classroom nature collections
- *Cultural Experiences:* Traditions, holidays, events, celebrations, history, and social movements
- *Media Experiences:* Television, film, music, video, and computers
- *Your Experiences:* Share yourself with your students

Supplies

As you plan to stock your classroom, think about acquiring the following materials. Some will be provided by your school, but you'll have to come up with others by scrounging around and by getting parents involved:

> Variety of paper: lined, unlined, art, wrapping and contact paper, butcher paper, paper bags, chartpaper
> Stationery and envelopes
> Pencils and crayons
> Tools: rulers, scissors, staplers
> Chart racks
> Art materials for a variety of media
> Science supplies and equipment
> Cooking equipment and utensils
> Rhythm and other musical instruments
> Costumes and properties for drama
> Puppet-making materials and stage
> Dry-erase board and markers
> Flannel board and material

Reference Books and Resources

Although your library will have reference books and resources, you should include as many as you can in your classroom, such as these:

> Dictionaries
> Thesauruses
> Encyclopedias
> Atlases
> Internet access and other electronic resources on CD–ROM
> File boxes for pamphlets, magazine clippings, articles

EXCELLENT SOFTWARE

CD-ROM Encyclopedias

Encarta (Microsoft)
Interactive Encyclopedia (Compton)
Multimedia Encyclopedia (Grolier)
Multimedia Encyclopedia (World Book)

Technology

An assortment of the following technology and media is essential for use in child and teacher creations, as instructional materials, and for self-expression and enjoyment:

> Computer with word-processing software, printer, and CD–ROM
> Internet access
> Tape and CD players, blank tapes, earphones
> Overhead projector, blank transparencies, and pens to write on them
> Television and VCR, video camera, blank videotapes, videotapes

Integrated Teaching: "Ripple Effects" of Response-Themed Learning

At the beginning of the year, teachers can plan appropriate experiences and choose books and materials for the classroom based on their knowledge of how children learn language arts. In making these plans, teachers can use standards-based state and district curriculum guides and current and seasonal events as sources of curriculum content. Recall from earlier in the chapter that these are some of the sources that Avril Font uses, as well. This approach to curriculum planning has been called various names: *thematic units, theme cycles, language across the curriculum,* and *integrated* or *cross-curricular teaching.* Regardless of the name used, the approach involves beginning with an interesting focal point (such as "Our Community" or "Favorite Authors") or a question asked by the teacher or students (such as "What can we do to improve the environment?").

Throughout the schoolyear, teachers can continue to plan based on students' responses to those initial experiences. For instance, the teacher might observe children's delight in a special book or note an individual's interest in a topic or related prior experience. Given these observations, the teacher lets the children make choices about what they want to talk, read, and write about or even act out or research in the library. The students then collaborate with the teacher on what response-themed projects they will work on, how they will form groups to do so, and how they will share what they learn with others. Recall that Avril uses students' ideas and interests as a third source in planning curriculum content.

This kind of teaching results in what I call a *"ripple effect"* of learning themes that flow out of the initial experiences that teachers plan and the books and materials they choose. The focus of each ripple effect is an idea, experience, or subject that becomes a theme and opens up a wealth of instructional possibilities. Think about what happens when you throw a pebble into a pond or lake: It enters the water at a certain point and from there, creates an ever-widening circle of rings. In the classroom, these "rings" are the ongoing responses of the children: their spontaneous comments after you read aloud from a book, their sharing a similar experience they've had, their enthusiasm or questions about a new topic, and their ideas about how to learn more about it.

Several "pebbles" were tossed out in Avril Font's room on the day we read about in the Snapshot. For instance, Shakespeare became a hot topic for a group

EXCELLENT SOFTWARE
Student Writing Center

WWW

For reviews of educational software, go to Way Cool Software Reviews at **www.ucc.uconn. edu/~wwwpcse/wcool.html**.

For more on thematic teaching, see Chapter 14, Language across the Curriculum.

of children who read and wrote about him and published a book on his life. Another group who were interested in guppies researched how to build an aquarium, created one, and stocked it with fish, which they also studied. And the groups who were learning about "St. George and the Dragon" and the maypole dance connected these topics of English culture with what other children were learning about Shakespeare.

A great part of the joy of teaching is watching this ripple effect occur and thinking of how to enhance it—that is, to help children experience, explore, and discover new ideas and ways to use language and construct meaning. Once you begin, it's an adventure. You and your class can boldly go where no class has gone before! And this is when children reach and stretch and grow in their use and control of language as well as their understanding of themselves and the world.

Model and Example of a Ripple Effect

A ripple effect occurred in Avril's class at the beginning of the schoolyear that originated from a combination of a state curriculum requirement in social studies and questions that came up during sharing and planning one morning of the first week of school. Here's how it happened:

During morning sharing, it became apparent to Avril that many of the children in her class were not sure that Baton Rouge (the city they lived just outside of) was actually the capital of Louisiana. Avril noted this and saw a teachable moment, since fourth grade is the year for which most states suggest a study of the local community and state history in social studies. Here was a chance for Avril to begin group workshops and for children to use language across the curriculum.

She began by asking them what they already knew about their community and state. They used the following *KWL chart* (Ogle, 1989) to begin the ripple effect, listing the things they already knew (K), what they wanted to learn (W), and what they learned (L, to be filled in later):

KWL Chart: Our Community and State

K What we know:	W What we want to learn:	L What we learned:
• Football teams—Southern University and Louisiana State University • Mississippi River floods • Hurricanes happen • Crawfish and alligators • Cajun and Creole foods	• What happens in Baton Rouge, the capital of Louisiana? • What is Louisiana's history? • Can we make a big map of Louisiana? • How can we track a hurricane? • Can we make jambalaya?	

GREAT BOOKS FOR CHILDREN

Flood: Wrestling with the Mississippi (Lauber, 1996a)
Hurricanes: Earth's Mightiest Storms (Lauber, 1996b)

Next, the students formed groups around topics that interested them and discussed how they could find out about these things. Avril suggested many ways the children could learn about their community, all of which were rich in opportunities for oral language, literacy, and cross-curricular experiences. Avril did some modeling with initiating lessons (like using an alphabet book as a frame for making an ABC book about Louisiana) and demonstration lessons (like how to develop interview questions). (Again, we'll look at these types of lessons more closely in the next section.) But most of the students' work was done in small groups using a variety of children's literature, reference books, the newspaper, and their own writing—notes, memoirs, interview questions, and reports. See page 32 for a model of a Ripple Effect about "Our Community and State" that would work in any class using language arts across the curriculum.

Bridget, a child in Avril's class, wrote, illustrated, and bound *My Louisiana Book* as a part of this ripple effect after Avril modeled an initiating lesson on how to write about a subject using an ABC pattern. The cover of the book shows a large, red crab (part of Louisiana's seafood bounty), and the book itself consists of a page with a letter, sentence, and picture for each letter of the alphabet (see Figure 1.5). Here's the complete text:

My Louisiana Book
by Bridget

A is for the Acadian people.
B is for Baton Rouge, the capital city.
C is for Creole food.
D is for downtown Baton Rouge.
E is for Exxon, where my Daddy works.
F is for Louisiana flag.
G is for Governor.
H is for Henry Shreve, who founded the city of Shreveport.
I is for the Indian mounds, where they buried people
   above ground.
J is for privateer Jean Lafitte.
K is for King Cotton.
L is for the city of Lake Charles.
M is for the Mardi Gras parade.
N is for the city of New Orleans.
O is for the Old State Capital.
P is for pelican, the state bird.
Q is for quay, where we tie up our boats.
R is for the Mississippi River.
S is for the Louisiana State seal.
T is for old Beauregard Town.
U is for the Louisiana State University.
V is for vegetable soybeans.
W is for the War of 1812, when the Battle of New Orleans
   was fought.
X is for Xavier University in New Orleans.
Y is for yams.
Z is for Zydeco music and dancing.

Figure 1.5 Cover and One Page from Student's Book

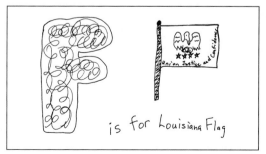

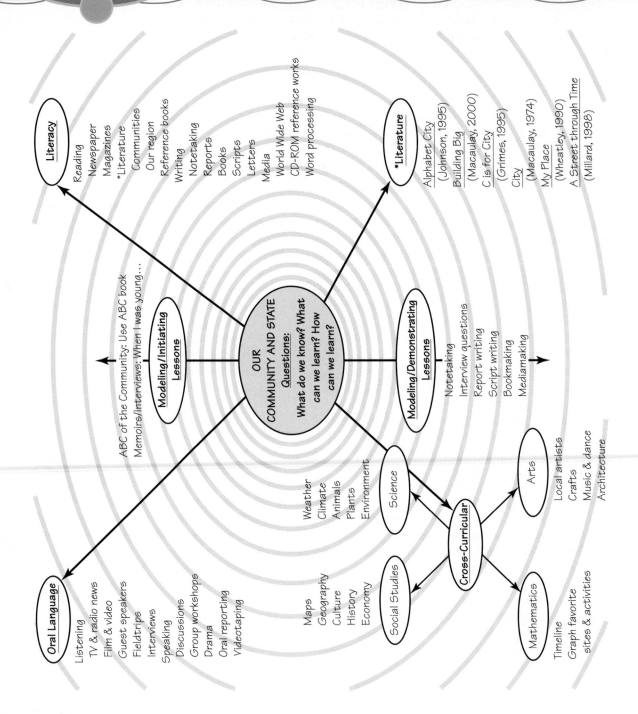

Literacy

Reading
Newspaper
Magazines
*Literature
Communities
Our region
Reference books
Writing
Notetaking
Reports
Books
Scripts
Letters
Media
World Wide Web
CD-ROM reference works
Word processing

OUR COMMUNITY AND STATE
Questions:
What do we know? What can we learn? How can we learn?

Modeling/Initiating Lessons

ABC of the Community: Use ABC book
Memoirs/Interviews: When I was young...

Modeling/Demonstrating Lessons

Notetaking
Interview questions
Report writing
Script writing
Bookmaking
Mediamaking

***Literature**

Alphabet City
(Johnson, 1995)
Building Big
(Macaulay, 2000)
C is for City
(Grimes, 1995)
City
(Macaulay, 1974)
My Place
(Wheatley, 1990)
A Street through Time
(Millard, 1998)

Oral Language

Listening
TV & radio news
Film & video
Guest speakers
Fieldtrips
Interviews
Speaking
Discussions
Group workshops
Drama
Oral reporting
Videotaping

Science

Weather
Climate
Animals
Plants
Environment

Social Studies

Maps
Geography
Culture
History
Economy

Cross-Curricular

Arts

Local artists
Crafts
Music & dance
Architecture

Mathematics

Timeline
Graph favorite sites & activities

Modeling with Initiating and Demonstrating Lessons

In a student- and response-centered classroom, much of what happens takes place in group workshops and depends on students' ideas, interests, and abilities. However, the teacher will model with *initiating lessons* to introduce a topic or type of literature and *demonstrating lessons* to teach students something they need to know to continue their work. Table 1.2 lists some examples of each type of lesson.

At the beginning of the year, the teacher should plan an initiating lesson about language and literacy experiences. The following Lesson Plan outlines such a lesson using an alphabet book. This book provides a source for reading and responding to literature as well as a frame for reporting on information learned across the curriculum on a topic like the community.

Example of Modeling with an Initiating Lesson

The alphabet books we have today are beautiful and exciting; they are definitely not "baby books." In fact, many are very sophisticated and appropriate for older students, including *The Z Was Zapped*, by Chris Van Allsburg (1987). This is a predictable book. Each right-hand page shows a large illustration of a letter having something done to it. Students can guess what's happening. The back of each page has a sentence about the letter: for instance, "The A was in an avalanche." What's nice about this book is that many interpretations are possible for each page.

TEACHER RESOURCES

For ideas on using alphabet books with middle-grade students, see Thompson (1992).

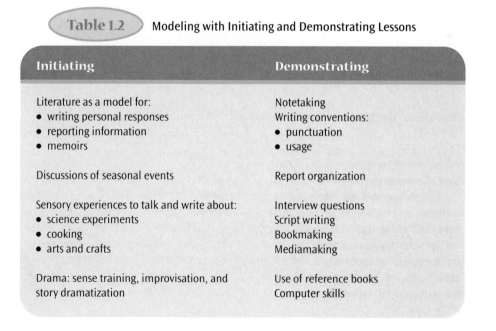

Table 1.2   Modeling with Initiating and Demonstrating Lessons

Initiating	Demonstrating
Literature as a model for: • writing personal responses • reporting information • memoirs	Notetaking Writing conventions: • punctuation • usage
Discussions of seasonal events	Report organization
Sensory experiences to talk and write about: • science experiments • cooking • arts and crafts	Interview questions Script writing Bookmaking Mediamaking
Drama: sense training, improvisation, and story dramatization	Use of reference books Computer skills

Reading and talking about an alphabet book like this one can lead to lively discussions about the objects and images presented for the letters. Children can talk about their favorite images or other images that start with certain letters of the alphabet, or they can reflect on what the book reminds them of. You could try this initiating lesson in your practice teaching or at the beginning of the schoolyear when you have your own class.

LESSON PLAN

Modeling with an Initiating Lesson Using an Alphabet Book

IRA/
NCTE

Topic: Reading and writing in response to *The Z Was Zapped,* by Chris Van Allsburg (1987)

Purposes: To listen to and enjoy literature through discussion and writing; to increase vocabulary; to understand and apply alliteration in writing.

Standard 3: Students apply a wide range of strategies to comprehend, interpret, evaluate, and appreciate texts. They draw on their prior experience, their interactions with other readers and writers, their knowledge of word meaning and of other texts, their word identification strategies, and their understanding of textual features (e.g., sound-letter correspondence, sentence structure, context, graphics).

Materials: *The Z Was Zapped*; paper; crayons; and pencils

Teaching Sequence:
1. Read *The Z Was Zapped* aloud. Ask children to predict what's happening to each letter. Encourage a variety of responses before you check to see what Van Allsburg wrote on the back of each page. Discuss *alliteration*, which is repeating the same letter or sound. (Note that the verb, or action word, in each sentence begins with the letter illustrated on that page.)
2. Discuss the book. Ask open-ended questions, which invite children to think about their own impressions while reading:
   "What did you think of the book?"
   "What was your favorite part?"
   "What things could happen to a letter?"
3. Record students' responses to the last question on chartpaper to create a "word wall" of their ideas. Pick one letter, or do several. Students could also do this activity in small groups after you demonstrate it with the whole class. Write this at the top of the chartpaper: "Word Wall for the Letter M."

The W was writting.

Figure 1.6 Student's Drawing and Writing in Response to *The Z Was Zapped*

4. Have each student pick a letter and draw and write something that's patterned after the book (see Figure 1.6). Encourage students to add alliterative sentences to their drawings and writings about certain letters. If they're interested, they could do more activities with alliteration, such as a storyboard. Younger students or language-minority students who are just learning to speak English could use the word wall for ideas. Or you could take dictation for them, writing their spoken words on their drawings.

Assessment:
1. Observe whether students listened to and enjoyed the book and were able to comprehend, interpret, evaluate, and appreciate the alliterative text pattern and relationship of text to illustrations.
2. Examine the "word wall" for evidence of children's increased vocabulary and understanding of new word meanings.
3. Note what individual students drew and wrote in response to the book and whether they were able to use an alliterative sentence structure. Figure 1.6 is an example of student drawing and writing in response to *The Z Was Zapped*.

Extending Activities:
1. Have students make a bulletin board with their work.
2. Bind the students' work into a class book, and place it in the class library.
3. Have the children dramatize the action for a certain letter by pantomiming it or creating a dialogue between two letters. Share this activity with the class.
4. Ask students to go to the library and find more books by Chris Van Allsburg:
    Jumanji (1981)
    The Polar Express (1985)
    The Sweetest Fig (1993)
    Bad Day at Riverbend (1995)
5. Have students go to the library and find more alphabet books that use alliteration:
    A, My Name Is Alice (Bayer, 1984)
    Allison's Zinnea (Lobel, 1990)
    Animalia (Base, 1986)
    Aster Aardvark's Alphabet Adventures (Kellogg, 1987)
    Away from Home (Lobel, 1994)
    Goodnight to Annie: An Alphabet Lullaby (Merriam, 1992)

GREAT BOOKS FOR CHILDREN

Alphabet Books

A, B, See! (Hoban, 1982)
Chicka Chicka Boom Boom (Martin & Archambault, 1989)
Eating the Alphabet (Ehlert, 1989)
Firefighters A to Z (Demarest, 2000)
Tomorrow's Alphabet (Shannon, 1996)

A nswers to Questions about Learning and Teaching Language Arts

● *What are the language arts?*

In simple terms, the language arts are listening, speaking, reading, writing, viewing, and visually representing. In broader terms, they include everything based on language, which is a system of communicating that offers countless possibilities for representation, expression, and thought. Oral language—listening and speaking in the classroom—includes activities such as sharing and planning; having conversations and conferences; reading aloud; dramatizing, singing, and storytelling; and media listening and viewing. Literacy activities focus on both reading and writing in the classroom. Reading activities involve the use of a variety of materials, from literature to environmental print. Writing activities address the conventions of written language—spelling, punctuation, grammar, and usage. Other literacy activities comprise handwriting, biliteracy, and word processing and computer literacy. Language arts provide a means to use language across the curriculum through integrated teaching.

● *How do children learn language arts?*

Learning is an active, constructive process that takes place when students are truly engaged in what they're doing and focused on the discovery of meaning. The constructivist learning theory of Jean Piaget explains that children learn by adding new experiences to old and constructing new understandings of themselves and the world. To use John Dewey's expression, they "learn by doing."

Learning is a social, interactive process that takes place when students work collaboratively with each other and the teacher. The social interactionist theory of Lev Vygotsky explains that children construct new knowledge by first interacting in context with adults, other children, and materials and tasks in the environment; then later, they internalize what they've learned. Teachers and more capable peers build "scaffolds," according to Jerome Bruner, to help learners construct new knowledge based on the foundation of what children already know.

In literature-based teaching, Louise Rosenblatt's transactional theory explains that reading and writing are two-way transactions between a reader and a text, during which meaning is created. Readers draw on prior experiences, and the stream of these images and ideas flows through their minds while reading. In response-centered teaching, the teacher initiates experiences with literature but also observes each student's personal response to a story.

● *How should we teach language arts?*

Children learn to use language by using it when they are surrounded by print and participate in rich and social interactive experiences with language that always focus on meaning. Curriculum content in this type of classroom comes from three sources: standards-based state and district curriculum guides; seasonal and special events through the year; and students' ideas and interests. Content is taught in "ripples" generated by response-themed learning, which emerge from topics of interest and student ideas. Lessons are used for initiating and demonstrating, but most of the time, the children are in a workshop atmosphere, in which they are in control of their own learning.

Looking Further

1. Start a journal. You might focus on your thoughts while reading this text, on experiences in your college class and elementary classrooms, or on your ideas and plans for your future as a teacher.

2. Make a list of the things you would take to your class to demonstrate to your students how to be Star of the Week. What would you tell them about yourself? Why?

3. Draw a floorplan of what you think your classroom might look like. Be sure to consider how you will create an environment for maximizing opportunities for student- and response-centered learning. Discuss your plan with others in your class, and compare yours to theirs.

4. Develop a lesson plan for using literature with a specific grade level. Use the initiating lesson example in this chapter as a model (see the Lesson Plan, pp. 34–35). Teach your lesson, if possible, and report to your class what happened.

Children's Books, Films, and Software

Base, G. (1986). *Animalia.* New York: Abrams.

Bayer, J. (1984). *A, my name is Alice.* New York: Dial.

Berger, M. (1999). *Chomp! A book about sharks.* New York: Scholastic.

Blume, J. (1972). *Tales of a fourth-grade nothing.* New York: Dutton.

Cerullo, M. (2000). *The truth about great white sharks.* New York: Holiday House.

Dahl, R. (1961). *James and the giant peach.* New York: Knopf.

Darling, M. K. (1997). *Komodo dragon on location.* New York: Lothrop, Lee & Shepard.

Demarest, C. L. (2002). *Firefighters A to Z.* New York: Simon & Schuster.

Donaldson, E., & Donaldson, G. (1979). *A book of days.* New York: A & W.

Dubowski, C. E. (1998). *Shark attack!* New York: DK.

Ehlert, L. (1989). *Eating the alphabet: Fruits and vegetables from A to Z.* San Diego: Harcourt Brace Jovanovich.

Grahame, K. (1980). *The wind in the willows* (M. Hague, Illus.). New York: Holt, Rinehart, & Winston.

Grimes, N. (1995). *C is for city.* New York: Lothrop, Lee & Shepard.

Hoban, T. (1982). *A, b, see!* New York: Greenwillow.

Johnson, S. (1995). *Alphabet city.* New York: Viking.

Kellogg, S. (1987). *Aster Aardvark's alphabet adventures.* New York: Morrow.

Lamb, C., & Lamb, M. (1957). *Tales from Shakespeare.* New York: Dutton.

Lauber, P. (1996a). *Flood: Wrestling with the Mississippi.* Washington, DC: National Geographic Society.

Lauber, P. (1996b). *Hurricanes: Earth's mightiest storms.* New York: Scholastic.

Lobel, A. (1990). *Allison's zinnia.* New York: Greenwillow.

Lobel, A. (1994). *Away from home.* New York: Greenwillow.

Lord, B. B. (1984). *In the year of the boar and Jackie Robinson.* New York: Harper & Row.

Macaulay, D. (1974). *City.* New York: Houghton Mifflin.

Macaulay, D. (2000). *Building big.* New York: Houghton Mifflin.

Martin, B., & Archambault, J. (1989). *Chicka chicka boom boom.* New York: Simon & Schuster.

Maynard, T. (1997). *Komodo dragons.* New York: Child's World.

Merriam, E. (1992). *Goodnight to Annie: An alphabet book.* New York: Hyperion.

Millard, A. (1998). *A street through time: A 12,000-year walk through history.* New York: DK.

Red balloon, The [Film]. (1956). Available from Macmillan Films, Inc.

Rowling, J. K. (1998). *Harry Potter and the sorcerer's stone.* New York: Scholastic.

Sarnoff, J., & Ruffius, R. (1977). *A great aquarium book: The putting it together guide for beginners.* New York: Charles Scribner's.

Shannon G. (1996). *Tomorrow's alphabet.* New York: Greenwillow.

Simon, S. (1977). *What do you know about guppies?* New York: Four Winds Press.

Simon, S. (1995). *Sharks.* New York: HarperCollins.

Soto, G. (1990). *Baseball in April.* San Diego: Harcourt Brace Jovanovich.

Spenser, E. (1984). *St. George and the dragon* (Retold M. Hodges; T. S. Hyman, Illus.). New York: Little, Brown.

Student writing center [Computer software]. Available from The Learning Company.

Timeliner [Computer software]. Available from Tom Snyder Productions.

Van Allsburg, C. (1981). *Jumanji.* New York: Houghton Mifflin.

Van Allsburg, C. (1985). *The polar express.* New York: Houghton Mifflin.

Van Allsburg, C. (1987). *The Z was zapped.* New York: Houghton Mifflin.

Van Allsburg, C. (1993). *The sweetest fig.* Boston: Houghton Mifflin.

Van Allsburg, C. (1995). *Bad day at Riverbend.* Boston: Houghton Mifflin.

Wheatley, N. (1990). *My place.* Australia in Print.

White, E. B. (1952). *Charlotte's web.* New York: Harper & Row.

Whiteley, S. (2000). *Chase's calendar of events.* Chicago: Contemporary Press.

Williams, V. B. (1981). *Three days on a river in a red canoe.* New York: Greenwillow.

Assessing Language Arts

chapter 2

Questions about Assessing Language Arts

- *What do we mean by* assessing language arts *in schools today?*
- *How should we assess language arts?*
- *How should we teach and assess students with disabilities and other special needs?*

REFLECTIVE RESPONSE

What comes to mind when you hear the terms *standardized tests, authentic assessment,* and *students with disabilities and other special needs*? Jot down your ideas and any personal experiences you have had related to these terms, and think about them as you read this chapter.

Guidelines for Assessment

Assessing language arts means collecting, analyzing, summarizing, and interpreting information about students to appraise their performance and achievement. Teachers use multiple forms of ongoing, authentic assessment daily to plan further instruction to meet each child's needs. Assessment that aligns with the social constructivist theory of learning, described in Chapter 1, focuses on meaningful language and literacy experiences. Such assessment follows these guidelines (adapted from Herman, Aschbacher, & Winters, 1992):

- *Learning is a process of personal construction of meaning.*
  Discuss new ideas and relate them to personal experience and prior knowledge.
  Encourage divergent thinking; there is no one right answer.
  Provide multiple modes of expression: role-playing, simulations, debates, explanations to others, and so on.
  Emphasize critical thinking: analyze, compare, generalize, predict, and hypothesize.

- *Learning isn't a linear progression of acquiring separate skills.*
  Focus on problem solving.
  Don't make learning contingent on mastering routine, basic skills.

- *Learning varies according to student diversity.*
  Provide choices in tasks (not all reading and writing).
  Provide time to think, revise, and rethink.
  Include concrete experiences and link them to personal experiences.

- *Learning is affected by motivation, effort, and self-esteem.*
  Motivate students with meaningful tasks that are related to personal experiences.
  Encourage students to see the connection between effort and results.
  Have students self-evaluate: that is, to think about how they learn, why they like certain work, and how to set new goals.

- *Learning is social; group work is valuable.*
  Provide group work, and use heterogeneous groups.
  Encourage students to take on a variety of roles.
  Consider group products and processes.

You are probably familiar with the current national debate about so-called high-stakes testing in U.S. schools (Barksdale-Ladd & Thomas, 2000; Moses, 2001). The No Child Left Behind Act, which became federal law in January 2002, requires all states to design and administer standardized reading and math tests for children in grades 3 through 8 by the 2005–2006 schoolyear. Fifteen states already do this; this will be the first time, however, that such testing is a national mandate. The "high stakes" involved are that standardized test results may be used to determine school funding or to make changes in school programs and faculty. But also at stake is whether schools will be guided more by a practice known as "teaching to the test" than by knowledge of how children learn in the development of curriculum and programs, in text adoption, and in teacher professional development.

Standardized Testing versus Authentic Assessment

Standardized tests are based on a *behaviorist* model, which describes learning as a set of subskills that can be separated, taught, mastered, and tested. Multiple-choice tests reflect this model of learning. They can pinpoint what skill a student has difficulty with and make a reliable comparison of his or her ability with that of other students. But these types of tests cannot explain what went wrong in the learning process. Moreover, they are not aligned with or instructionally sensitive to state, district, or school standards and curriculum and therefore do not provide information on whether the goals of standards-based programs have been met (Elmore & Rothman, 1999; Tierney, Johnston, Moore, & Valencia, 2000).

This has been particularly true in lower-performing schools, where more time has reportedly been spent on test preparation, than in higher-performing schools. (This is ironic, given that spending time on meaningful instruction may be more critical in lower-performing schools, which may also have specific goals and standards for progress that require more time to meet [Hoffman, Assaf, Pennington, & Paris, 2001].) There is an inherent conflict for teachers who strive to create the conditions that promote children's development and proficiency in language and literacy (such as think for themselves, take risks, be creative, pursue their interests, and think convergently) yet are expected to encourage divergent thinking during test preparation.

The International Reading Association (IRA, 1999) has issued this position statement on high-stakes assessment and literacy:

TEACHER RESOURCES

See *Assessing Student Performance* (Myers & Spalding, 1997) for ways to link standards-based teaching and assessment.

> *The International Reading Association strongly opposes high-stakes testing. Alarmingly, U.S. policy makers and educators are increasingly relying on single test scores to make important decisions about students. For example, if a student receives a high score on one high-stakes test, it could place him in an honors class or a gifted program. On the other hand, if a student receives a low score on one test, she could be rejected by a particular college. These tests can also be used to influence teachers' salaries, or rate a school district in comparison with others.*
>
> *The Association believes that important conceptual, practical, and ethical issues must be considered by those who are responsible for designing and implementing test programs. Assessment should be used to improve instruction and benefit students rather than compare and pigenhole them. (p. 2)*

Based on this position statement, the IRA (1999) makes the following recommendations to teachers about assessing language and literacy:

WWW

Go to **www.reading.org** for the IRA's complete position statement.

Teachers should:
- *Construct rigorous classroom assessments to help outside observers gain confidence in teacher techniques*
- *Educate parents, community members, and policy makers about classroom-based assessment*
- *Teach students how tests are structured, but not teach to the test*

Parents and child-advocacy groups should:

- *Ask questions about what tests are doing to their children and their schools*
- *Lobby for the development of classroom-based forms of assessment that improve instruction and help children become better readers and learners*

Policy makers should:

- *Design assessment plans that reflect the complexity of reading, learning to read, and teaching reading*
- *Rely on multiple measures of assessment for decision making*
- *Avoid using incentives, resources, money, or recognition of text scores to reward or punish schools or teachers.* (p. 7)

The dilemma is that while there is no single view of assessment today (Serafini, 2000; Tierney, 1998), high-stakes, federally mandated standardized tests are now required in all states. Moreover, all teachers will be expected to prepare students for them (Lawrence, 2002), even though they are not the kind of meaningful and useful assessment that enables teachers to determine children's achievement and, more importantly, to plan instruction to meet individual children's specific needs. Language arts and literacy assessment should be a blueprint for planning language arts and literacy instruction.

Language arts educators have come to believe that learning is a holistic process of the social construction of meaning. Students are actively engaged in authentic listening, speaking, reading, and writing experiences across the curriculum in the context of the classroom. This model of learning is reflected in *authentic assessment*, which is continuous, embedded in classroom contexts, and includes information from logs and journals, anecdotal records and observations, checklists and records, inventories and tests, rubrics, self-assessment and peer assessment, portfolios and work samples, and planning and progress forms (Calfee, 1999–2000; Cambourne & Turbill, 1990; Johnston, 1992; Leslie & Jett-Simpson, 1997; Paris, 1992; Roderick, 1991). Authentic assessment situates a student's development over time in the classroom and includes student reflection and collaboration between teacher and student (McMillan, 1997). In addition, it relies on information gathered by students and teachers during regular classroom activities, rather than on the results of paper-and-pencil tests.

The following list compares the principles of standardized testing with those of authentic assessment:

Standardized Testing

- Information is gathered with paper-and-pencil tests.
- Tests are given only periodically.
- One test, given at a single point in time, determines evaluation.
- Specific problems can be identified but not in context.
- Subskills are the focus, rather than process.
- Forms include multiple-choice, true/false, matching, and short-answer questions.
- Teachers make no decisions about which tests are used.
- Attempts to "teach to the test" may not support learning.
- Testing disrupts the classroom schedule.

Authentic Assessment

- Information is gathered by teachers and students.
- Ongoing, daily observations are made.
- Multiple sources of information are used.
- Information is considered in the context of process.
- Artifacts (writing, art, journals, tapes) and rich descriptions (anecdotal records, checklists) are used.
- Teachers and students make decisions about assessment.
- Information is gathered as part of the classroom schedule.

Authentic assessment allows students to demonstrate their understanding of language and literacy processes in several ways, and teachers can use these means to support, guide, and monitor students' learning and to plan for instruction (Cairney, 2000; Cambourne, 1995). The following Snapshot will show you how a teacher can do this from the first day of school in first grade.

SNAPSHOT Draft Books in Avril Font's First-Grade Class

In Chapter 1, you read a Snapshot called A Day in Avril Font's Fourth-Grade Class, which was about her teaching in Scotlandville, Louisiana. In this chapter, you will read about her first-grade class at the Louisiana State University (LSU) Laboratory School. This class has 26 students, among them 2 African Americans, 2 Asian Americans (1 Taiwanese Chinese American and 1 Korean American), and 3 Hispanic Americans (or Latinos), whose home language is Spanish.

Avril was named Louisiana Elementary Teacher of the Year in 2002–2003. She has many student observers in her classroom every day from LSU and a student teacher every semester. Avril also teaches a language arts methods course at LSU, in which she uses this text. She served as the Director of Reading in the Louisiana State Department of Education and has consulted widely for publishers, schools, and districts across the country as well as in other countries.

A first-grader's portrait of teacher Avril Font.

Avril uses multiple forms of ongoing, authentic assessment in her first-grade class so as to gather the information she needs to plan instruction to meet each child's needs. Her students still share every day and make choices about what to write about, and they publish prolifically. See how Avril uses *draft books* and conferences both to assess and teach writing from the first day of school in first grade.

See Avril model the writing process on the first day of school.

IRA/
NCTE
Standard 12

August 8

Avril models the writing process for her young students on the first day of school. She shows how to plan using pictures; how to create a title; and how to write a beginning, middle, and end. She also emphasizes that a piece of writing has to be *perfect* to be published. She believes her students are authors, and so she looks for *voice* in writing. That is her first standard.

Avril's students also start to write in draft books on the first day of school. These are bound composition books, so students have a continuous record of their writing and no papers are lost. For example, in his draft book, Alex writes his name and the date, August 8, on the first page. He draws a picture as his plan for writing, which he has seen Avril model, and then he writes several sentences. When Alex conferences with Avril later, she asks him about his plan, represented by the picture. They talk about what he has written, and she praises him.

Avril is able to both assess and teach writing through editing Alex's draft with him. They focus on the following areas:

- Upper- and lowercase letters: *WAS* versus *was* and *Bed* versus *bed*
- Spelling: *I HF TO TIUE HI AOUT* = *I have to take him out*

Avril created this chart to illustrate the writing process for her students.

12-2-2002   December 2, 2002

24 Hours With Gwenllian Margaret
December 3 2002
Sedley called me and asked
me to babysit for them on Friday
night I was excited. I was to have
Gwen for 24 hours They came at

Avril praises Alex again for writing a whole page, draws a heart and a happy face on his paper, and puts a "1." at the bottom to show that it is the first page. She also tells him to keep writing.

Avril has formed an initial assessment of Alex's writing:

- Uses drawing as a prewriting plan.
- Draws on his own experience for ideas to write about.
- Takes risks—not afraid to get his ideas down on paper or to try to write a word he doesn't know how to spell (such as *mnetng* for *morning*), a prerequisite for developing as both a speller and a writer.
- Knows that he needs to attend to the sounds of a word to write it.
- Based on this writing sample, he is approximately in the semiphonetic stage of developmental spelling, meaning that he has written letters for some of the sounds of words he has used.
- Needs more experience and help with using upper- and lowercase letters conventionally.
- Writes enthusiastically!

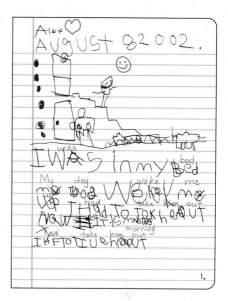

See Chapter 4, Emergent Literacy and Biliteracy, and Chapter 10, Spelling, for how to determine a child's stage of developmental spelling.

To help Alex become a competent, confident writer, Avril plans to do the following:

- Model writing daily for the whole class, including how to do the things that Alex needs.
- Plan time daily for writing in draft books.
- Conference with him several times a week to monitor his progress in his draft book.
- Begin a spelling journal—words he has used in his writing alphabetized under the correct letter, with a page for each letter (such as *morning*).
- Begin to publish his own books.
- Have him do peer editing with a fellow student.
- Read daily. (Avril will read aloud, and Alex will read his own books when he begins publishing, independent reading, and reading at home.)

September 1

Alex has been writing in his draft book and conferencing with Avril. On September 1, he writes a draft that Avril suggests would be a good book for him to publish. She helps him edit his spelling and sentence structure and writes a number in a circle next to the sentence or sentences that will be on each page of the book. For example, you can see number 1 circled in front of "I like to go to school" and number 2 circled in front of "It is cool."

Alex and a fellow classmate help edit one another's writing.

Comparing the pages from September 1 and August 8, Avril can assess Alex's progress in writing. This new draft is longer—two pages. Alex has more control over forming his letters (using upper- and lowercase letters) and forming sentences. He is still taking risks by writing words he is not sure how to spell and is still approximately in the semiphonetic developmental stage of spelling, but he is using some difficult words (*beks* for *because, owr* for *hour, kfrbool* for *comfortable*).

Avril teaches Alex writing with his draft, as well. She edits it with him and directs him to add several new words to his spelling journal. He copies the corrected draft into a blank book with a sentence on each page and then illustrates it. He reads his book aloud to the whole class and learns how good it feels to be a good writer. Avril has been able to both assess and monitor his progress and teach him to write through the use of draft books.

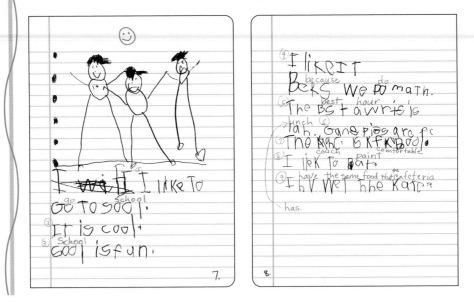

October 10

Alex writes another draft that he publishes into a book after revising and editing in a conference with Avril. She can see that he continues to improve his use of letters. His spelling is more phonetic, such that all the sounds in many words are represented (for instance, *woelers* for *wheelers*, *wend* for *wind*, and *mesttrjfskpe* for *Mr. Jeff's camp*). She shows him how to write an abbreviated title and name (*Mr. Jeff's*) and how to use a possessive apostrophe. She is especially pleased with Alex's strong voice in this draft and this excellent description: "I like the wind in my face. It feels good." Again, Alex publishes his book and reads it to the class.

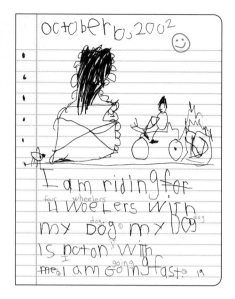

See Avril conference with Alex and share one of his books with the class.

November 15

Alex writes a draft that Avril thinks is excellent. He has filled four pages of his draft book. His first published book from September 1 had nine pages with a sentence on each page. This book has several sentences on each page and is thirteen pages long.

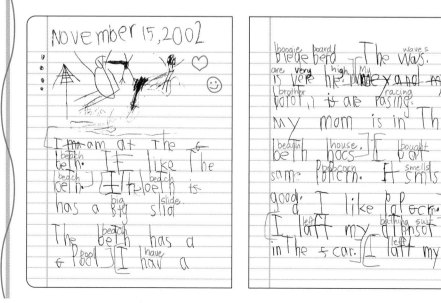

[Student writing sample — left notebook page:]

book in the he cr. [I did not my leave live my toell towell in the car.] [The The The beach is a good place to it. it had sand. on the way back me and my brother and I got in a fight. my sister did not.] [A My

[Student writing sample — right notebook page:]

mom had a fit. [my dad said shhhhh hhhh h.] [We got something samthing to eat. toe it.] [We had a good time.] bed bed

Avril likes the way Alex has used excellent descriptive language: "I bought some popcorn. It smells good. I like popcorn." She believes he has a very strong voice as a writer and is able to draw readers into the story, helping them feel and even smell what is happening. The story also has humor ("I left my bathing suit in the car. I left my book in the car. I did not leave my towel in the car.") and drama ("On the way back me and my brother got in a fight. My sister did not. My mom had a fit."). While he still needs careful editing for conventions, he is becoming a better writer through use of descriptive details.

Avril can assess that Alex has improved in fluency in writing, development of ideas, control of letters, and spelling. He is now between the phonetic stage (because he has a symbol for every sound he hears) and the transitional stage (because he now has a vowel in every syllable). The next stage will be conventional spelling. Alex has also learned to use dialogue complete with quotation marks: "My dad said, 'Shhhhhhhhhhhh'" (after Mom had a fit at the fight).

Because several of Alex's pages have more than one sentence on them in this book, Avril puts brackets around the sentences that should go on one page. She writes each set of sentences on a page in a blank booklet. Alex then illustrates each page and adds text in his own writing, like "YES NO YES NO" on

On the way back my brother and I got in a fight. My sister did not.

the page where it says he and his brother got into a fight and "SHHH" on the page where it says his dad says "Shhhhh." Finally, he creates a cover for the book, which he has titled *At the Beach.*

You can use an assessment tool called a *writing log* along with the draft books to assess, monitor progress, and plan for a child's writing. Assessment Toolbox 2.1 (p. 50) shows such a log filled in with assessment data from Alex's draft book, his conferences with Avril, and his published books from the preceding examples.

Assessment Tools

Avril Font uses draft books to assess and teach writing in her first-grade class. As a very experienced teacher, Avril now uses the draft books as her primary means of assessing and teaching each child; she does not use another form of record-keeping, either. However, as a preservice teacher doing field experiences or a beginning teacher developing your own system of assessment, you might want to use a recordkeeping tool based on activities like writing in draft books.

Assessment Toolbox 2.1, the Writing Log, is an example of a form on which to record assessment information about a child's progress in writing and in editing, illustrating, and publishing pieces of writing from his or her draft book. The log shows at a glance how a child is progressing in several areas over time and allows space for including appropriate standards and plans for further instruction. While all children need to learn to plan and organize their writing, to use descriptive language, to develop a strong written voice, and to master the conventions of English, each child will be different in terms of abilities. In addition, each will pick different topics to write about based on his or her own life or reading experiences. Teachers will assess children's strengths and needs using activities like writing in draft books and assessment tools like the writing log in order to monitor their progress and plan appropriate instruction to guide them in their language and literacy development.

Other types of assessment tools are described in the following sections, and some are illustrated with Assessment Toolboxes. See the marginal notes for other examples of Toolboxes and where they can be found in subsequent chapters of the text. The Toolboxes include formal and informal assessment tools that are related to the aspect of learning and teaching language arts discussed in that chapter. Each is something you can put to immediate use in your field experiences in elementary classrooms.

IRA/
NCTE

The standards shown in Assessment Toolbox 2.1 are the IRA/NCTE national standards, shown inside the front cover of this book.

ASSESSMENT TOOLBOX

2.1 Writing Log

This log has been filled in with assessment data about Alex's writing. You can modify the categories to address different grade levels, standards, and conventions for your own use with children in the classroom.

Writing Log

Name: Alex   Grade: 1   Starting Date: August 8

Date	Standard(s)	Genre/Title	Strengths	Conventions	Plans
Aug. 4	12	Draft book—First entry/dogs	Wrote name, date Drew plan Five sentences Uses experience Enthusiastic	Needs help distinguishing upper- and lowercase letters Spelling—semiphonetic stage of development; letters for some of the sounds (I hf to tiue hi out) and takes risks with unknown words (mnetng = morning)	Work on letters Start spelling journal Continue drawing a plan and writing
Sept. 1	12	Draft book—About liking school Published book—I Love School	Drew plan Nine sentences Improved upper-/lowercase letters and sentence structure Good voice	Spelling—still in semiphonetic stage but trying some difficult words— Sool = school beks = because owr = hour kaohc = couch kfrbook = comfortable pat = paint kafe = cafeteria	Spelling journal—add several new words Edit draft, add page numbers, illustrate and publish book: I Love School
Oct. 10	4 & 12	Draft book—Four wheelers Published book—Riding Four Wheelers	Date Drew plan Nine sentences More complex sentence structure Excellent voice—"wind in my face"	Spelling—more phonetic, all sounds represented— Woelers = wheelers Wend = wind Mesttrjfskpe = Mr. Jeff's camp Use of title for "mister" and possessive apostrophe	Spelling journal—add words Edit, illustrate, publish book: Riding Four Wheelers Read to class
Nov. 15	5 & 12	Draft book—Trip to beach Published book—At the Beach	Date Drew plan Twenty-two sentences Revised sentence structure Good descriptive language—"waves are very high" and "popcorn smells good" Excellent voice, humor, drama—"Mom had a fit"	Spelling—improved to phonetic stage; letter for every sound he hears with some transitional stage spellings; vowel in every syllable— Beige berd = boogie board Rasing = racing Bot = bought Use of quotation marks Added conclusion to a story	Spelling journal—add words Continue to use quotation marks Always write a conclusion Edit, illustrate, publish book: At the Beach Read to class

Logs and Journals

Writing Log (p. 50)

2.1

Assessment Toolbox 2.1, the Writing Log, is an example of how a teacher may use a log to record information from an observation or a conference, noting what a child is doing, adding some form of analysis, and planning next steps for instruction. Students can also use *reading logs* to record the books they have read and *double-entry journals* to respond to literature. Assessment Toolbox 2.2 shows the double-entry journal format, in which students note things that interest them

ASSESSMENT
TOOLBOX

2.2 Double-Entry Literature Journal

According to the transactional perspective, reading assessment should involve multiple measures that focus on students' responses to literature. Using a Double-Entry Literature Journal allows students to note topics or points of interest from their reading on the left-hand side and their interpretations of these topics on the right-hand side.

Name _____   Date _____

Book Title _____

Double-Entry Literature Journal

Page	Notes from Story	My Comments, Ideas, & Feelings

CW

Hear Paul Boyd-Batstone explain his method of ARA. Also see his article (2004) about using ARA.

while reading on the left-hand side of the page and note their interpretations on the right-hand side. Students can then bring these logs or journals to conferences with the teacher about their reading, and the teacher can keep anecdotal records of the conferences. Students can keep learning logs in other subjects, as well. In *dialogue journals,* the teacher, aide, or another child writes in response to the student's daily journal entry.

Anecdotal Records and Observations

In an *anecdotal record,* teachers make notes based on classroom observations or during conferences. These notes usually include not only what the students did but how the teacher interprets what they did. Anecdotal records can become the basis for further individualized instruction. They may be kept in notebooks with running entries, in computer files, on stick-on notes, or using sticky labels.

Checklists and Records

Teachers can create *checklists* and *records* to document a wide range of developing language and literacy behaviors or for specific activities and projects. For example, a writing checklist could be used to check a child's writing status (where he or she is in the writing process), and a revising and editing checklist could be used before a child publishes a piece of writing. For literature, a checklist could be used to determine how well a child is able to retell a story or what he or she learned from an informational text. A checklist can also be used to assess a child's level of understanding of information and library skills at several different grade levels.

Inventories and Tests

Inventories and *tests* have been developed most often by teacher educators and researchers for use as assessment tools in the classroom. You may see different variations of each test used across a school district or within an individual school. These assessment devices apply primarily to a child's level of development and progress in reading and spelling.

Rubrics

Rubrics can be created by teachers, students, or both together (Au, 2000; Skillings & Ferrell, 2000). They are scoring guides that list a range of writing features and describe a range of writing quality for each feature. A rubric can be *holistic* (a general list of writing features), *analytic* (a more detailed description of writing features), or *primary trait* (emphasizing a particular type of writing).

For example, for assessing a memoir like that of Benton, one of Avril Font's fourth-grade students (see Figure 2.1, pp. 54–55), the students and teacher could collaborate on creating a Writing Rubric, as shown in Assessment Toolbox 2.3.

2.3 Writing Rubric

This Writing Rubric can be used by teachers, students, or both if each individual uses a different colored pen or symbol to mark his or her ratings. After you have completed your assessment of Benton's book, compare your comments to mine (see p. 56).

Name _____ Date _____

Title _____

Writing Rubric

Criteria	Exceeds Expectations 4	Excellent 3	Satisfactory 2	Needs Improvement 1
•				
•				
•				
•				
•				
•				
•				
•				

Comments:

Strengths of Piece	Things to Work On
Writer	
Teacher	

Benton's memoir could also be assessed using a developmental continuum of general writing abilities generated from samples (or so-called *anchor papers*) of a group of students in the fourth grade. Schools and districts often develop such grade-level continuums for teachers to use throughout the year. Creating this

Figure 2.1   Student's Memoir, Published as a Book

SCAFFOLDING

Here are five strategies Avril Font recommends for students like Benton:

- Have them read aloud every day (both picture books and novels).
- Make sure they read at home (parent signature verifies).
- Have parent volunteers give oral book reports.
- Immerse them in language and literature.
- Respect them and what they can do.

Benton was repeating the fourth grade because he had been considered a nonreader and nonwriter, as well as immature and a behavior problem, in the third grade. Through Avril's teaching and with the strong support of his single mother, Benton was emerging as a reader and writer.

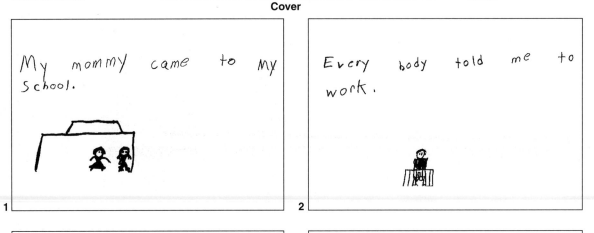

Cover

rubric can serve as both a prewriting activity, as the class discusses the memoir genre, and as an assessment tool for reviewing drafts and published pieces.

Teachers and students can co-create and use rubrics by following these three steps:

1. To introduce a type of genre writing, such as a memoir, the teacher can read several such pieces aloud, invite the children to respond, encourage independent reading of memoirs, and ask: What's important in a memoir? From this discussion, the students and teacher can generate a list of important features, such as these:

    Tells about a memorable event from his or her own experience

    Chooses a title that hooks the reader

    Writes about the event in an interesting, exciting or humorous, or surprising way

    Describes the event clearly

    Uses good description and details

A rubric can also address important writing conventions:

Uses complete sentences

Uses correct spelling

Uses correct punctuation

2. Create a form that lists the relevant criteria and provides an easy-to-use rating system for each feature (see Assessment Toolbox 2.2, p. 51). Make copies of the form. Space should also be provided for comments.

3. Students, teachers, or both can fill out the same form using different colored pens or symbols to rate each feature.

Take a minute now and quickly assess Benton's book using the criteria in step 1. Also make some comments. I have already done so (see below). When you are finished, compare your assessment to mine or to those of other students in your class.

Carole's Comments about Benton's Memoir

I love Benton's piece. On the five important features of memoirs listed, I'd give it 4's except on "Uses good description and details." I would give it a 3 on this one. I like the part about "doing my work and being quiet" but feel he could have added some visual imagery. I would also give it a 5 on "Writes about the event in a humorous way." Benton is a natural master of the brief memoir in the tradition of great humorists like Bill Cosby and Mark Twain. He tells you just enough, briefly, so that almost everyone listening or reading can connect it with their own experience in some way and be moved. I wish I'd written this myself. On writing conventions, I would give Benton a 2 for complete sentences (page 8 lacks a capital letter and the first *I* should be deleted), a 3 for spelling (on page 2 *every body* should be one word), and a 2 for punctuation (page 6 lacks a period).

Strengths of the piece are that Benton immediately engages the reader with his intriguing title, *The Lie That Mrs. Font Told My Mommy,* that he creates a suspenseful tone, and that he builds up to an unexpected ending with a real kick. Benton needs to work on being more careful about editing. But for a student who was classified as a nonreader and nonwriter the year before, Benton has emerged into a writer with a talent for creating a clear and vivid snapshot of a memorable event and for using tongue-in-cheek humor quite successfully.

Self-Assessment and Peer Assessment

Some assessment tools require students to take responsibility for their own activities and learning and also to work collaboratively and cooperatively with others. For example, students can self-assess their own projects to evaluate comprehensive skills and knowledge, cross-curricular understanding, and initiative and

ASSESSMENT TOOLBOX

2.4 Self-Assessment Form for Individual Work

Having each student assess his or her own contribution to group work is an example of authentic, contextualized assessment. This approach is rooted in the principles of constructivism.

Name _____ Date _____

Topic and Project _____

Self-Assessment of Individual Work

Directions: For your project, answer these three questions:

1. What was your project?

2. What was the best part of your project and why?

3. How could you improve your project?

Source: Adapted from Cox & Boyd-Batstone, 1997.

creativity. Assessment Toolbox 2.4, Self-Assessment Form for Individual Work, can be used to guide students' self-assessment.

Students can also demonstrate what they have learned by working in groups. A group project may be created by all the students, or each student may create part of a project in cooperation with others. Either way, students can assess each other's work. Assessment Toolbox 2.5, Peer-Assessment Form for Group Work (p. 58), can be used for this purpose.

Students can use either Toolbox to assess oral presentations such as sharing, interviews, storytelling, drama, puppets, and oral reports. And for writing, they can use these forms to self and peer edit. In self-assessment and peer assessment, students take control and responsibility for their own learning.

5.1 Peer Evaluation of Listening and Talking (p. 187)

9.4 PeerEditing Form (p. 313)

9.5 Self-Editing Checklist (p. 316)

12.1 Student's Media Critique Form (p. 404)

12.2 Drama Self-Assessment Form (p. 431)

ASSESSMENT TOOLBOX

2.5 Peer-Assessment Form for Group Work

Having students assess their peers' contributions to group work is an example of authentic, interactive assessment. This approach is rooted in social interactionist principles.

Name _____ Date _____

Peer Assessment of Group Work

Directions: For each member of your group, answer these two questions:
    A. What did you learn?
    B. What would you have done differently if you were that person?

Name _____
A.

B.

Name _____
A.

B.

Name _____
A.

B.

Source: Adapted from Cox & Boyd-Batstone, 1997.

CW

Go to the accompanying website for this text for examples of complete portfolios.

For more on writing portfolios, see Chapter 9, The Writing Process.

Portfolios and Work Samples.

Portfolios represent individual students' performances. They comprise samples of student work that are collected systematically over time. Those samples might include specific projects, such as a self-published book or drawing, or the samples might represent a skill that has developed over time. For example, the following work samples could be collected at the beginning, middle, and end of the kindergarten year: students write their name, write the numbers from 1 to 10, and draw a picture of themselves.

    Portfolios can take many different forms, and it is often the teacher's responsibility to plan what will be collected and when. This should be decided in collaboration with students and parents, as the teacher's dialogues, conferences, and reflections with them are integral to the process (Calfee, 1999–2000; Courtney & Abodeeh, 1999). It is key that students be engaged in this process and in self-reflection. They should ask themselves not only What am I doing? but Why am I doing it? How well did I do it? and Where will I go from here? The portfolio is a kind of emerging map of literacy learning and instruction. The student is making and following the map at the same time.

Portfolios can do any or all of the following: paint a portrait of a child, offer a history of a child's progress over the year, or engage a child in goal setting and self-reflection, among other things. Whatever the focus or design, a portfolio should be a means to conduct authentic, ongoing, meaningful assessment so as to document a child's growth and progress and plan for further instruction.

What kind of work samples should be included in a language arts portfolio? Here is a list of possibilities with examples, some of which you will recognize as the same assessment tools described earlier in this chapter:

- *Logs and journals:* Reading and writing logs, double-entry literature journal
- *Anecdotal records:* Conference notes and group-planning records
- *Checklists and records:* Writing status checklists and story and informational text retellings
- *Inventories and tests:* A writing sample analysis or developmental spelling inventory
- *Rubrics:* Teacher-created or student- and teacher-created for writing, such as a memoir
- *Self- and peer assessment:* Reflections on individual and group projects
- *Planning and progress forms:* Literature circles and similar activities
- *Writing drafts:* The draft books that Avril Font uses in her first-grade class
- Art projects with notes
- Projects from thematic units, either in literature or the content areas (or both)
- Media and videotaped drama productions with notes

WWW

Go to **www.state.vt.us/educ** to learn more about the use of writing portfolios and statewide assessment in Vermont.

The state of Vermont created the statewide Vermont Assessment Program for writing using portfolios for fourth- and eighth-grade students. This type of portfolio is a *showcase portfolio,* in which students choose materials to display samples of their best work and progress. These portfolios include the following elements:

- Table of contents
- "Best piece": Dated and chosen with the teacher's help
- Letter: Dated and annotated as to why it was chosen and what composition process was followed in creating it
- Poem, short story, play, or personal narration: Dated
- Personal response to cultural, media, or sports exhibit; a book; a current issue, math problem, or scientific phenomenon
- Fourth grade: Prose piece from any curriculum area other than language arts
- Eighth grade: Three prose pieces from any curriculum areas other than English

WWW

Go to **www.michigan.gov/mde** to see the Michigan English Language Arts Content Standards.

A student/teacher conference follows the assembly of a portfolio, in which the student explains his or her portfolio selections and progress to the teacher. Together, the student and teacher identify strengths and needs and plan for further instruction.

Portfolios are also a means for teachers to reflect on student work and progress by mapping it onto content standards. For example, Michigan teacher Sharon Martens Galley (2000) considered the connections between her teaching and her district's new standards-based curriculum using her students' portfolios. One of her fifth-grade students, Jenna, used the metaphor of a vine growing as an introduction to her portfolio presentation to other students, the parents, and her teacher:

> As I grow, I learn that you need reading and writing skills all through life, you need to vine around it. I have learned a lot this past year, and this portfolio will show how I have grown and bloomed. This will show the evidence of how I vined around every chapter, every topic, every stick and branch I can reach to become the best I can. (p. 121)

Galley used Jenna's portfolio to analyze assessment in her classroom and its relationship to the new standards-based curriculum because Jenna was an average student but had produced an outstanding portfolio. Galley and her students had designed the portfolio structure together to include the following sections: *Strategies and Thinking, Choices, Turning Points for Me as a Reader and Writer,* and *Quality Evidence.* Using minilessons, Galley demonstrated what a quality portfolio would look like, and during discussions, she and the class created rubrics.

Upon reflecting on the use of portfolios in her room, Galley (2000) created a graphic organizer to illustrate the connections among her teaching, the state standards, and her students as they unfolded over a year's time. To create this organizer, design a chart, and reflect on the data, Galley followed these steps:

1. *Decide on a question: Could I match evidence of student learning to a standards-based curriculum and the standards themselves?*
2. *Separate the question variables into explicit categories . . . student portfolio evidence . . . content standards . . . classroom lessons. These become the column headings.*
3. *List in the first column the total contents of the evidence. For ease in understanding, I wrote in bold the actual evidence piece and quoted the student whenever possible.*
4. *Match standards with listed evidence. What does evidence show about understanding the standards?*
5. *Analyze classroom activities. How did the student acquire the evidence?*
6. *Use the developed chart to assess teacher effectiveness. What is going well? What is missing? What will I do differently?* (p. 124)

Assessment Toolbox 2.6 (pp. 62–63) shows the results of Galley's analysis of Jenna's portfolio. While Galley did this analysis at the end of the year, her model could be modified and used throughout the year by entering data at the beginning, middle, and end of the year. Doing this would allow teachers to use students' developing portfolios to monitor their progress and inform instruction through the year. Unlike standardized tests, teachers have both the right and the responsibility to develop ways to use portfolios, including designing them and developing tools to assess them meaningfully.

Planning and Progress Forms

Planning and *progress forms* show not only an assessment of a child's progress but carefully detail what the teacher must do to meet the child's needs or to make adaptations for any identified special needs. For instance, a teacher may use a form to plan for each child participating in a literature circle. An example of such a form is provided in the next section, which considers assessing and teaching students with disabilities and other special needs (see Assessment Toolbox 2.7, p. 67).

Teaching and Assessing Students with Disabilities and Other Special Needs

When you teach language arts, you will be responsible for meeting the needs of *all* your students, including those with disabilities and other special needs. Your instruction should be based on each student's developmental, linguistic, functional, and age-appropriate needs. In other words, you should provide instruction at a level that meets the needs of the individual student.

4.3 Systematic Sampling of Emergent Literacy (p. 150)

7.2 Literature Portfolio Organizer (p. 262)

9.6 Self-Assessment Form for Student's Portfolio Selection (p. 322)

2.7 Classroom Activity Analysis Worksheet (p. 67)

7.1 Literature Circle Plan and Progress Sheet (p. 247)

Inclusive classrooms meet the criteria set by federal law for educating students with disabilities.

2.6 Portfolio Analysis Form

Teacher Sharon Martens Galley (2000) used this form to analyze a student's portfolio at the end of the year for the purpose of reviewing her own instruction and assessment. This form could be adapted and used to analyze students' portfolios throughout the year so as to monitor their learning and inform instruction.

Vine Connections

Jenna's Portfolio Contents	Content Standards and Benchmarks	Classroom Lessons or Connections
Intro. Vine metaphor and theme	9. Depth of Understanding A) Explore, reflect on universal themes B) Draw parallels, contrasts	Poetry discussions Portfolio models and lessons
Chapter 1 Strategies & Thinking "Here is a **journal** entry about strategies of a real author, Cynthia Rylant."	7. Skills & Processes 8. Genre & Craft D) Formulate author ideas	Author Study: Cynthia Rylant
"Here is another **journal** entry about strategies I use when I read . . . Old and New."	3. Meaning & Communication D) Multiple strategies	Teacher lesson on reading strategies
"Here are some strategies I use all the time in class." **Forms** for peer conferencing, permission to publish, brainstorming; Poetry **Rubric**	3. Meaning B) Read, write fluently, speak confidently, listen, interact appropriately 7. Skills & Processes 12. Critical Standards	Mini-lessons on peer conferencing Writers' Workshop Structure Rubric Development
Letter from R. L. Stine	6. Voice A) Practice elements of effective communication	Mini-lesson on writing to an author
"Here is where I get my ideas for reading and writing." Poetry Collection **cover, form** for ideas list and entire **journal**	7. Skills & Processes 8. Genre & Craft	Class Poetry Collection and discussions Writers' Workshop Structure Journal guidelines
"Here is a strategy I used to make my Reader Responses quality." Reader Response **Quality Scale**	5. Literature A) Respond thoughtfully 12. Critical Standards	Response Development lessons for journal: prompts . . . questions . . . Remind Notice React Rubric development
Chapter 2 Choices "See how I have Changed . . . Here is the **record** of the books I've read cover to cover this year in Readers' Workshop."	5. Literature 12. Critical Standards C) Choices based on aesthetic qualities with rationale	Readers' Workshop Structure
"Choices I've Made . . . Journal entry to poem." **Journal** copy change entry . . . Zoom in, zoom out **assignment** . . . poetry **drafts** (Jan, April) **form** for permission to publish . . . **published poetry** titled *Taste of Blackberries*	3. Meaning and Communication A) Integrate skills for multiple purposes F) Recognize and use texts as models 7. Skills & Processes D) Develop, use a variety of strategies	Writing lesson on copy change Revision mini-lessons Writers' Workshop Structure

Jenna's Portfolio Contents	Content Standards and Benchmarks	Classroom Lessons or Connections

	8. Genre and Craft
	    D) Identity and use aspects of the craft of the speaker
	9. Depth of Understanding
	10. Ideas in Action
	    B) Combine skills to reveal strengthening literacy	

Chapter 3 Turning Points
"The next three poems by Arnold Adolf were a turning point for me because they made me think about white space." **Poems** were from *In for Winter, Out for Spring.*
	3. Meaning and Communication
	    F) Recognize and use texts as models
	6. Voice
	    C) Identify styles, characteristics
		Class poetry collection and discussions

"This **worksheet** was a turning point for me because it helped me write metaphors and similes in my poetry"	8. Genre and Crafts D) Identify, use aspects of the craft of speaker	Teacher mini-lesson on similes and metaphors

"This **journal** entry (on reader response expectations) was a turning point for me because it made me think about doing better Reader Responses . . . Before turning point (**journal** entry on Barbara Park . . . After turning point (**journal** entry on *Bridge to Terabithia*)"	5. Literature
	    A) Respond thoughtfully
	    B) Describe, discuss shared human experiences
	6. Voice
	    C) Identify style, characteristics
	8. Genre and Craft
	    B) Identify, use narrative genre to convey ideas, perspectives
		Reader Response development lesson
		Whole class reading of *Kid in the Red Jacket* by Barbara Park
		Readers' Workshop Structure
		Reader Response expectations

"This was a turning point for me because it helped me revise and work with my poetry. (**Journal** entry in response to Barry Lane revision lesson.) See the difference on the next page" . . . **draft** and permission to publish **form** of *Things that Hide in the Dark* poem with label "Before the turning point" . . . **drafts**, permission to publish **form**, and **published poem** titled *Stars in My Eyes* with label, "After the turning point."	7. Skills and Processes
	    C) Apply new learning
	    D) Develop, use a variety of strategies
	8. Ideas in Action
	    A) Identify own experience influenced by key ideas
		Teacher revision lesson adapted from Barry Lane
		Writers' Workshop Structure

Chapter 4 Quality Evidence **Published Requirements** **Nonfiction:** Calvin Coolidge **Free Choice:** *I Am* (poetry) **Free Choice:** *Taste of Blackberries* (poetry) **Poetry:** *Stars in My Eyes* **Personal Narrative:** The First Time I Lost a Tooth **Free Choice:** Moving Changes (personal narrative)	11. Inquiry and Research 12. Critical Standards D) Create a personal collection of work	Social Studies unit on famous persons Writers' Workshop Structure Portfolio Expectations MEAP Month Lessons for personal narratives

Source: From "Portfolio as Mirror: Student and Teacher Learning Reflected through the Standards," by S. M. Galley, 2000, *Language Arts, 78,* 121–127. Copyright 2000 by the National Council of Teachers of English. Reprinted with permission of the NCTE.

A series of federal laws have mandated that education be responsive to students who have disabilities and other special needs: namely, Public Law (PL) 94-192, the Education for All Handicapped Children Act, or EHA (passed in 1975); PL 99-457, amendments to EHA (1986); PL 101-476, the Individuals with Disabilities Education Act, or IDEA (1990); and amendments to IDEA (1997). In sum, these laws require educational accommodations and individualized educational planning that provide each exceptional student with the least restrictive environment for learning. Classrooms that meet these criteria are described as *inclusive.*

Teaching Students with Special Needs

The law requires that students with special needs get the special services they require to learn. You should be aware of the types of special needs your students may have; the following list describes some of the most common exceptionalities (Hallahan & Kauffman, 2000; Smith, Polloway, Patton, & Dowdy, 1998):

● *Learning Disabilities:* Students with learning disabilities have great difficulties acquiring, organizing, and expressing specific academic skills and concepts. These problems are generally caused by factors other than lack of educational opportunity, emotional stress in the home or school, lack of motivation, and/or environmental, cultural, and economic differences. The largest group of students with learning disabilities have conditions such as dyslexia, perceptual and memory disorders, and attention-deficit hyperactivity disorder (ADHD). Students who are learning disabled often have difficulties in language processing and literacy learning. They are often referred to as poor readers or as having specific or developmental language disabilities. Their achievement is often significantly below their intellectual capacities.

● *Mental Retardation:* Students with mental retardation are at a low level of intellectual functioning, scoring less than 70–75 on individual intelligence tests. (A score/IQ of 100 is considered average intelligence.) In addition, these students have concurrent deficits in adaptive behavior, limited language abilities, and problems in learning, memory, problem solving, and social skills.

● *Sensory Problems:* Students have sensory problems if their auditory sensitivity/acuity or visual acuity or both adversely affect their educational performance, even with correction. Students may have varying degrees of impairment. For instance, those with hearing impairments may be hard of hearing or deaf, and those with vision impairments may be partially sighted or blind. These children will benefit greatly from proper diagnosis and the use of hearing aids, glasses, and other aids.

● *Giftedness:* The U.S. Office of Education defines *gifted* students as those "possessing demonstrated or potential abilities that give evidence of high performance capability in areas such as intellectual, creative, artistic, leadership capability, or specific academic fields, and who require services or activities not ordinarily provided by the school in order to fully develop such capabilities" (PL 97-35, 1981, sec. 582).

  • *Behavior Disorders:* Children with behavior and emotional disorders show patterns of situationally inappropriate personal behavior over an extended period of time, including unhappiness, depression, withdrawal, and development of physical symptoms or fear associated with personal or school problems. Behavior and emotional disorders cannot be explained by intellectual, sensory, neurological, or general health factors.

Assessing Students with Special Needs

In describing the inclusive classroom, Grenot-Scheyer et al. (1996) explain the importance of carefully assessing students with disabilities and other special needs. Assessment will determine each student's eligibility for special education services, the specific disability code necessary for him or her to receive federal and state funding, and the kinds of support that will most benefit him or her (Taylor, 2000). In general, students with disabilities are evaluated in similar ways to students without disabilities. However, an *individualized educational plan* (*IEP*) is also developed for each special-needs student to set specific goals and objectives for ongoing evaluation. The five areas that should be assessed by an IEP are as follow:

1. the child's individual qualities, such as cultural background, values, family, and interests
2. basic skills, including motor, communication, self-care, and medical
3. academic strengths and needs, for instance, the assessment of reading through standardized and authentic measures
4. ability to function in classroom and school routines, as demonstrated by behavior patterns
5. learning styles, as characterized by Howard Gardner's theory of multiple intelligences (Armstrong, 1994; Gardner, 1983)

Quality and comprehensive assessment occurs when teachers, support professionals, and parents team to accurately describe the student's performance level and strengths, interests, effective learning styles, and goals for intervention.

As suggested in item 1, assessment must also be sensitive to the student's culture and language. Students from diverse cultural backgrounds are over-represented in referrals for special education in all areas except giftedness (Rodriguez, 1982). This pattern is often attributed to the cultural bias against racial, ethnic, and economic minorities of the standardized tests used for the assessment and placement of students; possible causes of bias in tests include language

An *IEP* is a specific instructional plan designed to meet the needs of an individual student; it is often required to receive federal or state funding for special services.

TEACHER RESOURCES
For ideas, see *Guide to Writing Quality Individualized Education Programs* (Gibb & Dyches, 2000).

The Multiple Intelligences and Associated Means of Learning
• Linguistic: reading, writing, spelling
• Logical-mathematical: reasoning, math
• Spatial: drawing, art, charts
• Bodily-kinesthetic: sports, movement
• Musical: patterning, sequencing, music
• Interpersonal: interaction, social, empathy
• Intrapersonal: independence
• Naturalistic: environment

and dialect differences, content specific to the mainstream culture, and cultural differences regarding motivation and attitude toward testing.

Stanley (1996) describes a new approach to assessing students of diverse backgrounds called *advocacy-oriented assessment*. According to this approach, assessment is a blueprint for instruction that is based on looking for individual strengths, not weaknesses, and causes in the social and educational contexts, not just within the student. This approach is grounded in Vygotsky's (1978) social interactionist view that the child develops intellectually because of adult mediation, or guided social interaction.

SNAPSHOT An English Language Learner with Learning Disabilities in an Inclusive Classroom

Grenot-Scheyer et al. (1996) provide this description of Thang, a Cambodian American child whose native language is Khmer:

Thang is beginning sixth grade this year, and he is both excited and scared. Thang lives at home with his mother, his maternal grandmother, and his five brothers and sisters. Thang has a kind, gentle nature and is described by his peers as being quiet and shy. Thang is a talented artist, and he almost always chooses drawing as a free-time activity. Thang's peers will often ask for help from him with drawing or other artwork. Thang has a great deal of difficulty with school. With identified learning disabilities in reading, writing, and math, Thang struggles with many traditional school assignments. Short-term memory problems also compound his difficulty in learning new content and vocabulary. Thang is currently receiving support from the speech and language specialist, and extensive assessment was conducted to determine that Thang's academic difficulties were related to a specific learning disability rather than due to his second language acquisition. Thang's teachers are impressed with the fact that Thang wants to learn and that he continues to try hard to learn new material. It seems, however, that Thang frequently will cry or become withdrawn when he is frustrated with his schoolwork. Thang's teacher is consulting with the school counselor to see if there are additional strategies to help Thang be more successful at school. (pp. 6–7)

Thang's needs are being met in several ways in an inclusive classroom: His proficiency is assessed in his native language; he has asked not to sit by peers who talk a lot; an aide adapts academic materials for him (e.g., creating a spelling list of 10 words rather than 25); and he can draw, rather than write, to demonstrate understanding. The goals on Thang's IEP include to increase math computation skills using a calculator; to brainstorm ideas for use in paragraph writing; to use notes to share information in a group setting; and to ask for help when he doesn't understand the directions.

To assess and adapt instruction for students like Thang, who have special needs, teachers can use the worksheet shown in Assessment Toolbox 2.7.

2.7 Classroom Activity Analysis Worksheet

This Classroom Activity Analysis Worksheet has been completed for Thang, an ELL student with learning disabilities in reading, writing, and math. It identifies the steps involved in a classroom activity, the skills Thang demonstrates in completing it, the specific adaptations that have been made for him, and the skills that need further instruction.

Name of Student: Thang

Activity: Reports on Ancient Greece and Rome

Date: November 15, 1995

Teachers: M. Cook and J. Smith

Classroom Activity Steps	Student Skills	Specific Adaptations	Skills in Need of Instruction
1. Teacher gives directions.	Has difficulty with verbal directions. Does not maintain attention to task.	Teacher writes information on the board.	Follow verbal directions.
2. Students share outlines of their reports in small groups.	Same as peers.	None necessary.	None.
3. Students take notes from reference materials.	Has difficulty reading materials independently. Cannot locate main points.	Takes notes from highlighted material (prepared by aide).	Locate main points. Increase reading comprehension.
4. Students write individual reports.	Has difficulty writing. Copies without understanding.	Dictates information to a parent volunteer. Thang edits material.	Increase vocabulary in content area. Use correct spelling and punctuation.
5. Students share progress in whole group setting.	Same as peers.	None necessary.	None.

Source: From *The Inclusive Classroom,* by M. Grenot-Scheyer, K. A. Jubala, K. D. Bishop, and J. J. Coots, 1996, Westminister, CA: Teacher Created Materials. Copyright 1996 by Teacher Created Materials. Used with permission.

Adapting Language Learning

Instruction for students with special needs in inclusive classrooms may not always require modification. However, when it does, adjustments in goals, instruction, environment, and materials may be made to meet the needs of individual students. Table 2.1 (p. 68) is a checklist of options teachers can use to accommodate students' different learning styles and needs. Table 2.2 (p. 69) lists specific adaptations for teaching language arts to students with different types of special needs.

Table 2.1	Checklist for Accommodating Different Learning Styles and Needs

Instructional Strategies	Materials	Assignments
___ Advance organizers	___ Adaptive/assistive device	___ Adapted testing
___ Charted progress	___ Audiotapes of text	___ Advance assignment
___ Checklist of steps	___ Calculator	___ Alternate assignments
___ Computer activities	___ Captioned films	___ Extended time
___ Evaluation checklists	___ Coded text	___ Extra practice
___ Graphic organizers	___ Computer programs	___ Outlined tasks
___ Modeling	___ Games for practice	___ Partial outlines
___ Mnemonic guides	___ Highlighted text	___ Question guides
___ Multisensory techniques	___ Key term definitions	___ Reference access
___ Organization charts	___ Large-print texts	___ Scripted practice
___ Repeated readings	___ Manipulatives	___ Segmented tasks
___ Scripted demonstrations	___ Math number charts	___ Shortened assignments
___ Self-questioning	___ Multiple text	___ Simplified directions
___ Strategy posters	___ Parallel text	___ Simplified tasks
___ Verbal rehearsal	___ Simplified text	___ Structured notes
___ Video modeling	___ Summaries	___ Study guides
___ Visual imagery	___ Video enactments	___ Timed practice

Human Resources	Management Strategies
___ Co-teacher	___ Charted performance
___ Cooperative group	___ Checklists
___ Instructional coach	___ Contracts
___ Interpreter	___ Extra reinforcement
___ Peer advocate	
___ Peer notetaker	
___ Peer prompter	
___ Peer tutor	
___ Personal attendant	
___ Study buddy	
___ Volunteer tutor	

Source: From Joyce S. Choate, *Successful Inclusive Teaching,* 3rd ed. Published by Allyn & Bacon, Boston, MA.
Copyright © 2000 by Pearson Education. Adapted by permission of the publisher.

Answers to Questions about Assessing Language Arts

• *What do we mean by* assessing language arts *in schools today?*

Assessing language arts means collecting analyzing, summarizing, and inter-preting information about students to appraise their performance and achieve-ment. Teachers should use multiple forms of ongoing, authentic assessment on a daily basis to plan instruction to meet each child's needs.

Table 2.2 Adapting and Teaching Language Arts for Students with Special Needs

Students with Learning Disabilities

1. Focus on the meaning of language, rather than the parts.
2. Build on students' personal explanations of the world.
3. Use materials and tasks that are at students' levels of interest and ability.
4. In writing, emphasize students' intentions over the accurate use of conventions.
5. Focus on oral language experiences.

Students with Mental Retardation

1. Immerse students in a language-rich environment.
2. Read aloud daily.
3. Use the language experience approach and shared reading.
4. Model specific strategies, such as book selection and writing.
5. Use concrete, hands-on experiences.

Students with Sensory Problems

Hearing Impairments

1. Seat students where they can see your lips move; for group work, seat students where they can see other students' lips move.
2. Speak loudly and clearly, facing students.
3. Use written directions on the chalkboard and charts.

Visual Impairments

1. Seat students in the best places for them to see.
2. Use small-group work and have peers read directions.
3. Provide materials with large print and paper with darkened lines.

Students Who Are Gifted

1. Use activities that require independence and the synthesis of ideas, rather than structure and recall.
2. Provide high-level projects, for individuals or groups.
3. Let students self-select literature and reference materials to support their research.
4. Allow students to work at their own level and pace.
5. Encourage making connections among concepts, prior knowledge, and content.

Students with Behavior Disorders

1. Maintain a positive classroom atmosphere.
2. Establish close relationships with students' parents and caretakers.
3. Provide many ways for students to communicate their ideas and feelings.
4. Team students with buddies.
5. Make directions clear, provide structure when needed, monitor, and follow up.

Sources: Falvey et al., 1995; Grenot-Scheyer et al., 1996; Smith et al., 1998.

Schools today are affected by the national debate about so-called high-stakes testing. Federal law requires every state to design and administer standardized reading and math tests for children in grades 3 through 8 by 2005–2006, and the results will be used to determine school funding and changes in programs and faculty. Many educators are concerned that this mandate will mean "teaching to the test," rather than teaching based on how children learn. Standardized tests are based on a behaviorist model and most often measure a set of separate subskills, as in a multiple-choice test. The International Reading Association strongly opposes such high-stakes testing.

• *How should we assess language arts?*

The social constructivist model of learning is reflected in authentic assessment, which is continuous, embedded in the classroom context, and includes information from logs and journals, anecdotal records and observations, checklists and records, inventories and tests, rubrics, self- and peer assessment, portfolios and work samples, and planning and progress forms. These types of assessment are used by teachers to support, guide, and monitor students' learning and to plan for their instruction. Authentic assessment relies on information gathered by students and teachers during regular classroom activities. Language arts and literacy assessment should be a blueprint for language arts and literacy instruction.

● *How should we teach and assess students with disabilities and other special needs?*

Students with disabilities and other special needs shoud be provided with special services and support, adaptive instruction, and performance assessment that is sensitive to their culture and language diversity and that focuses on their strengths and goals for intervention. Federal law requires that students with disabilities and other special needs be provided with an individualized education plan (IEP) and specific plans for adapting instruction. In addition, that instruction must be provided in the least restrictive environment for learning; for example, a deaf child would be placed in a classroom with his or her peers, allowing for membership and development of a sense of community for all students. Classrooms that meet these criteria are described as inclusive. Teachers of students with disabilities and other special needs who are of diverse backgrounds practice advocacy-oriented assessment, which uses assessment as a blueprint for instruction based on a student's strengths, not weaknesses, and factors within the social and educational contexts, not just within the student.

Looking Further

1. Use one of the Assessment Toolboxes in this chapter with a group of children. Then share your experiences with your class as the beginning point of a discussion about the role of assessment in learning and teaching language arts.

2. Go online and review either the No Child Left Behind Act or the International Reading Association's position statement on high-stakes testing. Post a response on an online discussion board for your class, and respond to at least two other students' responses.

3. Collect several samples of one student's writing over time. Using Assessment Toolbox 2.1, the Writing Log, make three entries for this student in which you evaluate his or her writing. Bring your evaluation to class and share it with other students who have done the same thing. Make comparisions among students at the same grade level and then among those at various levels.

4. Use the Double-Entry Journal, Assessment Toolbox 2.2, to make notes about something you are reading (for example, this textbook).

5. Use Assessment Toolbox 2.3, the Writing Rubric, to review Benton's memoir (see Figure 2.1). Bring your results to class and compare and discuss them with other students in a small group. Also compare your assessments to mine (see p. 56). How are they alike and different?

6. Observe in a special education classroom (such as a special day class, a resource room, or an inclusive classroom), and note the following: categories of disabilities of the students being served, the numbers of students versus adults, and the credentials held by the teacher. Ask the teacher what opportunities the students in this class setting have to interact with their nondisabled peers. Describe the curriculum, materials, assessment, and instructional activities that are used for language arts and what adaptations or modifications are made to provide access for students with disabilities. Write down your observations and share them with your classmates.

First- and Second-Language Development

Questions about First- and Second-Language Development

- *How do children develop a first and a second language?*
- *What do we know when we know how to use language?*
- *How do teachers support and assess children's growing knowledge of language and vocabulary?*

REFLECTIVE RESPONSE

How did you learn your first language or English as a second language? Who taught you? Jot down your ideas, and think about them as you read this chapter.

First-Language Development

Studies of children's language development (Cattell, 2000; Cook-Gumperz, 1979; Snow, 1986; Strickland & Feeley, 2003; Tamis-LeMonda & Bornstein, 1994; Wells, 1981) show that caretakers of young children—mothers, fathers, older children, and teachers—constantly negotiate meaning as they communicate with them, responding to *what* they're trying to say more than *how* they say it. By doing this, caretakers help children develop what Hymes (1974) calls *communicative competence,* or the ability to really use language.

TEACHER RESOURCES

See *Language Development: A Reader for Teachers* (Power & Hubbard, 1996) for more on children's language development.

Consider the following Snapshot of four children learning English as their first language from a social constructivist perspective. As you may recall from Chapter 1, this perspective of cognitive development merges ideas from two viewpoints about how children learn and acquire language: (1) the constructivist theory and (2) the social interactionist theory. Each theory, as it pertains to language development, will be described in a following section, including examples from the Snapshot and suggestions for teaching.

SNAPSHOT   Four Children Talking

Elizabeth, Gordon, and Wyatt are my three children; the scene that is described in this Snapshot occurred in 1985, when I was writing the first edition of this text.

Let's take a look at four children of different ages and at different stages in their cognitive, language, and social development. Elizabeth is 9 months old, Gordon is 3 years old, Becky is 7 years old, and Wyatt is 14. Wyatt is taking care of his sister and brother, Elizabeth and Gordon, while his mother is at work writing a book in her home office. Becky, a neighbor, joins the group as Wyatt helps Gordon work a puzzle and tries to keep Elizabeth happy. Think about what each child is saying and why as well as how all the children interact.

> *Elizabeth* (crying): Fafafafafa.
>   *Wyatt:* How you doin', Elizabeth? (Singing.) Little Elizabeth. Pretty little lizard.
>   *Becky* (to Wyatt about Elizabeth's crying): Maybe it was something we said?
>   *Wyatt* (laughing at Becky's remark and helping Gordon with the puzzle): Gordon, do you think you could help Becky work this puzzle? Do the puzzle, Gor.
>   *Gordon:* Where dis go? Dis go?

Here are Gordon, Wyatt, and Elizabeth (left to right) *at the ages they were when I taped the conversation repeated here.*

Wyatt:	Do you want this one? This one goes right here. Here.
Becky:	This one goes here. There.
Gordon	(grabbing the piece from Becky): Dat my piece. My piece. My piece.
Wyatt:	Do the puzzle, Gordon.
Becky:	Did he do this? It's pretty good, though. Map of the world. If the world was that small, I know . . . I know how Christopher Columbus made it. But the world's flat. Hmmmmm.
Gordon:	Der. I di-i!
Wyatt:	Gordon, did you do that puzzle? All by yourself?
Elizabeth:	Ehehehehehehe!
Wyatt:	Elizabeth? You want to work a puzzle sometime by yourself?
Gordon:	Now I . . . goin' to find it. Becky! (pushing her to put in a puzzle piece).
Becky:	Huh?
Elizabeth	(crying): Fafafafafafa.
Wyatt:	Elizabeth (soothingly, picking her up, rocking her, and singing). Puff, puff, cocoa puff. Chocolate covered cocoa puffs.
Gordon:	Oh, wow!
Wyatt:	You have a little baby brother, Becky?
Becky:	Yeah!
Wyatt:	How old is he?
Becky:	About fo— . . . he's . . . uhm . . . almost a month.
Wyatt:	That's pretty small.
Becky:	Yeah, real.
Wyatt:	What's his name?
Becky:	Patrick.
Gordon:	Oh . . . we're missing dat piece!
Wyatt:	You like him?
Becky:	When he's happy! He gets happy!
Wyatt:	He cries a lot?
Becky:	Yeah, he's usually happy and like—"ooohhhhh" (imitating baby noise)—and sometimes he's only—and sometimes he, he—when he's in a sore mood—he always—and sometimes he's like this (imitates baby). Like he's ready to sock ya.
Wyatt	(laughing): Ha-ha-ha-ha!
Becky:	Once Mom goes "What you thinkin' about Patrick?" and he goes (makes face).
Gordon:	Right . . . one here. One. Let's do other side.
Wyatt:	Do the other side. Do the other side (of a double-sided puzzle).
Gordon:	O–KAY!!!

You can easily see the differences in linguistic structures used by these children of different ages while learning English as a first language. But did you also observe the way in which each child used language and the importance of the meaning of what he or she was saying? The role of the oldest child, 14-year-old Wyatt, is especially important. He was obviously taking care of the two youngest children. What may not be so obvious is how he supported their language development by communicating and negotiating meaning with them.

Continue to think about the Snapshot and what it illustrates about language development according to the following theories: constructivism and social interactionism.

Constructivist Theory

Piaget's ideas on cognitive development were introduced in Chapter 1.

Jean Piaget (1959) held that language development is an aspect of general cognitive development. Although he believed that thought (or cognition) and language were interdependent, he maintained that language development is rooted in the more fundamental development of cognition. In other words, conceptualization precedes language.

Piaget based this cognitive-constructivist view on his observations of children at play. Through manipulating objects, they demonstrate that they understand concepts and can solve problems without verbalizing them. In the Snapshot, Gordon illustrated this understanding as he worked the puzzle. Children learn to understand language as they first assimilate and then accommodate language symbols to their symbolic structures, or schema (as discussed in Chapter 1). In the search for meaning, children *symbolize* before they *verbalize*.

Piaget viewed the adult or other caretaker's role in teaching language as creating situations in which children discover meaning themselves. For example, Wyatt got out the puzzle for Gordon and encouraged him to work it. According to the constructivist view, language will follow experience. In order to support language development, teachers provide opportunities for self-discovery in the classroom, such as centers with materials for art, writing, and science. This isn't to suggest that language doesn't play a part in children's overall development. To the contrary, language is critical in children's social interaction with one another and adults, and this interaction is essential in order for children to grow and move away from a totally egocentric (self-focused) point of view.

Constructivist theory suggests that children are constantly forming and testing hypotheses about language structure. Linguist Noam Chomsky's ideas (1957, 1965, 1997) about the nature of language are relevant here (Menyuk, 1991). His *generative theory of language* suggests that each of us has an innate *language acquisition device (LAD)* that enables us to understand and produce sentences we have never heard before. Using a finite number of words, we can produce an infinite number of sentences. We do this by constantly testing hypotheses, not merely by imitating the speech of others. Making errors is an important part of this process, because we are testing what we know about language. The errors children make show their basic underlying understanding of how language works, a notion already explained in Piaget's theory of child development as an active process (Shatz & Ebeling, 1991). Although Chomsky maintained that each child is born with innate linguistic principles, Piaget disagreed with him in a famous debate (Piattelli-Palmarini, 1995).

Chomsky's generative theory prompted great interest in psycholinguistic research in children's language development in the 1960s and 1970s, particularly regarding the stages and rate of acquiring language structures (Cazden, 1972; C. Chomsky, 1969; Menyuk, 1963; Strickland, 1962).

TEACHER RESOURCES

See *Children's Language: Consensus and Controversy* (Cattell, 2000) for a comparison of the theoretical perspectives on language development.

Stages of Language Development

Each child in the Snapshot falls into one of Piaget's stages of cognitive and language development. Let's look at the development of language in each stage.

Sensorimotor Stage (0–2 years): Preverbal—Elizabeth. Elizabeth is 9 months old and in the sensorimotor stage of cognitive development. She is crying and babbling—repeating one-syllable sounds, usually beginning with a consonant, such as "fafafafafa." She also says "Ma-ma," "Da-da," and "bye-bye." She will probably speak her first words at about 1 year old and two-word sentences at about 2 years old. Did you notice in the Snapshot that the only person to speak directly to her was her older brother, Wyatt? He included her in the conversation as though she was really part of it. This kind of talk—called "motherese" or "caretakerese"—is essential to further language development.

Elizabeth spoke these words between 9 months and 1 year: *Oh-oh, Wyee* (her brother Wyatt), *wa-* (water), *Hi!, Mama, Dada,* and *Bye-bye.*

Preoperational Stage (2–7 years): Vocabulary and True Language—Gordon. Gordon is 3 years old and in the preoperational stage. He can name things and use two-word, or *telegraphic*, sentences and other simple sentences. He can't pronounce many words accurately, but he is able to make his meaning clear. He repeats a lot and is still pretty egocentric. In the Snapshot, he was focused on doing the puzzle that interested him and not very interested in anyone else, except when he thought that Becky was taking a puzzle piece away from him. Wyatt interacted with Gordon as a big brother/coach. He adjusted his speech according to what Gordon said in the same way that studies show mothers do with even very young children (Akhtar, Dunham, & Dunham, 1991; Fernald, 1993; Lindfors, 1987). Wyatt didn't correct Gordon's speech approximations; instead, he responded to the meaning of what he knew Gordon was trying to say. Wyatt offered guidance and suggestions. He used simple, short, concrete sentences and repetition, specific directions, and exaggerated intonation. He also offered encouragement while sharing in Gordon's attempts to work the puzzle and talk.

Gordon spoke these phrases and sentences between 18 months and 2 years: *All gone* (and twists hands), *Uh-oh hat* (when he dropped it), *I'm tired,* and *Go car!*

Concrete Operational Stage (7–11 years): Logical Reasoning and Socialized Speech—Becky. At age 7, Becky is in the concrete operational stage. Her speech is remarkably like adult speech. Although her language will continue to develop in complexity of form and function, she has pretty much mastered her native language of English. You probably observed in the Snapshot that Becky

Becky was in the second grade at this time.

was much more social than Gordon. She was primarily interested in talking to Wyatt, who would talk back to her, yet she still commented on Elizabeth and tried to interact with Gordon (who had only limited, self-serving interest in her). Note that Wyatt listened to Becky, laughed at her jokes, asked her questions, and invited her to talk about herself and family.

Wyatt was in the eighth grade at this time.

Formal Operations Stage (11–15): Abstract Reasoning and World of Symbols—Wyatt. Wyatt is 14 years old and in the formal operations stage. Essentially, his speech can't be differentiated from that of an adult, as illustrated by the ways he used language to interact with the three younger children. He acted as their coach: negotiating meaning with them and helping them interact with each other in ways that both accepted and expanded their individual levels of cognitive and language development. What Wyatt did naturally as a caretaker is a good model for teachers in the classroom who wish to support their students' language development.

See Table 3.1 for an overview of Piaget's stages of cognitive and language development.

Social Interactionist Theory

Environment plays a more prominent role in social interactionist theories than in constructivist theories. Social interactionist theory assumes that language development is determined by the interaction of physical, linguistic, and social factors—any and all of which may vary greatly for each individual child. Lev Vygotsky (1978, 1986) believed that interaction with the environment, especially with adults and older children, plays a critical role in children's language development.

TEACHER RESOURCES

Vygotsky's ideas on learning were introduced in Chapter 1. For more information, see *Vygotsky in the Classroom: Mediated Literacy Instruction and Assessment* (Dixon-Kraus, 1996).

Babies hear language used around them and begin to use language to communicate their needs. Caretakers are sensitive to children's needs and developing language and try to understand both, making their langauge understandable to children. Caretakers aren't concerned with pointing out errors or correcting them; instead, they pay attention to the meaning of what children are trying to communicate. Messages are important; mistakes are not. Caretakers therefore provide an environment in which children are willing to test new hypotheses about language structure and use through social interaction that's founded on a need to negotiate and establish meaning. Sociolinguistic research of the 1970s and 1980s began to focus more on this social aspect of language development (Cook-Gumperz, 1979; Halliday, 1975; Lindfors, 1987; Tough, 1977; Wells, 1981), and Vygotsky's theory continues to provide a framework for research on language and learning (Schallert & Martin, 2003).

As summarized by Vygotsky, "Language is a major stimulant for conceptual growth, and conceptual growth is also dependent on interaction with objects in the environment. Moreover, adults (and older children) have a role in stimulating language growth through a variety of means" (p. 11, quoted in Pflaum, 1986).

Table 3.1   Piagetian Stages of Cognitive and Language Development (ages 0–15)

Stage	Age	Characteristics
Sensorimotor	Birth–6 months	Crying: • undifferentiated and differentiated Babbling: • makes random sounds, then selective and repeated (e.g., "fafafafafa") • associates hearing and sound production • imitates sounds of self and others selectively (e.g., "eheheheh")
	12–18 months	One-word stage: • speaks and duplicates single syllables (e.g., "Ma-ma," "Da-da") • has communicative intent • speaks one-word (holophrastic) sentences (e.g., "Juice" means "I want juice") • 10 word vocabulary
Preoperational	18–24 months	Two-word stage: • meaningful expressive language • speaks telegraphically, using two or more mainly content words (e.g., "Bye-bye car" means "I want to go somewhere in the car—now!") • 150–300 word vocabulary; mainly nouns, verbs, and adjectives; adds plural -s
	3–4 years	Simple and compound sentences, becoming more complex: • understands present and past tenses but may overgeneralize (e.g., uses -ed as in "He goed") • knows numerical concepts (*few* and *many; one, two, three*) • negative transformations • 1,000–1,500 word vocabulary; adding more adjectives, adverbs, pronouns, and prepositions
	5 years	Grammatically correct complex sentences: • has acquired most basic rules of language • uses present and past tenses and pronouns correctly • 2,500–8,000 word vocabulary and growing
	6 years	Begins to read and write: • uses adjectival and conditional clauses, beginning with *if*
Concrete operations	7 years	More symbolic language use: • understands concepts (e.g., time and seasons)
	8–10 years	Very flexible language use: • subordinates clauses beginning with *when, if, because* • articulates most sounds correctly
Formal operations	11–15 years	More complex sentences and subordination

Zone of Proximal Development

This stimulation should take place in what Vygotsky (1978) calls the *zone of proximal development*. As defined in Chapter 1, this zone is the center around which the child forms *thought complexes* (similar to schema) or *symbolic structures*. Piaget also identified the importance of connecting new experiences to prior knowledge and organizing that new information. However, his ideas differ from those of Vygotsky in that Piaget believed children verbalize structures that have already developed through firsthand experiences with objects in their environments. Vygotsky sees the verbal interaction between the adult and child as the primary means by which children achieve potential meaning through language. He clearly puts great emphasis on the role of the caretaker or teacher in the cognitive and linguistic development of the child.

Wyatt's interaction with Elizabeth, Gordon, and Becky is an example of Vygotsky's theory. This interaction also illustrates what Jerome Bruner (1978) describes as a *scaffold*, or a temporary frame for constructing meaning from language (see Chapter 1). When Wyatt talked to the younger children, he often repeated himself but used slightly more complex language than that of the children.

Language Structure and Systems

What do children like Wyatt, Becky, Gordon, and Elizabeth actually know when they use language? Language is constructed of interacting systems of sounds, meanings, sentence formation, and use. You know a language when you know whether a sentence sounds right or not. You have a feel for the language, which is an underlying knowledge of the language systems. That underlying knowledge represents your linguistic competence. Competence in any language includes knowledge of the following systems:

- phonological rules, which specify the sound patterns of the language
- semantic rules, which characterize the meanings of words and sentences
- syntactic rules, which specify how to combine words in sentences
- pragmatic conventions, which define how language is used

Let's examine each system more closely.

Phonology

When you know how to use a language, you're able to make sounds that have meanings and are able to understand the meanings of sounds that other people make. *Phonology* is the study of the patterns and systems of human language. *Phonetics* is a system of classifying these speech sounds. *Phonics* is a method of teaching unfamiliar words in print based on the sound/letter correspondences in spoken language.

See Chapter 6, Reading, for more on teaching phonics.

The phonology of each language includes a set of basic building blocks called *phonemes*. A phoneme is the smallest unit of sound that distinguishes between the meanings of words in a certain language—for example, *fan* versus *pan*. Only certain sequences of these segments make sense in a language. There are about 40 phonemes in the English language but only 26 letters in the English alphabet to represent these sounds. In written language, sounds in words are represented by *graphemes*.

Semantics

When you know a language, you're also able to produce sentences with certain meanings and to understand the meanings of sentences that other people make. *Semantics* is the study of linguistic meaning. *Morphemes* are the smallest units of meaning in each language; they are sequences of phonemes that can't be divided without losing meaning. Morphemes combine to form *words*, which can be made up of more than one morpheme. For example, the word *puzzle* can't be reduced without losing meaning. It's called a *free morpheme*, because it functions as a unit of meaning by itself. To create the plural word *puzzles*, we add another morpheme: *-s*. The *-s* is called a *bound morpheme*, because it cannot function as a unit of meaning by itself.

When you know a language, you know the morphemes, their meanings, how they may be combined to form words, and how to pronounce them. The vocabulary of morphemes and words in a language is called the *lexicon*.

Syntax

Knowing a language also involves knowing the rules of *syntax*. When you know these rules, you can combine words in sentences that express your ideas and are able to understand the sentences produced by other people to express their ideas. Meaning in a *sentence* is partly determined by *word order*, one of the things that syntactic rules determine.

Pragmatics

When you know a language, you know how to use the rules that govern its use for different functions, which are called *conventions*. We can't discuss these conventions without referring to how language is used by specific people or in specific situations. For instance, you can probably think of examples of the manipulative use of language in commercial advertising and political rhetoric (sometimes called *doublespeak*). Language also can be used to perpetuate racial or gender bias, unknowingly or intentionally. You may have noticed in reading this book that whenever a personal pronoun is needed, *he or she* is used, rather than just *he*. The latter was considered conventional until recently, when the use of *he* by itself was acknowledged as sexist. Awareness of gender fairness in language has also led to the use of *police officer* instead of *policeman* and *chairperson* instead of *chairman*. Because these usages are considered appropriate in most situations today, they have become new conventions.

How language is used in given societies or cultures is studied by *sociolinguists*. One such scholar, Michael Halliday (1975), defines *language* as "'meaning potential,' that is, as sets of opinions, or alternatives, in meaning, that are available to the speaker-hearer" (p. 63). Based on that definition, Halliday has created a model that shows the functions of language that children have

Table 3.2   Halliday's Model of Language Functions

Function	Example	Classroom Experiences
Instrumental: "I want" Language to get things done	"Dat my piece!"	Problem solving Gathering materials
Regulatory: "Do as I tell you" Language to control	"This one goes here."	Giving instructions Making rules, as in games
Interactional: "Me and you" Language in social relationships	"Let's do the other side."	Talking in groups Dialogue and discussion
Personal: "Here I come" Language to express individuality	"Oh, wow!"	Making feelings public Discovering through interacting
Heuristic: "Tell me why" Language as a means to learn	"Did he do this?"	Question/answer routines Metalanguage (language about language; words like *question, answer, knowing*)
Imaginative: "Let's pretend" Language to create and explore	"Puff, puff, cocoa puff."	Stories and dramatic games Rhymes, poems, and riddles Nonsense and wordplay Metalanguage (stories, make-believe, pretending)
Representational: "I'll tell you" Language to communicate content	"This one goes right here."	Telling about the real world Expressing propositions Conveying messages with specific references to real things (people, qualities, states, etc.)

Source: Based on Halliday, 1975.

developed by the time they come to school. Table 3.2 lists these functions along with examples from the Snapshot of four children talking. The table also shows the types of language arts classroom experiences that can help children expand their "meaning potential."

Second-Language Development

Many students in the United States speak a first language other than English. These students are often referred to as *English language learners* (*ELL*) or *limited English proficient* (*LEP*). LEP students become *FEP,* or *fluent English proficient,* when they reach an advanced level of English proficiency.

The United States is fast becoming a multilingual society. Today, language-minority students make up 15 percent of the K–12 (kindergarten through twelfth grade) enrollment. In the last 10 years, the general school population has grown 12 percent but the LEP population has grown 105 percent (Kindler, 2002). By the year 2026, they will make up almost 25 percent of school enrollment and there will be 47 percent more Hispanic children in kindergarten through eighth grade than there are today (Hoffman & Pearson, 2000). Given these increases, it's likely that you will teach language-minority students at some time during your career.

Educational goals for ELL include achieving social and psychological success, academic success across the curriculum (e.g., mathematics, social studies, science, etc.), and spoken fluency and literacy in English. These are important goals for all students, whatever their primary languages. But when children come to school with little or no proficiency in English, how are these goals to be met? Theories of second-language acquisition, development, and education provide some answers to this question.

Second-Language Acquisition Theories

In Chapter 1 and at the beginning of this chapter, you read about the theoretical perspectives of constructivism and social interactionism. These theories underlie the approach to learning, teaching, and assessing language arts in this book. While these theories go a long way toward explaining how children learn, in general—and more specifically, how they learn language—other theories also have contributed to our understanding of how children acquire a second language. One key idea that joins these theoretical perspective is the notion of context-embedded communication.

Context-Embedded Communication

The theories and research of Canadian linguist James Cummins (1979, 1980, 1984, 1986, 1989, 1991, 1992) have greatly influenced the education of language-minority students in the United States. Cummins maintains that *context-embedded communication*—which is the amount of contextual support present when someone is learning a second language—determines his or her proficiency in two important dimensions of language:

1. *Basic interpersonal communication skills (BICS)* are used daily in social speaking situations, such as children talking together on the playground. These skills require 0 to 3 years of practice for proficiency.
2. *Cognitive academic language proficiency (CALP)* involves those language skills used in school tasks, such as taking notes on a lecture and writing a report using the information. CALP skills require 5 to 7 years of use for proficiency.

Cummins uses the metaphor of an iceberg to explain the relationship between BICS and CALP. BICS represent only the tip of the iceberg in that we can see and hear basic communicative competence. We can be misled, however, in thinking that a student has also developed CALP, the language skills required for success in complex academic tasks.

In context-embedded communication, meaning is actively negotiated between speakers and supported by many contextual clues, like when deciding whose turn it is in playing a game. In *context-reduced communication*, there are few

WWW

Go to **www.ncela.gwu.edu**, the National Clearinghouse for English Language Acquisition and Language Instruction Educational Programs, for information on these and related topics:

Most Commonly Spoken Languages

Spanish
Vietnamese
Hmong
Chinese (Cantonese)
Korean
Haitian Creole
Arabic

States with the Most LEP Students

California
Texas
Florida
New York
Illinois
Arizona

The Iceberg Model

- *Multicultural/cross-cultural strategies:* Study content in terms of multiple perspectives, and select resources that represent the cultural fabric of the group. Have students share their experiences regarding the learning. For example, when studying immigration, draw on the experiences of the immigrants in the classroom. Also conduct "we"-search projects, such as interviews with family members that focus on certain issues or experiences (e.g., immigration).

- *Accommodating "teacher talk":* Use a slower rate of speech, speak clearly, and avoid idioms. Mirror back to students their words with model speech. Also make frequent use of cognates (English = *mode*; Spanish = *moda*), and try to contextualize speech using gestures and facial expressions.

- *Assessment:* Formative, or ongoing, assessment should measure understanding and mastery of the lesson for the day. Useful assessment tools include anecdotal records and teacher observations. Summative, or final, assessment should make use of project evaluations, rubrics, and exams.

3.3

Anecdotal Record Assessment
(p. 106)

Hear Paul Boyd-Batstone explain how how to do anecdotal record assessment for a second-language learner.

LESSON PLAN

Teaching English and Mathematics to Spanish-Speaking Students

Jaqui Denenberg, one of my students, put many of the ideas of second-language acquisition theory and instruction into practice during her field experience in a third-grade class composed primarily of English language learners. The classroom teacher, Linda Malone, had two years' experience and was not bilingual. Jaqui worked with a group of nine students throughout the semester, all of whom were native Spanish speakers and classified by the school district as limited English proficient.

Linda helped Jaqui plan three lessons for these students: (1) ELD, (2) content-based ELD, and (3) specially designed academic instruction in English (SDAIE). First, they decided on the content learning outcomes that were to be met in addition to English language development. They chose a content standard in the area of mathematics—place value—and a problem to solve: "How much is a million?"

Jaqui thought carefully about planning these lessons and adapting them for second-language learners so as to provide comprehensible input in low-anxiety, context-embedded learning experiences and to align content instruction with each student's level of English language development. The rest of this Lesson Plan describes the lessons and related means of assessment. The marginal notes show specifically how Jaqui adapted each lesson for her ELL students. Figure 3.2 shows a model for lesson planning to align language lessons in ELD and content lessons, or SDAIE, with each child's stage of language proficiency using standards along with both formal and informal assessment.

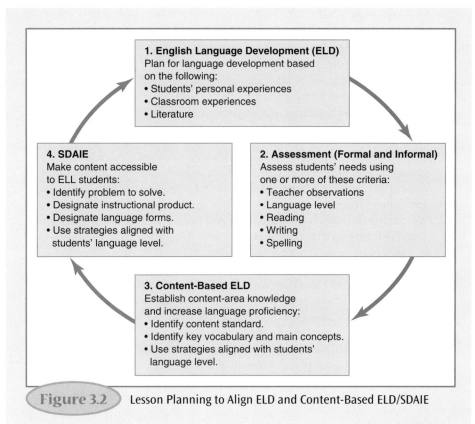

1. English Language Development (ELD)
Plan for language development based on the following:
• Students' personal experiences
• Classroom experiences
• Literature

4. SDAIE
Make content accessible to ELL students:
• Identify problem to solve.
• Designate instructional product.
• Designate language forms.
• Use strategies aligned with students' language level.

2. Assessment (Formal and Informal)
Assess students' needs using one or more of these criteria:
• Teacher observations
• Language level
• Reading
• Writing
• Spelling

3. Content-Based ELD
Establish content-area knowledge and increase language proficiency:
• Identify content standard.
• Identify key vocabulary and main concepts.
• Use strategies aligned with students' language level.

Figure 3.2 Lesson Planning to Align ELD and Content-Based ELD/SDAIE

ELL

Adapt this lesson for English language learners by using these tools and strategies:

• Drawing
• Student's primary language
• Interactive, shared book experience
• Highly illustrated book
• Props
• Visual aids
• "Word wall"
• Dramatic voice
• Facial expressions
• Gestures
• Student's prior experience
• Student interaction: buddies, groups

Lesson 1: Literature-Based ELD Using *Millions of Cats,* by Wanda Gag

Jaqui taught the following lesson using Wanda Gag's classic picture book *Millions of Cats* (1928/1956). She chose this book for several reasons. First, it is a beautifully illustrated and engaging story with a repeated language pattern. In addition, Jaqui loves cats and knew her students had experiences they could share about cats and other pets. As an extending activity, she read David Schwartz's nonfiction book *How Much Is a Million?* (1985).

Level: Primary-grade students with limited English proficiency

Purpose: Children will listen to and enjoy good literature; respond to literature through a variety of means, drawing and writing in Spanish or English or both; and develop concepts and vocabulary in the context of a shared book experience.

Standard 10: Students whose first language is not English make use of their first language to develop competency in the English language arts and to develop understanding of content across the curriculum.

IRA/
NCTE

(continued)

Materials:
1. *Millions of Cats,* by Wanda Gag (1928/1956)
2. Props: stuffed animals (cats)
3. Pictures: photographs of real cats
4. Chartpaper and marking pens for a "word wall"
5. Plain white drawing paper and crayons and pencils

Teaching Sequence:
1. Read *Millions of Cats* aloud to students, using a dramatic voice and facial expressions and gestures. Use illustrations from books and photographs of real cats to clarify the language. Use stuffed animals as props when cats are speaking in the story.
2. Use aesthetic, open-ended questions and prompts to discuss the book:
   "What did you think of the story?"
   "What was your favorite part of the story?"
   "What kind of pets do you have?"
   "Have you ever found a stray animal? What did you do?"
3. Discuss the children's responses and record them in marking pen on chartpaper, making a "word wall." In the center, write "Our ideas about *Millions of Cats.*"
4. Give students the following response options after the discussion:
   a. Draw or write anything you want about the story.
   b. Reread *Millions of Cats* with the teacher or a buddy.
   c. Talk about the book in small groups.

Extending Activities:
1. Read other books by Wanda Gag:
   ABC Bunny (1933)
   The Funny Thing (1929)
   Gone Is Gone (1935)
2. Read other English language books about cats:
   Catch That Cat! A Picture Book of Rhymes and Puzzles (Beisner, 1990)
   The Fat Cat (Kent, 1971/1990)
   Have You Seen My Cat? (Carle, 1987)
3. Read Spanish language books about cats:
   El Gato Cui (Gonzalez de Tapia, 1984)
   El Gato Sabio de Juanito (Vanhalewijn, 1980)
   Gatos (Petty, 1991)
4. Dramatize part of *Millions of Cats.*
5. Do a puppet show using stuffed animal cats or student-made puppets.
6. Create a chart of everybody's pets.
7. Invite a pet store owner in the community to talk to the class about cats. Ideally, ask someone who speaks Spanish.

8. Read *How Much Is a Million?* by David Schwartz (1985) to develop concepts and vocabulary about large quantities like *millions, billions,* and *trillions.*

After conducting this lesson with the ELL students, Jaqui described how she felt it went:

> The outcomes of this lesson were so overwhelming. I have been a substitute for 9 months, and it is amazing to see the differences in responses from the students when they are read to from a basal reader versus a literary book. It is always positive when a literary book is read. The students went on to so many different tangents and experiences from each of the stories, and even the shyest of students was sharing his experience with the dogs he had in Mexico. It was so exciting to hear all the different stories that the students had about themselves. They spoke in Spanish and English and helped each other out in English.
>
> They really responded in individual ways. Only one of their drawings had to do with the actual story. The rest all had to do with experiences that they have had with their own animals. Juan V. did a wonderful drawing of his farm in Mexico, showing all the animals that were on the farm, including a cat that used to love to climb on top of him to sleep [see Figure 3.3]. Oscar and Juan L. decided to draw a picture of the class pet, Pumpkin the bunny. When they finished, they read the book the class had written earlier in the year about Pumpkin. Mario, the shyest student, started telling me about his dog, which helped him fight off other dogs one day when he was playing in Mexico.
>
> What was so great about all this was that the students were learning new things about each other that they had not known all year long. I think it helped that I brought in a picture of my cat and stuffed animals. They were so eager to talk in English and Spanish. All the students wanted me to draw pictures of their pets.

Figure 3.3 Student's Drawing of Animals on Grandfather's Farm in Mexico

(continued)

Linda Malone, the classroom teacher, believes in using a lot of literature and hands-on experiences with her ELL students, so she was very pleased that the children were so involved with the story. She praised Jaqui on bringing in props like stuffed animals and pictures to provide visual support and clues for understanding the story. Linda also praised the "word wall" technique (see Figure 3.4) and asked to see students' drawings and writings. She told Jaqui that these are the types of things she includes in students' portfolios for assessment or makes notes about in an anecdotal record she keeps about each student.

See Chapter 2, Assessing Language Arts, and Chapter 9, The Writing Process, for more on portfolios.

Several important principles can be learned from Jaqui's lesson using literature-based instruction with ELL students:

1. Children learn a second language best when instruction draws on their prior experiences, which occurs naturally in response-centered, literature-based lessons.
2. Children will respond in different ways, no matter what their native language or level of English proficiency. They should be allowed to respond in their native languages, in English, or using a combination of the two. What's important is that students are actively engaged in a learning experience (as explained by Piaget's [1973, 1977] cognitive-constructivist theories).

Figure 3.4   "Word Wall" for *Millions of Cats*

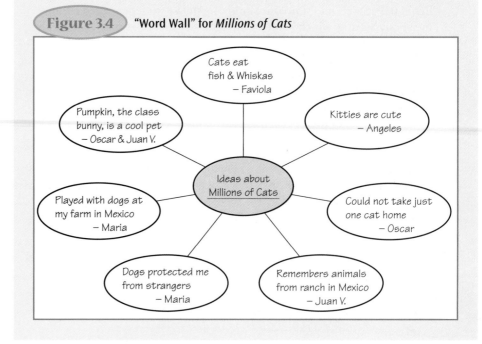

3. Children are empowered to use language for meaningful purposes when the teacher focuses on what they are trying to say (as explained in Vygotsky's [1962, 1978] social interactionist theories), rather than on a text.

See Chapters 1 and 2 for more on the theories of Piaget and Vygotsky.

Assessment: Assessment Toolbox 3.1, Stages of English Language Proficiency, has been filled in for Jaqui's students (see Assessment Toolbox 3.2, p. 96). It includes descriptions of each stage, observations of the children, and differentiations made for children at different stages to learn the same content. Jaqui used her observations of these students during the lesson to fill in the assessment form at the appropriate stage. She adapted further instruction to match the levels of English proficiency of her nine students with strategies appropriate for each stage.

Lesson 2: Content-Based ELD about Place Value in Mathematics

The next step for Jaqui was to plan a content-based ELD lesson on place value in mathematics. The relevant content standard was from the numbers and operations standard for Grades 3–5: "In grades 3–5 all students should understand numbers, ways of representing numbers, relationships among numbers, and number systems (NCTM, 2000, p. 148)."

The etymology of the term *place value* comes from the French *place*, which means "street" or "real estate value."

Conducting the literature-based ELD lesson on *Millions of Cats* provided Jaqui with an opportunity to assess her students' level of language acquisition (see Assessment Toolbox 3.2). Now, she would use that data to adapt a lesson on key vocabulary and main concepts for place value. Figure 3.5 (p. 97) is a planning form for content-based ELD lesson differentiation. Note the key vocabulary and main concepts Jaqui chose and how she adapted this lesson for different stages of language proficiency.

Lesson 3: SDAIE about Problem Solving: "How much is a million?"

Next, Jaqui planned a lesson to meet a national content standard from *Principles and Practices for School Mathematics* (NCTM, 2000) from the section Numbers and Operations, Standards for Grades 3–5 (p. 148): "Understand numbers, ways of representing numbers, relationships among numbers, and number systems." One of the specific expectations of this standard for grades 3–5 is that students should "recognize equivalent representations for the same number and generate them by decomposing and composing numbers." The standard maintains that "students' study and use of numbers should be extended to include larger numbers." Moreover, students "need to develop strategies for judging the relative sizes of numbers" and "explore whole numbers using a variety of models and contexts." For example, a third-grade class could "explore the size of 1,000 by skip-counting to 1,000, building a model of 1,000 using ten hundred charts, gather 1,000 items such as paper clips and developing efficient ways to count them, or using strips that are 10 or 100 centimers long to show the length of 1,000 centimeters."

(continued)

ASSESSMENT
TOOLBOX

3.2 Stages of English Language Proficiency for Jaqui's Students

Here, Assessment Toolbox 3.1 has been slightly adapted and completed for students in Jaqui Denenberg's class. Jaqui used her observations of nine ELL students during a lesson to identify the appropriate stage for each child and to adapt further instruction for him or her.

Stage	Assessment/Comments	Strategies
3. Extending production		
• **Advanced fluency**	All: Understand story when read in English without relying on pictures. Oscar: Speaks comfortably in English. Interrupted story for other students. Can write in English but prefers Spanish. Proud when his responses put on "word wall."	Self-selected reading Independent textbook reading Independent notetaking Leading discussions Completing independent or collaborative projects
• **Intermediate fluency**	Faviola: Knows many English words. When comfortable, speaks and writes in English.	Self-selected reading Jigsaw textbook reading Guided notetaking
• **Speech emergent**	Juan L.: Responds in both English and Spanish. Uses Spanish when doesn't know English word. Likes to talk a lot so prefers Spanish. Doesn't write in English. Magdalena: Understands English and speaks some. Not comfortable speaking English.	Self-selected reading Using language experience approach (LEA) Guided reading Journal writing
2. Early production	All: Understand directions in English, and follow story with help of pictures. Mario: Once understood story, was eager to share experiences with dogs in Mexico. Can identify certain words in book relying on pictures. Angeles: Understands that "millions" is large quantity. Listens and relates to pictures in book. Can identity certain words in book she knows. Juan V.: Generally responds and writes in Spanish. Curious about English words and asks for meanings. Dixar: Spoke these English words when talking about story: cat, dog, bird, fish.	Listing objects in picture Illustrating words and concepts Classifying and labeling categories
1. Preproduction	Veronica: Limited understanding of directions in English. Knows meanings of some English words. Aware of what was happening in parts of story by relying on pictures.	Using total physical response (TPR) Using visual aids Using realia

Figure 3.5 Planning Form for Content-Based ELD Lesson Differentiation

Planning Form

Content Area _Mathematics_   **Lesson Focus/Concept** _Place value up to 1 million_

Stage of Language Proficiency	ELD Adaptation of Lesson	Content Instruction: _Key Vocabulary and Main Concepts_
3. Extending production	Follow the same procedures as outlined below for Preproduction and Early production PLUS these tasks: Have students write paragraphs about how the manipulatives relate to the numbers and these words: _one/1/bean, ten/10/stick, hundred/100/flat, thousand/ 1,000/stack_.	**Key Vocabulary** <u>one</u>: "a unit" <u>ten</u>: "a unit of 10 ones" <u>hundred</u>: "a unit of 10 tens" <u>thousand</u>: "a unit of 10 hundreds" <u>million</u>: "a unit of 10 hundred thousands" **Main Concepts** <u>Place value</u>: The value of a digit in a number changes according to its position.
2. Early production	Follow the same procedure as outlined below for Preproduction PLUS these tasks: Show students the chart with place value and key vocabulary and direct them as follows: "Talk to your neighbor. What do you see?" Write down students' responses on an LEA chart, and point to the place value chart. Have students draw pictures of 1 (bean), 10 (stick), 100 (flat), and 1,000 (stack). Draw pictures on the board while the students draw their own.	
1. Preproduction	Begin with whole class. Do TPR with manipulatives, as follows: "Pick up 1 (bean)." "Pick up 10 (10 beans glued on a Popsicle stick)." "With a partner, let's count 10 sticks together to make 100 (10 sticks glued together to make a flat)." "Let's count by 100s to make 1,000 (each of 10 students brings a flat to the front of the room to construct a 1,000 stack). We will show 1,000,000 (10 hundred thousands) on graph paper)." Students draw a unit of 1 (bean) in their math journals.	

Since her content-based ELD lesson taught key vocabulary and main concepts, Jaqui planned this SDAIE lesson to solve the original problem that began this sequence of lessons: "How much is a million?" Her ELL students explored the relative sizes of numbers in two ways. First, they showed 1 million by photocopying graph paper with a grid of 10,000 $\frac{1}{8}$-inch squares. They made 100 copies and taped them together on the classroom wall to show the relative size of 1 million. Second, they showed 1 million by building a millions cube. To do so, they first made base-10 sticks by gluing 10 beans onto a popsicle stick. Next, they glued 10 sticks on a piece of cardboard to form a raft of 100. Then, they stacked 10 of these rafts on top of each other and held them together with rubber bands to form a 1,000 block. Eight of the students formed a cube shape—four on the ground and four standing—and used a ruler to measure the space needed for 10,000 cubes up and across each side of the cube. The students held yarn to show the dimensions of the cube and once again demonstrated their solution to the problem: "How much is a million?" Finally, they all wrote about what they had done in their mathematics journals, each child according to his or her stage of language acquisition. Figure 3.6, Planning Form for SDAIE Lesson Differentiation, shows how Jaqui developed this lesson.

Figure 3.6 Planning Form for SDAIE Lesson Differentiation

Planning Form

Content Area Mathematics   **Lesson Focus/Concept** Place value up to 1 million   **Problem** "How much is a million?"

Stage of Language Proficiency	SDAIE Adaptation of Lesson	Focus/Problem
3. Extending production	Journal Writing Students write or the teacher takes dictation for creating a manual on how to construct a "millions wall" or "millions cube."	"How much is a million?" 1. Show 1 million using graph paper or the classroom wall. 2. Build a "millions cube."

2. Early production	Journal Writing
	1. Diagram and label:
	   (a) a "millions wall"
	   (b) a "millions cube"	

1. Preproduction	Journal Writing 1. Draw a "millions wall." 2. Diagram a "millions cube."	

Teaching and Assessing Vocabulary Development for First- and Second-Language Learners

Our discussion of social constructivist theory has illustrated that teachers can play a very important role in children's development of vocabulary. One way to do so is to provide many interesting, hands-on experiences in the classroom, encouraging children to experiment with and discover things for themselves. Another way is to create many opportunities for interaction between the teacher and students and between students, as well.

Semantic Mapping

Johnson and Pearson (1984) define *semantic maps* as "diagrams that help children see how words are related to one another" (p. 12). Other terms you'll encounter that describe this visual means of relating many ideas to a central one are *cluster, web,* and *"word wall."* (I use the last term throughout this book.) To create a semantic map, use the following strategy (Johnson, 2001; Johnson & Pearson, 1984):

1. Choose a key word related to students' ideas, interests, or current studies or just any word.
2. Write the word in the middle of the chalkboard or a large piece of chart-paper.
3. Brainstorm other words that are related to the key word, or classify the new words in categories that you or the students suggest and label them.
4. Discuss the words and their relationships and meanings.

See Figure 3.7 for an example of a semantic map created around the word *beds,* which was drawn by Gordon in the fifth grade.

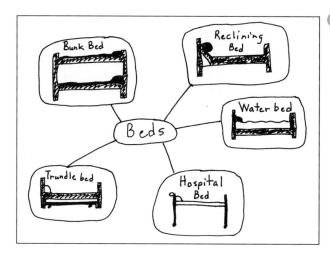

Figure 3.7 Semantic Map for *Beds*

Semantic Maps with Armenian-Speaking Students

One of my students, Jennifer Howard, did a semantic mapping activity with a group of children who were primarily English language learners (ELL); they spoke Armenian as their first language. Jennifer read Mary O'Neill's (1961) book of color poems, *Hailstones and Halibut Bones,* which she thought would be a good choice for an English language development activity.

Jennifer read the poems and talked about them with the students. She modeled a semantic map (or "word wall") by writing the word *yellow* in the middle of the chalkboard. Then she asked the students to mention all the other words for *yellow* they could think of and to name *yellow* things; she wrote down all these words. Next, each child wrote or drew in response to the poems. Aris did a semantic map for the word *green* because he said it was his favorite color (see Figure 3.8).

Jennifer tells how the activity went:

I began reading, and they really liked the poems. They wanted to express their opinions about the colors and other objects they thought of that were the same color. We created a word wall around the color *yellow.*

They loved it! They all stood up and encircled the word wall and me. They were excited to think up things that weren't in the original poem. Then they did their own semantic maps.

I was surprised at the level of writing of these students. I think the more English language learners are exposed to books, reading, writing, and lots of discussion, the stronger their achievements will become. This lesson was good because it was visual and hands on, two things that help lower the *affective filter* for English language learners.

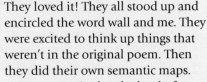

When walk in the park or at My backyard I see green and at the park all green. I see people wear shoes. We play monkey in the midell.

Figure 3.8 Semantic Map of the Color *Green*

See Chapter 14, Language across the Curriculum, for an entire thematic unit on colors that began with this book.

ELL

This Teaching Idea is effective for ELL students because it uses these strategies:

- *Visuals:* illustrated book
- *Interaction and modeling:* semantic map
- *Tapping prior experience:* colors
- *Hands-on experience:* drawing as prewriting

Word Play

From infancy, children naturally play with language and words. Kornei Chukovsky, a Russian linguist, collected language samples from children for many years to support his claim that children are linguistic geniuses. Consider these examples from his book *From Two to Five* (1971): "A bald man has a bare-foot head," "A mint candy makes a draft in your mouth," and "A grasshopper's husband is a daddy hopper" (p. 62).

Teachers who support this natural genius help children develop their own understanding and control over language (Pellegrini, Galda, Dresden, & Cox, 1991). Teachers can do this by recognizing and valuing children's playful inventions; by providing time, books, and materials for language play; and by displaying children's written examples of language play. Here are some suggestions for encouraging playing with language and words.

Synonyms and Antonyms

Synonyms are words that have the same or similar meanings. Make a game of searching for synonyms for color words. Places to look could be at home, in the crayon box, or on boxes of hair coloring at the store. (See the preceding Teaching Idea for semantic mapping with color words.) Encourage older children to use a thesaurus for writing.

- *Children's books*
  The American Heritage Children's Thesaurus (Hellweg, 1997)
  The Clear and Simple Thesaurus Dictionary (Wittels & Greisman, 1999)
  A First Thesaurus (Wittels & Greisman, 1985)
  Scholastic Children's Thesaurus (Bollard, 1998)

Antonyms are words that have opposite meanings. Start with a good children's book of antonyms, and brainstorm lists, which can be illustrated or acted out.

- *Children's books*
  Antonyms: Hot and Cold and Other Words That Are as Different as Night and Day (Hanson, 1972)
  Fast-Slow, High-Low (Spier, 1972)
  Push-Pull, Empty-Full: A Book of Opposites (Hoban, 1972)

Homonyms

These are words that look the same (*homographs*) or sound the same (*homophones*) but have different spellings or meanings—for instance, *bear* (meaning "an animal" or "to carry") versus *bare* (meaning "uncovered"). Brainstorm lists, such as *bear/bare, flour/flower, to/too/two.* Or write and illustrate cartoons using the wrong word from a homophone pair (see Figure 3.9, p. 102).

WWW

Students can find anything to do with words at this website: **www.wordwizard.com**.

See Chapter 11 for more on playing with words.

GREAT BOOKS FOR CHILDREN

Word Play

Chortles: New and Selected Wordplay Poems (Merriam, 1989)
Herds of Words (MacCarthy, 1991)
It Figures! Fun Figures of Speech (Terban, 1993)

For more on homonyms, see the Lesson Plan in Chapter 10 (pp. 347–348).

Figure 3.9   Example of Student's Homograph

CHIKEN Legs

- *Children's books*
  A Chocolate Moose for Dinner (Gwynne, 1976)
  The Dove Dove: Funny Homograph Riddles (Terban, 1988)
  Eye Spy: A Mysterious Alphabet (Bourke, 1994)
  Hey, Hay! A Wagonful of Funny Homonym Riddles (Terban, 1991)
  The King Who Rained (Gwynne, 1970)
  A Little Pigeon Toad (Gwynne, 1988)
  The Sixteen-Hand Horse (Gwynne, 1980)

Parts of Speech

See Chapter 11 for more on grammar.

Introduce students to the parts of speech through literature. Have them illustrate parts of speech or make their own grammar books.

- *Children's books*
  Add It, Dip It, Fix It (Schneider, 1995)
  A Cache of Jewels and Other Collective Nouns (Heller, 1987)
  Hairy, Scary, Ordinary: What Is an Adjective? (Cleary, 2000)
  Kites Sail High: A Book about Verbs (Heller, 1988)
  Many Luscious Lollipops: A Book about Adjectives (Heller, 1989)
  Mine, All Mine: A Book about Pronouns (Heller, 1997)
  A Mink, a Fink, a Skating Rink: What Is a Noun? (Cleary, 1999)
  Seeing, Saying, Doing, Playing: A Big Book of Action Words (Gomi, 1994)
  Up Up and Away: A Book about Adverbs (Heller, 1991)

Onomatopoeia

These are words that sound like the sounds they describe—for example, *snap, crackle, pop*. Brainstorm a list of words in class, and then continue to add to it. Each of these words can be dramatized.

- *Children's books*
  City Sounds (Emberley, 1989)
  Click, Clack, Moo: Cows That Type (Cronin, 2000)
  Click, Rumble, Roar: Poems about Machines (Hopkins, 1987)
  The Cow That Went Oink (Most, 1990)
  Gobble, Growl, Grunt (Spier, 1971)
  Rat-a-Tat, Pitter Pat (Benjamin, 1987)
  Thump, Thump, Rat-a-Tat-Tat (Baer, 1989)
  Zin! Zin! Zin! A Violin (Moss, 1995)

Palindromes

These are words or sentences that can be read forward and backward—for example, *Mom, Dad,* and *Bob* and *Able was I ere I saw Elba* (attributed to Napoleon). Start a list of palindromes in class, and add to it. One second-grade teacher started a palindrome craze in her school. Together, the children in the school found over 1,000 palindromes, which were displayed in a long list outside her class.

- *Children's books*
  Go Hang a Salami! I'm a Lasagna Hog! and Other Palindromes (Agee, 1992)
  Sit on a Potato Pan, Otis (Agee, 1999)
  So Many Dynamos! (Agee, 1994)
  Too Hot to Hoot: Funny Palindrome Riddles (Terban, 1985)

Similes and Metaphors

Similes are expressions that make comparisons using *like* or *as*—for instance, *eats like a bird* or *as blue as the sky. Metaphors* are expressions that compare one thing to another without using *like* or *as*—for instance, Shakespeare's Romeo said *Juliet is the sun.* Poets often use similes and metaphors, which are both examples of figurative language. Have children write, illustrate, or dramatize their own similes and metaphors.

See Chapter 14, Language across the Curriculum, for more on similes and metaphors.

- *Children's books*
  As: A Surfeit of Similes (Juster, 1989)
  As Quick as a Cricket (Wood, 1982)
  Owl Moon (Yolen, 1987)
  Silver Seeds: A Book of Nature Poems (Paolilli & Brewer, 2001)

Riddles, Puns, and Conundrums

Riddles are puzzling questions that are solved by guessing—for example, *What has four or more wheels and flies? A garbage truck.* Puns are plays on words using sounds and meanings, such as *Two coin collectors got together for old dime's sake.* A conundrum is a riddle based on an imagined likeness between things that are unlike: *What did the goblin say to the ghost? Spook for yourself.* Have children write and illustrate riddles, puns, and conundrums. To get started, see *Funny You Should Ask: How to Make Up Jokes and Riddles with Wordplay* (Terban, 1992).

- *Children's books*
  Batty Riddles (Hall & Eisenberg, 1993)
  Geese Find the Missing Piece (Maestro, 1999)
  I Spy: A Book of Picture Riddles (Marzollo, 1992)
  Pets in Trumpets and Other Word-Play Riddles (Most, 1991)
  Remember Betsy Floss and Other Colonial American Riddles (Adler, 1987)

  Here is a lesson plan for word play using children's literature.

LESSON PLAN

Word Play and Literature

Level: Middle 1, Upper grade

Purpose: Children will listen to and enjoy good literature; discuss the book by responding to open, aesthetic questions and prompts; play with words and increase vocabulary; and draw and write in response to the book.

IRA/
NCTE

Standard 4: Students adjust their use of spoken, written, and visual language (e.g., conventions, style, vocabulary) to communicate effectively with a variety of audiences and for different purposes.

Materials:
1. *ANTics! An Alphabetical Anthology,* by Cathi Hepworth (1992)
2. Chartpaper and marking pens for a "word wall"
3. Plain white paper and pencils or crayons

Teaching Sequence:
1. Read the book *ANTics! An Alphabetical Anthology* aloud. It's a humorous book that uses ants to illustrate words from A to Z that all have an ant in them—for example, *There's E for Enchanter.*

More *Ant* Words

antibiotic, antlers, buoyant, cantaloupe, contestant, deodorant, distant, elephant, elegant, fragrant, gigantic, hydrant, infant, lieutenant, nonchalant, panther, pants, quadrant, radiant, rant, servant, slant, tarantula, transplant, unpleasant, vacant, and *want*

2. Use aesthetic, open-ended questions and prompts to discuss the book. Ask students:
   "What did you think of the book?"
   "What was your favorite part?"
   "What did you notice that all the words in the book had in common?"
   "Can you think of other words the author/illustrator could have used?"
3. Create a word wall on chartpaper by writing down all the words the children suggest. Write "Ant Words" in the center.
4. Ask children to pick a word from the book or the word wall or to think of their own word to illustrate in a class book of antics.

Extending Activities:
1. Write and illustrate more *antics* (see Figure 3.10).
2. Dramatize a short scene based on one of their antics.
3. Write and sing a song for an antic.
4. Make a list of words that all have another small word in them, such as cat in *caterpillar, catastrophe, catalyst, cataclysmic,* and so on (see Figure 3.11).

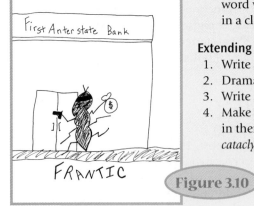

Figure 3.10 Example of Student's *Antic*

Figure 3.11   Example of Word Play Using *Cat*

decathlon

5. Make all the small words possible by using the letters in a big word.
6. Read a book about ants:
    Ant Cities (Dorros, 1987)
    Ants (Pascoe, 1999)
    I Wonder What It's Like to Be an Ant
        (Hovanec, 2000)
    Let's Take a Field Trip to an Ant Colony
        (Furgang, 2000)
    Two Bad Ants (Van Allsburg, 1988)
7. Make a simple ant farm. Fill a large jar about two-thirds full with sifted dirt, and put some ants in it. Add a small piece of damp sponge for water and a little food (try sweets, seeds, other insects). Cover the jar with a lid with holes in it. Keep the jar in a dark place, but bring it into the light to watch the ants.

Assessment:

1. Observe the children's reactions while you read the book. Did they listen and seem to enjoy it?
2. Were they able to play with words, brainstorm new *ant* words for the word wall, and write their own antics in response to the book? (See Figure 3.10, a sample child's antics drawing.)
3. Assess vocabulary development using Assessment Toolbox 3.3, the Anecdotal Record (p. 106), noting new words individual children use while writing on the word wall or creating their own antics.

Assessing Vocabulary

A useful tool for assessing vocabulary in an ongoing and authentic way is an anecdotal record assessment (ARA) using sticky labels and the form shown in Assessment Toolbox 3.3. This is also a very contextualized assessment tool, which makes it especially useful for children learning English as a second language (Boyd-Batstone, 2004). The ARA can be adapted to each child's level of English proficiency in a focused observation of his or her performance in a standards-based lesson. It can also be used to assess other areas of the language arts or in the content areas—again, especially for English language learners. The key idea is that each observation is focused on a particular standard. To use the ARA, follow these steps.

- Choose a focus—for example, language and vocabulary development.
- Add a standard.

WWW

Go to **ezra.mts.jhu.edu/ ~naomi/insects/ants.html**, a web project on insects created by a second-grade student.

(continued)

Teaching and Assessing Vocabulary Development for First- and Second-Language Learners

ASSESSMENT TOOLBOX

3.3 Anecdotal Record Assessment (ARA)

The use of sticky labels provides a simple, effective way of keeping standards-based* anecdotal records of children's language and vocabulary development. This form has been completed for a third-grade Cambodian American ELL student named Samrith, whose home language is Khmer.

Name _____ Samrith _____ Grade _____ 3 _____

Focus _____ English language and vocabulary development _____

Anecdotal Record

1 Samrith: Standard 3   9-10
   Answered questions about color poems from <u>Hailstones and Halibut Bones</u> with a few words. For word wall on "yellow" said: "Sun is yellow; stars is yellow; yellow is the sun."
	2 Samrith: Standard 3 9-17
	   Listened attentively to <u>Antics.</u> Volunteered and answered questions correctly. Said ants were "insects." Wrote "Inf<u>ant</u>" for his 'antic' and drew picture of ant in a diaper.

3 Samrith: Standard 3   9-24
   Responded to story <u>Two Bad Ants</u> in a complete sentence: "I like it when ants were bad." Repeated words on KWL chart on ants: "colony; queen; worker."
	4 Samrith: Standard 4 10-1
	   While making ant farm described ants as: "cute; black; shiny and fuzzy" and "looked like they were dancing to funny music" and started dancing saying: "Look at me—I'm a ant dancing"

5	**6**

Summary

Strengths: Listens well; enjoys stories read aloud; participates in discussions; understands wordplay and multiple   meanings of words; responds in multiple ways

Needs: Lots of read-alouds and literature discussions; opportunities to use language

Recommendations: Provide engaging activities with literature and language (loved making ant farm); give minilessons on subject-verb agreement; start personal dictionary; try songwriting

*The standards used here are the IRA/NCTE national standards, which are printed inside the front cover.

IRA/ NCTE

Source: Adapted from Boyd-Batstone (2004).

- Choose a group of children to observe each day. If you have 30 students, focus on 6 a day from Monday through Thursday; if you have 20, do 5 a day. Use Friday to work with children who have been absent or out of the room or any you would like to observe more closely.
- Prepare labels before making your observations. On each, write the date, the name of each child you will observe, and a standard.
- Conduct observations during an appropriate time—for example, during a literature discussion with a word wall, semantic map, KWL chart, or group work.
- Record observations. Note on a sticky label the language and vocabulary use for each of the children in a small group. Use a clipboard with a sheet of prepared lables attached.
- Place labels on a form for each child.
- File each form in a folder for each child.
- Summarize your observations and make recommendations. After several rounds of observations, use the records to summarize each child's language and vocabulary development over time and to make recommendations for next instructional steps.

Answers to Questions about First- and Second-Language Development

- *How do children develop a first and a second language?*

The social constructivist perspective of how children acquire a first language merges ideas from two viewpoints: the cognitive-constructivist theories of Jean Piaget and the social interactionist theories of Lev Vygotsky. Piaget maintained that children learn a first language as they first assimilate and then accommodate language symbols to their already existing symbolic structures, or schema. They do this through a process of self-discovery and through direct, hands-on experiences, like working puzzles and playing with clay. Vygotsky maintains that a first language is learned through the interaction of physical, linguistic, and social factors and that adults and older children play an active role in stimulating younger children's language growth. This stimulation takes place in what Vygotsky calls the *zone of proximal development*.

Children progress through approximately the same stages of first-language development but at surprisingly different rates. They speak their first words at around 1 year, and by the time they enter school at age 5, they are able to communicate effectively with others. Students with special needs learn language in inclusive classrooms that meet their needs through providing special services and support, adapting instruction, and performing assessment that is sensitive to culture and language diversity and focuses on student strengths and goals for intervention.

Cummins identifies two dimensions of proficiency in acquiring a second language: basic interpersonal communication skills (BICS), or informal, social speaking, and cognitive academic language proficiency (CALP), or language skills used in school tasks. Proficiency in both dimensions of language is determined by the amount of contextual support present, or context-embedded communication. The goal in educating language-minority students is for them to be able to use language in cognitively demanding, context-reduced instructional situations.

Krashen distinguishes between language acquisition and language learning. He maintains that we acquire a second language the same way in which we acquire a first: through successful communication of meaningful messages. This is language acquisition. Language learning is knowledge about the language, such as grammar. Krashen maintains that a communicative-based approach is the best way for language-minority students to develop basic skills in a second language; they do so through what he calls comprehensible input. Students acquire a second language when they obtain comprehensible input in a low-anxiety setting.

The approach advocated today is communicative-based instruction, which focuses on meaning, or students' ability to communicate messages. Learning English as a second language will be more successful when teachers assess students' individual levels of proficiency and then align language lessons and instructional strategies accordingly.

- ### What do we know when we know how to use language?

Language consists of four interacting systems: phonology (sounds), semantics (meanings), syntax (sentence formations), and pragmatics (use). Phonological information enables us to make sounds that have meanings and understand the meanings of sounds that other people make. Phonemes—the smallest units of contrasting sounds with different meanings—are the basic building blocks of the phonology of any language. Semantic information enables us to produce sentences with certain meanings and to understand those of others. Morphemes are the smallest units of meaning in each language; they cannot be divided without losing meaning. Syntactic information enables us to combine words in sentences to express our ideas and understand those of others. Word order is determined by the syntax of a language. Pragmatics is the set of the rules that govern the use of language for different functions, relating to other language users and specific situations. Halliday provides a good definition of language in terms of how people use it: as "'meaning potential,' that is, as sets of opinions, or alternatives, in meaning, that are available to the speaker-hearer" (1975, p. 64).

- ### How do teachers support and assess children's growing knowledge of language and vocabulary?

Teachers provide many opportunities for interaction and hands-on experiences. In addition, teachers create a print-rich environment, putting words on display and doing semantic mapping activities (also called *webbing, clustering,* or "*word walls*"). Many books, writing materials, and various types of technology and media are available in print-rich classrooms. Time for sharing and group work are important, as well. Teachers also create opportunities for wordplay by reading books that focus on words and encouraging children to respond to them through talking, reading, drawing, and writing. Anecdotal record assessment (ARA) with a focus on language and vocabulary development is an excellent authentic assessment strategy.

Looking Further

1. Check your baby book and find out when you spoke your first words, phrases, and sentences and what they were. Have a group of children find out the same information, and talk about how we learn language.

2. Describe three learning activities for kindergarten: (a) one that strictly reflects Piaget's notion of how children acquire language, (b) another that reflects Vygotsky's ideas, and (c) a third that combines the two views.

3. Observe in a classroom, and record children's language while they interact in large or small groups. Analyze and classify their language and how they use it according to Halliday's model of children's language (see Table 3.2), or keep an anecdotal

record using sticky labels (see Assessment Toolbox 3.3).

4. Develop a semantic map with others in your class or with a group of children. How could you use this map to plan further learning experiences?

5. Do the following activity with a small group of language-minority students: (a) Ask the teacher to identify each child's stage of language proficiency. (b) Read a picture book, discuss it, and ask children to draw and write in response to it. (c) Describe what happened.

6. Interview someone in a school or district office who's responsible for identifying students' stages of language proficiency. Ask him or her to describe the procedures used for doing this.

Children's Books and Software

Adler, D. (1987). *Remember Betsy Floss and other Colonial American riddles.* New York: Holiday House.

Agee, J. (1992). *Go hang a salami! I'm a lasagna hog! and other palindromes.* New York: Farrar, Straus, & Giroux.

Agee, J. (1994). *So many dynamos!* New York: Farrar, Straus, & Giroux.

Agee, J. (1999). *Sit on a potato pan, Otis.* New York: Farrar, Straus, & Giroux.

Baer, G. (1989). *Thump, thump, rat-a-tat-tat.* New York: Harper & Row.

Benjamin, A. (1987). *Rat-a-tat, pitter pat.* New York: Crowell.

Bollard, J. K. (1998). *Scholastic children's thesaurus.* New York: Scholastic.

Borns, M. (1981). *The hink pink book.* New York: Little, Brown.

Bourke, L. (1994). *Eye spy: A mysterious alphabet.* San Francisco: Chronicle.

Cleary, B. (1999). *A mink, a fink, a skating rink: What is a noun?* Minneapolis: Carolrhoda.

Cleary, B. (2000). *Hairy, scary, ordinary: What is an adjective?* Minneapolis: Carolrhoda.

Cronin, D. (2000). *Click, clack, moo: Cows that type.* New York: Simon & Schuster.

Dorros, A. (1987). *Ant cities.* New York: Harper & Row.

Emberley, R. (1989). *City sounds.* Boston: Little, Brown.

Furgang, K. (2000). *Let's take a field trip to an ant colony.* New York: PowerKids Press.

Gomi, T. (1994). *Seeing, saying, doing, playing: A big book of action words.* San Francisco: Chronicle.

Gwynne, F. (1970). *The king who rained.* New York: Windmill.

Gwynne, F. (1976). *A chocolate moose for dinner.* New York: Windmill.

Gwynne, F. (1980). *The sixteen-hand horse.* New York: Prentice-Hall.

Gwynne, F. (1988). *A little pigeon toad*. New York: Simon & Schuster.

Hall, K., & Eisenberg, L. (1993). *Batty riddles*. New York: Dial.

Hall, R. (1984). *Sniglets*. New York: Macmillan.

Hanson, J. (1972). *Antonyms: Hot and cold and other words that are as different as night and day*. New York: Lerner.

Heller, R. (1987). *A cache of jewels and other collective nouns*. New York: Grossett & Dunlop.

Heller, R. (1988). *Kites sail high: A book about verbs*. New York: Scholastic.

Heller, R. (1989). *Many luscious lollipops: A book about adjectives*. New York: Grossett & Dunlop.

Heller, R. (1991). *Up up and away: A book about adverbs*. New York: Grossett & Dunlop.

Heller, R. (1997). *Mine, all mine: A book about pronouns*. New York: Grossett & Dunlop.

Hellweg, P. (1997). *The American Heritage children's thesaurus*. Boston: Houghton Mifflin.

Hepworth, C. (1992). *ANTics! An alphabetical anthology*. New York: Putnam's.

Hoban, T. (1972). *Push-pull, empty-full: A book of opposites*. New York: Macmillan.

Hopkins, L. B. (Comp.). (1987). *Click, rumble, roar: Poems about machines* (A. H. Audette, Illus.). New York: Crowell.

Hovanec, E. M. (2000). *I wonder what it's like to be an ant*. New York: PowerKids Press.

Juster, N. (1989). *As: A surfeit of similes*. New York: Morrow.

MacCarthy, P. (1991). *Herds of words*. New York: Dial.

Maestro, G. (1999). *Geese find the missing piece*. New York: HarperCollins.

Marzollo, J. (1992). *I spy: A book of picture riddles* (W. Wicks, Photo.). New York: Scholastic.

Merriam, E. (1989). *Chortles: New and selected wordplay poems* (S. Hamanaka, Illus.). New York: Morrow.

Moss, L. (1995). *Zin! Zin! Zin! A violin*. New York: Simon & Schuster.

Most, B. (1990). *The cow that went oink*. San Diego: Harcourt Brace Jovanovich.

Most, B. (1991). *Pets in trumpets and other word-play riddles*. New York: Harcourt Brace Jovanovich.

O'Neill, M. (1961). *Hailstones and halibut bones* (L. Weisgard, Illus.). Garden City, NY: Doubleday.

Paolilli, P., & Brewer, D. (2001). *Silver seeds: A book of nature poems*. New York: Viking.

Pascoe, E. (1999). *Ants*. Woodbridge, CT: Blackbirch Press.

Schneider, R. M. (1995). *Add it, dip it, fix it*. New York: Houghton Mifflin.

Spier, P. (1971). *Gobble, growl, grunt*. New York: Doubleday.

Spier, P. (1972). *Fast-slow, high-low*. New York: Doubleday.

Terban, M. (1985). *Too hot to hoot: Funny palindrome riddles*. New York: Clarion.

Terban, M. (1988). *The dove dove: Funny homograph riddles*. New York: Clarion.

Terban, M. (1991). *Hey, hay! A wagonful of funny homograph riddles*. New York: Clarion.

Terban, M. (1992). *Funny you should ask: How to make up jokes and riddles with wordplay* (J. O'Brien, Illus.). New York: Clarion.

Terban, M. (1993). *It figures! Fun figures of speech*. New York: Clarion.

Tremain, R. (1979). *Teapot, switcheroo, and other silly word games*. New York: Greenwillow.

Van Allsburg, C. (1988). *Two bad ants*. Boston: Houghton Mifflin.

Vocabulary Challenge [Computer software]. Available from Learning Well.

Vocabulary Game [Computer software]. Available from J & S Software.

Wittels, H., & Greisman, J. (1985). *A first thesaurus*. Racine, WI: Western.

Wittels, H., & Greisman, J. (1999). *The clear and simple thesaurus dictionary*. New York: Grosset & Dunlap.

Wood, A. (1982). *As quick as a cricket* (D. Wood, Illus.). New York: Child's Play International.

Yolen J. (1987). *Owl moon*. New York: Philomel.

Emergent Literacy and Biliteracy

- *How do young children learn to read and write their first and/or second language?*
- *How should we teach young children to read and write when learning English as a first or second language?*

REFLECTIVE RESPONSE

Write a brief memoir of your own experiences in learning to read and write in English as your first or second language, both at home and in school. Compare them to the experiences of the children described in this chapter.

Emergent Literacy

Views of how children become literate have changed over the years. A study by Morphett and Washburne in 1931 concluded that children needed to reach the mental age of 6½ years before they could learn to read. So-called readiness teaching methods for young children were supposed to prepare them to read (Gates & Bond, 1936). Prerequisites included a range of skills, from knowing letter names to being able to walk on a balance beam. Children's writing was virtually ignored, as it was assumed that children had to be able to read before they could write.

WWW

For information and resources, in English and Spanish, see the website for the National Association for the Education of Young Children (NAEYC): **www.naeyc.org**.

The readiness view wasn't challenged until the 1960s and 1970s, when studies of children who were early "natural" readers (Clark, 1976; Clay, 1967; Durkin, 1966) and writers (Clay, 1975; Graves, 1978a) showed that literate behavior doesn't begin at a particular age but emerges continually. Specifically, literacy development begins with children's first experiences with print in the home and continues through preschool and the first few years of formal schooling (Clay, 1989; Goodman, 1986; Harste, Woodward, & Burke, 1984; Holdaway, 1979; Taylor, 1983; Teale & Sulzby, 1989). This research laid the groundwork for the emergent literacy perspective of how children learn to read and write (Sulzby & Teale, 2003). Sulzby (1989) defines *emergent literacy* as "the reading and writing behaviors of young children that precede and develop into conventional literacy" (p. 7).

SNAPSHOT   Apples and the First Week of First Grade

Marion Harris was in her second year of teaching first grade in Denham Springs, Louisiana, a small town near Baton Rouge. During the first week of school, some students brought her apples, which spontaneously provided active learning and literacy experiences for these emerging readers and writers. In reading this Snapshot, consider how Marion observed and listened to her students from day to day—their ideas, interests, and efforts at making meaning in reading and writing—and then used this information to plan further opportunities for meaningful literacy experiences. Take note of the teaching strategies she uses, which we'll return to later in this chapter in discussing ways to begin teaching young children to read and write.

WWW

Go to **http://michiganapples. com** for information from the Michigan Apple Committee.

Day 1. Apples for the Teacher during Sharing Time

It's the first day of school, and three of Marion's students bring her apples—really! She thanks the students and displays the apples prominently on her desk, but then she forgets about them. (Marion doesn't really like apples.) During sharing time, when some of the children ask why she hasn't eaten the apples, Marion hedges slightly on the truth and says that she wants to share the apples in a special way. This gets the children excited. Marion listens as they speculate about what she means, and she begins to think about how she might really use the apples.

Day 2. Reading Aloud and Writing and Drawing in Small Groups

Marion has planned literacy experiences around apples. She's found a story riddle in a file that she developed during her student-teaching days. She gathers the children on the rug for reading aloud:

> **An Apple Riddle Story**
> Once upon a time, there was a little star in the sky. This little star was not happy. It wanted to have a little, round, red house with no windows and no doors and a little, brown chimney. The star came down to earth.

It met a bear and asked, "Do you know where I can find a little, round, red house with no windows, no doors, and a little, brown chimney?" Mr. Bear said, "No, but why don't you ask Mr. Fox?" So the star asked Mr. Fox, "Do you know where I can find a little, round, red house with no windows, no doors, and a little, brown chimney?" Mr. Fox said, "No, but why don't you ask Mr. Owl?" So the star asked Mr. Owl, "Do you know where I can find a little, round, red house with no windows, no doors, and a little, brown chimney?" Mr. Owl said, "Don't you know, little star, of the perfect place you are looking for? Look under the big tree in the orchard."

This is a good flannel-board story. Use felt figures of the star, bear, fox, owl, apple tree, and apple that are big enough to fit over the star. Children can also dramatize the story or make puppets and props and tell it to others.

Marion tells the children that this is a riddle and they should guess the answer. A lively discussion follows, as the children try to guess the perfect place for the little star. Someone suggests an apple, but another child says that there aren't stars inside apples. Marion takes this as her cue to cut one of the apples in half horizontally and show the children the star-shaped seed pocket inside.

Next, Marion organizes the students in small groups, gives each group an apple, and asks each person to observe it: looking, touching, and smelling. After that, she asks the students to compare their observations with others in their group in order to come up with the most specific description possible. She tells them that if all the apples were together on the table, each group should be able to pick out its own.

Finally, Marion gives the children paper and pencils and an opportunity for writing and drawing by suggesting that they record their observations. The students excitedly begin to talk and look for things that will help them distinguish their own apples. They draw and write their observations, using combinations of pictures, letterlike forms, letters, and words to symbolize and record their experiences with apples (see Figure 4.1, p. 114).

Marion Harris's students observe and talk about apples so they are able to describe them before drawing and writing about the experience.

Figure 4.1

Children's Drawings and Writing about Apples

Michael

Darrell

Ashley

Leanica

Day 3. Planning to Make Apple Pies and a Whole-Class Writing Activity

After collecting all the apples in a bag, Marion asks a child from each group to find that group's apple and discuss the choice with the rest of its members. To help them, the students use the drawing and writing they did the day before. After much discussing, sharing of ideas, and comparing of notes, each group reclaims the apple it agreed was its own.

See Chapter 6, Reading, for more on language experience charts.

Someone suggests making pies with the apples. So the class makes plans for the next day, talking about how to do it and what they'll need. Marion writes the list of materials on a piece of chartpaper. This *language experience chart* is a text of the children's spoken language. Language experience charts and stories are frequently used in emergent literacy classrooms.

Things We Need to Make Apple Pies

1. Knives to cut the apples
2. Bowls for mixing
3. A pot for cooking
4. Sugar and cinnamon
5. Oil for frying
6. A frying pan
7. Pie dough from the store

Day 4. Making Apple Pies and Writing and Reading

The apples simmer slowly with some cinnamon and sugar on a hot plate, while Marion and the class make plans to bake apple pies. Marion writes down what the children say on another language experience chart as they watch the apples cook, and this becomes part of the "Morning Message" they write and read together.

Our Recipe for Apple Pies

Materials: Apples, sugar, cinnamon, pie dough, waxed paper, oil
Directions:
1. Cut up the apples and cook them in a pot with some sugar and cinnamon.
2. Mash the dough flat on waxed paper.
3. Put some cooked apples on it.
4. Pinch the dough together around the apples.
5. Fry the pies in oil.
6. Cool.
7. Eat.

Each child takes a piece of dough and some flour to keep it from sticking to his or her hands while flattening it out. The students talk in their small groups, and some of them start to imagine, rhyme, and play with the dough, flour, and language: "Yuck! Feels like Play-Doh. It's squishy. It's white. I like *flour* 'cause it's *powder*" (emphasizing the italicized words, as in a rhyme scheme).

Marion puts a dab of cooked apples on each child's piece of flattened dough. Then he or she folds the piece over, pinching its edges together. Next, each child cooks his or her pie in oil in a frying pan.

When the pies are cool, the children begin to eat them. Marion gets out more chartpaper to capture the children's ideas on a "word wall" of descriptive words that emerge from the children's experience of cooking and eating the little apple pies they've made themselves (see Figure 4.2). Marion sees that

Figure 4.2
"Word Wall" for Apple Pies

Apple Pies

Colors	Textures	Actions	Shapes
brown	icky	squashing	circle
white	yucky	frying	ball
yellow	slimy	patting	clam
	like Play-Doh	spooning	crab
	sticky	cooking	oyster
	stiff	rubbing	long
	greasy	sprinkling	hot dog
	smushy		round
	hot		turtle shell

Feelings	Sizes	Tastes	Sounds
happy	small	good	popping
sad	little	yucky	bubbling
glad	big	yummy	snapping
good	large	great	crackling
smiling	huge	delicious	sizzling
great		terrific	
jumpy		100% good!	

A cinquain follows this pattern:

Line 1:   Title
Line 2:   Description
Line 3:   Action
Line 4:   Feeling
Line 5:   Refers to title

October is officially known as the Apple Month.

many of these words fit into a pattern for writing called a *cinquain*. She adapts the pattern for her first-graders, and together, they write a cinquain about apple pies:

Apple Pies
Snapping, sizzling
Floating in the grease!
Yummy, great, delicious
100% good!

Day 5. Apple Books, Drama, and Centers

Over the past few days, the children's active involvement with apples has created a rich context of ideas and spoken language, which has provided a basis for emergent reading and writing experiences: drawing and writing, sharing time, and making language experience charts. Marion has provided more emergent literacy experiences by reading aloud about apples; by creating a print-rich environment, with lots of books, posters, and labels in the room; by dramatizing; and by establishing learning centers.

Since Marion practices integrated teaching, she uses the children's experiences with apples to provide a "ripple effect" of opportunities. What began with language and literacy experiences centered around the theme of apples now spreads to other subjects: social studies, science, mathematics, and art. Some of Marion's ideas are shown in the Ripple Effect chart on page 117. Many of these are excellent ways to begin the schoolyear, a time when some children still bring apples to their teachers—really!

The emergent literacy experiences that Marion Harris planned for her first-grade students reflect current views of how children in early childhood (birth–8 years) become literate. In addition to being involved and interested in their own learning, children use writing and reading for authentic purposes.

Emergent Reading

The studies of early natural readers (Clark, 1976; Durkin, 1966) clearly showed that young children are emerging as readers well before they come to school. Their early experiences with environmental print and storybook reading in the home or preschool are significant factors in their development of emergent reading.

Environmental Print

Children learn a great deal about print from the environment (Goodman, 1980; Harste, 1990; Sulzby & Teale, 2003). Children as young as 3 years old from various racial/ethnic and socioeconomic backgrounds are aware of what words in their environments mean. What's more, they understand more of these words

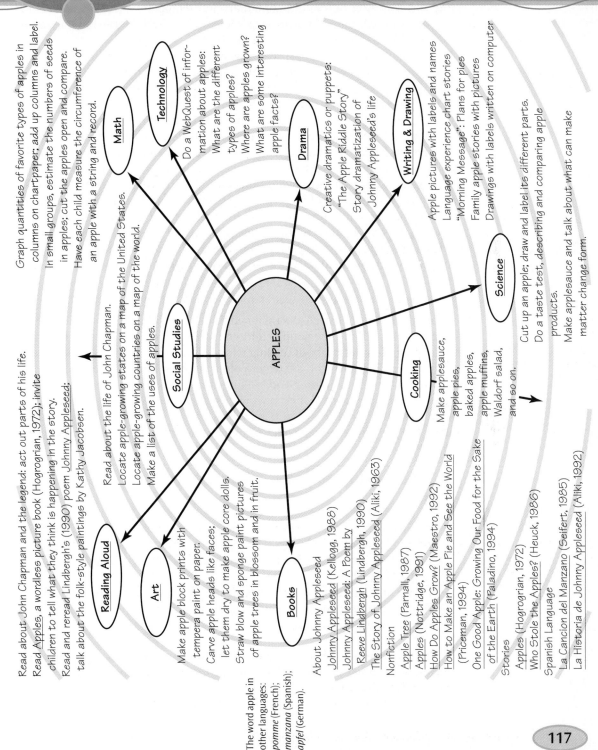

APPLES

Math
Graph quantities of favorite types of apples in columns on chartpaper; add up columns and label.
In small groups, estimate the numbers of seeds in apples; cut the apples open and compare.
Have each child measure the circumference of an apple with a string and record.

Technology
Do a WebQuest of information about apples:
What are the different types of apples?
Where are apples grown?
What are some interesting apple facts?

Drama
Creative dramatics or puppets:
"The Apple Riddle Story"
Story dramatization of Johnny Appleseed's life

Writing & Drawing
Apple pictures with labels and names
Language experience chart stories
"Morning Message": Plans for pies
Family apple stories with pictures
Drawings with labels written on computer

Science
Cut up an apple; draw and label its different parts.
Do a taste test, describing and comparing apple products.
Make applesauce and talk about what can make matter change form.

Cooking
Make applesauce, apple pies, baked apples, apple muffins, Waldorf salad, and so on.

Social Studies
Read about the life of John Chapman.
Locate apple-growing states on a map of the United States.
Locate apple-growing countries on a map of the world.
Make a list of the uses of apples.

Reading Aloud
Read about John Chapman and the legend: act out parts of his life.
Read *Apples*, a wordless picture book (Hogrogian, 1972); invite children to tell what they think is happening in the story.
Read and reread Lindbergh's (1990) poem *Johnny Appleseed*; talk about the folk-style paintings by Kathy Jacobsen.

Art
Make apple block prints with tempera paint on paper.
Carve apple heads like faces; let them dry to make apple core dolls.
Straw blow and sponge paint pictures of apple trees in blossom and in fruit.

The word apple in other languages:
pomme (French);
manzana (Spanish);
apfel (German).

Books
About Johnny Appleseed
Johnny Appleseed (Kellogg, 1988)
Apples (Nottridge, 1991)
How Do Apples Grow? (Maestro, 1992)
How to Make an Apple Pie and See the World (Priceman, 1994)
One Good Apple: Growing Our Food for the Sake of the Earth (Paladino, 1994)

Nonfiction
Apple Tree (Parnall, 1987)
Apples (Nottridge, 1991)
How Do Apples Grow? (Maestro, 1992)
How to Make an Apple Pie and See the World (Priceman, 1994)
One Good Apple: Growing Our Food for the Sake of the Earth (Paladino, 1994)

Stories
Apples (Hogrogian, 1972)
Who Stole the Apples? (Heuck, 1986)

Spanish Language
La Cancion del Manzano (Seifert, 1985)
La Historia de Johnny Appleseed (Aliki, 1992)

when they're presented in meaningful contexts. For instance, Harste et al. (1984) found that children understand complex concepts and words related to restaurants and common household containers and wrappers. These researchers explain that through understanding words in context, children develop the important expectation that language is meaningful.

My son Gordon demonstrated this expectation as a preschooler through his ongoing experiences playing with frozen yogurt containers. One day, he pointed at the lid, which had the acronym for the chain of stores on top—"TCBY!!" (i.e., "The Country's Best Yogurt")—and said, "Cream!" He had trouble saying "frozen yogurt," so he called it "i-cream" or "cream" for short.

Gordon's language learning continued. At 2½, he pointed at the yogurt container and said, "Yogurt eleven." He was learning numbers and thought the two exclamation points were the number 11. At the age of 3, he called it "TCBY" and laughed at himself for having said "cream" and "yogurt eleven." When he was almost 4, Gordon could read the words *chocolate* and *vanilla* in the daily list of flavors posted at the store, but he couldn't tell for sure if they had his favorite: *strawberry.* By 4 years and 3 months, though, he could read all the flavors listed— from *strawberry* to *papaya* to *kiwi.* And by age 5, Gordon was reading the store's brochure, which outlined the rules for owning a TCBY!! franchise.

Storybook Experiences

Perhaps the most extensively documented research finding (Sulzby, 1991; Sulzby & Teale, 2003) about how young children learn to read is a deceptively simple one: that children learn about reading when adults read aloud and talk to them about stories. Children who are read to often at home imitate reading behaviors like turning the pages, holding and looking at the book in certain ways, touching pages, retelling the story in their own words, and using booklike language. This pretend reading, or readinglike behavior, is in fact the beginning of reading. Sulzby (1985) calls these episodes of pretending *emergent storybook readings* or *independent reenactments.*

Taylor and Strickland (1986) have shown that parents of varying backgrounds do many of the same things with their children during storybook reading:

- talking with the child to further understand the story, its content, and print
- relating new information to what the child already knows
- expanding vocabulary by providing synonyms, brief explanations, and examples of words
- augmenting the story when a problem in understanding is anticipated
- listening to the child and answering questions about the storyline, characters, pictures, words, and letters

Laying this foundation is fundamental to emergent literacy. Research has shown that reading to children at home is associated with their later success in reading in school (Wells, 1985).

Concepts about Print

Based on her important research on emergent literacy, Marie Clay (1975, 1989, 1993) developed a Concepts about Print (CAP) observation instrument to find out what children are paying attention to in storybook reading experiences. With this information, teachers can monitor progress and guide their teaching of individual children. The CAP instrument assesses a child's concepts about orientation to books, directionality in reading, and concepts about letters, words, and sentences. It explores whether a child knows what is the front of the book, that print and not pictures tell the story, what a letter or word is, where the first or last letter in a word is found, the difference between upper- and lowercase letters, and some punctuation marks. Clay chose a booklet called *Sand* (1972) to be read to the child while administering the observation instrument, and she later added one called *Stones* (1979).

For the complete observational record, see Clay's *An Observation Survey of Early Literacy Achievement* (1993), which Clay says may be modified by teachers according to their students' backgrounds and needs. Assessment Toolbox 4.1, Concepts about Print (p. 120), is one such modification. It includes questions and directions you can use with a child while reading any storybook to him or her, and you may further modify and develop your own.

Emergent Writing

When given the materials and opportunities to write and an adult model to follow, young children experiment with and build a repertoire of knowledge about written language (Sulzby, 1992a). They draw on this repertoire to create what Holdaway (1979) and Clay (1975) call *gross approximations* of what will gradually become more and more like conventional writing.

Stages of Children's Emergent Writing

Sulzby (1989) describes a sequence of the forms of writing that mainstream U.S. children typically use as they begin to write: scribbling, drawing, nonphonetic letterstrings, invented spelling, and conventional orthography. In the next few sections, we'll discuss these forms or stages of writing by looking at examples from three children between 1 and 8 years old, the period of early childhood. You may remember these children—Elizabeth, Gordon, and Wyatt—from the Snapshot in Chapter 3.

Elizabeth, Gordon, and Wyatt are my children, and the mother is me.

Scribbling: Elizabeth at 1 year. Under the old chestnut table on which her mother writes at home, Elizabeth finds a pad of the smallest Post-its. She makes a mark on one with a pencil she's also found on the floor, pulls the Post-it off the pad, and sticks it to her arm. She repeats this process slowly until she's covered with notes, like a bird with square yellow feathers, each with its own curious marking. Then, as her mother watches with pride, she raises and flaps her paper-feathered arms and crows her pleasure in the marks she has made.

4.1 Concepts about Print

This tool is based on Marie Clay's Concepts about Print (CAP) observation instrument. It should be used to find out what children are paying attention to in storybook reading experiences. You can further modify this tool or develop your own to include specific questions and directions.

Name _____   Date _____

Book _____

Concepts about Print

Directions: Begin by saying, "Please help me while I read this story to you." Then give 1 point for each correct student response to a question or direction.

Question/Direction	Points	Comments
1. Where is the cover of the book?	_____	
2. Where do I start reading?	_____	
3. Where do I go after that?	_____	
4. Point to *a* word.	_____	
5. Point to *the* word _____.	_____	
6. Point to *a* letter.	_____	
7. Point to *the* letter _____.	_____	
8. Point to the first letter in a word.	_____	
9. Point to the last letter in a word.	_____	
10. Point to a capital letter.	_____	
11. Point to a lowercase letter.	_____	
12. Put your fingers around a sentence.	_____	
13. What is this [punctuation mark*] for?	_____	
14. Where is the end of the story?	_____	

Total Points _____

Summary:

* Period, question mark, comma, quotation mark, or exclamation point

Elizabeth is symbolizing her experience by making these marks. Just as she learned to speak by hearing words spoken to her and interacting with others around her, she is learning to write by watching others and having materials available.

Drawing: Gordon at 2–3 years old. Under the same old chestnut table, Gordon scribbles on a piece of paper. He holds it up to show his mother and talks to her about it:

Gordon:	Look! Kite!
Mother:	A cat?
Gordon:	No. Dat a kite. Like up in da 'ky. (He points to the picture and points up.) Like Mary Poppins. Like little boy in Mary Poppins. (He pretends to fly a kite.)
Mother:	I like that. (She writes the date in the corner of the paper as Gordon watches.)
Gordon:	I like dat. You write *Gordon?*
Mother:	Yes. (She writes *Gordon* in the corner of the paper as he watches.)
Gordon:	What dat? What you write?
Mother:	That's the date today: *November twentieth.*
Gordon:	Oh. You put dat on window?
Mother:	Yes. I'll put it on the window. (She tapes the drawing to the window next to some of her own papers.)
Gordon	(admiring his work on the window): Give me 'nother paper, Mama.

A year later, 3-year-old Gordon sits with his mother in a large armchair as she writes in a journal. He takes the pen out of her hand and vigorously makes marks on the page. He says, "Look, Mama. I write, too. I writing a building."

Gordon also takes pleasure in making symbols that signify his experience. He's able to tell his mother what his drawing means and to connect it to the story in a movie he's seen. He's also beginning to ask questions about writing. He reveals a *metalinguistic awareness* (Yaden & Templeton, 1986), which is the ability to talk about concepts of language by using the word *write* to describe what he's doing. Gordon shows that he understands some things about the writing process. For example, he knows that certain marks on a page mean something, like his name. He also wants to "publish" his writing, displaying it next to his mother's work on the window.

Vygotsky (1978) believes that when children engage in different types of symbol making, they do so by transforming shared social experience. This is true even of children as young as Elizabeth and Gordon. Piaget (1969) described this symbol-making function as "the ability to represent something—object, event, conceptual scheme—by means of a signifier—language, mental image, symbolic gestures" (p. 73).

Nonphonetic Letterstrings, Invented Spelling, and Conventional Orthography: Wyatt at 4–8 years old. At the age of 4, Wyatt draws pictures of his family. He then narrates what he's drawn to his grandmother while making large swirls with a red crayon next to the picture. He tells her the swirls are writing.

At 5, Wyatt draws a picture that he says shows Alice in Wonderland's sister reading a book to her. He draws a line around the picture and asks his mother for another piece of paper to glue next to it so he can make a book. He then carefully writes the letters and numbers he knows, explaining what's happening in the picture as he continues. Like other young children, he uses letter- and numberlike shapes to represent complex thoughts (Schickendanz, 1990). He tries many variations, experimenting with written language at this age. He can write his own name.

At age 6, as a first-grader, Wyatt writes about a trip to the zoo. At 7, as a second-grader, he writes a story about his dog. And at 8, as a third-grader, Wyatt writes about a family vacation.

Wyatt obviously learned a lot about writing over these 4 years. As a 4-year-old, he combined representational drawings and abstract swirls to tell a story. And as a 5-year-old, he used nonphonetic letterstrings and number shapes and gave meaning to his drawn and written symbols by talking about them. At age 6, Wyatt could write recognizable words and construct a story sequence. And at 7 and 8, he could write more elaborate stories and communicate his experiences to others using both invented spelling and conventional orthography.

by Wyatt

I he Zoo.

I am at the zoo. it is fun at the zoo. about 100 animals. at the zoo.

Arthur

I have a dog named Arthur He is a black tan and white Sheltie. He is fast and jumpy. We have to give him medicine every night because of skin dissease. He likes tobe petted and he is 8 moths old.

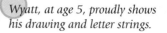

Wyatt, at age 5, proudly shows his drawing and letter strings.

Developmental Spelling

As children discover these concepts and principles, they are moving toward writing that can be read and understood by others without spoken explanation. In doing so, they will use letters and create wordlike forms. Their knowledge of abstract phonological categories and relationships will result in unconventional or *developmental spelling*. Charles Read (1975) calls this *invented spelling*. His research demonstrates convincingly that kindergartners can make sophisticated auditory predictions about the spellings of words and that certain patterns occur frequently in their spellings. For example, he found that children often do the following:

- use single letters to represent sounds of full letter names:
  PPL = people; BCAZ = because; LFNT = elephant

- omit nasal sounds before consonants:
  MOSTR = monster; NUBRS = numbers; PLAT = plant

- use single letters to stand for whole syllables:
  GRIF = giraffe; NHR = nature

One of the most revealing aspects of children's spelling that came out of Read's (1975) work is the sophisticated set of linguistic criteria children use for decoding which vowel sounds to use. Whereas adults are accustomed to the short/long vowel relationships found in spelling (e.g., the *a* in *nation* versus *national*), children are more sensitive to phonetic relationships between vowel sounds. Consider the vowel sounds in *feel* and *fill*, which are formed similarly in the mouth. A child might spell both *FEL.* Similarly, *like* and *lock* might both be spelled *LIK.*

During early childhood, children internalize what they learn about language, creating some very flexible rules based on that knowledge and applying these rules as they begin to spell. This is a developmental, systematic, sequential, and very slow process—one that's far too complex to teach through simplistic strategies like making word lists or learning rules in spelling books. Learning to spell is clearly rooted in children's abilities to articulate as well as hear and segment speech sounds in words. Their developmental spelling, therefore, is not random but systematic, even though it does not match conventional spelling.

Read (1975) suggests that teachers need to understand the underlying system of children's spelling in early childhood, to respect it, and to work with it, if only on an intuitive basis. Children move through relatively the same stages in learning to spell, and they know a great deal about English *orthography.* Using this knowledge, they create a hierarchy of concepts that guide their early spelling efforts. The sequence of stages children go through indicates that they're establishing internalized rules, moving from simple letter/sound correspondences to more complex phonological, syntactic, and semantic knowledge. They do this as they use spoken and written language in authentic, meaningful contexts: solving problems, testing hypotheses, and making mistakes as well as discoveries.

Orthography is the representation of sounds in a language by written or printed symbols; it's also the part of language study that deals with letters and spelling.

The stages of spelling through which children progress have been identified by several researchers (Beers & Beers, 1981 [summarizing Beers & Henderson, 1977]; Gentry, 1981; Henderson, 1980). Their different views are presented in Table 4.1. Next, we'll look more closely at the five stages identified by Gentry (1981):

1. *Precommunicative Stage:* Children are becoming aware that speech can be recorded by means of graphic symbols, even though they don't have a clear, objective understanding of the relationships between sounds and letters in words or of what words really are. Children make drawings that gradually become more representational and are often accompanied by spoken explanations. These drawings are gradually replaced with letter- or numberlike shapes or actual letters and numbers, often scattered randomly over a page (see Figure 4.3). Some children at this stage can write their names. This development occurs during preschool and kindergarten (4–5 years old).

2. *Semiphonetic Stage:* Children are still unable to spell many words conventionally, and they're still unclear about the concept of what a word is; however, they do know that letters make words, and they don't invent symbols as substitutes for letters, as in the earlier stage. Children know that letter names stand for elements of words (usually consonants), and they make one-, two-, and three-letter representations of specific, individual words. They have more control over the sounds at the ends of words than they do over the middles and the beginnings. This development occurs around kindergarten and the beginning of first grade (5–6 years old) for many children.

3. *Phonetic Stage:* Spellings at this stage include all the sound features of words as children hear and articulate them. That is, the written form contains all the speech sounds, recorded in the same sequence (e.g., *CHROBLE* = *trouble*). Children pass through this stage around the first grade (6–7 years old).

Figure 4.3

5-Year-Old's Drawing and Writing: Precommunicative Stage of Spelling

Table 4.1 Stages of Spelling Development

Stage*	Source		
	Gentry (1981)	Henderson (1980)	Beers & Beers (1981)
1. *Precommunicative* Preschool: 5 years old	Deviant btBpA	Preliterate Prephonetic dog candy bit Cinderella	Prereading Stage 1. Prephonetic level ABDG—Wally 11 + 02—cat 2. Phonetic level WTBO—Wally KT—cat HM—home GT—get
2. *Semiphonetic* Kindergarten and Beginning First: 5–6 years old	Prephonetic MSR	Preliterate Phonetic D or DJ K or KDE B or BT S	Phonetic Stage GAT—get TREP—trip FRMR—farmer SCARD—scared JUPT—jumped
3. *Phonetic* Midfirst: 6 years old	Phonetic MONSTR	Letter-Name Strategy DIJ KADE BET SEDRLI	
4. *Transitional* End First/ Beginning Second: 6–9 years old	Transitional MONSTUR	Vowel Transition DOG CANDE or CANDY BIT CINDARILA	Orthographic Stage GAETF—gate MAIK—make SPATER—spatter
5. *Conventional* Second–Fourth: 7–9 years old	Correct MONSTER	DOG CANDY BIT CINDERELLA	RIDDER—rider SITTIN—sitting CANT—can't
6. *Morphemic/ Syntactic* Fifth–Tenth: 10–16 years old			Morphemic & Syntactic Stage 1. Control of doubling consonants. HAPPY SMATTERING 2. Awareness of alternative forms. MANAGERIAL manage REPETITION repeat 3. Awareness of syntactic control or key elements in words. SLOWLY SAVED PASSED RESTED FASTER SLEEPING

*These stages correspond to those discussed in Chapter 10, Spelling.

Source: Adapted from Gentry, 1981.

4. *Transitional Stage:* Children include vowels in all recorded syllables and use familiar spelling patterns. Standard spellings are interspersed with invented, phonetic spellings (e.g., *HIGHCKED = hiked; TODE = toad*). Children seem to realize that it's necessary to spell words in order for them to be read and that all words have conventional spellings, used in print. Children also learn that there are various ways to spell many of the same speech sounds and that many words are not spelled entirely phonetically. This stage may occur around the end of first and the beginning of second grade (6–9 years old).

5. *Conventional Stage:* The points of change are less clear in this stage. Children are mastering word roots, past tense, and short vowels, although they still have problems with consonant doubling, word affixes, and the positions of letters (e.g., the silent *e* that determines long vowel sounds). This stage occurs anywhere between the second and fourth grades (7–9 years old).

In order to connect research findings (Templeton, 2003) on emergent literacy and invented spelling with real children, let's look at examples of writing by Michael, Alisha, and Anita. All three wrote these stories during a writer's workshop at the beginning of first grade. See if you can identify each child's stage of spelling development based on the writing sample and what he or she said about it (see the answers below):

• Michael reads his one-sentence story as "There is a plane." The words *is* and *a* are spelled correctly. He has written something to represent every word. Both *ThEHr/there* and *Plne/plane* include letters that represent some of the speech sounds heard in the word.

• Alisha reads her two-sentence story as "My cat is black and brown. He is cute." *Cat, black, and, he,* and *is* are spelled correctly, and the other spellings include all the sound features of the words: *mi/my, brwn/brown, cuty/cute.*

• Anita reads her four-sentence story as "My cat's name is Snow Paws. His last name is Fred. His middle name is Billy. And that is all." Most words are spelled correctly. Invented phonetic spellings use familiar patterns. A vowel is included in every recorded syllable: *Sno/Snow, Pous/Paws, mitul/middle, Bilee/Billy.*

Concept of a Word

Children in the precommunicative stage of spelling (usually kindergarten) may lack the concept of a *word*, or the relationship between sounds and letters. This is a benchmark concept for beginning to spell and write. Until children grasp this concept, they may simply use letter names to represent words. Since the unit of spelling is the word, children must understand this concept before receiving spelling instruction. To determine if children have the concept of a word (Henderson, 1990; Morris, 1993), use Assessment Toolbox 4.2, Concept of a Word, which uses a nursery rhyme and a simple pointing test.

Seven Ways to Begin Teaching Reading and Writing

The seven ways to begin to teach reading and writing that follow are founded on the assumption that from the very beginning, children learn language holistically for authentic, meaningful purposes. Moreover, they should continue to

ASSESSMENT TOOLBOX

4.2 Concept of a Word

The concept of a word—that is, the relationship between sounds and letters—is a benchmark for learning to spell and write. This tool uses a nursery rhyme and simple pointing test to determine whether children can distinguish separate words.

Concept of a Word

1. Teach a simple nursery rhyme that children can memorize—for example:

One, two, buckle my shoe;	OR	Hey, diddle, diddle!
Three, four, shut the door;		The cat and the fiddle,
Five, six, pick up sticks;		The cow jumped over the moon;
Seven, eight, lay them straight;		The little dog laughed to see such sport,
Nine, ten, a good fat hen.		And the dish ran away with the spoon.

2. When the children can recite the rhyme by memory, print it on a large poster. Recite the rhyme slowly, pointing to each word and asking the children to follow your finger with their eyes. Ask the children to recite the rhyme with you as you point to the words.

3. Then ask the children individually to point to each word as they recite the rhyme. Note when the following occur:
   a. The child moves his or her finger quickly across lines in a single movement.
   b. The child points to each word but loses rhythm on a two-syllable word, such as *buckle*.
   c. The child points to each individual word.
   The child who can distinguish each separate word (item c) has the concept of a *word* and is emerging as a reader, writer, and speller.

learn this way in the early years of school, as they each develop the inner control necessary to work with print (Clay, 1991). Each of the following recommendations begins with an example from Marion Harris's first-grade room and the "ripple effect" of apples that emerged there.

A Print-Rich Environment

When Marion's students became more and more interested in apples, she found and displayed posters with information about apples:

Different Types of Apples: Delicious (Red and Golden), Macintosh, Granny Smith, Gala, and Fuji

Apple Parts: Leaves, stem, core, skin, seeds, and flesh

Apple Products: Sauce, jelly, vinegar, cider, pies, and juice

Seven Leading Apple-Growing States: Washington, Michigan, New York, California, Pennsylvania, Virginia, and North Carolina

Young children learn a lot about written language through exposure to print in their environment. The term *environmental print* means print that is visibly situated in a context that will help children understand it.

    1. *Signs, Labels, Lists, and Charts:* These materials should be displayed prominently in the room, and the teacher should point to them when discussing what they label. Signs, labels, and the like should be functional, and children should be encouraged to use and read them. Examples:

The teacher's name and room number on the door
A "Welcome to Our Room" sign
Children's names on their desks
Labels for centers and supply storage
A "Morning Message"
A calendar with dates, school events, and birthdays
Poems, songs, and chants
Charts for classroom jobs
A list of classroom rules
A daily schedule

    2. *Books in the Classroom:* As many books as possible should be provided in the classroom. When you begin teaching, build your collection any way you can: Go to garage sales or request donations from parents, and use school and public libraries. Public library books should be kept on a separate shelf, and students should be involved in caring for them, keeping track of due dates, and so on. Teachers should look for books that that they will enjoy reading aloud and that children will enjoy looking at, such as great storybooks and single-concept books. For more ideas, also see the section on pattern books (pp. 130–131).

    3. *A Library/Reading Corner:* A place for books and reading should be created in a corner of the classroom, perhaps using bookshelves to define a space. Things to add might include a rocking chair or recliner for the teacher, a rug for the chil-

TEACHER RESOURCES

For more information on print-rich environments, see Leslie Morrow's (2001) *Literacy Development in the Early Years: Helping Children Read and Write.*

ELL

These items can be written in two languages:

- "Welcome" signs
- Labels
- Calendars
- Poems, songs, chants

dren to sit on while being read to, floor pillows, plastic crates for different types of books, plants, dolls or stuffed animals of characters from stories, and reading lamps.

Sharing Time and "Morning Message"

Sharing time was when Marion discovered her students' interest in apples and began to plan learning experiences around it. She wrote a "Morning Message" with the class recipe for making apple pies:

See the Snapshot in Chapter 1 for a description of how Avril Font uses sharing time with fourth-grade students.

> Today is Thursday, September 12. We are cooking apples with sugar and cinnamon to make pies. The apples smell good and sweet. We can't wait to eat the pies. We are having fun!

To get the most out of sharing time, consider these guidelines:

1. **When to Share:** Every day, time should be set aside for children to share what's important to them. Many teachers do so first thing in the day. By listening to the children, the teacher can find out more about them and thus come up with ideas for teaching.

2. **"Morning Message":** During sharing, the teacher models writing by jotting down upcoming events and news that students have shared on chartpaper, the chalkboard, or a white board. The teacher then models reading the message with students.

3. **Variations on Sharing**

   - Teachers can share, too, both school-related items, like announcements and plans for the class, and personal information, like favorite poems and things that are important to them.
   - Combine sharing time with other activities that begin the day, such as the calendar, weather, or thematic poetry, songs, or rhymes.
   - Designate a student as Star of the Day or Week. Plan ahead to have that child bring in special things to share with the class (e.g., pictures, artwork, or mementos), and create a bulletin board around them.

See Chapter 1 for more on Star of the Week.

Reading Aloud

After a few days of apple activities, Marion asked her school librarian to find books related to the apple theme. She read several aloud to the class; the first was Steven Kellogg's (1988) *Johnny Appleseed*. Here are suggestions for reading aloud:

1. **When to Read Aloud:** Teachers should read aloud to students several times every day, such as at the close of sharing time in the morning, before or after recess, to initiate a writing or drama activity, before or after lunch, or at the end of the day. In addition to serving a modeling purpose, reading aloud is one of the best ways to create a quiet, peaceful atmosphere in the classroom. Teachers who feel they need more control in the classroom should get out a good book and read it aloud to students.

Who else can read aloud besides the teacher? Try early readers, older student aides, bilingual adult and student aides, parents, and community volunteers.

2. *How to Read Aloud:* Teachers should share books they love. By doing so, they will be more likely to read dramatically and with enthusiasm. Others should be invited to read, too: principals, counselors, parents, and community members. Likewise, children should be encouraged to read aloud to each other (i.e., *buddy reading*), perhaps favorite books they have brought to share and even their own stories, read from the Author's Chair. Children learn to read by hearing stories read aloud and by reading aloud themselves. Time should be provided to do both often.

3. *Predictable Pattern Books:* Most predictable pattern books are based on familiar cultural sequences, like the alphabet, numbers, days of the week, and seasons. Other such books use repeated phrases that invite children to chime in. Remember "Sam I am, that Sam I am" from Dr. Seuss's *Green Eggs and Ham?* (Seuss, 1988). Some pattern books are cumulative tales, in which new parts of the story are continually added, as in the nursery rhyme "The House That Jack Built." Many pattern books are based on traditional rhymes, songs, or folktales; others are new and original. Predictable pattern books encourage children to participate in the reading experience by guessing what will happen next, by joining in a repeated phrase, or by repeating everything that's been said before. Books such as these should be read often with young children:

Familiar Sequences
Numbers: *Over in the Meadow* (Keats, 1973)
Days: *The Very Hungry Caterpillar* (Carle, 1969)
Months: *Chicken Soup with Rice* (Sendak, 1962)

Repeated Phrases
Caps for Sale (Slobodkina, 1940)
The Little Red Hen (Galdone, 1973)
Mary Wore Her Red Dress (Peek, 1985)
Millions of Cats (Gag, 1928/1956)
Whose Mouse Are You? (Kraus, 1970)

Rhyming Patterns
Chicka Chicka Boom Boom! (Martin & Archambault, 1989)
Green Eggs and Ham (Seuss, 1988)
Is Your Mama a Llama? (Guarino, 1989)
We're Going on a Bear Hunt (Rosen, 1989)
The Wheels on the Bus (Wickstrom, 1988)

Recurring Patterns
Are You My Mother? (Eastman, 1960)
Ask Mr. Bear (Flack, 1932)
Brown Bear, Brown Bear, What Do You See? (Martin, 1983)
The Doorbell Rang (Hutchins, 1968)
The Three Billy Goats Gruff (Brown, 1957)

Cumulative Patterns
I Know an Old Lady Who Swallowed a Fly (Hawkins & Hawkins, 1987)
If You Give a Mouse a Cookie (Numeroff, 1985)

The Mitten (Brett, 1986)
The Napping House (Wood, 1984)
Rooster's Off to See the World (Carle, 1972)

4. **"Big Books" and Shared Reading:** New Zealand educator Don Holdaway (1979) introduced the idea of using "big books" (i.e., books with oversized pages and print) and shared reading in emergent literacy classrooms. The purpose for doing so is to replicate the bedtime story experience and the good feeling children have when a parent or caretaker sits close to them and reads aloud. Today, many publishers have enlarged popular children's books to the "big book" size. Teachers can also create "big books" by copying stories on paper large enough so that children can see the words from up to 20 feet away.

See Chapter 6, Reading, for a Snapshot about shared reading.

Drama

In the weeks after Marion Harris told the apple riddle story, small groups of students dramatized it by acting it out and using props and puppets to retell it. The story was a natural for dramatizing; with a narrator, five children could easily plan and act it out. Other recommendations for using drama to teach reading and writing include the following:

See Chapter 5, Listening and Talking, for much more on creative dramatics in the classroom.

1. **Story Dramatization:** After the teacher has read a story aloud several times (to the entire class or a small group) or after children have read it aloud to each other, they can discuss dramatization: choosing what events to act out, characters and who will play them, and costumes or props that will be needed. The children might also practice the dramatization several times before sharing it with others; this is always optional.

2. **Props and Puppets:** A simple way to relive and retell a story is through the use of props or puppets. Students can make puppets out of construction paper, manila folders, or paper plates and attach tongue depressors to hold them up. Puppets can also be made out of paper bags and old (clean) socks. Dolls, stuffed animals, and real objects can be used as props. A box of prop and puppet supplies should be available in the room.

See Chapter 5, Listening and Talking, for more ideas on storytelling and puppetry.

Writing and Drawing

Marion's students wrote and drew in small groups to describe their apples. And as a class, they also wrote a list of things needed to make apple pies, a recipe, and a cinquain. After Marion read *Johnny Appleseed*, the class discussed it; then she told them to draw or write anything they wanted about the story. Here's a simple strategy for doing this:

1. **Read, Talk, Draw, Write:** The teacher should read a good story aloud and simply talk about it with the children, asking aesthetic questions. After that, the teacher should give students paper, crayons, and pencils and ask them to draw or write anything they want about the story. Following is a step-by-step lesson plan for doing this with any book.

Aesthetic questions direct children to what they were thinking and feeling while reading. This and other types of questions are reviewed in Chapter 5.

LESSON PLAN

Read, Talk, Draw, Write

IRA/
NCTE

Purpose: Children will listen to and enjoy literature; actively participate in a shared reading experience; talk in response to open and aesthetic questions and prompts; and draw and write in response to literature.

Standard 3: Students apply a wide range of strategies to comprehend, interpret, evaluate, and appreciate texts. They draw on their prior experience, their interactions with other readers and writers, their knowledge of word meaning and of other texts, their word identification strategies, and their understanding of textual features (e.g., sound-letter correspondence, sentence structure, context, graphics).

Materials: Children's book; props and realia (i.e., real objects); paper, crayons, and pencils

Procedure:
1. *Read*
   - Select a good children's book, based on these criteria: What you like and think children will like; good illustrations; predictable patterns; and "big books."
   - Read dramatically and slowly, vary intonation and voices for different characters, and use sound effects, facial expressions, and gestures.
   - Use props and realia, such as objects from the story and stuffed animals or dolls representing story characters.
   - Encourage participation in reading pattern books (e.g., repeating words or phrases).
   - Reread if children ask you to do so.

2. *Talk*
   - Ask open and aesthetic questions after reading to elicit children's individual responses:
     "What did you think of the book?"
     "What was your favorite part?"
     "Has anything like this ever happened to you?"
     "How would you feel if you were a character in the story?"
     "Is there anything in the story you wondered about?"
     "Is there anything in the story you would change?"
   - Base further questions and prompts on what the children say.
   - Encourage children to interact with each other.
   - Write children's ideas down on a "word wall," displaying it on a chalkboard, chartpaper, butcher paper, dry-erase board, or overhead projector.

3. *Draw*
   - Give children paper, pencils, and crayons.
   - Tell them, "You can draw anything you want about the story."

4. *Write*
   - Tell students to write, if they want to: their names, labels, captions, and so on.
   - Encourage all writing efforts (e.g., invented spelling).
   - Give assistance if students ask for it (e.g., write a word so they can copy it, take dictation for them, etc.).
   - Publish children's drawings and writings by sharing them, mounting them on the bulletin board, or making a group or class book.

See Chapter 9, The Writing Process, for ways to publish children's writing and book-making.

2. **Writing and Drawing Center:** Materials for drawing and writing should be kept in boxes, files, and baskets in one central location in the classroom, on or adjacent to a table. If the location is near a bulletin board, it will provide a natural place for children to publish their work. This writing and drawing center can be used when children need it: during small-group activity; for special purposes, like writing letters; and for special themes, like holidays. Children can also go to the center to draw and write simply because they have something they want to say. Here are some ideas for things needed in the center, which the teacher can collect or ask people to donate:

> Paper of any kind
> Pencils: plain lead, colored
> Erasers
> Crayons and crayon sharpener (baskets of these work well)
> Envelopes: legal, manila
> Post-its
> Stationery
> Index cards (for notes, to make postcards)
> Construction paper (save and use scraps)
> Tape: invisible, masking, colored
> Scissors
> Glue and glue sticks
> Hole punch (for joining paper)
> Yarn (for joining paper, book making)
> Paper clips

New multicultural crayons are available, offering a range of skin colors.

3. **Class Post Office:** Children should be encouraged to write notes and memos to each other and to "mail" them in class. A postal system can be created, with a mailbox for each child. Students' cubbies can be used, or mailboxes can be made out of clean half-gallon paper milk cartons. Cut off the tops, and staple the cartons together in stacks of five, with the open tops facing the same direction. Next, staple the five-carton stacks together, side by side, making enough so there's one for every child. Label the mailboxes with students' names.

4. *Language Experience Charts:* When Marion Harris made a list of what the children needed to make apple pies, recorded their recipe, and displayed the cinquain they wrote, she was using the *language experience approach* (Allen & Allen, 1968; Stauffeur, 1970). This approach involves recording children's ideas and spoken language and displaying them as written text in the classroom.

Language experience charts show children how written language works: that it involves words put on paper; that they're in order, from left to right; that letters have certain shapes and sounds; that when combined, letters make words; and that you can read what you've written. These charts become part of the print environment in the classroom or library. They can be displayed on bulletin boards or walls or bound into "big books."

Types of experiences such as these lend themselves to these charts:

Cooking experiences	Science experiments
Holidays	Class pets
Fieldtrips	Weather
Classroom visitors	Responses to literature
Current events	Class stories

5. *The Author's Chair:* The Author's Chair is where children can sit when they read aloud a story they have written (Graves & Hansen, 1983). Others can listen, ask questions, and make comments, discussing the story with its young author. This discussion can involve the whole class or just a small group during a writer's workshop.

6. *Interactive Writing:* Interactive or shared writing (Button, Johnson, & Fergerson, 1996; McCarrier, Pinnell, & Fountas, 2000; McKenzie, 1985) occurs when the teacher and young children share the writing experience. They talk about a class event or book they have read, and the teacher writes the group story on a piece of chartpaper or whiteboard as the children watch. This is similar to writing a language experience story, but with interactive writing, the children do some of the writing, taking turns writing words or even parts of the story as the others watch. The teacher can use this opportunity for modeling writing and presenting minilessons on spelling and language conventions.

Centers

In addition to the materials about apples in her writing center, Marion put tapes of the book *Johnny Appleseed* (Kellogg, 1988) in her listening center, materials for apple art in her arts and crafts center, and books and materials about growing things in her science center. All these types of centers provide many opportunities for reading and writing. Here's how each classroom center supports emergent literacy:

1. *Writing Center:* Given materials and opportunities, children can draw and write for authentic, specific purposes or simply to play and experiment with written language.

2. *Listening Center:* Tape and CD players and earphones and recordings of stories and books provide opportunities for young children to listen as they follow along with the pictures and print in books.

3. *Arts and Crafts Center:* Art supplies for drawing; for constructing puppets, props, signs, and labels; and for specific activities, like making apple head dolls, encourage children to use visual symbols and print to express meaning.

4. *Science Center:* Children can use nonfiction books and magazines (e.g., *Ranger Rick*) or write in observation logs about science experiments or displays (e.g., the class pet, seeds growing, or a collection of different types of apples).

5. *Thematic Center:* Centers can be developed around special themes, such as apples. A Center for the Study of Apples, for example, could include materials related to the "ripple effect": apple books, children's language experience charts about apples, and materials for apple projects.

Some centers, like the writing or listening center, will be set up permanently in the classroom. Others, such as thematic centers, will be temporary. Centers can be combined sometimes—for instance, the writing center with the classroom library and reading corner or the arts and crafts and science centers. Centers like the latter, which can get messy, should be located on a table or counter near a sink, where you may also locate cooking activities.

Integrated Teaching

In Marion's class, apples became a unifying theme that resulted in a "ripple effect" of learning experiences across the curriculum. This sort of integrated teaching is a natural outgrowth of developmentally appropriate, child- and response-centered classrooms, in which children have opportunities to explore, experiment, and discover things for themselves through many hands-on experiences. Suggestions for integrated teaching include the following:

For more on integrated teaching, see Chapter 14, Language across the Curriculum.

1. *Natural "Ripple Effects":* When teachers listen to children and note their ideas and interests, ripple effects occur naturally, as happened with the apples in Marion Harris's class. Other ripple effects stem from children's responses to literature, to seasons, or to what's going on in the world. Child-centered teachers notice these things, think about developmentally appropriate activities they can do in connection with them, and find a variety of resources to enhance the learning experience. Such teachers integrate these topics and activities with the ongoing classroom program of sharing, reading aloud, writing and drawing, drama, and learning centers.

2. *Theme Cycles:* Sometimes, teachers choose themes that are important and thus worth spending time on. But at other times, teachers select themes that lack a broad, conceptual base or that are trivial and not appropriate for extended study across the curriculum. For example, you could find ways to integrate the theme of teddy bears across the curriculum, but how important are teddy bears?

See the planner that accompanies this text for meaningful themes for each month of the year:

September: Me and My Family
October: Fall
November: We're All Pilgrims
December: Celebrations
January: Winter
February: Black History Month
March: Women's History Month
April: Spring
May: Ecology
June: The Future

(A kindergartner in a class loaded with teddy bears once confided to me, "I hope she can't find another bear book.") Instead, teachers should select themes that have big ideas behind them or that draw extensively on children's own experiences, such as these:

All about me	Native Americans	Martin Luther King, Jr.
Home and family	(e.g., Chumash of	Growing things
The community	California)	Animals and the zoo

Theory, research, and practice about emergent literacy are, in many ways, the same for teaching kindergartners as for teaching students in the first through third grades, the years of early childhood. Yet in other ways, supporting emergent literacy is different in teaching kindergarten (Fisher, 1998). Let's look at a day in a kindergarten class that uses the ideas for supporting emergent literacy discussed in this chapter.

In many parts of the United States, children attend kindergarten for just a half day.

SNAPSHOT   **A Day in a Kindergarten Class**

Mauretta Hurst teaches an all-day kindergarten class in Baton Rouge, Louisiana. Mauretta is African American, and so are all her students. In fact, over half the students in Baton Rouge are African American, whereas the majority of teachers are white. Baton Rouge has been under court order to desegregate for decades, and African American teachers are in demand so as to achieve a racial balance on each faculty. Given this and the fact that Mauretta is considered an outstanding teacher, with 20 years' experience, she could request a transfer to any school in town. She has chosen to teach at an urban school, where she feels she is a role model, brings unique cultural knowledge and understanding to her job, and relates well to parents.

Mauretta explains her approach to teaching, saying, "I draw on the children's own experiences and then relate language, literature, and lots of drama experiences to them." Here's how she does it:

Schedule for a Day in Kindergarten

Theme: The zoo

9:00–9:30	Sharing time and "Morning Message"
9:30–10:55	Writing and drawing and language experience story
10:55–11:15	Recess
11:15–12:15	Centers: Reading/writing, blocks/social studies, math, art, listening
12:15–1:15	Lunch/recess/P.E.
1:15–2:30	Reading aloud and drama
2:30–3:15	Rest/read aloud/review

In planning the day, Mauretta incorporates all the ways to begin teaching young children to read and write described in this chapter. She also integrates learning experiences across the curriculum. Here's an expanded description of what she does in a day:

9:00–9:30   Sharing Time and "Morning Message"

Children share about any subject they choose. Then Mauretta asks them to share about the fieldtrip they took to the zoo the day before. They excitedly talk about their many impressions of this fieldtrip, and Mauretta writes their ideas on chartpaper as they watch. This becomes the "Morning Message," which Mauretta reads back to them as they join in:

> Today is Tuesday, October 17. Yesterday we went to the zoo. We saw many animals at the zoo. We saw a baby elephant, giraffes, and tigers. We had fun.

9:30–10:55   Writing and Drawing and Language Experience Story

Next, the children draw about their experiences on the zoo fieldtrip. Some write their names on their pictures, and others write words, labels, and captions using invented spelling. The children talk to each other while working, and Mauretta moves from table to table, helping them get their ideas down on paper. Then she gathers the children together on the rug and asks them to tell about their pictures. On a large piece of chartpaper, she makes a list of all the animals the children drew about. She notices that the most popular animal was the baby elephant and suggests that they write a story together about it. She encourages them to share more, discusses what they say, and asks for ideas for the story, which she writes down on another large piece of chartpaper. Together, the class writes "The Adventures of a Baby Elephant." After they have finished the story, they read it aloud together; some students volunteer to read it solo.

10:55–11:15   Recess

11:15–12:15   Centers: Reading/Writing, Blocks/Social Studies, Math, Art, Listening

Children go to these different centers in groups of six. They will rotate, going to the other centers on one or several days throughout the week. Mauretta has used the theme of the zoo in several centers in the room. Here's what's happening in each center:

GREAT BOOKS FOR CHILDREN

The Baby Zoo (Macmillan, 1992)
A Children's Zoo (Hoban, 1985)
Color Zoo (Ehlert, 1989)

Also see the *Zoobook* series (Wildlife Education Limited), a full-color wildlife series full of photographs, articles, and games; published monthly, each issue focuses on a different animal.

   1. *Reading/Writing:* Some children are looking at picture books about animals and the zoo. Some children are gluing the drawings of animals they did earlier on bigger pieces of paper. Mauretta has provided yarn, feathers, and scraps of fake fur to glue on their animal pictures, if they want to. Other children continue to draw and write, putting their names on their pictures and using scribbling, letterstrings, and invented spellings. Children can also give dictation to Mauretta or an aide, who records their ideas on their pictures, or copy the names of their animals from the list Mauretta wrote down earlier. Students share ideas about their drawing and writing as they work and tell or read their stories to others.

2. *Blocks/Social Studies:* Children are building a zoo with wooden blocks and boxes. They're putting stuffed and plastic animals in their zoo and playing with them, pretending to be visitors, zoo keepers, or animals.

3. *Math:* Children are working on a class graph of their favorite animals in the zoo. Each person tells what was his or her favorite animal and draws it. Then all the children glue the animals in columns on a large piece of chartpaper, noting on the bottom the names of their favorite animals and their own names next to the ones they've made. Each group will add to the chart, and when everyone has contributed, the class will add up the number of animals in each column and write it at the bottom.

4. *Art:* Children are working at the easels and painting: animals, the zoo, or whatever they choose.

5. *Listening Center:* Children are listening to a recording of the story of "The Three Billy Goats Gruff," following along with several copies of the book as they listen.

6. *Computer Center:* Some children are taking an online tour of the San Diego Zoo by viewing photographs and videos of zoo exhibits. Others are visiting the *Zoobooks* website, where they experience a virtual zoo online; they look at pictures of animals, listen to the sounds they make, and "pet" an animal by clicking on a photograph (which takes them to more photographs and information).

12:15–1:15   Lunch/Recess/P.E.

1:15–2:30   Reading Aloud and Drama

Mauretta reads aloud Marcia Brown's (1957) picture book *The Three Billy Goats Gruff*. She reads dramatically, with a lot of facial expressions and gestures. When she's finished, the children applaud and ask her to read it again. She does, using as much expression as she did the first time. During the second reading, she encourages the children to fill in whatever words they remember from the first reading. Since this is a predictable pattern book, with a repeated phrase, many students join in, chanting with the troll, "Who's that tramping over my bridge?" The children begin to imitate Mauretta's gestures, such as making a long nose with her hand for the troll and patting the floor to make the "trip-trap" sound as the billy goats cross the bridge, one by one. The children make this noise softly for the first and smallest billy goat and loudly for the last and biggest one.

After reading, the class talks about what happened in the story. Mauretta asks open-ended, aesthetic questions:

"What did you think about the story?"
"What was your favorite part?"
"Who was your favorite character?"

Next, the class dramatizes the story. First, the children spread out around the room and pretend to be the different characters, imitating one at a time. Mauretta says she will take one volunteer to act out each character. The

WWW

Many zoos have online tours, such as the San Diego Zoo: **www.sandiegozoo.org**. The *Zoobooks* series has a website with pictures, sound effects, games, and information about animals: **www.zoobooks.com**.

rest of the students have rhythm sticks and will make the "trip-trap" sound effects. The scene is set with green carpet squares for grass and a bridge made of wooden blocks. A narrator is chosen to tell the story. The students dramatize the story this way several times. Mauretta promises she will read it again the next day, giving more children chances to play the characters.

2:30–3:15   Rest/Read Aloud/Review

After the children take a short rest, Mauretta reads aloud the language experience story they wrote earlier, "The Adventures of a Baby Elephant"; Brown's (1957) *The Three Billy Goats Gruff* again; and another zoo book, *A Children's Zoo*, by Tana Hoban (1985). The class ends the day by talking about their zoo trip, their favorite zoo animals, and what other things they can do around the theme of the zoo.

On following days, Mauretta continues the theme of the zoo in centers, dramatizing *The Three Billy Goats Gruff*, reading more books about animals, and drawing and writing. She integrates learning experiences through the unifying theme of animals and the zoo, an experience the children all shared and had many ideas and much enthusiasm about. Like Marion Harris did with her first-graders, Mauretta created a "ripple effect" in her kindergarten class.

Emergent Biliteracy

Research on *emergent biliteracy* has demonstrated the important role of teachers in helping second-language learners learn to speak English as well as learn to read and write English. In particular, teachers can support such learning by

1. *Creating an environment that both acknowledges and respects the language and literacy development of the child's home and community;*
2. *Providing multiple opportunities for language interactions that include oral and written experiences with both the teacher and the classmates;*
3. *Observing children's language interactions and planning instructional activities that reflect the reality of the idiosyncratic nature of literacy development in children; and*
4. *Allowing and valuing the use of the L1 in the language and literacy development of the L2.* (Hudelson, Poynor, & Wolfe, 2003, pp. 428–429)

This research has also suggested that emergent biliteracy is a social process in that young children need many opportunities to talk, share, and collaborate with each other in groups. Successful teachers of young second-language learners also provide extralinguistic clues for their speech through the use of gestures, acting out, facial expressions, and visual aids (Tabors, 1997). In addition, they are sensitive to young children's gradual development, allowing them time to be silent as well as providing extra time and support to facilitate their growth (Xu, 1996).

Learning to Read and Write in Two Languages

Young children who come to school speaking a native language other than English need multiple opportunities to use both languages in authentic contexts connected with their own lives through speaking, reading, and writing (Hudelson et al., 2003). Many studies have shown the importance of teaching young children to read and write in their native language—the language they already know—rather than a language they don't know well (Hudelson, 1987; Snow, 1990; Snow, Burns, & Griffin, 1998; Thomas & Collier, 1997). Edelsky (1986), for example, found that young children in a bilingual Spanish program used their knowledge of Spanish print to help them learn how to use English print; in fact, this knowledge enhanced their learning English. Basically, second-language learners draw on their knowledge of print in their first language as they learn to write in the second language (Lanauze & Snow, 1989; Townsend & Fu, 1998). For example, knowledge of Spanish orthography helps students learn to spell in English (Zutell & Allen, 1988).

The following Snapshot tells about the first day of school in Alicia Campos's kindergarten class at Furgeson Elementary School in Hawaiian Gardens, California. The student population at this school is almost 100 percent native Spanish speakers. Alicia is herself a native Spanish speaker who holds a bilingual teaching credential in California. She is teaching her young students how to speak English and to begin to read and write, and she is providing sheltered English instruction in content areas such as mathematics. While her class is designated bilingual, for the first 30 days of school, she teaches in English. After 30 days, parents can decide whether to leave their children in her bilingual class or move them to an English-only class. Alicia uses English primarily but also uses some Spanish when giving directions and to make her young students comfortable, especially on their first day of school.

 **The First Day of School for Spanish-Speaking Kindergartners**

 CW
See the first day of school in Alicia Campos's Spanish bilingual kindergarten class.

9:00   Greeting Children and Lining Up Outside the Classroom

Alicia calls the name of each child on her class list and greets each person in English and Spanish: "Good morning. Welcome" and "Buenos dias. Bienvenido." She gives the child a card with his or her name on it, shakes hands, and says something nice to him or her, such as "I like your new pink backpack." She asks each child to line up at the door.

9:10   In the Classroom on the Rug

Alicia has invited the children's family members to come into the classroom for the first few minutes today so they feel comfortable leaving their children in school. The children are seated on the rug, and the family members are standing in the back of the classroom. Only one child is crying, which Alicia discovers is easily explained: The girl had to hang her new pink backpack up on a rack and wanted to keep it with her. Alicia explains that the girl will be able to put it back on when she goes home, and that stops the tears. Alicia checks her class roll by saying "Buenos dias" and the child's name; when they respond with "Buenos dias," she says, "Gracias." She tells the class and parents, "We speak two languages in this class."

9:20   Counting from 1 to 10 in English

Alicia uses a *Sesame Street* "Count" puppet to count out the numbers from 1 to 10 in English. The "Count," on Alicia's hand, points to the numbers on cards that are strung across the room in front of the children. They see the numbers as well as say them in English. Then Alicia calls all the boys' names and asks them in English to "Stand up." She stands up herself and simultaneously gestures to them to do the same. Alicia says, "Help me count the boys" and points to each one as the class counts from 1 to 9. Alicia tells the boys in English to "Sit down"—again, sitting down herself and gesturing at the same time. She points to 9 on the number cards and says, "Nine boys." Then the class counts from 1 to 9 as she points one by one at the number cards. She repeats this process with the 10 girls. She asks in English, "How do I write 10?" The children make suggestions and she writes "9 boys and 10 girls" as an addition problem, adding them up to 19. She says, "Wow, we have boys and girls that know their numbers!"

9:30   "Morning Message"

On the same piece of chartpaper on which Alicia wrote the numbers, she writes the "Morning Message," saying each word as she writes:

Today is the first day of school. Welcome to kindergarten.

She says, "Let's read what I wrote," pointing to each word as she says it. Some children can read these English words, others are trying, and some are just watching and listening carefully.

Alicia Campos, herself a native Spanish speaker, teaches kindergarten in a school where the students are nearly all native Spanish speakers.

9:40 An Alphabet and Counting Book

Alicia reads the book *Blue Bug Goes to School* (Poulet, 1985) aloud in English. On each page, Blue Bug learns something new when he goes to school. He learns to read the alphabet, and Alicia's students read along with her. He learns to count from 1 to 10, and Alicia's students count along with her. He also learns to write his name, to use crayons to color, to play on the bars outside, and to do other things that kindergarten children do in school. Alicia asks the children to make predictions about the story as they look at the illustrations: "What do you think he's doing?" She shows them how to clap in appreciation at the end of a good story.

10:00 Nametags and Color Groups

Alicia has made a nametag for each child, which hangs around his or her neck with yarn. There are four different colors of yarn to identify the four groups of children. Children are also learning the names of the colors in English: *red, yellow, blue, green.* Alicia then arranges the children in rows by colors.

10:25 Singing "Head, Shoulders, Knees, and Toes . . . "

Now, it's time to stretch. Alicia asks the children in English to stand up, and they follow her lead as she points to different parts of her body. She says, "Touch your head," "Touch your shoulders," and so on. She sings the song and plays the piano while her aide leads the children in pointing to their own bodies to show each part as they sing about it. Alicia plays the song very slowly at first, but they end with a very fast version. This makes them laugh because they can't keep up.

10:25 Bryan Shares His Journal

One child, Bryan, walks up to Alicia and shows her a journal he made last year in preschool. He has drawn pictures and someone has added captions written in Spanish. Alicia asks Bryan to show the class the pictures and to read the captions. As he does, she says each one in English: *mi familia/my family, la escuela/my school, la piscina/my swimming pool, las letras/the letters.* She thanks Bryan for bringing his journal and tells the children they will start their own journals today in her class.

10:30 Nursery Rhyme Chart: "Humpty Dumpty"

The children sit on the rug and Alicia reads aloud the nursery rhyme "Humpty Dumpty" from an illustrated chart. She tells them, "He did something silly. He fell," and she pantomimes falling. When she asks "What happens when an egg falls?" one child answers, "Breaks!" Alicia reads the rhyme several times, pointing to each word, and some of the students join her in saying the rhyme. Others just watch and listen carefully.

10:45 Review

Before lunch, Alicia reads another book about the first day of school. She also reviews counting from 1 to 10 by having the children stand and snap their fingers for each number as they count forward and backward. And they sing the song "Head, Shoulders, Knees, and Toes . . ."—again, using gestures to review the names of the body parts.

11:00   Lunch

After lunch, the children rest on the rug with the lights off as Alicia plays "Fur Elise" softly on the piano.

11:45   Picture Book Reading

The children sit on the rug again as Alicia shows them the book *Brown Bear, Brown Bear, What Do You See?* (Martin, 1983). She asks them to make a prediction: "What do you think it's about?" Laura offers that she read that book in her prekindergarten class and that it is about a bear and that she likes pink. (Laura is the child who was crying because she had to hang up her new pink backpack.) Alicia tells them that the author of the book is Bill Martin, Jr., and that the pictures are by Eric Carle. Since this is a repeated-pattern book, Alicia invites the children to chime in and say the phrases with her. When the story is over, the children clap again. Alicia says, "This is my favorite book."

12:00   Picture Book Reading on Their Own

Alicia has several baskets of books ready. She picks Kevin from the yellow group to choose a basket and take it to a table, and she directs the other children in the group to follow him to the table. She shows them how to pick a book, open it, turn the pages, look at the pictures, and put it back in the basket. The red, blue, and green groups do the same. Alicia moves among the tables to help. Some of the children have obviously had experience in handling books. Nicholas, however, is just sitting there. Alicia gives him an ABC book and points to the picture on the "A" page and asks him in English, "What is it?" He says, "Airplane!" and flashes her a huge grin. Alicia says, "You can read it! You're a good reader!" Nicholas is mesmerized immediately. He devours each page with his eyes and mouths the words silently. He puts the book back and chooses another. He begins to turn the pages even faster and looks at several book in a row.

When Alicia tells the children it's time to come back to the rug and names a child at each table to be book monitor and collect all the books, Nicholas doesn't want to give his back. There is a slight tussle and the book monitor wins. Nicholas's eyes tear up but only for a minute. Alicia promises him that he can look at books later today and every day, all year. He wipes his eyes and joins his group on the rug. Alicia says, "Everybody in this class reads! I love to read!"

12:30   Journal Writing

Alicia shows the children a journal: sheets of paper stapled together with the words *My Journal* written on the construction paper cover and a blank line on which to write your name. She says, "I want to show you something we do every day. Maybe you have done it in prekindergarten or Head Start, like Bryan." Bryan jumps up again with his journal. He shows Alicia a picture of his birthday party and says, "Mira! ("Look!" in Spanish) and starts to sing "Happy Birthday to Bryan" in English. Alicia thanks him and says that each of the children in the class will begin drawing and writing in a journal.

On a piece of chartpaper, Alicia draws lines to look like a page in a journal. She begins to draw a picture of herself, naming the parts of her body she is drawing: "Here is my head, my leg, my arm," and so on. She also draws a picture of her vintage red Ford Falcon, which she drives to school. She asks, "What did I forget?" The children make suggestions: "Mouth, *ojos* (eyes), nose" and asks the students to describe what she is wearing and how she looks. When they answer in Spanish, she tells them what the words are in English—for example, *flores* (on her dress) is *flowers,* and *carro* is *car.* Then she writes a sentence under the picture on the blank lines that are provided, as they are in the students' journals: "Today, I came to school in my red Ford Falcon."

Alicia calls each child's name, and as the child comes up to her, she gives him or her a journal and says to write his or her name on it. Each child is also told to draw a picture with crayons and to write with a pencil. Doing this will produce a work sample that Alicia can use to assess each child's drawing and writing and whether the child can write his or her name on the first day of school. The children go to the tables assigned to their groups. At his table, Nicholas, the child who cried when he had to stop looking at books, draws a picture of himself in crayon and wants to write his name on it. He looks at his nametag and copies his name onto his journal, using letterlike shapes (see Figure 4.4). He holds it up for Alicia to see. When she asks him about his drawing, she writes a caption that sums up what he has said: "My mami and daddy." Alicia says, "You can write! Those are letters." She does the same with the other children.

Figure 4.4   Nicholas's Journal

12:45   Blocks and Centers

When the children finish their journals, they can play with blocks, tubs of plastic animals, and puzzles on the rug or go to following centers: housekeeping and dress-up, computers, or gerbils and fish tank.

1:00   Rhythm Sticks, Singing, and Dancing

Alicia gives each child two red rhythm sticks. She plays and the students sing in English "Humpty Dumpty," "Twinkle, Twinkle, Little Star," "Itsy Bitsy Spider," and the alphabet song. She has a chart for each song that the children can look at as they sing. They join in when they know the words, but they beat the rhythm sticks throughout the whole song.

Alicia comes back to the names of the parts of the body in English in another way. The children stand in a circle and she teaches them the song and dance "When Little Johnny Dances": "When little Johnny dances, he dances with his (pinkie, elbow, hip, knee, foot, and so on). Then she plays the piano and the children join in the singing when they can, pointing to and wiggling the body part they are singing about. Children participate at different levels. A few can remember most of the words; others watch those children and follow them. One little girl in pink just stands still, and one little boy gets on the ground and barks like a dog. It is, after all, the very first day of school! Alicia tells him to stand up and he does. Then she teaches the class the "Hokey Pokey," adding the words *right* and *left* to the names of the parts of the body the children are learning in English.

1:30   Planting a Learning Seed

Back on the rug, Alicia asks the children what they learned today. As they answer, she writes what they say in English to form a cluster on chartpaper that says in the middle, "Today in kindergarten, I . . ." She also draws a small picture to illustrate each statement. For example, they said "colored," "danced," "counted," and "read books." (Nicholas said "read books.") Then Alicia walks around, touches each child's forehead, and says one of the things on the list. She tells them she is planting a learning seed that will grow during the year.

1:50   Goodbye Song

Alicia sings a goodbye song to the children, and then they sing it together:

> Go home everybody, yes indeed, yes indeed, yes indeed,
> Go home and be happy, yes indeed.
> Yes indeed my friends! Cha, cha, cha!

After the song, the children get their backpacks. (The little girl who cried at the start of the day because she had to hang up her new pink backpack now hugs it tightly.) Alicia leads them outside to meet the family members who are picking them up.

This Snapshot describes a typical first day of school in kindergarten. Think about what Alicia did as an experienced teacher to make everything comprehensible to her Spanish-speaking students and how she introduced language and literacy activities in English on that first day of school. Her efforts are summarized in the box that follows. But what if you were an English-only preservice or beginning teacher teaching a group of Spanish-speaking kindergarten children?

SUPPORTING

Students Learning English as a Second Language

Alicia Campos used the following strategies for English language development (ELD) and sheltered content instruction (such as mathematics) for young children:

1. *Used the home or native language when possible and appropriate.* Alicia speaks Spanish and used it to greet the children and make them feel welcome and to give simple directions on the first day of school. She also translated answers that children give from Spanish into English because they speak two languages in her classroom. English-only teachers can learn commonly used words and phrases of greeting, welcome, and thank-you in languages other than English.

2. *Welcomed families.* Alicia invited those family members who brought their children to school to come in the classroom for the first few minutes.

3. *Used visuals, props, gestures, and engagement.* To teach the numbers from 1 to 10 in English, Alicia used large number cards (such that the numerals were strung across the front of the room), the *Sesame Street* "Count" puppet, and gestures (for instance, to have children stand up and sit down). She also made language visual by writing the numbers 9 and 10 on chartpaper, by writing the "Morning Message" in English, by reading a picture book showing the numbers and letters, and by using colored yarn for groups. All of these activities engaged the children in learning.

4. *Used rhyme, music, and song.* Alicia used the power of rhyme to teach English words—for example, in nursery rhymes and music and song. She accompanied rhymes with gestures to engage the children while learning English in the content areas (as in learning the names of the parts of the body).

5. *Modeled how to draw on personal experience.* To begin journal writing, Alicia drew a picture of herself and wrote a caption about her car, modeling what she wanted her young students to do: tap into their own personal experiences as a source for drawing and for writing and learning English.

6. *Read storybook and repeated-pattern books.* Alicia read several picture books, including a repeated-pattern book, and used colorful charts with nursery rhymes to introduce English in print to her students.

Common Words in Native Languages: *Hello, Welcome, and Thank-You*

Spanish: *Buenos dias, bienvenidos, gracias*

Vietnamese: *Kính Chào Qúy Vị* (king chow qwi ve), *Thành Thật Cám On Qúy Vị* (tine tat calm un qwi ve)

Hmong: *zoo siab txais tos, nyob zoo, va koj tsaug*

Chinese: *ni hao* (nee how); *huan ying* (wan ying); *xie xie* (shea shea)

Korean: *Ahn-Nyoung-Ha-Sae-Yo, Hwan-Young-Hop-Ni-Da, Gam-Sa-Hop-Ni-Da*

Haitian Creole: *byenvini, banjou, remesye*

Arabic/English: *Salamon Alaikom, Ahlan Va Sahlan, Shokran*

Marjorie Abbott, one of my students in a preservice, field-based language arts methods class, created a "Read, Talk, Draw, Write" lesson for use with a group of native Spanish-speaking kindergarten children at various levels of English language proficiency. She had a bilingual fifth-grader as an aide to provide primary language support in Spanish. Marjorie used the "big book" version of Audrey Wood's (1984) *The Napping House,* a cumulative story about a house and a bed. It has a lot of action, wonderful illustrations, and repeated phrases the children can join in on. Here's Marjorie's adapted lesson plan, along with her descriptions of the activities.

See pp. 132–133 to learn about the "Read, Talk, Draw, Write" lesson plan.

LESSON PLAN

Read, Talk, Draw, Write Adapted for Spanish-Speaking Kindergartners

Purpose: Children will listen to and enjoy an English, "big book" version of a pattern book; discuss the story; and draw and write in response to it.

Standard 3: Students apply a wide range of strategies to comprehend, interpret, evaluate, and appreciate texts. They draw on their prior experience, their interactions with other readers and writers, their knowledge of word meaning and of other texts, their word identification strategies, and their understanding of textual features (e.g., sound-letter correspondence, sentence structure, context, graphics).

IRA/ NCTE

Materials:
1. "Big book" version of *The Napping House,* by Audrey Wood (1984)
2. Props to act out the story, including stuffed dolls and animals: a granny; Dalmatian dog; tiger-stripped kitty; doll; catnip mouse; flea made from dryer lint; small, white quilt with a red, heart-shaped pillow for the bed
3. White construction paper
4. Crayons

ELL

To adapt this lesson for English language learners, follow these guidelines:

- Have students draw responses.
- Act out the story, using props/realia, sound effects, and dramatic voices.
- Use students' primary languages; accept their levels of language proficiency.
- Bring in native-speaking aides.
- Take dictation from students.

Procedure: Here's how Marjorie describes each step:
1. *Read*

   I sit in a small chair holding the "big book," and the children sit on the floor in front of me. I show them the cover and read the title page and author's name. Next, I make a little bed in front of me and tell them the reason I'm making the bed is because the story is about napping or sleeping. The children listen quietly, watching my every move. I start reading the first page, and then, while reading the second page, I put "granny" in bed. As I read the book and turn the pages, I (quite miraculously) am able to stack all the stuffed animals and dolls on top of each other without a

(continued)

single spill! I pretend to snore when I refer to the "snoring granny." (My fifth-grade aide, Norma, really laughed at seeing me act so silly! It's fun, and I don't mind because the children are so engrossed.) I make my voice sound dreamy when I put the "dreaming child" on top of the "snoring granny." I "meow" when I place the cat on the dog and "squeak" when I put the mouse on top of the cat. I had no sound effects for the flea— would you?

Norma, who has heard the story, hurries to my side at the end, when it's time for all the characters to jump up and off one another as each is clawed, bitten, scared, or whatever! She helps with the dramatic ending, while I excitedly read (and laugh) and turn the remaining pages frantically. The children *get* this! They laugh and cheer and catch some of the flying animals, speaking mainly in Spanish. It's wonderful!

2. *Talk*

I first ask the children their favorite part of the story. Eric replies, "The house" in English. Norma interprets my question for other children, and their answers come in Spanish. I hear "el ratón," "el perro," "el gato," "la abuela," and "la casa" (which mean the "mouse," "dog," "cat," "grandmother," and "house," respectively).

3. *Draw*

I give the children paper and crayons and ask them to draw their favorite part or anything they want about the story. Norma, the aide, repeats these directions in Spanish. I go around to the students individually, asking what they've drawn, or I ask (imitating the aide), "Que es esto?" They usually answer with one word—in Spanish or English. If I don't understand, the aide translates.

4. *Write*

I ask the students to write their names on their drawings. Most of them also allow me to write, in English, a sentence about what's going on in their drawing. They also say it's all right for me to write/spell the name of the object they have colored. Everyone thinks it's a good idea, except for Victor, who repeatedly says, "Nada, nada!" (i.e., "Nothing, nothing!"). He simply does not want *anything* written on his drawing! Eric has drawn all the animals and has me label each one and the granny. Then I ask him "Where's the child?" He answers in English, "Under Granny!"

Marjorie continues:

I see that this lesson could have expanded into the areas of the family and sleep, just to name a few. I was constantly aware of keeping the affective filter low, acting relaxed, friendly, and caring. The children behaved as if they felt safe and secure. With my heart pounding, and happy, I left the room where emergent literacy in two languages was experienced by all.

Assessing Young Children

The National Association for the Education of Young Children (NAEYC, 1991) opposes the use of standardized tests for young children, except as a way of screening for development and special services. Instead, teachers should use developmentally appropriate, constructive forms of observational and performance-based assessment for young children.

The National Board for Professional Teaching Standards (1995) has set standards for authentic assessment of young children. Teachers should continually monitor students' work and behavior and analyze this information to improve interaction with children and parents. A variety of approaches should be used: ongoing observations, questioning and listening, anecdotal records, and a systematic sampling of children's work and performance (e.g., writing, artwork, audiotapes of oral reading, dictated stories, literature-response logs, and records of group participation in projects). Teachers should consider this information against the unfolding picture of the individual child as a learner and person, keeping in mind what stage of development is typical for a child of that age.

Two such types of literacy assessment can be found in the Assessment Toolboxes presented thus far in the chapter: 4.1, Concepts about Print, and 4.2, Concept of a Word. Assessment Toolbox 4.3 (p. 150) shows a systematic sampling of children's work and performance that can be used to measure progress toward basic goals for each child. In this systematic sampling of emergent literacy, each child is directed to write his or her name, to write the numbers from 1 to 10, and to draw a picture of himself or herself at the beginning, middle, and end of kindergarten. The examples shown are by David, a non-English-speaking Cambodian American child who was placed in a Khmer transitional kindergarten in the fall with no previous school experience. In a *transitional* class, the teacher uses appropriate strategies for English language learners and has the help of a Khmer-speaking aide. None of the teacher's students speak English. The example on the left was completed at the beginning of the schoolyear, and the example on the right was completed at the end. You can see David's wonderful progress over the year in this developmentally appropriate, literature-based, student-centered kindergarten class. In this supportive atmosphere, David was able to keep up with district expectations of what a child should know at the end of kindergarten.

4.1
Concepts about Print (p. 120)

4.2
Concept of a Word (p. 127)

Answers to Questions about Emergent Literacy and Biliteracy

- *How do young children learn to read and write their first and/or second language?*

According to the emergent literacy perspective, young children learn to read and write as they use writing and reading for authentic purposes, actively constructing meaning. This view developed when studies of early natural readers

ASSESSMENT
TOOLBOX

4.3 Systematic Sampling of Emergent Literacy

In this systematic sampling of emergent literacy, each child is asked to write his or her name, to write the numbers from 1 to 10, and to draw a picture of himself or herself. This exercise is completed at the beginning, midpoint, and end of the kindergarten year. The example here shows the work of David, a non-English-speaking Cambodian American student, at the beginning and end of his kindergarten year.

Give these directions to the child: (1) Print your name, (2) Print the numbers 1 through 10, and (3) Draw a picture of yourself.

Name David	**Name** David
Date September 10	**Date** June 10
1. Print your name.	1. Print your name.
T⌐?E ⌐dᴀᴦ	David
2. Print the numbers 1 to 10.	2. Print the numbers 1 to 10.
ᴦEn ᴧᴧᴧᴧ	1 2 3 4 5 6 7 8 9 10
3. Draw a picture of yourself.	3. Draw a picture of yourself.

challenged the previously held readiness view by showing that literate behavior does not begin at a certain age but is constantly emerging. Children know a great deal about literacy when they enter school. Even though literacy experiences in the home may vary across families and cultures, all children have them. Important influences on emerging reading are environmental print and storybook experiences. Emergent writing develops in a series of predictable stages: scribbling, drawing, nonphonetic letterstrings, invented spelling, and conventional orthography. Children also go through predictable stages in spelling development: precommunicative, prephonetic, phonetic, transitional, and conventional.

Reading and writing are interactive processes and emerge together. Young children who come to school speaking a language other than English need multiple opportunities to use both languages in authentic contexts connected with their own lives through speaking, reading, and writing.

- *How should we teach young children to read and write when learning English as a first or second language?*

Seven ways to begin teaching young children to write include (1) creating a print-rich environment, (2) having a regular sharing time, (3) reading aloud, (4) dramatizing, (5) writing and drawing, (6) establishing centers, and (7) integrating teaching.

Teachers of young children who speak a home language other than English can use these same strategies but should adapt instruction by including and emphasizing (1) the home language when possible and appropriate, (2) by welcoming families into the classroom, (3) by using visuals, props, gestures, and engagement, (4) by using rhyme, music, and song, (5) by modeling how to tap into personal experience, and (6) by reading storybooks and repeated-pattern books.

Authentic, ongoing literacy assessment for young children should be developmentally appropriate and help the teacher determine appropriate instruction by finding out what each child knows (e.g., assessing concepts about print and a word). A systematic sampling can be conducted to determine progress toward appropriate goals for the end of kindergarten: ability to write his or her name, to write numbers, and to draw a representational, detailed self-portrait.

Looking Further

1. Diagram a possible "ripple effect" of learning and teaching experiences for a specific grade level from kindergarten through third grade. Make sure that it's based on a worthwhile topic appropriate for that grade level and that it provides many opportunities for authentic reading and writing experiences.

2. Do a lesson plan for "Read, Talk, Draw, Write," described in this chapter, and try it out with a group of young children in grades K–3. Describe the experience.

3. Adapt a lesson plan for "Read, Talk, Draw, Write" for ELL students. Describe your experience trying it out with children.

4. Compare experiences in items 2 and 3, if you were able to do both lesson plans.

5. Administer one of the Assessment Toolboxes in this chapter (4.1, 4.2, or 4.3) to an English-only kindergarten or first-grade student and then to a second-language learner. Compare results and report your findings to your college class.

6. Observe and participate in both a kindergarten and a first-grade class that include second-language learners. In terms of their approach to emergent literacy and biliteracy, how were they alike? How were they different?

Children's Books and Software

Aliki. (1963). *The story of Johnny Appleseed*. New York: Prentice Hall.

Aliki. (1992). *La historia de Johnny Appleseed*. New York: Lectorum.

Brett, J. (1986). *The mitten*. New York: Putnam's.

Brown, M. (1957). *The three billy goats gruff*. New York: Harcourt Brace Jovanovich.

Carle, E. (1969). *The very hungry caterpillar*. Cleveland: Collins-World.

Carle, E. (1972). *Rooster's off to see the world*. Saxonville, MA: Picture Book Studio.

Eastman, P. D. (1960). *Are you my mother?* New York: Random House.

Ehlert, L. (1989). *Color zoo*. New York: HarperCollins.

Flack, M. (1932). *Ask Mr. Bear*. New York: Macmillan.

Gag, W. (1956). *Millions of cats*. New York: Coward, McCann. (Original work published 1928)

Galdone, P. (1973). *The little red hen*. New York: Clarion.

Guarino, D. (1989). *Is your mama a llama?* New York: Scholastic.

Hawkins, C., & Hawkins, J. (1987). *I know an old lady who swallowed a fly*. New York: Putnam's.

Heuck, S. (1986). *Who stole the apples?* New York: Knopf.

Hoban, T. (1985). *A children's zoo*. New York: Greenwillow.

Hogrogian, N. (1972). *Apples*. New York: Macmillan.

Hutchins, P. (1968). *The doorbell rang*. New York: Morrow.

Keats, E. J. (1973). *Over in the meadow*. New York: Scholastic.

Kellogg, S. (1988). *Johnny Appleseed*. New York: Morrow.

Kraus, R. (1970). *Whose mouse are you?* New York: Macmillan.

Lindbergh, R. (1990). *Johnny Appleseed: A poem by Reeve Lindbergh*. Boston: Little, Brown.

Macmillan, B. (1992). *The baby zoo*. New York: Scholastic.

Maestro, B. (1992). *How do apples grow?* New York: HarperCollins.

Martin, B. (1983). *Brown bear, brown bear, what do you see?* (Eric Carle, Illus.) New York: Henry Holt.

Martin, B., & Archambault, J. (1989). *Chicka chicka boom boom!* New York: Simon & Schuster.

Nottridge, R. (1991). *Apples*. Minneapolis, MN: Carolrhoda.

Numeroff, L. J. (1985). *If you give a mouse a cookie*. New York: HarperCollins.

Paladino, C. (1999). *One good apple: Growing our food for the sake of the earth*. New York: Houghton Mifflin.

Parnall, P. (1987). *Apple tree*. New York: Macmillan.

Peek, M. (1985). *Mary wore her red dress*. New York: Clarion.

Poulet, V. (1985). *Blue bug goes to school*. Chicago: Children's Press.

Priceman, M.(1994). *How to make an apple pie and see the world*. New York: Knopf.

Rosen, M. (1989). *We're going on a bear hunt*. New York: McElderry.

Seifert, J. (1985). *La cancion del manzano*. Madrid, Spain: Ediciones S. M.

Sendak, M. (1962). *Chicken soup with rice*. New York: Harper's.

Seuss, Dr. (1988). *Green eggs and ham*. New York: Random House.

Slobodkina, E. (1940). *Caps for sale*. New York: Harper & Row.

Stickybear's reading room [Computer software]. Available from Optimum Resource.

Wickstrom, S. K. (1988). *The wheels on the bus*. New York: Crown.

Wood, A. (1984). *The napping house*. San Diego: Harcourt Brace Jovanovich.

Zoobooks [series]. San Diego: Wildlife Education Limited.

chapter 5

Listening and Talking

Questions about Listening and Talking

- *Why is it important to teach listening and talking?*
- *How should we teach and assess listening and talking?*

REFLECTIVE RESPONSE

Listening and talking seem like such natural language acts. Babies listen before they speak, and young children come to school already speaking their native languages. Perhaps we don't really need to worry about teaching listening and talking when it's so important to teach reading and writing. What do you think? Jot down your ideas.

Listening and Talking in the Classroom

Listening: The Neglected Language Art

A well-known study done by Paul Rankin in 1928 showed that 68 percent of each schoolday is spent in communication, and during that time, listening is the most prevalent activity (45 percent). Next is speaking (30 percent), followed by reading (16 percent) and writing (9 percent) (see Figure 5.1A, p. 154). More recent studies have verified similar breakdowns of classroom time (Chaney & Burk, 1998; Hunsacker, 1989). Yet relatively little attention has been paid to teaching

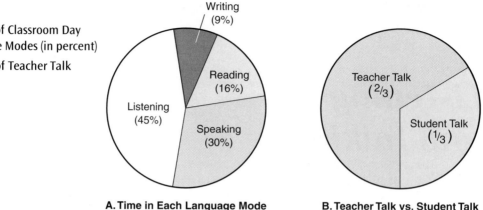

Figure 5.1

Part A: Amount of Classroom Day Spent in Language Modes (in percent)

Part B: Amount of Teacher Talk vs. Student Talk

A. Time in Each Language Mode

B. Teacher Talk vs. Student Talk

IRA/ NCTE

Listening, as defined in the *Standards for the English Language Arts* (1996), is "attending to communication by any means; includes listening to vocal speech, watching signing, or using communication aids."

listening, even though active approaches to doing so have been demonstrated to improve students' listening ability (Brent & Anderson, 1993; Devine, 1978; Funk & Funk, 1989; Winn, 1988). Listening is the neglected language art.

Opportunities for teaching listening, as well as talking, have been limited because educators have traditionally used reading and writing performance as measures of student achievement. Research has shown, however, that listening comprehension can be improved in a variety of ways when it's taught in the context of meaningful oral language experiences (Goodlad, 1984; Jalongo, 1991; Pearson & Fielding, 1982).

Talking: The Suppressed Language Art

Talking in the classroom has more often been associated with behavior problems and a teacher's lack of classroom management skills than as the important language art that it is (Helper, 1991). Talking is the suppressed language art. In general, students have fewer opportunities to talk in school than they do at home. Schools don't always provide a linguistically rich environment, compared to homes, where children have more opportunities to learn through talking (Wells & Wells, 1984).

This may seem surprising in light of research that has shown (Flanders, 1970; Wilt, 1974) that during the schoolday, someone is talking from one-half to two-thirds of the time (which is more than twice the amount of time teachers estimated). The problem is that the *teacher* talks more than all the students combined. In fact, two-thirds of the time someone is speaking, it's the teacher (see Figure 5.1B). Teacher talk tends to dominate activities involving explaining and evaluating, which limits student talk in terms of both quantity and meaningful purpose. As a result, children spend more time listening to teacher talk than engaged in active language interaction with either teachers or other students (Fox, 1983).

www.ablongman.com/cox5e

Literacy and Listening and Talking

Walter Loban's (1976, 1979) well-known longitudinal study of how children from kindergarten through grade 12 (K–12) use and control language had several significant findings about the connections between literacy and listening and talking. Children who are proficient in oral language—listening and talking—use more complex language and better understand the conventions of language, score higher on vocabulary and intelligence tests, and perform better in reading and writing than students who are less proficient in oral language. Reviews of research on the connections between literacy and listening and talking confirm that children's experience with and knowledge of the linguistic organization of spoken language is a fundamental prerequisite to their learning to read (Cox, 1984; Pinnell & Jaggar, 2003; Sticht & James, 1984).

Listening and talking are integral to writing as well as reading. For young, emergent writers, writing is "as much an oral activity as a written one" (Dyson & Genishi, 1982, p. 126), since talking works in concert with *composing,* or expressing ideas in writing (Dyson, 1994). Writing is one aspect of the total process of language development and thus interrelated with listening, talking, reading, and thinking. All of these abilities develop simultaneously and in concert, not in isolation. James Britton's famous metaphor—"Writing floats on a sea of talk" (1970, p. 164)—helps us picture the importance of listening and talking as a basis for literacy.

Considering the great importance placed on literacy instruction today, teaching listening and talking in your classroom will have a significant impact on your students' achievement in reading and writing. Keep this in mind as you read the ideas presented in the rest of this chapter.

SNAPSHOT Teacher Talk and Student Talk about a Book and a Film at Halloween

In this Snapshot, we'll look at what kinds of listening and talking went on in a second-grade class the week before Halloween, when teacher Kathy Lee read books, showed films, and then led discussions with students. This should give you ideas about how to start teaching listening and talking.

While reading the Snapshot, let's do simple analyses of several things: (1) the ratio of teacher talk to student talk and (2) the types of questions the teacher asked, closed versus open. Use Figure 5.2 (p. 156) to keep tallies of how many times the teacher and the students each spoke in the book and film talks as well as how many open and closed questions the teacher asked. We'll add up the totals and calculate ratios later, after reading the Snapshot, when we'll also discuss the implications of these observations for starting listening and talking in your classroom.

Open questions, which have many possible answers, lead to richer language interactions and higher levels of thinking than *closed questions,* which have simple, often one-word answers, such as "yes" and "no" (Barnes, 1992).

Figure 5.2 Language Interaction Analysis Chart

Date/Time _____

Activity _____

	Type of Talk		Type of Question	
	Teacher	**Student**	**Open**	**Closed**
Book Talk				
Total	_____	_____	_____	_____
Ratio	_____	_____	_____	_____
Film Talk				
Total	_____	_____	_____	_____
Ratio	_____	_____	_____	_____

Book Talk: *Where the Wild Things Are*

It was Halloween, and Kathy Lee was reading her second-graders Maurice Sendak's (1963) well-known Caldecott Medal–winning book *Where the Wild Things Are*, which is about a little boy's adventures on an island with some wild, monstrous creatures. Kathy was reading the book in the way teachers often do with young children: reading the text, showing the illustrations, and asking questions about the story as she went along. While reading the book, she engaged the students in the following book talk (remember to analyze this language sample using Figure 5.2):

Teacher (points to title):   What does it say?

Child (reading):   Where the wild things are.

Teacher: That's right. And the picture looks like . . . ?

Child: A monster.

Teacher: What kind of feet does it have?

Child: Human feet.

Teacher: Maybe this can be for one of the days we're celebrating this month. What day is that?

Child: Columbus Day?

Teacher: Well, this (points to monster) can be for Halloween, and this (points to boat) can be for Columbus Day.

(Noise from the children.)

Teacher (reading):   "The night Max wore his wolf suit and made mischief of one kind . . ." What is he doing?

Kathy continued to read the rest of the book in this way.

Film Talk: *Clay*

Kathy showed the film *Clay: The Origin of the Species* (1964), a clay animation, film in which things constantly change into other things at a frenzied pace. After the film was over, the class discussed it:

Teacher: Well, what did you think of it? What did you think of all those creatures?

Child: I liked the animals and people and boats and the Statue of Liberty.

Child: And a president. President Lincoln.

Child: A man eating. Something that eats everything that comes by. A lizard.

Child: And a whale and an elephant and a deer.

Child: Yeah, and a cow and a gingerbread boy.

Teacher: What do you think was the most unbelievable thing that happened in the movie? We saw a lot of funny things, but what really made you go "wow" or something?

Child: I know. When the dinosaurs were playing and they kissed.

(Many children laugh.)

Child: I like that, uh, that, um, one dinosaur, um, ate the other one.

Teacher: Do you think you could make things like you saw in the film?

Many Children: YEAH!

Teacher: What would you like to make?

Child: You could make anything you wanted to.

Child: Mrs. Lee, could we make something together?

Teacher: Would you like to make something together?

Child: Yeah. We'd like . . . two people to work in a group, you know, work together.

Child: Could we do it right now?

Teacher: I think maybe later on today we'll make some clay things.

Child: We're gonna make something good. We're gonna make a clown and a football player.

Child: See, I could bring a ball.

Child: We could make our own movie!

Child: Will we have prizes? Let's say they all get a prize.

Child: Yeah! Me included.

Child: We'll run the movie through again.

Child: We'll have prizes and show the movie and make our own movie and then we'll have it all together!

Now, add up your tallies (see Figure 5.2) and for each discussion, calculate the ratios of (1) teacher to student talk and (2) open to closed questions. Also think about what the children said. Here's a comparison of students' responses in the closed-question book talk versus the open-question film talk:

Closed-Question Book Talk	*Open-Question Film Talk*
Read title, words	Described parts they liked in the film and also the most unbelievable thing
Described pictures	
Answered with single words	Brainstormed ideas for making things out of clay
Named holidays	Asked to watch the movie again
	Suggested they make a movie
	Offered to work together in groups
	Requested having prizes for their movie

During the book talk, did you notice the following?

- Kathy talked more and asked more closed questions, and the students' responses were limited to one-word answers or trying to read words.
- In order to correctly answer the questions Kathy asked, the children just had to listen as she read the book. (The answers could be verified by the text.)
- The children didn't interact with each other, and they made noise unrelated to the book talk.

And did you notice these things during the film talk?

- Kathy asked more open questions and did less talking—and consequently, more listening to what her students said.
- She invited more than one possible response and then built new questions on each response received.
- The students listened to and interacted with each other and led the discussion in new and interesting ways.

In sum, when Kathy asked closed questions, her teaching was teacher and text centered and the discussion was impoverished. As a result, very little happened in terms of developing language. When Kathy asked open questions, however, her teaching was student and response centered and the discussion was rich and full. She scaffolded on students' ideas, and the result was a "ripple effect" of language and literacy experiences that actually occurred in her room; for instance, the class made a clay animation film called *The Greatest Clay Movie on Earth*.

Teaching Listening and Talking

In a summary of recent research, Gay Sue Pinnell and Angela Jaggar (2003) suggest that five principles should underlie teaching oral language, or listening and talking:

1. *The English language arts classroom must engage students in talk.*
2. *Classroom contexts must provide a wide range of learning contexts that require the development and use of a wide range of language.*
3. *Education should expand the intellectual, personal, and social purposes for which children use language.*
4. *A constructivist view of learning requires a curriculum that involves language interactions of many different kinds.*
5. *Context plays a central role in oral language learning.*
6. *Oral language is a means to learning.* (pp. 902–904)

Pinnell and Jaggar further recommend that in order to teach oral language, teachers should avoid "narrow lessons, isolated drills and exercises" (p. 903). Instead, oral language is best taught and learned using "small-group student discussions and project work, informal conversations between students and their peers and teachers, language games, storytelling, creative dramatics, role-playing, improvisation, and for older students, more formal drama" (p. 903). The rest of this chapter will describe these and other strategies for promoting oral language development.

Questions and Prompts

The kinds of questions and prompts teachers use are critical to oral language development as well as thinking and understanding. Given that, we might assume that teachers would most often choose to use open questions. But in *A Place Called School*, John Goodlad (1984) explains that this isn't the case:

> A great deal of what goes on in the classroom is like painting-by-numbers—filling in the colors called for by numbers on the page. . . . [Teachers] ask specific questions calling essentially for students to fill in the blanks: "What is the capital city of Canada?" "What are the principal exports of Japan?" Students rarely turn things around by asking the questions. Nor do teachers often give students a chance to romp with an open-ended question such as "What are your views on the quality of television?" (p. 108)

Unfortunately, teachers spend more time engaging students in closed discussions than open ones. Moreover, students often learn to give only the answers they think teachers want to hear (Short, 1995) and that fall within the traditional boundaries of classroom activities (Rowe, 1998a). Wells and Wells (1984) suggest that the problem may be that we as teachers have a

> less than wholehearted belief in the value that pupils' talk has for their learning. Many of us have years of being talked at as students and have probably unconsciously absorbed the belief that, as teachers, we are not doing our job properly unless we are talking, telling, questioning, or evaluating. But all the time we are talking, we are stopping our pupils from trying out their understanding in words. We are also depriving ourselves of valuable information about the state of their understanding and thus of an opportunity to plan future work to meet their specific needs. (p. 194)

The questions and prompts that teachers ask during and after reading aloud are extremely important, because they direct children's stance toward literature. According to Louise Rosenblatt's (1978) *transactional theory,* readers take a *stance* on a continuum of efferent to aesthetic responses. An *efferent* response focuses on information that can be taken away from the text—for instance, reading a story to learn facts. An *aesthetic* response focuses on personally experiencing the text—for instance, reading a story to examine personal values or attitudes. Rosenblatt (1980) suggests that children should be directed toward aesthetic stances during experiences with literature, rather than efferent ones.

Efferent and aesthetic stances toward literature will be explained more fully in Chapter 7, Teaching with Literature.

Nonetheless, research on aesthetic versus efferent questions has shown that even teachers who describe themselves as literature based tend to direct children to take efferent stances (Zarrillo & Cox, 1992). This is the case even though studies with fifth-grade students (Cox & Many, 1992a) and sixth- through eighth-grade students (Many, 1991) have shown that students who respond aesthetically to literature develop higher levels of understanding. Longitudinal research on young children's responses to literature has led to development of the types of

Both during and after reading aloud, teachers can direct children's stance toward literature with the questions they ask and the prompts they use.

questions and prompts that reflect children's natural aesthetic responses to literature (Cox, 1994c). And classroom studies have demonstrated how efferent questions can follow and develop from the initial open, aesthetic questions and prompts, keeping instruction student and response centered (Many & Wiseman, 1992).

Here are examples of both aesthetic and efferent questions (developing from aesthetic):

Aesthetic	Efferent
What do you think about the story?	What was the main idea of the story?
Tell anything you want about the story.	What did the author mean by —?
What was your favorite part? Tell about it.	Retell your favorite part. Tell the order of the story events.
Has anything like this ever happened to you? Tell about it.	Describe the main characters. Explain the characters' actions.
Does the story remind you of anything? Tell about it.	What other stories are like this one? Compare and contrast the stories.
What did you wonder about? Tell about it.	What was the problem in the story? How did the author solve the problem?
What would you change in the story?	How did the author make the story believable?
What else do you think might happen in the story?	Is it fact or fiction?
What would you say or do if you were a character in the story?	How do you think the characters felt?

Asking open questions is among the most valuable tools teachers have to support children's oral language development, understanding, thinking, and achievement.

Instructional Conversations

Questioning strategies that are especially appropriate for English language learners (ELL) are used in a model called *instructional conversation*, or *IC* (Goldenberg, 1993). Goldenberg suggests that given the perception that ELL students only need to drill, repeat, and review in order to succeed academically, teachers often fail to move beyond low-level, factually oriented, closed questions. IC is an explicit instructional model designed to guide teachers in how to have discussions that are interesting and engaging; that are about focused, meaningful, relevant ideas; and that have high levels of student participation not dominated by the teacher. Characteristics of IC include fewer known-answer questions and responsiveness to student contributions. Saunders and Goldenberg (1999) have found that IC promotes a higher level of understanding of significant concepts without sacrificing literal comprehension and that IC can be a productive mode of teaching for language-minority students, whom research has shown are particularly likely to receive inordinate amounts of low-level, skills-oriented instruction. See the box below for a summary of how to use ICs with ELL students.

SUPPORTING

English Language Learners in Instructional Conversations

The following instructional and conversational elements of an instructional conversation (Goldenberg, 1993) are especially helpful in providing support for English language learners:

Instructional Elements

1. Thematic focus
2. Activation and use of background and relevant schemata
3. Direct teaching
4. Promotion of more complex language and expression
5. Elicitation of bases for statements or positions

Conversational Elements

1. Fewer known-answer questions
2. Responsivity to student contributions
3. Connected discourse
4. A challenging but nonthreatening atmosphere
5. General participation, including self-selected turns

Guidelines for Planning and Implementing an IC

1. Select a story or book that's appropriate for your students.
2. Read the story or book several times until you feel you understand it thoroughly.
3. Select a theme on which to focus the discussion, at least at first.
4. Identify and provide, as appropriate, background knowledge that students need in order to make sense of what they will be reading.
5. Decide on a starting point for the discussion to get things going.
6. Mentally plan and think through the lesson.
7. Consider suitable follow-up activities, particularly any that will help you gauge what students have learned from the IC.

Following is an example of two small-group lessons conducted in a classroom of fourth-grade students who spoke Spanish as a first language and were learning English. For one group, the teacher used an IC; for the other, she used a more conventional recitation or basal-reader-type lesson. Pay attention to whether the teacher's questions are open or closed and who talks versus listens, as you did when you read the Snapshot of Kathy Lee's class at the beginning of the chapter.

Instructional Conversation

Teacher: What should Rob have decided?

Karla: Oh, he should have told his friend Soup not to do that.

Rosa: But he said that he wanted to go into the barbershop. He wanted to go and Soup said, "No, I'll cut your hair free." And he goes, "FREE."

Karla: No, that didn't happen.

Teacher: So he—

Char: He said, "*If* I had a barbershop, I would cut your hair free."

Teacher: Now was that a good friend?

Recitation

Teacher: What was the problem in the story?

Maria: The haircut.

Teacher: The haircut. Okay. Albert?

Al: They wasted their money on candy.

Teacher: Wasted money?

Ricky: Rob wanted a haircut, but he wanted candy more.

Teacher: Good. Was Soup involved?

Ricky: Soup tricked him.

Teacher: Oh, Soup was tricky.

Marta: Yeah, he told him, "I'll cut your hair for free."

Teacher: Okay. And then what happened?

Graphic Organizers

Teachers can record students' ideas during discussions on chartpaper or the chalkboard using *graphic organizers,* or students can use them when working in small groups or individually.

Kathy Lee used a graphic organizer to record children's ideas when they thought of "what they could make with clay." The teacher can support discussions like this (or even initiate them) using graphic organizers such as *clusters* to record children's ideas. To do so, the teacher simply writes down the focal point

As you may recall, clustering and webbing were discussed briefly in Chapter 2.

of the discussion at the top or in the center of a piece of chartpaper or the chalk-board and then records students' ideas for discussing and as a basis for further activities. For instance:

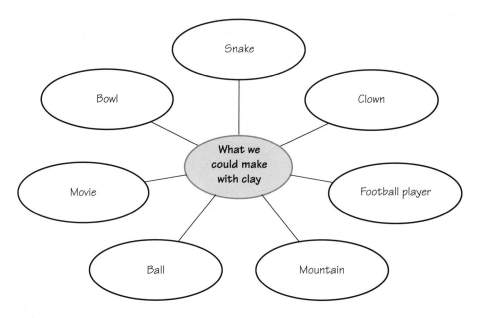

Different types of graphic organizers are useful for various purposes:

- *Cluster:* This is the type shown above, in which connections among ideas are shown.
- *List:* Characteristics or steps are listed (in order, if appropriate).
- *T-chart:* Characteristics or steps of two subjects or processes are listed in columns, side by side.
- *Venn diagram:* Relationships among ideas or parts are shown by overlapping items or putting one inside another.
- *Flowchart:* The order of elements is indicated, showing cause and effect.

Cooperative Learning

Cooperative learning is an instructional technique that uses students' own conversation as a vehicle for learning. Research has shown that cooperative learning also improves students' academic achievement, social skills, and self-esteem (Johnson, Johnson, & Holobec, 1991; Sharan, 1990; Slavin, 1990).

Kathy Lee used this technique when she formed her second-grade students into groups to work on some of the ideas that came from discussing what they could make with clay.

Cluster

List
Title
1.
2.
3.

T-Chart

Venn Diagram

Flowchart

Several cooperative learning strategies have been developed (Baloche, 1998; Kagan, 1992; Slavin, 1990):

1. *Jigsaw:* Students form teams, and each member of the team becomes an expert on one topic by working with members of other teams who are assigned the same topic. For example, if there are six teams and each has five members (A, B, C, D, E), topics would be assigned like this:

A   How long ago and how long did dinosaurs live?
B   Where and how did they live?
C   What are the types of meat-eating dinosaurs?
D   What are the types of plant-eating dinosaurs?
E   Why did dinosaurs become extinct?

When students return to their original teams, they share what they learned about their respective topics. All members of the teams are assessed on all topics.

2. *Think-Pair-Share:* In this type of cooperative learning strategy, students think about a question or topic, pair up with partners to discuss it, and share their thoughts with the rest of the class (Kagan, 1985).

3. *Three-Step Interview:* Students working in this strategy also form pairs; each partner interviews the other and then shares what he or she has learned with the whole class (Kagan, 1985).

ELL

ELL students may play roles like these in cooperative projects:

- Active listener
- Illustrator
- Encourager
- Materials manager

4. *Cooperative Projects, Co-op Co-op:* Students work together in small groups toward a single goal, but each individual must make an identifiable contribution. We've already seen several examples of this strategy in this book, including Avril Font's students working in group workshops to learn about the maypole dance or to build a dragon and dramatize the story of St. George and the dragon. Kathy Lee's students provided another example when they worked on cooperative projects in groups and made clay animation movies.

To work effectively, cooperative project groups should have the following features:

- heterogeneous composition (ability, gender, race/ethnicity)
- individual accountability
- group goals (positive interdependence)
- shared responsibility
- emphasis on social skills

5. *Gallery Walk:* Students work together in small groups to answer a question or solve a problem. Each group also creates some kind of artifact: a chart, graphic organizer, cluster, web, semantic map, illustration, model, or experiment. The artifacts are then displayed around the room. The student groups rotate to view the artifacts. They leave written feedback on a sheet of paper by each artifact or write their observations on Post-its and attach them to the artifacts. When each group returns to their own artifact, they discuss their peers' feedback about what they have done. All of the groups then reflect on the experience together.

SCAFFOLDING

Struggling readers and writers and students with disabilities gain independence through their contributions to group work.

6. *One-Minute Paper:* In response to a question or topic, students write or draw and write for one minute. Then they share their writings/drawings among themselves. The teacher can number off students (say, from 1 to 5), and they can find a number match to exchange papers with. Or students can sit in two concentric circles and share with the persons across from them.

7. *Group Interview:* In groups of three or four, students first think about a question or a problem to be solved. Then each student is interviewed by the rest of his or her group. All students have a chance to share, take turns, listen to each other, and ask questions to clarify their understanding of what other students have said.

8. *Corners:* This strategy works well if a group discussion has generated different points of view—for example, identifying a favorite season or character from a book or film or deciding what students would like to do in a class "ripple effect." The teacher designates one corner of the room for each option. Students first think by themselves about the choices and then go to the corner representing their choice, where they discuss ideas and plans with other students. They may use other cooperative learning activities, such as three-step interviews and group interviews. The group in each corner shares its ideas and plans with the other corner groups. Students may plan further experiences for a class project this way. For example, in Kathy Lee's class, students could decide what part of the animated clay movie they would work on and how.

9. *Find Someone Who Knows or Treasure Hunt:* The teacher or the teacher and students generate a list of questions or topics they would like to know more about. Topics may be about the students (e.g., "Find someone who has a family member that was born in another country and tell about it") or related to academic content (e.g., "Find someone who knows an animal that is a mammal and can tell some facts about it"). Each student records the topic or question on a piece of paper and then moves around the room, gathering information from other students. Students come together again to share what they have found out.

10. *K-W-H-L-S:* This approach is a variation on the K-W-L chart described in Chapter 1. The K-W-L chart usually describes an activity for a group: K (What we *know*), W (What we *want* to learn), and L (What we *learned*). The K-W-H-L-S is used by an individual to show differentiated goals and to build interdependence among students.

Cooperative learning strategies are well suited to students with individual differences, as described in the box on the next page.

Listening and Media Centers

A media center, offering listening and viewing activities, can be created in the classroom for use by small groups and individual children. In this center, children can listen to and view professionally recorded and filmed stories or their own media creations. The equipment needed includes a tape/CD player with earphones and a VCR or DVD player and television monitor.

English Language Learners, Struggling Readers and Writers, and Students with Disabilities in Cooperative Learning

Cooperative learning strategies support inclusion of all students in a classroom community (Graves, 1992). Differences among students—such as cognitive and learning styles, social class, race and ethnicity, language, and disabilities— are viewed as resources. Inclusion is rooted in frequent student-to-student interaction, in which students learn about each other as individuals, respect each other, and see each other as contributing members of the group.

Struggling readers and writers and students with disabilities may experience success in these ways:

- By filling a group role suited to their strengths
- By listening to material read aloud for information that others read for them
- By gaining independence through their contribution to group work

To accommodate individual differences, such as learning English as a second language, or to provide inclusion for a student with disabilities, a teacher may assign different roles to students in various groups based on their needs and strengths (Bennet, Rolheiser, & Stevahn, 1991; Daniels, 1994). Types of roles may include any or all of the following:

- *Active listener:* Repeats or paraphrases what has been said
- *Checker:* Makes sure everyone understands the work of the group
- *Discussion leader:* Directs the group to the main questions or important ideas
- *Encourager:* Acts as a cheerleader for group members; keeps enthusiasm up
- *Illustrator:* Captures ideas by drawing a picture or creating a graphic organizer
- *Materials manager:* Collects and organizes necessary supplies
- *Questioner:* Seeks ideas from everyone in the group
- *Reader:* Reads materials aloud to the group
- *Scout:* Gathers additional information from other groups
- *Summarizer:* Pulls together and presents the main ideas and/or group's conclusions
- *Timekeeper:* Monitors the time and keeps the group on task

GREAT BOOKS FOR CHILDREN

The Nutshell Library is a collection of four books by Maurice Sendak (1962): *Alligators All Around*, an alphabet book; *One Was Johnny*, a counting song; *Pierre*, a moralistic tale; and *Chicken Soup with Rice*, about the months of the year. All are available on tape, videotape, and filmstrip. The poems in *Chicken Soup with Rice* have also been set to music and sung by Carole King.

Teachers can also think of ways to extend media center experiences. For example, the only thing more joyful than listening to Carole King sing *Chicken Soup with Rice* would be to make hot chicken soup and eat it while listening, reading, and singing along. Other extending activities could be making puppets or dramatizing the poems, making costumes for use in presenting them, using them as patterns for more writing, or discussing how to make and eat chicken soup during a brainstorming session. Throughout these activities, students' ideas should be clustered and used as the basis for more extending activities.

Interviews and Oral Histories

Students can learn listening and talking skills by interviewing family members and people in the community and preparing oral histories (Ritchie, 1995). These are also effective strategies for ELL students. Haley-James and Hobson (1980) described a first-grade class in which all the children interviewed a police officer during a unit on "community helpers" and cited these benefits of doing so:

- Students assume adult language roles.
- The drive to communicate is encouraged, as students ask questions.
- Students are eager to write and read the results of the interview.
- Students are in control of their own language and learning.
- Every child can succeed.
- Interviewing unifies all the language processes.
- Children discover language rules and conventions about language based on their own experiences and observations.

Another observable outcome in this first-grade class was that the children wrote longer personal and group language experience stories. In addition, they used more sophisticated language and learned to spell words from the special vocabulary of the police officer. Finally, their desire to communicate was reinforced as they shared what they had written with others.

Haley-James and Hobson (1980) suggest the following guidelines for teaching students how to conduct interviews:

1. *Practice Interviews:* Simulate practice interviews, perhaps having students interview the teacher about one of his or her interests. The teacher should bring an object to prompt students' interest and questions.

   a. Give students only the information they ask for. If they ask only yes/no questions, give only yes/no answers. Help them to develop broader, higher-level questions.
   b. Evaluate the interview. Ask which questions solicited the most information, and develop more practice questions.
   c. Have the students interview each other in pairs, and evaluate their interviews the same way.

2. *Write Up Interviews:* Help students clarify meaning during conferences, and teach needed spelling and conventions in context.

3. *Share Interview Results:* Students can read interviews in class or at home. Other ways to share include through research reports, bookmaking, mediamaking (documentaries, audio recordings, or photo essays), and student-produced newspapers and magazines.

To conduct oral histories, students can identify, interview, and audio- or videotape members of their families or communities who have memories of special events in the past. In addition, students can research and collect artifacts, photographs, newspaper articles, and documents relating to the people they interview.

Students can report their oral histories in writing or audio- or videotape narration to go with recorded interviews. They can share their oral histories, along with any artifacts they may have collected, with wider audiences, such as the school or community, by publishing their accounts in the school or local newspaper or by creating their own newsletter or book.

TEACHING IDEA

Model for an Oral History

Read aloud Allen Say's (1994) Caldecott Medal–winning picture book *Grandfather's Journey,* a beautifully illustrated account of a Japanese grandfather's journeys to the United States and back to Japan over his lifetime. The story continues with the grandfather's child and grandchild. Discuss the book and make plans for children to write accounts of their grandparents' and parents' lives after interviewing them or other family members about them.

Children might also plan how they would interview other interesting persons about their lives or how they immigrated to the United States—for instance, famous or fictional figures from history. These oral histories could be written as stories or fictional journals, bound as books with illustrations, or recorded on audio- or videotape and presented to the class. Or children could write scripts and dramatize the lives of the people they've interviewed, dressing as them and playing scenes from their lives. The potential for cross-curricular teaching is obviously great here, extending to studies of U.S. immigration and history and even world geography and history.

ELL

Oral histories are effective with ELL students for these reasons:

- Draw on personal experience.
- Use cooperative learning techniques.
- Use two languages.

Reading Aloud

Reading aloud to children every day is essential for teaching them listening and talking as well as reading and writing. The benefits of reading aloud to children are well established: Young children whose parents have read to them gain in language development and literacy through expanded vocabulary, eagerness to read, and success in beginning reading in school (Schwartz, 1995; Sulzby, 1992b; Trelease, 1996; Wood, 1994). In school, teachers should read aloud every day, several times a day, to both younger and older students.

**GREAT BOOKS
FOR CHILDREN**

Wordless Books

The Adventures of Paddy Pork
    (Goodall, 1968)
A Boy, a Dog, and a Frog (Mayer,
    1967)

Picture Books

*Alexander and the Terrible,
    Horrible, No Good, Very Bad
    Day* (Viorst, 1976)
Frog and Toad Are Friends
    (Lobel, 1970)

Short Novels

The Reluctant Dragon
    (Grahame, 1953)
A Taste of Blackberries (Smith,
    1976)

Novels

Bridge to Terabithia (Paterson,
    1979)
*The Lion, the Witch, and the
    Wardrobe* (Lewis, 1970)

Poetry

The Golden Treasury of Poetry
    (Untermeyer, 1959)
Where the Sidewalk Ends
    (Silverstein, 1974)

Anthologies

The Fairy Tale Treasury
    (Haviland, 1980)
*Zlateh the Goat and Other
    Stories* (Singer, 1966)

Jim Trelease's (2001) book *The New Read-Aloud Handbook* suggests the following do's and don'ts:

Read-Aloud Do's

- Stop at a suspenseful spot each day.
- If reading a picture book, make sure the children can see the pictures easily.
- After reading, allow time for discussion and verbal, written, or artistic expression. Don't turn discussions into quizzes or pry interpretations from children.
- Use plenty of expression in reading, and read slowly.
- Bring the author to life by adding a third dimension when possible—for example, eat blueberries while reading *Blueberries for Sal*, by Robert McCloskey (1948).

Read-Aloud Don'ts

- Don't read stories that you don't like yourself.
- If it becomes obvious that a book was a poor choice, stop reading it.
- Don't feel that every book must be tied to something in the curriculum.
- Don't be unnerved by students' questions during the reading. Answer and discuss them.
- Don't use reading aloud as a threat or turn it into a weapon.

Trelease (2001) has also suggested selection criteria for a good read-aloud book. In sum, such a book should have these qualities:

- a fast-paced plot, which quickly hooks the children's interest
- clear, well-rounded characters
- crisp, easy-to-read dialogue
- minimal long, descriptive passages

Trelease thinks the best read-aloud book is *James and the Giant Peach*, by Roald Dahl (1978). He also recommends the books listed in the adjacent marginal note.

Drama in the Classroom

Since prehistoric times, people have used drama to express the human experience: to show feelings and ideas, recount past events, and tell the stories of their lives. Long before people wrote and read about their experiences, they danced and chanted and pantomimed and sang about them to tell others. Preliterate societies still do this. The word *drama* comes from a Greek word meaning "to do or live through."

In similar fashion, young children first learn to express their experiences through dramatic means such as voice, gesture, and movement. From an early

Drama offers many opportunities for teaching and learning about talking, listening, and literacy.

age, long before they actually speak words, babies use gestures and sounds to imitate things they observe in the environment. Piaget (1962) noted evidence of this innate human tendency during the first few days of his own son's life, when he observed his newborn child cry upon hearing other babies in the hospital cry. Piaget also found that his son would cry in response to his imitation of a baby's cry but not to a whistle or other kinds of cries. Piaget concluded that language development goes through three stages:

1. actual experience with an action or object
2. dramatic reliving of this experience
3. words that represent this whole schema verbally

Children are able to communicate successfully through dramatic means long before they can speak, read, and write. The mental images that children draw on during play are necessary for linguistic development. These symbolic representations also form the basis for the comprehension of text during what Piaget calls the *symbolic play period*, between the ages of 2 and 7. Based on Piaget's constructivist theory, drama is a natural part of the development of human thought and language. From Vygotsky's (1967) social interactionist perspective, *activity* is the major explanatory concept in the development of human thought and language. Play, then, is the primary learning activity of young children. The use of drama in the classroom reflects a social constructivist perspective of language learning—which is active, social, and centered in students' experiences—and provides an effective way to teach oral language as well as literacy (Wagner, 2003).

This section of the chapter will describe some of the many ways teachers can use drama in the classroom to teach listening and talking and to develop literacy. Storytelling, puppets, reader's theater, creative drama, and story dramatization, combined with a directed listening and thinking activity (DLTA), will all be considered.

See Chapter 12, Viewing and Visually Representing, for more on using drama in the classroom, along with related experiences in the visual arts, music, dance, and media viewing and making.

Storytelling

Even with the large number of books available for children today and the variety of stories they are exposed to on television and videos, children never seem to lose their fascination with storytelling. As one first-grade child put it, as I was about to read a picture book of a favorite folktale, "Tell it with your face!"

The tools of the storyteller are so deceptively simple and so basically human that storytelling is often neglected as a way of teaching listening and talking. It is, however, a powerful way for children to listen to and use spoken language (Nelson, 1989; Ralston, 1993; Roney, 1989). It's also a wonderful way to share traditional literature and stories of the past, whether historical events or even personal life stories—perhaps yours or your students'.

Here are some suggestions for storytelling by teachers and students:

1. *Finding Stories:* In addition to stories about personal experiences and those heard told by others, traditional folk literature is an excellent source for storytelling. Young children enjoy timeless tales, such as "The Three Billy Goats Gruff," "The Three Pigs," and other tales of three. Tales like "Jack and the Beanstalk" and "The Gingerbread Man" are sure winners, too.

2. *Telling Stories:* Storyteller Ramon Royal Ross advises that above all, the storyteller should know the story very well. In addition, he suggests the following approach for actually telling the story, which works well for him (Ross, 1980):

    a. Read the story aloud several times. Get a feel for its rhythm and style.
    b. Outline the major actions in the story, identifying where one ends and another starts.
    c. Picture the characters and setting in the story carefully. Describe them to yourself.
    d. Search for phrases in the story that you'd like to work into telling it.
    e. Practice gestures that add to the story.
    f. Prepare an introduction and conclusion before and after the actual telling.
    g. Practice telling the entire story—complete with intonation, colorful phrases, gestures, and sequence—in a smooth and natural fashion.
    h. Make an audio- or videotape of yourself telling the story, and listen and look for areas in which you might improve. Also time yourself.

3. *Props:* Even though props aren't necessary, some teachers like to use them for storytelling, especially with younger children. Props might be picture cards, flannel boards, puppets, or objects like a handful of beans for telling "Jack and the Beanstalk." Mood makers like candles and incense and background music and noisemakers (e.g., rattles and tambourines) effectively enhance the telling, too.

4. *Costumes:* When used with props, costumes can create a dramatic impact. For instance, wearing a black cape and witch's hat adds drama to telling scary stories in autumn. Even simple costumes, like hats and shawls, can be used in many creative ways.

Puppetry is a natural way for children to tell stories, respond to literature, or report what they have learned.

Puppets

Children are natural puppeteers. Watch any young child with a stuffed animal, toy car, or object that can become an extension of the body and voice, and you will see a born puppeteer. Rather than plan a specific, one-time puppet-making activity, teachers should make materials and books on puppets available in the classroom on a regular basis, seizing opportunities that arise in which puppet making is a perfect way for children to tell a story, respond to literature, or report on what they have learned. Folktales and picture books are great sources of stories for puppetry.

Teachers can collect puppet-making materials themselves or ask students and parents to do so. Many of the materials needed are everyday objects that would be discarded anyway. A box containing the following supplies should be made available to students and added to, as needed:

- *Tools:* scissors, tape, glue, paint, stapler
- *Bodies:* fingers, hands, feet
- *Paper:* construction, plates, bags, crepe, cups, envelopes, toilet paper rolls
- *Cloth:* scraps, yarn, socks, gloves, mittens, hats
- *Sticks:* tongue depressors, ice cream sticks, twigs, dowels, old wooden spoons
- *Fancy things:* buttons, feathers, beads, sequins, ribbons, old costume jewelry
- *Odds and ends:* boxes, milk cartons, Styrofoam, cotton balls, ping pong balls, fruits and vegetables, gourds, leaves, moss, pine cones, egg cartons, plastic bottles

Making puppets should be kept simple and left up to students. They should use their imaginations in creating puppets; their ideas are so much better than those of adults. For instance, children don't need patterns to trace around, which produce puppets that all look alike. Rather, they should draw directly on materials like tongue depressors and ice cream sticks, creating fingers, hands, and feet.

Try these methods of making simple puppets:

- *Stick puppets:* Attach a paper plate, cutout, or Styrofoam cup to a stick and decorate.
- *Paper bag puppets:* Draw directly on the bag and decorate.
- *Hand puppets:* Decorate a glove, mitten, sock, box, piece of fabric or handkerchief wrapped with rubber bands, or simply an envelope over the hand.

GREAT BOOKS FOR CHILDREN

See *Punch & Judy: A Play for Puppets* (Emberly, 1965), a picture storybook that includes a history of puppet drama along with a script for a puppet play.

TEACHER RESOURCES
How-To Puppet Books
Fantastic Theater (Sierra, 1991)
Pinocchio (Collodi, 1996)
Shadow Play (Fleischman, 1990)
Storytelling with Puppets (Champlin, 1997)

Drama in the Classroom   173

A puppet stage is nice but not necessary to fulfill the real purpose of puppetry: to encourage children's thinking, listening, talking, and imagination as they create oral texts to share with others. You can, however, create a simple stage in any of these ways:

- Turn a table on its side and drape it with a dramatic-looking cloth.
- Have two reliable students hold a sheet or drape a sheet over a broomstick balanced on two chairs.
- Put a cardboard box on a table and seat the puppeteers behind it on low chairs.

GREAT BOOKS FOR CHILDREN

Folk Literature

For Younger Children: "Chicken Little," "The Gingerbread Man," "The Little Red Hen," and "The Three Billy Goats Gruff."

For Older Children: "Cinderella," "East of the Sun, West of the Moon," "Rumpelstiltskin," and "Snow White."

Poetry

A Light in the Attic (Silverstein, 1981)
Where the Sidewalk Ends (Silverstein, 1974)

Fiction

For Younger Children: Amelia Bedelia (Parish, 1963), *Fish Is Fish* (Lionni, 1970), *Horton Hatches the Egg* (Seuss, 1940), *How the Grinch Stole Christmas* (Seuss, 1957), and *Leo the Late Bloomer* (Kraus, 1971).

For Older Children: The Lion, the Witch, and the Wardrobe (Lewis, 1950), *The Reluctant Dragon* (Grahame, 1953), and *Tales of a Fourth-Grade Nothing* (Blume, 1972).

See also other books by Crosby Bonsall and Judy Blume as well as others in the Narnia series by C. S. Lewis.

Other sources for reader's theater: newspaper and magazine articles and advertisements, letters and memos, and textbooks.

Reader's Theater

In *reader's theater*, participants read and interpret literature aloud from scripts adapted especially for this setting. The scripts can come from many types of literature: texts of picture books for younger children and novels for older children; folk- and fairytales and other types of traditional literature (e.g., fables, myths, and legends); poetry and songs; stories and poems from anthologies and basal readers; and even nonfiction, too (Young & Vardell, 1993). In presenting reader's theater, children hold the scripts, which may be read or glanced at by the performing readers. No special costumes, sets, props, lighting, or music are required, so once the scripts have been developed, reader's theater can be practiced and performed almost instantly in the classroom (Flood, Lapp, Flood, & Nagel, 1992; Hoyt, 1992).

Selecting Stories for Reader's Theater

Teachers should look for these qualities in selecting stories:

- dialogue and clear prose
- lively, high-interest, humorous stories, with children or personified animals as main characters
- a good balance of parts of nearly the same size
- short stories, especially the first time

See the adjacent marginal note for examples of stories that work well for reader's theater.

Adapting a Story or Text for a Reader's Theater Script

1. Add narrator parts for the following: identification of time, place, scene, and characters. One narrator can be added for the whole story, or separate narrators can be added for different characters.
2. Delete lines that aren't critical to plot development, that are peripheral to the main action of the story, that represent complex imagery or figurative

language difficult to express through gestures, that state characters are speaking (e.g., "He said . . ."), or whose meaning can be conveyed through characters' facial expressions or gestures, simple sound effects, or mime.

3. Change lines that are descriptive but could be spoken by characters or would move the story along more easily, if changed.

Putting Reader's Theater into Practice

This procedure may be used with a whole class or by a small group:

1. *Introduce the story:* Read or tell the story aloud to young children, or let older children take turns reading the story aloud. Encourage an extended response period to the story through discussion involving all children.

2. *Explain reader's theater:* If this is the first time students have done reader's theater, explain how it works: the physical arrangement and movements (turning in and out of the scene when not involved), the roles of narrators and characters, the uses of mime and expression, and the nature and use of scripts.

3. *Cast the story:* First, distribute prepared scripts: those the teacher has done alone or with children. An overhead projector is useful in displaying transparencies of the story and working through the adaptation with students. Revise it according to their suggestions as they watch on the overhead. Scripts can also be easily adapted by a few children or an individual using a word-processing program on the computer.

Next, take volunteers for all parts. In initial sessions, let many different children play each part. They should all become familiar with all the parts, as in improvised drama.

4. *Block, stage, and practice playing the script:* The teacher may plan the physical staging ahead with the group but should be ready to revise it according to how the script actually plays with the group. Suggestions for modifications should be accepted from students. Other guidelines are as follow:

- Narrators often stand, perhaps using a prop like a music stand for holding the script.
- Characters are usually seated on chairs, stools, or even tables.
- Floorplans should be decided ahead of time and changed as the play proceeds.
- There should be a minimum of movement around the floor in reader's theater.

5. *Sharing reader's theater:* By the time children have prepared and participated in reader's theater, they are so enthusiastic that they want to share it with others. To make this comfortable for them, avoid actual stages; instead, use a stage-in-the-round in the classroom or multipurpose room or library. Also, it's best to share with others in the classroom first, followed by classes of younger children and then classes of the same age. Work gradually toward sharing with adults, such as parents.

Reader's Theater Script Prepared for Children

This script adapts a traditional rhyme for young children about a mother chicken and her 5 baby chicks. It lends itself to reader's theater because it includes lines of dialogue. Subtle movements can be added for each chick to correspond to the dialogue: squirming, shrugging, squealing, sighing, moaning, and scratching. This script also works well for reader's theater because it allow 12 children to participate: Each of the 5 chicks and the mother speak a line, and each can be assigned his or her own narrator, as well. If you add an announcer to read the title, 13 children can participate.

Cast and Setting

Five chicks and the mother chicken (each standing in front of his or her narrator, backs to the audience)

Six narrators: one for each chick and the mother chicken (each standing behind his or her chick or mother, facing the audience)

Announcer (standing in the center, in front of everyone else)

Entire cast should form a semicircle

Announcer: Five Little Chickens (moves off to side).

First Chick Narrator: Said the first little chicken, with a queer, little squirm.
First Chick (turning in):   I wish I could find a fat, little worm.

Second Chick Narrator: Said the second little chicken, with an odd, little shrug.
Second Chick (turning in):   I wish I could find a fat, little slug.

Third Chick Narrator: Said the third little chicken, with a sharp, little squeal.
Third Chick (turning in): I wish I could find some nice, yellow meal.

Fourth Chick Narrator: Said the fourth little chicken, with a small sigh of grief.
Fourth Chick (turning in): I wish I could find a little, green leaf.

Fifth Chick Narrator: Said the fifth little chicken, with a faint, little moan.
Fifth Chick: I wish I could find a wee, gravel stone.

Mother Chicken (turning in):   Now, see here.
Mother Narrator: Said the mother from the green garden patch.
Mother Chicken: If you want your breakfast, just come here and scratch.

What makes this script particularly good for young children is its simplicity. No one has to say more than a single line of dialogue; the five chick parts are especially easy. Moreover, the rhyming nature of each chick/narrator pair of lines, the corresponding movements, and the repetitive nature of the entire script help readers understand and remember their parts. For the same reasons, a script like this would also work well with English language learners.

Creative Drama

www

Find teaching ideas and resources for creative drama at this website: **www.sites. netscape.net/buchananmatt/ lessons.html.**

The Children's Theatre Association (Davis & Behm, 1978) explains the purpose of *creative drama* as follows: "Creative drama may be used to teach the art of drama and/or motivate and extend learning in other content areas. Participation in creative drama has the potential to develop language and communication" (p. 10). Creative drama is a synthesis of sense training and pantomime and improvisation.

Sense Training

Sense-training activities help individuals become aware of their senses and encourage creativity and self-confidence through expressing that awareness. The key is the concentration ability children develop as they communicate through nonverbal means—facial expressions, gestures, and movements—and then add oral language.

Here are some ideas for activities that involve using the four senses:

1. Touch. The teacher should have children sit on the floor, each individual doing his or her own activity. Dimming the lights may help create a secure atmosphere. The teacher should give the following directions (one activity at a time):

See the following Lesson Plan on creatures (pp. 178–179).

- "There is a balloon on the floor in front of you. Pick it up. Blow it up. Tie a knot in the end of it and attach a string. Let it float in the air as you watch. Describe what you see."
- "There is a tiny creature crouched behind you. It is frightened. Pick it up. Pet it and comfort it. What would you say to it?"
- "There is a blob of sticky, gooey clay in front of you. Pick it up. Make something from it. Tell a buddy what you made."

2. Taste. For these activities, children should work in pairs, facing each other. The teacher should ask one partner to guess exactly what the other is pretending to eat and then tell the class what he or she saw:

- "Make your favorite sandwich and eat it."
- "Eat your favorite food."
- "Eat something you don't like."

3. Sight. Children should gather in small groups and sit in circles, everyone facing each other. The teacher should tell them that there is a collection of something in the middle of the circle; then going around the circle, each individual should take out an item and pantomime what he or she has selected. After everyone has finished, they should guess what one another did. Here are some ideas:

- "There is a trunk full of clothes in the middle of the circle. Take something out of it, and try it on. There is only one of each thing in the trunk."
- "There is a pile of presents wrapped in boxes in the middle of the circle. Choose one, open it, and take out and use what's inside."
- "Your favorite toy or game is in the middle of the circle. Pick it up and show how you play with it."

4. *Sound.* For these activities, children should stand in small groups (again, forming small circles). In response to the teacher's directions, each person should portray how a particular sound makes him or her feel. After everyone has finished, the students should try to tell what the others did. Here are some ideas:

- "I will make a sound. (Hit the table with a rhythmic beat.) Act out what it makes you think of."
- Give the same directions, but rub hands together to make a slithery sound.
- Give the same direction, but make a scraping sound with an object against the blackboard.

Pantomime and Improvisation

Pantomime and improvisation are natural extensions of sense training and may also follow from teachers' observations of children's spontaneous play. *Pantomime* uses facial expressions, body movements, and gestures to communicate instead of sounds and words, and *improvisation* adds speech to spontaneous movements and actions.

Here are some topics to focus on for pantomime and improvisation activities:

- *Animals:* Movements, interactions between children and pets, interactions among animals, and so on
- *Play:* Sports, games, toys, and fun places to visit
- *Children's literature:* Nursery rhymes, poems, picture books, folktales, and stories
- *Cross-curricular:* Social studies, science, math, or fine arts

Teachers may also use costumes and other props to motivate children's pantomime and improvisation (e.g., hats, capes, canes, buckets, baskets). Likewise, music provides a good source of motivation.

I like this drama-based lesson because it's student centered, highly interactive, and requires no special materials or preparation—just an imaginative teacher and students. I demonstrate it to students in my methods classes every semester and have included it here because the students who try it in their field experiences report to me how successful it is for teaching oral language, vocabulary and writing through drama, for English language development, and for beginning teachers.

 IRA/NCTE

LESSON PLAN

Creatures! Creative Drama and Listening, Talking, and Writing

Level: Any grade

Purpose: Visualize images; use pantomime and descriptive language to orally share images; expand concepts and vocabulary through group interaction and a "word wall"; visually represent ideas by drawing and writing

Standard 12: Students use spoken, written, and visual language to accomplish their own purposes (e.g., for learning, enjoyment, persuasion, and the exchange of information).

Materials: Paper, pencil, and crayons

Teaching Sequence:

1. Initiate the lesson by turning the lights down and lowering your voice to a dramatic whisper, saying:

   "I noticed that while you were busy working, a lot of little creatures came into the classroom. I noticed each creature was different. I'd never seen some of them before. Each creature is hiding under each one of your desks. Don't move and scare the little creature. Picture it in your mind. It's small enough to fit under your desk. What does it look like? What color is it? How big is it? What shape is it? Now reach down very slowly so you don't frighten it, and pick up the creature. Hold it carefully and comfort it. What does it feel like? What does it smell like? What is it doing?"

2. While students are holding, comforting, and observing their creatures, ask them:

   "Who would like to describe his or her creature? Tell what you see, feel, hear, and smell."

3. Take volunteers, and record students' descriptions of their creatures on a word wall cluster with "CREATURES" written in the middle of it.

4. Direct students first to draw pictures of their creatures and then to use describing words from the word wall to write about them (see Figure 5.3).

Extending Activities:

1. Students can write stories about their creatures, perhaps working in pairs or small groups on a story about what happens when their creatures meet.
2. Students can dramatize the meeting of their creatures.
3. Read poetry about *Creatures*, collected by Lee Bennett Hopkins (1985).

Assessment:

1. Observe whether students could visualize images and express them through pantomime and descriptive language.
2. Note the levels of concepts and vocabulary development on the word wall.
3. Record each child's ability to visually represent ideas through drawing as well as writing using an anecdotal record.

ELL

Adapt this lesson for English language learners by using these strategies:

- Dramatic voices and gestures
- Students' prior experiences
- Student interaction
- A "word wall" or other visual representation

SCAFFOLDING

Keep in mind these guidelines for students with disabilities in inclusive classrooms:

- All students can be successful.
- Use drawing as a way of demonstrating understanding.
- Active involvement is vital to success.

For books and films on creatures, see the Snapshot on Halloween earlier in this chapter (pp. 155–157).

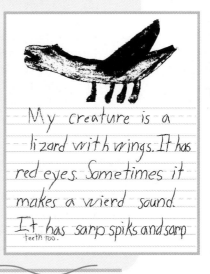

Figure 5.3 Drawing and Description of a Creature

My creature is a lizard with wings. It has red eyes. Sometimes it makes a wierd sound. It has sarp spiks and sarp teeth too.

3.3

See the Anecdotal Record Assessment (p. 106).

Story Dramatization

When children respond to a story through drama—portraying the actions as they play the characters—they are creating a *story dramatization*. This kind of drama is spontaneous and based on improvisation, but because it's based on an actual story, it follows a plot.

A two-step approach to story dramatization is shown on the following pages in two Teaching Ideas: first, by conducting a directed listening teaching activity (DLTA) of the classic children's picture book *Where the Wild Things Are*, by Maurice Sendak, and second, by bringing the story to life with mask making, mime, dance, and finally, the complete story dramatization, which teaches the literary elements of setting, characters, and sequence of events/plot and creating a story map. The Snapshot that follows describes how a preservice teacher in my language arts class did this with second-grade, Spanish-speaking English learners.

TEACHING IDEA

Directed Listening Thinking Activity (DLTA) with Literature

The purpose of a DLTA is to focus attention on stories read aloud. And since similar kinds of reasoning take place in both listening and reading comprehension, DLTA is an important strategy for teaching reading, as well. In this activity, questions are used first to activate students' prior knowledge and encourage their predictions and then to focus their attention on the story to verify those predictions, helping students construct meaning from the text (Stauffeur, 1980).

The teaching sequence outlined here presents sample questions using the book *Where the Wild Things Are* (Sendak, 1963); however, it can be used with any read-aloud story.

Before Reading

1. Introduce the book and tell something about it: "This is a book about a little boy and an adventure he had."
2. Encourage students to examine the cover and illustrations.
3. Discuss any experiences or concepts that come up.
4. Invite students to respond to the story while it's being read aloud with enthusiasm: "As I read, you can ask questions or share your ideas."

During Reading

1. Ask the children to make predictions about what will happen: "What do you think might happen to Max?"
2. Read but stop and give students opportunities to verify their predictions.
3. Continue to ask the children to make predictions and explain the reasons behind them: "What do you think will happen next? Why?"

4. Encourage students to respond openly to events, characters, and ideas in the book: "What do you think of Max, the Wild Things, or sailing away from home?"

After Reading

1. Talk about the book: "What did you think of the book?"
2. Ask for personal responses to the story: "Did you like the book? Why or why not? What was your favorite part?"
3. Talk about interesting concepts or words that come up: "How would you describe a *Wild Thing*? What's a *rumpus*?"

Extending the Reading

1. Read related books, such as *In the Night Kitchen* (Sendak, 1970) and *There's a Nightmare in My Closet* (Mayer, 1969).
2. Encourage further response-centered activities: drawing pictures, writing stories, making monster masks, dramatizing the story, and so on.

TEACHING IDEA

Bringing the "Wild Things" to Life

CW
See a student in my college methods class try this with a group of children.

Here's an example of how all the elements of drama can be integrated progressively in experiences in bringing Maurice Sendak's (1963) *Where the Wild Things Are* to life:

● *Monster Masks:* Making simple monster masks (see Figure 5.4, p. 182) will set the mood and help children establish distance between their real selves and monster selves. Making a mask will also help each student develop his or her own characterization for either Max or a "Wild Thing."

● *Monster Mime:* With masks in place, students can do sense-training, pantomime, and improvisational activities. After reading and discussing the book, the teacher should lead them through "A Day in the Life of a Monster," asking:

"Show me how you sleep, Monster, and how you wake up."

"How do you get ready for a new day, Monster? Do you brush your teeth (or tooth)? comb your hair (scales, fur, or tentacles)? wear clothes?"

"How do you move around when you are ready for a new day, Monster? Do you creep, crawl, slither, lumber, galumph, stagger, stumble, or fall down frequently?"

● *Monster Dance:* Using movements developed through mime, the "monsters" can dance. The teacher may suggest a series of movements for different

(continued)

2. *Take volunteers for the cast:* Delegate direction and leadership roles in the play to one child at a time. For example, begin with the narrator and rotate to other children.

3. *Have the cast plan how they will play the scene—who will do what action and where:* There are enough parts for trees, an ocean, a boat, and "Wild Things" to involve the entire class. Or half the students can play and the other half can watch; then reverse.

4. *Have the children play the scene:* Allow the narrator to provide direction for the story initially. Later, as the children play the scene several more times, this role will become less important.

5. *Discuss and evaluate after each playing with the children*: Everyone should become involved in this stage. Emphasize the positive by asking questions like these:

> What did you see that you liked?
>
> Who did something really interesting (or exciting, realistic, fantastic, etc.)?
>
> What can we do next time to make the play even better?

SNAPSHOT — English Language Learners Make Masks and Act Like "Wild Things"

Shelly Abesa, a student in a language arts methods class I teach, decided to dramatize *Where the Wild Things Are* (Sendak, 1963) with second-grade students. She did her field experience at Lincoln Elementary School in Long Beach, California, which is about 85 percent language-minority students— primarily Spanish-speaking Hispanic students and Khmer-speaking Cambodian Americans. Their teacher, Hope Zink, encouraged Shelly to do this activity because it is literature based and actively engages students in the types of experiences advocated for English language learners: hands-on, direct experiences and comprehensible input in a low-anxiety setting.

Here's how Shelly described the experience, which she did with the help of two other students, Patricia and Rachel:

> I began my lesson by reading *Where the Wild Things Are*. The students sat on the floor in a half circle as I read the story with lots of expression. I even growled like a monster. The students showed their gnawing teeth and sharp claws as we made monster faces at each other. After reading, we talked about the story. I asked them what they thought about it and their favorite part. Many said the "Wild Things" in the forest. Alexi liked when Max was crowned "King of All Wild Things."
>
> The students made file-folder masks next. They tore construction paper, glued cotton balls and feathers on, and colored them with crayons. They enjoyed wearing them and showing them to each other.

Students make masks and do a story dramatization of Where the Wild Things Are, *by Maurice Sendak.*

Now we were ready to begin the drama. I said, "Here is a magic line. Once you cross the line, you become the character in the book." I had made large signs with the characters' names to hang around students' necks. I began narrating the story and then put the "Max" sign around Alexi's neck. One student was the "forest growing," others were the "water" and "boat." Everyone else was a "Wild Thing." Their favorite part was the "wild rumpus"; we danced to the Monster Mash. We had so much fun bringing the story to life.

The students tried new things. One girl began to show us a dance from Cambodia. When she realized everyone was watching, she became shy. Patricia reminded her that she wasn't herself anymore but a character from a book. She said "Oh, yeah!" and began to show us the dance again. This led to a "ripple effect" of learning about Cambodia, which included having guest speakers from students' families and holding a cultural fair with dancing, music, and storytelling.

When the story dramatization was over, the students asked to do the whole thing again. Chametra and Alexi wanted to wear their masks out to recess. Three girls gave me a hug. Ms. Zink said it was a great lesson. *I will definitely use drama with reading in my own class!*

ELL

SCAFFOLDING

Drama in the classroom can be used to support the listening and speaking of students with disabilities and ELL students. See the box on page 186 for ideas.

Assessing Listening and Talking

Listening and talking have traditionally not been assessed to the same extent as reading and writing on either a formal basis (such as using nationally standardized tests) or an informal basis (such as using ongoing measures in the classroom) (Pinnell and Jaggar, 2003). A realistic approach to assessing listening and talking in the classroom would be to include many individual events, rather than

Students with Disabilities and English Language Learners in Drama

Teaching listening and speaking through drama in the classroom offers support for the inclusion of students with disabilities and those who are English language learners in the following ways:

Students with Disabilities

1. Students can all play active roles in drama activities—for example, from playing a character in a speaking or nonspeaking part to creating props or making costumes. Everyone is involved, which is key to an inclusive classroom and success for all students.
2. Students with disabilities can use different modes to demonstrate their understanding of a story or a concept. For example, they can draw a scene, make a costume, or pantomime an action.
3. Drama creates a spirit of community in a classroom among students with and without disabilities. For example, students with disabilities can be partners with other students in playing certain roles.

English Language Learners

1. English language learners can rely on actions, sound effects, and gestures to both understand and participate in drama—for example, showing how they would pet or comfort a small, imaginary creature.
2. All students must tap into prior experience, knowledge, and cultural experiences during drama, which is an especially important strategy to use for English learners. For example, students can pantomime playing with a favorite toy.
3. ELL students can interact with more proficient English speakers during dramatic activities, as in a sense-training activity in which children act out how to fix something to eat for one another.
4. Teachers can use visual representations of ideas during drama, such as a "word wall" to record children's ideas for a story dramatization.
5. Making props and costumes (such as masks) and using music and dance provides opportunities for English language learners to fully participate.

one single event (O'Keefe, 1995). Since oral communication is demonstrated through observable behavior, assessment should be performance based and conducted in authentic contexts; it should not be limited to paper-and-pencil listening comprehension tests or overly simplistic checklists.

A useful approach, especially for beginning teachers, is to include items in each student's portfolio that will document his or her listening and talking performance on an ongoing basis. You can use this information to drive your teaching of listening and talking. Here are suggested portfolio items:

1. *Graphic Organizers:* Examples from small-group brainstorming sessions may show you the level of interaction and communication each child is capable of. As discussed earlier in this chapter, different types of graphic organizers can be used for a variety of purposes. Which types students use and how well can give teachers insight into students' understanding of the relationships among ideas and topics.

2. *Audio- and Videotapes:* Periodically record group discussions, such as the ones you read about in the Snapshot earlier in this chapter (see pp. 155–157), describing oral communication in Kathy Lee's second-grade class. You can also assess your own teaching this way: Look at the kinds of questions you ask and the prompts you give. How much do you talk compared to your students? You can also record instructional conversations and other types of oral communication events, such as storytelling, puppetry, and oral histories.

2.4
2.5

See also the Self-Assessment Form for Individual Work (p. 57) and the Peer-Assessment Form for Group Work (p. 58).

3. *Peer Evaluation:* Students can evaluate each other's performance in listening and talking events. For example, students can use the simple open-ended form shown in Assessment Toolbox 5.1 to give each other feedback.

4. *Story Retelling:* Story retelling can be used after reading aloud, after storytelling, or after a DLTA story dramatization. See Assessment Toolbox 5.2 (p. 188).

ASSESSMENT TOOLBOX

5.1 Peer Evaluation of Listening and Talking

This simple form will guide students in evaluating one another's performance in listening and talking events.

Peer-Evaluation Form

Your name: _____

Name of listener/speaker: _____

Listening/speaking event: _____

How did the person show he or she is a good listener/speaker? (Give an example.)

_____

_____

How could the person improve next time?

_____

_____

5.2 Story Retelling Record

A story retelling record is an excellent strategy for teaching and assessing students' listening and talking. Use this form to record and score the retelling.

Story Retelling Record

Name _____   Date _____

Book Title _____

Read Aloud? _____   Read Silently? _____   Selected by: Teacher _____   Student _____

	Unprompted	Prompted
Setting		
1 point: Begins with an introduction	_____	_____
1 point: Gives time and place	_____	_____
Characters		
1 point: Names main character	_____	_____
1 point: Names other characters	_____	_____
Problem		
1 point: Identifies main story problem	_____	_____
Action		
1 point: Recalls major events	_____	_____
Outcome		
1 point: Gives problem solution	_____	_____
1 point: Gives story ending	_____	_____
Sequence		
Retells story in order—	_____	_____
2 points: Correct		
1 point: Partial		
0 points: No sequence		
Total Score _____ (10 points possible)	_____	

Comments:

Source: Adapted from Morrow, 1989.

● *Why is it important to teach listening and talking?*

Children listen more than they speak, read, or write in the classroom, yet most of the time, they're listening to the teacher. Schools do not always provide a linguistically rich environment compared to homes, in which children have more opportunities to actively listen and talk in authentic, meaningful interactions.

Oral language (listening and talking), thinking, and literacy are highly interrelated. Loban's well-known longitudinal study of the uses and control of language by children in grades K–12 found that those who are more proficient in oral language use more complex language, understand the conventions of language better, score higher on vocabulary and intelligence tests, and perform better in reading and writing. Listening, talking, reading, writing, and thinking are parts of a unified whole of language development.

● *How should we teach and assess listening and talking?*

Important strategies for teaching listening and talking include asking open and aesthetic questions and prompts, conducting instructional conversations with English language learners, using graphic organizers to record discussions, applying cooperative learning strategies, creating listening and media centers, doing interviews and oral histories, reading aloud, and performing drama in the classroom through storytelling, puppets, reader's theater, creative drama, directed listening thinking activity (DLTA), and story dramatization. Authentic assessment of listening and talking can include the use of graphic organizers, audio- and videotapes, peer evaluations, and story retelling records.

Looking Further

1. Observe in a classroom, and analyze a language sample according to the following criteria:
   ● Who talked and who listened? Count the number of times the teacher and children each talked during your observation period.
   ● How did the teacher talk and listen? Classify the questions the teacher asked as open or closed.

2. Pick a children's book, and develop a list of both aesthetic and efferent questions to ask about it. Read the book aloud to two different groups of children. Ask one group the aesthetic questions and the other group, the efferent questions. Compare responses from the two groups.

3. Write and carry out a three-step interview (cooperative learning) with another person in your class, and then let that person interview you. Each of you should share the results of your interview with the whole class.

4. Choose and prepare a story for storytelling according to the guidelines suggested in this chapter. Create a simple prop or costume for your story. Tell the story to a group of children.

5. Try out several of the sense-training activities with small groups of children. Brainstorm a list of other ideas for use with them.

6. List several stories suitable for dramatization with children. Choose one and develop an initiating lesson for a story dramatization. Try it out with children.

Children's Books, Films, and Software

Blume, J. (1972). *Tales of a fourth-grade nothing.* New York: Dutton.

Brink, C. R. (1975). *Caddie Woodlawn.* New York: Scholastic.

Carrick, C. (1971). *The dragon of Santa Lalia.* New York: Bobbs Merrill.

Champlin, C. (1997). *Storytelling with puppets.* Chicago: American Library Association.

Clay: The origin of the species [Film]. (1964). Available from Contemporary/McGraw-Hill Films.

Collodi, C. (1996). *Pinocchio* (E. Young, Adapt. and Illus.). New York: Philomel.

Dahl, R. (1978). *James and the giant peach.* New York: Bantam.

Dragon's tears, The [Film]. (1962). Available from Contemporary/McGraw-Hill Films.

Emberly, E. (1965). *Punch & Judy: A play for puppets.* New York: Little, Brown.

Fleischman, P. (1990). *Shadow play.* New York: Harper.

Goodall, J. (1968). *The adventures of Paddy Pork.* New York: Harcourt Brace Jovanovich.

Grahame, K. (1953). *The reluctant dragon.* New York: Holiday House.

Haviland, V. (1980). *The fairy tale treasury.* New York: Dell.

Hopkins, L. B. (Ed.). (1985). *Creatures.* New York: Harcourt Brace Jovanovich.

Kraus, R. (1971). *Leo the late bloomer.* New York: Windmill Books.

Lewis, C. S. (1970). *The lion, the witch, and the wardrobe.* New York: Macmillan.

Lionni, L. (1970). *Fish is fish.* New York: Pantheon.

Lobel, A. (1970). *Frog and toad are friends.* New York: Harper & Row.

Mayer, M. (1967). *A boy, a dog, and a frog.* New York: Dial.

Mayer, M. (1969). *There's a nightmare in my closet.* New York: Dial.

McCloskey, R. (1948). *Blueberries for Sal.* New York: Viking.

Parish, P. (1963). *Amelia Bedelia.* New York: Harper.

Paterson, K. (1979). *Bridge to Terabithia.* New York: Avon.

Say, A. (1994). *Grandfather's journey.* New York: Houghton Mifflin.

Sendak, M. (1962). *The nutshell library.* New York: Harper & Row.

Sendak, M. (1963). *Where the wild things are.* New York: Harper & Row.

Sendak, M. (1970). *In the night kitchen.* New York: Harper & Row.

Seuss, Dr. (1940). *Horton hatches the egg.* New York: Random House.

Seuss, Dr. (1957). *How the Grinch stole Christmas.* New York: Random House.

Silverstein, S. (1974). *Where the sidewalk ends.* New York: Harper & Row.

Sierra, J. (1991). *Fantastic theater: Puppets and plays for young performers and audiences.* New York: H. W. Wilson.

Silverstein, S. (1981). *A light in the attic.* New York: Harper.

Singer, I. B. (1966). *Zlateh the goat and other stories.* New York: Harper & Row.

Smith, D. B. (1976). *A taste of blackberries.* New York: Scholastic.

Untermeyer, L. (Ed.). (1959). *The golden treasury of poetry.* New York: Golden.

Viorst, J. (1976). *Alexander and the terrible, horrible, no good, very bad day.* New York: Atheneum.

Reading

Questions about Reading

- *What is reading?*
- *How should we teach and assess reading?*

REFLECTIVE RESPONSE

What are your memories of reading in school? When, what, and how did you read? What methods and materials did your teachers use? Jot down your ideas and reflect back on them as you read the chapter.

Reading Is a Language Art

When I was a graduate student at the University of Minnesota in the 1970s, my advisor was Robert Dykstra, co-author with Guy Bond of the first-grade reading studies in the 1960s (Bond & Dykstra, 1967). This landmark study comparing classroom teaching showed the need for many approaches to beginning reading as well as the value of early phonics instruction. My introduction to Dr. Dykstra (I still can't call him Bob) was as the instructor of the language arts methods course I took at the graduate level. He taught other courses with *language arts* in the title, as well, which I took along with courses with *reading* in the title. During one of our conversations regarding my program, I told him how interested I was in the language arts courses and those in children's literature and that I loved the courses in the English and speech departments in linguistics, language development, and language variation and dialects that he had advised me to take. But I was confused about whether to declare my area of focus as *reading* or *language arts*. I will never forget what he said: "Carole, reading is a language art."

This perspective is clearly reflected in the landmark book of the 1980s, *Becoming a Nation of Readers: The Report of the Commission on Reading* (Anderson, Hiebert, Scott, & Wilkinson, 1985), which characterized reading as an integral part of the language arts. As stated in the report, "It cannot be emphasized too strongly that reading is one of the language arts. All of the uses of language—listening, speaking, reading, and writing—are interrelated and mutually supportive. It follows, therefore, that school activities that foster one of the language arts inevitably will benefit the others as well. Writing activities, in particular, should be integrated into the reading period."

Becoming a Nation of Readers became an authoritative account of what we know about the theory and practice of teaching reading as the construction of meaning. Recommendations from the report for teaching reading included a greater focus on the following:

- getting meaning from print from the very beginning of school
- reading aloud to children
- providing a wide variety of experiences and talking together about them
- allowing more time reading self-selected books and writing and less time on worksheets

Providing children with a variety of reading experiences and talking together about them is vital to their development as readers.

- developing better libraries
- providing more comprehensive assessment
- making more use of good literature in reading instruction

In the 1990s, a national debate referred to as the "reading wars" in the popular press developed over the relative emphases that should be placed in reading instruction on the use of literature and other whole, meaningful texts and on the direct teaching of skills, especially phonics. The debate was frequently reduced to the phrase *whole language versus phonics. Whole language* and *phonics* tended to be associated with different models of reading that you should be familiar with; likewise, you should know about the methods and materials associated with these models. When you read about these and other models, think of what you wrote about how you read in school. Where does your experience fit?

Models of Reading

The International Reading Association website is an excellent place to learn about reading: **www.reading.org**.

Reading is primarily the construction of meaning. This is not as simple as it sounds, however. Reading theorists and researchers have wrestled for years with how to describe exactly how meaning is constructed during reading, and they have offered a variety of models of reading.

The Linear Model

The *linear model* of reading, familiarly called the *bottom-up model*, views reading as a part-to-whole process. First, the reader learns to recognize letters, followed by words, and then words in context, until he or she finally begins to understand what's read (Gough, 1976; LaBerge & Samuels, 1976). Thus, the reader's job is to figure out the meaning of the text as it was intended by the author.

The linear model is the theory behind the *commercial basal reader program's* sequential approach to teaching reading. According to this approach, the reading process is broken down into a series of smaller to larger subskills, which should be taught in a certain order. These skills are grouped under headings like *readiness, word recognition, word meaning,* and *comprehension.*

The commercial basal reader program was the dominant method of reading instruction in elementary schools throughout most of the twentieth century (Banmann & Heubach, 1996; Dole & Osborne, 2003; Hoffman et al., 1998; Langer, Applebee, Mullis, & Foertsch, 1990). A basal reader program consists of a set of graded books used by a class or by groups within a class. All the books include selections of stories, which form the core of the reading lessons. The teacher follows directions in the teacher's guide for covering the separate subskills thought necessary in learning to read. Students complete workbooks and skillsheets to practice the skills taught during the teacher-directed lesson planned in the teacher's guide. The method used with these materials is to form reading groups, usually on the basis of student ability. During a set reading period, the teacher works with one group at a time, while other groups do exercises in student workbooks or on skillsheets.

See how Avril Font uses basal readers in a different way in the Snapshot in Chapter 1.

Patrick Shannon (1988), among others, has criticized basal readers because they have reduced reading to a kind of management system that certifies students' minimum reading competence. As a result, reading instruction often becomes nothing more than the use of a set of commercial basals throughout a district. This approach clearly diminishes the role of the teacher in deciding goals, methods, and pace of teaching, which is another criticism of basal reading systems. Their use also clearly inhibits instructional innovations by predetermining teachers' instructional decisions.

A fundamental problem with basal reading systems was made clear by Durkin's research (1981), which showed that less than 1 percent of instructional time during basal reading lessons is devoted to comprehension, or understanding what's read. It's important to note, however, that newer basal reading systems emphasize reading as meaning construction. In fact, the newest basal series have recognized the widespread use of literature-based reading and used excerpts or intact selections of children's literature.

The Interactive Model

The *interactive model* is based on schema theory (Rumelhart, 1984) and views the reading process as an interaction between the reader and text. *Schema theory* explains how learners acquire, store, and use knowledge in the form of schema, which are like scaffolding, giving structure to how knowledge is organized in the mind. The reader's job is to make meaningful connections between new information and prior knowledge (or *schemata*) and to use personal reading strategies—developed and adjusted for each individual purpose in reading—while constructing meaning from print.

This theoretical model allows for both bottom-up and top-down processes and is reflected in teaching approaches that emphasize direct reading instruction of word identification skills, vocabulary, and word meaning and comprehension. These strategies include activating prior knowledge and concept development, teacher-questioning strategies and reader self-questioning strategies, summarizing, graphically representing ideas to teach story structure, and using patterned books that encourage predictions on the part of the reader.

Carefully planned questioning strategies for any kind of text—basal readers, children's literature, textbooks, or magazines—have developed from the interactive model of the reading process based on schema theory. The goal of this approach is to provide students with strategies that will help them become independent readers, who monitor their own thinking while reading and link their prior knowledge with the text they are reading.

The *question-answer relationship (QAR)* can be used to help students monitor their own reading comprehension with any type of text (Pearson & Johnson,

1978; Raphael, 1982, 1986). The QAR is based on a system of categorizing a question depending on where the reader will find information to answer it. Here's an example:

The Text: The beaver gnawed the tree. The tree fell to the ground.

Three Types of Questions	*Question-Answer Relationship:* *Where is the answer found?*
1. *Text-explicit question:* The answer is explicitly stated in the text.	1. *Right there:* The same words that make the question and the answer are found in the same sentence.
Q: "What did the beaver gnaw?"	A: "The beaver gnawed the tree."
2. *Text-implicit question:* The answer can be inferred from the text.	2. *Think and search:* The answer is there but not in the exact words used in sentence.
Q: "Why did the tree fall?"	A: "Because the beaver gnawed it."
3. *Script-implicit question:* The answer comes from the background knowledge of the reader.	3. *On my own:* The answer won't be found in the words in the story but in your own mind.
Q: "Why did the beaver gnaw the tree?"	A: . . .

The teacher explains these three types of questions to students in practice lessons and encourages them to use the questions independently as they read any type of text.

The Transactional Model

The *transactional model* of reading, developed by Louise Rosenblatt (1978, 1983, 1994, 2003), describes reading as a transaction between a particular reader and a particular text that occurs at a particular time and context. Meaning does not reside solely in the text or solely in the reader but comes into being during a transaction between the two. The reader is active; the text only consists of marks on the page until the reader transacts with it. The term *reader* implies a transaction with a text, and the term *text* implies a transaction with a reader. The two are not distinct entities but factors in a total situation. This view of the reading process has influenced approaches to teaching with literature that recognize the importance of the reader's response: student- and response-centered instruction, literature units and discussion groups, response journals, and the use of more open, aesthetic questioning.

See Chapters 5, 7, and 14 for more on the transactional model.

A Balanced Approach

While the debate over reading models and methods continues, many states, districts, and schools have taken what is called a *balanced approach* to teaching reading (Baumann & Ivey, 1997; Baumann, Hoffman, Moon, & Duffy-Hester, 1998; Mason, Stahl, Au, & Herman, 2003). This approach recognizes the importance of meaningful literature, language, and writing experiences *and* the value of incorporating direct instruction in word study and phonics (Fitzgerald, 1999). In fact, a large-scale survey showed that 89 percent of elementary teachers chose the following statement as most closely matching their approach to teaching reading: "I believe in a balanced approach to reading instruction which combines skills development with literature and language-rich activities (Baumann, Hoffman, Moon, & Duffy-Hester, 1998, p. 642).

Driving this debate has been concern about struggling readers with low standardized test scores. Research has shown that struggling readers have spent more time in lessons emphasizing skills, rote memorization, and often meaningless practice whereas more proficient readers have spent more time reading and discussing books (Rasinski & Padak, 2000). A balance could be achieved by including more social constructivist, interactive, literature-based experiences (Primeaux, 2000).

To guide your thinking about the controversy surrounding teaching reading today, Spiegel (1998b) offers these characteristics of a balanced literacy approach:

- It builds on research.
- Teachers are viewed as informed decision makers, therefore promoting flexibility.
- It takes a comprehensive view of literacy—one in which the goal is to develop lifelong readers and writers.
- Reading is not just word identification, but word identification is part of reading.
- Readers must be able to take aesthetic and efferent stances in reading.
- Writers must be able to express meaningful ideas clearly.
- Writing is not just grammar, spelling, and punctuation, but they are all part of effective writing.

The rest of the chapter will describe the classroom methods used in a balanced approach to reading instruction: shared reading, guided reading, reading workshop, student independent reading, writing to read, and word study and phonics.

Shared Reading

Shared reading is a natural outgrowth of the home bedtime story situation or the "lap method" of reading aloud with young children. An adult reads aloud to them, talks to them, and answers their questions. And perhaps more important, that adult is willing to read the children's favorite books over and over again.

Children can participate in a shared reading by doing role-playing, by reading along in unison, and by making predictions about the story.

Shared reading re-creates the natural ways that young children learn to speak and that many learn to read (Holdaway, 1979).

Holdaway (1982) describes components of the shared reading experience as including favorite poems, rhymes, and songs with enlarged text on chartpaper or words on sentence strips used in a pocket chart. A favorite story can be shared in an enlarged format, such as a "big book." While "big books" can be made by teachers, many publishers produce favorite children's books in a "big book" format to simulate the "lap method" and ensure that all children can see the book. The children can read along in unison participation and do role-playing and dramatization. They can make predictions about the story and discuss words in context. Skills are also taught in context during the reading. The children have fun with words and sounds in meaningful situations, play alphabet games, recite rhymes, and sing songs using letter names. Response options after a shared reading can include self-selected reading, art making related to the story, and writing, often using language structures from the new story.

The Snapshot that follows describes Nora Miller, an experienced teacher of struggling readers who had used a commercial basal reader for many years but decided to shift to teaching reading with literature and writing balanced with skills instruction. This shift represents a flexible, balanced use of strategies for before, during, and after a shared reading in a first-grade class of struggling readers (Tierney & Readance, 2000). As you read, think about your reading experiences in school along with the recommendations of *Becoming a Nation of Readers* and the characteristics of a balanced approach.

SNAPSHOT Shared Reading in a First-Grade Class of Struggling Readers

TEACHER RESOURCES
See the position statement of the International Reading Association on *Excellent Reading Teachers* in the October 2000 issue of *The Reading Teacher*.

Nora Miller is about to teach a shared reading lesson using literature to her first-grade class in Baton Rouge, Louisiana. She has the youngest, least mature first grade in the school. Many of her students are struggling readers, and two are repeating this grade. The majority have had limited experience with books and reading at home. Nora was chosen by her principal to teach this class because she is an excellent reading teacher.

As you read this Snapshot, note how she uses a balanced approach to teaching and assessing reading. Namely, Nora seeks a balance of skills, experiences with literature, and oral and written language in her teaching. Here's what she does during this shared reading experience—before, during, and after reading.

Before Reading

See Chapter 4, Emergent Literacy and Biliteracy, for a list of predictable pattern books.

Beni Montresor won the Caldecott Medal for illustrating *May I Bring a Friend?*

1. ***Choose Good Literature:*** Nora chooses the picture book *May I Bring a Friend?* by Beatrice Schenk de Regniers (1964). She believes her children will enjoy it and be motivated to join in the shared reading she has planned. This book is humorous and has a repeated pattern that students can predict and join in during the reading. The main character of the book is a child about the same age as Nora's students; other characters include zoo animals and a whimsical King and Queen, who keep inviting the child over to their house. The book is also colorful and has award-winning illustrations.

2. ***Link to Assessment of Students' Needs:*** Nora's students have usually done poorly on recognizing the names of the days of the week and sequencing in the statewide minimum competency tests. Even though Nora doesn't believe that succeeding on this test is the only way to measure students' progress, in her school system, students must pass this test in order to move on to the next grade. Since many of her students have been identified and placed as being "at risk," Nora planned this lesson to address their identified needs.

3. ***Gather Materials: Flannel Board, Word Strips, and Pictures:*** Nora has prepared word strips to use on the flannel board. On them, she's written the names of the animals in the story and also the names of the days of the week. These word strips are scattered on the flannel board next to her. She's also made pictures of all the animals and put these on the flannel board, too.

4. ***Set a Comfortable Mood:*** Nora gets the book and gets comfortable in a chair next to the flannel board. Then she invites the children to join her; they gather around her enthusiastically, settling on the floor. Nora reads aloud often and well. The mood is warm, and the setting is comfortable.

5. ***Introduce the Book Enthusiastically:*** Nora simply holds up the book and the children cheer. She's done repeated readings of this book (this is the third time this week), and her students enjoy it. It's like an old friend by now.

6. ***Word Study:*** The first two times Nora read this book, she simply read it and asked the children open and aesthetic questions: "What did you think of it?" and "What was your favorite part?" For this third reading, she wants the students to really join her, so she is drawing their attention to the words—animal names and names of the days of the week—and the sequence of both the appearance of the animals and the days of the week. She asks them if they remember the names of the animals, and as they call them out, she puts the

animal word strips on the flannel board. Then she asks if they remember the names of the days of the week, and as they call them out, she puts those words strips on the flannel board, too. They talk about the words; some children read them, and some come to the flannel board and touch them to show they recognize them.

During Reading

1. *Shared Repeated Reading:* Students join Nora in reading, chanting the parts of the story that they remember from the first two times she read it. They do this naturally and with pleasure. The text rhymes words such as *me* and *tea*, *King* and *bring*, and it has a predictable pattern.

2. *Make Predictions:* The page ends with "So I brought my friend," and before turning it, Nora dramatically asks the children to predict what will happen next:

Child: He'll bring a friend!

Nora: Do you know what friend he will bring?

Child: I know! A giraffe!

Nora: And what day of the week is it?

Child: Sunday?

3. *Confirm Predictions:* Nora turns the page slowly, mysteriously. The tension mounts. The children begin to bounce up and down in anticipation. Then they confirm their predictions when they see a picture of a giraffe. Nora continues reading about how the King and Queen meet the friend and everyone sits down to have a cup of tea.

4. *Talk about the Story:* Nora also asks the children aesthetic questions to encourage them to talk about the story and make more predictions:

Nora: Look at the picture of the king and queen. How do you think they're feeling?

Child: Sad.

Child: Amazed.

Nora: What do you think they'll do now? What would you do?

Child: I think she's gonna go (gestures with fist) wow! pow!

Nora: Why?

Child: She wouldn't take that. No way. I know I wouldn't.

Nora: Let's see what happens next.

Nora reads on, as the little boy brings a hippopotamus on Monday for dinner, monkeys for lunch on Tuesday, an elephant for breakfast on Wednesday, lions for Halloween on Thursday, a seal for Apple Pie Day on Friday, and on Saturday, they all go to the City Zoo for tea. As she reads, Nora asks the children to predict the story sequence, the day of the week, and the animal friend of the day. She also encourages them to respond aesthetically to the text and illustrations and discusses students' responses with them.

5. *Connect Ideas to Print:* After each new animal and day of the week, Nora asks a child to volunteer to find the name of that animal and day from among the word strips on the flannel board. Each is placed in order on one side of the flannel board.

See Chapter 3, First- and Second-Language Development, for more on semantic webbing and a Lesson Plan on finding words with *ant* in them.

After Reading

1. *Relive the Reading Experience:* Nora and her students talk about the experience of reading the book. Some of them chant parts of the story they remember. The children share their ideas and what they were thinking about while the story was being read. Nora encourages them to share all their ideas at this time, to listen to each other, and to interact. She does, too.

2. *Word Study—Vocabulary and Phonics:* When one child announces that she knows how to spell *Sunday,* many others want to spell other days and animal names. Nora takes this as a cue to talk about what they remember about words. After a lot of spelling outloud, she asks if anyone notices a way in which all the day words are alike. Someone notices that they all have the little word *day* in them. They talk about this for a while, and Nora guides the students through a semantic map of words that have *day* in them (see Figure 6.1). They also start a list of words that have the rime *-ay* in them, after Nora points out several examples. We'll discuss rimes more later in this chapter in the section Word Study (pp. 209–218).

3. *Response Options: Drawing and Writing:* Nora asks what the students would like to do next with the story during group time, and together, they come up with the following list (based on the kinds of things they're used to doing after reading):

(1) Read the book again. Select another book to read.

(2) Draw a picture of the castle where the King and Queen lived.

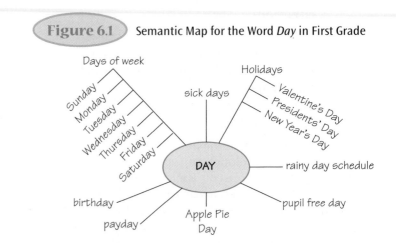

Figure 6.1   Semantic Map for the Word *Day* in First Grade

(3) Make a castle collage out of pieces of construction paper cut in shapes: circles, triangles, squares, rectangles.

(4) Write a story about animals.

(5) Write an "If I Were" pattern about animals.

(6) Draw or write anything you want about the story.

(7) Continue to do a "word hunt" for words with -<u>day</u> and the rime -<u>ay</u>.

The class had been talking about shapes in math.

"If I Were" Pattern
If I were a *lion*,
A *proud, loud lion*,
If I were a *lion*,
This is what I would do:
I would *roar, roar, roar!*

4. *Flexible Grouping:* Nora uses efficient, flexible grouping practices to accommodate the individual differences and needs of her students. She balances whole-class lessons with small-group and individual instruction, which are differentiated according to type of instruction, degree of support, and amount of practice. She does not have students spend time learning what they already know how to do. Her 20 students are grouped as follows, and response options are noted in parentheses:

- Five students who need more help with word study meet with Nora to write an "If I Were" pattern (5) and to start a word hunt (7), which they continue throughout the week.
- Eight struggling readers choose option (2) or (3) while Nora meets with the first group; then she joins them, takes dictation for them on the picture or castle collage they have created, and provides individual word study instruction based on the needs of each child.
- Four of her most independent readers do options (1) and (6) and take turns reading the book in a group; they respond by writing or drawing and then read on their own.
- Three of her strongest writers, who have recently shown an interest in independent writing, do option (4) seated at the same table for group support and interaction.

5. *"Ripple Effect" Extending Activity:* The children had talked about what they would fix for the little boy in the story, if he were coming to their house. Peanut butter and jelly sandwiches were suggested. Nora asked the children if they'd like to make edible clay out of peanut butter the next day, and the response was "Yeah!" Nora brought the materials for edible clay and wrote the recipe in enlarged format on a piece of poster paper; she posted it on the wall above the table where they worked. She helped students make clay during group time, working with each group individually; students made all kinds of shapes with the clay. The other students continued to work on one of the response options they had started the day before or on other reading and writing activities.

Edible Clay
½ cup peanut butter
½ cup dry milk
¼ cup honey
Mix and have fun!

The box that follows shows how Nora Miller provided support for struggling first-grade readers through shared reading in her balanced approach to reading instruction.

A Balanced Approach 201

See Avril Font do guided reading lessons with literature in her first-grade class.

See Chapter 5, Listening and Talking, for more on DLTA (directed listening thinking activity).

Guided Reading

Russell Stauffer (1975, 1980) coined the term *directed reading thinking activity* (*DRTA*) as a criticism of an approach used widely with basal readers called the *directed reading activity* (*DRA*). Stauffer argued that the DRA left children's *thinking* out of reading, instead relying too much on teacher direction, which was provided by carefully scripted lessons in the teacher's manual of the basal reading series. The DRTA focused on involvement with the text, as students made predictions and verified them as they read. Teachers used questions to activate prior knowledge, to introduce and expand vocabulary and word meaning, and to teach word study, comprehension, and critical thinking.

This general idea of teaching reading with literature in small groups has come to be called *guided reading* (Fountas & Pinnell, 1996, 1999). The key ideas behind it include the following:

- It is directed by the teacher, who provides support using scaffolding strategies.
- It is generally conducted in small groups, with all children reading at the same level and having their own copies of the book.
- Children read on their own, with a minimum of help from the teacher.
- Skills and strategies are taught in context.
- The books chosen can be slightly beyond the students' independent reading level, drawing on Vygotsky's idea of the zone of proximal development.

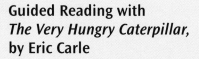

Guided Reading with
The Very Hungry Caterpillar,
by Eric Carle

The steps in a guided reading lesson can be broken down into before, during, and after reading, as you saw in the Snapshot about Nora Miller's first-grade class. Here is an example using *The Very Hungry Caterpillar,* by Eric Carle (1969).

See the author unit on Eric Carle in Chapter 7, Teaching with Literature.

Before Reading

1. *Choose Books:* Find multiple copies of a children's book appropriate for the group. Ask your school or public librarian for help in choosing and finding copies, or use "little books" or a selection from a literature-based reading series. For example, you could use Eric Carle's *The Very Hungry Caterpillar* from the first-grade level of Houghton Mifflin's series *Invitations to Literacy* (1997). It is a wonderfully illustrated story about a caterpillar who eats a different food each day of the week, gets a stomach ache, and then turns into a cocoon and finally a butterfly. This book uses the predictable patterns of numbers and days of the week and vocabulary about food and the life cycle of a butterfly.

2. *Introduce the Book:* Show the cover or an illustration, and read the title and the author.

3. *Make Predictions:* Ask students, "What do you think the story is about? Why?"

4. *Activate Prior Knowledge:* Ask students, "What do you know about caterpillars? What do you know about the author, Eric Carle? What else do you know that you want to share?"

5. *"Word Wall":* Write down the children's predictions, prior knowledge, and ideas on a word wall. Keep this simple. Use a small dry-erase board, chalkboard, or paper on a clipboard, since you will be working with a small group. Put the children's initials next to their comments to build self-esteem, encourage ownership, and remember who said them!

These children enjoy rereading Eric Carle's The Very Hungry Caterpillar *after first participating in a guided reading of the book.*

(continued)

During Reading

6. *Observe Reading:* Direct children to read the first two pages of the book silently, observing them and providing support by responding to any questions they have about the story or words in it. Tell students to look up when they have finished reading.

7. *Verify Predictions and Make New Ones:* Ask students to verify the predictions they made (which you may have noted on the word wall), and make further predictions about what will happen in the story. Ask "What do you think will happen next? Why do you think so?"

8. *Continue Reading and Predicting:* Continue to read the story as follows:
   a. Direct children to continue reading the next two pages, including the partial pages that tell about the days of the week and the food the caterpillar ate each day, and see what happens. Tell students to look up when they have finished reading.
   b. Again ask students to verify their predictions and make new ones (e.g., "What might the caterpillar do about his stomach ache?"). After each prediction, ask "Why do you think so?"
   c. Direct children to read the next three pages, which tell how the caterpillar ate a green leaf and felt better, was now a "big, fat caterpillar," and made himself a cocoon. Tell students to look up when they have finished reading.
   d. Again ask students to verify their predictions and make a new one: Ask "What do you think will happen when the caterpillar pushes his way out of the cocoon?" Also ask "Why do you think so?" Then read the last page to find out: "He was a beautiful butterfly!"

After Reading

9. *Discuss the Story:* Ask children to talk about their predictions, verifications, ideas, questions, and personal responses or connections with their own lives.

10. *Reread:* Encourage children to read sections aloud that confirm or disconfirm their predictions or that interested them. Talk about predictions that cannot be verified directly by the text but can be inferred. Discuss any differences among ideas the children may have.

11. *Teach Minilessons:* Focus on appropriate skills or strategies related to this story. For example:

   Have students read the last page in the story, and ask how they knew the word *butterfly* (i.e., by using the illustration as a context clue).

   Ask students to identify the unit (rime) in all the words for the days of the week (*-ay*), and make a list of other words with this rime.

Make a list of all the vocabulary words for food, and ask volunteers to read them (*apple, pears, plums, strawberries, oranges, chocolate cake, ice-cream cone, pickle, Swiss cheese, salami, lollipop, cherry pie, sausage, cupcake, watermelon,* and *leaf*—caterpillar food). These words can also be put on cards and sorted by type of food, number of syllables, compound words, and so on.

12. *Extend the Lesson through Writing:* Use a writing frame (as follows) for each student, and fill in the information on a language experience chart:

On _____ _____ ate _____ .
  (day of the week)   (name of child)   (number and food)

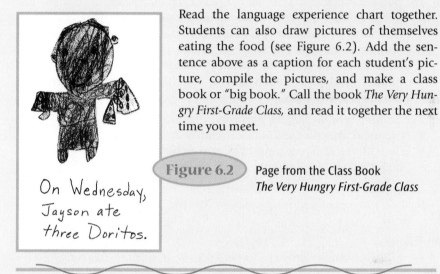

Read the language experience chart together. Students can also draw pictures of themselves eating the food (see Figure 6.2). Add the sentence above as a caption for each student's picture, compile the pictures, and make a class book or "big book." Call the book *The Very Hungry First-Grade Class,* and read it together the next time you meet.

On Wednesday, Jayson ate three Doritos.

Figure 6.2   Page from the Class Book *The Very Hungry First-Grade Class*

Writing to Read

Providing writing experiences is an important part of a balanced approach to reading. Writing is discussed in every chapter in this text and is the focus of Chapter 9. At this point, we'll look at a teaching method in which writing is closely associated with reading instruction: the *language experience approach (LEA).*

The language experience approach uses language experience charts, which are composed orally by the children and recorded by the teacher on a piece of chartpaper. We saw examples of language experience charts in Chapter 4, when first-grade teacher Marion Harris recorded students' descriptions of apples and kindergarten teacher Mauretta Hurst recorded the story "The Adventures of a Baby Elephant." Language experience charts based on interesting, shared experiences become part of the classroom print environment and student-composed texts for reading and rereading. These charts show the connections among reading, writing, experience, and meaning.

Here are the steps of the LEA:

See Chapter 3, First- and Second-Language Development, for more on vocabulary and concept development, and Chapter 5, Listening and Talking, for more on clustering and webbing.

1. ***Use experiences to develop language and concepts.***
   - Use experiences as the basis for thinking and talking.
   - Develop concepts through talking, clustering ideas, and semantic webbing.

2. ***Build vocabulary.***
   - Focus on words children already know and use during discussions, and add new words along the way.
   - Record and display these words on word strips or chartpaper.

3. ***The children compose and the teacher records on chartpaper.***
   - Choose a focal topic, such as an interesting classroom experience.
   - Discuss the topic and create a title. Record the title on top of the chart.
   - Continue to discuss; encourage children's comments; record them on the chart. Use questions like "What else can you tell me?"
   - Children watch as the teacher writes their ideas on the chart and read while he or she is writing.

4. ***The children read the language experience chart.***
   - Read the chart with the children, pointing to words.
   - Take volunteers to read parts or all of the chart.
   - Let another child point to the words while others read.

5. ***Integrate skills.***
   - Skills can be taught in a meaningful context, as children read their own words.

6. ***Publish.***
   - Writing through language experience is published instantly, as it's recorded by the teacher.
   - Display charts on bulletin boards and walls or bind them together, creating class books for further reading and rereading.

TEACHING IDEA

Struggling Readers Write about Bart the Crow

Here's an example of a teacher using the LEA with struggling readers. Their teacher, Gene Hughes, has found that LEA is a successful student- and response-centered method with students who have not succeeded with traditional reading instruction and who have low self-concepts as readers. Gene provides many interesting direct experiences, encourages students to talk about them, and uses LEA along with sustained silent reading, self-selected wide independent reading, and conferences. He builds vocabulary and teaches skills through these methods.

> **BART THE CROW**
>
> Bart is a baby crow. He has black feathres. He is soft. Bart lives in a nest. The nest is a plastic pail filled with hay. Sometimes we take him outside so he can exercise and get fresh air. He has a good appetite. We feed him grapes, baby food, dog food, and puppy chow. He drinks water. He is a good bird and we care about him.

Figure 6.3 Students' First Language Experience Story

For example, Gene was given a baby crow, which he brought to school each day. Figure 6.3 shows the first language experience story the students wrote about Bart the Crow. Gene's students read this story many times and published it by posting it on the wall outside their room; an article about Bart, which appeared in the education section of the local newspaper, was posted in their classroom. Given their interest in Bart, the students read books about birds and how to care for them.

When Bart had an accident, fracturing his leg, the students wrote a second language experience story about him and his injury (see Figure 6.4). It's shown here using the step-by-step LEA sequence:

1. *Share an Experience:* Gene gathers the children together on the rug:

   Teacher: When Bart comes out of his cage, he'll be excited.

   Child: Here he comes!

   Teacher: He needs to fly around for a while. His leg's doing better. He's not limping as badly as he was. What's he doing now?

   Child: Taking a bath kinda like.

   Teacher (picks Bart up and pets him soothingly): Just like a baby. Remember when he couldn't fly?

   Child: Broken leg.

   Teacher: Not exactly.

   Child: Fractured.

2. *Build Vocabulary:* The students watch Bart walking around them:

   Teacher: When babies are small, their bones are . . .

   Child: Tender.

   Child: Soft.

   Child: Weak.

> **BART'S ACCIDENT**
>
> Recently Bart had a little accident. Someone picked him up the wrong way. Bart fractured his leg. He limped and curled his toes up. We took him to the vet at LSU. The doctor gave him a shot and x-rayed his leg. The doctor said he needs rest. He's doing fine now.

Figure 6.4 Students' Second Language Experience Story

(continued)

Teacher:	What did we do when he had the accident?
Child:	Took him to the doctor.
Teacher:	What do you call a doctor for animals?
Child:	A vet.
Child:	A veterinarian.
Teacher:	What happened then?
Child:	They took a picture of him.
Teacher:	What's that called?
Child:	I know! An x-ray.
Teacher:	Let's talk about his accident. What happened?
Child:	He had a fraction.
Child:	No. He had a *fracture*.
Teacher:	It didn't happen too long ago, so we could start our story with the word *recently*. That means something that happened just a little while ago.

3. *Write and Read:* Gene uses a marking pen to write the story on chartpaper as the students dictate it. He's working on the floor, with the students around him:

Teacher	(writing and reading): "Recently Bart . . ."
Child:	Had an accident.
Teacher:	How do you spell that?
Child:	A-c-c- . . .
Child:	. . . i . . .
Child:	A-c-c-i-d-e-n-t.
Child:	Someone picked him up the wrong way.
Child:	Bart fractured his leg.
Teacher:	How did he act?
Child:	He limped.
Child:	He curled his toes up.
Teacher:	What did we do to make him feel better?
Child:	We took him to the vet at LSU.
Teacher:	Let's read what we have so far.

(Student reads.)

Teacher:	What happened next?
Child:	The doctor gave him a shot.
Child:	And x-rayed him.
Teacher:	What did the doctor prescribe for him?
Child:	The doctor said he needed rest.
Teacher:	How is he doing now?

Child:	Fine.
Teacher:	Let's put a sentence to tell that.
Child:	He's doing fine now.
Teacher:	Will someone read the story?

(Student reads the story; see Figure 6.4.)

4. ***Integrate Skills:*** Gene and his students check the story and focus on skills:

Teacher:	I see a little mistake. I wrote *need* here.
Child:	Write *needed.* Add *-ed.*
Teacher:	What should we add for a title?
Child:	"Bart's Accident."
Teacher:	This is an apostrophe. It means the accident happened to Bart. What does *LSU* stand for?
Child:	Tigers!
Teacher:	Yes, but the letters *LSU* are an abbreviation, or a short way to say something.
Child:	Louisiana State University.
Child:	*SU* is Southern University. Jaguars!
Teacher:	What do we call letters like *SU*?
Child:	Abbreviation.
Teacher:	You did a great job on this story. What's the new word that tells when?
Child:	Recently.
Teacher:	There's also a word that tells the name of a doctor for animals.
Child:	*Veterinarian.*
Teacher:	Which word tells about a special picture?
Child:	*X-ray.*

5. ***Publish:*** Gene talks with students about how to publish their story:

Teacher:	Now let's sign our names. You're the authors.
Child:	Let's put it in the hall so everybody can read it.
Child:	Put it by our other ones and the story they wrote about us in the newspaper.

Word Study and Phonics

EXCELLENT SOFTWARE

Word study that teaches the alphabetic principle, phonemic awareness, and whole-to-part phonics can be an integral part of a balanced approach to teaching reading with literature and writing. This section describes ways to do this and provides an overview of the current, continuing debate on the role of *phonics* in reading.

Reader Rabbit is a popular software program that focuses on word study in the form of a game: finding beginning, middle, and ending letters and making word matches.

The Alphabetic Principle and Phonemic Awareness

6.1

See the Test of Phoneme Segmentation (p. 213) for a tool to test phonemic awareness.

The *alphabetic principle* is that each speech sound, or *phoneme*, of a language will have a distinct graphic representation in the writing system of an alphabetic language. Proficient readers understand the alphabetic principle. They know that there's a correspondence between sounds and the letters that represent them. *Phonemic awareness* is "the awareness that spoken language consists of a sequence of phonemes" (Yopp & Yopp, 2000, p. 131). While this awareness is not necessary for learning and understanding spoken language, it is necessary for learning to read.

Simply put, a reader of an alphabetic language like English or Spanish must understand the relationship between the *letters,* or symbols of written language, and the *sounds,* or phonemes. There seems to be reciprocal relationship between being aware of speech sounds and learning to read. A certain knowledge of the sounds of language is necessary to learn to read, but reading increases a child's awareness of language. Moreover, young children who have learned their letters and are aware of the letter-to-sound correspondence between speech and print before coming to school have often begun to learn to read through literacy experiences at home or in preschool. These children will likely continue to be successful readers in kindergarten and first grade.

How do you know if a child is phonemically aware? A child who is phonemically aware can, for example, do these things:

- blend phonemes, or put together sounds and answer *pig* if you ask "What word does the sounds /p/-/i/-/g/ make?"
- isolate phonemes and answer /p/ if you ask "What is the beginning sound in *pig?*"
- segment phonemes and answer /p/-/i/-/g/ if you ask "What sounds do you hear in *pig?*"
- substitute phonemes and answer *big* if you ask "What word do you have if you change the /b/ for /p/ in *pig?*"

Some of these manipulations are harder than others. It is more difficult to segment phonemes in a word than it is to find a rhyme for a word, for example.

Even though phonemic awareness has been shown to correlate highly with learning to read (Nation & Hulme, 1997; Stanovich, 1986, 1994; Yopp, 1992, 1995), it is apparently a necessary but not sufficient condition of learning to read and spell (Adams, 1990). As you have already seen in this text, literacy instruction involves much more. Above all, children should have meaningful interactions with language and print in authentic, often social contexts that are guided and supported by the teacher—for example, reading aloud with the teacher, creating language experience charts, and joining in the reading of predictable pattern books. Drawing attention to the sounds of language should supplement, not replace, these experiences and can be done in a few minutes in the context of literature-based instruction.

Authentic activities that support the development of phonemic awareness in young children are storytelling, wordplay, nursery rhymes, riddles, songs, and reading books with an emphasis on sounds, such as those by Dr. Seuss. Some children will need more focused activities than others. Classroom activities for developing phonemic awareness in young children should center on oral language activities and wordplay that encourages actively exploring and manipulating the sounds of language (Yopp & Yopp, 2000). These activities can be integrated into literacy instruction in primary classrooms in the following ways (Yopp, 1992):

TEACHER RESOURCES
See *Oo-pples and Boo-noo-noos: Songs and Activities for Phonemic Awareness* (Yopp & Yopp, 1996).

1. *Songs:* Many songs rhyme and play with language and can be used to develop phonemic awareness. The teacher and children can sing "Down by the Bay," with the teacher drawing attention to the rhyming words and asking students to invent their own rhymes for the song. Other songs that work are "Willaby Wallaby Woo" and "Apples and Bananas" (Bishop, Yopp, & Yopp, 2000).

2. *Children's Books That Emphasize Speech Sounds and Wordplay:* Many children's books play with the sounds in words (Yopp, 1995). In *The Happy Hippopotami*, author Bill Martin, Jr. (1991), points out the sound phoneme substitution: *happy hippopotamamas* and *happy hippopotapapas*. In *There's a Wocket in My Pocket*, Dr. Seuss (1974) substitutes sounds at the beginnings of words naming familiar objects and creates nonsense objects: a child finds a *noonth grush on his tooth brush*. Teachers should look for books that feature sounds, sound substitutions, alliteration, songs and rhymes, and wordplay and tongue twisters. See Table 6.1 (p. 212), which lists children's books that emphasize speech sounds and wordplay.

3. *Routines:* When calling on children while taking roll, dismissing them, or passing out materials, the teacher should isolate the sounds in a child's name—for instance, /s/-/a/-/m/—and ask who it is. Another approach would be to substitute a letter at the beginning of children's names—for instance using /t/, *Sam* becomes *Tam, Jake* becomes *Take,* and so on.

Assessing Phonemic Awareness

The Yopp-Singer Test of Phoneme Segmentation (Yopp, 1995), shown in Assessment Toolbox 6.1 (p. 213), is a new tool to help teachers assess children's phonemic awareness, or the understanding that spoken language is made up of phonemes, or sounds. Children who understand this can hear separate phonemes in spoken words and discriminiate between spoken words on the basis of different phonemes. Phonemic awareness is associated with success in learning to read and spell and therefore should be assessed by the middle of kindergarten. It may be assessed through the third grade, unless the child is already reading fluently. Phonemic awareness is a prerequisite to reading. If a child is already reading, he or she is phonemically aware and there is no need for this type of assessment.

Table 6.1 — Children's Books That Emphasize Speech Sounds and Wordplay

Alliteration

All about Arthur (an Absolutely Absurd Ape) (Carle, 1974)
Alligators All Around: An Alphabet (Sendak, 1990)
Alphabears (Hague, 1984)
Dinosaur Chase (Otto, 1991)
Dr. Seuss's ABC (Seuss, 1963)
Zoophabets (Tallon, 1979)

Sounds

In the Tall, Tall Grass (Fleming, 1991)
The Listening Walk (Showers, 1991)
Roar and More (Kuskin, 1990)
Stop That Noise! (Geraghty, 1992)
We're Going on a Bear Hunt (Rosen, 1989)
Zin! Zin! Zin! A Violin (Moss, 1995)

Sound Substitution

Cock-a-Doodle-Moo! (Most, 1996)
Don't Forget the Bacon (Hutchins, 1976)
The Happy Hippopotami (Martin, 1991)
Henny Penny (Galdone, 1968)
The Hungry Thing (Slepian & Seidler, 1967)
The Hungry Thing Returns (Slepian & Seidler, 1990)
Moose on the Loose (Ochs, 1991)
Mrs. Wishy Washy (Cowley, 1990)
Old Mother Hubbard (Provensen & Provensen, 1977)
Pat the Cat (Hawkins & Hawkins, 1993)
There's a Wocket in My Pocket (Seuss, 1974)

Rhyme and Repetition

A Giraffe and a Half (Silverstein, 1964)
The Hungry Thing Goes to a Restaurant (Seidler, 1993)
"I Can't," Said the Ant (Cameron, 1961)
I Don't Care! Said the Bear (West, 1996)
Tasty Poems (Bennett, 1992)
Ten Cats Have Hats (Marzallo, 1994)

Wordplay and Tongue Twisters

Faint Frogs Feeling Feverish and Other Terrifically Tantalizing Tongue Twisters (Obligado, 1983)
Fox in Socks (Seuss, 1965)
Frogs in Clogs (Samton, 1995)
Moses Supposes His Toeses Are Roses (Patz, 1983)
Sheep on a Ship (Shaw, 1989)
The Teddy Bear Book (Marzollo, 1989)

Songs and Jump-Rope Rhymes

Down by the Bay (Raffi, 1987)
Hush, Little Baby (Zemach, 1976)
Jewels, Children's Play Rhymes (Harwayne, 1995)
The Lady with the Alligator Purse (Westcott, 1988)
Oh, A-Hunting We Will Go (Langstaff, 1974)
One Wide River to Cross (Emberley, 1992)
Tingalayo (Raffi, 1989)

Languages Other Than English

If I Had a Paka (Pomerantz, 1993)
Sing, Little Sack! (Jaffe, 1993)

The Yopp-Singer Test of Phoneme Segmentation (Yopp, 1995) assessess whether a child can separately articulate the sounds of a spoken word in English in order. Children are given the following directions for the test:

> Today we're going to play a word game. I'm going to say a word and I want you to break the word apart. You are going to tell me each sound in the word in order. For example, if I say "old," you should say "/o/-/l/-/d/." (Say the sounds, not the letters.) Let's try a few words together." (p. 21)

The practice words are *ride, go,* and *man.* The teacher should help the child with each word, separating the sounds, if necessary, and encouraging him or her to repeat the sounds.

ASSESSMENT TOOLBOX

6.1 Test of Phoneme Segmentation

Phonemic awareness is associated with success in learning to read and spell and therefore should be assessed by the middle of kindergarten. It may be assessed through the third grade, unless the child is already reading fluently.

Yopp-Singer Test of Phoneme Segmentation

Name _____ Date _____

Score (number correct) _____

Directions: Today we're going to play a word game. I'm going to say a word and I want you to break the word apart. You are going to tell me each sound in the word in order. For example, if I say "old," you should say "/o/-/l/-/d/." (*Administrator: Be sure to say the sounds, not the letters, in the word.*) Let's try a few together.

Practice items: (*Assist the child in segmenting these items as necessary.*)

    ride,   go,   man

Test items: (*Circle those items that the student correctly segments; incorrect responses may be recorded on the blank line following the item.*)

1. dog _____	12. lay _____
2. keep _____	13. race _____
3. fine _____	14. zoo _____
4. no _____	15. three _____
5. she _____	16. job _____
6. wave _____	17. in _____
7. grew _____	18. ice _____
8. that _____	19. at _____
9. red _____	20. top _____
10. me _____	21. by _____
11. sat _____	22. do _____

Source: From "Yopp-Singer Test of Phoneme Segmentation," by H. Y. Yopp, 1995, *The Reading Teacher, 49,* 22. Reprinted with permission of the International Reading Association and H. K. Yopp. Copyright © 1995 by the International Reading Association.

Note: The author, Hallie Kay Yopp, California State University, Fullerton, grants permission for this test to be reproduced. The author acknowledges the contribution of the late Harry Singer to the development of this test.

The teacher should give the 22-item test. If the child responds correctly to an item, the teacher should say, "That's right." If not, the teacher should provide the correct response. He or she should take notes about the child's response on the line next to each item. The test should take 5 to 10 minutes.

Correct responses are only those in which the child articulates each phoneme. For instance, /c/-/a/-/t/ is correct, but /c/-at/ is not. Saying letter names instead of sounds is incorrect. The teacher should be aware that item 7 on the test, *grew*, has three phonemes, /g/-/r/-/ew/, because /ew/ is a blend. Similarly, the digraphs /sh/ in item 5, *she*, and /th/ in item 15, *three*, are also single phonemes.

A child will be assessed as *phonemically aware* if he or she segments all or nearly all the words correctly, as *emergent phonemically aware* if he or she segments some words correctly, and as *lacking appropriate levels of phonemic awareness* if he or she segments only a few or no words.

The Current and Continuing Debate on Phonics

Phonics is "a way of teaching reading and spelling that stresses symbol-sound relationships, used especially in beginning instruction" (Harris & Hodges, 1995, p. 186). Phonics has traditionally been a controversial topic in literacy education, and never more so than today. Newspapers and national news magazines report on the so-called reading wars between advocates of whole language and advocates of phonics, making it appear as though these were the only two simple and clearly defined methods for teaching beginning reading. As you know from having read this much of the text, becoming literate depends on an entire array of complex and interrelated cognitive, linguistic, cultural, social, and personal factors. As a beginning teacher, however, you should be familiar with this current and continuing debate.

Certain historical landmarks are noteworthy. Early reading instruction in the United States taught the *code* and reflected reading materials available at the time, which were organized around the *alphabetic principle: A is for apple.* In the midnineteenth century, Horace Mann challenged the emphasis on the code, or phonics, and argued for an emphasis on comprehension by introducing whole words first. This "meaning first" method grew in popularity and dominated instruction by the 1940s. Whole words were taught using flashcards, the Dolch list of sight words, and basal readers with stories using the same words. These stories were hardly literary. You may have heard about or even remember these "look-say" basal readers with characters such as Dick and Jane, who said things to each other like "Look, Jane, look. See Spot run." In 1955, Rudolph Flesch's book *Why Johnny Can't Read* created a national stir by suggesting a return to the code emphasis, arguing that since English is an alphabetic language, children must learn letter/sound correpondences before learning to read. The debate was now between the phonics and the look-say (or whole-word) advocates.

In 1967, Jeanne Chall wrote a landmark book called *Learning to Read: The Great Debate* (revised in 1983), in which she looked at research to determine the best way to teach beginning reading. The now famous first-grade studies (Bond & Dykstra, 1967), funded by the U.S. Office of Education (USOE) Cooperative Research Program in First-Grade Reading Instruction, was another massive research project undertaken for the same purpose. Both the Chall and USOE projects reported the importance of a child's knowledge of letter names and sounds in learning to read but also noted that the teacher and the learning situation were more important than the method.

The debate continued with the publication of more research findings. *Becoming a Nation of Readers*, published in 1984, was funded by the National Institute of Education, and Marilyn Adams's book *Beginning to Read*, which appeared in 1990, was funded by the U.S. Department of Education to review research on phonics in beginning reading instruction. In general, these projects concluded that there is indeed research to support teaching the alphabetic principle and letter/sound correspondence in beginning reading. This is not, however, all that is needed. Adams has noted that "approaches in which systematic code instruction is included alongside meaning emphasis, language instruction, and connected reading are found to result in superior reading achievement overall . . . for children with low reading-readiness profiles . . . [as well as] for their better prepared and more advantaged peers" (1990, p. 49).

The most current debates in reading concern several issues: What kind of phonics should be taught and to what extent? How can the teaching of word skills be balanced with the literature and whole-language approaches?

To be sure, phonics is *not* a complete method for teaching reading. Teaching letter/symbol correspondences can be part of reading instruction that is grounded in a social constructivist perspective on how children learn, that is student and response centered, and that uses literature and other whole, meaningful texts (e.g., children's writing) as well as oral language (e.g., through language experience charts and reading aloud predictable pattern books).

Phonics Terms and Generalizations

Given the ongoing debate about the role of phonics, you should be familiar with what has characterized traditional phonics instruction. As noted in the previous section, phonics instruction has traditionally broken down language into parts. For example, phonics rules, or generalizations, were taught in a parts-to-whole approach. These rules are famous as well as controversial. Do you remember reciting "When two vowels go walking, the first one does the talking"? Rules like these were found in teachers' guides for basal readers and other commercial programs. The assumption was that if children learned these rules and how to apply them, they would learn to read. But do you also remember what often happened when your teacher asked for an example of a rule? Many times, the example didn't fit, and the teacher said, "That's an exception."

Theodore Clymer experienced this as a classroom teacher with a student named Kenneth. Clymer had been reviewing phonics generalizations with his class by presenting groups of words and analyzing them for similarities and differences; the purpose was to generalize about the relationships between certain sounds and letters and positions in words and pronunciations. But while Clymer was teaching these rules, Kenneth was poring over the dictionary, creating lists of words that were exceptions. Later, as a university researcher, Clymer (1963) followed Kenneth's example and did a study that has become another landmark in the debate over phonics. He analyzed the utility of phonics generalizations in four basal reading series that were widely used at the time. He found 121 generalizations and great variation in how and when they should be taught. He applied the generalizations to the words in a word list and found that most of these commonly taught rules were of limited value. In sum, those that did work did not pertain to many words, and those that pertained to many words were unreliable.

Teachers should be aware of the generalizations that are most useful (Clymer, 1996). They are discussed in the following sections, grouped under the heads Consonants and Vowels; other important terms used in traditional phonics instruction are introduced, as well.

Consonants. The consonants are *b, c, d, f, g, h, j, k, l, m, n, p, q, r, s, t, u, v, w, x, y,* and *z.* A *consonant blend* or *cluster* is comprised of two or more consonants whose sounds blend together but each consonant retains its own identity (e.g., *br* in *break*). A *consonant digraph* is comprised of two or more consonants that represent a single sound (e.g., *ch, sh, th, ph, gh, ng*). The most reliable consonant generalizations are as follow:

- *Soft and hard sounds of* c *and* g: When *c* is followed by *e* or *i*, it has the soft sound of *s* (*cent*), and when *g* is followed by one of these letters, it has the soft sound of *j* (*engine*). When *c* is followed by *o* or *a*, it has the hard sound of *k* (*cat*), and when *g* is followed by either letter, it has its own sound (*go*).
- *Two of the same:* When two of the same consonant appear side by side, only one is heard (*carry*).
- *Two sounds for* ch: When *c* and *h* occur next to each other, they make only one sound (*peach*), which is usually pronounced as it is in *kitchen, catch,* and *chair* but sometimes like *sh* (*machine*) or *k* (*chemistry*).
- *Silent* k *and* w: When a word begins with *kn* (*knife*) or *wr* (*write*), the *k* and *w* are silent.
- ck *at the end:* When a word ends in *ck*, it has the same last sound as in *look*.

Vowels. The vowels are *a, e, i, o, u,* and *w* and *y* at the end of a word or syllable or *y* in the middle of a word or syllable. A *vowel digraph* is comprised of two vowels that together make a single sound (e.g., *oo* in *book* and *ai, ay, ea, au, aw, oa, eigh*). A *vowel dipthong* is such a close blend of vowels that it can be considered one sound for word study (e.g., *oy* in *boy* and *oi, ou, uy, ee, ay, ough*). An *r* after a vowel gives it a different sound, as in *car*. The most useful vowel generalizations are as follow:

- *One vowel in a word:* If a word only has one vowel and it's at the end, the vowel usually has the long sound (*so*). If the vowel is not at the end of the word, it usually has the short sound (*pop*).
- *Vowel combinations:* The first vowel is usually long and the second is usually silent in the digraphs *ai, ea, oa,* and *ui*. The double vowels *oi, oy,* and *ou* usually form a dipthong, or one sound.
- *Two vowels and a final silent* e: If a word has two vowels and one is *e* at the end, the first vowel is usually long and the final *e* is silent (e.g., *make* and *like*).
- r-*controlled vowels:* The *r* gives the preceding vowel a sound that is neither long nor short (e.g., *horn*).

Syllables, Onsets, and Rimes

Researchers have also found it useful to teach onsets and rimes in word study. English can be broken down into syllables, onsets and rimes, and phonemes. Every syllable has a *rime,* or the vowel and any consonant after it, and may have an *onset,* or the consonant before the vowel in the syllable (e.g., *s-it*). Not every word has an onset (e.g., *I* and *it*). These are called *psychological units* because it is easier for children to break down a word into onsets and rimes and more difficult to break either down into the phonemic components (Goswami & Bryant, 1990; Treiman, 1983, 1985).

Furthermore, children use analogies from words they do know for words they don't know (Goswami & Mead, 1992; Moustafa, 1995), and they do this at the onset/rime, rather than the phonemic, level. Consider the example of *small* and *smile*. Children understand that the onset *sm-* is the same in *small* and *smile* and use this knowledge to read other words that begin with *sm-*. Children's ability to analogize known to unknown words is more useful to them in reading than knowing letter/sound correspondences, and the more words they know, the better they will be able to make these analogies. Wylie and Durrell (1970) have isolated 37 rimes that when combined with onsets produce 500 words that beginning readers can recognize. Words like these can be incorporated into wordplay, language games, and teaching with literature.

Rimes Beginning Readers Will Know

-ack	-ay	-p
-ail	-eat	-ir
-ain	-ell	-ock
-ake	-est	-oke
-ale	-ice	-op
-ame	-ick	-ore
-an	-ide	-or
-ank	-ight	-uck
-ap	-ill	-ug
-ash	-in	-ump
-at	-ine	-unk
-ate	-ing	
-aw	-ink	

Whole-to-Parts Phonics

Margaret Moustafa (1997) describes *whole-to-parts* phonics instruction, based on recent research, that differs from *parts-to-whole* phonics instruction in several ways:

1. It begins with what children know.
2. It teaches word study after a story has been read—for example, in a shared reading experience.
3. It teaches letter/sound correspondences using units of spoken language that are already familiar to children, such as onsets, rimes, and syllables in English and Spanish.

The whole-to-parts approach is like traditional phonics instruction in that it can be explicit and systematic. It is based on research that suggests children generally recognize whole words in print first and do so best in the context of familiar language, such as their names, a favorite story that has been read repeatedly, and environmental print (Moustafa, 1995).

TEACHING IDEA

Whole-to-Parts Phonics Instruction with "The Eeensy, Weensy Spider"

1. *Shared Reading:* This type of instruction begins with a story. The teacher reads a predictable pattern book, presents a poem, or teaches a song in a shared reading lesson, with an emphasis on enjoyment, understanding, and personal response. The second time through, the teacher reads and points to words so children see the connection between print and speech. The teacher and students could also create a language experience story. For example, the familiar children's rhyme "The Eensy, Weensy Spider" could be written on a large chart and individual copies could be provided for children.

2. *"Word Wall":* The teacher asks each student to tell his or her favorite word in the rhyme, such as *spider*, and writes them all on a piece of paper. Letters are highlighted to represent:

   a. Onset: *sp-* in *spider*, saying "These letters say /sp/."
   b. Rime: *-er* in *spider*, saying "These letters say /er/."
   c. Syllable: *-der* in *spider*, saying "These letters say /der/."

These techniques can be used to teach prefixes (e.g., *re-* and *un-*), suffixes (e.g., *-ly* and *-tion*), root words (e.g., *climb* in *climbed*), and words in compound words (e.g., *base* in *baseball*). Children should be directed to make generalizations as they add words to the word wall; for example, with *water, washed,* and *went,* the letter representing the initial onset, *w,* should be highlighted. Words can be grouped and regrouped in a pocket chart or on a sheet of plastic, such as a painter's drop cloth or a shower curtain. Not all the words in every poem or story should be emphasized, however. The point is to teach the alphabetic principle and letter/sound correspondences that occur frequently using words the children have heard and understand in the context of shared reading.

3. *Guided Reading:* As children move from shared to guided reading, this same strategy may be used in small groups, focusing on more and more complex letter/sound correspondences, such as *-ent* in *went* and *-own* in *down*.

Student Independent Reading

Children learn to read by reading. *Student independent reading* of self-selected books and reading across the curriculum takes place throughout the day—for instance, during literature circles and in literature units and shared reading experiences. Student independent reading is also known as *wide independent reading* (Morrow, 1992b), *free voluntary reading* (FVR) (Krashen, 1993), and *individualized reading* (Stuaffer, 1980; Veatch, 1959, 1978). Students in independent reading programs have become successful readers and writers and have succeeded on standardized tests (Bond & Dykstra, 1967; Duker, 1968; Krashen, 1993; Zarrillo, 1989). Student independent reading has been shown to be the most important factor in success in reading and vocabulary development (Nagy & Herman, 1985).

One approach to student independent reading that's used as a method of reading instruction is *sustained silent reading (SSR)*. SSR is based on the constructivist idea that children learn to do things by doing them. SSR means a period of uninterrupted reading of self-selected books and other reading materials in the classroom. The teacher reads, too. Other acronyms for SSR include *USSR* (uninterrupted sustained silent reading) and *DEAR* (drop everything and read).

SNAPSHOT **Sustained Silent Reading in a First-Grade Class**

Phyllis Crawford, a former classroom teacher and reading specialist (who's now a principal), explains the steps she used to initiate SSR in her first-grade classroom each year:

1. *Provide Reading Materials:* The only materials I use are good for reading at many levels and for many interests: picture books, chapter books, poetry, nonfiction, magazines and newspapers, and so on. I like to have at least 100 different things to read in my room.

2. *Introduce Books to Whole Class:* I put a pile of 40 to 50 books on the rug in the reading center, with the children seated around the edge. I choose a book, read a few pages aloud, make a comment, and put the book back in the pile. I do this three to five more times and then read at least one entire book aloud. This takes 20 to 30 minutes.

3. *Introduce Approach:* I say, "Today we're going to read silently and we're going to sustain ourselves in silent reading. This means that you're going to spend some time with one book, paying attention only to it, reading and rereading it or looking at the pictures carefully."

4. *All Select Books:* All the children scramble into the middle of the pile and immediately grab the book I read all the way through; next, they choose

the ones I've read a few pages from. After they all have books, they can go anywhere in the room to read. I find a book, too.

5. *All Read Silently:* No one can interrupt anyone, including the teacher. All the children must stay in the places they have chosen. If they finish looking at their books, they should reread or look at the illustrations.

6. *Share Books:* I signal the end of reading. (I note children's behavior to determine when to stop. If they are all absorbed in reading, I let them continue.) After SSR, I share something to give them an idea of how they might share about their book: what I thought about, my favorite part, how it relates to something in my life. I might read a passage aloud, share interesting words, phrases, ideas, or illustrations, or tell how I felt about reading it. Children then have a model for sharing their own books.

Usually four or five children share daily. I sometimes ask questions or invite other students to ask questions, which encourages them to think about and personalize their reading experience.

Reading Workshop

Reading workshop is an instructional approach for organizing the teaching of reading. It is especially appropriate for middle- and upper-grade students who are reading independently. It follows the same guiding principles as writing workshop, which will be discussed in Chapter 9, The Writing Process. In fact, reading and writing workshops are organized in similar ways and can be taught on alternate days. Some teachers combine reading and writing workshops in a single, large block of time.

In reading workshop, the students and teacher work in a group, or workshop, setting and plan experiences with these characteristics:

1. based on mutual interests (one book, several, or a theme)
2. flexible so that groups can change membership, the amount of time they meet, or their focus
3. social, cooperative, and collaborative
4. led by the teacher or students
5. student and response centered
6. allow ample time and opportunity to read, talk, plan, write, and carry out further experiences with literature

See Chapter 7, Teaching with Literature, for ways to organize instruction that could blend with reading workshop—for example, literature circles.

Reading workshop is based on the idea of teaching reading as a process of meaning construction similar to that of writing, where readers think, rehearse, draft, and revise their experiences with texts (Atwell, 1987; Calkins, 1983; Graves, 1983). Reading workshop is planned with a large block of time—for example, an hour or more—during which students read books of their own choice independently. They may read fiction or nonfiction and don't necessarily have to finish a book if they don't like it. In this way, reading workshop more closely approximates reading experiences in the real world. Finally, students respond to their reading in a variety of ways—through discussion, more reading, writing, drama, and so on—with other students and the teacher in flexible grouping patterns. They may also work on their own. Reading workshop gives the teacher great flexibility in meeting the needs of a diverse group of students and classes in which reading ability may vary greatly.

Reading workshop can also be combined with other instructional approaches to teaching reading with literature and writing. For example, reading workshop can be scheduled on alternate days with writing workshop and in combination with reading aloud, shared reading, guided reading, language experience approach, word study, sustained silent reading, and independent reading. Assessment can be based on how well students participated and following reading workshop guidelines as well as writing in reading-response journals and any other group work produced.

A reading workshop follows these steps:

1. *Minilesson:* Each reading workshop begins with a 5- to 7-minute minilesson on reading workshop procedures, literary concepts such as story structure, or reading skills and strategies that the teacher feels are important for students. In some cases, the minilesson could be reading literature aloud to encourage interest in a book, a genre of literature, or an author. In others, the minilesson could focus on a specific strategy, such as understanding symbolism in stories or using an index in a nonfiction book.

2. *Reading Status:* The teacher briefly checks each student's reading status—what he or she is planning to do. This can be done by creating a grid with the students' names in a vertical list on the left and the days of the week listed horizontally across the top. A simple activity code can be used to indicate the daily status: CR = continue reading, NB = new book, TC = teacher conference, and BR = buddy reading.

3. *Reading and Responding:* The majority of the period—say, 45 minutes of a 1-hour period—is spent reading and doing reading-related activities. Students can also write in reading-response journals or work in groups on projects. The teacher can circulate and guide discussions for students in literature circles reading the same book or several books on a theme or conference with individual children. During this time, students are expected to read for real purposes and enjoyment and to reflect on and respond to what they are reading. The teacher can also read aloud to an individual or group, if appropriate, or students can listen to tapes of books and follow along in their own copies.

See Chapter 7, Teaching with Literature, for ideas about response options after reading.

4. *Conferences with the Teacher:* During reading workshop, teahcers can conference with students. These conferences can be scheduled in a variety of ways. A

simple rotation system might be used, in which the teacher conferences with four or five students a day, or students can sign up to request conferences. The teacher may decide to conference more frequently with those students who seem to benefit more than others or schedule conferences on an as-needed basis. It's good to check in with each student every 2 weeks or so.

During a reading conference, several things can occur:

- The child reads to the teacher.
- The teacher reads to the child.
- Both ask questions of the other and talk about the book and their reading of it.
- Both make plans for further reading or response options.
- The teacher provides support for word recognition and meaning, author's style, or story structure, relating reading to the child's experience and cross-curricular connections.

5. *Sharing:* The last 5 to 10 minutes of the period can be for sharing: perhaps a response to a book, writing, or the results of a discussion.

TEACHER RESOURCES

To see which books children like best, see the October issue of *The Reading Teacher* each year for a list of "Children's Choices," based on a poll of 10,000 children across the United States.

To begin to implement reading workshop, build a classroom library of 100 to 150 books of interest for the grade level. Supplement this selection with books from the school and public libraries. Good sources for inexpensive books are garage sales, flea markets, library book sales, PTA funds, and donations from parents. Children can bring books from home and order books from paperback book clubs. Add magazines, pamphlets, brochures, and other reading material of interest to students. Choose many high-interest books for students using these guidelines (Purves & Beach, 1972):

1. Children prefer a literary to nonliterary presentation of materials, books that tell good stories with suspenseful plots and much action, and stories of others their own age.
2. Content (What's it about?) is the major determinant of reading interests.
3. Primary (K–3) students see reading as entertainment and like folk- and fairytales and stories with fantasy figures (often animals) representing childlike experiences.
4. Middle- and upper-grade (4–6) students also see reading as a way of finding out about the world and like stories of daily life as familiar experience, animals and nature, and adventure.

Remember that students spend most of their time during reading workshop actually reading books of their choice. Individual response options discussed with the teacher during conferences might include reading another book (by the same author or about the same subject or something totally new), writing in response journals, self-selected projects, writing, artmaking, drama, mediamaking, or working in a group with other students who share similar reading interests. The teacher should plan time for students to share ideas or projects about their reading with one another.

Assessing Reading

Assessing reading as a language art in a student- and response-centered classroom means using alternative means to standardized tests: that is, naturalistic, authentic, ongoing assessment by observing, interacting, and analyzing students' reading experiences. This kind of assessment should include five interactive components: "the observation, activity, test, or task must be relevant, authentic, and part of the teaching-learning process by informing the learner and furthering instruction" (Routman, 1991, p. 305).

A running record documents what a child says and does while reading a book chosen by the teacher (Clay, 1993). It is a useful tool for assessing strengths and weaknesses in reading strategies, especially for beginning readers, while reading a real text. Running records have been used successfully in the Reading Recovery Program in New Zealand (Clay, 1985) and the United States (Pinnell, Fried, & Estice, 1990). They can be used any time teachers meet with children—for example, during reading workshop while other students are reading independently or working in small groups.

Here are guidelines for creating and using a running record, such as that shown in Assessment Toolbox 6.2 (p. 224):

1. Prepare a record with the child's name, the book title, and the date across the top. List the pages to be read vertically down the lefthand side.

2. Choose a book the child has read before. Use a 100-word sample for a longer book.

3. Have the child read aloud. Make a checkmark for each word read correctly on each page.

4. Mark miscues as follows:
   - Misreads: Write the correct word with the misread word above it.
   - Omits word: Write the omitted word and circle it.
   - Self-corrects: Write the word with *SC* above it.
   - Teacher tells word: Write the word with *T* above it.

5. Scoring formula:

   Total words read correctly (including self-corrections) __ × 100 = __%
   Number of words in book/sample __
   Good progress = 90%

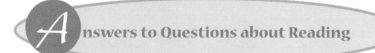

Answers to Questions about Reading

- ### *What is reading?*

As explained in *Becoming a Nation of Readers,* reading is an integral part of the language arts. Reading is primarily the construction of meaning. Various theoretical models have been proposed to explain what that means. The *linear model*

6.2 Running Record

A Running Record is a useful tool for assessing both strengths and weaknesses in reading strategies, especially for a beginning reader, while reading aloud a real text. The text should be a book the child has read before. For a longer book, use a 100-word sample.

Name _____ Date _____

Book Title _____

Running Record

Pages to Be Read	Words Read Correctly and Miscues* (one checkmark per word)
_____	_____
_____	_____
_____	_____
_____	_____
_____	_____
_____	_____
_____	_____
_____	_____
_____	_____
_____	_____
_____	_____
_____	_____

Total read correctly   _____

Total self-corrections _____

Scoring Formula: Total words read correctly (including self-corrections) ___ × 100 = ___%
Number of words in book/sample = ___
Independent level = 5% error rate
Instructional level = 6% to 10% error rate
Frustrational level = more than 10% error rate

*Key for Miscues:
  Misreads: Write the correct word with the misread word above it.
  Omits word: Write the omitted word and circle it.
  Self-corrects: Write the word with *SC* above it.
  Teacher tells word: Write the word with *T* above it.

explains that reading is a bottom-up, or part-to-whole, process. The child first recognizes letters, then words, and then sentences; a sequence of smaller to larger subskills must be learned before the reader gets meaning from print. The *interactive model* is based on schema theory, which explains that learners acquire, store, and use knowledge in the form of *schema*. The reader makes meaningful connections between prior knowledge, or schemata, and uses personal reading strategies (developed and adjusted for each individual purpose in reading) while seeking to construct meaning from print. The *transactional model* describes each reading act as a transaction between the reader and text, occurring at a particular time and in a particular context. Meaning comes into being during the transaction, in which the reader is active. The reader makes predictions about the meaning of what is read, testing and confirming hypotheses while reading.

- ### How should we teach and assess reading?

The balanced approach to teaching reading used by many teachers today combines skills development with literature- and language-rich activities. Classroom methods used in the balanced approach include shared reading; guided reading; writing to read, with strategies such as the language experience approach (LEA), direct instruction in word study, phonemic awareness, and phonics; and student independent reading using organizational strategies such as sustained silent reading (SSR) and reading workshop. Teachers are responsible for decision making and for planning a balanced approach to reading in a student- and response-centered classroom. That includes using authentic, ongoing means of assessment such as anecdotal records, the test of phoneme segmentation, and running records.

Looking Further

1. With others in your class, describe, discuss, and compare memories of reading instruction in elementary school. Which of the models of reading did it most reflect? How so?

2. Pick a children's picture book you like, and plan what you would do before, during, and after a shared reading of that book.

3. Read a book aloud to a group of children, and ask them open and aesthetic questions: What did you think of it? What was your favorite part? Make a list of response options, based on what the children said.

4. Plan a guided reading lesson for students in the primary grades and then teach it. Share what happened with your college class.

Children's Books and Software

Bennett, J. (1992). *Tasty poems.* New York: Oxford University Press.

Cameron, P. (1961). *"I can't," said the ant.* New York: Scholastic.

Carle, E. (1969). *The very hungry caterpillar.* New York: Philomel.

Carle, E. (1974). *All about Arthur (an absolutely absurd ape).* New York: Franklin Watts.

Cowley, J. (1990). *Mrs. Wishy Washy.* San Diego: Wright Group.

Emberley, B. (1992). *One wide river to cross.* Boston: Little, Brown.

Emberly, E. (1992). *Ed Emberly's thumbprint drawing box.* New York: Little, Brown.

Fleming, D. (1991). *In the tall, tall grass.* New York: Henry Holt.

Galdone, P. (1968). *Henny Penny.* New York: Scholastic.

Geraghty, P. (1992). *Stop that noise!* New York: Crown.

Hague, K. (1984). *Alphabears.* New York: Holt, Rinehart, & Winston.

Harwayne, S. (1995). *Jewels, children's play rhymes.* New York: Mondo.

Hawkins, C., & Hawkins, J. (1993). *Pat the cat.* New York: Putnam's.

Hutchins, P. (1976). *Don't forget the bacon.* New York: Greenwillow.

Jaffe, N. (1993). *Sing, little sack!* New York: Bantam.

Kuskin, K. (1990). *Roar and more.* New York: Harper Trophy.

Langstaff, J. (1974). *Oh, a-hunting we will go.* New York: Atheneum.

Lobel, A. (1980). *Fables.* New York: HarperCollins.

Lobel, A. (1983). *The book of pigericks.* New York: Harper & Row.

Martin, B., Jr. (1991). *The happy hippopotami.* Orlando, FL: Harcourt Brace Jovanovich.

Marzollo, J. (1989). *The teddy bear book.* New York: Dial.

Marzollo, J. (1994). *Ten cats have hats.* New York: Scholastic.

Moss, L. (1995). *Zin! Zin! Zin! A violin.* New York: Simon & Schuster.

Most, B. (1995). *Cock-a-doodle-moo!* San Diego: Red Wagon.

Obligado, L. (1983). *Faint frogs feeling feverish and other terrifically tantalizing tongue twisters.* New York: Viking.

Ochs, C. P. (1991). *Moose on the loose.* Minneapolis, MN: Carolrhoda.

Otto, C. (1991). *Dinosaur chase.* New York: Harper Trophy.

Patz, N. (1983). *Moses supposes his toeses are roses.* San Diego: Harcourt Brace Jovanovich.

Pomerantz, C. (1993). *If I had a paka.* New York: Mulberry.

Provensen, A., & Provensen, M. (1977). *Old Mother Hubbard.* New York: Random House.

Raffi. (1987). *Down by the bay.* New York: Crown.

Raffi. (1989). *Tingalayo.* New York: Crown.

Reader rabbit [Computer software]. Available from The Learning Company.

Rosen, M. (adapter). (1989). *We're going on a bear hunt* (H. Oxenburg, Illus.). New York: McElderry.

Samton, S. W. (1995). *Frogs in clogs.* New York: Crown.

Schenk de Regniers, B. (1964). *May I bring a friend?* New York: Atheneum.

Sendak, M. (1990). *Alligators all around: An alphabet.* New York: HarperCollins.

Seuss, Dr. (1963). *Dr. Seuss's ABC.* New York: Random House.

Seuss, Dr. (1965). *Fox in socks.* New York: Random House.

Seuss, Dr. (1974). *There's a wocket in my pocket.* New York: Random House.

Shaw, N. (1989). *Sheep on a ship.* Boston: Houghton Mifflin.

Showers, P. (1991). *The listening walk.* New York: HarperCollins.

Silverstein, S. (1964). *A giraffe and a half.* New York: HarperCollins.

Slepian, J., & Seidler, A. (1967). *The hungry thing.* New York: Scholastic.

Slepian, J., & Seidler, A. (1990). *The hungry thing returns.* New York: Scholastic.

Slepian, J., & Seidler, A. (1993). *The hungry thing goes to a restaurant.* New York: Scholastic.

Tallon, R. (1979). *Zoophabets.* New York: Scholastic.

West, C. (1996). *I don't care! Said the bear.* Cambridge, MA: Candlewick.

Westcott, N. B. (1988). *The lady with the alligator purse.* New York: Little, Brown.

Zemach, M. (1976). *Hush, little baby.* New York: E. P. Dutton.

chapter 7

Teaching with Literature

Q **uestions about Teaching with Literature**

- *How do young readers respond to literature?*
- *How should we teach with literature?*

REFLECTIVE RESPONSE

Think about a book that you read as a child. What did you think of it? What was your favorite part? Jot down your responses.

Reader Response to Literature

The *reader-response perspective* on teaching with literature is primarily concerned with how a reader makes meaning from an experience with a text (Beach, 1993; Marshall, 2000; Rosenblatt, 2003). This perspective shifts the focus from *finding meaning* in the text to more fully understanding the process by which readers, as critics, go about *making meaning*. According to this perspective, readers are actively engaged in the construction of meaning while reading. And because meaning is created by unique, individual readers, there is no single correct meaning of any text. The underlying assumption is that meaning is not found solely in the stance. The children in this nine-year study responded predominantly from an aesthetic stance (71 percent) rather than an efferent stance (28 percent). The frequency of each type of response is shown in the figure as a percentage. As you can see, the most frequent types of responses were more aesthetic than efferent.

As Rosenblatt suggests and my research confirms, there is an interplay between both types of stances. But the more efferent types of responses—such as considering print and language, explaining, and analyzing, which are most emphasized in traditional reading instruction—are invariably embedded in broader aesthetic responses. For example, a typical response pattern was for a child first to question part of the story he or she wondered about and then hypothesize (aesthetic) an explanation (efferent), drawing on personal associations (aesthetic) as well as print, language, and content to analyze it (efferent). Younger children often did this through performing by acting or talking like a character (aesthetic). Figure 7.2 shows how the efferent responses can be embedded in the aesthetic.

Let's look at an example of how one third-grade child responded to the book *Ira Sleeps Over* (Waber, 1972). In one part of the story, Ira is spending the night at his friend Reggie's house. The two are telling ghost stories. Ira has been afraid to go to Reggie's house, even though they are best friends and live next door to each other, because Ira sleeps with a teddy bear and is afraid that Reggie will laugh at him. First, the child reader questions one part, also making associations and performing:

> What if it's a *good* ghost story? Ghosts don't have to be scary. I *love* ghost stories. (She makes ghost sounds and tells about a ghost book she is reading.)

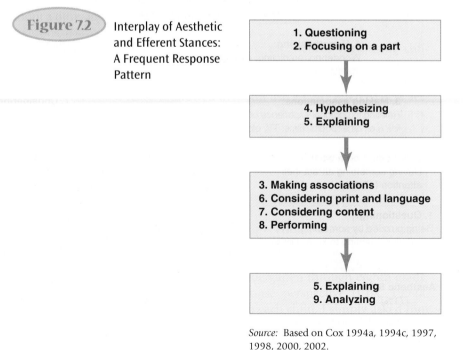

Figure 7.2 Interplay of Aesthetic and Efferent Stances: A Frequent Response Pattern

1. Questioning
2. Focusing on a part

4. Hypothesizing
5. Explaining

3. Making associations
6. Considering print and language
7. Considering content
8. Performing

5. Explaining
9. Analyzing

Source: Based on Cox 1994a, 1994c, 1997, 1998, 2000, 2002.

Then, the child questions a key part again, considering the content, and she begins hypothesizing and explaining:

> Is he hard of hearing? No. I don't think so. He just doesn't want to answer because he thinks they'll make fun of him because he didn't want to talk anymore about his teddy bear. And maybe he thought Ira wasn't going to get his teddy bear.

The child makes associations with her own life, hypothesizing and explaining some more:

> I think that's *dumb!* What's wrong with a teddy bear? I *like* taking my teddy bear to my friend's house. You know what I think he should do? I think he should—even though he's just *saying* that so his sister won't make fun of him—he should every night practice sleeping without his teddy bear. So he'll get used to it.

In student- and response-centered classrooms, teachers focus on students' responses, rather than their own predetermined ideas or those found in a teacher's guide to using literature (Commeyras & Sumner, 1998). Children are encouraged to respond openly, drawing on their own experiences and funds of knowledge (Hemphill, 1999). In transactional teaching with literature, teachers begin by asking open questions—"So what did you think of it?"—and directing children to take an aesthetic stance toward literature.

Now that you have seen how children respond to literature, consider your own response to the children's book that I asked you to think about at the beginning of the chapter. What stance did you take? And how might knowledge of stance influence teaching with literature and literacy development? The Snapshot and discussion of approaches that follow should help you answer these questions.

TEACHER RESOURCES

For excellent ideas about response-centered teaching with literature, see *Making Meaning in the Response-Based Classroom* (Hunsberger & Labercane, 2002), including a chapter I wrote on my research on children's stance and a chapter by Paul Boyd-Batstone, a Spanish bilingual teacher you will read about later in the chapter.

SNAPSHOT How to Find a Lost Mine and Other Treasures in Children's Books

Student- and response-centered, transactional teaching with literature is a powerful means to actively engage children in experiences with literature and reading, to focus on the personal construction of meaning, and to integrate the curriculum. I discovered this almost by chance during my first year of teaching. As my fourth-grade class and I quietly pored over paperback book club order forms, three students approached me excitedly, saying, "Miss Shirreffs, there's a book in here with your name on it!" "Impossible," I countered, "No one has a name like that except my family." "It's true," they insisted, and they were right. My father was Gordon D. Shirreffs, an author of Western novels who had also written many books of historical and regional fiction for children and young adults.

By now, the entire class was interested. Many students ordered their own paperback copies of *The Mystery of the Haunted Mine* (Shirreffs, 1962), a con-

See Cox (1986), "Gordon D. Shirreffs: An Interview with a Western Writer," *English Journal*, 75, 40–48.

GREAT BOOKS FOR CHILDREN

By Gordon D. Shirreffs

Mystery of Lost Canyon (1963); *Mystery of the Lost Cliff Dwelling* (1968); *The Secret of the Spanish Desert* (1964) (sequel to *The Mystery of the Haunted Mine*); *Son of the Thunder People* (1957); and *Swiftwagon* (1958).

See Chapter 5, Listening and Talking, for more on reading aloud.

temporary tale of mystery and adventure set in the rugged Arizona mountain country. In it, three young people search for an elusive lost Spanish gold mine that's supposedly been guarded by the spirit of the outlaw Asesino for over 50 years.

The day the books arrived was exciting for the children and significant for me in terms of how I began to perceive the role of literature in teaching language arts. Before this experience, I wasn't fully aware of how simultaneously easy and essential it is to base language and literacy learning across the curriculum on literature. Now, I can't imagine it any other way. And the children showed me how it should be done.

Here's a step-by-step review of what happened in this fourth-grade class and others that I taught, when one book set off a "ripple effect" of literature-based, response-themed learning:

1. *Reading Aloud, Along, and Alone:* I read a chapter of *The Mystery of the Haunted Mine* aloud every day, and it soon became the high point. Some students read along in their own copies (and some read ahead on their own, because they couldn't wait to find out what happened next). Others put their heads down on their desks and became lost in listening to the story of Gary, Tuck, and Sue, as they unraveled the mystery of the lost map and mine.

2. *Talking Together:* Time for talking after reading gave children the opportunity to reflect and respond, focus their thinking, clarify feelings, develop concepts, and share ideas as they thought aloud and talked with others—students and the teacher. I started each discussion with an open, aesthetic question: "What did you think?"

3. *Writing in Literature-Response Journals:* Students wrote in their literature-response journals each day when something about the book struck them, raised a question, or prompted a personal association. They could write while I read (or they read) or before or after our discussions. These journals became records of students' responses to the book.

4. *Response Options:* In addition to talking and writing in literature-response journals, I offered other options for response: talking in groups or with buddies; other types of writing; drawing, artmaking, or mediamaking; and drama. These optional responses became the basis for further integrated activities across the curriculum.

5. *Focal Topics of Interest:* The questions from students that emerged during whole-class discussions and other times gave us many ideas about how to extend literature reading and responding as well as experiences across the curriculum. I wrote down the following focal questions:

Put checkmarks next to the questions in this list you think are aesthetic. Put circles next to those you think are efferent.

> What would we do if we were Gary, Tuck, and Sue? How would we go
>   about looking for the map and the treasure?
> How would we feel if we were them?
> Was there really a treasure? Whose was it?
> What are the desert and mountains in Arizona like?

What were the Native Americans like there?
Are there other mines and treasures in Arizona?
Was this one really haunted?

Through further discussions and planning times, these questions became focal topics for more experiences and reading related literature.

6. *Literature Circles:* We formed groups to read other books and find out more about what questions interested students most. Each group developed their own questions and ideas for further reading and learning experiences with literature across the curriculum.

7. *Gathering Related Books and Resources:* When one child brought in a map of Arizona, saved from a family trip, I invited others to do the same. Soon, a table and bookshelf were crowded with maps, postcards, rock collections, Native American artifacts, and a snakeskin and some real rattlesnake rattles. This area became our Center for Study of the Desert of the Southwest United States. I began to look for related children's fiction and informational books and media to build our classroom study and literature center.

WWW

Visit these websites on the Southwestern desert: **www.desertusa.com** and **arizona.cacti.home.att.net/ cacti.htm**.

8. *Wide Independent Reading:* I learned to help students find books they were interested in or that related to the focal topic for wide independent reading. From discussions about the book, I discovered that some students had a real interest in mysteries; others, in stories about the supernatural; and still others, in adventure stories. I asked the school librarian for ideas and books lists.

9. *Integrating Teaching across the Curriculum:* Reading *The Mystery of the Haunted Mine* started a ripple effect of response-themed experiences about the desert of the Southwest United States that included social studies (history, geography, and Native American, Hispanic, and Anglo cultures), science (geology and ecology of the desert), the arts, and mathematics. The Ripple Effect chart on page 235 shows the range of possible focal topics, learning experiences, and related books for research and wide independent reading by individuals or literature groups. Ever since my first experience with literature-based teaching, the beginning of any theme cycle or unit of study has been the time for me to gather a nucleus of good children's books—both nonfiction and fiction—around which to center opportunities for response-centered experiences related to students' interests. And well into the cycle or unit, I've continued to add books, based on my ongoing observation of students' responses.

Keep a record of theme-related books, making brief annotations on notecards or in a computer file.

A Visit from the Author

A highlight of the ripple effect that came from reading *The Mystery of the Haunted Mine* was a visit from the author (my father), Gordon D. Shirreffs. When he agreed to come and talk to my class, he warned me he wasn't going to answer impossible questions like "Where do you get ideas for your stories?" But he did just that as he told my students more stories drawn from his knowledge about the culture and history of the Southwest. From time to time during his narrative, he reached into an old shoebox full of arrowheads, old nails, and special rocks—things we'd found on family trips to the desert.

My father, Gordon D. Shirreffs, was the 1995 recipient of the Owen Wister Award, given by the Western Writers of America for lifetime contribution to the literature of the West. He died in 1996.

This snapshot from the 1950s shows my father, my brother, and me on a research trip in the desert.

First, my father told the class the following seriously stated (but tongue-in-cheek) rules for how to find a lost mine:

1. Travel to a remote part of the desert Southwest that is unmapped and unexplored.
2. Be chased by bandits, desperadoes, or outlaws.
3. Lose your food and water.
4. Become completely lost.
5. Discover a gold mine but not a way of taking the gold with you.
6. Fill an empty tin can (shoe, canteen) with a few gold nuggets.
7. Head for civilization.
8. Be caught in a fierce desert sandstorm and stagger or crawl along.
9. Be found unconscious with the can (shoe, canteen) of gold nuggets clutched in your hand but unable to find your way to the gold mine.
10. You have found a lost mine!

More stories followed about mysterious mountains, strange glyphs and signs carved in rough canyon rock, and spirits of long-dead patrons. As my father spoke, he spirited these mesmerized fourth-grade students out of their classroom and over the twisting trails of the Southwest, sharing a curious blend of the truth and legend of the Native, Spanish, and Anglo American cultures. With my father as their beckoning guide, the children trudged through an imaginary desert, searching for gold.

My father also gave the children insight into the process of writing historical or regional fiction by telling them that everything in his books and stories was based on fact. For instance, he didn't create his formula for finding a lost gold mine out of his fertile imagination; rather, it grew from countless tales of prospectors about finding and losing mines under those very circumstances. And the Espectros Mountains, which appear in my father's books, are modeled closely after the Superstition Mountains in Arizona, the real site of many mysterious disappearances and unsolved murders documented in local records. Perhaps the most tempting nugget of Western lore that my father tantalized the children with was a description of the old Spanish miner's code: symbols that early miners carved in rock to mark their way back to mines. When he explained that these symbols were really used and might even still be out there—somewhere in the wild canyons and rugged foothills of the Southwest, just waiting to lead someone to a lost mine—many young eyes in the class lit up with a gleam that can only be described as "gold fever."

Espectros means "ghosts" in Spanish.

Old Spanish Miner's Codes

There is gold here.

Various meanings: Church treasures; a Christian passed this way; treasure trail.

Various meanings: Head points to treasure; death, defeat, or destruction.

Treasure is in tunnel directly below.

Treasure is on opposite side.

Follow trail to mine or treasure; travel on.

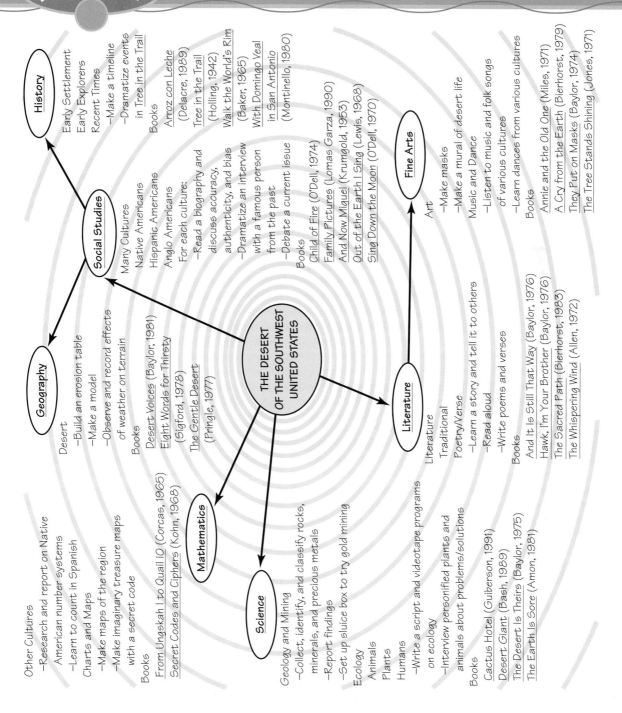

THE DESERT OF THE SOUTHWEST UNITED STATES

History
Early Settlement
Early Explorers
Recent Times
—Make a timeline
—Dramatize events in Tree in the Trail
Books
Arroz con Leche (Delacre, 1989)
Tree in the Trail (Holling, 1942)
Walk the World's Rim (Baker, 1965)
With Domingo Veal in San Antonio (Montinello, 1980)

Social Studies
Many Cultures
Native Americans
Hispanic Americans
Anglo Americans
For each culture:
—Read a biography and discuss accuracy, authenticity, and bias
—Dramatize an interview with a famous person from the past
—Debate a current issue
Books
Child of Fire (O'Dell, 1974)
Family Pictures (Lomas Garza, 1990)
And Now Miguel (Krumgold, 1953)
Out of the Earth I Sing (Lewis, 1968)
Sing Down the Moon (O'Dell, 1970)

Fine Arts
Art
—Make masks
—Make a mural of desert life
Music and Dance
—Listen to music and folk songs of various cultures
—Learn dances from various cultures
Books
Annie and the Old One (Miles, 1971)
A Cry from the Earth (Bierhorst, 1979)
They Put on Masks (Baylor, 1974)
The Tree Stands Shining (Jones, 1971)

Geography
Desert
—Build an erosion table
—Make a model
—Observe and record effects of weather on terrain
Books
Desert Voices (Baylor, 1981)
Eight Words for Thirsty (Sigford, 1978)
The Gentle Desert (Pringle, 1977)

Literature
Literature
Traditional
Poetry/Verse
—Learn a story and tell it to others
—Read aloud
—Write poems and verses
Books
And It Is Still That Way (Baylor, 1976)
Hawk, I'm Your Brother (Baylor, 1976)
The Sacred Path (Bierhorst, 1983)
The Whispering Wind (Allen, 1972)

Other Cultures
—Research and report on Native American number systems
—Learn to count in Spanish
Charts and Maps
—Make maps of the region
—Make imaginary treasure maps with a secret code
Books
From Ungskah I to Quail IQ (Corcas, 1965)
Secret Codes and Ciphers (Kohn, 1968)

Mathematics

Science
Geology and Mining
—Collect, identify, and classify rocks, minerals, and precious metals
—Report findings
—Set up sluice box to try gold mining
Ecology
Animals
Plants
Humans
—Write a script and videotape programs on ecology
—Interview personified plants and animals about problems/solutions
Books
Cactus Hotel (Guiberson, 1991)
Desert Giant (Bash, 1989)
The Desert Is Theirs (Baylor, 1975)
The Earth Is Sore (Amon, 1981)

235

Response-Centered, Integrated Teaching with Literature

From this experience with my first class, I learned that the power of literature is to capture the imagination for a moment, to take it where it's never been before—to other times and places and even other worlds. Through experiencing literature, we can empathize with others and discover their needs and pleasures, joys and fears. And above all, through literature, we can feel, see, and understand things that would otherwise have remained unknown—about ourselves and the world.

In the classroom, literature extends students' interests and encourages listening, thinking, talking, responding, and sharing. Literature also extends students' independent reading on a wide variety of subjects of interest to them. Finally, literature extends language learning across the curriculum, integrating the language arts with the content areas.

To establish a student- and response-centered program and make the most of children's literature, follow the content and teaching strategies described in the following sections.

Choosing Children's Books

WWW

An excellent starting place for gathering resources is *The Children's Literature Web Guide* at **www.ucalgary.ca/ ~dkbrown/index.html**.

School librarians are willing to help teachers select books for their classrooms. Other ways of finding out about and choosing books are through journals, book lists, and specialized bibliographies, such as those selectively listed here:

- *Professional Journals:* Journals with websites, such as the following, include reviews of new books and articles about children's literature:

  Book Links: Connecting Books, Librarians, and Classrooms   www.ala.org
  Book List   www.ala.org
  Bulletin for the Center for Children's Books   www.ala.org
  Horn Book Magazine   www.hbook.com
  Language Arts   www.ncte.org
  The Reading Teacher   www.reading.org
  School Library Journal   www.sli.com

- *Bibliographies:* Resources like these can help in selecting children's literature:

  A to Zoo: Subject Access to Children's Picture Books (Lima & Lima, 2001)
  Adventuring with Books: A Booklist for Pre-K–Grade 6 (McClure & Kristo, 2002)
  Best Books for Children: Preschool through Grade 6 (Gillespie, 2001)
  Children's Books in Print (Bowker, annually)
  The Children's Catalog (Price & Yaakov, 2001)

- *Awards:* Many awards are also given to children's books, which may guide your choices. For example, to honor the most distinguished contributions of literature for children published in the United States each year, the American Library Association gives the Caldecott Medal to the illustrator of the best picture book and the Newbery Medal to the author of the best text.

While not everyone agrees on every book, a group of children's literature experts (Breen, Fader, Odean, & Sutherland, 2000) identified the 100 books they considered most significant in shaping the twentieth century, according to these criteria:

> We decided our list should include books with literary and artistic merit, as well as books that are perennially popular with young readers, books that have blazed new trails, and books that have exerted a lasting influence on the world of children's book publishers. (p. 50)

See the marginal note for the 23 books these experts selected unanimously.

Genres of Children's Literature

Teachers should be familiar with various types or categories of children's literature, which are *genres*. The following list identifies genres of children's literature along with examples of picture books for younger children and chapter books for older children (presented in that order):

- **Poetry:** Works of carefully chosen, condensed, and artfully arranged language that looks selectively at the world in unique and unusual ways:

  Read-Aloud Rhymes for the Very Young (Prelutsky, 1986)
  A Light in the Attic (Silverstein, 1981)
  Where the Sidewalk Ends (Silverstein, 1986)

- **Picture Books:** Works in which illustrations and text combine equally to tell a story:

  Tar Beach (Ringgold, 1992)
  Grandfather's Journey (Say, 1994)

- **Traditional Literature:** Stories that have been told for many years, across many cultures, first orally and then written down:

  Lon Po Po: A Red Riding Hood Tale from China (Young, 1990)
  The People Could Fly: American Black Folktales (Hamilton, 1993)

- **Fantasy:** Stories told in the real or an unreal world, with characters or events that probably don't really exist and events that may depend on magic or the supernatural:

  The Stinky Cheese Man and Other Fairly Stupid Tales (Scieszka, 1993)
  Harry Potter and the Sorcerer's Stone (Rowling, 1997)

- **Science Fiction:** Stories that explore the possibilities of science in our lives through invention or extension of the laws of nature:

  Tuesday (Weisner, 1992)
  The Giver (Lowry, 1990)

See the companion book to this text, *Schoolyear Activities Planner*, which includes lists of all the Caldecott and Newbery Medal winners and honor books.

GREAT BOOKS FOR CHILDREN

Books That Have Shaped the Twentieth Century

Tuck Everlasting (Babbitt, 1975); *Madeline* (Bemelmans, 1976); *Are You There, God? It's Me, Margaret* (Blume, 1981); *The Chocolate War* (Cormier, 1986); *Harriet the Spy* (Fitzhugh, 1964); *Anne Frank: The Diary of a Young Girl* (Frank, 1952); *Lincoln: A Photobiography* (Freedman, 1987); *Julie of the Wolves* (George, 1973); *The Snowy Day* (Keats, 1963); *From the Mixed-Up Files of Mrs. Basil E. Frankweiler* (Konigsburg, 1972); *A Wrinkle in Time* (L'Engle, 1962); *The Lion, the Witch, and the Wardrobe* (Lewis, 1986); *Frog and Toad Are Friends* (Lobel, 1970); *Sarah, Plain and Tall* (MacLachlan, 1985); *Winnie-the-Pooh* (Milne, 1926); *Island of the Blue Dolphins* (O'Dell, 1988); *Bridge to Terabithia* (Paterson, 1977); *The Tale of Peter Rabbit* (Potter, 1902); *Where the Wild Things Are* (Sendak, 1963); *The Cat in the Hat* (Seuss, 1976); *Charlotte's Web* (White, 1952); *Little House in the Big Woods* (Wilder, 1961)

- *Contemporary Realistic Fiction:* Stories of real people, living here and now:

  Smoky Night (Bunting, 1995)
  Maniac Magee (Spinelli, 1991)

- *Historical Fiction:* Stories set in a real time and place in history but with some or all fictional characters:

  Encounter (Yolen, 1992)
  Number the Stars (Lowry, 1990)

- *Biography:* Stories about the lives of real people:

  Duke Ellington (Pinkney & Pinkney, 1999)
  Eleanor Roosevelt: A Life of Discovery (Freedman, 1994)

- *Nonfiction:* Books of information about a variety of topics in the real world:

  Harlem (Myers, 1998)
  The Way Things Work (Macaulay, 1988)

TEACHER RESOURCES

For lists of *Notable Children's Trade Books in the Field of Social Studies* and *Outstanding Science Trade Books* chosen each year, write Children's Book Council, 67 Irving Place, New York, NY, 10003.

Literature Discussions

Teachers also need to provide time and opportunities to talk before, during, and after reading, involving the whole class, small groups, and individual students at various times. Eeds and Wells (1989) and others (Eeds & Peterson, 1991, 1995; Peterson & Eeds, 1990) describe these talks as "grand conversations." These moments are some of the richest times that students have to reflect on their own responses while reading and that teachers have to know more about those responses as a basis for planning further response-centered activities.

Questions: Aesthetic and Efferent

The types of questions teachers ask direct children to take aesthetic or efferent stances toward any text. Ideally, teachers should first direct students to take aesthetic stances toward literature. Think about the analysis of children's response types, described earlier. Their preferred types were aesthetic. They questioned, talked about favorite parts, hypothesized, and made associations. Out of these broad, rich, aesthetic responses (which were focused on the development of personal meaning), more efferent concerns will emerge, such as developing explanations or attending to print and language, content, and analysis (Cox, 2002).

Focus first on aesthetic questions and prompts. Begin with an open question or prompt that has many possible responses:

See also the list of aesthetic and efferent questions and prompts in Chapter 5, Listening and Talking.

1. *Questioning*
   - What did you think of the story?
   - Tell anything you want about the story.

Many times, children will state a preference, such as "I liked it," "I didn't like it," or "It was okay." Follow up on this response by asking the children to tell why they did or didn't like the story. Next, ask questions or prompts that are based on the children's comments or that invite them to respond first aesthetically and then more efferently. The following questions and prompts are based on characteristic responses of children described in the earlier section on aesthetic and efferent stances:

2. *Focusing on a part*
   - What was your favorite part of the story? Tell about it.

3. *Making associations*
   - Has anything like this happened to you? Tell about it.
   - Have you ever had feelings like a character in the story? Tell about them.
   - Does this story remind you of any other stories? Tell about them.

4. *Hypothesizing*
   - Was there anything in the story you wondered about? Tell about it.
   - Did something puzzle you? Tell about it.
   - What else do you think might happen?
   - Is there anything you would change in the story? What? How?

5. *Explaining*
   - Explain a character's actions.
   - What did the author mean by _____ ?

6. *Considering print and language*
   - What does this letter or word say? What does it mean? How is it used in the story?
   - Tell about how the author used language: words, sentences, rhyming patterns, and so on.

7. *Considering content*
   - What happened in the story? Tell the order of the story's events.
   - What happened in the beginning, the middle, and the end?
   - What was the main idea of the story?

8. *Performing*
   - If you were a character in the story, what would you say? Show how you would act.
   - If you could talk to a character in the story, what would you say?
   - What sounds would you hear in the story?

9. *Analyzing*
   - Is the story true (factual) or made up (fiction)?
   - Compare and contrast this story to other stories.
   - What did you think of how the story was written or illustrated?

Questions: Literary Elements

After students have had the opportunity to fully experience reading literature by responding aesthetically, teachers can also provide the opportunity to take a more critical, analytical approach. They can use efferent questions and prompts that emerge from responses to aesthetic questions and prompts (as just discussed). A framework for the critical analysis of a text can be developed by examining its literary elements.

Sloan (1984) suggests questions that teachers can use to guide children to better understanding the elements and structure of literature: namely, the story world and literary elements of setting and plot, characters, point of view, mood and theme, and finally, how these interrelate to create specific story structures:

1. *Story World*
   - What signs indicate whether a story will be more fanciful than realistic: talking animals? exaggeration? strange, improbable situations, characters, or settings? beginning with "Once upon a time . . ."?
   - If the story world created by the author is far different from the world we know, how does the author make the story seem possible and believable?

2. *Setting and Plot*
   - Where and when does the story take place? How do you know? If the story took place somewhere else or in a different time, how would it be changed?
   - What incident, problem, conflict, or situation does the author use to get the story started?
   - How is the story told or arranged: chronologically? by individual incidents? through flashbacks? through letters or diary entries?

3. *Characters*
   - Who is the main character in the story? What kind of person is he or she? How do you know?
   - Do any characters change in the course of the story? If so, how? What made them change? Does the change seem believable?

4. *Point of View*
   - Who is telling the story? How does this affect how it's told?
   - If one of the characters is telling the story, how does his or her personality or purpose influence what's told and how?

5. *Mood and Theme*
   - Does the story, as a whole, create a definite mood or feeling? What is the mood? How is it created?
   - What are the main ideas behind the story? How does the author get you to think of them?

6. *Comparison to Other Stories*
   - Even though this story is different in content, is it like any other story you have read or watched? How so?
   - Does the story follow a pattern? If so, what is it?

Literature Circles

Using *literature circles* is one way to organize your teaching with literature. The basic idea behind this approach is that children form small groups to read, discuss, and possibly develop projects related to a single book, author, genre, theme, or combination of these. For example, think back to the Snapshot at the beginning of the chapter. One of the things that happened when I read aloud one of my father's books to the class was that the children formed groups and read books related to *The Mystery of the Haunted Mine* (Shirreffs, 1962). In these groups, or literature circles, some children read other books by my father, some read other mysteries, and some read books related to topics of interest that had developed during our class discussions, especially in connection with the desert of the Southwest United States (which integrated nicely with our study of California history in social studies).

See Chapter 1, Learning and Teaching Language Arts, for the example of Avril Font's class, in which all work is done in small, cooperative groups during workshops throughout the day.

Literature circles have been widely used and written about (Daniels, 2002; Day, Spiegel, McLellan, & Brown, 2002; Harste, Short, & Burke, 1988). Other terms that have been used for the same idea are *literature groups* (Calkins, 1994), *literature study groups* (Eeds & Wells, 1989), and *book clubs* (Raphael, Goatley, McMahon, & Woodman, 1995). While literature circles can take many different forms, they usually share the following characteristics, as described by Daniels (2002):

- Children choose the books they will read.
- Small, temporary groups are formed around these book choices.
- Different groups read different books.
- Groups meet to discuss their reading on a regularly scheduled basis.
- Children write in journals and share these written notes in their groups.
- Topics and questions for discussion come from the children.
- Discussions are open, natural conversations centered around children's responses to, questions about, and personal connections to books.
- The teacher meets with groups on a rotating basis but serves as a facilitator, rather than a group member or instructor.
- Children may assume different roles.

Daniels (2002) has also described six roles that children can take. The teacher may simply note these roles or he or she may want to describe them to students, let each student choose a different role, and integrate the roles into literature circles as a way of organizing the discussions. In addition to these six, you can likely think of other roles:

1. *Discussion Director:* Keeps things moving along
2. *Connector:* Makes connections to personal experiences of other books
3. *Word Wizard:* Notes the author's specific word choices
4. *Illustrator:* Creates an illustration of a significant event in the book
5. *Passage Picker:* Chooses and reads aloud a special passage, explaining why it was picked
6. *Summarizer:* Summarizes the text and the literature circle discussion

Literature circles have been used effectively with children in multicultural classrooms (Samway & Whang, 1996) and with children learning English as a second language. Martinez-Roldan and Lopez-Robertson (2000) reported on

See Paul Boyd-Batstone use literature circles in a Spanish bilingual class.

their use of literature circles in a first-grade bilingual classroom and concluded that "young bilingual children, no matter their linguistic background, are able to have rich discussions if they have regular opportunities to engage with books from a transactional perspective."

The following Teaching Idea describes how Paul Boyd-Batstone put literature circles into action in his class of third-grade native Spanish speakers, some in the very beginning stages of learning to speak English.

For more on using literature with second-language learners, see the book that Paul and I co-authored, *Crossroads: Literature and Language in Culturally and Linguistically Diverse Classrooms* (Cox & Boyd-Batstone, 1997).

ELL

This Teaching Idea is appropriate for ELL students for these reasons:

- It uses context-embedded instruction.
- It taps into students' ideas and prior experiences.
- Reading is done in groups with peer support.
- The teacher reads aloud.
- Group discussion generates a cluster to help organization for writing.
- Poetry, metaphor, music, and language play are all used.
- Students take charge of their own projects.

TEACHING IDEA

Literature Circles with English Language Learners

Here's an example of how Paul Boyd-Batstone organized literature circles when teaching a bilingual Spanish third-grade class of English language learners. (This idea could be used with any class, however.) Paul explains that this idea grew out of his desire to structure the classroom for listening and responding to students' thoughts and ideas, creating a rich environment for what second-language theorist James Cummins (1989) calls *context-embedded instruction*. Incidentally, Paul sees strong connections between Cummins's concept and Rosenblatt's (1938/1978) transactional theory, which affirms the importance of the reader and the ideas and experiences they bring to the classroom (Cox & Boyd-Batstone, 1997).

Here are the steps Paul follows in organizing literature circles, how he helps each circle make an action plan based on their responses to the book, and how he schedules and assesses each child's progress in a literature circle. The examples shown are from literature circles organized around books about the tropical rainforest.

Steps

1. *Selection:* Students select what they want to read and form literature groups around the selected pieces: books about the tropical rainforest.

English language learners in Paul Boyd-Batstone's bilingual class actively engaged in experiences with literature during a literature circle.

2. *Reading:* Students spend the first week reading and rereading their books reading themselves (individually, in pairs, and in choral reading), by listening to the teacher read aloud, or by reading along with a taped version.

3. *Conferences:* Each group meets with the teacher to discuss the literature, focusing on that part of the story that gripped them. This is where the teacher listens for the background knowledge and prior experiences that the students bring to the text. Based on that point of contact between the text and the students' lives, writing is developed in the form of an essay, a poem, a song, or a story.

4. *Action Plan:* Figure 7.3, the Literature Circle Action Plan, shows a cluster of ideas generated in a literature circle about the book *The Great Kapok Tree* (Cherry, 1990).

5. *Writing:* Figure 7.4 (p. 244) shows the writing part of the plan, which is based on clustering students' responses to a book on a piece of chartpaper. Then they talk together and identify themes, circling the sentences that express similar

Figure 7.3 Literature Circle Action Plan for *The Great Kapok Tree*

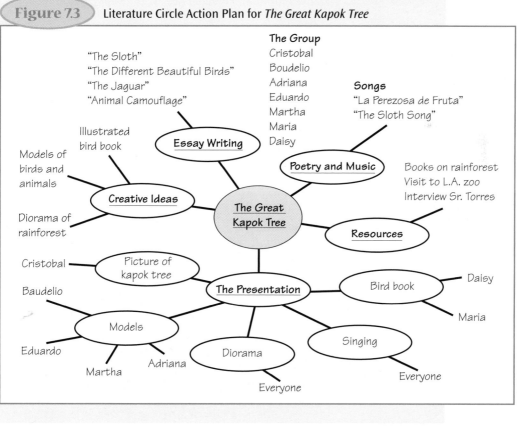

(continued)

Response-Centered, Integrated Teaching with Literature

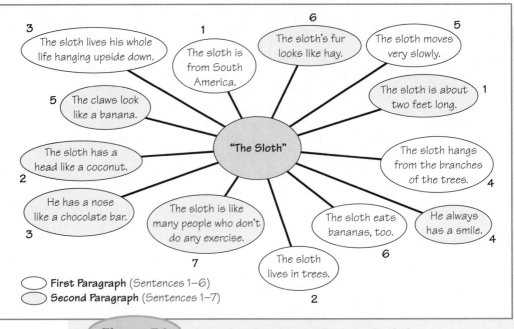

The sloth lives his whole life hanging upside down. 3

The sloth is from South America. 1

The sloth's fur looks like hay. 6

The sloth moves very slowly. 5

The claws look like a banana. 5

The sloth is about two feet long. 1

The sloth has a head like a coconut. 2

"The Sloth"

The sloth hangs from the branches of the trees. 4

He has a nose like a chocolate bar. 3

The sloth is like many people who don't do any exercise. 7

The sloth eats bananas, too. 6

He always has a smile. 4

The sloth lives in trees. 2

First Paragraph (Sentences 1–6)
Second Paragraph (Sentences 1–7)

Figure 7.4   Cluster for a Two-Paragraph Essay: *The Sloth*

Examples of Students' Writing

Story
Report
Biography
Script
Interview
Illustrated book

Examples of Students' Creative Ideas

Play
Mural or poster
Game
Model or diorama
Puppet show
Video

ideas with colored markers. (Usually, more than one theme emerges from their responses.) Each color identifies sentences that will go in the same paragraph. The students talk about the order of the sentences within each color code and use the color-coded, clustered ideas as an organizer for writing a first draft. Each student takes his or her work to another student to be edited, after which both editor and writer meet with the teacher for the final edit. The students finish by writing final drafts of their two-paragraph essays (see Figure 7.5). Three to four such essays are usually generated this way in each literature circle.

6. *Creative Ideas:* As the teacher conferences with a group to talk about the story, ideas begin to germinate—the better the story, the richer the sharing of ideas. During this brainstorming, ideas rarely come to light in sequential order. For example, a group might be discussing some aspect of a character, when suddenly a student will jump up

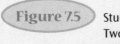

Figure 7.5   Student's Two-Paragraph Essay

The Sloth

The Sloth is from South America. The sloth live in trees. The sloth lives his whole life hanging up-side-down. The sloth hangs by the braches of the trees. The sloth moves verry slow. The sloth eats bananas too. The sloth is about two feet long. The sloth has a head like a coconut. He has a nose like a chocolate bear. He always has asmiel. The sloth's fur looks like hays deer's eyes. The Sloth is in people who don't do eny exercise.

and say, "Hey! Why don't we put on a puppet show?" The teacher can affirm the student's thinking by incorporating it into the literature action plan on the spot. The creative ideas section is restricted only by the group's imagination of some project related to the story. The responsibility to produce the project, however, falls on the students' shoulders: how to make it, obtain the materials, and assign various tasks to complete the project. Some examples are making an illustrated book, a mural, a model, or a diorama or even putting on a play. Figure 7.6 shows the creative project completed by Cristobal, a student with learning disabilities.

7. *Poetry and Songs:* Poetry and songs focus students' attention on the cognitively demanding features of language arts: metaphor, rhyme, meter, melody, and language play. Given their importance, students are encouraged to find or compose poetry and music related to the story. They write the selected or composed poetry or music on chartpaper and teach it to the whole class.

For example, the children in the literature circle reading *The Great Kapok Tree* wrote two songs about one of their favorite animals: the tree sloth. They had already done a cluster of ideas about the sloth during a discussion with Paul, and he had recorded these ideas on a piece of chartpaper as a basis for writing a two-paragraph essay (see Figure 7.4). During the discussion, the students compared the body parts of the sloth to fruits found in the rainforest, and these metaphorical images led to writing one of the songs, "La Perezosa de Fruta" ("The Fruit Sloth"). It was written first in Spanish and then in English and put to music. Both songs were performed by all the students in the literature circle during the presentation. They also made a "fruit sloth" out of foods found in the tropical rainforest, which they later ate.

Here is the English version of the song:

The Fruit Sloth
The fruit sloth, the fruit sloth.
It has the head of a coconut
that can never, ever be opened.

The fruit sloth, the fruit sloth
has the body of a watermelon
just like a ripe melon.

The fruit sloth, the fruit sloth
has a chocolate nose
that I would love to eat.

(Chorus)
The fruit sloth
has a body of fruit
the entire body of fruit
from the tropical rainforest.
Cha, cha, cha.

In the *Schoolyear Activities Planner* that accompanies this text, see the month of May for ideas for a story dramatization of *The Great Kapok Tree* and more teaching ideas, books, and resources.

Examples of Students' Poetry and Songs

Similes and metaphors
Free verse
Haiku
Concrete poetry
New version of an old song
New song put to an old tune

Figure 7.6   Cristobal's Creative Idea

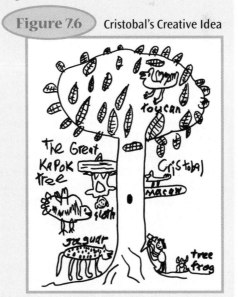

(continued)

The children in one literature circle wrote and performed English and Spanish versions about one of their favorite animals in The Great Kapok Tree.

WWW

For resources related to rainforests and *The Great Kapok Tree*, go to **www.sdcoe.K12.ca. us/score/kapok/kapoktg.htm**.

Examples of Students' Presentations to Class

Perform the play.
Explain the mural or poster.
Recite the poem.
Sing and/or play the song.
Show how to play the game.
Explain the model or diorama.
Perform the puppet show.
Show the filmstrip or video.

2.4
2.5

See the Self-Assessment Form for Individual Work (p. 57) and the Peer-Assessment Form for Group Work (p. 58).

SCAFFOLDING

A student with learning disabilities can fully participate in a literature circle with these special adaptations:

• The teacher takes dictation for the first part of writing.
• Another student "buddy" assists with the completion of writing.
• The teacher provides frames for writing.

8. *Resources:* Each group identifies the resources they need to put their plan into action: books related to the theme or that will help them with creative ideas or presentations, materials for their projects, field trips, and people with special knowledge they can interview or ask for information. The groups can continue to add to their lists of resources as they develop their plans.

9. *Presentation:* The culmination of the literature circle is a demonstration of the learning. Parents are invited to this presentation. Each student reads a selection of his or her writing and demonstrates creative idea projects, and they all teach the whole group their poetry and songs. At this point, the students are the experts in the given area of study, so time is also set aside for questions and answers about their work. Students write an assessment of their group participation, what they have learned, and what improvements they would suggest for the next cycle.

Schedule

Here's a possible daily and weekly schedule for using literature action plans and literature circles:

Daily	*Weekly*		*Focus*
1–2 periods	M	10:30–12:00, 1:00–2:00	Initiating writing
	Tu	10:30–12:00	Writing development
60–90 minutes each	W	10:30–12:00	Initiating projects
	Th	10:30–12:00	Project development
90–150 minutes total	F	10:30–12:00, 1:00–2:00	Closure to projects

The strength of using literature circles for organizing literature-based language arts instruction is that by listening and responding to students' thoughts, context-embedded instruction occurs naturally. The role of the teacher changes from being the sole resource of knowledge to being a co-creator with students. Thus, the responsibility for learning is shared, rather than imposed. And while working with students on a literature action plan, the teacher learns that they are the classroom's greatest resource.

The Literature Circle Plan and Progress Sheet shown in Assessment Toolbox 7.1 can be used with the approach described in this Teaching Idea for literature circles with English language learners. This tool has multiple functions: It can be used by the student to plan individual activities for the literature circle or

7.1 Literature Circle Plan and Progress Sheet

The progress sheet shown here has been completed for Cristobal, a student with learning disabilities. He was able to participate fully in the literature circle once adaptations were made for his special needs. For example, he joined other students in the group discussion and idea cluster, but to write the subsequent two-paragraph essay, he needed the help of another student and the teacher, who took down dictation for the first part. The teacher also provided a frame for Cristobal to use in making his own copy of one of the songs, but he worked in the same group as the other students as they dictated the second song to the teacher. Cristobal independently completed his creative idea of a picture of the kapok tree, which included writing labels of the animals' names. He then shared his picture in the group presentation and sang the two songs with his classmates. This progress sheet monitors Cristobal's learning activities, noting where he needed adaptations to participate and where he was able to complete tasks similarly to other students.

Name ___Cristobal_____   Book _____The Great Kapok Tree_____

My Literature Plan and Progress Sheet

Directions: Check off each step after you have completed it.

Step	**Comments**
Writing: List titles.	
☑ 1. The Sloth	Did with help of another student.
☑ 2. The Jaguar	Teacher took dictation for first part.
Creative Ideas: List ideas.	
☑ 1. Drew picture of The Great Kapok Tree.	Completed independently; used book as resource; drew animals and wrote title on picture.
☑ 2. Labeled animals in picture.	Completed independently.
Poetry and Songs: List titles.	
☑ 1. La Parezosa de Fruta	Used frame to make own copy.
☑ 2. The Sloth Song	Worked in groups and teacher took dictation.
Presentation: Describe responsibilities.	
☑ 1. Shared picture and read labels of animal names.	
☑ 2. Sang two songs with group.	

---

with other students and the teacher. It can also be used to monitor each student's progress and for a final, summative evaluation of his or her activities. However it's used, the form should be attached to the cover of a folder in which all work related to the literature circle is kept. The teacher should review the sheet to monitor progress and to discuss further planning with each child and the group.

All of Paul's students were native Spanish speakers learning English as a second language. In addition, Paul's student Cristobal had an identified learning disability. You saw Cristobal's creative idea in Figure 7.6, where he was able to draw his response to the book *The Great Kapok Tree* and add labels with help from Paul. This was a modification of the response option of writing in a response journal or doing another type of writing. Paul also had students who were struggling with reading and writing in both Spanish and English. The box on page 249 summarizes how the use of literature circles helped all these groups of students.

Literature Focus Units

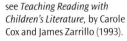

TEACHER RESOURCES

For more on literature units, see *Teaching Reading with Children's Literature*, by Carole Cox and James Zarrillo (1993).

Using *literature focus units* is another way to organize for teaching with literature. A literature focus unit can be organized around a core book, an author, a genre, or a common theme for the purpose of not only experiencing and enjoying literature but for integrating multiple language and literacy experiences. The result can be a "ripple effect" of student ideas and experiences that spreads across many areas of the curriculum, as you saw in the Snapshot at the beginning of the chapter. That particular experience, which occurred during my first year of teaching, actually began with a core book, *The Mystery of the Haunted Mine* (Shireffs, 1962), which happened to be written by my father. My students noticed his name while looking at a book order form. We ordered multiple copies and were off on a journey of discovery about the desert region of the Southwest United States. That experience blended aspects of core book, author, and genre literature focus units, as well as thematic, integrated, literature-based teaching.

Many literature focus units will evolve this way, generating their own "ripple effects." But to get started using literature focus units, begin to plan using any of three popular approaches: core book units, author units, and genre units. Table 7.1 (p. 250) gives some examples of children's literature to use for these three types of units with children at different grade levels.

Core Book Units

Core book units focus on single books. James Zarrillo's research on teachers using the core book model (Zarrillo, 1989; Zarrillo & Cox, 1992) found the following characteristics of effective teaching with core books:

1. Teachers built teaching around students' responses.
2. The teacher loved the book, and his or her interest and enthusiasm were communicated to students.

English Language Learners, Students with Disabilities, and Struggling Readers and Writers through Literature Circles

Literature circles can be used to help students who are learning English as a second language, students with disabilities, and struggling readers and writers, as outlined here:

English Language Learners

1. The students and teacher listen and respond to other students' ideas, which meets the goal of context-embedded instruction (Cummins, 1989).
2. Creating a literature circle action plan establishes a collaborative atmosphere that honors all students' voices.
3. Students' prior knowledge and experience are tapped, employing a key strategy in learning a second language.
4. Reading is done with the peer support of other students in the literature circle.
5. The teacher or another student may record the information from a discussion on a chart with a graphic organizer to provide visual support for those learning English.
6. Music, rhyme, poetry, metaphor, and language play can all be used and are all important genres with which to learn a second language.

Students with Disabilities

1. Students are fully included in the group discussion and creation of projects.
2. Each child's creative project varies according to his or her interests and abilities.
3. Group projects such as drama and puppetry allow students with disabilities to participate in specific roles (such as acting out part of the story, if reading and writing are difficult).
4. A student "buddy" may assist with the completion of writing.
5. Students are able to present their projects along with all the other students in the class.
6. The teacher may provide writing frames for support.

Struggling Readers and Writers

1. The teacher may read aloud to the group, or an individual in a literature circle may read aloud.
2. The teacher or another student records discussion ideas on chartpaper in a cluster, which the teacher color codes to identify leading sentences and describing sentences as a guide for students to later write two-paragraph essays.
3. The teacher may take dictation for the first part of a writing activity.
4. Students take charge of their own projects with the support of both the teacher and their peers in the literature circle.
5. Assessment is individualized and targets each child's specific strengths and needs so as to plan for further instruction.

Table 7.1 Ideas for Three Types of Literature Units

Primary Grades (K–2)	Middle Grades (3–4)	Upper Grades (5–6)
Core Book		
Abuela (Dorros, 1991)	*Charlotte's Web* (White, 1952)	*Catherine, Called Birdy* (Cushman, 1995)
Grandfather's Journey (Say, 1994)	*Number the Stars* (Lowry, 1990)	*The Giver* (Lowry, 1994)
Miss Rumphius (Cooney, 1982)	*Sarah, Plain and Tall* (MacLachlan, 1985)	*Joyful Noise* (Fleischman, 1989)
Tar Beach (Ringgold, 1992)	*Tales of a Fourth-Grade Nothing* (Blume, 1976)	*Julie of the Wolves* (George, 1973)
The Very Hungry Caterpillar (Carle, 1969)	*The Way Things Work* (Macaulay, 1988)	*The Watsons Go to Birmingham— 1963* (Curtis, 1996)
Author		
Marcia Brown	Judy Blume	Russell Freedman
Eric Carle	Eve Bunting	Virginia Hamilton
Donald Crews	Beverly Cleary	Katherine Paterson
Patricia Pollaco	C. S. Lewis	Gary Soto
Allen Say	Lois Lowry	Laurence Yep
	Andrea Davis Pinkney and Brian Pinkney	
Genre		
Alphabet books	Humorous fiction	Mystery
Animal stories	Fairytales	Adventure
Cumulative tales	Nonfiction	Science fiction
Pattern books	Fantasy	Biographies
"Tall tales"	Historical fiction	Poetry

3. Core books were presented dramatically. Teachers read with flourish or presented books through reader's theater, using audiotaped versions read by professional actors, or through film or video. Children eagerly looked forward to each new reading.
4. Children could read core books independently. Those who couldn't wait for the inclass reading could read ahead and then listen to or reread chapters; they could also read other books by the same author or books on related topics. Teachers did not try to hold anyone back from reading.

Keep in mind these characteristics of effective teaching with core books as you read the following Snapshot, which describes a core book unit.

Core Book Unit on
Treasure Island

As a teacher of average- to high-achieving fourth-grade students, Margaret Mattson felt that using basal readers as the core of her reading program was inadequate: "Students never really got into the stories as one does with a really good book. The only rationale for using a certain story was to teach a certain skill. Although students were able to score well on skills tests after completing the prescribed activities, I never felt that they had learned anything that they actually integrated into their own personal reading processes. Rather, they learned the format, to give the expected answers. It is a superficial type of learning."

At the same time Margaret was struggling with the value of basal readers, she was aware that her students were not at all familiar with classic books. In addressing these two concerns, she decided not to use a basal reader but to teach reading through a core book unit on Robert Louis Stevenson's (1947) classic *Treasure Island*. Here's how she did it:

- *Selecting the Book:* Margaret chose *Treasure Island* because she loved it, none of her students had read it, and she felt a fantastic classroom environment could be created around it: pirates, mysterious maps, hidden treasure, and so on. She used PTA funds to order paperback copies for all students from a book club.

- *Planning the Unit:* Margaret tried to be discriminating. "I didn't want to dissect the book until its magic was gone, but I wanted it to be a productive learning experience." In addition to encouraging students to respond aesthetically, she felt this book would be a good one to discuss characterization, plot and story structure, setting, and point of view in literature.

- *Scheduling Reading and Activities:* Reading and activities were conducted during at least 1-hour blocks of time, three times a week. Students were also given 30 to 60 minutes a day to read the book; any unfinished reading was done at home. Impromptu sessions were also held as students' interest grew or when discussions or activities took longer than expected. The general schedule was as follows:

Daily	Students read book in class Unfinished reading at home	30–60 minutes
Weekly (3 times)	Whole-class and group work	60–90 minutes
As needed	Impromptu sessions, depending on interest or more time needed	30–60 minutes

- *Organizing Groups:* Students worked together in groups, and the groups changed for different activities.

Treasure Island was first published in installments entitled "The Sea Cook" in *Young Folks* magazine; it appeared in book form in 1883.

- *Creating a Classroom Environment:* Students drew a large map of Treasure Island on brown wrapping paper so it looked ancient. This map was displayed on one wall, a colorful paper parrot hung from the ceiling, and a bulletin board was covered with a labeled cross-section of a sailing ship, complete with a Jolly Roger. Each child had a paperback copy of the book.

- *Initiating the Unit:* Margaret told students that Robert Louis Stevenson was a sickly person who felt the function of literature was to supply adventure to people who lead unexciting lives. She asked them to respond to that idea. She also told them that *Treasure Island* was the outcome of his adding a story to a map of an imaginary island drawn by his 12-year-old stepson. Stevenson entertained the boy and himself with stories of pirates and buried gold.

Here's a day-by-day description of what Margaret and her students did during the core book unit for *Treasure Island:*

Day 1. Reading Aloud and Talking Together

Margaret read the first 19 pages aloud. The story begins with a flashback and sets the mood with a vivid description of Billy Bones:

> I remember him as if it were yesterday, as he came plodding to the inn door, his sea chest following behind him in a handbarrow; a tall, strong, heavy, nutbrown man; his tarry pigtail falling over the shoulders of his soiled blue coat; his hands ragged and scarred, with black, broken nails, and the saber-cut across one cheek a dirty, livid white.

Margaret stopped and asked students what they thought about the story so far. They talked about the description of Billy Bones. One student remarked that she knew exactly what he looked like because she had seen the movie. This led to an interesting discussion about adapting books into movies and selecting actors to play the roles. Students talked about their feelings about Billy Bones and how the author created those feelings. They drew portraits of Billy Bones.

The only vocabulary Margaret talked about before reading were the words used on the labeled cross-section of the ship and a chart of nautical and geographical terms, which students added to throughout the unit. Vocabulary words were talked about after students read.

Reading for next day: The rest of Part I, "The Old Buccaneer," Chapters 1–4.

Day 2. Making Treasure Maps and Writing Summaries in Groups

Each group made a token treasure out of cardboard and hid it on the schoolgrounds; then they created maps to guide treasure seekers in other groups. Compasses and yellowed paper added authenticity. As Margaret had hoped, doing these activities helped students get into the mood of the book. On their maps, they referred to Margaret as "One-Eyed Mattson" and the teacher next door as "Peg-Leg McGraw." Groups traded maps and went looking for treasure tokens. When the tokens were found, students traded them for real treasure: candy coins covered in gold foil.

Back in their groups, students talked together about the first four chapters and wrote summaries; then all the groups talked about the story. Margaret noted, "This was a clarifying experience for them and me. They really interacted and challenged each other. I find group activities to be very productive as it forces students to form an opinion and defend it."

Reading for next day: Part II, "The Sea Cook," Chapters 7–9.

Day 3. Recognizing and Discussing the Technique of Foreshadowing in Literature

The class talked about what they'd read and discussed foreshadowing (i.e., how authors give clues of what is to come) and how Stevenson used it.

Reading for next day: Part II, Chapters 10–12.

Day 4. Dramatizing a Scene from the Story

Groups picked scenes and planned dramatizations of them. Margaret noticed, "The room buzzed with the creative noise of students who were involved and excited about what they were doing, and a much deeper analysis of the story was occurring than any workbook or teacher's guide could inspire. One student said, 'Long John oughta be kind of like two different people, you know? All friendly and polite around the Captain but real mean and bragging when he's not.'" That student's group dramatized the scene with a trembling Jim hiding in the apple barrel while a freckle-faced Long John Silver boasted of his infamous past.

See Chapter 5, Listening and Talking, for how to adapt a story for dramatization.

Students were very excited after their dramatizations and began to plan a play based on the whole story, which they wanted to perform on stage for the rest of the school.

Reading for next day: Part III, "My Shore Adventure," Chapters 13–15.

Day 5. Painting and Writing Descriptions

Margaret reread the description of the island and asked students to close their eyes and imagine that they could really see it. They used watercolors to paint pictures of what they saw in their minds and wrote descriptions, as well.

Day 6. Discussing Cliffhangers

Margaret asked the children how many kept reading after Chapter 14, which ends in a cliffhanger. Many hands shot up, so she asked, "Why? Isn't the end of the chapter a good place to stop?" They discussed how a cliffhanger makes you want to keep reading and how this writing technique is used elsewhere in the book, in other books they've read, and in film and television.

Reading for next day: Part IV, "The Stockade," Chapters 16–18.

Day 7. Discussing and Using Point of View in Writing

The three chapters the class read are told from the Dr. Lively's point of view, rather than Jim Hawkins's. Groups talked about why Stevenson might have changed the point of view in the middle of the story. The whole class talked about advantages and disadvantages of first-person, omniscient, limited-omniscient, and objective points of view.

Students rewrote an episode in the book from a different point of view. One student wrote a journal for Long John Silver, complete with a tattered paper cover and blots of red ink (blood stains?) on the pages. Part of an entry reads:

> My Journal, by Long John Silver
> Today me and my friends plotted to take over the Hispanola. But I said we're going to let them find the treasure and get it on board and wait till we're halfway back to England. Then we would take over. I was so happy just thinking how rich I was going to be.

Reading next day: Part IV, Chapters 19–21.

Day 8. Student-Selected Group Projects

Each group brainstormed ideas for a project and started it. Group 1 decided to make a papier-mâché model of the island, and group 2 created a board game based on the book. Group 3 wrote an etiquette book for pirates, and group 4 taped an interview with Long John Silver.

Reading next day: Part V, "My Sea Adventure."

Day 9. Discussing Jim's Character

Students discussed Jim's character in their groups: What kind of person was he? If he were transplanted to a different setting, like our classroom, what kinds of problems might he have? If we were transplanted to the setting of *Treasure Island*, what kind of problems might we have? Students also continued work on their projects.

Reading next day: Part VI, "Captain Silver."

Day 10. Group Projects

With the book finished, groups concentrated on their projects. They went back and mined the story for ideas:

Group 1: Island model: They skimmed the story for descriptions of the island, made a list of ideas, talked about them, and decided how their model would look.

Group 2: Game: They sequenced events in the story to lay out the game board.

Group 3: Etiquette book: They reread about pirates' actions and used informational books about real pirates and privateers to create a spoof, with chapters like "What to Do If You Receive the Black Spot."

Group 4: Interview with Long John Silver: They spent a lot of time rereading and talking about his complex character in preparation for writing the interview.

Days 11–15. Group Projects and Discussions

The groups continued to work on their projects, talk about the story, and respond to it. Margaret said they couldn't be stopped. Here are some of the things they did:

> *Writing:* Wrote accounts of the adventure for a Bristol newspaper, secret codes, journals for various characters, and sequels about another trip to the island to recover the remaining treasure. Students also adopted many of Stevenson's conventions in their writing.

> *Artmaking:* Made "Wanted" posters for pirates, designed book jackets for the story, and drew illustrations of unillustrated scenes.

> *Dramatization and media*: Added costumes and replayed the scenes they had created, dressed as pirates and had a pirate party; watched the Disney movie *Treasure Island* and acted like pirates; and ate duff (a dessert mentioned in the book; see the recipe in the adjacent note).

Margaret is enthusiastic about teaching with literature because of the excitement and enthusiasm it generates, because she is able to teach all the language arts as an integrated whole, and because many of the skills associated with reading or critical analysis of literature occur naturally. In the *Treasure Island* core book unit, students learned new words, looked at idioms and figures of speech in context, identified and understood literary elements, and recognized and appreciated elements of style. After completing this unit, students formed literature circles, each of which chose a new book to read and explore.

By tradition, duff was not properly cooked until it could be dropped from the cross-gallant crosstrees, the highest point on the ship, and not break.

A Recipe for Duff
Beat: 2 eggs well
Add & blend:
1 cup brown sugar
1 1/2 cup raisins
1/3 cup shortening
Sift & add:
1 cup flour
1/2 teaspoon salt
1 teaspoon baking soda

Pour mixture into well-greased 1-quart mold (1-pound coffee can is ideal). Cover pudding with waxed paper and then cover can with double layer of aluminum foil, tied on tightly with string to prevent water from seeping in. Place can in large pot of boiling water, which should come 3/4 of the way up the side of the can. Cover pot loosely and boil for 3 1/3 to 4 hours, adding more water as needed. Serve warm with whipped cream.

Author Units

In an *author unit,* the unifying element is the author. The teacher reads aloud books by a single author, and students work together in groups and read books of their own choice independently. In picking an author, the teacher should choose one who has written a substantial number of books appropriate for the grade and of interest to many students.

WWW

To find information for author units, go to *Ask the Author* at **www.pl.sils.umich.edu/youth/AskAuthor/**.

TEACHING IDEA

Author Unit on Eric Carle

Eric Carle would be a good choice for a 1- to 2-week author unit in the primary grades. He's written many books, including predictable pattern books and books on topics like insects and animals, which lend themselves to cross-curricular activities. Here are some ideas:

Books

The Grouchy Ladybug (1977)   *The Very Lonely Firefly* (1995)
The Very Busy Spider (1984)   *The Very Quiet Cricket* (1990)
The Very Hungry Caterpillar (1969)

Resources

- Kit to hatch butterfly eggs in the classroom
- Crickets in a cage
- Chart of names of days of week
- "Big book" versions of Eric Carle's books
- Recordings of the books
- Food from *The Very Hungry Caterpillar*
- Collage materials: paint, wrapping paper, tissue paper, yarn, fabric

Response Options

- Draw and write anything they want about the stories.
- Make collages using Eric Carle's illustrating style.
- Following the pattern of *The Very Hungry Caterpillar*, make a "big book" called *The Very Hungry Class*, with pages for all the children to draw or write what they would eat, on what day of the week, and so on.
- Act like a grouchy ladybug, a busy spider, a quiet cricket, and the like.
- Make a story map of *The Grouchy Ladybug*.
- Throw a "Hungry Caterpillar" party with food from the book; write a language experience story about it.

Genre Units

A type of children's literature can be used as the basis of a *genre unit*—for example, traditional literature, poetry, picture books, fantasy, science fiction, contemporary realistic fiction, historical fiction, biography, or nonfiction. Again, teachers choose and read aloud good examples of the genre and encourage children to form literature circles to read and respond through projects and to continue self-selected reading.

Zarrillo (1989) uses the example of a genre unit on fairytales. All students listened to the same 10 stories read aloud and talked, wrote, drew, painted, or acted in response to them. The teacher presented lessons on fairytale language patterns (e.g., "Once upon a time . . ."), characters, and settings. All students wrote letters to a fairytale character, who wrote back (channeled through the teacher or aide). But in addition, students could choose from many response options to do on their own or in groups with common interests.

TEACHING IDEA

Genre Unit on "Cinderella"

"Cinderella" may be the world's best-loved tale, with almost one thousand variants in existence. The rags-to-riches theme appeals to something basic in human nature and makes it an excellent choice for reading the same story across cultures and times. The issue of "Cinderella" perpetuating a sexist stereotype should be considered, as well. Here are some ideas for planning a 2- to 3-week literature unit about fairytales—specifically, "Cinderella":

Books

Cinderella, or The Little Glass Slipper (Brown, 1954)
Mufaro's Beautiful Daughters: An African Tale (Steptoe, 1987)
The Rough-Face Girl (Martin, 1992)
The Talking Eggs (San Souci, 1989)
Yeh-Shen: A Cinderella Story from China (Louie, 1982)

Resources

- Chart for comparing different versions of the tale
- World map to locate where different versions originated
- Bookmaking materials for creating own version of "Cinderella"
- Costumes and props for dramatizing different versions of the story
- Films: *The Tender Tale of Cinderella Penguin* (1982) and *Ashpet: An American Cinderella* (1989)
- Music: Rodgers and Hammerstein's musical theater and Masenet's opera of "Cinderella"

Response Options

- Draw and write anything they want about the stories.
- Brainstorm ideas, create a new version of the tale, and write it.
- Compare and contrast different tales, looking at literary elements: setting, characters, plot, mood, and theme.
- Write an invitation to a ball after reading the European version of "Cinderella."
- Read *The Jolly Postman* (Ahlberg & Ahlberg, 1986), which includes a letter to Cinderella, asking permission to publish her life story.
- Do group dramatizations of different stories.

Response Options

Whether you use literature circles or focus units, it's important to provide children with many options for responding to literature along with flexibility in using them. However, after reading a book, children should not *always* have to write or do a project about it. Probably the best thing to do after reading a book is to read another one.

Here are some response options:

See Chapter 4, Emergent Literacy and Biliteracy, for an example of using Read, Talk, Draw, Write with Spanish-speaking kindergartners.

● *Read, Talk, Draw, Write:* After the teacher reads aloud to the class or a group or one child reads to a buddy, students talk together about the book, draw a picture, and either write or give the teacher dictation.

● *Read Another Book:* If students enjoyed a book, talk to them about it and help them find another one with similar content, in the same genre, or by the same author. Adults and children alike are usually excited to find out that a book they loved is part of a series.

● *Response Journals:* Post a list of aesthetic questions and prompts in the classroom to suggest ways students can begin writing in response journals. For example:

What were you thinking about while reading? Tell about it.
What was your favorite part of the story? Tell about it.
Was there anything you wondered about? Tell about it.

2.2

See the Double-Entry Literature Journal (p. 52).

Some teachers prefer to use double-entry journals: In one column, students write down the parts of the story that interested them, and in the second column, they write down what they thought about those parts.

See Chapter 14, Language across the Curriculum, for examples of using literature as a model for writing, and Chapter 4, Emergent Literacy and Biliteracy, for a list of pattern books that are excellent models for young children.

● *Literature as a Model for Writing:* Children use the book as a model for their own writing. For example, after reading *When I Was Young in the Mountains* (Rylant, 1982), students might write about when they were young.

● *Role-Playing:* Students pretend to be characters in the book, either doing what the characters actually did or something the students think they might do. Books with two main characters are good for this, such as *Frog and Toad Are Friends* (Lobel, 1970).

See Chapter 5, Listening and Talking, for a step-by-step approach for dramatizing *Where the Wild Things Are,* by Maurice Sendak (1963).

● *Story Dramatization:* Students talk about the characters and how they act, analyze the story structure and decide which are the important events (in order), and play the story. Use the questions in the section on story structure, earlier in this chapter.

See Chapter 5, Listening and Talking, for how to do reader's theater.

● *Reader's Theater:* Any printed text can be adapted for reader's theater, including both fiction and nonfiction. The poetry in Shel Silverstein's *A Light in the Attic* (1981) and *Where the Sidewalk Ends* (1986) is great for reader's theater.

See Chapter 5, Listening and Talking, for how to do story-telling and puppet shows.

● *Storytelling:* Students retell the story in their own words and also use flannel boards, props, and music. Storytelling can be an individual or group project. Traditional tales, like *The Gingerbread Boy,* by Paul Galdone (1983), are excellent selections for storytelling.

- *Puppetry:* By making puppets, students can play a part of or an entire story or create their own story based on a story's characters. Again, traditional tales are good choices, especially those with several characters, like *The Bremen-Town Musicians* (Plume, 1987).

- *Mediamaking:* Students enjoy creating filmstrips of the story or their version of it. Stories with simple plots and sequences of action work well for mediamaking, such as *Rosie's Walk* (Hutchins, 1968).

See Chapter 12, Viewing and Visually Representing, for more on mediamaking.

- *Videotaping:* Students are motivated to respond to literature in a variety of ways by making videotapes—for example, role-playing characters, playing scenes or whole stories, creating their own versions of stories, or doing mock interviews with story characters. Books that present real conflicts, told from different points of view, are good candidates for videos. Consider using *The True Story of the Three Little Pigs* (Scieszka, 1989), which is told from the wolf's point of view.

- *Dioramas:* Students make three-dimensional constructions of the story world on a cardboard or Styrofoam base or in a box with one side cut away. They would have great fun creating a house for *Stuart Little* (White, 1954), the mouse child of normal-sized human parents.

- *Bookmaking:* Students retell a story or make a new version of it by creating books out of construction paper or contact paper or by making fold-a-books or pop-up books. See *The Jolly Postman* (Ahlberg & Ahlberg, 1986) for a book made with letters and envelopes inside.

See Chapter 9, The Writing Process, for how to make books in the classroom.

- *Create a Character:* Students talk about characters in a book and create characters of their own to write about. For example, fifth-grade students read *The Egypt Game* (Snyder, 1967), a contemporary story about a multicultural neighborhood, after they had also read and learned a lot about ancient Egypt. As a class, they created a web for different kinds of characters living in ancient Egypt. Then each student picked one type of person from ancient Egypt, did his or her own web, and wrote a story about that character (see Figure 7.7, p. 260).

- *Story Boxes:* Students find or create objects related to the story and put them in boxes. Then each student uses his or her box and the objects in it to tell others about the story. A good book for this activity is *Angel Child, Dragon Child* (Surat, 1983), which is about a young immigrant to the United States whose mother is still in Vietnam. The child carries a box with a picture and mementos of her mother.

- *Story Maps:* Students map the structure of a story or a character's journey through a story. Story maps can be created by the teacher with a class or group, or students can make their own.

See Chapter 5, Listening and Talking, for an example of a story map.

- *Make-Believe World Maps:* Children create maps of their own make-believe worlds after reading a book set in a fictitious world that can only be entered in a special way—for instance, *Bridge to Terabithia* (Paterson, 1977) and *The Lion, the Witch, and the Wardrobe* (Lewis, 1986). In addition to drawing this world, children can also write about it, addressing these questions: What's your world like? Where is it? How do you get there? How do you get back? Why would you like to go there?

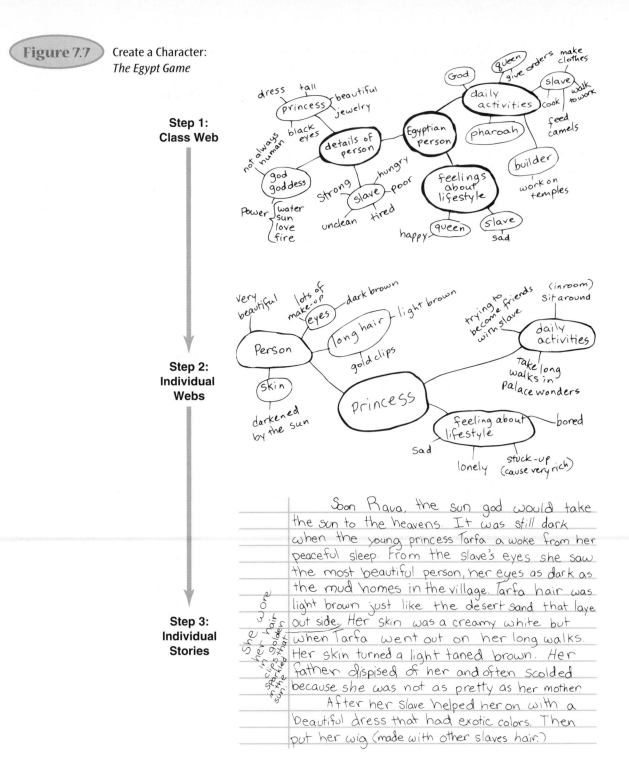

Figure 7.7 Create a Character:
The Egypt Game

Step 1:
Class Web

Step 2:
Individual
Webs

Step 3:
Individual
Stories

Soon Rava, the sun god would take the sun to the heavens. It was still dark when the young princess Tarfa awoke from her peaceful sleep. From the slave's eyes she saw the most beautiful person, her eyes as dark as the mud homes in the village. Tarfa hair was light brown just like the desert sand that laye out side. Her skin was a creamy white but when Tarfa went out on her long walks. Her skin turned a light taned brown. Her father dispised of her and often scolded because she was not as pretty as her mother.

After her slave helped her on with a beautiful dress that had exotic colors. Then put her wig (made with other slaves hair.)

She wore her hair in golden clips that sparkled in the sun.

- **Story Quilts:** Children can draw pictures, for example, of their favorite parts of the story, glue them to construction paper for backing, punch holes around the edges, and weave them together with yarn. The result is a class quilt of responses to a story. For an example, look at Faith Ringgold's (1991) childhood memoir *Tar Beach*, which uses books as a quilt motif.

See the companion book, *Schoolyear Activities Planner*, March: Women's History Month, for more books with quilt motifs.

- **E-mail Dialogues with "Keypals":** Two or more students read the same book and start an e-mail dialogue about it with keypals in the same class, with keypals in classes in the same school or other schools in the district, or with keypals in other states or countries. A teacher or a preservice teacher could also be a keypal with a child.

See Chapter 13, Technology in the Classroom, for more on second-grade keypals e-mailing between an American school and a Chinese school where children were learning English as a second language.

Assessing Teaching with Literature

When teaching transactionally with literature, the focus should be on students' lived-through experiences. Assessment must be designed to tap into those experiences and provide ongoing information for planning further experiences with literature for each child. In addition, teaching with literature can often be social and done in groups, such as literature circles. Both individual and group experiences require ongoing authentic assessment.

Each child's experiences with literature can be assessed in several ways:

1. Reading Logs: Have each student keep a log of the books he or she has read with space to record each book's title and author, dates reading started and finished, and perhaps a summary or comment. Students' logs can be kept in their portfolios. Teachers should keep in mind, however, that logs are only useful to give them an idea of what and how much students are reading. More in-depth forms of assessment are necessary to reveal the kinds of experiences students are having with literature.

2. Response Journals: As discussed earlier, these journals provide ongoing accounts of what students are thinking while reading. A double-entry journal (described earlier) can be used to show (1) what part of the book attracted the student's attention (in the left-hand column) and (2) what he or she was thinking while reading that part of the book (in the right-hand column). Journals that are kept on a regular basis can provide teachers with richly detailed accounts of students' personal responses to literature.

 2.2

See the Double-Entry Literature Journal (p. 52).

3. Portfolios: Any of the response options listed earlier in the chapter can be included in students' portfolios as artifacts that document the kinds of experiences they have had with books. And these artifacts can be catalogued using Assessment Toolbox 7.2, the Literature Portfolio Organizer (p. 262). This organizer should be stapled to the front of each child's literature portfolio as a way to identify what should go in the portfolio and to monitor the student's progress. The portfolio items should be kept in the folder for analysis by the teacher and for review and discussion among the teacher, student, and parents.

ASSESSMENT TOOLBOX

7.2 Literature Portfolio Organizer

This Literature Portfolio Organizer has been used by Paul Boyd-Batstone, the third-grade bilingual teacher described in the Teaching Idea. Paul maintains that the keys to using portfolios effectively are knowing what artifacts should go into them and when artifacts should be collected and keeping careful records of this information. This Assessment Toolbox provides a way to accomplish these goals.

Student _____   Date _____

Literature Portfolio Organizer

Artifact   **Date Collected**

1. Written responses to literature   **Rubric Score**
- _____   _____   ☐ October
- _____   _____   ☐ February
- _____   _____   ☐ June

2. Journal samples (list books)
- _____   ☐ October
- _____   ☐ February
- _____   ☐ June

3. Anecdotal records (attach sticky labels)   **Analyses**
_____   ☐ October
_____
_____
_____   ☐ February
_____
_____
_____   ☐ June
_____
_____

4. Literature circle/Unit activities
- _____   ☐ October
- _____   ☐ February
- _____   ☐ June

Answers to Questions about Teaching with Literature

● *How do young readers respond to literature?*

Reader-response theorists explain that readers are actively engaged in constructing meaning while reading, and because meaning is created by individual readers, no text has a single correct meaning. Among reader-response theorists, Louise Rosenblatt's *transactional model* has interested elementary educators. She calls the reading process a transaction, during which a "live circuit" is created between the reader and text. Meaning is discovered during this transaction.

The reader assumes a *stance*, or focuses his or her attention selectively in different ways, ranging between two points on a continuum. During an *efferent* reading, the focus is on the information to be taken away, or the more public aspects. During an *aesthetic* reading, the focus is on what the book arouses in the reader, or the more private aspects. Rosenblatt suggests that teachers' primary responsibility for most experiences with literature is to encourage children to take an aesthetic stance. Research has shown that children naturally assume a predominantly aesthetic stance toward literature. More efferent responses emerge from the richer, broader, more fluent aesthetic responses.

● *How should we teach with literature?*

Teachers should provide a classroom environment with many books, time, and opportunities for children to read or listen to books read aloud. Children should have time to hold literature discussions, work in literature circles using related books and resources, and participate in literature focus units. Literature should be integrated across the curriculum and become the primary source of reading and information. Students' should choose from among response options, and their own responses should determine much of what they will learn about.

Looking Further

1. Keep a double-entry literature-response journal to write about your own reading.

2. Read a book aloud to a group of children, and ask them what they think of it. Prompt them to draw or write anything they want in response to it. Analyze their responses to determine the stance they take toward literature: efferent or aesthetic.

3. Develop a graphic organizer for a core book that should be used with a specific grade.

4. Try one of the response options for literature with a child or a group of children in one of your field experiences in an elementary school. Share what happened in your college class.

5. Start an e-mail dialogue about a book. Perhaps read a picture book to a group of children and start an online group discussion with them, or e-mail another student in your college class about a book you have both read (such as this text).

Children's Books and Films

Ahlberg, J., & Ahlberg, A. (1986). *The jolly postman.* New York: Little, Brown.

Aliki. (1979). *Mummies made in Egypt.* New York: Harper-Collins.

Amon, A. (1981). *The earth is sore: Native Americans on nature.* New York: Atheneum.

Arnold, C. (1992). *The ancient cliff dwellers of Mesa Verde.* New York: Clarion.

Ashpet: An American Cinderella [Film]. (1989). Available from Davenport Films.

Babbitt, N. (1975). *Tuck everlasting.* New York: Farrar, Straus, & Giroux.

Banks, L. R. (1982). *The Indian in the cupboard.* New York: Avon.

Bash, B. (1989). *Desert giant.* Boston: Little, Brown.

Baylor, B. (1976). *Hawk, I'm your brother.* New York: Scribner's.

Bemelmans, L. (1976). *Madeline.* New York: Viking.

Bierhorst, J. (1979). *A cry from the earth.* New York: Four Winds Press.

Bierhorst, J. (1987). *Doctor Coyote: A native American Aesop's fables.* New York: Macmillan.

Blume, J. (1976). *Tales of a fourth grade nothing.* New York: Dell.

Blume, J. (1981). *Are you there, God? It's me, Margaret.* New York: Bantam.

Brown, M. (1954). *Cinderella, or the little glass slipper.* New York: Scribner's.

Bruchac, J. (1995). *Gluskabe and the four wishes.* New York: Cobblehill.

Bunting, E. (1995). *Smoky night.* New York: Harcourt.

Burch, J. J. (1994). *Chico Mendes: Defender of the rain forest.* New York: Milbrook Press.

Burks, B. (1998). *Walks alone.* New York: Harcourt.

Carle, E. (1969). *The very hungry caterpillar.* New York: Philomel.

Carle, E. (1977). *The grouchy ladybug.* New York: Harper-Collins.

Carle, E. (1984). *The very busy spider.* New York: Philomel.

Carle, E. (1990). *The very quiet cricket.* New York: Philomel.

Carle, E. (1995). *The very lonely firefly.* New York: Philomel.

Cherry, L. (1990). *The great kapok tree.* San Diego: Gullive Books.

Cherry, L., & Plotkin, M. J. (1998). *The shaman's apprentice: A tale of the Amazon rain forest.* San Diego: Harcourt Brace Jovanovich.

Cleary, B. (1982). *Ramona the pest.* New York: Dell.

Cooney, B. (1982). *Miss Rumphius.* New York: Viking.

Cormier, R. (1986). *The chocolate war* (Ed. B. Horowitz). New York: Bantam.

Crichton, M. (1990). *Jurassic park.* New York: Knopf.

Curtis, C. P. (1996). *The Watsons go to Birmingham—1963.* New York: Delacorte.

Cushman, K. (1995). *Catherine, called Birdy.* New York: Clarion.

de Paola, T. (1973). *Nana upstairs & Nana Downstairs.* New York: Putnam's.

Dewey, J. O. (1996). *Stories on stone: Rock art: Images from the ancient ones.* New York: Little, Brown.

Dorros, A. (1990). *Rain forest secrets.* New York: Scholastic.

Dorros, A. (1991). *Abuela.* New York: Dutton.

Dorros, M. (1997). *Tales from the rainforest* (Ed. J. W. Carter). New York: HarperCollins

Dunphy, M. (1995). *Here is the southwestern desert.* New York: Hyperion.

Fitzhugh, L. (1964). *Harriet the spy.* New York: Harper & Row.

Fleischman, P. (1989). *Joyful noise: Poems for two voices.* New York: Harper.

Frank, A. (1952). *Anne Frank: The diary of a young girl.* New York: Doubleday.

Freedman, R. (1987). *Lincoln: A photobiography.* New York: Clarion.

Freedman, R. (1994). *Eleanor Roosevelt: A life of discovery.* New York: Clarion.

Gag, W. (1977). *Millions of cats.* New York: Putnam.

Galdone, P. (1983). *The gingerbread boy.* New York: Houghton Mifflin.

George, J. C. (1973). *Julie of the wolves.* New York: Harper-Collins.

George, J. C. (1990). *One day in a tropical rain forest.* New York: Crowell.

Gibbons, G. (1994). *Nature's green umbrella: Tropical rain forests.* New York: Morrow.

Goodman, S. E. (1998). *Stones, bones, and petroglyphs: Digging into Southwest archaeology.* New York: Simon & Schuster.

Guiberson, B. Z. (1991). *Cactus hotel.* New York: Henry Holt.

Hamilton, V. (1993). *The people could fly: American black folktales.* New York: Knopf.

Hirschi, R. (1992). *Discover my world: Desert.* New York: Bantam.

Holling, H. C. (1942). *Tree in the trail.* New York: Literary Classics.

Hutchins, P. (1968). *Rosie's walk*. New York: Macmillan.

Joyce, W. (1988). *Dinosaur Bob*. New York: HarperCollins.

Keats, E. J. (1963). *The snowy day*. New York: Viking.

Keister, D. (1995). *Fernando's gift: El regalo de Fernando*. San Francisco: Sierra Club Books for Children.

Kellogg, S. (1988). *Johnny Appleseed*. New York: Morrow.

Kent, J. (1971). *The fat cat: A Danish folktale*. New York: Parent's Magazine.

Konigsburg, E. L. (1972). *From the mixed-up files of Mrs. Basil E. Frankweiler*. New York: Simon & Schuster.

L'Engle, M. (1962). *A wrinkle in time*. New York: Farrar, Straus, & Giroux.

Lesser, C. (1997). *Storm on the desert*. San Diego: Harcourt Brace Jovanovich.

Lewis, C. S. (1986). *The lion, the witch, and the wardrobe*. New York: Macmillan.

Lobel, A. (1970). *Frog and Toad are friends*. New York: HarperCollins.

Louie, A.-L. (1982). *Yeh-Shen: A Cinderella story from China*. New York: Philomel.

Lowry, L. (1990). *Number the stars*. New York: Houghton Mifflin.

Lowry, L. (1994). *The giver*. New York: Houghton Mifflin.

Macaulay, D. (1988). *The way things work*. New York: Houghton Mifflin.

MacLachlan, P. (1985). *Sarah, plain and tall*. New York: Harper.

MacLachlan, P. (1985). *Sarah, plain and tall*. New York: Harper.

Marrin, A. (1997). *Empires lost and won: The Spanish heritage in the Southwest*. New York: Simon & Schuster.

Martin, R. (1992). *The rough-face girl*. New York: Putnam's.

McCloskey, R. (1941). *Make way for ducklings*. New York: Viking.

Miles, M. (1971). *Annie and the old one*. New York: Little, Brown.

Milne, A. A. (1926). *Winnie-the-Pooh*. New York: Dutton.

Mora, P. (1994). *Listen to the desert/Oye al desierto*. Boston: Clarion.

Myers, W. D. (1998). *Harlem*. New York: Scholastic.

Norton, M. (1953). *The borrowers*. New York: Harcourt Brace.

O'Dell, S. (1970). *Sing down the moon*. Boston: Houghton Mifflin.

O'Dell, S. (1974). *Child of fire*. Boston: Houghton Mifflin.

O'Dell, S. (1988). *Island of the blue dolphins*. New York: Dell.

Paterson, K. (1977). *Bridge to Terabithia*. New York: HarperCollins.

Pinkney, A. D., & Pinkney, B. (1999). *Duke Ellington*. New York: Hyperion.

Plume, I. (1987). *The Bremen-town musicians*. New York: HarperCollins

Politi, L. (1973). *The nicest gift*. New York: Scribner's.

Potter, B. (1902). *The tale of Peter Rabbit*.

Prelutsky, J. (1986). *Read-aloud rhymes for the very young*. New York: Knopf.

Provensen, A., & Provensen, M. (1987). *The glorious flight: The story of Louis Bleriot*. New York: Puffin Books.

Ringgold, F. (1991). *Tar beach*. New York: Crown.

Rowling, J. K. (1997). *Harry Potter and the sorcerer's stone*. New York: Levine.

Rylant, C. (1982). *When I was young in the mountains*. New York: Dutton.

San Souci, R. (1989). *The talking eggs*. New York: Dial.

Say, A. (1994). *Grandfather's journey*. New York: Houghton Mifflin.

Scieszka, J. (1989). *The true story of the three little pigs*. New York: Viking.

Scieszka, J. (1993). *The Stinky Cheese Man and other fairly stupid tales*. New York: Viking.

Sendak, M. (1963). *Where the wild things are*. New York: HarperCollins.

Seuss, Dr. (1976). *The cat in the hat*. New York: Random House.

Shirreffs, G. D. (1957). *Son of the thunder people*. New York: Westminster.

Shirreffs, G. D. (1958). *Swiftwagon*. New York: Westminster.

Shirreffs, G. D. (1961). *The gray sea raiders*. New York: Chilton.

Shirreffs, G. D. (1962). *The mystery of the haunted mine*. New York: Scholastic.

Shirreffs, G. D. (1963). *Mystery of lost canyon*. New York: Chilton.

Shirreffs, G. D. (1964). *The secret of the Spanish desert*. New York: Chilton.

Shirreffs, G. D. (1968). *Mystery of the lost cliff dwelling*. New York: Prentice-Hall.

Siebert, D. (1988). *Mojave*. New York: Crowell.

Silverstein, S. (1981). *A light in the attic*. New York: HarperCollins.

Silverstein, S. (1986). *Where the sidewalk ends*. New York: Dell.

Simon, S. (1998). *Deserts*. New York: Morrow.

Slobodkina, E. (1947). *Caps for sale*. New York: Harper & Row.

Snyder, Z. K. (1967). *The Egypt game*. New York: Macmillan.

Spinelli, J. (1991). *Maniac Magee*. New York: Little, Brown.

Steig, W. (1969). *Sylvester and the magic pebble*. New York: Windmill.

Steptoe, J. (1987). *Mufaro's beautiful daughters: An African tale.* New York: Lothrop, Lee, & Shepard.

Stevenson, R. L. (1947). *Treasure Island.* New York: Putnam.

Surat, M. (1983). *Angel child, dragon child.* Racine, WI: Carnival/Raintree.

Taylor, B. (1992). *Desert life.* New York: Dorling Kindersley.

Taylor, M. (1976). *Roll of thunder, hear my cry.* New York: Dial.

Tender tale of Cinderella Penguin, The [Film]. (1982). Available from National Film Board of Canada.

Van Allsburg, C. (1979). *The garden of Abdul Gasazi.* Boston: Houghton Mifflin.

Van Allsburg, C. (1981). *Jumanji.* Boston: Houghton Mifflin.

Van Allsburg, C. (1983). *The wreck of the Zephyr.* Boston: Houghton Mifflin.

Van Allsburg, C. (1984). *The mysteries of Harris Burdick.* Boston: Houghton Mifflin.

Viorst, J. (1972). *Alexander and the terrible, horrible, no good, very bad day.* New York: Atheneum.

Waber, B. (1972). *Ira sleeps over.* New York: Houghton Mifflin.

Waber, G. (1977). *An anteater named Arthur.* New York: Houghton Mifflin.

Wallace, M. D. (1996). *America's deserts: Guide to plants and animals.* Golden, CO: Fulcrum.

Wegman, W. (1993). *Cinderella.* New York: Hyperion.

Weisner, D. (1992). *Tuesday.* New York: Clarion.

White, E. B. (1952). *Charlotte's web.* New York: HarperCollins.

White, E. B. (1954). *Stuart Little.* New York: HarperCollins.

Wilder, L. I. (1961). *Little house in the big woods.* New York: HarperCollins.

Yashima, T. (1958). *Umbrella.* New York: Viking.

Yep, L. (1975). *Dragonwings.* New York: HarperCollins.

Yolen, J. (1992). *Encounter.* New York: Harcourt Brace Jovanovich.

Yolen, J. (1993). *Welcome to the green house.* New York: Putnam's.

Yolen, J. (1996). *Welcome to the sea of sand.* New York: Putnam.

Yorinks, A. (1986). *Hey, Al.* New York: Farrar, Straus & Giroux.

Young, E. (1990). *Lon Po Po: A Red Riding Hood tale from China.* New York: Philomel.

chapter 8

Multicultural Education and Children's Books

Questions about Multicultural Education and Children's Books

- *How should we approach multicultural education?*
- *How can we use children's books in multicultural education?*

REFLECTIVE RESPONSE

Jot down answers to the following questions now, and continue to think about them as you read this chapter: What is your culture? Where are you from? Can you speak more than one language? Does your family communicate in more than one language? Was one of your parents or grandparents born in another country? Do you celebrate holidays not common to all Americans? Do you usually socialize with people of your own religious or ethnic identity? Have you ever personally experienced prejudice?

Multicultural Education

The questions in the Reflective Response ask you to explore your own experiences so you will be aware of the importance of cultural knowledge and ethnic identity as you consider multicultural education. As defined here by James and Cherry McGee Banks (Banks & Banks, 2003), *multicultural education* is

> *a reform movement designed to change the total educational environment so that students from diverse racial and ethnic groups, both gender groups, exceptional students, and students from each social-class group will experience equal educational opportunities in schools. . . . A major assumption of multicultural education is that some students, be-*

267

cause of their particular racial, ethnic, gender, and cultural characteristics, have a better chance to succeed in educational institutions as they are currently structured than do students who belong to other groups or who have different cultural and gender characteristics. (pp 429–430)

Today, classrooms in most parts of the United States are made up of students of many different racial, ethnic, religious, and cultural groups. To understand this cultural diversity, we need to understand culture. Nieto (2000) defines *culture* as "the ever-changing values, traditions, social and political relationships, and worldview created and shared by a group of people bound together by a combination of factors (which can include a common history, geographic location, language, social class, and/or religion), and how these are transformed by those who share them" (p. 390). Student cultural diversity, as explained by Au (1993), has three distinguishing features:

1. *Ethnicity:* national origin, such as African American, Asian American, Hispanic American, and Native American or, more specifically, Haitian, Cambodian, El Salvadoran, or Ojibwe
2. *Class:* socioeconomic status or parents' occupation and family income
3. *Language:* whether a dialect of English, such as Black English, or a language other than English, such as Spanish

Yet despite the great diversity among students in today's classrooms, the curriculum and teaching materials and methods used most often still reflect the experiences of what are called *mainstream Americans*—White Americans of European descent. This mainstream-centric curriculum often ignores or marginalizes the experiences, histories, and cultures of other groups. Banks (2003) maintains that this focus on the mainsream culture has had a negative effect on both mainstream American students and those of other cultural groups because it has reinforced ethnocentrism and racism.

Approaches to Multicultural Education

According to Grant and Sleeter (2003), *multicultural education* is the term most widely used by educators to describe educating for pluralism. This can be achieved through several approaches, each with different goals (Grant & Sleeter, 2003; Sleeter & Grant, 1999):

1. *Exceptional and Culturally Different Students Approach:* preparing students who are exceptional and culturally different to fit into mainstream society
2. *Human Relations Approach:* helping students learn to live together harmoniously
3. *Single-Group Studies Approach:* studying a particular group of people to raise its social status
4. *Multicultural Education Approach:* promoting pluralism and equity to bring about social reform
5. *Multicultural and Social Reconstructionist Approach:* seeking to reconstruct society toward greater equity in race, class, gender, and disability

Grant and Sleeter (2003), along with many other educators, advocate this fifth approach to multicultural education. On a broader scale, this approach is aimed at reforming all schools, whether all-white suburban or multiethnic urban, around principles of pluralism and equity, hopefully leading to broader social reform. It deals more directly than the other approaches with oppression and social structural inequality based on race, social class, gender, and disability. Four practices are unique to this reconstructionist approach:

- Democracy is actively practiced in the schools. Students are given opportunities to direct their own learning and to be responsible for it.
- Students analyze institutional inequality in their own lives. They learn how to question how society works and to look at problems in order to prepare themselves to change unfair social processes—for example, gender and racial inequities for people with the same educational level.
- Students learn to use social action skills. For example, elementary-age children can read multicultural books about issues involving discrimination and suggest ways to deal with these issues, and middle school students can learn to identify sexist advertising and suggest ways to stop it.
- Students build bridges to connect various oppressed groups (e.g., people who are poor, people from racial/ethnic groups, and white women) so they can advance common interests together.

On a more general level, the key ideas that underlie multicultural education include the following:

1. *Curriculum:* Planning is still organized around the content areas, but texts and teaching materials are used that reflect the full range of experiences and perspectives of diverse cultural groups. When teaching with literature, teachers should choose works written by members of diverse groups who write about the struggle for identify in a white-dominant society—for example, a Puerto Rican girl in *Felita* (Mohr, 1990), a Chinese boy in *Dragonwings* (Yep, 1975), an African American boy in *Scorpions* (Myers, 1990), and a European American girl in *The Great Gilly Hopkins* (Paterson, 1987).

2. *Perspectives:* The material that's taught about a given cultural group should reflect perspectives that the group itself would choose and that show it as dynamic and active. To choose such material, teachers must learn about different groups and discover what's important and meaningful to them. For example, members of Native American tribes should be asked whom they would like to see studied instead of historical figures like Pocahontas, Kateri Tckakwitha, and Sacajawea, who are often perceived as having served white, rather than Native American, interests. Likewise, to eliminate the focus on African Americans as athletes and entertainers, examples of individuals from fields such as science and literature should be presented.

3. *Instruction:* Teachers should assume that *all* students can learn, try to find each student's individual learning style, and draw on the extensive personal knowledge each student brings to school. Cooperative learning should be fos-

Average annual salaries for U.S. high school graduates (U.S. Bureau of the Census, 1999):

Males
White: $26,125
Black: $18,525
Latino: $19,667

Females
White: $15,078
Black: $14,333
Latino: $14,313

tered, and both boys and girls should be treated equally in a nonsexist manner. The cultural makeup of the school staff should be diverse, and jobs should be assigned based on individual merit, not stereotypes. More than one language should be taught, and bilingualism for all students should be identified as a goal.

GREAT BOOKS FOR CHILDREN

Here are some examples of children's books appropriate for each of Banks's approaches to integrating multicultural content (Rasinksi & Padak, 1990):

1. Contributions: *Grandfather's Journey* (Say, 1993)—The immigration of a Japanese American
2. Additive: *Roll of Thunder, Hear My Cry* (Taylor, 1976)—The true story of an African American family in the Depression-era South
3. Transformation: *Johnny Tremain* (Forbes, 1946) and *My Brother Sam Is Dead* (Collier & Collier, 1974)— Two contrasting views of the American Revolution
4. Social Action: *Number the Stars* (Lowry, 1989)—A New-bery Medal–winning book about a Christian family who hides a Jewish family in Nazi-occupied Denmark

Integrating Multicultural Content

Banks (2003) identifies four approaches to the integration of multicultural content into the curriculum:

1. *Contributions Approach:* This approach focuses on heroes and heroines, holidays, and discrete cultural elements. It's used as a first attempt to integrate ethnic and multicultural content into the curriculum. The mainstream curriculum remains unchanged; rather, ethnic figures and artifacts similar to those in the mainstream culture are inserted into it. For example, people are chosen for study because of their success within the mainstream, rather than the ethnic, community.

2. *Additive Approach:* In this approach, content, concepts, themes, and perspectives are added to the curriculum without changing its structure. For instance, books and units on ethnic content are added to the existing curriculum. However, as with the contributions approach, ethnic content is still seen from a mainstream perspective.

3. *Transformation Approach:* The structure of the curriculum is changed in this approach to enable students to view concepts, issues, events, and themes from the perspectives of diverse ethnic and cultural groups. Students view issues and concepts from different ethnic perspectives, only one of which is the mainstream perspective. This approach goes beyond looking at how ethnic and cultural groups have contributed to mainstream culture and society, however. Instead, the emphasis is on how the common U.S. culture and society emerged from a complex synthesis and interaction of the diverse cultural elements that originated within the various cultural, racial, ethnic, and religious groups that make up U.S. society. Banks (2003) calls this process *multiple acculturation*, which describes how various ethnic and cultural groups have been an integral part of shaping U.S. society.

4. *Social Action Approach:* Following this approach, students make decisions on important social issues and take actions to help solve them. This goes beyond the transformation approach, educating students for social change and decision making. The result is a synthesis of knowledge and values.

In reality, these approaches are mixed and blended when applied in the classroom. A teacher might begin with the contributions approach and then move to other levels, for example. Or perhaps becoming aware of the importance of moving to higher levels of integrating multicultural content into the curriculum will help a teacher recognize opportunities when they occur.

In teaching language arts, teachers can integrate multicultural content in several ways:

1. *Children's Books.* Use tradebooks and children's books as the main sources of reading material and integrated teaching. Use multicultural books that feature the following:

- different races, exceptionalities, socioeconomic classes, and disabilities
- males and females doing traditional as well as nontraditional activities
- both urban and rural settings

See Chapter 7, Teaching with Literature, and the section on multicultural children's books later in this chapter for ideas about using these books.

2. *Computers.* Computers should be available in the classroom in addition to the school computer lab. Cooperative learning and responsibility are fostered when children use computers in groups, and students become accustomed to supporting each other's learning, regardless of their race, ethnicity, or gender.

See Chapter 13, Technology in the Classroom.

3. *Writing.* Letter writing is an excellent way for children to advocate for oppressed groups and to challenge social issues they want to change.

4. *Viewing and Visually Representing.* By critically analyzing media (such as magazines, newspapers, advertisements, television, film, video, and so on), children will come to understand the effects of media on their lives and ways to deal with them.

See Chapter 12, Viewing and Visually Representing.

5. *Projects.* Children can choose a topic of interest (say, in social studies) and work in groups to develop a comprehensive perspective on that topic that they may not discover in a textbook. Children will also learn to critically analyze textbooks by looking at information across a range of sources, such as tradebooks, the Internet, and interviews with people.

Teaching Speakers of Nonmainstream English

An important dimension of multicultural education is *language diversity.* You have read elsewhere in this book about students who come to school speaking a language other than English. However, Americans also speak many varieties of English, as seen in regional accents, vocabularies, and styles. For instance, there are many Native American varieties of English. There are also many Creole languages, including Gullah (of English and West African origin), Louisiana French Creole, and Hawiian Creole (influenced by Hawaiian, Japanese, Chinese, Portuguese, English, and Ilocano). Black English is a dialect, rather than a Creole language, and carries influences from British and American English as well as sixteenth-century, English-based West African pidgin (Ovando, 2003).

See Chapter 3, First- and Second-Language Development, and Chapter 4, Emergent Literacy and Biliteracy.

Thus, even among native English speakers, language varies in many ways. To identify the different ways we can look at each person's language, sociolinguists describe the phenomenon of a *language community.* Members of a language community regard themselves as speakers of the same language. Each speaker within the community has a personal speech pattern called an *idiolect.* Systematic variations in speech patterns among speakers that stem from differences in social status or geographic region are called *dialects.* When speakers choose from the range of varieties of use within a dialect, they are using a *register.* Among the many factors that determine a person's idiolect, dialect, and register are age, gender, health, size, personality, emotional state, grammatical idiosyncrasies, profession, racial/ethnic heritage, family situation, geographic region, and social group.

Understanding how language is used in varying social and cultural contexts is equally important to understanding how language is acquired. In her book *Ways with Words* (1983), Shirley Brice Heath reported the results of a study she did in South Carolina that looked at the ways language was used in a poor, African American community and in a working-class, European American community. In particular, she found differences in how language was used in the home versus the school in these communities. To characterize these differences, Heath identified *language genres,* or descriptive units into which different types of language events fit. Different cultural groups use certain genres more frequently, and not all groups use the same genres. The language of school has its own genres—language that doesn't occur naturally in the home.

Heath argues that in order for children to succeed, they must be able to use these school language genres:

1. *Label quests:* Teachers ask questions about the names and attributes of things: What is this? What color is it?
2. *Meaning quests:* Teachers ask students to explain the meanings of words, pictures, and events: What did the author mean? (Heath says this should be done with books from "the basal to Shakespeare.")
3. *Recounts:* Teachers ask children to summarize information or recount facts they already know.
4. *Accounts:* Students provide new information or new interpretations. Show-and-tell and creative writing are types of accounts. (Schools generally allow for few accounts.)
5. *Eventcasts:* These are narratives of events that are happening or will happen. For instance, teachers tell students how to solve a math problem or do a science experiment.
6. *Stories:* This is the most familiar language genre and includes fictional stories in basal readers as well as children's literature.

The language of schooling has its own genres, and children must be able to use them to succeed.

Teachers should not make assumptions and try to "fill in the gaps" in students' language use differences. Rather, teachers should model the use of language genres in the classroom. In the classroom, Heath suggests that teachers do the following:

1. Provide children with experiences with the full range of language genres typically used in school. Expand the number of language genres that students can use.
2. Go beyond traditional school texts and use texts or types of narratives that are more familiar to children, such as jokes, comic books, and television.
3. Do not expect that children will learn to use genres in any kind of linear order. Some children will use certain genres better than others, and use and progress will differ among individuals.

Many speakers of English language varieties have difficulty in school, and their language variation is often seen as the cause of that difficulty. However, educators, cognitive psychologists, linguists, and anthropologists tell us that students develop cognitively and academically by building on their prior knowledge, experiences, attitudes, and skills (Ogbu, 1999; Perry & Delpit, 1998). Teachers should build on what students bring to school, adding the school experience to what children already know (Ovando, 2003).

Black English is widely spoken among African Americans; its use spread throughout the United States as African Americans migrated to urban areas in the North during the last century (Ovando, 2003). Some aspects of Black English stigmatize its speakers—for example, the practice of using multiple negation, or double negatives. (Interestingly enough, using multiple negations was an integral part of English up to Shakespseare's time [Whatley, 1981].) Among the most common speech markers of this dialect are using *be* to denote an ongoing action ("He be going to work"), dropping linking verbs ("You crazy"), shortening plurals ("Twenty cent"), dropping some final consonants ("firs" instead of "first"), and substituting some pronouns ("That's the man got all the money"). The language varieties spoken by African Americans, however, are valid, rule-governed linguistic systems with internal infrastructures and sets of grammar rules, just like all other languages (Perry & Delpit, 1998; Smitherman, 1999).

Sociolinguists in the 1960s and 1970s began to systematically describe dialects, particularly those of African Americans, and the relationship between dialectal difference and learning to read and write (Labov, 1972; Shuy, 1969). Ample evidence suggested that the use of a dialect didn't critically interfere with learning to read (Goodman, 1978; Ruddell, 1965). In fact, other studies suggested that teachers' limited knowledge of dialectal differences was perhaps what made the difference in students' literacy learning. Specifically, teachers with limited knowledge were more likely to mistake differences in pronunciation for reading errors (Cunningham, 1976–1977) and have lower expectations, estimates of intelligence, and ratings of performance for nonstandard dialect speakers (Harber & Beatty, 1978; Politzer & Hoover, 1977).

Lisa Delpit (1995; Perry & Delpit, 1998) is an African American educator who has maintained the need for a balance of both skills and attention to

GREAT BOOKS FOR CHILDREN

Jokes

Clifford's Riddles (Bridwell, 1974)

Invisible Oink: Pig Jokes (Phillips, 1993)

Old Turtle's 90 Knock Knock Jokes and Riddles (Kessler, 1991)

Tyrannosaurus Wrecks: A Book of Dinosaur Riddles (Sterne, 1979)

learning mainstream English with child-centered, process approaches to literacy in educating children who are linguistically different. She recommends that teachers help nonmainstream speakers of English acquire standard English. Teachers need to support the language children bring to school and its intimate association with family, community, and personal identity; provide them input using standard English; and give them opportunities to use this new language in safe, real communicative contexts. It's important, however, that any standard English language activities be conducted without implying that any child's native dialect is inadequate.

Some successful literacy programs have modified reading and writing instruction to be more congruent with local speech; for example, there's a reading program based on the Hawaiian "talk story" (Au, 1980; Au & Jordan, 1981). Other programs have successfully incorporated children's family values and life histories, or "funds of knowledge," as the basis for literacy instruction (Diaz, Moll, & Mehan, 1986), and still others have used dialogue journals, in which writing isn't evaluated but serves as a natural form of communication between student and teacher (Staton, Shuy, Kreeft Payton, & Reed, 1988).

Children are aware of and sensitive to teachers' attitudes to their speech and may be reluctant to use their natural dialects in teachers' presence (Lucas, 1983). Labov (1978) reminds teachers that progress in English language development and literacy may be less tied to language differences than to cultural conflicts between the child's own language and culture and those of the classroom. Teachers should be knowledgeable about language differences and variations

SUPPORTING

Speakers of Nonmainstream English

Teachers can support the language children bring to school while providing input in standard English and opportunities to use it in safe, real communicative contexts. Suggested activities include the following:

1. Students create bidialectal dictionaries using both their own dialect and standard English.
2. Students use standard English by role-playing or scriptwriting in drama or media productions.
3. Students produce and videotape a news program, taking on the role of a famous newscaster.
4. Students explore language differences—for instance, finding out the many ways a certain expression can be used or what a particular word may mean depending on who's using it.
5. Students and teachers write in dialogue journals, in which the writing is not evaluated.
6. Teachers modify literacy activities to be more congruent with local speech and to incorporate family values and life histories.

See Chapter 5, Listening and Talking, and Chapter 12, Viewing and Visually Representing, for more on drama and media productions.

TEACHER RESOURCES
See *Speech, Language, and the African American Child* (VanKeulen, Weddington, & DeBose, 1998) for an in-depth discussion.

and be able to make the fundamental distinction between a difference in pronunciation and a mistake in reading and writing (Farr & Daniels, 1986; Labov, 1978). The box on page 274 offers suggestions for supporting students who speak nonmainstream English.

Ethnosensitivity is the most important principle of effective literacy instruction for students from minority groups (Baugh, 1981). Teachers' attitudes toward students who are culturally and linguistically different are crucial to those students' academic success. As James Baldwin so aptly put it, "A child cannot be taught by anyone whose demand, essentially, is that the child repudiate his experience and all that gives him sustenance" (1981, p. 51).

Multicultural Children's Books

Literature Focus Units

See Chapter 7, Teaching with Literature, for more on literature focus units.

Literature focus units can be developed with multicultural children's books, organizing these units as core book, author, and genre units. Table 8.1 (p. 276) shows examples of multicultural books that can be used for each type of unit

It is important in today's classrooms to use *culturally conscious literature*—which depicts the diversity in human society, including ethnic, linguistic, religious, socioeconomic, and gender differences—as literature written primarily by but not limited to authors who are members of such groups and thus accurately portray and reveal their groups' cultures (Bishop, 1992; Harris, 1997). Valerie Pang (Pang, Colvin, Tran, & Barbra, 1992) provides the following criteria for selecting culturally conscious multicultural children's books:

1. *Culturally pluralistic themes:* Literature should value diversity and treat cultural assimilation with sensitivity.
2. *Positive portrayals:* Characters from diverse groups should be portrayed as empowered, not stereotyped.
3. *Settings in the United States:* Characters should be portrayed in American settings. Keep in mind that many Hispanic and Asian Americans are native-born citizens whose families have lived in this country longer than those who may have immigrated from Europe and Great Britain.
4. *Plot and characterization:* Well-developed and accurately portrayed characters, a well-constructed plot, and good writing should characterize *all* children's literature.
5. *Accurate illustrations:* Portrayals of physical features, dress, and mannerisms should not be stereotypical.

Table 8.2 (pp. 280–281) is a selective list of books focusing on cultural groups that have historically been underrepresented in children's literature. Some of them are traditional tales and biographies, but most are contemporary stories. Teachers should go beyond using just traditional tales, which depict Native Americans in ways of life that really don't exist anymore. It's also important to show Native Americans as they live today. Multicultural literature should include the present, as well as the past, which means looking at issues of racism,

Native American Authors and Illustrators: Joseph Bruchac, Michael Dorris, Jamke Highwater, Virginia Driving Hawk Sneve, White Deer of Autumn

African American Authors and Illustrators: Ashley Bryan, Lucille Clifton, Eloise Greenfield, Virgina Hamilton, Julius Lester, Patricia McKissack, Walter Dean Myers, Faith Ringgold, John Steptoe, Mildred Taylor

Hispanic American Authors and Illustrators: Alma Flor Ada, George Ancona, Pura Belpre, Sandra Cisneros, David Diaz, Arthur Dorros, Carmen Lomas Garza, Nicholosa Mohr, Pam Munoz Ryan, Gary Soto, and Victor Villasenor

Asian American Authors and Illustrators: Betty Bao Lord, Allen Say, Yoshiko Uchida, Taro Yashima, Paul Yee, Laurence Yep, Ed Young, Yangsook Choi

EXCELLENT SOFTWARE

In My Own Voice: Multicultural Poets includes poetry collections, some read in the poet's own voice or with the poet telling how they were created; related art and music; and a student tool to write poetry and add music and a visual representation.

Table 8.1   Literature Focus Units Using Multicultural Children's Books

Core Book Units	Author/Illustrator Units	Genre Units
Primary/Middle Grades	George Ancona	Picture book
Grandfather's Journey (Say, 1993)	Joseph Bruchac	Poetry
The Keeping Quilt (Pollaco, 1988)	Sandra Cisneros	Traditional tale
The Name Jar (Choi, 2001)	Walter Dean Myers	Historical fiction
People (Spier, 1980)	David Dìaz	Contemporary realistic
Tar Beach (Ringgold, 1991)	The Pinkneys	Informational
Too Many Tamales (Soto, 1993)	Patricia Pollaco	Biography and
	Faith Ringgold	autobiography
Middle/Upper Grades	Allen Say	Memoir
The Birchbark House (Erdich, 1999)	Gary Soto	
Bud, Not Buddy (Curtis, 1999)	Mildred Taylor	
Dragonwings (Yep, 1975)	Laurence Yep	
The House on Mango Street (Cisneros, 1991)		
Number the Stars (Lowry, 1989)		
Shabanu, Daughter of the Wind (Staples,1989)		

**TEACHER
RESOURCES**

See *Multicultural Children's
Literature: Through the Eyes of
Many Children* (Norton, 2001)
for more multicultural
children's books.

resistance, and violence, not just talking animals and happy villagers. Also, the books listed here come, as much as possible, from the experience of people in the Americas. For instance, traditional African tales are not included under the "African American" heading but rather as African American traditional tales.

This list of books provides a good start but is certainly not exhaustive. Many of the titles mentioned have been used by my students when teaching with literature in field experiences. And I have annotated the list because some titles, like *Tar Beach* and *Amazing Grace*, don't really tell about the multicultural content of the book or how it might be used with children.

Core Book Units

The use of core book units in teaching with literature was described in Chapter 7, Teaching with Literature, and illustrated with an example unit done with fourth-graders on *Treasure Island*, by Robert Louis Stevenson. The following lesson plan outlines a core book unit for kindergartners through second-graders using the multicultural picture book *People*, by Peter Spier (1980). This is a good book to use for several reasons. In particular, many of the students I have taught in language arts methods courses over the years have successfully used *People* with children in their field experiences in elementary schools from grades K–5 and written core book units with it. Also, many experienced teachers and principals use it year after year to begin the schoolyear. It is a great multicultural book to begin with because it doesn't focus on any one culture; instead, it takes a global perspective, showing how people are alike and different all over the world. Most important for children, it emphasizes that everyone is unique.

I recommend getting as many copies of *People* as possible from the library. It also comes in a "big book" version and in multiple languages. In a core book unit, however, you are not limited to using just one book, especially in the primary grades. You can put together a set of related books for the unit, which you can also read aloud and which children can read. Keep in mind that the purpose of a core book unit is to use literature to teach language arts; in this case, you will be using a multicultural book. This unit is not intended to be a cross-curricular or social studies unit exploring global diversity, although children may certainly learn about that. Instead, you should take an aesthetic approach, tapping into children's experiences of the book as well as their personal experiences to teach listening, speaking, reading, writing, and viewing and visually representing.

LESSON PLAN

Core Book Unit on *People*

Subject: This is a three-day core book unit plan for *People* (Spier, 1980) that can be adapted for use with children in grades K–2 and can also result in a continuing "ripple effect" of literature-based language and literacy experiences.

Purposes: To listen to and respond to multicultural literature; to talk about how people are both alike and different; to draw and write about how each child is special or unique.

Standard 1: Students read a wide range of print and nonprint texts to build an understanding of texts, of themselves, and of the cultures of the United States and the world; to acquire new information; to respond to the needs and demands of society and the workplace; and for personal fulfillment. Among these texts are fiction and nonficition, classic and contemporary works.

Materials:
- "Big book" edition of *People;* multiple copies of *People,* including in languages other than English
- Copies of *How My Parents Learned to Eat* (Friedman, 1984) and *Cleversticks* (Ashley, 1991); text set of multicultural books
- Chartpaper; paper, pencils, crayons; chopsticks and cotton balls
- Optional: bookmaking materials; 5" × 7" blank index cards and yarn; videocamera and tape

See one of my education students try this lesson with children.

IRA/
NCTE

This bulletin board shows the text set of related books that students read in the core book unit on People.

(continued)

Teaching Sequence: Here are the activities for the three days in this lesson.

Day 1

20 minutes: Read *People* aloud. Encourage the children to respond during the reading.

10 minutes: Discuss the book, asking open, aesthetic questions:
"What did you think of the book?"
"What was your favorite part?"
"How are people alike (e.g., they all eat) and different (e.g., they eat different things)?"
"What is unique about you?"

10 minutes: Record students' responses on chartpaper as a cluster or other graphic organizer.

15 minutes: Have each student draw a picture and write a caption about something that is unique about him or her.

5 minutes: Have a book talk about a text set of related books that students can self-select to read during independent reading time in addition to copies of *People:*
Amazing Grace (Hoffman, 1991)
Bread, Bread, Bread (Morris, 1989)
Cleversticks (Ashley, 1991)
Everybody Cooks Rice (Dooley, 1992)
The Name Jar (Choi, 2001)
Salt in His Shoes (Jordan & Jordan, 2000)
This Is the Way We Go to School (Baer, 1990)

Reread *People* during read-aloud time over the next two days.

Day 2

20 minutes: Read *How My Parents Learned to Eat,* which is about how John (an American) learned to eat with chopsticks and Aiko (a Japanese schoolgirl) learned to eat with a knife and fork in Japan before they got married; their daughter learned how to use both.

5 minutes: Discuss the book, first asking open, aesthetic questions.

10 minutes: In "buddy" pairs, have children use chopsticks to pick up cotton balls. Children who know how to use chopsticks can demonstrate.

5 minutes: Have "buddies" talk to one another: "Tell about something that was hard for you to learn and something you've learned to do well."

10 minutes: Have each student draw a picture and write a caption about something that was hard or easy for him or her to learn.

10 minutes: Read aloud *Cleversticks,* which is about a little boy who starts school thinking that he can't do anything but finds that he is better than anyone at using chopsticks.

Suggest that students read other books in the related text set during self-selected independent reading time.

What things are unique about . . .

All People	Our Class	Each Person

Figure 8.1 Chart for Core Book Unit

Day 3

15 minutes: Create a three-column chart with students to record their ideas about the books *People, How My Parents Learned to Eat,* and *Cleversticks* (see Figure 8.1). Responses could include things students have discovered from one of the books, things they have learned about the class, and special things about each one of them.

10 minutes: Create a semantic map for the word *unique.* Record ideas on chart-paper to make a graphic organizer—for instance, unique things (knowing how to eat with chopsticks), different forms of the word (*uniqueness, uniquely*), and words with the root *uni-* (*universal, uniform, united*).

20 minutes: Have students write about things that are unique about them, such as their characteristics, things they do well, and things they learned that were easy or hard. Each student should illustrate his or her writing with crayons (see Figure 8.2). Publishing options are as follow:

- A class book or bulletin board: Unique People in Our Class
- A quilt: Students write on blank 5'' × 7'' cards with holes punched in all of the corners; tie together with yarn to form a paper quilt.
- A video: Record children in pairs reading each other's writing.

Assessment:

1. Observe whether students listened to and responded to the books during reading aloud and talking about them.
2. Note students' responses on a "word wall."
3. Assess students' writing.
4. Use an Anecdotal Record Assessment form to assess students' language use, vocabulary, and writing.

3.3
Anecdotal Record Assessment (p. 106)

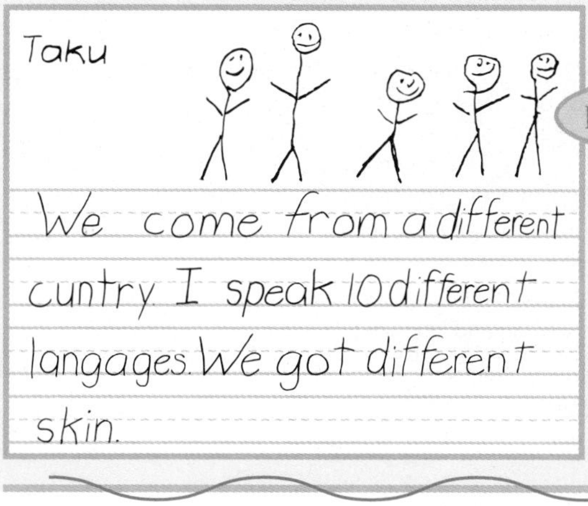

Taku
We come from a different
cuntry I speak 10 different
langages. We got different
skin.

Figure 8.2 Taku's Response to *People:* How He's Special

Table 8.2 Annotated List of Multicultural Children's Books

Native American

Anpao: An American Indian Odyssey (Highwater, 1977)—A history of traditional Native American tales in North America; a Newbery Honor Book. (U)

The Birchbark House (Erdrich, 1999)—This National Book Award finalist tells the story of an Ojibwe girl's life in 1847. (M/U)

Dogsong (Paulsen, 1985)—Tells of a contemporary Inuit boy who leaves a modern life to discover his traditional heritage; a Newbery Honor Book. (U)

The Girl Who Loved Wild Horses (Goble, 1978)—The Caldecott Medal was awarded to this traditional tale of a girl's powerful connection with horses. (P/M)

Hawk, I'm Your Brother (Baylor, 1976)—A contemporary story set in the Southwest that explores the relationship between a Native American boy and a hawk. (P/M)

Mama, Do You Love Me? (Joosse, 1991)—A young native American girl tests her mother's love. (P)

Sweetgrass (Hudson, 1984)—The story of a young Blackfoot girl living through a deadly smallpox epidemic, or "white man's sickness"; winner of the Canadian Library Associations Book of the Year Award. (U)

Walk Two Moons (Creech, 1994)—This Newbery Medal winner is about a 13-year-old who learns about her Native American mother. (U)

African American

Amazing Grace (Hoffman, 1991)—The story of Grace, a young African American girl with a talent for acting, who perseveres to win the part of Peter Pan in the school play, despite resistance because of her race and gender. (P/M)

Big Mama's (Crews, 1992)—A warm family story about visiting Big Mama's in Florida. (P)

Bud, Not Buddy (Curtis, 1999)—This well-written story tells of a 10-year-old homeless orphan, struggling to survive during the Great Depression of the 1930s, and his experiences with a famous jazz band; winner of both the 2000 Newbery Medal and the Coretta Scott King Award. (U)

Flossie and the Fox (McKissack, 1986)—An African American folktale retold in a storytelling style. (P/M)

Harlem (Myers, 1997)—A Caldecott Honor Award went to Christopher Myers for illustrating his father's book of poetry. (P/U)

Jonathan and His Mommy (Smalls-Hector, 1992)—A young boy and his mother walk through the neighborhood. (P)

The Patchwork Quilt (Flournoy, 1985)—Creating a quilt brings an African American family together. (P/M)

The People Could Fly: American Black Folktales (Hamilton, 1993)—A collection of 24 folktales from the African American experience, retold by the author. (M/U)

Roll of Thunder, Hear My Cry (Taylor, 1976)—The Depression-era story of an African American family in segregated Mississippi. (U)

Tar Beach (Ringgold, 1991)—A childhood memoir of family and hot summer nights in the city on the roof, which is the "tar beach." (P/M)

The Watsons Go to Birmingham—1963 (Curtis, 1995)—During the civil rights movement, an African American family from Michigan travel to Birmingham, where they experience racial hatred and a church bombing; winner of a Newbery Honor Award. (U)

Working Cotton (Williams, 1992)—A Caldecott Honor Award went to Carol Byard for illustrating this memoir about a migrant worker family in California. (P/U)

Hispanic Americans

Arroz con Leche: Popular Songs and Rhymes from Latin America (Delacre, 1989)—Songs and poems from several Latin American cultures. (P)

Barrio: Jose's Neighborhood (Ancona, 1998)—Photographs illustrate this story, which is set in the Mission District of San Francisco. (P)

Baseball in April and Other Stories (Soto, 1990)—A collection of stories about young Mexican Americans in California. (U)

Big Bushy Moustache (Soto, 1998)—A contemporary Cinco de Mayo story. (P)

Cendrillon: A Caribbean Cinderella (San Souci, 1998)—Creole words and phrases are used in this retelling of the Cinderella story. (P/U)

The Crossing (Paulsen, 1987)—A boy living in a border town in Mexico longs to go to the United States. (U)

Esperanza Rising (Ryan, 2000)—The 2002 Pura Belpre Award was given to this book.

Family Pictures/Cuados de Familia (Garza, 1990) and *In My Family/En mi Familia* (Garza, 1996)— The story, told in Spanish and in English, is illustrated by paintings of the author's memories of growing up in Brownsville, Texas. (P)

Note: P = Primary grades, M = Middle grades, U = Upper grades

The House on Mango Street (Cisneros, 1991)—A young girl's memoir. (U)

Too Many Tamales (Soto, 1993)—A family Christmas dinner and losing Mother's ring means that the children eat too many tamales looking for it. (P/M)

Under the Royal Palms: A Childhood in Cuba (Ada, 1998)—The 2000 Pura Belpre Award was given to this memoir.

Asian and Asian American

Baseball Saved Us (Mochizuki, 1993)—A young boy learns to play baseball in an internment camp during World War II. (P/M)

Dragonwings (Yep, 1975) and *Dragon's Gate* (Yep, 1993)—*Dragonwings* tells of the Chinese American experience at the time of the San Francisco earthquake, and *Dragon's Gate* is the story of Chinese Americans building the transcontinental railroad; both were Newbery Honor Books. (U)

Grandfather's Journey (Say, 1993)—Say won the Caldecott Medal for illustrating the tale of his grandfather's immigration to the United States from Japan. (P/M)

How My Parents Learned to Eat (Friedman, 1984)—A humorous memoir of a child who learns to eat with both chopsticks and knives and forks because her mother was Japanese and her father, American. (P/M)

Hush: A Thai Lullaby (Ho, 1996)—A lullaby for young children, with illustrations inspired by Thai art forms; won the Caldecott Honor Award. (P)

In the Year of the Boar and Jackie Robinson (Lord, 1984)—Baseball helps a Chinese girl adjust to life in the 1940s United States. (M-U)

Journey to Topaz (Uchida, 1971) and *Journey Home* (Uchida, 1978)—Stories of a Japanese American family that was interned during World War II. (U)

The Lotus Seed (Garland, 1993)—A Vietnamese woman brings a lotus seed to the United States to remind her of her homeland. (P/M)

The Name Jar (Choi, 2001)—A young Korean girl must decide whether to pick a new American name. (P)

Nim and the War Effort (Lee, 1998)—A young Chinese American girl in San Francisco does her part in World War II. (P)

A Single Shard (Park, 2001)—The Newbery Medal was awarded to this story, set in twelfth-century Korea. (U)

Tales from the Rainbow People (Yep, 1989) and *Tongues of Jade* (Yep, 1991)—Traditional stories collected from Chinese Americans, who told them not only to remind themselves of China but how to survive in a new country. (M-U)

Other Cultures

The Day of Ahmed's Secret (Heide & Gilliand, 1990)—A young boy in Cairo shares a secret with his family: He can write his name. (P)

The Golem and the Dragon Girl (Levitin, 1993)—A Chinese American girl and a Jewish American boy compare their cultures. (M)

Habibi (Nye, 1997)—A Palestinian American family moves from St. Louis to the village between Jerusalem and Palestine, where the father was born. (U)

The Keeping Quilt (Polacco, 1988)—A Jewish American family passes down a quilt, made from clothes of their Russian ancestors, through each new generation.

Number the Stars (Lowry, 1989)—Set during World War II, this is the story of a family in the Danish resistance who shelters a Jewish girl; won the Newbery Award.

People (Spier, 1980)—A global look at how people are alike and different; emphasizes how each of us is unique. (P/M)

Shabanu, Daughter of the Wind (Staples, 1989)—The daughter of a nomad in Pakistan is pledged to marry an older man for her family's benefit; a Newbery Honor Book. (U)

Three Cheers for Catherine the Great! (Best, 1999)—A Russian grandmother and American granddaughter exchange language lessons. (P/M)

People with Exceptionalities

Be Good to Eddie Lee (Fleming, 1993)—A child learns to appreciate a peer with Down syndrome. (P/M)

Mandy (Booth, 1991)—The thoughts of a young girl with a hearing loss. (P/M)

Mind's Eye (Fleischman, 1999)—Paralyzed at 16, a young girl learns to adapt with the help of her 88-year-old roommate. (U)

Stuck in Neutral (Trueman, 2000)—A 14-year-old with cerebral palsy, who is perceived to have the mental age of 3 to 4 months, narrates the story of his life. (U)

Well Wished (Billingsley, 1997)—A fantasy about two friends, one of whom is in a wheelchair, who switch bodies through magic. (M/U)

Author/Illustrator Unit

The author/illustrator unit approach to teaching with literature was also described in Chapter 7, Teaching with Literature, and an example was given in the Teaching Idea: Author Unit on Eric Carle. Here is another example of an author/illustrator unit for the primary through intermediate grades about an entire family of notable, award-winning, African American authors and illustrators, the Pinkneys. While they have tended to focus on the African American experience, their collective works truly celebrate the human spirit and thus have universal appeal.

GREAT BOOKS FOR CHILDREN

Jerry Pinkney has won Caldecott Honor medals for *Mirandy and Brother Wind* (McKissack, 1988), *The Talking Eggs: A Folktale from the American South* (San Souci, 1989), *John Henry* (Lester, 1994), and *The Ugly Duckling* (Andersen, 1999). Brian Pinkney has won the same award for *The Faithful Friend* (San Souci, 1996).

Jerry Pinkney's work as an illustrator working primarily in the medium of watercolor spans 40 years. In his distinguished career, he has received four Caldecott Honor medals, and he is the only illustrator to have won the Coretta Scott King Award five times. Jerry Pinkney's wife, Gloria Jean Pinkney, has written books of personal memoirs, such as *Back Home* (1992), which Jerry has illustrated. Their son Brian is an illustrator working primarily in the medium of scratchboard painting, and his wife, Andrea Davis Pinkney, has written books that Brian has illustrated. Like his father, Brian has won a Caldecott Honor award and a Coretta Scott King Award. Another son, Myles Pinkney, is a photographer who has illustrated poetry collections, such as *It's Raining Laughter* (Grimes, 1997).

I chose the Pinkneys for this author/illustrator unit because I love their work, and so did my children. *The Talking Eggs* was one of Elizabeth's favorite read-aloud books. It is a Creole-based, Cinderella-type tale set in Louisiana, where she was born. When I read it to her, she would say, "That looks like our house," referring to a house raised on piers because of the rainy climate and to the large trees draped in Spanish moss. But Elizabeth loved the luminous watercolor illustrations best. She would tell me they were magic and that she thought they were moving. We would put on music and she and Gordon would dance around like the little girl and magic rabbits in fancy party dress in the story; I would be the conjure woman. That is the magic that a beautiful book can conjure up in the mind of a child!

Jerry Pinkney

I also chose the Pinkneys because their books represent a major contribution to the field of multicultural literature and because they have illustrated and written a large number of books that cut across almost all genres of children's literature—not only multicultural literature but also biography, historical fiction, picture books, poetry, traditional literature, and even science fiction. Their books also are illustrated using different art mediums: watercolor, scratchboard painting, and photography.

A text set of Pinkney family books offers children many choices for self-selected reading that will tap their personal interests and provides a great opportunity for group work. For example, a group could focus on one of the Pinkneys—say, Jerry Pinkney, who has by far the most titles. (In fact, more than one group could focus on him.) A group could also choose a genre as their focus—for example, the biographies written by Andrea Davis Pinkney and illustrated by her husband, Brian.

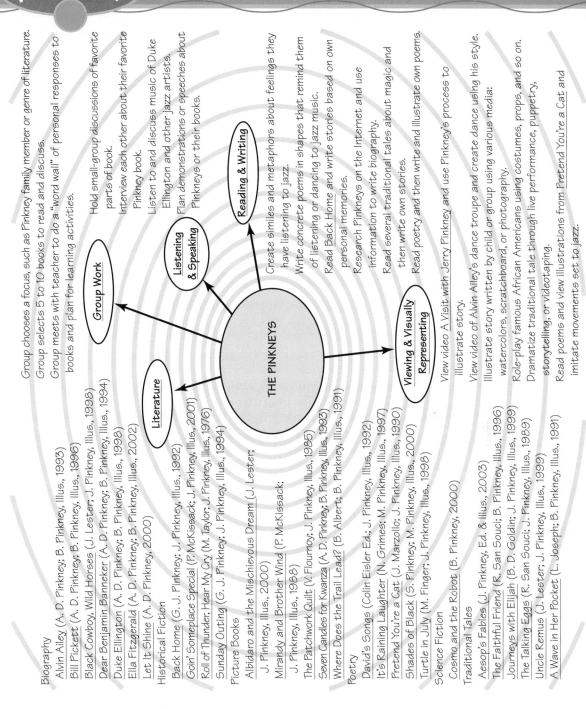

THE PINKNEYS

Group Work
- Group chooses a focus, such as Pinkney family member or genre of literature.
- Group selects 5 to 10 books to read and discuss.
- Group meets with teacher to do a "word wall" of personal responses to books and plan for learning activities.

Listening & Speaking
- Hold small-group discussions of favorite parts of book.
- Interview each other about their favorite Pinkney book.
- Listen to and discuss music of Duke Ellington and other jazz artists.
- Plan demonstrations or speeches about Pinkneys or their books.

Reading & Writing
- Create similes and metaphors about feelings they have listening to jazz.
- Write concrete poems in shapes that remind them of listening or dancing to jazz music.
- Read Back Home and write stories based on own personal memories.
- Research Pinkneys on the Internet and use information to write biography.
- Read several traditional tales about magic and then write own stories.
- Read poetry and then write and illustrate own poems.

Viewing & Visually Representing
- View video A Visit with Jerry Pinkney and use Pinkney's process to illustrate story.
- View video of Alvin Ailey's dance troupe and create dance using his style.
- Illustrate story written by child or group using various media: watercolors, scratchboard, or photography.
- Role-play famous African Americans using costumes, props, and so on.
- Dramatize traditional tale through live performance, puppetry, storytelling, or videotaping.
- Read poems and view illustrations from Pretend You're a Cat and imitate movements set to jazz.

Literature

Biography
Alvin Ailey (A. D. Pinkney; B. Pinkney, Illus., 1993)
Bill Pickett (A. D. Pinkney; B. Pinkney, Illus., 1996)
Black Cowboy, Wild Horses (J. Lester; J. Pinkney, Illus., 1998)
Dear Benjamin Banneker (A. D. Pinkney; B. Pinkney, Illus., 1994)
Duke Ellington (A. D. Pinkney; B. Pinkney, Illus., 1998)
Ella Fitzgerald (A. D. Pinkney; B. Pinkney, Illus., 2002)
Let It Shine (A. D. Pinkney, 2000)

Historical Fiction
Back Home (G. J. Pinkney; J. Pinkney, Illus., 1992)
Goin' Someplace Special (P. McKissack; J. Pinkney, Illus., 2001)
Roll of Thunder; Hear My Cry (M. Taylor; J. Pinkney, Illus., 1976)
Sunday Outing (G. J. Pinkney; J. Pinkney, Illus., 1994)

Picture Books
Albidaro and the Mischievous Dream (J. Lester; J. Pinkney, Illus., 2000)
Mirandy and Brother Wind (P. McKissack; J. Pinkney, Illus., 1988)
The Patchwork Quilt (V. Flournoy; J. Pinkney, Illus., 1985)
Seven Candles for Kwanza (A. D. Pinkney; B. Pinkney, Illus., 1993)
Where Does the Trail Lead? (B. Albert; B. Pinkney, Illus., 1991)

Poetry
David's Songs (Colin Eisler Ed.; J. Pinkney, Illus., 1992)
It's Raining Laughter (N. Grimes; M. Pinkney, Illus., 1997)
Pretend You're a Cat (J. Marzollo; J. Pinkney, Illus., 1990)
Shades of Black (S. Pinkney; M. Pinkney, Illus., 2000)
Turtle in July (M. Finger; J. Pinkney, Illus., 1998)

Science Fiction
Cosmo and the Robot (B. Pinkney, 2000)

Traditional Tales
Aesop's Fables (J. Pinkney, Ed. & Illus., 2003)
The Faithful Friend (R. San Souci; B. Pinkney, Illus., 1996)
Journeys with Elijah (B. D. Goldin; J. Pinkney, Illus., 1999)
The Talking Eggs (R. San Souci; J. Pinkney, Illus., 1989)
Uncle Remus (J. Lester; J. Pinkney, Illus., 1999)
A Wave in Her Pocket (L. Joseph; B. Pinkney, Illus., 1991)

A teacher could easily spend two weeks doing an author/illustrator unit on the Pinkneys, as shown in the Ripple Effect on the Pinkney family on page 283. Ideas are provided for learning experiences in all six areas of the language arts—listening and speaking, reading and writing, and viewing and visually representing—and a selection of their many books are included, as well.

Genre Unit

The third type of literature focus unit is the genre unit, which focuses on a specific type of literature, such as science fiction or poetry. The following Snapshot shows how a genre unit using informational books and biographies emerged as a "ripple effect" from discussing Christopher Columbus in the Americas in a literature circle in a third-grade Spanish bilingual class. The Snapshot also illustrates how teacher Paul Boyd-Batstone recognized the opportunity to integrate multicultural content into the curriculum by organizing it around a genre unit using informational books and biographies based on his students' responses to a controversial issue.

"Somebody's Lying": Discovering the Truth about Columbus and the Taino People

TEACHER RESOURCES

See *Crossroads: Literature and Language in Culturally and Linguistically Diverse Classrooms* (Cox & Boyd-Batstone, 1997).

See Chapter 7, Teaching with Literature, for more on literature circles.

In Edison Elementary School, which has many ELL students and several bilingual classrooms, teachers team teach and Latino bilingual and monolingual English students from different classes are combined regularly during the year to promote intercultural understanding. One of the third-grade bilingual teachers, Paul Boyd-Batstone, used a literature-based, response-centered approach literature circle to integrate language arts across the curriculum. Students worked in groups, choosing books or themes of interest to them to form the basis of language and literacy activities developed through a literature plan.

One year, all the literature circle groups in Paul's class were reading books about the people, history, and culture of the Americas. One of the groups had brought two books about Columbus back from the library: *Columbus* by the d'Aulaires (1955), a biography written from a Eurocentric perspective, and *Encounter* by Jane Yolen (1992), written from the first-person perspective of a Taino (the native people who lived on the island of San Salvador when Columbus landed there in October 1492). Specifically, *Encounter* tells how the Taino people and their culture were devasted as a result of their encounter with Columbus and his men.

Elizabeth—a white, native English speaker of European descent—joined the literature circle on the day it wanted to read *Encounter*. Paul suggested that Elizabeth read it aloud, since it was written in English and she was "an expert

English user." (Actually, he wanted to make her feel part of a community of learners.) Elizabeth read aloud to Paul's Latino students: Antonio, Fabiola, Eddie, Sammy, Natalie, and Gerardo. During this time, Paul conferenced with students in other literature circles. When Elizabeth finished reading *Encounter*, Paul told the group to take some time and talk about it—anything they wanted. Paul joined the group after a while. (The discussion was in English, because Elizabeth didn't speak Spanish.) Here's part of that discussion:

Paul:	Tell me about the book.
Antonio:	It's a sad story. Columbus took the Taino people as slaves to Spain. Many died. Only one survived in the story.
Elizabeth:	He was little. A child. The little boy had a bad dream about Columbus coming and he woke up. Nobody believed him when he said bad things would happen.
Antonio:	He was sad because he had his people and his land taken away.
Paul:	Have you ever had things taken from you?
Elizabeth:	We were robbed. They took my Dad's tools and our bikes.
Eddie:	My mom was washing, and they stole all the clothes from the line.
Fabiola	(to Elizabeth): How did they get in your house?
Elizabeth:	Don't know. But it's happened twice.

(Other children told about being robbed. Every child in the group had had such an experience.)

Bilingual teacher Paul Boyd-Batstone and a small group of students discuss multicultural literature: the book Encounter, *by Jane Yolen.*

Paul:	So you've all been robbed, and the boy in the story was robbed.
Elizabeth:	Yeah, of his own people.
Gerardo:	They took him away from his land.
Paul:	Did he ever come back?
Natalie:	No.

Then Paul read aloud the other book, *Columbus*. It didn't mention the Taino by name but referred to them as "red-skinned savages" and said, "The Spaniards did not mind being treated like gods by these gentle heathens to whom they had come to bring the Christian faith" (d'Aulaire & d'Aulaire, 1955, p. 40). This book didn't tell what happened to the Taino after Columbus left, either. A lively discussion followed, comparing the two different perspectives on Columbus and his visit to the New World. The students were most interested in what happened to the Taino described in *Encounter*. Paul recorded their ideas on a "word wall" (see Figure 8.3).

The students in the literature circle read other books about Columbus and the native people of the Americas. The question the students kept asking as they read these books was: "What happened to the Taino people when Columbus came to the Americas?" Depending on which perspective the book was written from, the information was presented differently. Antonio finally summed it up: "Somebody's lying."

Based on this experience, the students' understanding of history changed. They realized how important it is to look at people and events from multiple perspectives and to read multiple books on controversial issues. The

Figure 8.3 "Word Wall" for Two Perspectives on History

What happened to the Taino people when Columbus came to the Americas?

In <u>Encounter</u> by Jane Yolen	In <u>Columbus</u> by the d'Aulaires
Taino welcomed Columbus with feast.	Didn't mind being treated like gods.
Took Taino's gold and gave them beads.	Thought gold was his to take for Spain.
Took Taino as slaves to Spain.	Thought Taino should be converted.
He lied to them.	They were cold in Spain.
They lost land, language, and religion.	Doesn't say what happened to them.
300,000 Taino in 1492—only a few today.	Taino didn't seem important to them.

children wrote a report about what they learned, "La vida de los Indios Tainos" ("Life among the Taino Indians"). And they also wrote a script based on the book *Encounter*, which they presented as a play for the whole school. They wanted to tell the story of Columbus's arrival in the Americas from the point of view of the Taino and to make it clear that the entire Taino people and culture were devastated because of their encounter with Columbus and his men.

This Snapshot is a real-life illustration of how multicultural content can be integrated into the curriculum. What's more, it illustrates how a school can promote intercultural understanding and how a perceptive teacher can use a literature genre unit to do this.

Historical Fiction and Biographies

By locating children's books with various perspectives on multicultural content, you and your students can read, discuss, and compare different views on historical figures, events, and issues such as gender, race/ethnicity, disabilities, social class, and language and cultural diversity. Here are examples of historical fiction and biographies about Columbus and the native people of the Americas that offer three different points of view: the European perspective, Columbus's personal perspective, and the perspective of the Taino people.

European Perspective

Columbus, by Ingri and Edgar Parin d'Aulaire (1955)—This well-illustrated picture book biography portrays the native Taino people as simple "heathens," who worshipped Columbus and his men as gods; the book also shows Columbus's intentions to convert the Taino to Christianity and to teach them Spanish. As mentioned earlier, this book doesn't tell that the Taino ceased to exist as a people after they were taken to Spain.

The Columbus Story, by Alice Dalgliesh (1955)—This is another well-illustrated picture biography. Its only mention of the Taino says that Columbus "took with him some Indians." They were not regarded as having equal status with the Europeans.

Columbus's Perspective

I, Columbus: My Journal, 1492–1493, edited by Peter and Connie Roop (1990)—Adapted from a copy of Columbus's log, this book shows that he wanted the native people to develop a friendly attitude so they could be converted to Christianity, as they seemed to have no religion. Columbus wanted to take them to Spain so they could learn Spanish, even though he recognized that they had their own culture and language.

The Log of Christopher Columbus, by Christopher Columbus, selections by Steve Lowe (1992)—In this picture book, also adapted from Columbus's log, the explorer mentions meeting friendly native people on arrival in San Salvador, which is where the book ends.

See Chapter 7, Teaching with Literature, for more children's books with different perspectives on multicultural topics.

TEACHER RESOURCES

For stories, interviews, and lesson plans that re-evaluate the legacy of Columbus in North America, see *Rethinking Columbus: The Next 500 Years* (Bigelow & Peterson, 1998).

GREAT BOOKS FOR CHILDREN

Columbus

The First Voyage of Christopher Columbus 1492 (Smith, 1992)

Follow the Dream: The Story of Christopher Columbus (Sis, 1991)

In 1492 (Marzollo, 1991)

A Picture Book of Christopher Columbus (Adler, 1991a), also available in Spanish: *Un Libro Ilustrado Sobre Cristobal Colon* (Adler, 1991b)

Westward with Columbus (Dyson, 1991)

Where Do You Think You're Going, Christopher Columbus? (Fritz, 1980)

Taino Perspective

Encounter, by Jane Yolen (1992)—This dramatically illustrated historical fiction picture book shows that Columbus encountered native people who had an established culture and civilization, which challenges the idea that he "discovered" a new world. Events are seen through the eyes of a Taino boy, who escapes from Columbus's ship (which is taking his people to Spain) and lives to old age. During his life, he sees colonization by the Spanish result in the loss of his land, religion, language, and people. This boy is the last Taino.

Morning Girl, by Michael Dorris (1992)—This short novel is a historical fictional perspective about what the community of Taino people that Columbus met in the fifteenth century might have been like. We meet Morning Girl and her family and see that they live in a community striving to co-exist with the natural world, not dominate it. The community also expects visitors to be friendly, not dangerous. The book ends with the arrival of Columbus.

A nswers to Questions about Multicultural Education and Children's Books

• *How should we approach multicultural education?*

A *culture* is a system of knowledge that produces behavior and is used to interpret experience. People in a particular social group share a culture. Student cultural diversity has three features: race/ethnicity, class, and language.

According to Grant and Sleeter, multicultural education means working with students who are different because of race/ethnicity, gender, class, or disability. The goal is to reduce prejudice and discrimination and provide equal opportunities for all students. Multicultural education attempts to reform the total schooling process for all children, whether at an all-white suburban school or a multiracial, multilingual urban school.

Banks identifies four approaches to integrating multicultural content into the curriculum: the contributions, additive, transformation, and social action approaches. The latter approach is the highest level, which educates students for social change and decision making. In reality, the approaches are mixed and blended, but teachers should always be aware of the importance of moving to higher levels.

Teachers should be aware of how language is used in students' homes, give students the full range of genres typically used in school, and accept students' use of native languages and dialects. Ethnosensitivity is the most important principle of effective literacy instruction for students from cultural and language minorities and for speakers of nonmainstrean English.

- ● *How can we use children's books in multicultural education?*

Culturally conscious literature—which depicts the diversity in human society, including ethnic, linguistic, religious, socioeconomic, and gender differences—is written primarily by but not limited to authors who are members of such groups and thus accurately portrays and reveals their groups' cultures. In selecting culturally conscious children's books, teachers should look for culturally pluralistic themes, positive portrayals of characters from diverse groups, settings throughout the United States, well-developed and accurately portrayed characters, and illustrations that are not stereotypical. Every classroom library should have many of these types of books available for self-selected reading. Using literature focus units based on a multicultural core book unit, author/illustrator unit, or genre unit is an effective way to teach language arts with multicultural children's books.

Looking Further

1. Create an activity that would fit each of Banks's four approaches to integrating multicultural content for either a primary- (K–3) or upper-grade (4–6) class.

2. Find two children's books that present different perspectives on multicultural content (e.g., gender, disabilities, immigrant status, or ethnic/race relations), and compare them for any biases they may contain.

3. Bring five multicultural children's books from the list in the chapter to your college class. In groups, use the criteria for selecting culturally conscious books to evaluate them (see p. 275). Share what your group discussed with the rest of the class.

4. Plan a one-day lesson using one of the core books listed in Table 8.1 (p. 276) Teach the lesson to a group of children, and then describe what happened with your college class.

Children's Books, Films, and Software

Ada, A. F. (1998). *Under the royal palms: A childhood in Cuba.* New York: Atheneum.

Adler, D. A. (1991a). *A picture book of Christopher Columbus* (J. & A. Wallner, Illus.). New York: Holiday House.

Adler, D. A. (1991b). *Un libro ilustrado sobre Cristobal Colon* (por J. Y. A. Wallner, Illus.). Traduccion de Teresa Mlawer. Madrid, Spain: Editorial Everest.

Albert, B. (1991). *Where does the trail lead?* (B. Pinkney, Illus). New York: Simon & Schuster.

Ancona, G. (1998). *Barrio: Jose's neighborhood.* San Diego: Harcourt Brace.

Anderson, H. C. (1999). *The ugly duckling* (J. Pinkney, Illus.) New York: Morrow.

Arnoff, A. (1991). *In for winter, out for spring* (J. Pinkney, Illus.). New York: Harcourt Brace.

Ashley, B. (1991). *Cleversticks* (D. Brazell, Illus.). New York: Crown.

Baer, J. (1990). *This is the way we go to school.* New York: Scholastic.

Baylor, B. (1976). *Hawk, I'm your brother.* New York: Scribner's.

Best, C. (1999). *Three cheers for Catherine the Great!* New York: Kroupa/DK Ink.

Billingsley, F. (1997). *Well wished.* New York: Atheneum.

Booth, B. D. (1991). *Mandy.* New York: Lothrop, Lee & Shepard.

Bridwell, N. (1974). *Clifford's riddles.* New York: Scholastic.

Choi, Y. (2001). *The name jar.* New York: Knopf.

Cisneros, S. (1991). *The house on Mango Street.* New York: Vintage Books.

Collier, J. L., & Collier, C. (1974). *My brother Sam is dead.* NY: Four Winds Press.

Columbus, C. (1992). *The log of Christopher Columbus,* selected by S. Lowe (R. Sabuda, Illus.). New York: Philomel.

Creech, S. (1994). *Walk two moons.* New York: HarperCollins.

Crews, D. (1991). *Big Mama's.* New York: Greenwillow.

Curtis, C. P. (1995). *The Watsons go to Birmingham—1963.* New York: Delacorte.

Curtis, C. P. (1999). *Bud, not Buddy.* New York: Delacorte.

d'Aulaire, I., & d'Aulaire, E. P. (1955). *Columbus.* New York: Doubleday.

Dalgliesh, A. (1955). *The Columbus story* (L. Politi, Illus.). New York: Scribner's.

Dalokay, V. (1994). *Sister Shako and Kolo the Goa: Memories of my childhood in Turkey.* New York: Lothrop, Lee, & Shepard.

Delacre, L. (1989). *Arroz con leche: Popular songs and rhymes from Latin America.* New York: Scholastic.

Dooley, N. (1992). *Everybody cooks rice.* Minneapolis: Carolrhoda Books.

Dorris, M. (1992). *Morning girl.* New York: Hyperion.

Dunbar, P. L. (2000). *Jump back, honey* (B. Pinkney, J. Pinkney, et al., Illus.). New York: Hyperion.

Dyson, J. (1991). *Westward with Columbus* (P. Christopher, Photographer). New York: Scholastic.

Eisler, C. (Ed.). (1992). *David's songs: His psalms and their story* (J. Pinkney, Illus.). New York: Dial.

Erdrich, L. (1999). *The birchbark house.* New York: Hyperion.

Finger, M. (1998). *Turtle in July* (J. Pinkney, Illus.). New York: Macmillan.

Fleischman, P. (1999). *Mind's eye.* New York: Holt.

Fleming, V. (1993). *Be good to Eddie Lee.* New York: Philomel.

Flournoy, V. (1985). *The patchwork quilt* (J. Pinkney, Illus.). New York: Dial.

Forbes, E. (1946). *Johnny Tremain.* New York: Houghton Mifflin.

Friedman, I. (1984). *How my parents learned to eat.* New York: Houghton Mifflin.

Fritz, J. (1980). *Where do you think you're going, Christopher Columbus?* (M. Tomes, Illus.). New York: Putnam's.

Garland, S. (1993). *The lotus seed.* New York: Harcourt Brace Jovanovich.

Garza, C. L. (1990). *Family pictures/Cuadro de familia.* San Francisco: Children's Book Press.

Garza, C. L. (1996). *In my family/En mi familia.* San Francisco: Children's Book Press.

Goble, P. (1978). *The girl who loved wild horses.* New York: Bradbury.

Goldin, B. D. (1999). *Journeys with Elijah: Eight Tales of the Prophet* (J. Pinkney, Illus.). New York: Harcourt.

Greenfield, E. (1994). *Mary McLeod Bethune* (J. Pinkney, Illus.). New York: HarperCollins.

Grimes, N. (1997). *It's raining laughter* (M. Pinkney, Illus.). New York: Dial.

Hamilton, V. (1993). *The people could fly: American black folktales.* New York: Knopf.

Heide, F. B., & Gilliand, J. H. (1990). *The day of Ahmed's secret.* New York: Lothrop, Lee & Shepard.

Hicyilmaz, G. (1992). *Against the storm.* New York: Little, Brown.

Highwater, J. (1977). *Anpao: An American Indian odyssey.* New York: Lippincott.

Ho, Minfong. (1996). *Hush: A Thai lullaby.* New York: Orchard.

Hoffman, M. (1991). *Amazing Grace.* New York: Dial.

Hooks, W. (1990). *The ballad of Belle Dorcas* (B. Pinkney, Illus.). New York: Knopf.

Hudson, J. (1989). *Sweetgrass.* New York: Philomel.

Hughes, L. (1994). *The dream keeper and other poems* (B. Pinkney, Illus.). New York: Knopf.

In My Own Voice: Multicultural Poets [Computer software]. Available from Sunburst Communications.

Joosse, B. M. (1991). *Mama, do you love me?* New York: Chronicle.

Jordan, D., & Jordan, R. M. (2000). *Salt in his shoes.* New York: Scholastic.

Joseph, J. (1991). *A wave in her pocket: Stories from Trinidad* (B. Pinkney, Illus.). New York: Clarion.

Kessler, L. (1991). *Old Turtle's 90 knock knock jokes and riddles.* New York: Greenwillow.

Lee, M. (1997). *Nim and the war effort*. New York: Farrar, Straus & Giroux.

Lester, J. (1994). *John Henry* (J. Pinkney, Illus.). New York: Dial.

Lester, J. (1996). *Sam and the tigers* (J. Pinkney, Illus.). New York: Dial.

Lester, J. (1998). *Black cowboy, wild horses* (J. Pinkney, Illus.). New York: Dial.

Lester, J. (1999). *Uncle Remus: The complete tales* (J. Pinkney, Illus). New York: Dial.

Lester, J. (2000). *Albidaro and the mischieveous dream* (J. Pinkney, Illus.). New York: Penguin Putnam.

Levitin, S. (1993). *The golem and the dragon girl*. New York: Dial.

Lord, B. B. (1984). *In the year of the boar and Jackie Robinson*. New York: Harper & Row.

Lowry, L. (1989). *Number the stars*. New York: Houghton Mifflin.

Marzollo, J. (1990). *Pretend you're a cat* (J. Pinkney, Illus.). New York: Dial.

Marzollo, J. (1991). *In 1492* (S. Bjorkman, Illus.). New York: Scholastic.

McKissack, P. (1986). *Flossie and the fox*. New York: Dial.

McKissack, P. (1998). *Mirandy and Brother Wind* (J. Pinkney, Illus.). New York: Knopf.

McKissack, P. (2001). *Goin' someplace special* (J. Pinkney, Illus.). New York: Atheneum.

Mochizuki, K. (1993). *Baseball saved us*. New York: Lee & Low.

Mohr, N. (1990). *Felita*. New York: Bantam.

Morris, A. (1989). *Bread, bread, bread*. New York, Lothrop.

Myers, W. D. (1997). *Harlem*. New York: Scholastic.

Nye, N. S. (1998). *Habibi*. New York: Simon & Schuster.

Orlev, U. (1991). *The man from the other side*. New York: Houghton Mifflin.

Park, L. S. (2001). *A single shard*. New York: Clarion.

Paulsen, G. (1985). *Dogsong*. New York: Bradbury.

Paulsen, G. (1987). *The crossing*. New York: Doubleday.

Phillips, L. (1993). *Invisible oink: Pig jokes*. New York: Viking.

Pinkney, A. D. (1993). *Alvin Ailey*. (B. Pinkney, Illus.). New York:Hyperion.

Pinkney, A. D. (1993). *Seven candles for Kwanzaa* (B. Pinkney, Illus.). New York: Dial.

Pinkney, A. D. (1994). *Dear Benjamin Banneker* (B. Pinkney, Illus.). New York: Harcourt.

Pinkney, A. D. (1996). *Bill Pickett: Rodeo-ridin' cowboy* (B Pinkney, Illus.). New York: Harcourt.

Pinkney, A. D. (1998). *Duke Ellington: Piano Prince and his orchestra* (B. Pinkney, Illus.). New York: Hyperion.

Pinkney, A. D. (2000). *Let it shine: Stories of Black Women Freedom Fighters*. New York: Harcourt.

Pinkney, A. D. (2002). *Ella Fitzgerald: The Tale of a Vocal Virtuosa* (B. Pinkney, Illus.). New York: Hyperion.

Pinkney, B. (2000). *Cosmo and the robot*. New York: Greenwillow.

Pinkney, G. J. (1992). *Back home* (J. Pinkney, Illus.). New York: Dial.

Pinkney, G. J. (1994). *Sunday outing* (J. Pinkney, Illus.). New York: Dial.

Pinkney, J. (Author & Illus.). (2000). *Aesop's fables*. New York: North South.

Pinkney, J. (Author & Illus.). (2002). *Noah's ark*. New York: Sea Star.

Pinkney, S. (2000). *Shades of black: A celebration of our children* (M. Pinkney, Illus.). New York: Scholastic.

Polacco, P. (1988). *The keeping quilt*. New York: Simon & Schuster.

Ringgold, F. (1991). *Tar beach*. New York: Crown.

Roop, P., & Roop, C. (Eds.). (1990). *I, Columbus: My journal: 1492–1493* (P. E. Hanson, Illus.). New York: Avon.

Ryan, P. M. (2000). *Esperanza rising*. New York: Scholastic.

San Souci, R. D. (1989). *The talking eggs* (J. Pinkney, Illus). New York: Dial.

San Souci, R. D. (1992). *Sukey and the mermaid* (B. Pinkney, Illus.). New York: Four Winds.

San Souci, R. D. (1996). *The faithful friend* (B. Pinkney, Illus.). New York: Four Winds.

San Souci, R. D. (2001). *Cendrillon: A Caribbean Cinderella*. New York: Simon & Schuster.

Say, A. (1993). *Grandfather's journey*. Boston: Houghton Mifflin.

Schami, R. (1992). *A handful of stars*. New York: Dutton.

Schroeder, A. (1996). *Minty: A story of young Harriet Tubman* (J. Pinkney, Illus.). New York: Dial.

Sis, P. (1991). *Follow the dream: The story of Christopher Columbus*. New York: Knopf.

Smalls-Hector, I. (1992). *Jonathan and his mommy*. New York: Little, Brown.

Smith, B. (1992). *The first voyage of Christopher Columbus 1492*. New York: Viking Penguin.

Soto, G. (1990). *Baseball in April and other stories*. New York: Harcourt Brace Jovanovich.

Soto, G. (1993). *Too many tamales*. New York: Putnam.

Spier, P. (1980). *People*. New York: Doubleday.

Staples, S. F. (1989) *Shabanu: Daughter of the wind*. New York: Knopf.

Sterne, N. (1979). *Tyrannosaurus wrecks: A book of dinosaur riddles*. New York: Crowell.

Taylor, M. (1976). *Roll of thunder, hear my cry* (J. Pinkney, Illus). New York: Dial.

Trueman, T. (2000). *Stuck in neutral*. New York: Harper-Collins.

Uchida, Y. (1971). *Journey to Topaz*. New York: Scribner's.

Uchida, Y. (1978). *Journey home*. New York: Atheneum.

Visit with Jerry Pinkney, A. [Video]. (1995). Available from Penguin Author Series.

Williams, S. A. (1992). *Working cotton*. New York: Harcourt Brace Jovanovich.

Yep, L. (1975). *Dragonwings*. New York: Harper & Row.

Yep, L. (1989). *Tales from the rainbow people*. New York: Harper & Row.

Yep, L. (1991). *Tongues of jade*. New York: Harper.

Yep, L. (1993). *Dragon's gate*. New York: HarperCollins.

Yolen, J. (1992). *Encounter* (D. Shannon, Illus.). New York: Harcourt Brace Jovanovich.

chapter 9

The Writing Process

Questions about the Writing Process

- *What is the writing process?*
- *How should we teach and assess writing as a process?*

REFLECTIVE RESPONSE

Choose one thing you remember about learning to write in elementary school and write about it. Think about how it might have influenced your feelings about yourself as a writer today and how you will teach and assess writing.

What Children Do in the Writing Process

The notion of teaching writing as a process, which developed during the 1970s and 1980s, is based to a great extent on Donald Graves's (1983) influential book *Writing: Teachers and Children at Work*. With this approach, the focus of writing instruction shifted from the product to the process. The *process* of writing refers to what children do, which Graves describes as having five stages—(1) prewrite, (2) draft, (3) revise, (4) edit, and (5) publish—each of which involves children in a number of different activities (see Figure 9.1, p. 294).

Figure 9.1
What Children Do in the Writing Process

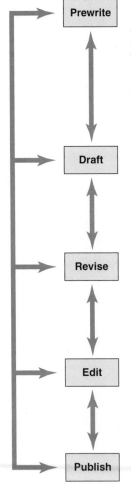

Prewrite
Draw on their own experiences
Read or listen to stories read aloud
Generate ideas
Organize thinking
Talk over ideas with others
Choose what type of writing they'll do: journals,
  letters, expressive writing, literature as a model
Consider the audience they're writing for
Brainstorm ideas: make a list, cluster, quickwrite
Rehearse: draw, talk, map, plot, diagram, act out

Draft
Put their ideas down on paper
Focus on meaning, rather than conventions
Feel free to experiment
Understand that writing can change
Try out different possibilities
Talk over their drafts with others
Rehearse some more

Revise
Reread during and after writing the draft
Rethink what they've written
Share with others in the reader's circle
Talk to the teacher in a conference
Change, add, delete, or modify their draft
Clarify meaning
Expand ideas

Edit
Proofread their revised piece
Talk to the teacher in an editing conference
Ask for help in a peer-editing conference
Rephrase and refine
Check: spelling, punctuation, capitalization, usage, form, legibility
Identify and correct their own pieces

Publish
Choose the form: book, displayed in room, drama, reader's theater,
  electronic media, letter, "big book," newspaper, posters, advertisement
Share their published pieces by reading aloud: reader's circle, Author's
  Chair, writing workshop

Terms like *prewriting, drafting, revising, editing,* and *publishing* are useful for talking about the parts of the writing process, which don't necessarily occur in a fixed order for individual writers in specific situations (Graves, 1994). However, teachers shouldn't think of these terms as comprising steps in a rigid, linear fashion. Writing is a recursive process. Writers don't always do things in the same order. For instance, they may change the topic of a piece in the middle of writing it, rather than definitely deciding it at the beginning. They may think of an ending first and then add a beginning and a middle. Or they may change ideas as they revise, in no particular order.

Graves suggests the idea of multiple starts in writing. Children may write down several possible opening sentences, with the understanding that only one or perhaps none of them will be used. They realize that first drafts can be tentative, and they can choose and change things at any time. Children need to know that they can take chances, make and test hypotheses, and experiment and that teachers will accept their approximations in writing (Cambourne & Turbill, 1987). To gain this confidence, children must be allowed to explore ideas through writing freely, to discover for themselves how the process works rather than follow a daily writing schedule, established by the teacher. Different aspects of the writing process occur simultaneously and even randomly. Teachers should exercise caution about turning a personal, creative, fluid, and even messy process like writing into a daily routine that must be followed.

Writing is a way of knowing, of discovering what you know as you put it down—not only in the form of words and phrases but of scribbles and drawings, ideas and images, and all the other wonderful stuff in your mind that may only become clear as you engage in the process of writing it down. Just as you may not know what you're going to say until you say it, so you may not know what you're going to write until you write it. Thus, as you write, writing becomes a way of knowing.

Viewed in this way, writing is a rather messy process. And as children freely use their innately human symbol-making power, they certainly make a lot of messes. They mark and scribble, gesture and talk and act out, draw and write and rewrite, crumple paper and make holes in it as they erase and break pencil points, and then write some more as they revise. All these activities are part of discovering what they know about the world and communicating it to others. Think of children as attempting to interpret the world by hypothesizing, taking chances, and testing new experiences.

Writing Workshop

Writing workshop is based on the ideas behind writing as a process (Atwell, 1987; Calkins, 1983; Graves, 1983; Solley, 2000) and reflects a social constructivist point of view about learning, as well (Lensmire, 2000). From a Vygotskian perspective, students collaborate with the teacher and other students to initiate writing. From a Piagetian perspective, they respond to tensions within themselves, within the environment, and with others to discover meaning.

See Chapter 1, Learning and Teaching Language Arts, for further discussion of these key ideas.

The student's role is to exercise his or her choice of topic and genre in writing and time for writing. Students use their own voices and learn to take control and responsibility for their own learning. The teacher's role is to provide a regular block of time for children to write and to initiate the process approach to writing in a student- and response-centered classroom. The teacher's role also involves modeling, observing students' activity, assessing progress, demonstrating the writing process and needed skills, collaborating through conferences and serving as an audience for young writers, and expecting that children will succeed as writers. Teachers and other students respond to student writing to help them rethink, revise, and edit. Students write for real purposes and real audiences. Writing conventions and skills are taught in the context of this real writing and adapted to meet individual needs (Graves, 1994).

Writing workshop may appear loosely structured, but it requires excellent organization and observation and ongoing, authentic assessment on the part of the teacher. Part of students' responsibility is to learn the procedures of the writing process and writing workshop. Each session begins with a brief minilesson to initiate or demonstrate a procedure, concept, or skill relevant to students' writing and needs. This lesson is followed by a very brief planning period. The bulk of the period is reserved for writing, during which the teacher circulates, providing support, observing students' needs, and holding individual conferences. The teacher can also write during this time, modeling writing for students. The session can end with an open sharing in which students read their writing to the whole group and request feedback. Assessment is ongoing and authentic, and students do self-assessment. Students keep their work in progress in folders and use notebooks to jot down ideas to write about (Calkins, 1991).

Writing workshop is especially well suited to classrooms in which students' abilities vary. Likewise, this method is effective when students would seem to benefit from one-to-one conferences with the teacher and a cooperative, collaborative learning environment.

Writing Workshop in a Fourth-Grade Class of English Language Learners

ELL

See Chapter 3, First- and Second-Language Development, for more on teaching English language learners.

See Chapter 6, Reading, for a discussion of reading workshop.

Sheila Kline teaches fourth grade at Lincoln Elementary School, in Long Beach, California, in which over 80 percent of the students come to school speaking a language other than English. About half are Latino and Spanish speaking, and another half are Cambodian American and Khmer speaking; a few speak other languages.

Many of Sheila's fourth-grade students are still developing fluency in English and are emerging readers and writers. She uses writing and reading workshops every day because she believes in the writing process approach and the ongoing authentic assessment it requires. She takes a social constructivist perspective on learning and teaching language arts and feels her English language learning (ELL) students benefit greatly from the one-to-one individual conferences with her and the cooperative environment that exists.

Sheila schedules hour-long writing workshops on Mondays, Wednesdays, and Fridays and reading workshops on Tuesdays and Thursdays, although reading and writing go on in both. Since two new students just joined Sheila's class, she's brought out handmade posters that describe writing workshop in her class and reviewed them with students (see Figure 9.2).

A Minilesson (7 minutes)

Sheila starts with a minilesson on expressive writing. She's made another poster to provide visual support for what she's saying and so students can refer to it later (see Figure 9.3). She goes over the ideas on the poster:

Figure 9.2	Class Poster: Writing Workshop

In writing workshop, writers:

1. Think about what they want to write about. Use their idea list to find a subject.
2. Prewrite. Organize everything you want to say. Use a cluster, list, or outline.
3. Write a first draft.
4. Read the draft to at least two other people in reader's circle.
5. Revise. Make changes, add new information. Check to see if there is a topic, supporting details, and a conclusion. Writers listen to see if they used interesting sentences and good descriptions. Will the words put a picture in the reader's mind?
6. Read the piece in reader's circle.
7. Edit. Check your spelling, punctuation, margins, and indenting.
8. Turn in your paper for either an editing conference or a score.
9. Publish what is perfect!

Figure 9.3	Class Poster: Minilesson for Expressive Writing

Can you express yourself? Follow these easy steps, and you will succeed:

1. Introduction
   - Can you tell a little about the subject?
   - Why is this scene, person, object, or memory important? Give a clue or hint.
2. Body Paragraphs
   - Have you described the person, scene, object, or memory?
   - Have you told what you see, think, or feel about it?
   - Have you used details, names, and everything you can remember?
3. Conclusion
   - Tell again why this subject is important to you.

Sheila: I will do a minilesson to help make your writing stronger, more powerful. You're already doing lots of this. After we talk, you can look at the poster and think, "Oh, yeah! That's what I'm doing." Can you express yourself? Get those wonderful ideas out? From your brain to your hand and out your pencil? Sometimes it's *hard*. I know it is for me. Is it hard for any of you, too? (She raises her hand and several students do, too.)

If you follow these steps I think it will help.

1. *Introduction.* Give a little clue or hint: "I'm going to tell you about something that changed my life" or "I'm going to tell you about the scariest thing." Throw out a fishing line with a little hook for the reader.
2. *Body Paragraphs.* Describe a lot. Now you have so much more to say than when we started school!

Child: In July, we knew a little. Now we know a lot.

Child: You could write more now.

Sheila: Check these off. Ask yourself, "What are your feelings?" Give details. Have you used names? What did he look like? Then . . .

Child:	Conclusion. End.
Sheila:	Yes! Wrap it up with a ribbon. "I told you about my plant because it's the neatest thing you've ever seen." Should you end with "the end" in 2 inch bubble letters?
Child:	No. Write more.
Child:	They'll be bored. Write more.
Sheila:	Make it juicy!

Checking Writing Status (3 minutes)

To get organized, Sheila checks with each student to see what he or she is planning to do. She uses the Writing Status Checklist shown in Assessment Toolbox 9.1. Each student uses the same list as a record of what he or she has done and is going to do. Some answer with the symbols shown on the sheet or note other things they might be doing: "Rough draft on vacations," "Computer," or "Pen pal." Some of the symbols on the checklist correspond to a list Sheila has posted on a bulletin board, showing things children might do in the writing process: prewrite, draft, reader's circle, revise, edit, and publish.

Sheila's students correspond with pen pals at another school all year.

ASSESSMENT TOOLBOX

9.1 Writing Status Checklist

Each student uses this checklist to record what he or she has done or is going to do. Some students use the symbols below the chart; others jot down notes.

Name _____   Date _____

Writing Status Checklist

Monday	Tuesday	Wednesday	Thursday	Friday

Symbols to identify writing process:

PW = Prewrite	TC = Teacher Conference
D = Draft	ED = Editing
RC = Reader's Circle	FC = Final Copy

Establishing writing status this way means that each child knows what he or she is doing. Each child also knows that Sheila knows, and Sheila knows that he or she knows. This is an example of how the student's role in a student- and response-centered classroom was described in Chapter 1—choice, voice, control, and responsibility. The teacher's corresponding role involves initiation, observation, demonstration, and expectation. These roles must constantly be negotiated, which they are each time a writing workshop takes place in Sheila's class.

Writing (45 minutes)

Everyone is getting ready to write or is already writing. Sheila circulates, talking to students about what they're doing, helping with questions, and finding things for them. Here are the things that happen during this writing workshop:

• *Conference:* Sheila conferences with one child who had placed a writing piece in one of the two files in the writing center: "Needs Editing" and "Grade." La Phin—a Cambodian American student who is learning to speak, read, and write in English—had placed hers in the "Needs Editing" file. Sheila took the story and went to La with an *editing strip:* a piece of lined paper cut in 2½" strips. Sheila uses these strips to write comments on because she doesn't like to write on students' drafts. She wants them to do it on their own and take ownership of their writing.

Sheila sits close to La Phin and asks her to read her story, which was written in response to *The Hundred Dresses* (Estes, 1974) (see Figure 9.4, p. 300). Sheila offers encouragement and support to La, who's very shy and speaks softly because she's often unsure of her English. Here's their conversation about La's story:

Sheila had read aloud *The Hundred Dresses*, by Eleanor Estes (1974), which is about a girl who's rejected by others. The class talked about whether that had ever happened to them or whether they'd seen it happen and what they did or would do.

Sheila:	What do you need here (where it says *teas*)?
La:	Teach.
Sheila:	Do you mean *tease?* (La nods.) OK, what do we need on the end?
La:	A *d.*
Sheila:	Do we need something else?
La:	An *e.* (Sheila writes this on the editing strip.)
Sheila:	Right! You have the rest of the word. Read the rest to me. (La reads very quietly; Sheila leans to listen.) That's good! You talked about feelings and what they did and how they needed to fix it. About Octavia, do we need something here? (La had started the second sentence with *teas.*)
La:	She. (Sheila writes it next on the editing strip.)
Sheila:	Yeah. Put a period and *she.* (Reading.) "She teased her and then she *said* . . ." What do you need to put around the words?
La:	Marks. Quotation marks.

Sheila explains her beliefs about writing workshop as a part of learning and teaching language arts:

> In writing workshop, we don't move as a herd, doing everything the same at the same time. Today, some are writing to pen pals at another school, but others are doing different things. Sometimes, we are all over the place and my job is to coordinate. It's like a big, multilane freeway, where we shift lanes constantly. It's not linear but spiral, even amorphous. I do a lot of reading aloud, and we talk, and they might write about what I read and we talked about. I want to get the language flowing for my English language learners. My aides provide primary language support in Spanish and Khmer. I throw out something each time in minilessons—procedure, terminology, types of writing, writing conventions—and some will use it right away and others take more time. Writing is like that. I find things to encourage them to put their "toe in" writing.

ELL

See Chapter 3, First- and Second-Languge Development, for more on teaching language arts in culturally and linguistically diverse classrooms.

Writing in English as a Second Language

Teachers must be concerned about how to teach writing effectively to culturally and linguistically diverse students, which means viewing writing as a sociocultural act (de la Luz Reyes & Halcon, 2000). In a student- and response-centered classroom, teachers pay attention to students' prior experience and situate writing in real and sensible contexts. And for nonnative English speakers who are learning to write in English as a second language, teachers must make careful plans to provide the kind of support and guidance these students need. In particular, this means frequent modeling of writing behaviors and needed skills related to language conventions (Reyes, 1991). It's also important to make expectations about writing clear to students (Delpit, 1988) and to connect the skill instruction and actual writing students do.

In a review of research on the writing development of students learning English as a second language, Hudelson (1986) found that their development parallels that of native English speakers. See the box on page 303 for suggestions on teaching writing to ELL students.

Children who are learning to write in English as a second language can benefit from a process approach to writing, especially through the use of teacher modeling and minilessons in skills and language conventions, literature as a model for language, sharing and talking together, peer-response groups, cooperative and collaborative learning, dialogue journals (in which the teacher writes back), and drawing on their prior knowledge and experience.

Culturally responsive teachers like Sheila Kline encourage their students to draw on what Luis Moll calls *funds of knowledge*, or resources and experiences that ELL students have access to outside school. Moll's (1992b) research has shown that when teachers tap into English language learners' funds of knowledge, their intellectual development and academic achievement exceeds those of students

English Language Learners in the Writing Process

Keep these points in mind about English language learners:

1. They can begin to write in English before they have complete control over all the other aspects of language conventions (e.g., grammar, spelling, and sounds). That is, they can use what they know at the time to write.
2. ELL students can do different kinds of writing for different purposes and should have opportunities to do so—for instance, journals, dialogue journals, expressive writing, literature as a model for writing, and writing across the curriculum.
3. They can revise their writing with feedback and support from teacher conferences and peer conferences. ELL students' revision processes are similar to those of native English speakers, and they benefit from cooperative, collaborative peer revision and editing conferences.
4. They are greatly affected by the teacher's attitude and the classroom context for writing. Taking a process approach to writing indicates to children that their experiences, ideas, and writing are important.
5. ELL students vary greatly in their writing development because of individual differences in ability as well as cultural background and language development. This is also true of native English speakers.

Teachers of ELL students can support and guide their writing in these ways:

1. By reading aloud often and talking about stories
2. By providing encouragement to get language flowing
3. By conducting minilessons connected to students' actual writing
4. By using graphics and visuals
5. By suggesting that students write about personal experiences and knowledge
6. By encouraging collaborative writing (e.g., "buddies," small groups)
7. By holding one-on-one conferences with students for assessment and instruction
8. By providing primary language support (e.g., aides who speak students' native languages, print materials in home languages)

Source: Based on Hudelson, 1986.

whose teachers held low expectations for their performance and focused on low-level literacy experiences, such as rote memorization and drill.

Moll (1988b) also found that effective teachers of Latino students encouraged them to use personal experiences to make sense of school experiences. Even though such topics might have been considered controversial in the classroom, they were commonplace in the community and could be used effectively to expand students' literacy. Teachers' accommodations, using students' social and

Figure 9.5 Fernando's Writing about a Personal Experience

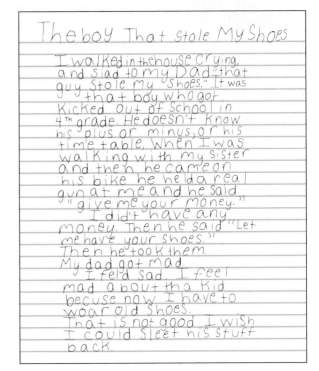

> **The boy That stole My Shoes**
>
> I walked in the house crying, and siad to my Dad "that guy stole my "shoes." It was that boy who got kicked out of school in 4th grade. He doesn't know his "plus or minus, or his time table. When I was walking with my sister and then he came on his bike he held a real gun at me and he said "give me your money." I did't have any money. Then he said "Let me have your shoes." Then he took them. My dad got mad. I feld sad. I feel mad about tha kid becuse now I have to woar old shoes. That is not good. I wish I could sleet his stuff back.

linguistic resources, have been shown to improve students' academic achievement and growth as bilingual and bicultural individuals (Diaz, Moll, & Mehan, 1986; Moll, Saez, & Dworin, 2003). Recall from the Snapshot how Sheila Kline encouraged La Phin to write about an experience with language discrimination she had on the playground. Even though this was a sensitive issue, the incident really happened and so La Phin chose to write about it. Another similar example from Sheila Kline's classroom involved Fernando, who wrote about an important personal experience in his piece "The Boy That Stole My Shoes" (see Figure 9.5). Fernando had shared this experience with Sheila, and she encouraged him to write about it. It was the first extended piece of writing he had done in her class, and he chose to place the final, revised version in his portfolio. Sheila continues to encourage her students to draw on their own personal funds of knowledge.

Teaching and Assessing Writing as a Process

Here are key ideas about teaching and assessing writing as a process based on current research, theory, and best practices of teaching writing (Dyson & Freedman, 2003; Indrisano & Squire, 2000). These ideas are illustrated with examples from Sheila Kline's fourth-grade class of predominantly English language learners.

Authentic Assessment

The shift in elementary education to teaching writing as a process has meant questioning traditional means of assessing writing: namely, multiple-choice tests based on questions and answers about subskills and timed essays that require specific prompts. Alternative means of writing assessment have emerged that more closely approximate the actual writing process—for instance, essay exams done in two sittings (one for prewriting and drafting and the second for revising and editing) and large-scale portfolio assessment.

The model of writing assessment used by many schools, districts, and states is based on that of the Educational Testing Service (ETS). Students write on an assigned topic in a timed testing situation. Teachers score these pieces based on a rubric of scoring standards; usually more than one teacher reviews each paper. More than one writing test is often given. Similarly, national writing assessment is done through the writing portion of the National Assessment of Educational Progress (NAEP) for 9-, 13-, and 17-year-olds and the College Entrance Examination Board's Achievement Test in English Composition. They also evaluate short pieces of writing done in formal testing situations.

These more holistic testing and scoring procedures are an improvement over multiple-choice grammar tests and may help schools, districts, and states come to a consensus on what is good writing. However, these tests and procedures are not able to assess students' writing in real situations for real purposes on topics of their own choosing—the real goal of writing instruction. Constraints such as assigned topics (which may be of little interest or unfamiliar to students), a formal testing situation, and a short period of time are not conditions under which people really write.

The best way to assess students' writing on an ongoing basis is through contextualized, authentic assessment. Students should be involved in the authentic assessment of writing, deciding which of their pieces should be edited and graded. Through this type of assessment, patterns of students' progress are revealed over time (Newkirk & Atwell, 1988). These patterns will not always be regular and will vary from child to child and among different types of writing.

Types of authentic assessment used by Sheila Kline include the following:

3.3

See the Anecdotal Record Assessment (p. 106).

1. *Anecdotal Records:* Keep a log for each child based on observations and conferences. Use a loose-leaf notebook, providing a page for each child; note the date, topic, and observation or score. Assessment Toolbox 9.2 (p. 306) shows the Writing Record Sheila Kline uses for pieces she scores.

2. *Rubrics:* Teachers, schools, and districts have developed scoring rubrics, which are used to look at a piece of writing as a whole and evaluate it on the basis of criteria with a scoring scale and a descriptor of what each point on the scale means. A rubric allows the teacher to look at a given student's progress compared to that of others whose writing has been scored by the same scale. Numbers can be attached to points on the rubric. Rather than use rubrics only to show students what's expected of them, teachers should develop rubrics in collaboration with students, identifying what criteria will be assessed and why (Wiener & Cohen,

2.3

See also Chapter 2, Assessing Language Arts, for ideas about co-creating a writing rubric with students (pp. 52–56).

ASSESSMENT TOOLBOX

9.2 Writing Record

This Writing Record is a good example of contextualized, authentic assessment of students' writing. The teacher keeps this record based on his or her observations of and conferences with individual students.

Writing Record

NAME	Date/Title	Date/Title	Date/Title	Date/Title
Albarron, Hugo $3/3$	9/23 Mountain $3/3$	9/19 School $3/3$	10/17 Math Grade $3/3$	
Barragan, Rolando $3/3$	9/23 The Mall $3/3$	10/17 Disneyland $3/3$		
Caro, Taina $4/3$	11/3 Babysitter $4/3$	10/17 Chuck E Cheese $4/3$		
Casarez, Hugo $2/3$	9/16 Baseball $2/3$			
Chann, Ry $2/3$	9/23 Beach $2/3$	9/23 Like to Write $2/3$	10/17 $2/3$	10/17 Like School $2/4$
Chavez, Susana $4/4$	9-17 Baby Cousin Fell $4/4$	10/12 Window Hurt Finger $4/4$	10/12 Mom in Hospital 4/4	10/17 Mexico $2/3$

9.4

Peer-Editing Form (p. 313)

9.1
9.5

See the Writing Status Checklist (p. 298) and the Self-Editing Checklist (p. 316).

9.6

See the Self-Assessment Form for Student's Portfolio Selection (p. 322).

1997). Assessment Toolbox 9.3 shows the holistic scoring rubric Sheila Kline and her students developed to score their writing.

3. *Conferences:* Teacher/student and peer conferences are also important means of authentic assessment. See the upcoming section on Conferences (pp. 310–313) for types of questions teachers can ask as a guide for developing a conference record form. In addition, review the Peer-Editing Form, Assessment Toolbox 9.4, for use in peer conferences of small groups of students assessing each other's writing.

4. *Checklists:* Checklists allow quick spotchecks of various writing experiences and are useful in guiding both teachers and students in assessing progress. See how Sheila Kline uses the Writing Status Checklist (Assessment Toolbox 9.1) in the previous Snapshot, and see also the Self-Editing Checklist (Assessment Toolbox 9.5) in the upcoming section on Revising and Editing (pp. 315–317). Both of these tools help students assess and monitor their own progress.

5. *Portfolios:* Ideas about portfolio assessment were introduced in Chapter 2. See a continuation of this discussion as it pertains especially to writing in the upcoming section on Portfolios (pp. 320–323), including Assessment Toolbox 9.6, the Self-Assessment Form for Student's Portfolio Selection.

9.3 Writing Rubric

By using a Writing Rubric, the teacher can review a piece of student writing as a whole and evaluate it on the basis of criteria with a scoring scale and a descriptor of what each point on the scale means. It allows the teacher to look at a given student's progress compared to that of others whose writing has been scored by the same scale.

Writing Rubric

Content

0	1	2	3	4	5	6
No attempt or impossible to decipher.	Collection of words with little sentence structure. Minimum of coherent organization.	Words and simple sentences. Mainly lists. No feelings or insight evident.	Fairly complete ideas. May use main idea sentence. Uses few supporting details. Writes with some feelings or sense of audience. Some descriptive language. Little evidence of insightful thinking.	Generally well thought out and arranged. Uses main idea/ supporting details/conclusion formula. May have several supporting details. Writes with some evidence of feelings and sense of audience. Good clear descriptions. Some evidence of insight in place.	Well thought out and arranged. Many supporting details. Definite feelings and sense of audience. Clear, vivid descriptions. Much reflective, insightful thinking.	Well thought out and arranged. Many supporting details. Definite feelings and sense of audience. The overall impact of the piece is of a thoughtful, reflective author who has confidence in their writing.

Conventions

0	1	2	3	4	5	6
No recognizable words.	Almost all spelling invented. Use of random upper-case and lower-case letters. Extremely hard to decipher. No margins.	Spelling mostly invented, interferes with reading the piece. Little sense of sentence or paragraph structure. May be written like a "list." Punctuation missing or randomly inserted. May use margins. Paragraphs may be indented.	Much invented spelling, but still easily readable. Some evidence of checking for correct spelling. Most common punctuation used correctly (, ' .). Uses fairly simple sentences. May use margins. Paragraphs may be indented.	Some invented spelling. Most words checked for correct spelling. Uses quotation marks, question marks, and exclamation points correctly most of the time (" ? !). Must use margins. Paragraphs are indented.	Almost all words spelled correctly. Most punctuation marks used correctly. Uses more complex sentences. Uses margins. Indents paragraphs.	Words have been checked and are spelled correctly. Punctuation is used correctly. Uses more complex sentences. Uses margins. Indents paragraphs.

A Literate Environment

For more ideas on creating a literate environment in the classroom, see the section in Chapter 1, Learning and Teaching Language Arts, on classroom environment and that in Chapter 4, Emergent Literacy and Biliteracy, on a print-rich environment.

Sheila has a writing center in her class as part of the literate environment she has created. There's a sign over it, "Writing Center," and this area contains materials for writing and bookmaking:

Stacking file with different kinds of paper: blank, lined, colored, stationary, note, Post-its
Paper clips and rubber bands
Paste and glue
Scotch tape, masking tape, wide tape for book binding
Pencils, colored pencils, crayons, and erasers
Scissors, staplers, hole punch, rulers
Construction paper for book covers
Decorations for book covers: yarn, wrapping paper, and so on

Sheila uses a plastic file crate, divided in two, to contain the files "Needs Editing" and "Grade," in which students put their work. If they file a piece in "Needs Editing," Sheila knows they would like a conference with her, so she plans it. If they file a piece in "Grade," they've edited it themselves or with the help of other students in reader's circle.

Sheila has created a literate environment in her classroom in other ways, too. She has a large classroom library of books, including a file of books written by the students. The walls of the room are covered with student writing, posters made by Sheila about writing or other subjects, and labels, lists, and directions.

Modeling

Sheila Kline believes that modeling writing is an important part of teaching it. She models writing primarily as she responds to students' writing in conferences but also tries to find other times to do so.

See Avril Font model by writing her own piece.

Teachers can model the enjoyment and practice of writing just as they model the enjoyment and practice of reading:

1. *Provide examples:* Do so during minilessons or when the class is writing a language experience story. Share your ideas, ask questions about what's being written, and offer examples and options.
2. *Write your own pieces:* If you have used literature as a model or prompt for writing, write about it yourself. In October, when everyone else is writing Halloween stories, try it yourself.
3. *Keep a journal:* Start one now. It will become a thread that connects your future as a student teacher and teacher with your past, which will help you understand the present. Keep your journal going in your own classroom.
4. *Write curriculum:* Participate in professional writing like curriculum development, school self-study reports, inservice preparations, and other projects that require expository writing. You may find you have a great deal to

say and learn when you're writing about children, teaching, and learning—things you know well.

5. *Write for publication:* Try it. Many of the journals of professional organizations, such as *Language Arts* (National Council of Teachers of English) and *The Reading Teacher* (International Reading Association), encourage classroom teachers to write articles.

6. *Join a writing project:* Through the National Writing Project, teachers participate in summer workshops, in which they learn to teach writing by writing themselves. Find out if your state has a writing project and become involved.

Minilessons

Minilessons is a term often used in connection with writing workshops. Sheila Kline uses minilessons to initiate writing workshops. They usually last 5 to 10 minutes and focus on procedures in the workshop, the writing process, and skills. On the day described in the Snapshot, Sheila did a minilesson on expressing yourself in writing using a poster she made. She often uses class posters that summarize the ideas presented in minilessons so that children can refer to them. For example, see Figure 9.6, a class poster showing that a paragraph has four parts.

Here's the actual schedule of the minilessons Sheila uses from July to January:

Sheila's school is on a year-round calendar, starting in July.

July

Procedural Lessons

Folders	Conduct in reader's circle
Idea list	When papers are turned in: where and how
How to make a cluster	Scoring rubric
Skills list	

A paragraph has 4 parts:

1. <u>Topic</u>
   - Topic sentence
   - Ask a question, make a wish, state an opinion
2. <u>Describe</u>
   - Explain
   - Detail sentences
3. <u>Support</u>
   - Prove
   - Detail sentences
4. <u>Conclusion</u>
   - Repeat or restate topic sentence
   - Can be a WOW!

 Figure 9.6 Class Poster: Parts of a Paragraph

Procedures	September	
Folders	9/8	Reviewed procedures
Idea list	9/10	Main idea: reviewed questions to ask in reader's circle
Clustering	9/12	Main idea and topic sentence
Reader's circle	9/14	Conduct in reader's circle
Conferences		Who, what, when, where, and why/how should be
Filing papers		covered in writing
Revising and Editing	9/16	Editing strips, "P" means to indent new paragraph
Editing strips	9/23	Reviewed editing strips, recopying for publication
Margins		All week talked about feelings and making the reader
Parts of a paragraph		see what the author saw
Parts of a sentence		
Spelling	9/28	Margins
Editing checklist	9/30	When do you publish? How do you publish?
Writing	**October**	
Main idea	10/3–10/5	Publishing tips
Topic sentence	10/7	All capitals for loud voices; review of quotation marks
Who, what, where, when, why	10/10–10/31	Worked together to develop a Halloween scary story;
Detail sentences		emphasized topic, topic sentence, detail sentences,
Conclusion		and conclusion
Making the reader see;		
describing		
Publishing	**Jaunary**	
When do you publish?	1/4	Developed list of 9 items to check before turning in
How do you publish?		a piece
Illustrations	1/6	Reviewed parts of a paragraph
Computer publishing	1/9	Reviewed scoring rubrics
Drama and media	1/11	Reviewed writing workshop procedures for new students
Collaboration		

See the adjacent marginal notes, which list some of the many possibilities for minilessons for writing workshop.

Conferences

See Avril Font conference with a student.

Teacher Conferences

Sheila Kline conferences with students during writing workshops when they put their pieces in the "Needs Editing" file, which she checks at the beginning of each workshop. She also holds on-the-spot conferences with students who ask for or appear to need them.

Conferences are an important part of the process approach to writing (Calkins, 1994; Graves, 1994). Graves's (1983) research has shown that language exists in meaningful contexts and that composing is an activity of literate communities for purposes of self-expression and communication, rather than the teaching of separate skills. Integral to this approach is the idea that teachers are knowledgeable adults who interact and guide children, who are the decision makers about their own writing (Bury, 1993).

Children use conferences as a means to do this, asking *responsive questions,* which Graves (1983) defines as those teachers don't know the answers to. Teachers guide students through the decision-making process needed to bring a text to publication during these conferences. Graves advises keeping conferences short by focusing on one thing, teaching only one thing per conference, avoiding rushing, and not talking too much. Here are other guidelines for teacher conferences:

1. *Scheduling Conferences:* Conferences can occur at any time—during writing workshop or writing in other subject areas. They can be scheduled by students (e.g., through signing up or placing their papers in a certain place) or occur spontaneously, as the teacher circulates while children write. With regard to scheduling conferences, Graves (1983) offers "answers to the toughest questions teachers ask about conferences":

- *"How do I find the time?"* You don't have to correct every paper for every child every time you meet. Writing and conferences are ongoing processes. A timetable for a 37-minute writing period, accommodating about 17 students, might look like this.

    First 10 minutes: After reviewing writing folders, the teacher circulates the room and helps children who need it.

    Next 15 minutes: The teacher holds regularly scheduled conferences with certain children.

    Next 12 minutes: The teacher holds a conference either with a small group who are applying a common skill or with children who are at an important point in their writing.

- *"How often should I hold conferences?"* This will vary, but you should confer with each child at least once a week.

- *"What are the other children doing?"* The others should be writing, finding more things to write about as they do. It's important to create experience and interest centers in the classrooms to engage children, keep writing materials accessible, and keep children from interrupting. Class discussions will help children cope by themselves with certain problems, such as spelling, what to write about next, and so on.

2. *Questions for Writing Conferences:* Calkins (1983) lists questions for conferences that can apply to any kind of writing:

See Chapter 5, Listening and Talking, for more on teacher questions.

- "What is your favorite part?"
- "What problems are you having?"
- "How did you feel?"
- "Do your paragraphs seem to be in the right order?"
- "Can you leave out parts that repeat or that fail to give details about your subject?"
- "Can you combine some sentences?"
- "Can you use more precise verbs in some places?"
- "What do you plan to do next with this piece of writing?"

Peer Conferences

Children can work in groups to read and respond to each other's writing (Calkins, 1994). As discussed earlier, Sheila Klein's class uses a *reader's circle* during writing workshop. Students write their names on the board inside a circle, and when several names are listed, students meet together to read what they have written to each other. The emphasis here is usually on listening and responding to the ideas and having an audience.

Another approach is *peer-editing groups,* in which children work together closely to edit each other's work, revising without the teacher's help (Elbow, 1973). This may work best with older students. Here are some guidelines for peer-editing groups:

- Editors should make positive comments and emphasize strengths as well as places for improvement.
- Writers and editors should respect everyone in the group.
- Writers should not apologize or feel what they have written isn't good enough. The purpose of the group is to help.
- Rather than arguing, writers should discuss suggestions and then make their own decisions about revision.
- Writers should appreciate the comments and help offered by editors.

Students should follow these techniques for working in peer-editing groups:

- *Summarizing:*

    Give a one-sentence summary of what the writing is about.

    Give a one-word summary. Pick a word from the writing that best summarizes it, or pick a word of your own that you feel best describes it.

In peer editing, students work closely together to edit each other's work, revising without help from the teacher.

- *Pointing:*

    As you listen to the writer read, note words and phrases that make an impression on you.

    As you respond, point to the words and phrases.

- *Telling:*

    Tell the writer how you felt as you listened.

To help students follow these guidelines, they can use Assessment Toolbox 9.4 during and after peer-editing groups.

Journals

Students in Sheila Kline's class can write in their journals during writing workshop and also at other times during the day. Sheila sometimes writes in students' journals (as in a dialogue journal, described later) and sometimes dictates students' entries. Some entries are personal and some are about class activities, such

ASSESSMENT TOOLBOX

9.4 Peer-Editing Form

In peer-editing groups, students work together to edit each other's writing, revising without the teacher's help. This Peer-Editing Form guides students in formulating specific comments that will provide useful observations and suggestions.

Peer-Editing Form

The piece I read was _____

by _____ .

The best thing about this piece is _____

_____ .

If the writer wanted to change something, I would suggest _____

_____

_____ .

Peer Editor _____   Date _____

---

as watching a bean plant grow. Many drawings are included, too. Here are some variations of journals:

● **Personal Journals:** Students can write in personal journals every day, both during a regular journal-writing period and throughout the day. All they need to get started is a notebook and support from the teacher.

● **Kindergarten Journals:** Even the youngest students can write in journals. Kindergarten teacher Hipple (1985) has children write in journals during the first 30 minutes of every day, when they're eager to communicate. The journals she uses consist of five pieces of paper stapled together—a page for each day of the week. Children write their names and the date on each page (copied from the chalkboard). They all receive new journals every Monday, and the old ones are saved in their portfolios. Students can draw, write, dictate to the teacher, and talk about and share their journals with the rest of the class.

● **Community and Content Journals:** Not all journals are individual. Open, community journals may be kept in the room for all children to write in. Good places to keep these are at windows, encouraging children to write about what they see (e.g., the weather), or by class pets, helping children observe what they're doing.

● **Literary Journals:** Journals and diaries are an ancient form of recording the events in people's lives and have also become a literary form. Children who read books written in diary or journal form may choose to write in this form themselves. Read aloud one of the books listed in the margin to introduce children to this form.

● **Dialogue Journals:** Dialogue journals are written conversations. The children make journal entries on any topic, and the teacher writes back in response. These journals may be exchanged one or more times a week or on an individual basis. They are valuable because they make connections between thinking and language, speaking and writing, and teacher and child. In addition, dialogue journals help students unlock the literacy puzzle (Bode, 1989). Here are suggestions for dialogue journals (Staton, 1984):

Use small, bound notebooks (not spiral ones), which can be filled quickly enough so that children feel success when they get a new one to fill. Decorate the covers.

Establish regular places and times to turn in and pick up journals.

Teachers should write back immediately, taking the journals home to do so, if needed.

Writing more frequent, brief entries seems to work best.

Return journals first thing in the morning the day after students have written in them, and give students ample time to read and respond in return.

Teachers responding to journal entries of ELL students should indicate that the *meaning* of what they are saying is the most important thing, rather than lan-

GREAT BOOKS FOR CHILDREN

Journals

Anne Frank: The Diary of a Young Girl (Frank, 1952)
The Diary of a Churchmouse (Oakley, 1987)
Diary of a Rabbit (Hess, 1982)
Dorrie's Book (Sachs, 1975)
The First Four Years (Wilder, 1971)
A Gathering of Days: A New England Girl's Journal, 1830–1832 (Blos, 1979)
Harriet the Spy (Fitzhugh, 1964)
I, Columbus: My Journal, 1492–1493 (Roop & Roop, 1990)
Marco Polo: His Notebook (Roth, 1990)
Nettie's Trip South (Turner, 1987)
Off the Map: The Journals of Lewis and Clark (Roop & Roop, 1993)
On the Frontier with Mr. Audubon (Brenner, 1977)
Pedro's Journal: A Voyage with Christopher Columbus (Conrad, 1991)
Three Days on a River in a Red Canoe (Williams, 1981)

guage conventions like spelling or punctuation. Dialogue journals are nonthreatening and private types of writing, but teachers still need to model the writing process and use of language conventions (Peyton & Reed, 1990).

Revising and Editing

The writing process is as individual as a fingerprint. Some students write easily and prolifically; others write more slowly, spending more time revising. Revising and editing can be done in reader's circle in writing workshops, teacher conferences, and peer-editing groups, all described earlier in this chapter. Students can also do self-editing, relying on reminders in a poster like the one Sheila had over the writing center (see Figure 9.7) or using a self-editing checklist (see Assessment Toolbox 9.5, p. 316).

While keeping in mind that revising and editing are not ends in themselves, consider the following guidelines for editing children's work:

1. *The self-image of the young writer:* How does the writer feel about himself or herself? With some children—particularly young or reluctant writers—suggesting changes may discourage them from writing at all. Teachers must consider the effects that their comments will have on students' feelings as well as their writing.
2. *The needs of the young writer:* Why is the child writing and for whom? The more real writing is to students, the less they may need the teacher to tell them what it might be like. Teachers should take their cue from the degree of students' involvement in their writing.
3. *The purposes of the young writer:* What is the child's intent? The teacher's suggestions for changes in a student's newspaper article, in which information needs to be clearly communicated, would be different from those made for a poem or some other personal piece.

Figure 9.7

Class Poster: Self-Editing

Before I turn in a piece of writing for a score, I check to see if:
1. Paragraphs are indented.
2. Margins are correct.
3. Punctuation is correct: periods, commas, quotation marks, apostrophes, question marks, and exclamation points.
4. The right words are used.
5. Words are spelled correctly.
6. It has a topic sentence, detail sentences, and conclusion.
7. Capital letters are used correctly.
8. It is neat.
9. The prewrite and rough draft are stapled to it with <u>one</u> staple.

9.5 Self-Editing Checklist

To be successful at self-editing, students need reminders of what they should look for as they revise and edit their work. This Self-Editing Checklist provides those reminders in a simple, specific format.

Name _____   Date _____

Title _____

Self-Editing Checklist

____ 1. Each sentence begins with a capital.

____ 2. Names of people and places are capitalized.

____ 3. Each sentence ends with a (.), (?), or (!).

____ 4. I have used (") to show when someone is talking.

____ 5. Each new paragraph is indented.

____ 6. I have corrected all misspelled words.

____ 7. I have chosen the words that best describe what I want to say.

____ 8. I have reread my writing and checked it.

---

4. *The style of the young writer:* What is the writer's approach? Some children write factual stories based on their experiences and can easily answer questions about what really happened. Others prefer writing fiction; fantasy emerges strongly in some students. When they're writing about a person or place in their minds, which they may still be trying to visualize, it may be hard for them to explain it to someone else. The teacher can help by providing plenty of opportunities to discuss writing with others to clarify ideas.

My experience has been that when children care about what they are writing and have a strong sense of their purpose as well as their audience, they will readily seek revision as they need it. But keep in mind that not every piece needs revising or even finishing. When children have a wide audience in mind and the writing is important to them, they may want to make changes to make it as effective as possible. Their concern for conventions like spelling, punctuation, and grammar will reflect their concern for communicating with that audience.

Perhaps revision should be seen as answering the need for children to say clearly what they want to say, rather than answering the need for teachers to have writing fit their own or someone else's model of the writing process. Consider yourself an active listener, a practice audience. Let children come to you to discover through rehearsal what they're trying to say.

Publishing

Ways to Share and Publish Writing
Take the Author's Chair.
Read aloud.
Make a speech.
Do a videotaped reading.
Display on a bulletin board, chart stand, or clothesline.
Make a class book or "big book."
Produce drama or media scripts.
Create a class newspaper.
Give a report.
Create greeting cards and letters.

Publishing is an important part of establishing a sense of ownership for young writers as well as a feeling of authorship. Sheila Kline's students publish regularly: Stories they have written are displayed in the classroom and hallway, letters are exchanged with pen pals, and books they've made of their stories go in the classroom library. Children can publish their writing in countless ways, many of which we've already described.

Bookmaking is another way of publishing students' work. It can be as simple as stapling a construction paper cover over a piece of writing or more involved. See Figures 9.8 and 9.9 (pp. 318 and 319), which show two types of bookmaking techniques: fold-a-book and hardcover book.

Scheduling

WWW

Students can publish their work at these websites: Kid Pub **www.kidpub.org/kidpub/** and KidStuff Children's Publishing **www.worldchat.com/public/ kidstuff/a.htm**.

As mentioned earlier, Sheila Kline scheduled hour-long writing and reading workshops on alternating days of the week. Here's what the class does during each 60-minute period:

- *Minilesson (5–10 minutes maximum):* Procedures, process, skills, reading as a source of writing (ideas, clustering, chart stories).
- *Writing Status (5 minutes):* Uses a checklist of each child's focus; keeps terminology up; serves as an oral contract as part of management.

Students should have opportunities to write throughout the day—for instance, when they are not involved with other subjects or have some free time.

Figure 9.8 Making a Fold-a-Book

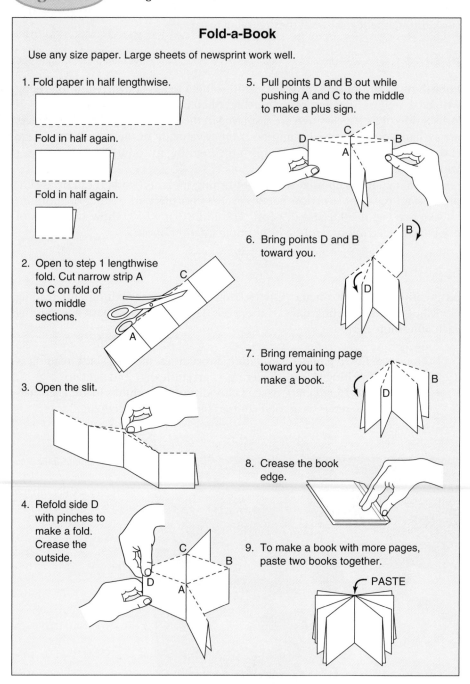

Fold-a-Book

Use any size paper. Large sheets of newsprint work well.

1. Fold paper in half lengthwise.

   Fold in half again.

   Fold in half again.

2. Open to step 1 lengthwise fold. Cut narrow strip A to C on fold of two middle sections.

3. Open the slit.

4. Refold side D with pinches to make a fold. Crease the outside.

5. Pull points D and B out while pushing A and C to the middle to make a plus sign.

6. Bring points D and B toward you.

7. Bring remaining page toward you to make a book.

8. Crease the book edge.

9. To make a book with more pages, paste two books together.

   PASTE

Figure 9.9 Making a Hardcover Book

Hardcover Book

1. Stack the completed book pages, and add an extra page each to front and back. Sew or staple the pages together on the binding edge. (Sewing creates a more durable binding.)

2. Cut two pieces of cover cardboard 1/4" larger in each dimension than the page size.

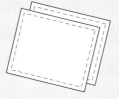

3. Tape the two pieces of cardboard together with a 1/4" separation in the hinge.

4. Place the cardboard on the cover Con-Tact paper spaced far enough apart for the cover to fold shut. Cut the Con-Tact paper to extend 1/4" beyond each edge of the cardboard. Peel the backing off the paper; center the cardboard on the cover. Press into place.

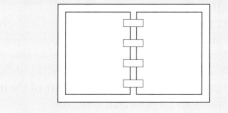

5. Fold the edges of the cover material around the cardboard by folding down first the corners and then the sides.

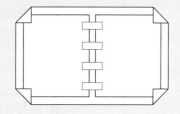

6. Tape the bound edges of the book into the cover. Masking tape will do.

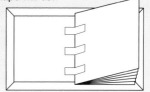

7. Cut two pieces of Con-Tact paper the height of the pages and more than twice the width of the pages.

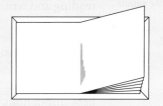

8. Place the peeled Con-Tact paper (inside cover piece) on the inside of the cover to overlap the tape in the hinge, and adhere to the extra page in front and the hardcover front. Repeat this step with the back inside cover.

7.2

See the Literature Portfolio Organizer (p. 262) for an example of a useful means of tracking portfolio items.

Here are the items that Sheila Kline's students collect in their portfolios:

1. Completed writing folder after all pieces have been scored
2. Student selection of best pieces, at least four in different modes: observation, expressive, expository, and persuasive
3. Writing across the curriculum: math, science, social studies
4. Published books

Students, as authors, should have choices about what goes into their portfolios. Moreover, they should be able to explain what they want to include and

ASSESSMENT TOOLBOX

9.6 Self-Assessment Form for Student's Portfolio Selection

Students should have choices about what pieces of writing go into their portfolios. This Self-Assessment Form asks students to explain what they want to include and why. In addition, it asks them to think about goals for future writing, given the work they have already done.

Name _____ Date _____

My Portfolio Selection

I chose this piece for my portfolio because

_____

_____

Something special about this piece is

_____

_____

I scored this piece with a _____ for rhetoric and a _____ for conventions.

My goal for writing in the future is to:

_____ Try a different type of writing, like poetry or fiction.

_____ Spell more words correctly.

_____ Write more sentences.

_____ Write more interesting sentences.

_____ Other ideas: _____

---

why. To help students assess their work, Sheila Kline developed Assessment Toolbox 9.6. She has each student fill out this form whenever he or she selects a piece of writing to include in his or her portfolio. Note that the form also asks the student about goals for future writing.

Answers to Questions about the Writing Process

● *What is the writing process?*

The notion of teaching writing as a process, which developed during the 1970s and 1980s, is based on Donald Graves's influential book *Writing: Teachers and Children at Work* (1983). With this approach, the focus of writing instruction shifted from the product to the process. The stages of the writing process are prewriting, drafting, revising, editing, and publishing. These terms are useful for talking about the parts of the writing process, which don't necessarily occur in a fixed order for individual writers in specific situations. Teachers shouldn't think of these terms as comprising steps in a rigid, linear fashion. Writing is a recursive process.

● *How should we teach and assess writing as a process?*

The writing workshop is based on the principles of writing as a process and reflects a social constructivist point of view about learning, as well. The emphasis is on providing time and choices for students' writing. The teacher presents a short minilesson at the start of the workshop, students write individually or meet in reader's circles or conferences with the teacher, and share their writing briefly at the end.

Keys to a process approach to writing include using authentic, ongoing, informal assessment (e.g., anecdotal records, rubrics, journals, and portfolios); creating a literature environment; teacher modeling; minilessons for procedures and language conventions; teacher and peer conferences; journal writing; student-controlled revising and editing; publishing and establishing ownership and authorship; and flexible scheduling.

Looking Further

1. Share with a small group of classmates what you wrote in the Reflective Response at the beginning of the chapter. Talk about your feelings about writing, how you were taught writing, and how you plan to teach writing.

2. Observe writing instruction in an elementary classroom. Compare what you saw with how teaching writing as a process is described in this chapter.

3. Plan a minilesson for a writing workshop. Do the lesson with a group of students, if possible.

4. In your college class, write a short piece and share it in a reader's circle. Or conduct a peer-editing group, according to guidelines described in this chapter.

5. Collect several papers written by children and score them using Sheila Kline's writing rubric (see Assessment Toolbox 9.3). Then create a rubric you might use in your own class, in collaboration with students, if possible.

Children's Books and Software

Blos, J. (1979). *A gathering of days: A New England girl's journal*, 1830–1832. New York: Scribner.

Brenner, B. (1977). *On the frontier with Mr. Audubon*. New York: Coward.

Conrad, P. (1991). *Pedro's journal: A voyage with Christopher Columbus (August 3, 1492–February 14, 1493)*. Honedale, PA: Boyds Mills Press.

Estes, E. (1974). *The hundred dresses*. New York: Harcourt Brace Jovanovich.

Fitzhugh, L. (1964). *Harriet the spy*. New York: Harper & Row.

Frank, A. (1952). *Anne Frank: The diary of a young girl*. New York: Doubleday.

Hess, L. (1982). *Diary of a rabbit*. New York: Scribner's.

Inspiration [Computer software]. Available from Inspiration Software.

Oakley, G. (1987). *The diary of a churchmouse*. New York: Atheneum.

Roop, P., & Roop, C. (Eds.). (1990). *I Columbus: My journal, 1492–1493*. New York: Avon.

Roop, P., & Roop, C. (1993). *Off the map: The journals of Lewis and Clark*. New York: Walker.

Roth, S. L. (1990). *Marco Polo: His notebook*. New York: Doubleday.

Sachs, M. (1975). *Dorrie's book*. New York: Doubleday.

Turner, A. (1987). *Nettie's trip south*. New York: Macmillan.

Wilder, L. I. (1971). *The first four years*. New York: Harper & Row.

Williams, V. B. (1981). *Three days on a river in a red canoe*. New York: Greenwillow.

Spelling

uestions about Spelling

- *How do children learn to spell?*
- *How should we teach and assess spelling?*

REFLECTIVE RESPONSE

How do you think you learned to spell? Think back to how you were taught to spell. If you can remember things that you definitely will or will not do when you're a teacher, write them down, too.

The English Writing System

In order to understand spelling, teachers should know something about the origins and characteristics of the English writing system (Templeton, 2003). The language conventions of spelling, as well as punctuation and handwriting, represent the rather monumental efforts of literate humans to put the living sounds of language into the symbols of print. Writing first emerged from early people's efforts to record their experiences and leave messages for others; they drew on the walls of caves and carved marks in stone. Later, these pictures and marks became symbols, such as the pictograms of prehistoric cultures and the hieroglyphics of

325

the ancient Egyptians. Different cultures developed different forms of recording spoken language in writing.

These writing systems, or *orthographies,* have evolved over time. An *orthography* is a code that consists of a set of graphemes (written symbols that stand for a word, syllable, or speech sound in a language). There are several types of orthographies: *logographic,* or word writing, such as Chinese; *syllabic,* or syllable writing, such as Japanese; and *alphabetic,* or sound-to-letter writing, such as English. When we know how to spell, we know how to produce these graphics correctly and we know what they mean.

The most widespread type of writing is alphabetic. The alphabet used for English derives from the ancient Hebrew, Greek, and Roman languages. Some alphabetic codes—such as Finnish, Turkish, and Spanish—have a one-to-one correspondence between sounds and letters. English, however, has a many-to-many correspondence. More specifically, English has over 40 speech sounds but only 26 letters in the alphabet to represent them. One, two, or more of these letters may function as *graphemes*—for example, the *-gh* in *laugh,* which represents the *phoneme* /f/. Many graphemes can represent single phonemes (e.g., the long *a* sound in *way, weigh, wait, fate, ballet, fiancée, lady*), and many phonemes can represent single graphemes (e.g., the *o* in *one, do, dot, open, oven, women*).

Why does English have a many-to-many correspondence, which often makes it highly irregular? The answer lies in a basic characteristic of language: that it changes. Some types of changes have made great differences in how English is spoken and written:

1. *Sound Changes:* The pronunciations of sounds and words have changed over the centuries, but their spellings have not always changed accordingly. For example, the transition from Old to Middle English rendered the *k* sound silent when it preceded a consonant at the beginning of a word, but the grapheme *k* remained in the orthography, resulting in irregular spellings like *knife* and *knight.*

2. *Borrowed Word Changes:* Many invasions and occupations of the British Isles (notably, by the Romans, the Danes, and the Norman French) as well as British exploration and colonization around the world have made English the "borrowingest" language in the world. For example, the Vikings brought with them the Danish words *tree, birth, egg,* and *reindeer,* and the Normans brought the French words *ballet, bouquet, restaurant,* and *lieutenant.* This type of borrowing has continued with more recent additions to English from Spanish, such as *mesa, junta,* and *macho.* Numerous words from other languages have been added to English without changing their spellings. The adjacent marginal note shows some interesting examples.

3. *Etymological Changes:* An example of this type of change comes from the influence of classical studies during the Renaissance. Writers of that era wanted to give classical languages a rebirth, so they resurrected some Latin spellings. Many of these spellings reinstated voiced letters that had been deleted in the French pronunciations from which the English words were derived. For example, *dette* was changed to *debt* (from the Latin *debitum*), and Latin spellings such as *allusion, external,* and *meditate* became common.

Words Added to English from Other Languages

Native American: *raccoon, squash*
Norse: *knife, hut*
Arabic: *algebra, zero*
Gaelic: *slogan, clan*
Italian: *umbrella, piano*
Portuguese: *banana, molasses*
Chinese: *tea, mandarin*
Hindu: *pajama, gymkhana*
Japanese: *kimono, typhoon*
Dutch: *wagon, yacht*

Learning about the complex orthography of English not only provides a fascinating history lesson, but it also suggests the importance of learning about the relationship between words and meaning, rather than simply writing single words in isolation. And although English may seem highly irregular to anyone learning to spell it, the most common words in English have regular spellings about 80 percent of the time (Hanna, Hanna, Hodges, & Rudorf, 1966). What's most important to remember about spelling is that it is a graphic representation of writing. And writing is for constructing and communicating meaning.

SNAPSHOT   A Child Learns to Spell

I've watched many children learn to spell, but none more closely than my own three children. I'm going to tell you about my daughter, Elizabeth, and I will use examples of her writing in the next section to illustrate the stages that children go through in their spelling development. I chose Elizabeth because she has always been a prolific writer—partly by nature and partly by experience. She has always been around writing—mine, in particular. It seems that she has played with paper and pencils on or under my desk almost from birth.

As you may recall, I've talked about Elizabeth in other chapters. For instance, in Chapter 4, Emergent Literacy and Biliteracy, I described her first writing at about 1 year old, when I gave her a pad of small Post-its to keep her busy while I was writing; she made marks on them, one by one, with a pencil she found on the floor and slowly covered herself with these Post-its until she looked like a little yellow bird. When Elizabeth was older, paper and crayons were her toys of choice. I also made her little blank books out of scrap paper, which she delighted in. I remember one time, she filled a book with page after page of squiggly lines, brought it to me, and said, "Read it." Trying to be tactful, I asked, "Why don't you read it to me?" She looked stunned and said, "I don't know how to read. I know how to write."

Sometimes, Elizabeth asked how to spell words, but she usually figured them out herself. Everyone around her learned not to suggest that her spelling was incorrect. She took great offense at this and usually argued with whomever was correcting her. Does this mean she confused *invented* with *correct* spelling? I don't think so. I think it demonstrates her risk-taking ability and confidence as a writer along with her focus on the meaning of what she wanted to say. Does that mean she has grown up spelling incorrectly? To the contrary, she is an excellent speller and a prolific writer.

Above all, Elizabeth has always enjoyed writing and used it as a way to communicate her ideas and feelings. She has had a lot of reading and writing experiences at home, where books and paper, crayons, and pencils were plentiful. She has also had adult and older sibling models of reading and writing and a lot of encouragement to experiment. And to be sure, she has always had confidence. Luckily, her teachers in preschool and the primary grades provided similar types of experiences at school and understood the importance of a developmental approach to literacy.

Stages of Spelling Development

Learning to spell is a constructive developmental process, like learning to speak. Children move from the simple to the more complex, making increasingly sophisticated approximations of correct spelling. Individual children seem to move through the same sequence of stages in learning to spell, regardless of when they begin to write. Moreover, they intuitively know a great deal about English orthography, which they use as a foundation in creating a hierarchy of concepts that guide their initial spelling efforts.

See Chapter 4, Emergent Literacy and Biliteracy, to review Charles Read's research on the development of young children's spelling and the description of early stages of spelling.

Other terms for *invented* spelling: *temporary, creative, emergent, developmental,* and *phonics-based.*

Recall from Chapter 4 the discussion of Charles Read (1971, 1975, 1986), who looked at the way children 4 to 8 years old used their knowledge of phonology (i.e., how words sound) to spell. Preschool children were able to name the letters of the alphabet and relate the letter names to the sounds of words. Then they "invented" spellings for words. Read found that even very young children could do this, and although they misspelled most words, they tended to misspell them in the same ways. There was a logic to their system of invented spelling. For example, they spelled the sounds of words with the letters that were like those sounds: *BOT* for *BOAT, FAS* for *FACE, LADE* for *LADY.*

Three important ideas were demonstrated by Read's research:

1. Children are trying to make sense of spelling, applying their intuitive knowledge of the sounds of English to writing words.
2. Their understanding of the relationship between sound and writing is qualitatively different than that of adults. Thus, learning to spell and write, like learning to speak, is a developmental process.
3. The spelling errors young children make tell us about the developmental stages of their mental processes.

Also recall from Chapter 4 the description of how young children begin to hypothesize about spelling based on their knowledge of spoken English. The focus there was on young children, including examples of three first-grade students who were all writing but at different stages of spelling development. The following sections describe these stages for school-age children, kindergarten through middle school, as identified by Gentry (1981, 1982, 2000). These stages have also been described by other researchers (Beers & Beers, 1981, summarizing Beers & Henderson, 1977; Gentry & Gillet, 1993; Henderson, 1980, 1990; Henderson & Templeton, 1986; Templeton, 1979; Zutell, 1979), and I have used the different names they have given to these stages. Each stage is illustrated with a spelling of the word *MONSTER* (Gentry, 1981) and an example from my daughter Elizabeth's writing over the years.

1. *Precommunicative Stage (Preschool to Midkindergarten, age 2–5 years):* This stage is also called *preliterate* and *prephonetic.* Children in it are aware of the purposes of writing but lack the concept of *word* and that words can be divided into phonemes. At first, children use scribbles, letterlike forms, and alphabet

symbols to represent words. But because they don't know what sounds match the symbols, their writing isn't readable.

Examples: A child in the precommunicative stage spells *MONSTER* as *btBpA.* You can see that Elizabeth uses scribbles, letterlike forms, and even alphabet symbols—*MR* and lots of capital *B*'s. She's aware that speech can be recorded through grahic symbols but obviously doesn't have a concept of what a word is or how to match speech sounds with symbols.

2. Semiphonetic Stage (End of Kindergarten through Beginning of First Grade, age 5–6 years): This stage is also called *prephonetic.* Children at this stage understand that letters represent sounds in words. They begin to use letter name spellings to make the association between letters and sounds, making closer approximations to true spelling but omitting major sounds. They also make associations with letters and sounds that are alike. They may use only one or two letters to represent a word (e.g., *D* or *DJ* = *DOG* or *K* or *KDE* = *CANDY*).

Examples: A child in the semiphonetic stage spells *MONSTER* as *MSR.* You can see from Elizabeth's writing that she knows that letters make words; she has used two- to three-letter representations of words, although she doesn't spell many words correctly. At the bottom of the page, you can see that she can spell her name. I dictated the words *Kitty named Fluffy* to her, which she wrote from bottom to top next to a picture of the kitty she had drawn.

3. Phonetic Stage (Middle of First Grade, age 6 years): Children are able to represent all the surface sound features of words and spell words the way they sound to them (*CHROBLE* = *TROUBLE*). They have invented a system of phonetic spelling, based on their awareness that letters and words represent sounds. This system is consistent and reflects a highly sophisticated understanding of the relationship of sounds of speech to symbols of writing. Spelling in this stage can be read by others. Children include all the sound features of the words (e.g., *KADE* = *CANDY; SEDRLI* = *CINDERELLA*).

Examples: A child in the phonetic stage spells *MONSTER* as *MONSTR.* Elizabeth can now represent in her spelling all the sounds she hears in a word. Although none of the words are spelled conventionally, you can—with a little imagination— read all of them. Elizabeth wrote this list after complaining to me that we didn't have any food she liked in the house. I told her, "Write a list of what you want." Can you read it?

4. *Transitional Stage (End of First through Beginning of Second Grade, age 6–9 years):* Children begin to spell conventionally in this stage. In addition to being able to spell based on their awareness of how words sound, children can now spell based on their awareness of how words look. (Good adult spellers are expert at this when they're able to tell if a word is spelled correctly by whether it "looks right.") At this stage, children put a vowel in every syllable and use e-marker and vowel digraph patterns. They can also use inflectional endings of words correctly as well as letter sequences that occur frequently. Their invented spelling is interspersed with correct spelling (e.g., *DOG* = *DOG* and *CINDARILA* = *CINDERELLA*). Children at

Elizabeth as a first-grader

this stage are able to use their morphemic knowledge by comparing one word to another; they can also use their visual memory of words they know how to spell and apply it to new words (e.g., *HIGHCKED* = *HIKED*).

Examples: A child in the transitional stage spells *MONSTER* as *MONSTUR*. Conventional spelling is mixed with invented phonetic spelling in this Mother's Day card Elizabeth wrote to me. Note that a vowel is included in every syllable and familiar spelling patterns are used.

5. *Conventional Stage (Second through Fourth Grade, age 7–9 years):* In this stage, children are beginning to spell correctly. Their knowledge of word meanings is growing, and they are better able to use complicated vowel patterns in English. They have basically mastered the complexities of English orthography. However, the characteristics and points of change in their spelling in this stage are more difficult to discern now than in earlier stages. They are probably still struggling with consonant doubling and word affixes but may have mastered word roots, past tense, and short vowels; they may still have trouble with the positions of letters, as in the silent *e* that controls vowels. Children's vocabulary is growing, and they understand the meanings of many more words. They have greater familiarity with vowel patterns in relation to stress and meaning in words.

Examples: A child in the conventional stage spells *MONSTER* as *MONSTER*. In this fold-a-book about a puppet show at her school, Elizabeth's spelling is generally conventional. She had some trouble with consonant doubling in *Petter;* used a silent *e* inappropriately at the end of *clime (climb)*, perhaps overgeneralizing the rule to add a silent *e* in a one-syllable word with a long vowel; and substituted *c* for *k* in *cept*, although phonologically, that is correct. Note, however, that she managed not to be sexist by using the pronoun *he/she*.

6. *Morphemic and Syntactic Stage (Fifth through Tenth Grade, age 10–16 years):* By the fifth grade, children increasingly understand how meaning and grammatical structure control spelling in English. They are better at doubling consonants and spelling alternate forms of the same word and at using word endings (e.g., *MANAGERIAL/MANAGE; REPETITION/REPEAT*). Children in this stage are increasingly able to use word meaning (or morphemic) and sentence structure (or syntactic information) (e.g., *SLOWLY; PASSED; FASTER; SLEEPING*). In addition to understanding the underlying phonological rules they gained as young children, older youths now understand and are able to use knowledge about the importance of meaning and syntax in spelling in English.

Example: Look how Elizabeth has demonstrated her knowledge of word meaning as it pertains to spelling in this note to me. She is playing with the homonyms *you* and *ewe* when she writes *I love you (ewe) not I love sheep* to explain her rebus picture of a sheep; this also illustrates her knowledge of the relationship of sound, symbols, and meaning in English.

We'll look at these stages of spelling development later in the chapter as a basis for assessing and teaching children. Understanding these stages is especially important in assessing and teaching children who are ELL, who have disabilities, or who struggle with spelling. See the box on page 332 for guidelines in supporting these children.

Spelling and Literacy Development

In the past, spelling has often been treated as a separate subject and thus taught with spelling books. Using such books as a guide, teachers taught and tested weekly lists of spelling words, usually the same list for all students. However, as you learned from the previous discussion on stages of spelling development, students in the same class could be at varying stages in their ability to spell, so one list would not be appropriate for all of them. This means that in the past, students often practiced words they already knew how to spell or were tested before they reached the stage of conventional spelling (anywhere between second and fourth grade), when they could reasonably be expected to spell words correctly (Genry & Gillet, 1993; Zutell, 1994).

As an alternative to spelling books and weekly practice and testing of isolated words and skills, Routman (1996) recommends teaching spelling and

Struggling Students, Students with Disabilities, and English Language Learners in Spelling

Understanding the stages of spelling development is especially important when working with students who are struggling with spelling or who have disabilities and may be delayed in their development. Teachers should do the following:

1. Carefully assess each student to determine what spelling stage best identifies his or her skill level.
2. Find appropriate instructional activities that match the student's stage.
3. Provide ample encouragement and opportunities for success.

Teachers of English language learners should keep in mind these guidelines about teaching and assessing spelling:

1. Be sure to understand the comparisons and contrasts ELL students make when learning to spell in English.
2. ELL students move through the same stages of spelling development as native English speakers, even if their native language is nonalphabetic.
3. Knowing the traits of specific languages is valuable in understanding ELL students' frame of reference (e.g., Spanish is much more phonetically regular than English).
4. Focus instruction on vocabulary expansion and enrichment and also on semantic relationships among words.
5. Draw attention to English words that have been borrowed from other languages.
6. Encourage second-language learners to share their first language with the class and to compare it with English.
7. Compare synonyms across languages by using dictionaries in various languages.
8. Be aware of semantic differences in the literal translations of words.

other language skills in the context of using language for meaningful purposes. This can be accomplished through modeling, setting high expectations for student work, teaching minilessons using children's books and their own writing, and giving students the tools to be responsible for their own work (e.g., self-assessment and proofreading). Specifically, teachers should plan a daily spelling program based on their knowledge of the stages of spelling development, such that spelling is integrated with student writing, reading, and word study. Research has demonstrated the effectiveness of teaching spelling every day as part of a student- and response-centered approach to teaching language skills (Wilde, 1990, 1993).

Spelling and Writing

Children learn to spell most words by reading and using invented spelling in their writing. Clarke (1988) found that first-grade children who were encouraged to use invented spelling were able to write more independently at the beginning of the year, wrote longer stories with more word variety, and did better when given spelling tests than those children who were prompted to use only words they knew how to spell correctly. Gettinger (1993) observed the same results for third-graders who used invented spelling.

Additional research looked at students in an *embedded spelling program*—namely, one in which students learned to spell inductively while writing, with scaffolding provided by the teacher and other students (about 97 percent of the time) and some explicit teaching of skills (about 3 percent of the time). These students scored as well on tests of isolated skills as students in a traditional spelling program but outperformed them for overall writing quality (O'Flahavan & Blassberg, 1992; Varble, 1990). Another study (Jongsma, 1990) of 28,000 essays written by American students from second grade through college found that most could spell correctly when they wrote: from 87 percent in second grade increasing steadily to 98 percent in college.

Teachers need to remember that invented spelling isn't taught. It's something that children do and should be encouraged to do as a means of discovering spelling conventions. Recall how Elizabeth made first gross and then closer and closer approximations to conventional spelling. Children learn to do this through frequent, daily experiences with writing, as described throughout this text and as recommended by the International Reading Association (IRA) and the National Association for the Education of Young Children (NAEYC) in their joint position statement, "Learning to Read and Write: Developmentally Appropriate Practices for Young Children" (IRA, 1998).

But what about cases in which children ask how to spell certain words? Telling a child to go to the dictionary will not help if he or she cannot spell the word well enough to look it up; doing so also interrupts the flow of the writing process. Telling a child to spell a word the way it sounds is not necessarily useful, either; the child would have done that if he or she could have.

Try these simple steps in helping a child "fix it." First say:

1. "Try spelling it yourself, and I'll help you fix it."

Next (then or later), say:

2. "What do you hear at the beginning of the word? Does it start like . . ." (referring to an alphabet chart)
   or
3. "Does it sound like any words you know?"
4. "Have you seen this word anywhere before?"
5. "What do you hear at the end of the word?"

Help the student do these things:

A *personal dictionary* is an individual's collection of words he or she has trouble spelling, perhaps on a regular basis.

6. Identify the sounds in the words using aids like an alphabet chart, "word wall," or personal dictionary.
7. Discover visual similarities to known words.
8. Recognize root words, prefixes, affixes, and the like.
9. Add new words to his or her personal dictionary.

Two other strategies to incorporate spelling in writing activites include proofreading and peer editing.

SNAPSHOT   **Peer-Editing Group in Writing Workshop**

See Chapter 9, The Writing Process, for how to do writing workshop.

Five children are editing and revising writing in a fourth-grade writing workshop peer-editing group. Robert is the student author who's going to read his story, "Mystery of the Witch and Warlock Continues," which is written in a journalistic style for a fictional class newspaper on Halloween. He's new to the class, so Nathan explains to him how peer editing works. After Robert reads, the other students respond to his writing and make suggestions. (The marginal notes indicate what steps in the writing process and what language conventions are being used and learned.)

1. *Explaining Editing in a Writing Workshop*

Editing

    Nathan: Robert, editing means to look through it and see if there's any mistakes, and revising is like changing the words to make it easier to understand.

    Robert: It's not going to be the final copy?

    Nathan: No.

    Robert: After we revise it, do we rewrite it again?

    Nathan: Yeah.

In this peer-editing group, students respond to and help revise one another's writing.

2. *Author Reads in a Peer-Editing Group:* Robert prefaces his reading by explaining, "This is like a newspaper story about what might happen at Halloween." Then he reads his story: Revising

Mystery of the Witch and Warlock Continues

In Baton Rouge, on the 31st of October which is Halloween, Robert Troll said he saw an evil witch and warlock on a magic broomstick. "It was a scary sight," he said. Robert says that at 8:00 at night while he was taking his son and daughter trick-or-treating he saw the witch and warlock. "My children thought it was scary," says Robert Troll. It was a full moon when the witch and warlock came. They made a scary laughing sound and flew away. His wife said that she had seem something fly up in the sky and she . . . (pause) . . . outside to look at it . . . (pause) . . . outside to see it better but she couldn't see anything. When she came inside it looked like her house had been robbed. "My diamond ring and necklace has been stolen," she screamed. Every Halloween people look outside to see what this flying object is and something gets stolen. Only the most valuable stuff gets stolen. So if you see a flying object do not look outside 'cause if you do something will get stolen.

3. *Peer Editors Respond to the Author:* After Robert finishes reading, the other students make suggestions for editing and revising his story, and Robert asks them questions: Author reads

Melissa:	*Evil.* I don't think that word should be there. Maybe you could find a better word to describe them.	Peers edit
Robert:	Or maybe I should leave *evil* out?	
Melissa:	That might sound better.	
Jason:	Why don't you put *jewelry* instead of *stuff?* It sounds kinda . . . babyish or something.	Word choice
Robert:	OK. Let's see (looking at story). *Jewelry.* Should I put "'Only the most valuable *jewelry*" or "Her most valuable *jewelry*"? How do you spell *jewelry?*	Sentence structure
Melissa:	J-E-W-E-L-R-Y.	Spelling
Kim	(looking at the story): I think you need to indent here to make another paragraph.	Paragraph
Melissa:	He could give a name to the son and daughter. It could be anybody. You know, it's sorta . . .	
Kim:	How about using adjectives to describe them? Or grades in school? Or specific ages?	
Melissa:	Like *evil.* It describes witch.	Descriptive words
Robert:	OK. How about "His fourth-grade son and baby daughter"?	
Jason	(looking at story): You need a comma in the middle there. This sorta looks like a period or something.	Punctuation
Robert:	Well, it shouldn't. I'll write it neater.	Handwriting
Kim:	I couldn't really understand the part about his wife. But it's good. It's a good story.	Meaning

Spelling and Literacy Development

The students in this fourth-grade peer-editing group continue to discuss all aspects of the story: meaning, word choice, sentence structure, style (it's supposed to be a newspaper article), spelling, punctuation, and handwriting. Their discussion shows that they're aware of the language conventions of spelling, punctuation, and handwriting and know how to apply them when getting a piece of writing ready to publish. These language conventions become important and meaningful when students are writing to communicate to a real audience.

The other peer-editing group members—Nathan, Melissa, Kim, and Jason—all shared their pieces in the same way that Robert did. With the editing and revising advice they received from each other, they spent the next day in writing workshop, rewriting their pieces.

Spelling and Reading

Spelling and reading have a close relationship (Anderson, 1985). Children who are good at invented spelling when writing are also good at figuring out, or *decoding*, words when reading. This amounts to self-directed phonemic awareness in young readers and writers (Davidson & Jenkins, 1994; Richgels, 1995). Put another way, decoding words and inventing spellings of them both involve the same process but working in opposite directions. The use of phonological knowledge in both reading and writing correlates highly with invented spelling (Adams, 1990). By looking at children's invented spellings, teachers can "assess and teach not only spelling, but also important aspects of phonemic awareness, phonics, writing, and other essential elements of literacy" (Gentry, 2000, p. 318).

See Chapter 6, Reading, for more on phonemic awareness in young children and independent reading.

Older students who are good spellers and recognize many words in print use visual as well as phonological knowledge. They have acquired these types of knowledge through reading to spell words correctly, and the more words students learn—through listening, speaking, and reading—the better they will be able to read and spell. In fact, one difference between poor and good spellers in the middle and upper grades is that good spellers use this visual information along with morphemic and syntactic knowledge about words (such as root words, prefixes and affixes, and semantic relationships among words), while poor spellers still rely on phonological information. They are stuck on sounding out words, rather than using the visual information that good spellers are able to access.

Word Study

Word study integrates spelling, phonics, and vocabulary into the larger picture of literacy instruction, or reading and writing. In doing word study, children analyze the meanings, structures, and sounds of words and then apply what they learn to new words they encounter in reading and use when writing (Bear & Templeton, 1998). Word study activities should be a part of the daily spelling program; specific activities by stage of spelling development are described in the section Assessing and Teaching Spelling in Grades K–8 (pp. 340–349), from simple to more complex levels of knowledge about the alphabet, patterns of words, and meaning.

Here's an assortment of effective word study strategies:

Semantic Maps. When introducing new words or words in content areas, teachers can use graphic organizers such as clusters and webs to relate words. For example, if studying a topic in biology, students could do a semantic map of words that include *bio-* in them. For older students, understanding how these words are related by meaning is fundamental to understanding the orthographic relationship among them.

See Chapter 3, First- and Second-Language Development, for more on semantic maps.

"Word Walls." *"Word walls"* are used to record ideas and words on topics such as special events, holidays, and those in the content areas. When the teacher records students' ideas on a word wall, he or she is modeling writing for them and establishing the importance of their ideas. Children can do word walls with each other in small groups. Moreover, word walls can be added to over time, as children come up with new ideas and words. Any time words are put on a paper that can be displayed on the wall, a word wall is being created—along with a print-rich environment. Try these variations:

The concept of a "word wall" was introduced in the Lesson Plan in Chapter 1, Learning and Teaching Language Arts.

- *Alphabet:* Some word walls have a space for each letter of the alphabet, and words related to the topic at hand are written under the appropriate letter. Teachers can record children's words, or children can write on the word wall themselves.

See the month September in the *Schoolyear Activities Planner* for a lesson that uses an alphabet "word wall."

- *Graphic organizers:* Word walls can be presented as clusters, Venn diagrams, T-charts, and flowcharts.

- *Post-its:* Words can also be added on Post-its or on small pieces of paper with tape. For example, a fifth-grade class brainstormed a word wall of synonyms for the word *said* using Post-its to avoid using it over and over again and to make their writing more interesting (see the marginal note). A list like this could be added to throughout the year.

Synonyms for *Said*

asked, spoke, told, begged, stated, declared, pleaded, complained, whined, complimented, informed, screamed, yelled, shouted, hollered, advised, warned, and *cautioned*

Word Lists. Lists of high-frequency words and useful words for spelling and writing can be displayed in the classroom or duplicated so children have their own copies for reference. See Table 10.1 (p. 338) for a list of these words.

Dictionaries, Thesauruses, and Word Journals. A traditional dictionary or thesaurus is most useful to students who are in at least the conventional (second through fourth grade) or morphemic and syntactic (fifth through tenth grade) stages of spelling development. However, students at other stages of development can create their own personal word journals and dictionaries. They can reserve a page for each letter of the alphabet, and on each, they can list words they have learned how to spell and are using in their writing. Children can add words at home, as well. When students regularly update their journals/dictionaries, they can be used for future reference. These lists can also be kept on file cards in a box or envelope or on a metal ring.

A picture dictionary for younger students, with versions in several languages (e.g., Spanish-English) is available at **www.enchantedlearning.com/Dictionary.html**. And Roget's Internet Thesaurus of English can be accessed at **www.thesaurus.com/**.

Table 10.1	Most Useful Words in Reading and Writing

Before beginning a formal spelling program, students need to be able to spell the following words automatically.

The ten words listed below make up 25% of all running words. One of these words will be found in every four words:

a be of we and I the you in to

The words on the following list make up 50% of all running words. This means that one of these words will occur, on the average, in every two words:

a	ever	how	more	out	their	very
after	for	I	most	part	them	was
all	from	if	must	said	then	were
an	get	into	my	say	there	what
and	give	is	no	see	these	when
any	go	it	not	shall	they	where
are	good	know	now	she	this	which
as	great	leave	of	should	those	who
at	had	letter	often	so	though	will
been	has	like	on	some	time	with
but	have	made	one	such	today	would
by	have	make	only	take	under	you
can	he	many	or	than	upon	yours
come	him	may	other	that	us	
do	his	me	our	the	use	

Source: From *Word Knowledge Continuum*, Office of Curriculum and Resources, Long Beach Unified School District, 1996, Long Beach, CA. Reprinted with permission.

TEACHER RESOURCES

For an extensive list of ideas for word study and word sorts, see *Words Their Way: Word Study for Phonics, Vocabulary, and Spelling Instruction* (Bear, Templeton, & Invernizzi, 1999).

EXCELLENT SOFTWARE

For information on the software program Word Sort, go to the website **www. hendersonedsoft.com**.

Word Sorts. Another way to show the relationships among words is to sort words into categories—for instance, how words are alike or different. Students can do this by building on what they already know about word meanings and use; they also gain knowledge about orthograhic word patterns as they do so. Word sorts are an important word study activity for spelling and can be organized in three ways: (1) by conducting them in learning centers, (2) with small groups of children, and (3) with the teacher.

Here are some suggestions for conducting word sorts (Bear & Templeton, 1998; Beers & Beers, 1981):

1. Gather a collection of words that the child knows from sources such as books he or she has read, his or her own word journal, words from language experience charts and writing, labels in the classroom, or words used in the content areas. The only materials required are index cards (or small cards you cut yourself) with the appropriate words printed on them.

2. The child can be seated on the floor or at a table and work individually or with a few peers. He or she can begin to practice sorting objects (e.g., buttons) or picture cards (e.g., animals) and move into sorting words. The child may sort the items in piles or use a sorting card with categories on it.

3. Ask the child to categorize the words under various headings. You may provide the headings based on the child's spelling or encourage the child to name the headings. Examples of headings include the following:

> Short-vowel words
> Long-vowel words
> One-syllable words
> Describing words (adjectives or adverbs)
> Verbs ending in -*ing*
> Past-tense verbs
> Words with prefixes or suffixes
> Words conveying the same meaning

4. Once a category has been filled by the child, ask and discuss why he or she grouped these words and what similarities and differences he or she found. Help children generalize about these word categories and form hypotheses about patterns among words that they can test with new words they come across in reading and then use in writing.

In addition, there are several kinds of word sorts:

- *Closed Sorts:* The teacher chooses the words and states the criteria in advance—for example:
    1. *Letters and sounds:* initial letters; consonants, vowels; blends; vowel sounds and patterns (short, long digraphs, *r*-controlled); homophones
    2. *Structure:* prefixes; affixes; inflection; number of syllables; consonant doubling; dropping *e*
    3. *Function:* parts of speech; inflectional endings (-*ed*, -*ing*)
    4. *Meaning:* root families; etymology; types of words

- *Open Sorts:* Children establish their own criteria. This can be done in a gamelike situation. For example, to play Guess My Group, the children sort their own cards into several categories and the other players try to guess what the categories are. For the game of Concentration, 16 cards are placed face down on the table. A child turns 2 cards over and tries to create and justify a category for them; if the others accept it, he or she picks up these cards and chooses 2 more. If the others do not accept the categories, another child plays. The child with the most cards at the end of the game wins. Go Fish, Rummy, Old Maid, and other traditional card games can also be played with word sort cards.

- *Word Searches:* Children search for words that fit a category and circle, underline, or write them down. Younger students may do this with pages copied from a book, with teacher-created text, or with their own writing. These texts can also be laminated and written on with nonpermanent markers so they can be used more than once. An answer key can be written on the back of each card so the children can self-check their work. Older students can go on word searches using dictionaires, thesauruses, textbooks, newspapers, or anything that might contain a word that fits a category. The teacher can suggest a word teaser, such as the phonogram (i.e., word part) *mne,* to see if the students can find other words with this element (e.g., *amnesia* and *mnemonic*). Or they might look up word origins to explore common roots or words—for example, *psych,* as found in *psychology, psychiatrist,* and *psychiatric*. These searches can be linked to content areas or literature study, such as Greek and Roman mythology.

- *Word Constructions:* Make a deck of letter cards (you will need at least 200), and then use them to play the following games, which use letters to construct words:

  1. *Scrambled Words:* Playing in pairs, children try to stump each other by posing scrambled words that their partners try to unscramble.
  2. *Building Words:* Each child in a small group receives the same number of letter cards and uses them to make as many words as possible.
  3. *Attaching Words:* Older children may attach the words they build in horizontal and vertical strings, as in Scrabble.
  4. *Anagrams:* Children make as many words as possible by rearranging the letters of a given word.

Word Study Minilessons

Formal instruction in spelling can be done through minilessons, especially during writing workshop. These minilessons should be 5 to 10 minutes in length, and additional time should be provided for children to practice what they're learning. See the minilessons for students of various grades and stages of spelling development in the next section, Assessing and Teaching Spelling in Grades K–8.

Assessing and Teaching Spelling in Grades K–8

When spelling is taught from a developmental perspective, teachers must take into account what research says about the stages of spelling that children go through. Thus, the first step in assessing spelling is to determine what stage each child is in and what he or she can be expected to do. Table 10.2 summarizes the characteristics of each stage, based on researchers' observations of children's invented spelling.

Teachers should plan their spelling programs according to the grade levels they teach and, even more so, according to the stages of spelling development that characterize their students. To determine each child's level of development, authentic and ongoing assessment should be used. The following sections describe assessment and minilessons on word study for the developmental stages of spelling for kindergarten through second grade, second through fourth grade, and fifth through eighth grade.

Table 10.2 Stages of Spelling Development and Teaching

Kindergarten through Second Grade

Precommunicative (Preschool–Midkindergarten, age 2–5 years)

- Scribbling can be representational.
- Understand speech can be written.
- Lack concept of *word*, or relationship between sounds and letters.
- Make letterlike shapes or actual letters and numbers.
- May write name.

> *Examples:*
> MONSTER = *btBpA*
> Elizabeth: *MR, B*, and letterlike forms

Semiphonetic (End of Kindergarten–Beginning of First Grade, age 5–6 years)

- Spells few words correctly but knows letters make words.
- Still invents symbols for letters and words.
- Makes one- to three-letter representations of words, usually consonants.
- Has more control over beginnings and ends of words than middles.
- Predicts words auditorially in sophisticated ways with frequently occurring patterns.

> *Examples:*
> MONSTER = *MSR*
> Elizabeth: *BEBHT, ELISA, RPB, EB*

Phonetic (Middle of First Grade, age 6 years)

- Spellings include all sound features of words as heard.
- Invents system of phonetic spelling that is consistent.
- Understands relationship of sounds in speech to symbols in writing.
- Spelling can be read by others.

> *Examples:*
> MONSTER = *MONSR*
> Elizabeth: *ISECREM (ice cream), PENOTBOTR (peanut butter)*

Transitional (End of First–Beginning of Second Grade, age 6–7 years)

- Begins to spell conventionally and knows it is necessary for others to read their writing.
- Uses knowledge of how words look as well as sound and applies to other words.
- Includes vowels in every syllable.
- Uses familiar spelling patterns.
- Intersperses conventional spelling with invented spelling.

> *Examples:*
> MONSTER = *monstur*
> Elizabeth: *Mothers/Moters, Fredome (freedom), Becaues (because)*

Assessment	Activities
Concept of a Word	Writing and invented spelling
Writing Sample Analysis	Reading and word study
Developmental Spelling Inventory	Learning sounds, letters, word patterns

4.2

See the Concept of a Word (p. 127).

10.2
10.3

See the Writing Sample Analysis (p. 344) and the Developmental Spelling Inventory (p. 346).

(continued)

Table 10.2   Stages of Spelling Development and Teaching (continued)

Second through Fourth Grade

Conventional (Second–Fourth Grade, age 7–9 years)

- Begins to spell correctly.
- Displays characteristics that are less clear.
- Has probably mastered root words, past tense, and short vowels.
- Still struggles with consonant doubling, letter position (e.g., silent *e*, controlled vowels), and word affixes.
- Has growing knowledge of word meanings and complicated vowel patterns.

> *Examples:*
>   MONSTER = MONSTER
>   Elizabeth: *school, puppet, favorite, Petter (Peter), clime (climb), cept (kept)*

Assessment	*Activities*
Writing Sample Analysis	Writing and reading
Developmental Spelling Inventory	Test-corrected-test technique
	Word study and sorts

Fifth through Eighth Grade

Morphemic and Syntactic (Fifth–Eighth Grade, age 10–13 years)

- Increasingly understands how meaning and grammatical structure control spelling.
- Adds morphemic and syntactic to phonological knowledge gained when younger.
- Is better at doubling consonants, spelling alternative forms of words, and word endings.

> *Examples:*
>   Elizabeth: *you* (sounds like) *ewe* (which means) *sheep*

Assessment	*Activities*
Writing samples	Reading and writing
	Content-area literacy
	Word study and games

10.2
10.3

See the Writing Sample Analysis (p. 344) and the Developmental Spelling Inventory (p. 346).

Kindergarten through Second Grade

For children in these grades, learning to spell should be an integral part of free writing for meaning; invented spelling should be encouraged. Research has shown that formal instruction in spelling can begin only when children understand the concepts of *word* and *word structure* through numerous experiences with words in their own writing and reading (Beers, Beers, & Grant, 1977). Characteristic errors of beginning spellers are using letter names for sounds, omitting nasals before consonants, and confusing vowel sounds with similarly articulated letter names. Few of these errors occur after second grade (Read, 1971; Zutell, 1979).

Assessment

To assess the knowledge of beginning spellers, use Assessment Toolbox 10.1 or 10.2 (pp. 343 and 344).

4.2

See also the Concept of a Word (p. 127), which is appropriate for beginning spellers.

10.1 The Camel Test

Gentry (2000) recommends this simple way to use invented spelling to assess the benchmark of full phonemic awareness by the middle of first grade.

The Camel Test

1. Ask the child to spell *camel*—a word he or she has heard but most likely has not seen in print. If the child writes C-A-M-L, it demonstrates awareness of the four phonemes and the ability to match letters to phonemes in this word.

2. If the child spells *camel* correctly, substitute another word. Gentry recommends using *eagle* (EGL), *bacon* (BAKN), or *magic* (MAJEK).

3. Assess the results. If the child is a Stage 3 Phonetic Speller (letter name), he or she is phonemically aware.

Source: Based on Gentry, 2000.

Word Study Minilessons

● *Picture and Object Sorts:* Young children can practice classifying related pictures and objects according to similar properties (various buttons, seashells, dry pasta). The teacher can make picture cards by cutting up file cards or manila folders and adding an image (animals, objects, fruit) on each card. The students can sort the cards into piles or arrange them in labeled columns or boxes on a sort of gameboard. (A token object or picture can be used to label each column or box.)

● *Onsets and Rimes:* Teachers of young children should use *onsets* (any consonant that precedes a vowel in a syllable) and *rimes* (a vowel and any consonants after it in a syllable) as a decoding strategy for reading. In doing so, they are also teaching children necessary spelling patterns for writing. Children can make many words using the same rime but different onsets—for example, *-ake* can become *cake, rake,* or *lake* using letter cards or magnetic letters. The teacher should make a list of onsets and rimes and display it in the room.

See Chapter 6, Reading, for more on onsets and rimes.

● *Analogies:* This is another reading strategy that can be applied to spelling. Children decode unknown words by using rimes from words they already know and use this same knowledge to spell new words. For example, if a child can read and write *cat*, he or she can analogize that to reading and spelling more words, like *rat* and *sat*.

● *Word Building:* The teacher should provide children with manipulatives that have individual letters and rimes on them (such as letter titles) and encourage the children to build new words from them. This can also be done by simply writing the words.

10.2 Writing Sample Analysis

This Writing Sample Analysis provides a simple means to analyze student spelling; the sample included for analysis is a first-grade student's letter to a friend. The teacher should use this form to categorize student spelling by stage of development and then figure the percentage of words spelled correctly in each stage. This form can be used until students are in the conventional stage, between second and fourth grade, when they spell about 90 percent of the words in their writing correctly.

Writing Sample Analysis

Directions: Classify words by stages of spelling development. List repeated words together and count them as one word. Note the number of words in each category.

Student _____   Date _____

Stage of Spelling Development	Number of Words	Percent
1. *Precommunicative*	0	—
2. *Semiphonetic* yro kap	2	8%
3. *Phonetic* pichr ws	2	8%
4. *Transitional* hop lik haw bo lic mad mlsalf drivf hap hav camq haw	11	46%
5. *Conventional* Dear Graham I you it fun the love Bryce I you I you	9	38%

Dear Graham.
I hop you lik kaP.
haw bo you lic The
Pichr. I mad it m!
Salf haw ws
yro drivf. I
hop you hav fun.

LOVe
Bryce
cam q

- *Letter and Word Sorts:* Follow the same procedure as for picture and object sorts, but use small cards with sounds, letters, and word patterns printed on them: initial letters, consonants, vowels, and so on. The cards used for sorts can also be used for games like Bingo, Concentration, and Rummy.

Commercial word games that enhance spelling: Boggle, Perquackey, Hugger Mugger, Scrabble, Spill & Spell, and Word Yahtzee.

Second through Fourth Grade

Children at this stage should still be learning to spell as a part of writing. They may also engage in simple activities using high-frequency irregular words and difficult words from their own writing and spelling journals. Children typically misspell common words and don't apply generalizations about orthographically regular words.

Assessment

Teachers can continue to use Assessment Toolbox 10.2, the Writing Sample Analysis, and also introduce Assessment Toolbox 10.3, the Developmental Spelling Inventory (p. 346).

Word Study Minilessons

Minilessons can take a variety of forms at this stage, including some formal spelling instruction:

10.3

See the Developmental Spelling Inventory (p. 346), which is based on Richard Gentry's (1985) study asking children in different stages of spelling development to spell the word *monster.*

- *Spelling Tests:* Gentry (1987) recommends the following research-based instructional strategies for spelling tests, which usually begin in the second grade, when students are somewhere between the phonetic and transitional stages in their spelling development:

  1. Allow 60 to 75 minutes per week.
  2. Present words in a list or column format.
  3. Pretest students to determine unknown words; then have them study those words; and then posttest students to determine what they have learned.
  4. Have children correct their own spelling tests, with guidancce.
  5. Teach systematic techniques for studying unknown words.
  6. Use word study to teach words.

- *Spelling Rules:* The following useful spelling rules can be introduced through minilessons in writing workshop:

  1. Y rule: For words that end in a consonant plus *y,* change the *y* to *i* before adding *-es* or *-ed* (e.g., *try/tries/tried*).
  2. Final, silent *e* rule: For words that end in silent *e,* drop the *e* before adding a suffix beginning with a vowel and keep the *e* when adding a suffix that begins with a consonant (e.g., *skate/skating/skates*).
  3. Doubling rule: For words in which the final syllable ends in a consonant preceded by a single vowel, double the consonant before adding a suffix beginning with a vowel (e.g., *hit/hitting*).
  4. Plurals rule: Most single nouns become plural by adding an *-s* or *-es* (e.g., *cat/cats; dress/dresses*).

ASSESSMENT TOOLBOX

10.3 Developmental Spelling Inventory

Gentry (1985) developed a Developmental Spelling Inventory based on his research on how children learn to spell. This inventory is a list of words that can be used to evaluate the spelling skills of children from kindergarten through fourth grade. In sum, the teacher reads aloud each word, uses it in a sentence, and asks the student to write it. The teacher then analyzes the student's spelling errors, characterizing each according to the developmental levels of spelling. A pattern will become evident, identifying the level the student is in.

Developmental Spelling Inventory

- Read the following 10 words. Use each in a sentence. Ask the child to write down each word.

1. monster	5. hiked	8. closed
2. united	6. human	9. bumped
3. dress	7. eagle	10. typed
4. bottom		

- Analyze the child's spelling.

  a. Find the error type in the scoring chart below that best matches the child's spelling. This does not have to be exact.

  b. Write an abbreviation of the developmental level beside each word.

  c. Look for the abbreviation that occurs most frequently to determine the child's developmental level.

- Scoring Chart

Precommunicative	Semiphonetic	Phonetic	Transitional	Conventional
1. random	mtr	mostr	monstur	monster
2. random	u	unitid	younighted	united
3. random	jrs	jras	dres	dress
4. random	bt	bodm	bottum	bottom
5. random	h	hikt	hicked	hiked
6. random	um	humm	humun	human
7. random	el	egl	egul	eagle
8. random	kd	klosd	clossed	closed
9. random	b	bopt	bumpped	bumped
10. random	tp	tip	tipe	type

Source: Adapted from Gentry, 1985, p. 50. Reprinted with permission of the publisher, *Teaching K–8*, Norwalk, CT. From the 1985 issue of *Teaching K–8*.

5. *Q rule:* The letter *q* is followed by *u* in English spelling (e.g., *quit, queue*).
6. *V rule:* Words in English never end in *v*.
7. Rules for using periods in abbreviations, possessive apostrophes, and capitals for proper names and adjectives

● *Test-Corrected-Test Technique:* This technique can account for almost all spelling words learned by students in testing situations. In fact, recent research has shown that this technique alone may account for the upper one-third of all third-grade students' achievement in spelling (Wirtz et al., 1996). Gentry (1987) suggests the following two ways to learn new words or words students have missed on tests using the test-corrected-test technique:

Fitzgerald Method	Horn Method
1. Look at the word carefully.	1. Pronounce each word carefully.
2. Say the word.	2. Look carefully at each part of the word as you say it.
3. Visualize the word with eyes closed.	3. Say the letters in sequence.
4. Cover the word and write it.	4. Try to recall how the word looks; then spell it.
5. Check the spelling.	5. Write the word.
6. If the word is misspelled, repeat steps 1–5.	6. If the word is misspelled, repeat steps 1–5.

● *Word Sorts:* Focus on the structure of words, analyzing compound words; the number of syllables; prefixes, suffixes, and affixes; homphones and homographs; and inflectional endings (e.g., *-ed* and *-ing*). Use word cards to play games like Old Maid, Go Fish, and Rummy.

WWW

Spelling games can be found on the Internet at **www.funbrain. com/index.html**.

EXCELLENT SOFTWARE

Word Muncher is a word game that uses sounds and patterns in words.

LESSON PLAN

Word Study of Homophones

Children's literature is still the best source of words and ideas for reading, writing, spelling, and word study. Many children's books focus specifically on language. Some of my favorites are by Fred Gwynne, who has written and illustrated several around the idea that some words in English have different meanings and spellings but sound the same. Try one of his books for children in second grade and above, such as *The King Who Rained*, using this Lesson Plan as a guide:

Level: Second grade and up

Purpose: Children will listen to and enjoy good literature, discuss the book by responding to open/aesthetic questions and prompts; play with words; increase vocabulary; understand homophones; generate a list of homophones and continue to add to it; use homophones in writing.

Homophones are words that sound alike but look different (e.g., *bear* and *bare*).

Homographs are words that look alike but sound different (e.g., *read*).

GREAT BOOKS FOR CHILDREN

By Fred Gwynne

A Chocolate Moose for Dinner (1976)
The King Who Rained (1970)
A Little Pigeon Toad (1988)
The Sixteen Hand Horse (1980)

(continued)

Homophone Pairs

*sail/sale, tail/tale, pane/pain,
plain/plane, night/knight,
pair/pear, made/maid,
cheap/cheep, meat/meet,
hare/hair, dye/die, days/daze,
eye/I, been/bin, red/read,
way/weigh, flour/flower,
Mary/marry/merry, no/know,
mail/male, to/too/two,
great/grate, right/write,
seem/seam, threw/through,
cent/scent, hair/hare,
knew/new, son/sun, stair/stare,
heard/herd, lie/lye,
their/they're/there, see/sea,
waist/waste, led/lead,
stake/steak, sore/soar, pole/poll,
piece/peace, main/mane,
forth/fourth, creek/creak,
flare/flair, strait/straight,
sweet/suite, mist/missed,
sore/soar, fir/fur,
manor/manner, flee/flea*

**GREAT BOOKS
FOR CHILDREN**

Homophones

*Eight Ate: A Feast of Homonym
    Riddles* (Terban, 1992)
*Night Knight: A Word Play Flap
    Book* (Ziefert, 1997)
Two-Way Words (Kudrna, 1980)
*What's Mite Might? Homophone
    Riddles to Boost Your Word
    Power* (Maestro, 1986)

www

For more on words that are
spelled the same but have
different meanings when
pronounced differently, go to
**www-personal.umich.edu/
~cellis/heteronym.html**.

Standard 6: Students apply knowledge of language structure, language conventions (e.g., spelling and punctuation), media techniques, figurative language, and genre to create, critique, and discuss print and nonprint texts.

Materials:

1. *The King Who Rained,* by Fred Gwynne (1970)
2. Chartpaper and marking pens for a "word wall"
3. Plain white paper and pencils or crayons

Teaching Sequence:

1. Read aloud *The King Who Rained.* It's based on homophones; each page has an illustration of what it would look like if a homophone were used incorrectly. For example, "There once was a king who rained" shows a king horizontally in the air, *raining* like a cloud (as opposed to *reigning*, a homophone for *raining*).
2. Use aesthetic, open-ended questions and prompts to discuss the book:
    "What did you think of the book?"
    "What was your favorite part?"
3. Ask directed questions leading to a generalization about homophones:
    "What did you notice about the words and the pictures in the book?"
4. Explain homophones, and ask students to give an example from the book and explain it.
5. Ask students to give examples of other homophones.
6. Create a T-chart or "word wall" on chartpaper, and write down homophone pairs the children suggest.
7. Ask students to pick one of the pairs and draw an illustration to demonstrate their understanding of homophones.

Extending Activities:

1. Write and illustrate more homophones.
2. Bind students' illlustrations of homophones in a class book.
3. Add to the T-chart or word wall of homophones.
4. Read more homophone books.

Assessment:

1. Observe children's reactions while you read the book. Did they listen to and enjoy it?
2. Were they able to identify, explain, and give an example of a homophone from the book?
3. Were they able to create a list of homophones not found in the book or on the word wall?
4. Were they able to illustrate and explain a homophone pair?

Fifth through Eighth Grade

Research has shown that providing no formal instruction in spelling is just as effective as providing a formal program for teaching students beyond the fourth grade (Hammill, Larsen, & McNutt, 1977; Manolakes, 1975). Students at this level should focus on better understanding how meaning and form are related in English spelling by studying words that have related forms and roots, especially those in the content areas.

Assessment

Spelling should be assessed as part of ongoing, authentic assessment of writing and writing portfolios.

Word Study Minilessons

- *Word Sorts:* Focus on exploring word meaning, examining root families, word origins (or etymology), and types of words (e.g., grammatical function such as parts of speech).

- *Word Searches:* In pairs or groups, students can search for words in dictionaries, the thesaurus, or textbooks—anywhere they might find words to fit a certain category. The teacher can suggest one, such as the phonogram (word part) *mne*, and students can look for words using this element (e.g., *amnesia* or *mnemonic*). While reading Greek myths, the whole class can search for words with the Greek root *psych* (e.g., *psychology, psychiatrist, psychiatric,* and so on).

- *Mystery Words:* This is a game for the whole class, which should be divided into groups or teams. The teacher should compile a list of words students are not likely to know (e.g., *xenophobia, quaff, pyre, mein, entail, cayuse*). In groups, students guess or create meanings for the words and write them down. They can then look up each word in the dictionary and compare their guesses to the real meanings. Once the teacher has introduced this game, students can play it on their own in pairs or groups.

Answers to Questions about Spelling

- *How do children learn to spell?*

Learning to spell is a constructive, developmental process, like learning how to speak. Spelling is learned best when considered part of the writing process. In learning to spell, children move from the simple to the more complex, making increasingly sophisticated and similar approximations of correct spelling based on how they hear words. From kindergarten through the eighth grade, children move through the same six stages: precommunicative, semi-phonetic, phonetic, transitional, conventional, and morphemic and syntactic. Individual children seem to move through the same sequence, regardless of when they begin to write.

- *How should we teach and assess spelling?*

Children should be taught spelling as part of the writing process. Individualized instruction using students' own writing is more effective than whole-class instruction in skills. The teacher's role is to provide time and opportunities to write, to encourage invented spelling, and to organize the classroom to provide for whole-class, small-group, and teacher- and peer-editing conferences. A variety of word study strategies can be used to teach spelling minilessons, including "word walls," personal spelling journals and dictionaries, test-corrected-test method, word games, word sorts, semantic maps, and self-editing.

Looking Further

1. Collect at least three samples of writing from children in the same class. Analyze the stage of spelling development each child is at according to the Writing Sample Analysis, Assessment Toolbox 10.2. If possible, do this for two different grade levels more than one year apart.

2. Plan appropriate spelling instruction for one of the children you assessed in item 1.

3. Observe a group of students in a peer-editing group in a writing workshop. Make notes about ideas you have for teaching spelling using writing workshop.

4. Play one of the word study games described in this chapter with a group of children. Talk about it, and see if you can all create a new word game.

Children's Books and Software

Cole, J. (1989). *The magic school bus, inside the human body.* New York: Scholastic.

Gwynne, F. (1970). *The king who rained.* New York: Prentice-Hall.

Gwynne, F. (1976). *A chocolate moose for dinner.* New York: Windmill.

Gwynne, F. (1980). *The sixteen hand horse.* New York: Prentice-Hall.

Gwynne, F. (1988). *A little pigeon toad.* New York: Simon & Schuster.

Kudrna, C. I. (1980). *Two-way words.* New York: Abingdon.

Maestro, G. (1986). *What's mite might? Homophone riddles to boost your word power.* New York: Clarion.

Showers, P. (1970). *What happens to a hamburger?* New York: Clarion.

Terban, M. (1992). *Eight ate: A feast of homonym riddles.* New York: Clarion.

Word muncher [Computer software]. Available from MECC.

Word sort [Computer software]. Available from Henderson Educational Software.

Ziefert, H. (1997). *Night knight: A word play flap book.* New York: Houghton Mifflin.

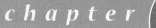

Grammar, Punctuation, and Handwriting

Questions about Grammar, Punctuation, and Handwriting

- *What is* grammar, *and why should we teach it?*
- *How should we teach and assess grammar, punctuation, and handwriting?*

REFLECTIVE RESPONSE

Write down your ideas about what you think *grammar* is. Then write any memories you have of learning grammar, punctuation, and handwriting. What do you think you learned, and how did it affect your education?

Grammar

Defining Grammar

You may or may not have a firm idea of what *grammar* is, depending on how you were taught it. The role of grammar in instruction is an elusive and loaded concept, with a long history linking it to everything from philosophy, logic, and rhetoric during the time of the ancient Greeks to literature, writing, and usage today. Few people agree on any one description.

The word *grammar* has been used by different people for different purposes and in different periods of history (Weaver, 1979, 1996, 1998a):

1. *Sentence Structure:* Grammar often simply refers to word order, the functions of words, and the grammatical endings of words in a language.
2. *Usage:* Socially acceptable and prestigious language use is often referred to as "good grammar"; "bad grammar" often means the use of language forms and constructions that are not acceptable to many people.
3. *Description:* Many linguists have attempted to classify and describe the syntactic structure of a language, which they call a "grammar."
4. *A Process:* Psycholinguists have tried to describe how people are able to create and understand sentences in a language; they refer to this process as "grammar."
5. *A Set of Rules:* In education, grammar has often been thought of as a set of rules for teaching students about some combination of the meanings above as well as pronunciation and whatever else teachers thought would help students speak and write "correctly."

Which of these descriptions best fits the definition of *grammar* you wrote down earlier? That likely depends on your age, the kind of school you went to, the English books you used, and the beliefs of your parents, English teachers, and school administrators regarding the purpose and importance of teaching grammar. Regardless, chances are that you were definitely taught something called "grammar."

Types of Grammar

Given the long tradition of teaching grammar and the likelihood that it will remain an educational issue, teachers should know what it is and how to teach it. Their decisions as to how to approach teaching grammar should be based on information about grammar, grammar teaching, and language development and learning.

Grammarians have developed different models for explaining how language works. The three main types of grammar described in the following sections—traditional, structural, and transformational—have different histories and theoretical frameworks. Teachers should be familiar with them in order to put grammar in proper perspective. The following comparison considers the features of these three types of grammar, including a historical perspective, main characteristics, educational implications, and some terms, rules, and definitions. See also Table 11.1, which provides an overview of these three types of grammar.

Traditional Grammar

Traditional grammar began as a prescriptive grammar for teaching English in medieval times; its roots can be traced to the study of classical languages. Traditional grammar provided a commonly used terminology for talking about language and a tradition of analyzing and describing the grammar of a language. Eventually, however, traditional grammar became a set of rules for writing English

IRA/ NCTE

Definition of Grammar

"The means by which the different components of language can be put together in groups of sounds and written or visual symbols so that ideas, feelings, and images can be communicated; what one knows about the structure and use of one's own language that leads to its creative and communicative use."

Table 11.1   Comparison of Types of Grammar

Traditional Grammar	Structural Grammar	Transformational Grammar
Grammar as rules for socially correct usage.	Grammar as a description of how language is used.	Grammar as a theory of how language is produced.
Originally provided a basic terminology that teachers and students could use to discuss language.	Looks at different languages and differences among language uses: idiolect, dialect, and other varieties of language form.	Meaning is tied to a theory of language that gives it explanatory and predictive power and a way to understand language competence and performance.
but	**but**	**but**
The terms and rules are inadequate and inaccurate and cannot explain how language works. Prescribes rather than describes and does not account for learners with language differences.	It does not attempt to explain how meaning is related to use in language.	It is difficult to understand and apply rules, which sometimes sound like algebraic equations.

Eight Parts of Speech
noun
pronoun
verb
adjective
adverb
preposition
conjunction
interjection
	Form Class Words
	Nouns, verbs, adjectives, and adverbs—words that carry most meaning and are inflected or change form.
	
	Function Words
	Noun determiners, auxiliary verb forms, subordinators, prepositions—words that are important for structural relationships but have little meaning and do not change form.
		Phrase Structure Rules
		Noun $N \rightarrow T + N$
		
		where N = noun and
		T = determiner.
		
		Noun Phrase NP Det N
		           Prop N
		           Pronoun
		
		where Noun phrase = determiner plus a noun, proper noun, or pronoun.
		
		Transformational Rules
		Movement, deletion, insertion, and substitution.

Sentence A group of words expressing a complete thought and possessing a subject and a predicate.	*Sentence* Each sentence is an independent linguistic form, not characterized as a grammatical construction in any larger linguistic form.	*Sentence* $S \rightarrow NP + VP$, or where S (sentence) equals NP (noun phrase) plus VP (verb phrase).

correctly, based on rules of Latin grammar. But English is not a Latin language; thus, Latin categories and terms don't fit English or accurately describe it.

During the eighteenth century, traditional language scholars classified the parts of English speech in the same way classical languages were classified. These parts of speech are still found in schoolbooks today. In the nineteenth century, linguists began to focus on describing how language forms, such as those that had been studied for centuries before, were related to language use.

Structural Grammar

Structural grammar was an attempt by linguists to distinguish between spoken and written language and to analyze the patterns unique to English, taking into account language differences among geographical regions and social classes, dialects of different groups, and individual idiolects. These linguists provided much information about how language is really used, in nonstandard as well as standard usage, and about the many varieties of language use, such as literary, formal, colloquial, and slang.

Anthropological interest arose when the structuralists described Native American languages, for example, and throughout the 1950s, as linguists sought to accurately describe how English was actually spoken. Unlike earlier linguists, however, these structuralists didn't relate meaning to their descriptions, given the impreciseness of the terms, and used categories (or form classes), rather than the traditional parts of speech, to classify relationships among words.

Transformational Grammar

Transformational grammar is a more recent attempt to describe not only how language is used but also what psycholinguistic processes are at work when we use it. This type of grammar also makes the most complete attempt to establish the relationship between sound and meaning in language. Noam Chomsky (1957) and other linguists challenged the structuralist view, which left meaning out of descriptions of language, citing examples such as *John is eager to please* and *John is easy to please.* These two sentences can't be explained without reference to their meanings.

The transformationalists were most interested in the intuitive knowledge that allows speakers—even very young ones—to create, use, and understand sentences that they have never heard before but that are nonetheless grammatical. The transformationalists maintain that grammar should be more than just a description of speech. It should be a description of the process of how language is produced.

Chomsky (1957) made an important distinction between *competence* and *performance. Competence* is what we know; *performance* is what we say. In order to explain this distinction, Chomsky described two levels of language:

1. Language competence is characterized by *deep structure,* or meaning: understanding the underlying propositions and relationships among them.
2. Language performance is characterized by *surface structure,* or form: the string of sounds, letters, words, phrases, and clauses.

The transformationalists were not as interested in defining terms as they were in explaining the relationship between surface structure and deep structure. They were also concerned with understanding the innate "sentence sense" that tells us when a sentence in our native language is grammatical and when it is not—in other words, when it just sounds right.

Transformational grammar is not a set of prescriptive rules of how to speak and write correctly (traditional grammar) or simple descriptions of the language (structural grammar). Instead, transformational grammar attempts to describe the relationship of form to meaning and how any speaker is able to produce language. According to Chomsky (1957), a grammar should explain how a language user is able to make infinite use of finite means. The rules should explain why speakers can create and use sentences they have never heard before and why others, who may never have heard these sentences either, will understand them. Even very young children are able to do this because they have internalized these rules of language. And even though children learn much about language through imitation, the process they draw on to use language is innate.

Reasons for Teaching Traditional Grammar

Weaver (1979) has described the reasons people have given over the centuries as to the great importance of teaching traditional grammar. It is a way of learning how to do these things:

- use a language
- approach other topics that require a scientific, investigative approach
- think, since language is a reflection of thought
- learn a second language more easily
- speak and write in a socially acceptable and even prestigious way
- become a better speaker and writer

The fact is, however, that researchers have explored these six reasons for teaching traditional grammar over the past 90 years and consistently failed to find support for them (Cramer, 2001; Hillocks, 1987; Hillocks & Smith, 2003; Weaver, 1996, 1998a). Furthermore, researchers have shown that students don't even remember aspects of the formal study of grammar very long after they've been taught them. Although some exposure to the rules of grammar may benefit students, it is not a prerequisite for learning to write effectively (Smith & Elley, 1997).

These research findings certainly support current social interactionist beliefs that children learn by doing, not by learning rules about doing. That is, children learn to speak by speaking, to read by reading, and to write by writing in meaningful transactions with others using texts they experience or compose themselves.

Research has failed to support the argument that learning formal rules of grammar and practicing skills in isolation transfers to learning actual language use or to knowledge in other subjects. Actually, research supports an argument *against* the teaching of traditional grammar, since time spent learning rules takes away from time spent using language for meaningful purposes. Furthermore, in an examination of compositions written by 9-, 13-, and 17-year-olds as part of the National Assessment of Educational Progress (NAEP), Applebee, Langer, and Mullis (1987) found that "most students make only a few errors and the frequency of errors is less at the older ages" (p. 3).

So, if extensive, long-term research has failed to support the arguments for teaching traditional grammar and even suggested that doing so has a negative effect, why do we persist in teaching it? Teachers must be aware of and able to deal with many historical, philosophical, social, cultural, and even political reasons in facing the issues of whether and how to teach grammar and usage. Consider the following:

- *Teaching grammar has a long tradition:* Of all the subjects, grammar has the longest unbroken tradition as an essential subject in school. This tradition goes back to the time of the ancient Greeks and Romans, who taught rhetoric as a means to analyze and understand poetry and speak effectively in public, to the current generation of parents and teachers, who were taught grammar in schools and may have a deeply embedded belief that it was a necessary part of their education.

- *Teaching grammar is viewed as a basic skill:* Nationwide concern has arisen over teaching and learning what are called "basic skills," and in many people's minds, grammar is traditionally one of those skills. These people believe that grammar provides a foundation for learning correct language usage and writing, which are vital to success in school and the world. Again, this view is not supported by research.

- *Teaching grammar is a part of textbooks:* In a survey of representative elementary school English textbooks over a 60-year period, three major trends appeared: (1) less emphasis on writing, (2) more emphasis on oral language, and (3) no change for grammar and sentence construction exercises. The latter reflects "those nineteenth century die-hards, . . . plodding unerringly along, oblivious to changing times . . . and educational currents" (von Bracht Donsky, 1984, p. 797).

- *Teaching grammar lends itself to testing:* It's much easier to test and grade students' knowledge of rules of grammar using objective, multiple-choice tests than it is to test the quality of their actual writing or the sophistication level of their speech. Standardized tests of language are still used extensively as measures of students' success.

SNAPSHOT Arguing about Grammar in Writing Workshop

In a *rebus story*, a letter, number, or picture replaces a word using the same sound (e.g., a picture of an eye = the word *I*) or meaning (e.g., a picture of an eye = the word *eye*).

Faith and Barbara are in Phyllis Fuglaar's fifth-grade class. The girls are best friends and like to work together, but they often fight. I observed them one day during writing workshop. They were in a group with their friend Lillian, writing a rebus story they wanted to publish as a book and read aloud to the kindergarten classes. Barbara had misplaced several days' worth of ideas, notes, and drafts for the story. Faith was annoyed, Barbara was defensive, and Lillian was very quiet as the other two criticized each other's attempts to reconstruct the story and write a new draft.

Faith is annoyed because Barbara has misplaced the draft of a story they are writing with Lillian. What does this have to do with grammar?

As you read about the three friends arguing about grammar and writing, think about these key issues of language learning and literacy development:

1. the primary role of meaning in writing
2. children's intuitive knowledge of the rules underlying language production and of the formal rules of grammar
3. the teaching of grammar and writing

> *Barbara* (reading a draft): "In Lancaster, Wisconsin, a small 8-year-old boy found a lost cat." *Found* is past tense.
>
> *Faith:* I think it should be in the present tense because, see, he says, "How long will I have to stay?"
>
> *Barbara:* How about "While they're gone, Tommy started walking around"?
>
> *Faith* (sarcastically): Yeah. That's what we put on the draft *you* lost. (She makes a face at Lillian in front of Barbara.)
>
> *Barbara* (visibly upset): It doesn't matter, Faith. You don't have to look at Lillian that way.
>
> *Faith* (to Lillian): What do you like: past or present?
>
> *Lillian:* I like 'em both.
>
> *Barbara:* Oh, I hate it! Now she's gonna say majority rules 'cause she doesn't care. Faith, uh . . . how come you always use majority rules when you want to get your own way? OK, if we use present tense, how am I gonna say "You tripped over him"?
>
> *Faith:* We had that part, and you were supposed to have proofread it, but now we don't know because you can't find it!
>
> *Barbara:* There's no time to argue.

> *Faith*   (sarcastically):   I'm sorry. OK. You can just redo it all again.

The conversation continues a little later, when they're adding rebus pictures to the story:

> *Faith:*   Draw an eye for *I*.
>
> *Barbara:*   *I* is a pronoun. I don't think kindergartners would think about an eye.
>
> *Lillian*   (quietly):   Anybody have any marking pens?
>
> *Faith*   (loudly):   I don't like the eye!
>
> *Barbara*   (more loudly):   Then *you* change it!
>
> *Faith*   (loudest):   OK! I'LL CHANGE IT!

They continue to talk—and argue—about the types of rebus pictures that kindergartners will understand the meanings of:

> *Barbara*   (reading back what she has just written):   "The cats came back . . . came back . . . came back . . . came back?" Maybe we should say *returned.*
>
> *Faith:*   Come on, Barbara! They don't know what that means.
>
> *Barbara:*   OK. "Came back . . . accidentally."
>
> *Faith*   (sarcastically):   *Accidentally?* Are they going to know what that means? What's another word for *accidentally?*
>
> *Barbara*   (laughing):   *Not-on-purposely!* "The cats came back not-on-purposely."
>
> *Faith*   (sighing resignedly):   Barabara. Please. Tomorrow, will you just bring your work?

Grammar in Proper Perspective

In order to put grammar in proper perspective in the context of teaching language arts, think about the girls in the Snapshot arguing about grammar and writing. They made references to grammatical terms and to many of the meanings associated with the word *grammar*. When I asked them "What is *grammar?*" they gave the following answers:

> *Faith:*   Grammar is dots and things that make sense. So that it sounds right. Also so that people can understand what you wrote. I know spelling, periods, commas, colons, semicolons, pronunciation, exclamation points, question marks, quotations, parentheses, capital letters, paragraphs, complete sentences, adverbs, adjectives, subjects, noun predicate, verb, preposition, prepositional phrase, infinitive, gerund, present tense, past tense, participles, spaces, letters, punctuation, usage.
>
> *Barbara:*   Grammar is the way that you use words. Slang is bad grammar. I know the parts of speech, how to use words properly, when to use words.

How did the girls' answers compare to the one you wrote in the Reflective Response at the beginning of the chapter? Clearly, Barbara and Faith can talk about grammar. Both have had many years of instruction in the formal rules of grammar using textbooks and skill exercises, and they have been successful at completing such exercises on grammar tests. What's important to note, however, is that Barbara and Faith would be able to talk and write effectively *without* knowing how to talk about grammar or do exercises or pass tests on it. Like all children, they come to school with an underlying intuitive knowledge of the rules that govern language production. They are able to communicate meaning.

To illustrate, let's examine what Faith and Barbara were really doing during their writing workshop:

ELL

See the Snapshot in Chapter 9, The Writing Process, to see how Sheila Kline used writing workshop to teach writing and language conventions to ELL students.

- In arguing over whether to use the present or past tense, they were really talking about meaning: Will it make sense to the reader? Present and past were not the real issue. Rather, the issue was what they wanted their story to mean and how to communicate that to whomever reads it.
- When they were arguing about proofreading and paragraphs, the girls were checking for the organization of their ideas, the sequence of chunks of meaning—or paragraphs—and how they relate to one another.
- When they were arguing about using a drawn eye for an *I* and about nouns and pronouns, they were really talking about the ambiguities of word meanings in English, because many words that sound alike are written differently.
- When they were talking about word choice—for instance, whether to use *came back, return, accidentally,* or *not-on-purposely*—they were concerned about using the right words to say precisely what they meant and so others would understand them.

So even though Barbara and Faith used grammar terms in talking about their writing, the real focus of their session was on communicating meaning. Think again about what the girls were doing while talking and writing together in writing workshop:

- learning to write by writing
- using talking, writing, and reading together in a group formed for a social purpose as well as a language purpose
- writing for a purpose: to make a rebus book for kindergartners
- exercising choices in their writing: they picked a topic and decided what to write about it
- solving a problem: how to do a rebus story
- focusing on meaning: how to tell the story
- interacting: arguing and revising and editing their story
- being creative and using their own voices: composing the story and playing with language by making up words like *not-on-purposely*
- exercising control: revising and editing their story so it made sense
- being responsible: they started a new draft when the old one was lost

Above all, the girls were focusing on *meaning* and learning to use language by using it.

www

The University of Illinois at Urbana–Champaign Writers' Workshop provides ideas for teachers on writing techniques along with resources for editing and revising stages of writing. See the online grammar book and information on teaching parts of speech, phrases, clauses, and general usage at **www.english.uiuc.edu/cws/wworkshop/writer.html**.

Teaching and Assessing Grammar

Research on both grammar and writing suggests that the most effective way to teach and assess grammar and language conventions is in the context of meaningful reading and writing (Hillocks, 1987; Noguchi, 1991; Noyce & Christie, 1983; Weaver, 1996, 1998b). In the next few sections, we will look at various ways of incorporating grammar in reading and writing experiences. In addition, we will look at the use of minilessons in word and sentence study.

Grammar and Writing

Grammar and language conventions can be taught and assessed as part of the writing process. Doing so is most meaningful during the editing and revising stages of writing. Recall the Snapshot earlier in this chapter, in which Barbara, Faith, and Lillian were arguing about grammar during writing workshop. The next Snapshot returns to that classroom and finds the girls under happier circumstances, revising and editing the book they had argued about earlier and learning grammar and writing conventions, as well. This Snapshot also shows how nonlinear the writing process really is. Note that these students spend a lot of time experimenting with ideas, leaving things blank, moving things around, and making changes.

SNAPSHOT Revising and Editing in Writing Workshop

I visited Phyllis Fuglaar's class on another day and found Barbara, Faith, and Lillian in better spirits than during my first visit. And this time, I could trace the development of the whole story, which by now had gone through several weeks of revising and editing, session by session in writing workshop:

Session 1. Generating Topics. During the first of several sessions of writing a rebus story for kindergartners, Faith, Barbara, and Lillian talk, interact, doodle, draw, write, rewrite, and reject several topics, words, and names for characters. Think about the process they're going through. They cross out many rejected ideas, combine other ideas, create new choices, and finally settle on a main idea: Tommy finds stray cat; Tommy takes care of cat.

Session 2. Expanding and Elaborating on Ideas. During this session, the three girls revise as they write, making needed decisions yet leaving their options open.

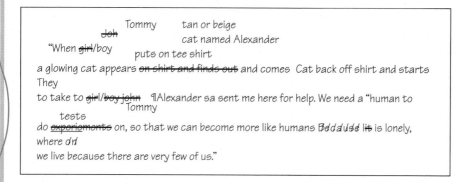

Session 3. Moving Sentences and Leaving Blanks for Future Ideas. Now, the girls begin to write a dialogue for their characters, rather than just a narrative of what's happening to them (as they did in Session 2). The girls are also moving whole sentences around within the text. When they're not sure where the story is going next, they leave a space and make a note to themselves about possible options for next time.

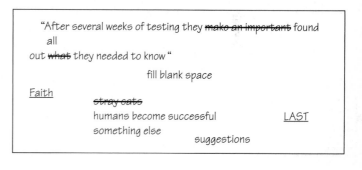

Sessions 4 and 5. More Generating, Expanding, Combining, Changing, Moving, and Leaving Blanks. Session 4 is a period of intense writing, during which the girls pause and break when their ideas seem to stop. And Session 5 is another idea-generating period, during which they come up with a recipe for a magical mixture of bat's blood, flies, fingernails, toes, eyeballs, and water.

Session 6. Reconstruction. This is the session described in the first Snapshot: Faith and Barbara argue about grammar during writing workshop, while they try to reconstruct their draft.

Sessions 7 through 9. Reworking a Complete Draft and Teacher Conference. Barbara has found the missing notes and draft! Each girl works at home on the final draft, and then they work together at school to refine their ideas. They make changes, fill in blanks, change some more, and finally produce a final draft. They also ask Phyllis for a teacher conference to resolve a few questions they have about grammar and usage.

Session 10. Peer-Editing Group, Self-Editing, and Final Proofreading. The girls ask some of their classmates to form a peer-editing group to check for spelling, grammar, and punctuation. They also make their own final review before publishing.

Sessions 11 and 12. Publishing the Story. During these two sessions, the girls plan their book, breaking it up into logical chunks for page breaks. Then they lay it out; copy it in large, neat print; and add illustrations and rebus symbols. The final step is binding the story into a book.

Session 13. Sharing Published Writing. The three young authors read their book to all the kindergarten classes in the school and present it to the kindergarten teachers to place in their class library.

This Snapshot illustrates why students need time and opportunities to write and talk when learning to use written language conventions. This time for talking and revising and editing writing isn't practice for learning how to master language usage; it's actually language in use.

Proofreading Marks for Editing

∧   Add, insert

⌐   Delete, take away

t̲   Capitalize

✗   Make lowercase

(e̯i)   Reverse order of letters

⊙   Add a period

⋏   Add a comma

∨′   Add an apostrophe

(sp)   Check spelling

How do teachers know what and when to teach grammar if students spend most of their time writing, as in writing workshops? It depends on the grade and developmental level of the students. The best guideline is to teach the skills students need when they need them but to always provide opportunities for students to apply skills in writing. Here are ways to do that:

- ***Minilessons:*** There are two ways to use minilessons in writing workshop:
  1. *Teach One Skill to the Whole Class:* Do this either with a skill that should be introduced to the whole class or one that almost everyone is struggling with. Discuss the skill with the class, take volunteers to talk about it in their writing, and do a minilesson for everyone.
  2. *Teach One Skill to a Small Group:* Do this when only some students need help, refinement, or special instruction in a skill. For example, if a group is having difficulty with tense (like Barbara, Faith, and Lillian were), that would be a good time to do a minilesson with them. Graves (1996) suggests these topics for minilessons: how to use verbs, nouns, and adjectives and how to combine sentences. Another good topic for a minilesson is how to use common proofreading marks for editing. Make a poster identifying the marks shown in the adjacent marginal note. After conducting the minilesson, hang the poster on the wall in the writing center, or make reduced copies of it so each student has his or her own.

- ***Teacher Conferences:*** The bulk of the teacher's time will focus on assessing individual children's needs and will take place in conferences. Students will master the conventions of writing when they have a real need to get them right—for example, if they're writing a newspaper article that will be published. Conventions gain importance as children develop audience awareness. Thus, the focus of teacher conferences should move from content to editing, as described by teacher Mary Ellen Giacobbe:

> Content Conference: *I assume the role of learner and by careful listening encourage the writer to teach me about the topic. Once it is established what the writer knows, I ask general questions to help the writer to discover he or she knows even more: "Gee, I didn't know about . . . Could you tell me more about . . . ?" After expanding the topic, I ask questions to help the writer focus.*

> Editing Conference: *When the content is as the writer intends it to be, the child is taught one skill in the context of his writing. . . . If the child uses that skill in the next piece of writing, I ask about the usage, and the child decides if it should be added to the list of skills he or she is responsible for during the editing stage of future writing.* (Cordeiro, Giacobbe & Cazden, 1983, p. 324)

- *Peer-Editing Groups and Self-Editing:* In peer-editing groups, children work together to edit each other's writing. Students should also edit their own work. Post a list of questions children can ask themselves as they revise and edit their work, whether self-editing or in peer-editing groups.

Observe peer-editing groups in action in the Snapshot in Chapter 10, Spelling.

Grammar and Reading

When the language of literature sings in children's ears, they will not only understand and enjoy a different kind of language, but they will use a different kind, too. Carol Chomsky (1972, 1980) found that the knowledge of complex language structures varies greatly among children from 6 to 10 years old and that this knowledge is not necessarily related to age. The children in her study who developed the greatest facility with language structures sooner were those who had had more exposure to the language of books—both those they had heard read aloud and those they had read themselves.

Teachers in student- and response-centered classrooms can support students' growing acquisition of syntactic structures and use of words by reading aloud. They should do so frequently and from a range of different types of books. Literature provides a model of language, which students will use in their own speaking and writing. For example, when writing about a cemetery at Halloween, Faith (described in the Snapshot) came up with the term *blood curdling*, which impressed her friend Barbara. Then Faith sheepishly confided that she had found the words in a less-than-literary but ever-popular *Nancy Drew* book.

Language Structure and Style in Literature. Children's books are full of wonderful words and language, which makes them excellent resources for teaching about the style and structure of written language:

- *Form:* Children's literature contains sleek but deeply embedded sentence structure forms. This is true even of books for the very young, like the classic *The Tale of Peter Rabbit* (Potter, 1902): "'Now, my dears,' said old Mrs. Rabbit one morning, 'you may go into the fields or down the lane, but don't go into Mr. McGregor's garden: your Father had an accident there; he was put in a pie by Mrs. McGregor.'"

GREAT BOOKS FOR CHILDREN

By Beatrix Potter

The Tale of Benjamin Bunny (1904a)

The Tale of Flopsy Bunnies (1909)

The Tale of Jemima Puddle-Duck (1908)

The Tale of Mr. Jeremy Fisher (1906)

The Tale of Tom Kitten (1904b)

GREAT BOOKS
FOR CHILDREN

By William Steig

Abel's Island (1976)
Dominic (1972)*
The Real Thief (1973)
Rotten Island (1984)
Sylvester and the Magic Pebble
   (1969)*
*Also available in Spanish

By Natalie Babbitt

Bub, or the Very Best Thing
   (1994)
Phoebe's Revolt (1968)
The Search for Delicious (1969)
Tuck Everlasting (1975)

By Paul Goble

Beyond the Ridge (1989)
Death of an Iron Horse (1987)
The Friendly Wolf (1974)
I Sing for the Animals (1991)
Love Flute (1992)

An example of kindergartners
dramatizing "The Three Billy
Goats Gruff" is included in
Chapter 4, Emergent Literacy
and Biliteracy. See also
Chapter 5, Listening and
Talking, for ideas about story
dramatization.

See Chapter 4, Emergent
Literacy, for more on repeated
patterns in children's books.

GREAT BOOKS
FOR CHILDREN

**Sentences Repeated in a
Repeated Plot**

A Dark, Dark Tale (Brown, 1981)
Do You Want to Be My Friend?
   (Carle, 1971)
Have You Seen My Duckling?
   (Tafuri, 1984)
I Went Walking (Williams, 1990)
The Little Red Hen (Galdone,
   1973)
Sheep in a Jeep (Shaw, 1986)

● *Description:* William Steig has a wonderful way with descriptive words in *Amos and Boris* (1971), a picture book about an improbable friendship between a mouse and a whale who learn to appreciate their differences. Amos, the mouse, is characterized by phrases like "quivering daintiness" and "gemlike radiance," and Boris, the whale, is described as having "abounding friendliness."

● *Imagery:* Natalie Babbitt is a master of the use of imagery in children's books. In her book *The Eyes of the Amaryllis* (1977), she describes the ocean at low tide, saying that "it sparkled in the early sunshine, flicking tiny, blinding flashes of light into the air." She characterizes a beautiful day as "a mermaid morning—a morning for sitting on the rocks and combing your long red hair."

● *Similes:* Children are aware of how authors use language. For example, in voting for *The Girl Who Loved Wild Horses* (Goble, 1978) to receive a Children's Choice award (given to children's favorite books each year), readers cited use of this simile to describe a herd of wild, running horses: "They swept like a brown flood across hills and through valleys."

Language Patterns in Literature. Many traditional rhymes, songs, and stories use sentence and story patterns that are repetitive and predictable. Exposing students to such patterns through listening and reading and then responding is a powerful means of promoting facility with different grammatical forms and uses of language.

● *Sentences Repeated in a Repeated Plot:* A familiar example of sentences repeated in a repeated plot is the Scandinavian folktale "The Three Billy Goats Gruff." There are three billy goats in three different sizes, and each repeats the same dialogue in three encounters with a troll when he asks, "Who's that tripping over my bridge?" Marcia Brown's (1957) version of this tale is an excellent story for reading aloud and inviting children to join in on the repeated sentences. This is also a great story for dramatizing by young children. See the adjacent marginal note for a list of children's books that have sentences repeated in a repeated plot.

● *Sentences Repeated in a Cumulative Plot:* Other books use cumulative plots, in which characters, objects, and actions are introduced and then added to previous ones as the story unfolds. A classic example is the nursery rhyme "The House That Jack Built." Here's an adaptation written by first-graders:

This Is the School We Learn In

This is the school we learn in.
These are the children that go to the school we learn in.
This is the book that is read by the children that go to the school
   we learn in.

See the marginal note on the next page for a list of books with sentences repeated in a cumulative plot.

- **Storyframes:** Even very young children understand and use conventional story structure, which includes elements like formal openings and closings and the past-tense voice. Children can brainstorm examples of these conventions and write them on separate file cards, which can be classified and kept in separate envelopes (e.g., for openings, characters, closings, etc.). Then, by choosing one card from each envelope and putting them all together, students create correctly constructed but nonsensical stories. The cards provide a *storyframe:* something for the students to build on. Here are a few examples:

The Three Bears (Galdone, 1972)
The Three Billy Goats Gruff
   (Brown, 1957)
The Three Little Pigs (Galdone, 1970)
Whose Mouse Are You? (Kraus, 1970)

Sentences Repeated in a Cumulative Plot

The Cake That Mack Ate (Robart, 1986)
Drummer Hoff (Emberley, 1967)
The Elephant and the Bad Baby (Vipoint, 1969)
The Fat Cat (Kent, 1971)
Four Fur Feet (Brown, 1989)
The Gingerbread Boy (Galdone, 1975)
The Little Old Lady Who Was Not Afraid of Anything (Williams, 1986)
The Napping House (Wood, 1984)
Rum Pum Pum (Duff, 1978)
This Is the Bear (Hayes, 1986)

Openings	Characters
Once upon a time . . .	A poor woodcutter
Long, long ago . . .	A wicked queen
In a galaxy far, far away . . .	A young starfighter pilot

Problems	Closings
Didn't have enough food for his children	. . . and they lived happily ever after.
Hated the beautiful princess	. . . and was never seen again.
Set out to discover his destiny	. . . and saved the universe.

Word and Sentence Study

Minilessons in word and sentence study are another means to teach grammar. Much of word and sentence study in the classroom is like the wordplay children do naturally as they learn to use language. For example, in the Snapshot in which the girls argued about grammar, Barbara was playing (and really annoying Faith) when she made up the word *not-on-purposely* as a synonym for *accidentally.* Children will do this on their own, but teachers can build on this natural tendency by introducing minilessons on word and sentence study.

Classifying Words. This is a variation of semantic mapping in which children look for relationships among words and do visual maps of them. When they classify words, students also look for differences. Words for classification can come up in discussions, be related to learning in content areas, or be introduced by the teacher. Here are several approaches:

See Chapter 3, First- and Second-Language Development, for more ideas on semantic mapping and language play.

1. *Contrasting Pairs of Words:* Here are simple dual classifications:

Feelings	*Happy/sad; good/bad; nice/mean*
Descriptions	*Ugly/beautiful; big/little; smooth/rough*
Old and new words	"A word I used to think meant something else . . . but now I know it means . . ."
Personal choices	Favorite words/disliked words

Children often have personal choices of words they love or hate. My son Wyatt has kept a running list of words he hates, including *nougat, snorkel,* and *yawn* (which he says "may be the most mindless word in the world"). Ask children to make their own personal choice lists.

2. *Groups of Words:* Here are simple ways to classify related words:

- *The Four Seasons:* Brainstorm ideas for a chart like the one shown in Figure 11.1.
- *The Five Senses:* Instead of a chart, do a minilesson on a triante pattern for writing. The following example was written by third-graders about spring, after doing a chart about each of the seasons:

Triante Pattern	Senses	Poem
Line 1: One word (Title)		Spring
Line 2: Two words	Smell	Fresh Sweet
Line 3: Three words	Touch	Warm Soft Wet
Line 4: Four words	Sight	Green Colorful Sunny Lively
Line 5: Five words	Sound	Singing Laughing Whispering Gurgling Buzz

3. *Comparisons:* Children can classify words by making comparisons—for example, about what they're able to do in a "You Are Too . . ." pattern. Here are examples from second-graders:

You are too <u>large</u> to:	You are too <u>small</u> to:	You are <u>just right</u> to:
fit into a mouse house	fly to the moon	climb upstairs alone
swim in a fish bowl	lift a whale	swing up high in a
live in a bird cage	eat a watermelon whole	swing

Parts of Speech. It's a simple step from classifying words, in general, to classifying them by their functions and using their traditional names as parts of

Figure 11.1   Classifying Words: The Four Seasons

Name	Winter	Spring	Summer	Fall (or Autumn)
Temperature	Cold	Warm	Hot	Cool
Weather	Snow	Wind	Sunny	Frost
	Ice	Rain	Humid	Chilly
Holidays	Hanukkah	St. Patrick's Day	Memorial Day	Halloween
	Christmas	Passover	Flag Day	Day of the Dead
	Kwaanza	Easter	Fourth of July	Rosh Hashanah
	Chinese New Year	Cambodian New Year	Labor Day	Yom Kippur
	Martin L. King, Jr., Day	Cesar Chavez Day		Thanksgiving
	Presidents' Day	(in California)		
Play	Sledding	Kites	Swimming	Leaves
	Snowmen	Puddles	Beach	School
Sports	Hockey	Basketball	Baseball	Football
Colors	White	Green	Blue	Brown

speech. A few simple writing patterns use and expand on the classifications of words using traditional terms for the parts of speech and the order of sentences:

1. *Nouns and Adjectives:* For the "What Next?" pattern, choose a noun and find three adjectives that start with the same letter:

Noun	Adjectives
cave	cold, clammy, creepy
dungeon	dark, damp, dreary
swamp	sticky, slimy, slippery

2. *Verbs:* For the "My Hands, My Feet" pattern, choose the name of something that can do an action (e.g., hands or feet), and write verbs for what it can do. First-graders wrote these:

My Hands	My Feet
squeeze a mop	walk on floors
mess with slop	go through doors
do the dishes	step on bugs
scoop up fishes	play on rugs

3. *Nouns, Adjectives, and Verbs:*

- For the "Concentric Circle" pattern, pick a noun and use three adjectives and five verbs to make a spiral. Fourth-graders created this one:

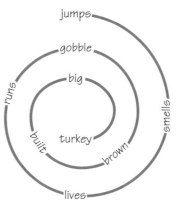

- For the "Diamante" pattern, create a verse in the shape of a diamond, which shifts topic or shows a change in the fourth line. Here's an example written by a fifth-grader, showing his bike before and after he had a wreck on it:

Line 1: Noun	My Bike
Line 2: Adjective, adjective	Black, rubber
Line 3: Verb, verb, verb	Turning, squeaking, fixing
Line 4: Noun, noun/*noun, noun	Wheel, handlebars, chain, pedals
Line 5: Verb, verb, verb	Crashing, bounding, smashing
Line 6: Adjective, adjective	Broken, bent
Line 7: Noun	Bike

* Marks shift in topic or show of change

Table 11.2 Children's Books about Parts of Speech

Nouns

Merry-Go-Round: A Book about Nouns (Heller, 1990)
Your Foot's on My Feet! and Other Tricky Nouns
   (Terban, 1986)

Collective Nouns

A Cache of Jewels and Other Collective Nouns
   (Heller, 1987)
Herds of Words (MacCarthy, 1991)
A Kettle of Hawks and Other Wildlife Groups
   (Arnosky, 1990)

Verbs

Dig, Drill, Dump, Fill (Hoban, 1975)
I Think I Thought and Other Tricky Verbs
   (Terban, 1984)
Kites Sail High: A Book about Verbs (Heller, 1988)

Kitten Can . . . (McMillan, 1984)
*Seeing, Saying, Doing, Playing: A Big Book of Action
   Words* (Gomi, 1994)

Adjectives

Many Luscious Lollipops: A Book about Adjectives
   (Heller, 1989)
Super, Super, Superwords (McMillan, 1989)

Adverbs

A Snake Is Totally Tail (Barrett, 1983)
Up, Up and Away: A Book about Adverbs (Heller, 1991)

Prepositions

Over, Under, and Through and Other Spatial Concepts
   (Hoban, 1973)
Rosie's Walk (Hutchins, 1968)

See Table 11.2 for a list of children's books about language, which focus on parts of speech as well as other language conventions.

Constructing Sentences. When children know the names of the parts of speech and what they do, teachers should use patterns that begin with a word or words and build sentences:

1. *Noun, Verb, Adverbial Phrase:* For the "Do What, When, and Where" pattern, write a simple sentence using a noun, verb, and adverbial phrase. These rhyming ones were written by third-graders:

Noun	Verb	Adverbial Phrase
Snakes	crawl	down the hall.
Kittens	sleep	while I eat.
Witches	zoom	on their brooms.
Bats	soar	outside my door.

2. *Adjective, Noun, Verb, Adverb:* Read *Aster Aardvark's Alphabet Adventures* (Kellogg, 1987) and show students this syntactical pattern:

Letter	Adjective	Noun	Verb	Adverb
A is for the	angry	alligator	acting	ambidextrously.

3. *Adjective, Noun, Verb, Adverb:* To form a sentence pyramid, begin with a noun and add a word for each line, working down from the top with the base as the whole sentence:

Noun	Rock
Adjective/Noun	Big rock
Adjective/Noun/Verb	Big rock sits
Adjective/Noun/Verb/Adverb	Big rock sits quietly

4. *Name Sentences:* Choose a name or a special word, and use its letters to start the first words in a sequence of sentences. For variation, use a theme: an advertisement, a slogan, a newspaper headline, or a song, book, or movie title. Here's an example about the movie *Babe,* which is about a pig:

B̲eing a pig wasn't what he wanted to be.
A̲ll the other animals thought he should act like a pig.
B̲ut he proved that he could herd sheep, like the dogs.
E̲ven the boss thought he was a great herding pig!

5. *ABC Sentences:* Each word in a sequence must begin with the next letter in the alphabet. Second-graders wrote this one:

Doughnuts eaten frantically give heartburn.

6. *Alphabet-All Sentences:* Challenge children to write ABC sentences using all the letters in the alphabet. Here's an example written by two fifth-graders:

A bear catches dogs, eats frogs, goads horses into jumping kangaroos, likes making new orangutans pretty; "quite right" said the unicorn verifying with x-rays, yams, zebras.

7. *Alliterative Sentences:* Read an alliterative alphabet book like *Animalia* (Base, 1987), which contains examples written by fourth-graders. Make a class book, providing a page for each letter along with an alliterative sentence (see Figure 11.2).

Figure 11.2 Fourth-Grader's Illustration of an Alliterative Sentence

8. *Newspaper Cut-Up Sentences:* Have children find interesting words in the newspaper, cut them out, and arrange them in sentences. Variations on this idea include writing ransom notes, nonsense recipes, and hidden messages.

9. *Mad Libs:* Mad Libs are an adaptation of a commercial word game, consisting of a series of partially completed sentences in a story. Only one student sees the story, and he or she asks another student for a type of word to fill in a blank: a noun, verb, adjective, and so on. Since the student giving the word doesn't know what the story is about, the result is a nonsense adaptation of the original.

Students can write their own stories, make the deletions by inserting blanks with the names of the parts of speech written under them, and play Mad Libs with others. Here is an example written by a fifth-grader (bracketed inserts show where the blanks go):

Babies

Most [plural noun] think babies are cute. They are [adjective] if they don't belong to [pronoun]. If you live with one, you find they [verb] and [verb adverb] and when you [verb] them they smell [adjective]. I am just glad I don't have a [noun], because I think they are [adjective].

Sentence Combining. Sentence combining is a technique used to increase students' syntactic maturity by having them combine *kernel sentences*—the simplest statements of ideas—to form more complex sentences (O'Hare, 1973; Straw, 1994). Doing so provides a way for students to develop increased control over language conventions and complexity in writing. Three important concepts underlie the technique of sentence combining:

1. *The Model of Transformational Grammar:* Recall from earlier in this chapter that Noam Chomsky (1957) proposed a model of grammar with an underlying deep structure, or meaning (language competence), and surface structure, or form (language performance). Understanding the form of language requires awareness of the meaning of language. As Chomsky explains, "To understand a sentence, it is necessary to reconstruct its representation on each level, including the transformational level where the kernel sentences underlying a given sentence can be thought of, in a sense, as the 'elementary content elements' out of which this sentence is constructed" (pp. 107–108).

2. *A Definition of Syntactic Maturity:* Kellogg Hunt (1965) created a definition of *syntactic maturity* and a measure called a *T-unit,* which is a "minimal terminable unit," or a main clause plus all modifiers. Using the T-unit, Hunt researched the development of syntactic maturity, showing that as students mature, their written language becomes more complex.

3. *A Study of Sentence-Combining Exercises:* John Mellon (1969) did a study using sentence-combining exercises, based on the transformational model of grammar, which showed students' gains in writing maturity and quality.

Materials for sentence-combining practice are available commercially, but children can also work on strategies of sentence combining, changing, and expanding using their own words, phrases, sentences, and ideas (Strong, 1986). This is what Faith, Barbara, and Lillian were doing in the Snapshot, when they worked together to revise their writing—combining, adding to, expanding, moving parts, and changing their sentences. The word and sentence games described earlier are also excellent ways of teaching students how to combine sentences.

Teachers can also use minilessons and writing conferences to make students aware of the three basic types of sentence transformations: changing, combining, and reducing. The best way to encourage children to develop facility with language structures in real writing contexts is to use their own ideas and writing. In the list that follows, examples from children's writing are used to illustrate each type of sentence transformation. And those examples come from a prewriting idea list brainstormed by Barbara, Faith, and Lillian (the students in the Snapshot) in preparing to write their story for a kindergarten rebus book. Here's their list:

Boy finds lost cat.
Boy is small.
He's 8 years old.
The cat is a stray.
Cat came from street.
It's in Lancaster, Wisconsin.
The boy's name is Tommy.
Tommy takes care of cat.
Tommy finds out cat is magical.

1. *Changing:* This type of transformation involves turning one type of sentence into another, such as a question or negation:

Basic Sentence: A boy finds a stray cat.

Changed into a:
   Question: Does a boy find a stray cat?
   Negation: A boy doesn't find a stray cat.

2. *Combining:* This is putting together several sentences to form a compound sentence:

Basic Sentences: A boy finds a stray cat.
                     The boy is small.
                     He's 8 years old.
                     The cat came from the street.
                     The cat is magical.

Combined into a Compound Sentence:
                     A small, 8-year-old boy finds a stray cat from the street, and the cat is magical.

3. *Reducing:* This transformation involves changing some sentences into smaller parts and inserting them into or combining them with other sentences:

Basic Sentences: A small, 8-year-old boy finds a stray cat from the street, and the cat is magical. The boy's name is Tommy, and it's in Lancaster, Wisconsin. Tommy takes care of the cat.

Combined with Other Sentences: Tommy, a small, 8-year-old boy in Lancaster, Wisconsin, finds a stray, magical cat from the street. He takes care of it.

TEACHING IDEA

Content-Centered Sentence Combining

Of course, the best way to practice sentence combining is with students' own writing, but a useful alternative is to integrate sentence combining with content-based text. This is also an effective way to adapt both grammar and content for students with special needs. Borrowing an idea from special education teacher Dave Nielsen, William Strong (1986) recommends beginning with fact sheets related to content. Here's how it works:

1. *Write a Fact Sheet:* A *fact sheet* is a list of facts that can be quickly written and used to introduce content vocabulary and concepts, to reinforce comprehension, and to improve writing. The facts are first written out in predicate phrases. Each phrase can then be turned into a sentence by adding a topic word, or noun. For example:

WWW

Whales: A Thematic Web Unit is an excellent example of integrated teaching across the curriculum, including writing. Go to **www.curry.edschool. Virginia.EDU/go/Whales**.

Fact Sheet on Whales

Whales . . .
are among the most intelligent animals
range from 4 feet to 100 feet in length
may become extinct
live in all the world's oceans
are social animals
are mammals

Fact sheets can be adapted to individual students' abilities and special needs. Several fact sheets can be written on the same topic for the same class and can be used as assessment tools to monitor students' progress in mastering the syntactic manipulations required of good writing.

2. *Combine Phrases into Sentences:* This can be done as a class or group activity, with the teacher modeling sentence combining, or students can work individually or in groups. Students must read carefully and discriminate between essential and less important facts:

> Whales are among the most intelligent animals.
>
> Ranging from 4 feet to 100 feet in length, they live in all the world's oceans.
>
> Whales are mammals.
>
> This social animal may become extinct.

3. *Arrange Sentences into a Paragraph:* It may be necessary to make small wording changes to combine the sentences such that they make sense in a paragraph. To do so, students need to understand sentence types, sequencing, and paragraph structure. Here's an example:

> Whales are animals. Ranging from 4 feet to 100 feet in length, they live in all the world's oceans. These mammals are among the most intelligent animals. This social animal may become extinct.

Arranging sentences also provides students with valuable practice in report writing: paraphrasing notes into sentences and paragraphs.

This Teaching Idea can be used with any content topic and adapted for different grade levels, student abilities, English language learners (ELL), and students with disabilities. And it's fun! I used fact sheets extensively when I began teaching in very overcrowded schools in California. My first fourth-grade class had 42 children, including 26 boys and 4 nonreaders—numbers I will never forget. One set of content texts or even library books couldn't meet the needs of all these students. I wrote fact sheets in social studies and science and adapted them to the many levels of students in my class. Students can create their own fact sheets, too.

SCAFFOLDING

See the box on page 375 for strategies to adapt sentence-combining activities for struggling writers and students with disabilities in the middle and upper elementary grades and in middle school.

Teaching Grammar to Students with Language and Dialect Differences

Students who are English language learners should be taught grammar just as they are taught other language skills: through real and meaningful experiences with using language. The *monitor model* supports the idea that a second language is best learned using a communicative-based, natural approach. Based on that model, Stephen Krashen (1981; Krashen & Terrell, 1987) argues that learning the rules of grammar is only effective as a monitor of language use—and even then, the speaker or writer has to know the rule, be thinking about it, and have time to apply it. This happens infrequently in speaking and may not be effective in

ELL

See Chapter 3, First- and Second-Language Development, for lessons for ELL students.

writing, either. What's most important is providing *comprehensible input* (i.e., language that's just a little bit beyond the child's current level of language acquisition) in a low-anxiety environment (what Krashen calls a *low affective filter*).

See Chapter 8, Multicultural Education and Children's Books, for more on teaching speakers of nonmainstream English.

Sensitivity to language differences is particularly important when working with students who use dialects. Variations in use within the same language are found among different language communities in which unique speech standards have developed. For example, Labov (1972) describes what he calls *Black English Vernacular* (*BEV*) and argues that it's not a mass of errors in speaking Standard English. Instead, it is a "distinct subsystem within the larger grammar of English" (pp. 63–64), with it's own regular conventions and rules for language production. For example, "I been knowin' your name" means "I have known for a long time, and still know, your name" (pp. 53–55).

Heath (1983) has shown that a teacher's lack of knowledge of the rules of BEV can cause misunderstanding when interpreting what a student speaking in this dialect is saying:

> A teacher asked one day: "Where is Susan? Isn't she here today?" Lem answered: "She ain't ride de bus." The teacher responded: "She doesn't ride the bus, Lem." Lem answered: "She do be ridin' de bus." The teacher frowned at Lem and turned away. Within the system of Black English Lem used, ain't was used as equivalent to didn't, the negative of the past tense of the auxiliary do; thus his answer had to be interpreted as "She didn't ride the bus." The teacher heard the ain't as equivalent to doesn't and corrected Lem accordingly; he rejected this shift of meaning and asserted through his use of do be ridin' that Susan did indeed regularly ride the bus. (pp. 277–278)

Labov's (1972) work has shown that BEV has an internal logic and its own language conventions. Nonetheless, Heath's (1983) work has shown that conflicting conventions in the language used within the same community can lead to misunderstanding for both teachers and students and thus failure to learn. Sensitivity to differences in native languages and dialects are essential to teaching language arts.

See Chapter 3, First- and Second-Language Development, to review the theories on teaching and learning a second language.

Teachers must consider these issues when they make choices between focusing on teaching isolated skills versus authentic writing experiences. Research by Sperling (1996) looked at students who were learning English as a second language or spoke a dialect or who were in schools characterized by cultural and linguistic diversity as well as low scores on standardized tests. It was found that these students were more likely to receive direct instruction in isolated skills of grammar, punctuation, and spelling rather than be taught by methods used with native-English-speaking students or those who were in schools characterized by high scores on standardized tests.

Current theory and practice for teaching English language learners and developing skills for all students advocate teaching language skills in authentic and meaningful contexts, such as reading and writing workshops and other activities that involve listening, speaking, reading, and writing for real purposes. See the following box for guidelines on teaching grammar to ELL students as well as students with disabilities and struggling writers.

Struggling Writers, Students with Disabilities, and English Language Learners in Learning Grammar

For struggling writers and students with disabilities in the middle and upper elementary grades, teachers should use these sentence-combining strategies:

- Work through each exercise orally in heterogeneous student groups before having students write it down.
- Use contextual clues and oral prompts to help students understand how language fits together.
- Have students work in pairs, but have only one student write down their responses.
- Be sure to focus activities on each student's assessed needs.

For students who are learning English as a second language or who use a dialect, teachers should keep these points in mind in teaching grammar:

- Learning will be more successful if students' anxiety about correctness is kept to a minimum.
- Qualities and variations of students' native languages might lead to misunderstandings or unconventional uses of English.
- Teaching grammar in context through meaningful writing experiences, rather than in isolation through drills and exercises, is particularly important for ELL students.

Punctuation

Development of Punctuation Skills

Children develop control over punctuation as they develop overall writing ability (Cramer, 2001; Hodges, 2003). Thus, knowledge about punctuation develops gradually. From the middle elementary grades on, the majority of U.S. students make few punctuation errors. Results from *The Nation's Report Card* (Applebee et al., 1987) showed that even at age 9, 25 percent of students made no errors and 50 percent averaged 1.5 or fewer errors per 100 words in writing.

Another study by Calkins (1980) compared the way two third-grade teachers taught punctuation: One taught punctuation conventions as isolated skills, using daily drills and worksheets; children corrected their incorrect sentences but did little writing per se. The other teacher taught punctuation as part of the writing process; children wrote for one hour a day, three times a week, and were encouraged to use their own ideas and experiment with punctuation. At the end of the year, the students with the teacher who emphasized daily drills could use an average of 3.85 kinds of punctuation correctly. By contrast, the children with the teacher who emphasized writing could use an average of 8.66 kinds of punctuation correctly. In short, the children in the second group learned more about punctuation because they needed it to write.

Cordeiro et al. (1983) took an even closer look at how children develop the use of punctuation by studying a first-grade class in which students wrote extensively. For a year, these researchers analyzed children's writing and the nature of writing conferences between the teacher and children. They found that the punctuation marks the teacher explained most often were periods, possessive apostrophes, and quotation marks. Although direct instruction helped some children learn to use possessive apostrophes and quotation marks, many learned them with only half the amount of instruction. Periods were taught and retaught more than any other kind of punctuation but were still used only about half the time they were required.

All the children in the class progressed at about the same rate, but those who didn't receive direct instruction in the correct use of periods actually did better using them correctly. They relied on other sources of information about punctuation, like reading and their own underlying knowledge of how written language works. Even though students didn't always use punctuation by adult standards of correctness, they were developing an intuitive and untaught understanding of phrases and clauses.

Teaching and Assessing Punctuation

These research findings show the value of teaching punctuation as part of writing. When students need to work on specific skills, they can participate in minilessons as well as self-editing and peer-editing groups (Hall & Robinson, 1996).

Minilessons

Minilessons provide direct instruction in punctuation during writing workshop. Table 11.3 shows the appropriate grade levels at which to introduce and reinforce the teaching and practice of types of punctuation in the context of writing (Fearn & Farnan, 1998).

Children should be encouraged to edit their own writing for punctuation and other language conventions.

Table 11.3 Topics for Minilessons on Punctuation by Grade Level

Topics	Grade Levels							
Beginning in Kindergarten	K	1	2	3	4	5	6	7
Capital Letters								
For names	■	■	■					
To begin sentences	■	■	■					
For days and months	■	■	■	■				
For place names	■	■	■	■				
End Punctuation								
Periods	■	■	■					
Question marks	■	■	■					
Exclamation marks	■	■	■					
Commas								
In dates	■	■	■					
In abbreviations	■	■	■	■				

Topics	Grade Levels							
Beginning in First Grade		1	2	3	4	5	6	7
Capital letters in people's titles		■	■	■	■			
Periods in abbreviations		■	■	■	■			
Apostrophes in contractions		■	■	■	■			

Topics	Grade Levels							
Beginning in Second Grade			2	3	4	5	6	7
Commas in compound sentences			■	■	■			
Apostrophes in possessives			■	■	■			
Quotation marks and other punctuation in dialogue			■	■	■	■		

Topics	Grade Levels							
Beginning in Third Grade				3	4	5	6	7
Commas								
In series of adjectives and complex sentences				■	■	■		
With quotation marks and underlining in titles				■	■	■		
After introductory words and phrases				■	■	■	■	
Capital Letters								
For titles, trade names, and names of commercial products, companies, institutions, associations, and events				■	■	■	■	■
For nationalities, ethnicities, and languages				■	■	■	■	■

Topics	Grade Levels							
Beginning in Fourth Grade					4	5	6	7
Punctuation to set off parenthetical expressions (i.e., dashes, parentheses, commas)					■	■	■	■
Colons and semicolons in sentences					■	■	■	■

Source: Adapted from Fearn & Farnan, 1998.

Self-Editing and Peer-Editing Groups

Teachers should encourage children to edit their own writing, both as they go along and before publishing their pieces. A chart of commonly used punctuation marks should be displayed in the writing center so students can check their work against it (see Figure 11.3). The teacher should also post a list of questions children can ask themselves as they conduct self-editing or peer-editing groups:

> Did I start each sentence with a capital?
> Did I capitalize the names of people and places?
> Did I punctuate the end of each sentence?
> Did I use punctuation in other appropriate places?
> Did I use quotation marks when someone was talking?
> Did I spell correctly or check spelling I wasn't sure about?
> Did I indent paragraphs?
> Did I use my best handwriting?

In addition, teachers should encourage children to discover and use punctuation as they need it for writing (Graves, 1995, 1996). Punctuation conventions should be explained based on their functions and meanings, rather than as rote-memory rules (e.g., "a sentence is a complete thought").

Teachers should not rely on language arts texts, commercial programs, or worksheets or workbooks. Nor should they become discouraged with themselves or their students if even after direct instruction in minilessons and using correct forms in their writing, some children make the same errors again. While they gain mastery over one aspect of writing, they may temporarily lose it over another. Progress is real but not always even.

Figure 11.3

Commonly Used Punctuation Marks

Period .
1. A period ends a statement.
2. A period is used for an abbreviation and initials.

Question Mark ?
1. A question mark ends a question.

Exclamation Point !
1. An exclamation point shows strong feeling.

Comma ,
1. A comma separates words in a series.
2. A comma comes between a date and year and between a city and state.
3. A comma comes after the greeting and closing in a friendly letter.

Apostrophe '
1. An apostrophe shows where letters have been left out in contractions.
2. An apostrophe shows ownership.

Quotation Marks " "
1. Quotation marks enclose direct quotations.

Handwriting

Despite the wide use of computers for writing by adults, most children begin to write by hand and continue to do so through most of elementary school. Thus, the development of legible handwriting is important to their schooling. Keep in mind, however, that handwriting is for writing and writing is for *communicating meaning* (Graves, 1994).

Development of Handwriting Skills

Graves (1983) has described five general phases in children's handwriting development, all of which can occur and overlap during the first grade:

1. *Get-It-Down Phase:* Children want to get something down on paper, so they make letterlike forms, letters, and words, often in random order. They have a general idea of writing from left to right.

2. *First Aesthetics:* Children are aware of how words are placed on the page and the amount of space needed for their stories. The like to have clean, fresh pages to write on and try hard to get rid of mistakes, which can lead to problems with erasing (e.g., smudging, tearing the page, frustration).

3. *Growing Age of Convention:* Children may be less interested with getting their message written down and more concerned with how it looks to others; they take more care with word spacing, margins, and writing exactly on the lines. This concern for appearance also affects spelling and mechanics, as they become more aware of their audience.

4. *Breaking Conventions:* As children gain more control over handwriting, spelling, and punctuation, they continue to deal with the content of their writing. Teachers can help them learn that it's all right to change, move, or mess up parts of their writing in the drafting stages.

5. *Later Aesthetics:* When children discover they can scratch out rather than erase errors and move and add parts to their writing, they're on their way to understanding that their writing is a work-in-progress. The published piece is where they'll use their best handwriting or word processing, correct spelling and punctuation, clean or special paper, special writing tools (e.g., colored pencils), and illustrations and binding.

During all these phases and throughout their further development in handwriting, children are trying to control the motion of making letters and words on a page and to arrange the page space. Teachers may be tempted to compare children's handwriting to the models in commercial handwriting series, as it seems logical to do so. But unlike spelling, there isn't an agreed on form for handwriting. Legibility should be the standard each child's writing development is viewed against. Students' handwriting may even become less conformist as they get older, which seems to be a natural outgrowth of the preadolescent drive for personal expression. In the fourth and fifth grades, students may adopt a backhand style or a large scrawl with flourishes—perhaps dotting the letter *i* with little circles or even hearts, flowers, or smiley faces. The issue isn't whether it's correct for an 11-year-old to add these personal touches; rather, the issue is whether his or her writing is legible and allows him or her to communicate effectively with others.

Teaching and Assessing Handwriting

Handwriting is typically taught beginning with manuscript (i.e., printing) in the first grade and shifting to cursive (i.e., connected letters) between the second and fourth grades. Handwriting charts and books for copying are frequently used, as are minilessons, in which the teacher models letter formations for the whole class.

Modeling Handwriting

Teachers model handwriting when they write on the board, make posters, take dictation on language experience charts, write to students in dialogue journals, and make editorial comments on writing. Handwriting can also be modeled with wall charts of manuscript for first- and second-graders and cursive for third-graders and up. These charts often come in long horizontal strips, which can be mounted above a chalkboard. Students can also look at handwriting books for models of handwriting.

Materials for Handwriting

Teachers should provide many materials for handwriting in the classroom, along with materials for drawing and painting: pens, pencils (including colored pencils), crayons, paints, and brushes and a variety of types of paper (plain, colored, lined, journal). Teachers should also provide other surfaces to write on: wipe-off slates, paper plates, folders, and the like. As mentioned above, handwriting books may also be used.

There are two commonly used programs, which use materials that present different types of handwriting:

1. *Parker Zaner-Bloser* is the traditional ball-and-stick style.
2. *D'Nealian* is an italic style, which attempts to make the transition from manuscript to cursive easier by teaching students to form slightly slanting manuscript letters.

Minilessons

Handwriting is a tool for writing, so children should spend most of their time learning handwriting by using it in writing. Enough direct instruction should be given to enable children to write freely, as they develop fluency and legibility. Topics for minilessons for the whole class or groups in writing workshops include the following:

1. *Demonstrate Writing Position:* Writers of all ages should have comfortable spaces, with tables and chairs at correct levels and enough room to move their arms freely without bumping their elbows. The teacher should demonstrate a

good position for the relationship of paper to writer and how to hold a pencil. Guide students to take comfortable and relaxed positions with pencil and paper.

2. *Introduce Manuscript Letter Forms:* Figure 11.4 (p. 382) shows a good order and techniques for doing this.

3. *Demonstrate Transition from Manuscript to Cursive:* Show the same words written in both styles; then show how cursive letters are connected and the change in slant.

4. *Introduce Cursive Writing:* Figure 11.4 also shows a good order and techniques for introducing cursive writing.

5. *Name Game:* Encourage children to experiment writing their names as many different ways as possible, making letters that are large and small, fat and thin, overlapping, colored, and so on.

6. *Creating Codes:* Try the following activities:

- Write a story in which a letter, number, or picture replaces a word.
- Create a secret code and write a message in it. Some simple formulas include substituting numbers for letters of the alphabet in order, reversing the alphabet, using the next letter of the alphabet, and creating new symbols for letters.
- Create culture codes by finding symbols from the past or other cultures (such as hieroglyphics), and write messages using them.

In teaching handwriting, teachers should observe children's handwriting development as they write. They should also keep handwriting in the proper context of writing for real purposes. Legibility is not the only goal of handwriting. Children need many opportunities to explore space: art, constructions, drama, dance, as well as writing; their use of writing materials should not be restricted (e.g., letting them use only wide-ruled paper or primary pencils without erasers). Instead, teachers should stock a variety of materials in the writing center and provide plenty of time for children to write on topics of their own choices.

Teachers should be cautious about using a set of commercial materials with a rigid sequence of isolated drills. Handwriting should not be taught as though it were an end in itself. A strong connection is made by learning handwriting in the context of real writing.

GREAT BOOKS FOR CHILDREN

Codes

Codes for Kids (Albert, 1976)
Doubletalk: Codes, Signs, and Symbols (Hovanec, 1993)
The Kids Code and Cipher Book (Garden, 1981)
Loads of Codes and Secret Ciphers (Janeczko, 1984)
Super Secret Code Book (Pickering, 1995)

Hieroglyphics

The Beginning of Writing (Warburton, 1990)
Egyptian Hieroglyphics for Everyone (Scott & Scott, 1968)
Hieroglyphs: The Writing of Ancient Egypt (Katan, 1980)
The Riddle of the Rosetta Stone: Key to Ancient Egypt (Giblin, 1990)

Assessing Grammar, Punctuation, and Handwriting

So, how well do most U.S. students actually control the conventions of written English? Results of analyses of the writing of 9-, 13-, and 17-year-old students in *The Nation's Report Card* were encouraging (Applebee et al., 1987). They showed that "even though American schoolchildren have difficulty organizing and expressing their ideas in a thoughtful manner, they have reasonable control over

Figure 11.4 Teaching Sequence for Handwriting

Manuscript

Simple Letters

1. Straight line | and line with another stroke   t i j k u

2. Circle O and circle with another stroke   a d b p g q

Letters with Similar Patterns

1. Open circle C and open circle with another stroke   e f

2. Lines and humps   n m h r

3. Angles   x y v w z

4. A unique letter   s

Uppercase

1. Like lowercase   C O S T K P U V X Z

2. In between   F J M N W

3. Unlike lowercase   A B D E G H I L R Q Y

Transition from Manuscript to Cursive

Show same words in both styles, how they are connected, and the change
in slant.

Cursive Writing

1. The numbers and arrows on commercial materials show the order and
direction of the formation of each letter.

2. Letters with an undercurve   ∕- b e f g h i k l r s t u w

3. Overcurve ⌒ or hump letters   m n v x y z

4. Downward curve   ⟨- a c d g o

5. Lower loop   j p g

6. Uppercase letters with similarities

7. Note that only six letters are really formed differently in cursive: *b, e, f, r, s, z.*

the conventions of grammar, punctuation, and spelling" (p. 6). Here's a summary of the report's other findings:

1. Students learn to control the conventions of written English.
2. Older students are more proficient than younger ones at both sentence and word levels; likewise, older students use more complex sentences and fewer fragments and run-ons.
3. Spelling improves significantly as children grow older.
4. Students make few errors in word choice and capitalization.
5. Students make very few punctuation errors.
6. There is no consistent profile of a poor writer.

Given these findings, the report made these recommendations:

Students are learning the conventions that they need for writing. . . . However, . . . learning writing conventions is an individual process, with particular skills being learned and practiced by particular children at particular times. . . . Hence, asking an entire class to focus on a particular convention of written English seems unnecessary, even inappropriate. Instead, instruction may be more effective if it treats students as individual language learners, with the teacher relying on each student's own written papers for information about what that student knows and is in the midst of learning. (p. 45)

The revising and editing stages of writing provide excellent opportunities to assess students' skills in grammar, punctuation, handwriting, and other language conventions. Children should learn how to proofread and assess their own work, whether through self-editing, in peer-editing groups, or in conferences with the teacher. Assessment Toolbox 11.1 (p. 384) can assist them in self-assessment, as it provides a list of things to check during the revising and editing stages. This form can be adapted for students of different grades and skill levels as well as for English language learners.

Answers to Questions about Grammar, Punctuation, and Handwriting

● *What is* grammar, *and why should we teach it?*

There are three types of grammar: (a) *traditional,* a prescriptive grammar dating back to medieval times; (b) *structural,* an attempt to describe differences among languages; and (c) *transformational,* an attempt to explain the relationship between language and meaning. Current social constructivist and child development theory and research suggest that children learn language and its conventions by using them. Communicating meaning is the purpose of language use.

Historically, teaching traditional grammar has been considered essential because doing so supposedly helps students learn how to use language, conduct an investigative approach, learn a second language, and speak and write in a more socially prestigious way. Even though research over the years has failed to support these reasons for teaching traditional grammar, many educators persist in doing so, for several reasons: Grammar has a long tradition, is viewed as a basic skill, is integral to many textbooks, and is easy to test.

ASSESSMENT TOOLBOX

11.1 Student's Revising and Editing Checklist

This checklist guides students in revising and editing their writing, asking them specific questions about grammar, punctuation, and handwriting.

My Checklist for Revising and Editing

Name _____ Date _____

Reader's Name _____

Title of Writing _____

Revise   **Comments**

Read the piece to yourself.

  1. Does it make sense? _____

  2. Is it well organized? _____

  3. Does it have a main idea? _____

  4. Should any words or parts be added or subtracted? _____

  5. Could it be improved in any way? _____

Make revisions.

Edit   **Comments**

Reread the revised writing.

  1. Does each paragraph have one main idea? _____

  2. Are all of the sentences in each paragraph related to the main idea? _____

  3. Are all of the paragraphs indented? _____

  4. Do the sentences have variety? _____

  5. Does each sentence begin with a capital letter? _____

  6. Does each sentence end with a period, a question mark, or an exclamation mark? _____

  7. Are all of the names and proper nouns capitalized? _____

  8. Are quotation marks used to show when someone is talking? _____

  9. Are all of the words spelled correctly? _____

  10. Is the handwriting neat? _____

Source: Adapted from Leslie & Jett-Simpson, 1997; O'Malley & Valdez Pierce, 1996.

- *How should we teach and assess grammar, punctuation, and handwriting?*

Grammar, punctuation, and handwriting are best taught and assessed through talking and writing in meaningful contexts, in which language is used for real purposes. Teachers can help students develop awareness of the form and structure of language in several ways. Students can play with words and sentences, through classification, forming patterns, and combining sentences. Children's literature is an excellent model for language use; students should be encouraged to play with the forms and structures of stories. It is during the revising and editing stages of writing that students apply their underlying knowledge of grammar, punctuation, and handwriting. Children learn to use language by using it. Teachers must keep in mind, however, that the purpose of all these experiences should be to communicate meaning.

Looking Further

1. Create a pattern based on the functions of words, or find a pattern in literature that does the same thing. Try it out with children.

2. Start a file of children's books that you feel are outstanding examples of how words can be used in literature. Create your own classification for the books, including categories like books with interesting sentence structure, description, figurative language, and imagery.

3. Observe children revising their writing while working in peer-editing groups. Note how they use their underlying knowledge of grammar.

4. Collect at least three samples of handwriting from children in the same class. Analyze them according to Graves's phases of handwriting development, described in this chapter (pp. 379–380). If possible, do this for children in two different grade levels more than one year apart.

5. Ask several teachers how they teach punctuation. Comment on their answers in light of the research findings discussed in this chapter (pp. 375–376).

6. Using the approach outlined in the Teaching Idea on pages 372–373, create a fact sheet for sentence combining and use it with a group of children.

Children's Books and Software

Albert, B. (1976). *Codes for kids*. New York: Whitman.

Arnosky, J. (1990). *A kettle of hawks and other wildlife groups*. New York: Lothrop, Lee & Shepard.

Babbitt, N. (1968). *Phoebe's revolt*. New York: Farrar, Straus, & Giroux.

Babbitt, N. (1969). *The search for delicious*. New York: Farrar, Straus, & Giroux.

Babbitt, N. (1975). *Tuck everlasting*. New York: Farrar, Straus, & Giroux.

Babbitt, N. (1977). *The eyes of the amaryllis*. New York: Farrar, Straus & Giroux.

Babbitt, N. (1994). *Bub, or the very best thing*. New York: HarperCollins.

Barrett, J. (1983). *A snake is totally tail*. New York: Atheneum.

Base, G. (1987). *Animalia*. New York: Harry N. Abrams.

Brown, M. (1957). *The three billy goats gruff*. New York: Harcourt Brace Jovanovich.

Brown, M. (1989). *Four fur feet*. New York: Watermark.

Brown, R. (1981). *A dark, dark tale*. New York: Dial.

Carle, E. (1971). *Do you want to be my friend?* New York: Harper & Row.

Correct grammar [Computer software]. Available from Writing Tools Group, WordStar International.

Duff, M. (1978). *Rum pum pum*. New York: Macmillan.

Emberley, B. (1967). *Drummer Hoff*. New York: Prentice-Hall.

Galdone, P. (1970). *The three little pigs*. New York: Clarion.

Galdone, P. (1972). *The three bears*. New York: Clarion.

Galdone, P. (1973). *The little red hen*. New York: Clarion.

Galdone, P. (1975). *The gingerbread boy*. New York: Seabury.

Garden, N. (1981). *The kids code and cipher book*. New York: Holt, Rinehart & Winston.

Giblin, J. C. (1990). *The riddle of the Rosetta Stone: Key to Ancient Egypt*. New York: Crowell.

Goble, P. (1974). *The friendly wolf*. New York: Bradbury.

Goble, P. (1978). *The girl who loved wild horses*. New York: Bradbury.

Goble, P. (1987). *Death of an iron horse*. New York: Bradbury.

Goble, P. (1989). *Beyond the ridge*. New York: Bradbury.

Goble, P. (1991). *I sing for the animals*. New York: Bradbury.

Goble, P. (1992). *Love flute*. New York: Bradbury.

Gomi, T. (1994). *Seeing, saying, doing, playing: A big book of action words*. San Francisco: Chronicle Books.

Grammatic [Computer software]. Available from Reference Software, Computer Centerline.

Hayes, S. (1986). *This is the bear*. New York: Lippincott.

Heller, R. (1987). *A cache of jewels and other collective nouns*. New York: Grosset & Dunlap.

Heller, R. (1988). *Kites sail high: A book about verbs*. New York: Scholastic.

Heller, R. (1989). *Many luscious lollipops: A book about adjectives*. New York: Grosset & Dunlap.

Heller, R. (1990). *Merry-go-round: A book about nouns*. New York: Grosset & Dunlap.

Heller, R. (1991). *Up, up and away: A book about adverbs*. New York: Grosset & Dunlap.

Hoban, T. (1973). *Over, under, and through and other spatial concepts*. New York: Macmillan.

Hoban, T. (1975). *Dig, drill, dump, fill*. New York: Greenwillow.

Hovanec, H. (1993). *Doubletalk: Codes, signs, and symbols*. New York: Bantam.

Hutchins, P. (1968). *Rosie's walk*. New York: Macmillan.

Janeczko, P. (1984). *Loads of codes and secret ciphers*. New York: Macmillan.

Joyce, W. (1986). *George shrinks*. New York: Harper & Row.

Katan, N. J. (1980). *Hieroglyphs: The writing of Ancient Egypt*. New York: Atheneum.

Kellogg, S. (1987). *Aster Aardvarks alphabet adventures*. New York: Morrow.

Kent, J. (1971). *The fat cat*. New York: Parent's.

Kraus, R. (1970). *Whose mouse are you?* New York: Macmillan.

Lionni, L. (1967). *Frederick*. New York: Pantheon.

MacCarthy, P. (1991). *Herds of words*. New York: Dial.

McMillan, B. (1984). *Kitten can . . .* New York: Lothrop, Lee & Shepard.

McMillan, B. (1989). *Super, super, superwords*. New York: Lothrop, Lee & Shepard.

Pickering, F. (1995). *Super secret code book*. New York: Sterling.

Potter, B. (1902). *The tale of Peter Rabbit*. London, England: Warne.

Potter, B. (1904a). *The tale of Benjamin Bunny*. London, England: Warne.

Potter, B. (1904b). *The tale of Tom Kitten*. London, England: Warne.

Potter, B. (1906). *The tale of Mr. Jeremy Fisher*. London, England: Warne.

Potter, B. (1908). *The tale of Jemima Puddle-Duck*. London, England: Warne.

Potter, B. (1909). *The tale of Flopsy Bunnies*. London, England: Warne.

Robart, R. (1986). *The cake that Mack ate*. New York: Little, Brown.

Scott, H. J., & Scott, L. (1968). *Egyptian hieroglyphics for everyone*. New York: Funk & Wagnalls.

Shaw, N. (1986). *Sheep in a jeep*. New York: Houghton Mifflin.

Steig, W. (1969). *Sylvester and the magic pebble*. New York: Farrar, Straus, & Giroux.

Steig, W. (1971). *Amos and Boris*. New York: Farrar, Straus, & Giroux.

Steig, W. (1972). *Dominic*. New York: Farrar, Straus, & Giroux.

Steig, W. (1973). *The real thief*. New York: Farrar, Straus, & Giroux.

Steig, W. (1976). *Abel's island*. New York: Farrar, Straus, & Giroux.

Steig, W. (1984). *Rotten island*. New York: Godine.

Tafuri, N. (1984). *Have you seen my duckling?* New York: Greenwillow.

Terban, M. (1984). *I think I thought and other tricky verbs*. New York: Clarion.

Terban, M. (1986). *Your foot's on my feet! and other tricky nouns*. New York: Clarion Books.

Vipoint, E. (1969). *The elephant and the bad baby*. New York: Coward McCann.

Warburton, L. (1990). *The beginning of writing*. New York: Lucent.

Williams, L. (1986). *The little old lady who was not afraid of anything*. New York: Harper.

Williams, S. (1990). *I went walking*. New York: Harcourt Brace Jovanovich.

Wood, A. (1984). *The napping house*. New York: Harcourt Brace Jovanovich.

chapter 12

Viewing and Visually Representing

Q uestions about Viewing and
  Visually Representing

- *What are the roles of viewing and visually representing in
  the integrated teaching of language arts?*
- *How should we teach and assess viewing and visually representing?*

REFLECTIVE RESPONSE

Make a list of elementary classroom activities that you think represent
viewing and visually representing. Also jot down any memories you have
of these types of activities from your own elementary school years. What
did you do? How did you feel about these activities—then and now?
How do you think you will use viewing and visually representing in your
classroom when you teach?

The New Language Arts

Viewing and *visually representing* have been officially added to the traditional four
language arts—listening, speaking, reading, and writing—in the IRA/NCTE *Standards for the English Language Arts* (1996). However, teachers have always included these areas in their teaching of language arts because they are such natural parts of human experience and communication. We are surrounded by visual as well as auditory media. In fact, the United States is the most mass-mediated country in the world. Moreover, children learn through viewing and visually representing from a very early age, and doing so is an essential aspect of the natural approach to learning English as a second language.

I was recently reminded of how powerful viewing and visually representing can be in the classroom when I received this e-mail:

See Chapter 14, Language across the Curriculum, for a description of this student's class and performing the *Ramayana* (India's epic poem about Prince Rama) and making *chapattis*, a type of Indian bread.

I hardly know where to begin. I was a third-grade student of yours in Madison, Wisconsin. Most of my elementary education is now a complete blur, but I remember that year with astonishing clarity. We performed *Julius Caesar* and the *Ramayana*, we learned to make chapattis and movies, and to see the difference between Braque and Picasso. You introduced us to the idea that a book could be read for more than plot and character, that a picture could depict more than meets the eye, if we only took the time to work at understanding. As you can imagine, these are ideas I use every day of my working life at the museum, and when I have time, in my life as a reader.

I have my own children now, my son is in his last year of preschool and my daughter is in third grade. I know from my experience as a parent that the right teacher can make or break a year, but also make a difference for a lifetime, and I just wanted to thank you. I'm sure you've taught hundreds of kids over the course of your career, so of course I don't expect you to remember me. I was in your summer Shakespeare program for a couple of years, and have a vague memory of watering your plants once when you were on vacation. I hope things have gone well for you.

All the best,

Sarah Kianovsky

Assistant Curator of Paintings,
Sculpture and Decorative Arts,
Harvard University Art Museums

Well, you can imagine how pleased I was when I received this e-mail. And of course I remember Sarah! She played one of the conspirators in our class's drama production of Shakespeare's *Julius Caesar*. She was a ferocious Roman conspirator who stabbed Caesar to death. I remember trying to figure out what to do with her long, brown, very curly hair. She did not look the part she was going to play. She finally put her hair in a bun and added a dark hood to her white toga so she would look more sinister. How could I forget that?

Notice that Sarah's memories are of experiences that fall within the realm of *viewing and visually representing*, such as drama performance, media production, the visual arts, and critical viewing. These experiences were integrated with the traditional language arts in our third-grade classroom. And according to Sarah, that's what made them meaningful, effective, and therefore memorable.

Throughout this text, you have seen how viewing and visually representing are essential parts of teaching language arts across the curriculum. In this chapter, we will focus on the following viewing and visually representing experiences, which are appropriate for integrating the teaching of language arts: critical viewing and media literacy; film, video, and television; the visual arts, media production, and drama performance. But first, let's take a look into a third-grade class of

English language learners (ELL) in the following Snapshot to see how teacher Audrey Eldridge taught a unit on the solar system by integrating it through the language arts of viewing and visually representing.

SNAPSHOT Introducing the Solar System to Third-Grade English Language Learners

One of my former students, Audrey Eldridge, teaches native-Spanish-speaking and Khmer-speaking students at International School in Long Beach, California. Here's a day-by-day description of how she introduced a science unit on the solar system, used viewing and visually representing experiences to teach it, and integrated content and language teaching using English language development (ELD) and specially designed academic instruction in English (SDAIE) techniques.

Day 1. Introduce Content Material through Nonfiction Literature

Audrey introduced the topic *space* with the book *The Magic School Bus, Lost in the Solar System* (Cole, 1990). The *Magic School Bus* series is extremely popular and a great way to introduce content material through literature. These books use a visual media-influenced fantasy format to present accurate factual information. A miniaturized school bus goes on impossible fieldtrips led by the teacher, Ms. Frizzle. Students' comments are shown in speech bubbles, like the comics. Their reports on what's happening are shown in inserts, like a split screen on film, and the dialogue takes a humorous tone, like a TV situation comedy.

Audrey read the book aloud, and students discussed it. She said her students were mesmerized by the story and very excited about learning about the solar system.

Days 2 and 3. Using Informational Books and Photographs

Audrey located a lot of informational books about the solar system and put them in a plastic tub in the class library. She read some aloud, and students read others on their own and in pairs and groups. Audrey also displayed a set of black-and-white photographs of the solar system. Students found more photos, along with other information, on the Internet and a CD–ROM encyclopedia.

Days 4 and 5. Writing Frame for an Informational Report

Audrey provided a writing frame for an informational report on the solar system (see Figure 12.1, p. 390). Students read and did research to find answers to these six questions:

1. What is your planet's name?
2. How many kilometers is your planet from the sun?
3. How many planets is it from Earth?

GREAT BOOKS FOR CHILDREN

The Magic School Bus Series (by J. Cole)

The Magic School Bus, at the Waterworks (1986)
The Magic School Bus, Inside the Earth (1987)
The Magic School Bus, Inside the Human Body (1989)
The Magic School Bus, Lost in the Solar System (1990)
The Magic School Bus, on the Ocean Floor (1992)
The Magic School Bus, in the Time of the Dinosaurs (1994)

The Magic School Bus Media

On television, see the animated series on PBS, featuring Lily Tomlin as the voice of Ms. Frizzle, and the *Reading Rainbow* series. The books are also available on CD–ROM.

GREAT BOOKS FOR CHILDREN

Informational Books on the Solar System

Discovering Mars: The Amazing Story of the Red Planet (Berger, 1992)
Journey to the Planets (Lauber, 1993)
Meteors and Meteorites: Voyagers from Space (Lauber, 1989)
Sun Up, Sun Down (Gibbons, 1983)

4. What does it look like?
5. What is special about it?
6. What is the most interesting thing about it?

After they had finished doing reading and research, students proceeded to write their reports. Some worked on computer and included hypertext graphics in their reports; others wrote out their reports by hand and pasted in photographs they had downloaded from the Internet. When the reports were finished, students were even more motivated to learn about the solar system. Audrey noticed this and planned more activities.

Days 6 through 10. Multimedia Projects

With Audrey's help, the class brainstormed ideas for the following multimedia group projects, which they researched and carried out:

- *Planet model:* papier-mâché model and written report
- *Planet posters:* picture, written report, and title
- *Plan for a rocketship:* labeled diagram and materials needed to build it (see Figure 12.2)

See Chapter 14, Language across the Curriculum, for more on research and report writing.

WWW

The NASA home page at **www.nasa.gov** offers information and resources for teachers. A special section NASA for Kids: Mars Thermal Emission Spectrometer Project has a K–12 educational program and a virtual tour of the solar system: **www.esther.la.asu.edu/asu_tes**.

Figure 12.1   Writing Frame for an Informational Report

Reporters 1. _____   Date _____

2. _____

3. _____

4. _____

We are writing about _____. It is a _____.

It is _____ miles/kilometers from the sun. It is _____ miles/kilometers from Earth.

_____ looks like _____

_____.

_____ is special because _____

_____.

The most interesting thing we learned about _____ is _____

_____

_____.

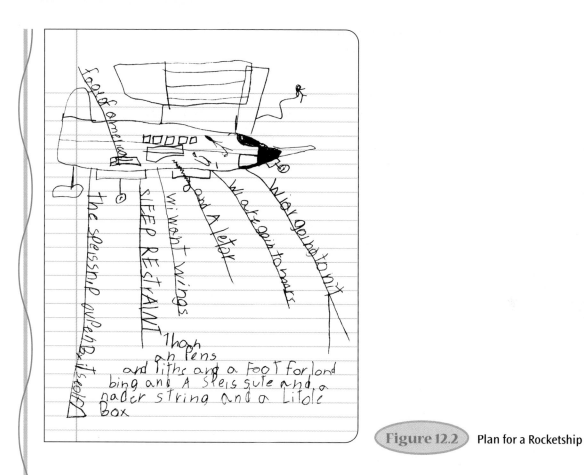

The drawing contains the following handwritten labels:

food or america
the sleessnP orPenBuit siolf
SLEEP RESTRANT
wi want wings
and A letor
what goin to mars
whay going to nix

Thoph
an Pens
and lithe and a foot for lond
bing and A sleis sule and a
nader string and a Litole
Box

Figure 12.2 Plan for a Rocketship

- *Rocketship model:* construction and written report on how it works
- *Model of solar system:* drawn in colored chalk on black butcher paper, with a written description
- *Space suit:* construction and written description
- *Astronaut training video:* video and written script

Days 11 through 15. Science Fiction Scriptwriting on the Computer and Making a "Big Book"

Mikey started this next wave of activities when he researched and made a space suit for his project. He was the only one who chose this, and when he did, the other students were very excited. Others wanted to make space suits, so they made costumes for outer space characters. Now that the students no longer felt confined to the facts, fiction took over. A group began calling themselves "Super Mikey and the Evil Aliens."

This round of science fiction projects included writing science fiction stories, doing a puppet show (called "The Cool Aliens"), writing and illustrating a "big book" (*Miss Eldridge on Mars*), and making a film (*Super Mikey and the Evil Aliens*). Here are samples from the "big book" and the film script:

<u>Miss Eldridge on Mars</u>
An Original Science Fiction Book
Written and Illustrated by The Kids in Room 20

Once upon a time Miss Eldridge went to Mars. Seda and Dina were with her in her spaceship. The spaceship turned around and around, and they landed on Mars. All of a sudden an alien saw their spaceship. Then the aliens jumped on their spaceship.

The girls screamed because they were scared of the alien. The alien had four hands, and three legs, and two eyes at the ends of his long antennas and he was green. The girls asked the alien what his name was. He answered, "My name is Tukataka." He wanted to be their friend. Then they all flew back to Earth together.

Video Script for <u>Super Mikey and the Evil Aliens</u>

Super Mikey: We are going to fight the evil aliens.

Hamza: Were are going to go west and we're going to Jupiter and then to Mars, too.

Narrator: Then they got to Jupiter. When they got to Jupiter they saw the aliens diging for tresure.

Super Mikey: Oh no. There stiling the gold.

Hamza: We need that gold for the good king.

Narrator: Super Hamza and Super Mikey wen to the good alien king.

King Alien: You need to get that gold.

Queen Alien: We need the gold to pay the rent on the castle.

Narrator: Super Mikey and Super Hamza went to get the treasure on Mars. Thay went to the evil aliens castle. When Super Mikey and Super Hamza went in the castle the aliens saw Super Mikey and Super Hamza fly to get the gold so that the king and the queen could pay the rent.

Alien: Don't move one step.

Narrator: So they did not move a step.

Hamza: Let's fly up.

Narrator: They fly up. They brak the window and went throu the window. They went to the good king and they gave the treasure to the good king and queen. Then Super Mikey and Super Hamza went to thir onw world.

See page 394, a Ripple Effect of the solar system and science fiction, which shows what happened in Audrey's class, along with other possibilities for teaching language arts with this focal topic. And here's how Audrey described the children's experience making this videotaped science fiction film, which was their first. What she learned about using multimedia and viewing and visually representing with her third-graders is shown in the marginal notes:

It hardly took any instruction. They wanted to make up a story with the characters of Super Mikey and Evil Aliens and film it on videotape. They wrote the story and then the script. They were ready to film in about a week. I brought the camera, showed them how to start and pan, right to left. They figured the rest of it out as they needed it, made more props and costumes as they needed them. I didn't really know how to do it, so we figured it out together.

Students are self-directed.

We experimented with things like close-ups. I realized they needed to experience it, try things out, and change things—to just do it. Once the initial excitement was over, they got very professional. I saw lots of good things happening. They practiced hard making their dialogue clear with lots of expression. With video, they get immediate feedback on how they sound or facial expressions. We shot it and played it and made changes immediately. Many times the second take was 100 percent better.

Students learn by doing.

They were excited, and I really got work out of them. When I said "If you want to do a video, write the script," they were really writing!

Students work hard.

Another plus is that these children are entering a world full of technology, and they will be lost without experience. Many of my students come from very low-income families. They don't have computers and video cameras at home. It's not fair to limit their experiences. They will lose out.

Students need experiences with multimedia and viewing and visually representing in school.

The beauty of multimedia and viewing and visually representing is that it is authentic, genuine, and self-created. That's when I learn about my students, their talents. I plan to do more media projects because they're active and students figure things out on their own.

Students are in control.

I have expectations. I ask them what they can do; then I expect them to do it. They will always surprise you. I have also learned to let myself off the hook, that I'm not pounding information into them. Just like the students, teachers have to discover their own way rather than just being this rehearsed person. I have learned to give my students freedom of thought and to let them talk. I encourage them to be risk takers and try to be one myself.

Teachers have expectations, take risks.

Viewing

IRA/
NCTE

Viewing—one of the six language arts in the national *Standards for the English Language Arts* (1996)—is defined as "attending to communication conveyed by *visually representing.* Students with visual impairments might 'view' tactile drawings, charts, or diagrams" (p. 76). The third-grade English language learning students

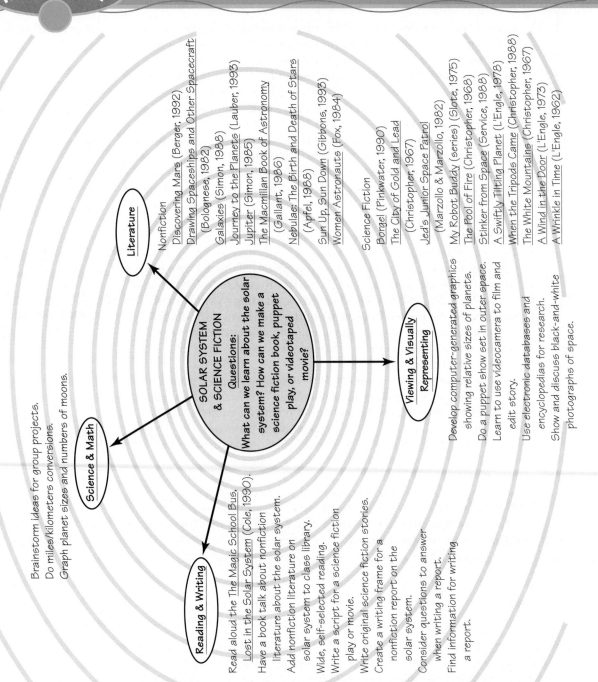

Literature

Nonfiction
Discovering Mars (Berger, 1992)
Drawing Spaceships and Other Spacecraft
   (Bolognese, 1982)
Galaxies (Simon, 1988)
Journey to the Planets (Lauber, 1993)
Jupiter (Simon, 1985)
The Macmillan Book of Astronomy
   (Gallant, 1986)
Nebulae: The Birth and Death of Stars
   (Apfel, 1988)
Sun Up, Sun Down (Gibbons, 1993)
Women Astronauts (Fox, 1984)

Science Fiction
Borgel (Pinkwater, 1990)
The City of Gold and Lead
   (Christopher, 1967)
Jed's Junior Space Patrol
   (Marzollo & Marzollo, 1982)
My Robot Buddy (series) (Slote, 1975)
The Pool of Fire (Christopher, 1968)
Stinker from Space (Service, 1988)
A Swiftly Tilting Planet (L'Engle, 1978)
When the Tripods Came (Christopher, 1988)
The White Mountains (Christopher, 1967)
A Wind in the Door (L'Engle, 1973)
A Wrinkle in Time (L'Engle, 1962)

Science & Math

Brainstorm ideas for group projects.
Do miles/kilometers conversions.
Graph planet sizes and numbers of moons.

SOLAR SYSTEM & SCIENCE FICTION
Questions:
What can we learn about the solar system? How can we make a science fiction book, puppet play, or videotaped movie?

Viewing & Visually Representing

Develop computer-generated graphics showing relative sizes of planets.
Do a puppet show set in outer space.
Learn to use videocamera to film and edit story.
Use electronic databases and encyclopedias for research.
Show and discuss black-and-white photographs of space.

Reading & Writing

Read aloud the The Magic School Bus, Lost in the Solar System (Cole, 1990).
Have a book talk about nonfiction literature about the solar system.
Add nonfiction literature on solar system to class library.
Wide, self-selected reading.
Write a script for a science fiction play or movie.
Write original science fiction stories.
Create a writing frame for a nonfiction report on the solar system.
Consider questions to answer when writing a report.
Find information for writing a report.

in Audrey Eldridge's class attended to communication through viewing illustrated picture books like *The Magic School Bus, Lost in the Solar System* (Cole, 1990), illustrated informational books on the solar system, and photographs and other images on the Internet and a CD–ROM encyclopedia.

What is the relationship between viewing media and learning? Cognitive psychologist Gabriel Salomon (1997) has conducted research that suggests that the role viewing media plays in learning is determined by (1) the amount of mental effort invested in learning from media and (2) the attention paid to how the unique symbol system of each medium structures messages. Visual media are eclectic symbol systems that merge characterisitcs of photography, music, cultural codes, and speech. The meaning of a visual media message is not intrinsic in the message itself, however. It is determined by the interaction between the viewer's prior knowledge and the message. Viewing is active communication that requires the support of other students and teachers in order for learning to occur. For example, when *Sesame Street* was first introduced in Israel, Salomon's research (1983) showed that mothers who watched with their children caused the children to invest more mental effort in the viewing experience and to learn more as a result.

This finding that active engagement in viewing experiences increases learning with media echoes constructivist (Piaget, 1969), social interactionist (Vygotsky, 1986), and transactional (Rosenblatt, 1978) perspectives on learning and understanding texts. Media and learning theory and research (Cox, 2003; Frost & Hobbs, 1998; Luke, 1999; Smagorinsky, 1995) make clear the need for the active teaching of critical viewing in schools.

Critical Viewing and Media Literacy

Critical viewing is the rational analysis of visual texts such as television, film, and photography. In order to become critical viewers, students should learn to ask and answer questions about the images used in constructing these visual texts (Fuller, 1994):

- What are the purposes of the images?
- What is real or not real in these images?
- What are the sources of the images?
- What techniques are used to create the images in each visual medium?
- What other kinds of texts and genres do the images draw on?

When reflecting on these questions, students should also be aware of the characteristics specific to each different medium. All media differ according both to content and form (Cox, 1994). Content may also vary across media. For instance, a news event may be seen live on television, heard later on the radio, read about the next day in the newspaper, seen the next week in a photo-illustrated magazine, read within a few months as a fictionalized paperback, and finally viewed the next year as a television docudrama or feature film based on the original event. The forms of media differ, as well. A media such as television may use several symbol systems, including live-action images or animation, speech, sound effects, music, and print. In sum, critical viewing requires understanding that each type of visual image uses a particular code to convey content from the viewpoint of the individuals who created that image.

Commercial advertising language also cuts across all mass media: television, radio, newspapers, and magazines. Children need to understand how ads make the following types of claims and should be interpreted critically:

- *Testimonial:* having a famous person or organization endorse a product
- *Transfer:* applying the qualities of one thing to another
- *Plain folks:* talking down to people to appear to be one of them
- *Bandwagon:* saying that everybody's doing it
- *Snob appeal:* suggesting that better people are buying it
- *Facts/figures:* suggesting that there are statistics to prove it
- *Hidden fears:* playing on people's insecurities
- *Repetition:* saying a message so often that it won't be forgotten
- *Magic:* suggesting that a special ingredient makes a product effective
- *Weasel words:* misleading customers to think a product is good

Active engagement with various forms of media in meaningful classroom experiences is necessary for students to learn how content is conveyed through media codes. And that understanding is essential for students to acquire critical-viewing skills as well as media literacy.

TEACHING IDEA

Examining Advertising Language

Here's a simple strategy to teach critical viewing using advertising language across a range of mass media:

1. Make an overhead transparency or poster to introduce these common types of advertising claims.
2. Have children work in groups to find examples of the claims in at least three types of mass media: magazines, newspapers, television, and radio. (Students can tape record or write down examples from the last two.)
3. Have each group make a poster to display and interpret ads to share with the class.
4. Have children create their own advertisements using the types of claims discussed. They can write and illustrate, use a graphics program on the computer, or videotape or tape record their ads and then share them with the class.

Teaching Media Literacy

I have defined *media literacy* in the *Encyclopedia of English Studies and Language Arts* (Cox, 1994b) as follows:

> *Media literacy refers to composing, comprehending, interpreting, analyzing, and appreciating the language and texts of the multiple symbol systems of both print and nonprint media. The use of media presupposes an expanded definition of "text" in the English language arts classroom. Print media texts include books, magazines, and newspapers. Nonprint media include photography, recordings, radio, film, television, videotape, videogames, computers, the performing arts, and virtual reality. On the full range of media channels, all these types of texts constantly interact. They are all texts to be experienced, appreciated, and analyzed and created by students.* (p. 13)

The term *media literacy* is part of an expanded definition of *literacy* in general. The *Standards for the English Language Arts* (1996) have acknowledged this expanded definition of literacy and therefore newly defined what students should learn in the English language arts as "reading, writing, listening, speaking, viewing, and visually representing" (p. 1). Thus, viewing and visually representing have been added to the more traditional language arts. Other terms have also been redefined in the standards: *Text* includes spoken language, graphics, and technological communications; *language* encompasses visual communication; and *reading* refers to listening and viewing.

Traditionally, teachers of English language arts have been concerned with students' ability to read and write print texts. Electronic and artistic media have been used primarily to motivate students to read or to supplement print content. For example, recordings of current songs might be used to introduce a unit on poetry, or a film adaptation of a short story might help students visualize setting and character. But today, students obviously live in a world where more and more information is communicated through listening and viewing. As a result, the meaning of literacy has broadened to include direct education in both print and nonprint texts.

The following model (Cox, 1994b) provides a framework for teaching about and through the media:

1. *Experiencing media:* Students should experience works in a wide range of print and nonprint media to enjoy, reflect on, discuss, study, and relate works in various media to their own lives. Experiencing media means that students do these things:

   - Use their experiences with media outside the classroom (e.g., print and electronic news, television, advertisements, music, videogames, etc.) as a common experiential basis for classroom exploration through talk and writing.
   - Use their experiences with media in the classroom (e.g., film and videotape, audio recordings, computers, etc.) as a common experiential basis for classroom exploration through talking and writing.

I was Director of the Commission on Media of the National Council of Teachers of English from 1992–1995; this definition emerged from many discussions with the commission (NCTE, 1994).

IRA/ NCTE
See inside the front cover for a list of the twelve IRA/NCTE *Standards for the English Language Arts;* note that seven of them make it clear that today's students will become media literate (standards 1, 3, 4, 6, 7, 8, and 12).

TEACHER RESOURCES
For a review of the research on media and teaching language arts, see Carole Cox (2003), "The Media Arts," in *Handbook of Research on Teaching the English Language Arts* (3rd ed.).

- Gain a more equitable access to language-learning experiences through talking and writing about media events outside the classroom and both print and nonprint texts in the classroom.

2. *Analyzing media:* Students should analyze forms of mass media and other symbolic systems to understand and appreciate their structure and effects. Appreciating and critically analyzing media means that students do the following:

- Discuss and analyze their own transactions with media texts.
- Discuss and analyze texts in various media to understand their distinctive versus shared characteristics.
- Analyze media to understand biases and values inherent in public media.

3. *Creating media:* Finally, students should create their own works in a variety of media, including print, drawings, graphs, diagrams, photographs, films, videos, and performing arts. Creating media means that students do the following:

- Create works in varied media so that they have direct knowledge of how language and communications are shaped through different symbol systems.
- Use varied media, such as the visual and performing arts, along with print, in order to extend and express their understandings and feelings.
- Understand the process of creating within a given media through experience and practice with media making.

Film and Video

Students should have experiences with good children's films just as they do with good children's books. In an article I wrote with Joyce Many (Cox & Many, 1989), we discussed children's responses to both literature and film in the context of Rosenblatt's transactional theory:

> *In her transactional model of reader response, Rosenblatt (1985a) also takes an eclectic view of the various literary forms and their potential as lived-through experiences. She uses the term "poem" to stand for any literary work of art which she describes as ". . . not an object but an event, a lived-through process or experience" (p. 35). The formal differences between stories, poems, and plays, which she classifies together as literary events, are not less great than the differences between literature and film. Indeed, she suggests that the transactional theory, which seeks to account for the question of "'literariness' or 'poeticity'—i.e., of 'the aesthetic' in 'literature'—has implications for aesthetic education in general" (1986, p. 122). An aesthetic transaction, where the focus of attention is on the lived-through experience and the accompanying ideas, sensations, feelings, and images, can occur between any perceiver and any artifact, as between any reader and any text. Thus, the value of the role of the reader, as stressed in reader response theories, can be analogized to the role of the viewer and the same perspective can be used to describe how understanding and literary discourse is created in response to film narrative as well as literature. (p. 289)*

Children's Film Interests

Children like the same kinds of things in films that they like in books: storylike narratives, rather than nonnarratives, and live-action films with real-life characters, rather than animated, abstract films (Cox, 1982). Children can be encouraged to respond to films, just as they are to respond to literature, and the same kinds of response options are possible: discussion, writing, drama, and art and mediamaking (Cox & Many, 1992b).

Table 12.1 (p. 402) provides a selection of good children's films that teachers might use to introduce this media to students of different grade levels.

Film Response Guide

Here's a model for using a film in the classroom:

1. *Previewing:* Teachers should always preview films for suitability and interest; to note concepts, themes, and vocabulary; and to plan how to extend the viewing experience.

2. *Viewing:* Children are already enthusiastic about films, so simple introductions are best. Perhaps include a few initiating questions, or suggest that students each remember one thing they saw or heard to talk about after viewing. Teachers should avoid long explanations, vocabulary lists, and questions that sound as if they plan to give a test on the film after showing it. As film critic Pauline Kael put it, "If you don't think you can kill the movies, you underestimate the power of education."

3. *Postviewing:* After viewing the film, let children talk about it in small groups. Observe their responses and then use them for planning activities. The children's interests should be the basis for planning experiences with drawing, writing, drama, and media.

The following Teaching Idea shows a film response guide for *The Tender Tale of Cinderella Penguin*, an animated, humorous retelling of the familiar tale. I showed this film to two classes of first-graders who rated and responded to it, as shown in the guide. I based the postviewing ideas on their responses.

GREAT BOOKS FOR CHILDREN

See *Martha the Movie Mouse*, by Arnold Lobel (1966), a children's book in rhyme about a mouse who loves movies.

The steps *previewing, viewing,* and *postviewing* for teaching with film correspond to the steps *before, during,* and *after* reading for teaching with literature. See the Snapshot in Chapter 6, Reading, to review these steps for teaching with literature.

TEACHING IDEA

Film Response Guide for *The Tender Tale of Cinderella Penguin*

1. Previewing

Title: *The Tender Tale of Cinderella Penguin*

Distributor: National Film Board of Canada

Rating: 4.96 out of 5 for 51 first-graders

Length: 10 minutes

(continued)

Producer/Director: Janet Perlman   **Level:** Kindergarten–third grade

Circle: (color) / b&w   live-action / (animation)
               narration / dialogue / nonverbal music

Awards and Reviews: Academy Award Nominee; *Booklist; EFLA Evaluations; Language Arts*

Annotation: The familiar story of Cinderella receives an unfamiliar film treatment. Unforgettable images: a flipper-shaped glass slipper; Cinderella's roly-poly penguin shape asleep on a narrow shelf; a reverse, cabaret-style tango as Cinderella lofts the prince into the air and catches him again, never losing the grip on the rose between her teeth. Perlman has added humor without subtracting from the graceful poignancy of this traditional tale. The castle is regal, the fairy godmother magical, and the prince smitten. Medieval furnishings, music, and costumes (refitted for penguins) complete the fairytale picture. Excellent for ELL students since no words are used.

2. Viewing

Questions
- Who knows the story of Cinderella and can tell us about it?
- What do you think of the story?
- How would you change the characters in the story?

Prompts
- Watch the film.
- Remember your favorite part to talk about with others.
- Enjoy the film.

3. Postviewing

Watch-and-Talk Groups

Students meet in groups of four or five to talk about the film. They may begin with telling their favorite parts. I noted these responses while listening to two classes of first-graders after watching the film: "Great, funny, and liked it because it was a Cinderella story." Favorite parts: mean stepsisters and how they ordered Cinderella around, Cinderella sleeping on a shelf, getting the invitation to the ball, the fairy godmother making magic, the dragon at the ball, dancing, kissing her hand, when she was locked in the basement, the slipper/flipper flying up in the air and landing on her foot, getting married. One child disliked that the characters didn't talk.

Drawing and Writing
Have students do any of the following activities:

- *Draw Your Favorite Part:* Write a caption on the drawing, ask someone to take dictation and write it for you, or write "speech bubbles" for what a character might be saying.
- *Point of View:* Write the story from the point of view of a character other than Cinderella: one of the stepsisters, the stepmother, or the fairy godmother.
- *Invitation:* Write one for the ball or for the wedding of Cinderella and the prince.
- *Dialogue:* Draw a storyboard of what happened in the film, and write dialogue for what the characters might be saying. Use quotation marks when a character speaks.
- *Script:* Write one for a humorous version of a familiar tale like Cinderella.

Drama and Media
Have students try these activities:

- *Creative Drama:* With a partner, pick a character and mime his or her actions. Let your partner guess which character you are portraying. Then switch, and let your partner mimic another character.
- *Story Dramatization:* Plan a story dramatization for the story and then play it.
- *Viewing:* Watch another Cinderella film and compare it to this one. How were the stories, settings, and characters in the films alike or different? Which version did you like the best? Why?
- *Visually Representing:* Make your own Cinderella film, video, or filmstrip.

Television

Neil Postman (1961) has described television as "the first curriculum," given children's experience with this medium before coming to school. Teachers can help children develop critical viewing habits without planning inclass television viewing by simply drawing on students' experiences at home or when an important event is televised (e.g., a presidential inauguration or space mission). Try these activities for critical viewing:

- **Survey Students' Viewing Habits:** Have students keep logs for 2 weeks of when, what, and how much (total time) television they watch each day. Based on students' records, discuss their viewing habits. Repeat this activity periodically to note any changes.

- **Television Journals:** Have students keep television journals as a basis for thinking and talking about viewing in class. Suggest double-entry journals, in which students note what they watched in one column and their reaction to it in

| Table 12.1 | A "Top Ten" List of Children's Films (in alphabetical order) |

Film Title/Description	Suitable Grade Level
Apples (1997): A glowing tribute to the shiny, red fruit presents science, history, and folklore in the context of an energetic, out-of-the-ordinary investigation of the reproduction, propagation, uses, and legends of apples (30 minutes).	Grades K–7
Ashpet: An American Cinderella (1989): Set in the rural South in the early years of World War II, this is a humorously touching, live-action version of "Cinderella." *Ashpet* is one of the many fine films by Tom Davenport contained in his series *From the Brothers Grimm,* all of which are set in the South in different historical periods (45 minutes).	Grades 2–5
Dr. Seuss's My Many Colored Days (1999): In this creative melding of art forms, a little boy's many feelings are effectively evoked through sophisticated computer animation and an emotional, original orchestral score (45 minutes).	Grades K–5
Fat Monroe (1994): A live-action, childhood memoir rich in visual imagery and characterization, this film is based on a story by Kentucky writer Guerney Norman. Actor Ned Beatty, himself a Kentuckian, stars in the drama (30 minutes).	Grades 3–8
Molly's Pilgrim (1985) and *Make a Wish Molly* (1996): The classic film *Molly's Pilgrim,* based on Barbara Cohen's sensitive children's book of the same name, is the story of a young Russian Jewish immigrant girl and how she overcomes the insensitivity of her classmates and gains acceptance in her new American environment. The sequel, *Make a Wish Molly,* depicts how other students learn to respect the diverse heritages of others (24 minutes and 30 minutes, respectively).	Grades 2–5
Quilt (1998): This dazzling, animated film offers an exquisite, computerized melding of high-tech and homemade. An ever-changing kaleidoscope of geometric designs, inspired by traditional quilt patterns, is set to a rollicking score of flute and strings (7 minutes).	All grades
The Snowman (1982): Haunting original music by George Winston accompanies this unnarrated, animated film version of Raymond Brigg's worldless picture book, *The Snowman* (26 minutes).	Grades K–2
The Sweater (1983): A young French Canadian boy in the 1940s idolizes professional hockey player Maurice Richard in this animated film filled with humor, nostalgia, and the universal fears and joys of childhood. Based on an original memoir by Roch Carrier, the film was adapted to picture book form in *The Hockey Sweater* (10 minutes).	Grades 3–8
The Tender Tale of Cinderella Penguin (1982): A wonderful animated spoof of the familiar tale, this nonverbal film is both poignant and humorous: The glass slipper is webbed, and Cinderella tosses Prince Charming in the air during a torrid tango (10 minutes).	Grades K–5
Zea (1981): Viewers are held in suspense while this live-action, minimystery unfolds. It begins slowly to the strains of soothing classical music; the camera then slowly follows a large, moist, red-gold, and round form as it slowly rotates. The true identity of the form isn't revealed until the end of the film, much to the viewer's surprise and delight (5 minutes).	All grades

another. Students can write in class as part of regular journal writing. Journals are especially effective as response options to targeted viewing—for example, a documentary related to a content area or an adaptation of literature read in class (e.g., *Sarah, Plain and Tall* [MacLachlan, 1985]).

- **Television Fact and Fiction:** Pick a topic and compare how it's depicted on television with what students know about it from their own experience. Use the following frame:

Television Fact and Fiction Frame

Topic	TV Image	Real Experience	Explanation of Difference
Moms	*I Love Lucy:* Lucy stays at home and get into troubles with crazy schemes.	My Mom works and would never do all those crazy things; she'd be too tired.	Exaggeration is funny sometimes when it's not real.

"Moms" in the frame was written by two of my children—Gordon, then 13, and Elizabeth, then 10—both great fans of *Lucy* reruns.

- **Television and Literature:** Pick a show or special that's been adapted from a book or a certain genre (e.g., humor, adventure, mystery). Compare how the original book and adapted TV versions are alike and different. Use the following frame:

TV/Book Comparison Frame

	Book	Television
Setting		
Characters		
Plot		
Theme		
Mood		

Assessing Media Literacy

Portfolios can easily be expanded to include things written by students about media as well as students' own media productions. For example, journals provide ongoing records of students' television and film viewing experiences and responses to them. When teachers carry on dialogues with students in their journals, they are constantly assessing students' viewing, thinking, and writing about the media.

Teachers can use videos to document projects, puppet shows, and dramatizations or to compose by creating and producing film stories, storyboards, and scripts. All these items can become part of students' portfolios. Teachers can also use videos to assess the language development of ELL students (O'Malley & Valdez Pierce, 1996).

Students should become enlightened, critical consumers as well as users of all media. And just as they critique and interpret literature, they can evaluate

12.1 Student's Media Critique Form

I originally developed this critique form as a film preference instrument for children to use when viewing and responding to film (Cox, 1985a). However, it is equally adaptable to all visual media: film and video, television, photography, and computer displays using graphics and imagery.

Rate the Media!

Name _____   Date _____

Media Title _____

1. How do you rate this media (circle one)?

   1 = I didn't like it at all. (I would rather have done something else.)
   2 = I didn't like it very much. (I wouldn't want to see it again.)
   3 = It was OK. (I wouldn't mind seeing it again.)
   4 = It was good. (I would like to see it again.)
   5 = It was great! (I could see it many times without getting tired of it.)

2. Why did you give it this rating?

---

both print and nonprint forms of media. Assessment Toolbox 12.1 is both an instructional and an assessment tool. For instructional purposes, teachers can use it to have children respond, think about, and rate media, which should include giving reasons for their ratings in writing. For assessment purposes, teachers can use this tool to monitor student appreciation, analysis, and interpretation of a media work.

In addition, a copy of this tool could be put in the front of a media log that each student keeps as an ongoing response record of his or her listening and viewing experiences; the student could refer to it as a guideline in making each entry. Students' logs can be brought to discussion circles, similar to literature circles, to talk about current experiences with media: perhaps a television special everyone watched, a recent film of interest, a new piece of software in use in the classroom, or a new online database or electronic book in use.

Visually Representing

IRA/ NCTE

Visually representing—another of the six language arts in the national *Standards for the English Language Arts* (1996)—is defined as follows:

> *Conveying information or expressing oneself using nonverbal visual means, such as drawing, computer graphics (maps, charts, artwork), photography, or physical performance. For students with visual impairments, this language art might also include communicating by means of tactile drawings or diagrams, as well as by gesture and performance.* (p. 76)

As indicated in the Snapshot at the start of this chapter, the third-grade ELL students in Audrey Eldridge's class conveyed information and expressed themselves through visual representation by making "big books," illustrated written reports using images downloaded from the Internet, models, posters, diagrams of plans, puppet shows, and a science fiction video they wrote and produced. This section of the text will further explore several types of visually representing experiences: the visual arts, media production, and drama performances.

The Visual Arts

Drawing, painting, and other graphic arts are used by children to communicate throughout the elementary and middle school curriculum. Young children draw before they write, kindergartners go to easels to paint, and drawing illustrations is a prewriting and postwriting activity in grades K–8.

In addition, works of art are integrated across the curriculum on a daily basis—for instance, illustrations in picture books, animation in children's films, and computer graphics in software and online. Art history can be integrated naturally across the curriculum as children learn social studies. For example, much of what we know about early civilizations is through the artworks that have survived: the cave paintings in Lascaux, France; the pyramids, the Sphinx, and the treasures of the pharoahs in ancient Egypt; the bronze sculptures of the Benin empire in Africa; and Mayan temples in Mexico and Central America. Art history also informs children's understanding of subjects across the curriculum. For example, the Bayeux tapestry is an embroidered record of the Norman invasion of England, which culminated in the victory of the French army at the Battle of Hastings in 1066. The tapestry shows specific historical events related to social studies and tells about the role of the anonymous women artists during the Middle Ages who created the 75 embroidered scenes. Interestingly, it also records the appearance of Halley's Comet in the same year, which is related to the study of science.

You have seen numerous examples of visually representing through the visual arts throughout the text, including the activities described in the Snapshot at the beginning of this chapter. You may teach a lesson at any time by simply picking a visual art, finding an example by an artist, and combining it with a traditional language art, as shown in the following Lesson Plan. I have used this

Lesson Plan not only with children but with my preservice language arts students, who have in turn done the same lesson with their own students in their field experiences. I picked the artist Frida Kahlo as representative of both a great woman artist and a great Mexican artist. Also, many of my students and many of their students have become familiar with her and her work through the recent film *Frida*, starring Selma Hayek.

LESSON PLAN

Self-Portraits and Poetry

Level: All grade levels, K–8

Subject: Creating self-portraits and poems is a wonderful way for children to tap into their own experience and self-knowledge. In doing so, they can experience beautiful children's books and paintings, use technology, visually represent themselves, acquire a vocabulary of descriptive words, and create an illustrated face poem.

Purpose: To experience and respond to literature and paintings (via the Internet) through discussion, creating self-portraits, acquiring adjectives/descriptive vocabulary, and writing a poem.

IRA/
NCTE

Standard 12: Students use spoken, written, and visual language to accomplish their own purposes (e.g., for learning, enjoyment, persuasion, and the exchange of information).

Materials:
- Text set: *Frida* (Winter, 2002), *Portraits of Women Artists for Children: Frida Kahlo* (Turner, 1993), *Paths: Jose Marti, Frida Kahlo, Cesar Chavez* (Ada, 2000), and *Inspirations: Stories about Women Artists* (Sills, 1989)
- Website: To see Kahlo's self-portraits, go to one or both of these websites: www.artchive.com or www.proa.org
- Writing frames: Face feature chart and face poem
- Hand mirrors
- Paper and crayons, colored markers, watercolors, or tempera paint

Teaching Sequence:
1. Read *Frida* (Winter, 2002), and discuss it by asking open-ended, aesthetic questions:
   What did you think of the book?
   What was your favorite part?
   How would you describe your own face?

Eyes	Nose	Mouth	Hair
1. _____	1. _____	1. _____	1. _____
2. _____	2. _____	2. _____	2. _____
3. _____	3. _____	3. _____	3. _____
4 _____	4. _____	4 _____	4. _____
5. _____	5. _____	5. _____	5. _____

Figure 12.3   Face Feature Chart

2. Show examples of Frida Kahlo's self-portraits, which can be downloaded and printed out from the Internet or located in an art history text or collection of art prints. Students can also view them in groups on the Internet at either of the websites listed in the previous section, depending on the availability of computers.
3. As a class, create a face feature chart for Frida, using the writing frame in Figure 12.3. Feel free to add or change the features shown in the chart (e.g., add ears or change the mouth to show teeth).
4. Model writing a face poem for Frida with the class, using the writing frame shown in Figure 12.4.
5. Create a semantic map of facial features for the class, with each child suggesting an adjective to describe one of his or her features.
6. Have the children use hand mirrors to view their own faces, and ask them to draw or paint their own self-portraits.

Figure 12.4   Template for a Face Poem

_____
(First Name)

Feature _____   _____   _____   _____
                    Adjective   Adjective   Adjective

Feature _____   _____   _____   _____
                    Adjective   Adjective   Adjective

Feature _____   _____   _____   _____
                    Adjective   Adjective   Adjective

Feature _____   _____   _____   _____
                    Adjective   Adjective   Adjective

_____
(Last Name)

(continued)

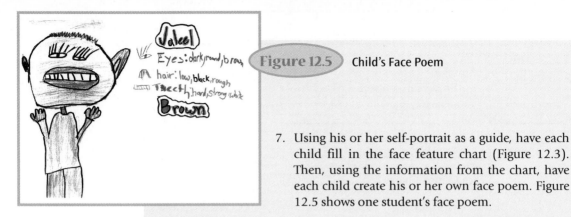

Figure 12.5   Child's Face Poem

7. Using his or her self-portrait as a guide, have each child fill in the face feature chart (Figure 12.3). Then, using the information from the chart, have each child create his or her own face poem. Figure 12.5 shows one student's face poem.

Extending Activities:

1. Create an "art gallery" on a bulletin board by posting a picture of Frida Kahlo and the face poem the class wrote about her along with the children's self-portraits and face poems.
2. Bind the children's drawings and poems into a book, or take digital photos and display them on a class website.
3. Send the students' self-portraits to www.artcontest.com, a website where students can view art by other students in multiple genres and vote on their favorites. Weekly winners are posted.
4. Read the picture book *Diego* (Winter, 1991) or the fictionalized biography *Diego Rivera: Artist of the People* (Neimark, 1992), both of which are about Frida Kahlo's husband, who was also an artist. Write a scene from their life together and dramatize it.
5. In groups, have children learn about other artists who are famous for their self-portraits, such as Rembrandt, Van Gogh, and Gaughin. Have them report what they find to the class using the visual arts (e.g., a poster, an illustrated book, a hypertext or PowerPoint project, a video drama, and so on).
6. Create a text set of books in the classroom about other Hispanic American artists—for instance, *A Piece of My Heart: The Art of Carmen Lomas/Pedacito de mi corazon* (Lomas Garza, 1994), *Pena on Pena* (Pena, 1995), and *Steps: Rita Moreno, Fernando Botero, Evelyn Cisneros* (Ada, 2000).

Media Production

The sequence outlined here for producing media will be further illustrated with examples of slides, transparencies, photograms, video, photographs, and xerography. This producing process can also be applied to any other visual or auditory form of media (Cox, 1985, 1987). Here are the steps:

   1. *Envisioning:* Children can discover ideas and visions for mediamaking anywhere, both in the classroom (e.g., children's literature and films, holidays, content areas, field trips) and outside the classroom (e.g., personal experiences, mass media, special events, dreams).

GREAT BOOKS FOR CHILDREN

See *Ida Makes a Movie*, by Kay Chaoro (1974), about a personified cat who makes a movie and wins an international student film contest.

2. *Arranging:* Brainstorming and recording ideas using a graphic organizer, such as a cluster or web, is an excellent starting point for children to clarify their ideas and visions (see Figure 12.6). Children can work in cooperative groups to discuss and take notes through drawing and writing.

3. *Storyboarding:* After noting and sketching a central idea on paper or on the computer, each student must break this idea up into meaningful chunks of images and action (if using a moving medium) and then record these images and actions on a storyboard that will become the script for production. As shown in Figure 12.7 on page 410, a *storyboard* has three or four squares running vertically down the center of a page to show images and space on either side of each square for a description of the content, production notes, narration, music, or dialogue or sound.

4. *Producing:* After composing a successful storyboard, children can use it to guide video production to make a live-action or animated film.

5. *Editing:* For video production, the story is shot in sequence and thus edited in the camera.

6. *Presenting:* Young mediamakers require an audience with which to communicate. Children's media creations can be publicized and presented to other students, classes, parents, and members of the community.

Figure 12.6 Students' Idea Cluster for a Science Fiction Film

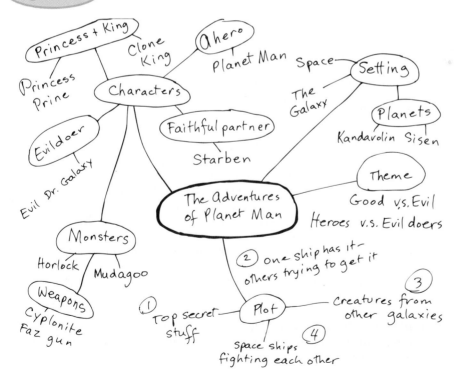

Figure 12.7 Storyboard for *The Adventures of Planet Man*

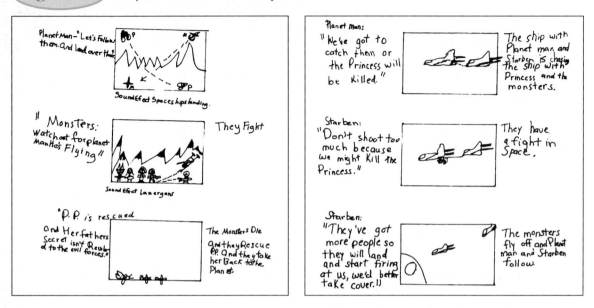

Mediamaking with a Camera

Students can create media using videocameras for live-action and animated films and 35 mm and Polaroid cameras for still photographs.

Video Production. Children can make live-action and animated films with a videocamera. Live-action films can take any of three forms:

1. *documentary,* or filming a real event or interview in a realistic, real-time style
2. *drama,* or telling a fictional narrative story
3. *docudrama,* combining a real event with a narrative story

Animated films can take either of two forms:

1. *three dimensional,* or filming objects such as puppets, toys, or clay figures one or a few frames at a time and moving the object between shots
2. *flat animation,* or filming a series of drawings, paper cutouts, or cut-up photographs that are moved between shots

Students making videos can follow the steps in the sequence for producing media described in the previous section. For example, a group of fourth-grade students made an animated space film called *The Adventures of Planet Man.* Here is a description of what they did in each step:

1. *Envisioning:* The students were great fans of science fiction films, especially *Star Wars,* and wanted to make a science fiction film of their own.

EXCELLENT SOFTWARE

Animation Programs

Grades 1–4: Students can create animated stories with Storybook Theatre.

Grade 4–12: Students can use Hollywood and Hollywood High to create their own animated movies.

GREAT BOOKS FOR CHILDREN

See *Make Your Own Animated Movies and Videotapes,* by Yvonne Andersen (1991), a how-to book for children.

2. *Arranging:* See Figure 12.6 (p. 409), Students' Idea Cluster for a Science Fiction Film, for their ideas.

3. *Storyboarding:* They created the storyboard from the cluster made in Step 2. See Figure 12.7 (p. 410), Storyboard for *The Adventures of Planet Man.*

4. *Producing:* Students made backgrounds using 22" × 28" poster paper. One background was black with yellow stars cut out of construction paper, which could be moved. Another was blue with the inside of Planet Man's spaceship painted on it. A background for a fight scene on a planet's surface was also blue with mountains painted on it. Shapes to be animated were cut out of construction paper: black letters for the title and credits, yellow stars and comets, and grey spaceships. Characters such as Planet Man had separate body parts that could be moved. For example, facial expressions could be shown by substituting several different mouth shapes in different positions (e.g., a smile, a frown, a big "O" for surprise). Backgrounds were placed on the floor, and the camera, attached to a tripod, was angled down. The animators sat on the floor and moved the objects and the characters' body parts between shots.

5. *Editing:* The students shot this film in sequence and edited it in the camera. There were a few "bloopers"—such as hands that didn't get out fast enough before the cameraperson started—but the students thought they were funny and left them in.

6. *Presenting:* A world premiere was announced with posters and invitations, and several viewings were shown to other students and families. Popcorn and Tang were served.

Audrey Eldridge's students used a combination of live-action and animation in making the film *Super Mikey and the Evil Aliens.* Some scenes were shot live as the students played characters and spoke lines. Other scenes were animated to show spaceships moving against a backdrop of planets and even Super Mikey himself flying through space in his magical spacesuit. Audrey's students followed the steps in the sequence of composing media described above and through the example of *The Adventures of Planet Man.*

Video Projects. Most schools today have videocassette recording (VCR) systems that allow students to make videos. Even young children can visually represent their ideas with this user-friendly medium. Here are some video projects to try:

- *Self-Portraits:* Young children can do simple self-portraits in the classroom as part of an "All about Me" project at the beginning of the schoolyear. Older students can do full-blown autobiographies and videotape interviews with family members (who can be recorded at home or can come to school). A buddy system works well for this project, with one child serving as cameraperson and crew for another. Self-portraits are great to show to parents at Back-to-School Night.

- *Role-Playing:* Improvisational situations of all kinds can be videotaped: real-life situations, such as resolving conflicts between friends; scenes from the past, such as interviews with famous explorers or scientists; or scenes from literature, such as the "wild rumpus" in *Where the Wild Things Are* (Sendak, 1963).

- *Dramatic Readings:* Tape a reader's theater presentation of a poem or a story or of students reading their own writing.

- *Plays:* Tape story dramatizations or plays written by students.

- *TV Shows and Commercials:* Encourage children to create original TV shows, TV show spin-offs, or commercials. Commercials can be spoofs or advertise real products, favorite books, or school events.

- *News Reports:* Have students plan and tape a newscast, including headlines, sports, weather, commentary, and commercials. The newscast could have a special focus, such as humor or fantasy (e.g., *News from the Moon*), or relate to one of the content areas (e.g., *News from the Santa Fe Trail, Dateline 1890*).

- *Oral Histories:* Have students choose topics and collect first-person accounts about them, creating oral histories of their school or community or a local historical event.

- *Portraits:* Ask students to pick special individuals about whom to do documentaries: a family member, classmate, teacher, or community figure.

Photography. Children can use 35 mm and Polaroid cameras to experience and learn about photography with a camera. Try activities such as these:

- *Photo Stories:* Children can write stories about events that take place in the classroom (e.g., the class gerbil has babies) and photoillustrate them. They can do idea clusters and storyboards, as outlined in Steps 2 and 3 in the section on producing media (p. 409). Students can shoot needed pictures and write captions and then publish their stories as books or on posters, which can be displayed in the room.

- *Photo Essays:* Children can pick topics that interest them (e.g., the environment), research and write essays, and photoillustrate their writing. These could be group essays on a topic of interest related to the curriculum (e.g., the history of our community).

- *Photo Portraits:* Each child can pick a person and create a photo portrait of him or her. The person can be another student, another teacher in the school, the principal, or a friend or family member. He or she could be interviewed for information about himself or herself and photographed to provide illustrations of the written portrait.

Mediamaking without a Camera

Students also can visually represent their ideas by mediamaking without a camera (Cox, 1980a). Several kinds of media can be made by drawing directly on film acetate with thin-tipped, permanent marking pens. These images can then be projected in the same way as those made with a camera. Other media—such as still photographs from magazines, newspapers, the Internet, or home as well as photograms and xeroxed copies of images—can be manipulated to represent children's ideas visually. The same process described earlier for producing media can be applied for a wide range of projects. The following sections describe ideas for each of these forms of mediamaking without a camera.

Draw-On Media. Draw-on media require a form of acetate media to draw on and permanent pens to draw on the acetate. Table 12.2 shows the materials needed for making slides and transparencies. Figure 12.8 (p. 414) shows the film gauge to use with slides. Transparencies do not require a gauge.

Here's an overview of each medium:

- *Slides:* Children can use clean 35 mm gauge blank film or cut up a blank transparency to fit the size of a plastic slide mount (see Figure 12.8). They can draw an image on each slide to create a slide show. An advantage to this medium is that the order of the slides can be changed. Thus, several groups can work on a larger themed project and content-area topics. For example, young children could do a slide show on spiders, with each group working on one type of spider (e.g., trap door, wolf, Black Widow). Put together, all the slides would be a *Spider Extravaganza.* Older students could do a slide show on a period of history, with each group working on one aspect (e.g., early California: Chumash Indians, Father Serra and the missions, the ranchos).

- *Transparencies:* One child or a group can use this easy medium to visually represent their ideas for a variety of purposes (e.g., as a visual aid for reporting research or book sharing). Several transparencies can be used for storytelling, using one at a time or by making a *tryptych* (i.e., several transparencies are attached at the edges, which, when laid over the others, adds more images and ideas to the

Good Markers for Drawing on Film

Staedtler Lumocolor S313 permanent thin-tip markers are available in eight colors.

Sources for Clear 35 mm Film Stock

Eastman Kodak, New York, NY (800-634-6101) and Christy's Editorial Film Supply, Burbank, CA (818-845-1755).

Table 12.2   Materials for Mediamaking without a Camera

For all acetate media: pens and pencils designed to draw and write on acetate

For each specific acetate media:

Slides	Transparencies
35 mm negatives or film roll or blank transparency	Blank transparency
Plastic slide mounts	Mounts
Slide gauge	
Slide projector	Overhead projector

Source: Based on Cox, 1987.

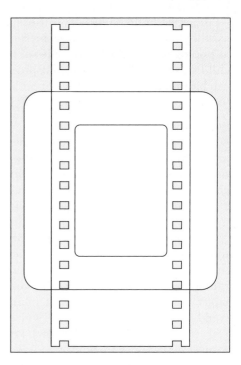

Figure 12.8 Slide Gauge with 35mm Film Superimposed to Show Relative Size

story). Attached transparencies can be cut into smaller pieces to make even more possible additions. This format works well for retelling cumulative tales like *The Napping House* (Wood, 1985), in which a little boy and a lot of animals end up on top of a sleeping granny and then all fly off when the one on top is bitten by a flea. This story can be depicted by adding and then removing images of the boy and animals.

Two of my students in a preservice language arts methods class used this mediamaking experience with a group of fifth-graders who made a transparency tryptych to share an episode of the book *Pippi Longstocking* (Lindgren, 1981) with the rest of the class. Here's how it worked:

Transparency 1   A picture of Pippi with two children watching her

Transparency 2   An overturned bucket and water spilled all over the
(Laid over 1)   floor

Transparency 3   Pippi says, "Who needs a holiday to scrub floors?" in a
(Laid over 2)   speech bubble, and two scrub brushes are attached to
                     her feet like skates to clean the floor.

Transparencies can be stored in manila folders. Each folder can also be cut on one side with an opening for the transparency, which is taped on the back. Shapes such as hearts and pumpkins can be cut out for holidays and other themes. The manila folder will black out the space around the shape, creating a dramatic effect.

Photography. Three good sources of still photographs include the following:

1. magazines, newspapers, and advertisements
2. photographs downloaded from the Internet
3. family pictures from home

And here are ideas for visually representing using photographs that have already been taken:

- *Elements of a News Photograph:* Select several photographs from the newspaper. Discuss the following elements for each one: choice of subject, details in background, camera angle, and caption. How do these affect the reader? Why?

- *News Captions:* Cut out photographs from newspapers with the captions removed. Give the photos to groups of students and ask them to discuss what the stories the photos are from might be about. Then write new captions and compare them to the real captions.

- *Photo Ads:* Cut out ads with photographs from magazines. Group them by the products they are selling: soap, shampoo, cars, or whatever. For each group, discuss the features of the photographs highlighted to sell the item.

- *Collages:* Have students cut out photographs and ads from magazines and make collages on poster paper. Encourage them to put images together that aren't usually seen together. Students should share their collages in groups and talk about the impact of combining various photographic images, especially if they're not expected to be together.

- *Historical News Photographs:* Order duplicated copies of photographs of special events from September 1851 to the present from The New York Times Information Office (207 West 43rd Street, New York, NY 10036), or access the archives at www.nytimes.com. Discuss these photos while studying the historical period they were taken in.

- *Self-Collages:* Have children bring photos from home and compose collages about themselves with titles, captions, poetry, and so on. Each collage can be made using a sheet of 8½" × 11" paper or 22" × 28" poster paper.

- *Photo Bodies:* A variation on the self-collage is the photo body, in which each student traces his or her body outline on a piece of butcher paper and makes a collage within it—again, with titles, captions, poetry, and the like.

- *Baby Photo Boards:* Ask children to bring in baby pictures, writing their names on the backs of the photos, but keep them secret from each other. Put the pictures on a bulletin board and number them. Make a folder with a page with each number. Students can write who they think is in each picture and why.

Photograms. Students can make photographs without a camera, or *photograms,* by placing small objects on light-sensitive paper and exposing it to sunlight. The image, captured on paper, will appear white, and the background will be black. The sharpest images are made from small objects with clearly defined edges: keys, scissors, leaves, and paper clips, for example.

Light-sensitive paper can be purchased at camera stores or where art supplies are sold.

Begin by reading *A, B, See!* (Hoban, 1982), an alphabet book of photograms. Each page shows objects to illustrate a given letter. Talk about the book and how students could make their own photograms or alphabet books. Identify and find objects that fit the theme chosen. Students can write captions and make photo exhibits or a class book of images.

Xerography. Students can be creative with duplicated copies of photographs: reducing or enlarging size, changing the tone from dark to light, cutting them up and making collages, and so on. Stories can be created to go with these xerographies (based on the word *Xerox*). Filmmaker and teacher Andrew Garrison (1998) suggests the following xerography projects:

- *Personal Object Collage:* Ask students to bring to class objects that will tell something about who they are and that will fit on a flatbed copier. Photocopy one or a group of objects, and have students write about them on the copy or another sheet of paper. These illustrations can also be colored or cut up to create a collage, which students can write about.

- *Xerography Mask:* Students can also create masks by making photocopies of their faces (with their *eyes closed*). The copy can then be colored, cut up, or reconfigured to make a mask representing a persona of the child. Each student should write a description of his or her self-created persona. An extension would be to make a color slide of each student's mask and tape record him or her talking about the mask/persona. All the slides and the tape recording could be put together to create a slide show.

Drama Performance

You have already read about drama in the classroom in Chapter 5, Listening and Talking. The focus there was on storytelling, puppets, reader's theater, creative drama, and story dramatization—the more improvised and spontaneous drama forms. While these drama forms may be performed and integrated with other forms of visual representation, such as creating sets, props, and costumes, it is not necessary to do so. The focus in this chapter will be on *drama performance,* which *does* require rehearsal and integration with the other forms of visually representing: scriptwriting (and performing it), adapting and performing dramatic literature (such as Shakespeare), and curriculum drama.

Scriptwriting

As an extension of improvised, spontaneous drama in the classroom, children can create scripted drama (Chapman, 1984; Sklar, 1991). Preferably, these scripts are those the children write themselves from original concepts or based on cross-curricular topics, adaptations of fine children's books, or dramatic literature. Children who write original scripts—perhaps in response to topics they're pursuing in school or recent events or experiences of high interest to them—have unique opportunities to put their feelings, thoughts, and language to work, as they draw on these responses as a source of inspiration.

Writing scripts for plays on subjects they choose puts students to work, building ideas by using language as a tool and constructing their own dramas in written form. The real reward is when they are able to communicate their original ideas (which have gone through a period of revision and refinement through the composing process) to an audience of significant others. Through this experience, children literally act on what they know and bring their words and ideas to life, visually representing them as they produce and perform their own plays.

One approach to scriptwriting evolves from the entire class being interested in a topic and wanting to explore it further, learning what they know about it through selecting, organizing, elaborating, and performing a script they have written (Cox, 1988). Follow these steps:

1. *Select a topic:* The suggestion to write a play for the first time may come from the teacher, *after* a topic of interest has emerged in the classroom. Some types of topics that may trigger playmaking include these:

- Children's books read aloud to the whole class
- Social studies or science units of study
- Current events of interest
- Popular films and other media events
- Fieldtrips

2. *Extend the response to the topic through writing:* Younger children may dictate a group story to the teacher, who can record it as part of a language experience story, or students may write their own stories. Older students may come up with their own ideas and extend them through personal writing. Many ideas for scripts will also emerge from writing activities.

3. *Share stories:* At some point, children may choose to share what they are writing, and their stories may become focal points for discussing and extending their ideas into a dramatic script.

4. *Brainstorm ideas:* Begin with small-group discussions of the focal ideas, and then move to a whole-class sharing of these ideas.

5. *Block a script:* Again, begin with small-group discussions, followed by a whole-class discussion of group ideas. One way to organize these discussions is to group ideas under the following types of headings, writing them on the board or a large wall chart. These new terms may be defined and explained and added to children's growing vocabulary of drama and script terms:

Synopsis (story idea)
Plot
Setting
Characters
Sequence of actions and events

6. *Record results:* One child can record the ideas under one heading, and a small group can put them on a chart for the whole class to use as a framework for future discussions and writing.

7. *Divide the sequence of events and actions into numbered acts:* Then divide the class into groups according to their interests and ability to work together.

8. *Write acts in small groups and add dialogue:* This will be an extended period of discussing and revising until each group has a working draft it can share with the class. This is a good opportunity to introduce, teach, and reinforce the many specialized writing skills children will need to produce a working draft. For example:

- Ordering and sequencing events and actions
- Writing in script form (scene notes, stage directions, narration, dialogue and quotation marks, etc.)
- Ensuring continuity of time and place
- Maintaining consistency of character behavior and language

9. *Come together as a large group to share act drafts:* Read the drafts together, and discuss the sequencing of acts and ways to smooth transitions between them.

10. *Revise the acts in multiple small groups:* Groups should now collaborate on transitions between acts: the group for Act 1 with Act 2, Act 2 with Act 1 and Act 3, and so on.

11. *Review and revise the script as a group:* Leave a copy of the emerging working script available in a writing center, so that children can read and respond to it between periods of writing.

12. *Synthesize the final script:* Changes will undoubtedly occur as the play goes into production. Nonetheless, a working script, which has gone through an extended period of talking and writing, is the beginning point for producing a scripted play.

 ### Third- and Fourth-Graders Write and Perform an Original Play

See Chapter 7, Teaching with Literature, for more about how I used *The Mystery of the Haunted Mine* across the curriculum.

I had read aloud *The Mystery of the Haunted Mine* (Shirreffs, 1962), a book written by my father, to my third- and fourth-grade combination class, and it generated a "ripple effect" of ideas, interests, and activities. Working in small groups, my students created a play. Not only was the play a natural outgrowth of several interests that were organized, clarified, and communicated through dramatization, but in addition, it demonstrated how natural it is to integrate the curriculum through visually representing as drama performance.

My students were excited about the three main characters in the book—Gary, Tuck, and Sue—and were spontaneously playing them. I noticed somewhat uncomfortably that Sue began to take on mannerisms I knew were my own after my father visited the class and suggested that this character might be me. (Children often "act out" their teachers, imitating voice and speech patterns when they don't think the teachers are listening.) These characters also began to appear in students' writing, so it seemed only natural to suggest scriptwriting and organizing these improvisational character sketches into dramatic form.

We began with the three main characters, but we still needed a setting, a plot, and a lot of action. Because the class was studying the moon and plants in science, the play's setting became another planet peopled by two races: the Plant People and the Humanoids. The conflict in the play came from another interest: a social studies unit on elections, since it was a presidential election year. The play began to take form when the children titled it *The Tale of an Unfair Election.*

Here's the plot, as summarized in a promotional release for the performance:

> An election takes place on the planet Zot. The election has been rigged by the Humanoid presidential candidate, Taylor. The Humanoids are invaders from a dying planet and have enslaved the native Plant People. Trailing Arbutus, the other presidential candidate, sends his vice-presidential candidate, Leaf, to Earth for help to restore free elections for Plants and Humanoids alike.
>
> Leaf meets the Metzenberg children, Gary, Tuck, and Sue, who take him to their father, a famous space scientist who is going on a scientific expedition to Zot. He takes Leaf along and promises to help. The children stow away on the spaceship *U.S.S. Moonbeam* and join their father for many adventures on Zot.

The play was performed in-the-round on the floor of the gym. The audience sat in a circle of chairs around the action. Spaces were left at intervals in the circle for the entrances and exits of performers, who waited behind screens, outside the circle. To create an effect of deep space, the room was dark, except for spotlights on the action. During scenes with political rallies and revolt, the audience was invited to participate, becoming part of the crowd and the drama itself.

Although this play was special for everyone, one student in particular appeared to benefit. Jan was the shyest child in the class and often struggled to look people in the eye when she spoke. She was large for her age and self-conscious about it, which compounded her shyness and desire to remain unnoticed.

Surprisingly, Jan became extremely involved with her scriptwriting group. When we called for volunteers for the cast, she asked to play the important role of the presidential candidate of the Plant People, Trailing Arbutus. When Jan donned the imperial-looking robes of the leader of the Plant People—a long, flowing, hooded garment, covered with plastic leaves attached with safety pins—no one was prepared for the transformation that took place. She suddenly stood straighter, to the full advantage of her larger size. And as she gripped her robe and swished it about for emphasis, a voice emerged from inside the hood that none of us had ever heard before. It was similar to the voice of the quiet and very dignified Jan, but it had a new edge of authority and volume. Jan had become Trailing Arbutus!

Jan outdid herself in this role and came to relish all drama. The other children recognized her special talent and the transformation that took place when she worked on a script or put on a costume, visually representing herself. For Jan, composing a play in the relative safety of a small group and then acting on it by assuming another persona was a special way to find her own voice—one barely audible during whole-class activities but strong and clear during dramatizations.

Adapting and Performing Dramatic Literature

www

Go to the Folger Shakespeare Library website for resources, teaching ideas, and lesson plans for teaching Shakespeare through performance with children: **www.folger.edu/ education/teaching.htm**.

Children can also adapt dramatic literature, like the works of Shakespeare, and visually represent them by performing the plays. However, some people question whether Shakespeare belongs in the language arts curriculum.

"Doesn't He Know Who Shakespeare Is?"

A surprised principal once hastily posed the question "Does Shakespeare really belong in the language arts curriculum?" while leading a group of college students to observe language arts in my third-grade class. They arrived in the middle of our production of *Julius Caesar*, just as an active Roman mob came pouring out of the classroom, screaming "Burn, burn!" and "Kill, kill!" They had been fired up by Carolyn's impassioned delivery of Mark Antony's famous speech, "Friends, Romans, countrymen, lend me your ears," delivered over the dead body of Caesar (played by Bart).

Jeff, leader of the Roman rabble, heard the principal's question to the university students and stopped dead in his tracks. He turned to me dramatically and asked with amazement, "Mrs. Cox, doesn't he know who Shakespeare is?"

All Jeff really knew about Shakespeare was that he's considered a literary master and one of the world's greatest storytellers. All I really knew about doing Shakespeare with children was that it generated tremendous enthusiasm and extended possibilities for "ripple effects" across the curriculum. My third-grade class had already had extensive experiences with drama. When I added Shakespeare, I found that his language and ideas were not too difficult for the children to read and understand at their own level. They demonstrated this by their ability to perform his plays with great feeling, style, and energy.

No one will every grasp all of Shakespeare at one time; his plays are too rich in thought and emotion to be understood quickly and easily. But we can return to him at different times in our lives and always find new meaning. Children are able to find this meaning, as well. In fact, I can think of no way to make elementary-age children read, memorize, characterize, rehearse, and present a Shakespearean play without their understanding what they're doing or their wanting to do it.

Top 10 Shakespearean Plays for Children

I recommend adapting these Shakespearean plays for children: *A Comedy of Errors; Hamlet; Julius Caesar; Macbeth; A Midsummer Night's Dream; Richard III; Romeo and Juliet; The Taming of the Shrew; The Tempest;* and *Twelfth Night.*

Shakespeare for Children

And just how do you adapt and perform Shakespeare's plays with children? Here's my approach (Cox, 1980b, 1985c):

Adapting a Script

First, a script is needed. To prepare it, I work with a paperback copy of the play and underline what I think are the most important and manageable parts for the age of children who will use the script. I delete scenes and characters that are peripheral to the main plot, as well as long soliloquies, but try not to underestimate the children. I am constantly amazed at their capacity to comprehend and act on Shakespeare's words. And I have never changed his words or thought that I should. Children love to roll the words and phrases of Shakespeare off their tongues. Reading and dramatizing Shakespeare is one way to develop children's taste for a gourmet vocabulary.

A script condensed for children should play about 30 minutes. (The original would run 2 or more hours.) While rehearsing, add or subtract lines. Many children will be able to add to their parts as the play and their confidence develop.

Here are examples of three scripts for the two witches' scenes from *Macbeth*, adapted for three levels: two versions of Act IV, Scene 1, for grades K–1 and 2–3, and one version of Act I, Scene 1, for grades 4 and above:

Grades K–1

Scene: A cavern. In the middle, a boiling cauldron. Thunder. Enter the three Witches.

First Witch: Round about the cauldron go.
All: Double, double, toil and trouble; Fire burn and cauldron bubble.
Second Witch: Fillet of a fenny snake; In the cauldron boil and bake.
All: Double, double, toil and trouble; Fire burn and cauldron bubble.
Third Witch: Scale of dragon, tooth of wolf; Witches' mummy, maw of the shark.
All: Double, double, toil and trouble; Fire burn and cauldron bubble.

Grades 2–3

Scene: A cavern. In the middle, a boiling cauldron. Thunder. Enter the three Witches.

First Witch: Round about the cauldron go; In the poison'd entrails throw.
All: Double, double, toil and trouble; Fire burn and cauldron bubble.
Second Witch: Fillet of a fenny snake; In the cauldron boil and bake. Eye of the newt and toe of frog; Wool of bat and tongue of dog.
All: Double, double, toil and trouble; Fire burn and cauldron bubble.

GREAT BOOKS
FOR CHILDREN

Shakespeare

Shakespeare and Macbeth: The Story Behind the Play, by Stewart Ross (1994).

Add these sound effects: wind blowing, lightning crackling, thunder rumbling, owls hooting, and wolves howling.

(continued)

Third Witch: Scale of dragon, tooth of wolf; Witches' mummy, maw of the salt-sea shark; Root of hemlock digged i' the dark.

All: Double, double, toil and trouble; Fire burn and cauldron bubble.

First Witch: Cool it with a baboon's blood.

Second Witch: Then the charm is firm and good.

Third Witch: By the pricking of my thumbs; Something wicked this way comes; Open, locks, whoever knocks!

Grades 4 and Above

Scene: Scotland. A deserted place. Thunder and lightning. Enter three Witches.

First Witch: When shall we three meet again, In thunder, lightning, or in rain?

Second Witch: When the hurly-burly's done, When the Battle's lost and won.

Third Witch: That will be ere the set of sun.

First Witch: Where the place?

Second Witch: Upon the heath.

Third Witch: There to meet with Macbeth.

All: Fair is foul, and foul is fair; Hover though the fog and filthy air.

(Drum within)

Third Witch: A drum, a drum! Macbeth doth come.

All: The weird sisters, hand in hand; Posters of the sea and land; Thus do go about, about; Thrice to thine, and thrice to mine; And thrice again, to make up nine. Peace! the charm's wound up.

(Enter Macbeth and Banquo)

Macbeth: So foul and fair a day I have not seen.

Banquo: What are these, So wither'd and so wild in their attaire?

Macbeth: Speak, if you can: what are you?

First Witch: All hail, Macbeth! hail to thee, thane of Glamis!

Second Witch: All hail, Macbeth! hail to thee, thane of Cawdor!

Third Witch: All hail, Macbeth! thou shalt be King hereafter!

First Witch: Hail!

Second Witch: Hail!

Third Witch: Hail!

First Witch: Lesser than Macbeth and greater.

Second Witch: Not so happy, yet much happier.

Third Witch: Thou shalt get kings, though thou be none; So all hail, Macbeth and Banquo!

First Witch: Banquo and Macbeth, all hail!

Macbeth: Stay, you imperfect speakers, tell me more; I know I am thane of Glamis; But how of Cawdor? The thane of Cawdor lives, A prosperous gentle man; and to be king stands not within the prospect of belief; No more than to be Cawdor. Say from whence you owe this strange intelligence? Speak, I charge you.

(Witches vanish)

Playing Scenes from Shakespeare

To play these scenes from *Macbeth*, read and discuss them with the class. Then begin to turn a corner of the room into a witches' cavern on a deserted heath in Scotland. Use murals and art created by the children and add a large black pot (a trash can works well); assorted rags, capes, hoods, and brooms; and child-made ingredients for the witches' brew (e.g., "eye of newt and toe of frog," etc.).

Begin to move students through scenes of the play as the atmosphere develops and their interest mounts. With younger children, three witches can take turns saying their lines, as the rest of the class sit in a circle and chant the refrain for "All": "Double, double, toil and trouble; Fire burn and cauldron bubble." Here's one way to play the adapted witches' scene with an entire class in grades K–3:

1. Divide the whole class into three groups, and seat them in a semicircle around the cauldron.
2. Speak the lines to all the children, while they repeat them softly.
3. Practice chanting the lines softly and with expression until students are fairly comfortable with them. Enthusiasm and energy are important here, not exactness or enunciation. The lines can be divided such that students in the three groups recite the respective witches' lines together; the entire class can respond for the "All" lines.
4. Ask for a volunteer from each group to come forward to play a witch around the cauldron. Repeat the lines in step 3 again with all the children: the standing witches and their seated classmates.
5. When the children appear confident, let the standing witches say their lines alone, while the seated children chant the refrain along with them.
6. After this succeeds, dim the lights and put dry ice in the pot. Have students add motions, gestures, and sound effects.
7. Repeat the above steps over several periods, continuing to add motions, gestures, and sound effects as well as costumes and props. Do so until every child who wants to be a witch has had the opportunity.

Fourth- through sixth-grade children can play the scene with the witches as well as the characters of Macbeth and Banquo. When children are not playing speaking parts, they can support the players by making sound effects, such as the beat of the drum. Every child should have the chance to play the role of a witch, Macbeth, or Banquo and to serve as a member of the chorus, crew, and audience.

Casting an Entire Play Adapted from Shakespeare

Describe the play and each part while the children have scripts in hand. Ask them to think about which part they would most like to play, if they could choose. Students usually have questions at this time:

How big is the part?
How many lines and how many scenes does the character play?

See children performing scenes from Shakespeare.

Safety Tips for Handling Dry Ice

1. Store it in a metal container.
2. Don't touch it with bare hands.
3. To create a bubble effect, slowly pour room temperature water over the ice.

(continued)

What kind of costume does the character wear?
What are some things the character does?

One fourth-grader described what he liked about Shakespeare: "The things I like best is when swords bust or someone goes mad."

After discussing these issues, have students put their heads down and raise their hands as you call the name of the part they would most like to play. If no one else raises a hand, the part is theirs. Most parts can usually be cast in this way. If more than one student wants a certain part, give them a chance to pick one of the remaining parts. If they still want the same one, have them look over a few lines and read them on the spot for the rest of the class. The class can then vote secretly for the person they feel should have the part.

Children invariably want to play the parts they feel they're most suited for, and they all want to do their best and enjoy the experience. Letting them self-select parts virtually guarantees this. Furthermore, this means of selection helps develop children's tolerance for sharing and cooperating.

Perhaps understandably, the "heavy" parts aren't always the most desired. No one may select the role of Hamlet, for instance, although several may want to play his father's ghost. Likewise, it may require some coaxing to get someone to play Macbeth, but there's never a lack of volunteers to play the three witches. No distinction according to gender needs to be made when casting characters in Shakespeare. Some of my best Hamlets have been wonderfully intense girls, and Lady Macbeth was once a perfectly ruthless fourth-grade boy. Supernatural creatures—such as witches, fairies, ghosts, and monsters—are always open to both genders, too.

In the case of a large class, major parts can be split between students. Macbeth can be divided neatly in two: before and after the murder of King Duncan. Lady Macbeth, usually a highly desired part, can also be divided in two: before and after she goes mad. Splitting roles like this solves the problem of having more children than parts and gives more children the chance to play a meaty role.

Rehearsal

In drama, *blocking* means staging the movements and positions of the characters.

Blocking the play relies heavily on working together as a group and making decisions. Children may also rehearse scenes in small groups and at different times, depending on the class schedule. It's not necessary to come together as a whole group at each rehearsal.

Costumes, Sets, and Properties

GREAT BOOKS FOR CHILDREN

Shakespeare and the Renaissance

Bard of Avon: The Story of William Shakespeare (Stanley & Vennema, 1992)

Favorite Tales from Shakespeare (Miles, 1985)

One Day in Elizabethan England (Kirtland, 1962)

Shakespeare and His Theatre (Brown, 1982)

Shakespeare Stories (Garfield, 1985)

Creating costumes, sets, and props requires that children research and read to get ideas from many sources. But when the information they're seeking will help them create a Renaissance ball gown for Juliet or a rapier for Tybalt, children are highly motivated to do extensive reading with attention to meaning. During this research, students glean ideas from a great range of sources and thereby extend their reading beyond the script of the play.

The children's imagination is perhaps the best resource in creating sets and costumes. Items found at home are more than enough to outfit a play. Children

Third- and fourth-grade students enjoy performing this scene from Romeo and Juliet: *the sword fight between Romeo and Tybalt, in which Tybalt is killed.*

are quite adept at transforming materials like cardboard room dividers into an impenetrable castle and branches and twigs into the surrounding forest. Similarly, a pair of black tights and a belted blouse changes anyone into a Renaissance rake, whereas a child in leotard and tights decorated with colored nylon net becomes a midsummer fairy.

Performances

When performance day arrives, the teacher can do several things to put the emphasis on children and their language, rather than on technical difficulties. As mentioned earlier, a real stage should be avoided. Children are visually lost and too far removed from the audience on a stage, and their voices don't carry well. The classroom, multipurpose room, or playground are ideal places to produce Shakespeare-in-the-round with room for chairs or sitting on the floor. Curtains are also unnecessary; a door or tree can be the exit/entrance. Shakespeare's theater was actually performed this way: curtainless, in the open, on a thrust stage with an entrance/exit or two in the rear. Prompting students during performance should be avoided, too. They should be encouraged to think on their feet. If someone forgets a line, he or she should improvise another to take its place.

A Renaissance festival may precede the play, with strolling performers in costume playing recorders or guitars and passing out flowers or gingersnaps, an Elizabethan treat. Children will enthusiastically enter the time of William Shakespeare, throwing aside their inhibitions and fear of work. Or as one youngster exclaimed when asked what he thought about doing Shakespeare, "I liked everything about it except for when we took breaks."

Shakespeare's Theatre (Hodges, 1966)
Stories from Shakespeare (Chute, 1976)
Tales from Shakespeare (Lamb & Lamb, 1979)
Will Shakespeare and the Globe Theatre (White, 1955)
William Shakespeare and His Plays (Haines, 1968)
The World Awakes: The Renaissance in Western Europe (Brooks & Walworth, 1962)

Recipe for Gingersnaps

1. Cream ¾ cup shortening and 1 cup sugar (brown or white).
2. Add 1 egg and 4 tablespoons molasses.
3. Sift and add 2 cups flour, 2 teaspoons baking soda, 1 teaspoon each ginger, cloves, and cinnamon.
4. Roll into balls and then in sugar.
5. Arrange evenly on a cookie sheet.
6. Bake at 350–375° for 10–12 minutes.

Curriculum Drama

Drama is a powerful means to enrich, enliven, and expand learning across the curriculum (Combs & Beach, 1994; Nelson, 1988; Putnam, 1991; San Jose, 1988). *Curriculum drama* is a term used to "describe a method by which potentially dramatic moments within required studies are identified and developed in order to heighten emotionally the students' response to the curriculum, thus deepening the learning experience" (Kelly 1981, p. 102). Potentially dramatic moments in the curriculum could include the following:

- acting out problems of social living
- contemporary social problems and current events
- reliving events in history
- stepping into the lives of people of other cultures
- becoming characters in favorite books
- dramatizing biographies of famous people
- bringing myths, legends, and folktales to life
- writing and adapting scripts of fantasy or spin-offs from subjects in the content areas

For more on these examples, see Chapter 1, Learning and Teaching Language Arts (group workshops), and Chapter 4, Emergent Literacy and Biliteracy (*Three Billy Goats Gruff* in kindergarten and *Johnny Appleseed* in first grade). Later in the book, see Chapter 14, Language across the Curriculum ("ripple effect" of colors in third and fourth grades).

In this text, we've looked at several examples of such moments of curriculum drama and drama as an integrating force in the curriculum:

- Avril Font's fourth-grade class dramatizing the life of St. George, creating a TV documentary on Shakespeare's life, and dancing around the maypole as part of their social studies small-group study
- Marion Harris's first-grade class acting out the life of Johnny Appleseed after she read a biography of his life, which was done in conjunction with a study of how things grow and what foods we eat
- Mauretta Hurst's kindergarten class's story dramatization of the *The Three Billy Goats Gruff* after reading the book by Marcia Brown (1957) and in connection with a visit to the zoo and a study of animals

In this chapter, examples of visually representing and integrating drama across the curriculum have included a science fiction film and puppet show; students' writing inspired by literature and content-area study in social studies and science in the fantasy *The Tale of an Unfair Election*; and adaptations of dramatic literature, such as Shakespeare. The latter is an example of how to integrate learning in all subjects throughout an entire school.

Drama embraces virtually all other arts and humanities. It forms a link with the past and with culture. As a mixed art, drama is a tool for integrated teaching across the curriculum.

Language	*Content Areas*
Responding to literature	Content as the subject of drama:
Expressing personal experiences	Multicultural education
Organizing and clarifying experiences	Social studies
	Science
Listening	Mathematics
Speaking	Current events
Reading	Physical education and dance
Writing	The arts
Nonverbal language	

A Schoolwide Renaissance Fair

One year, I directed a cross-curricular study of the Renaissance in an entire school at the invitation of the principal, Orlena MacKenzie, a strong believer in visually representing and the arts in education. The result was 2 weeks of concentrated schoolwide and classroom activities that culminated in a Renaissance Fair held in conjunction with the school Book Fair. The gym was decorated with the children's art and writings, and teachers, children, and parents came to the fair in Renaissance dress. Renaissance theater treats of mead and gingersnaps were served, and a Renaissance recorder group from Louisiana State University played.

During the fair, each class visually represented what they had learned about the Renaissance or a scene from a Shakespearean play. For instance, fourth-grade classes presented reports on William Shakespeare and Renaissance weapons, complete with visual displays, murals, and demonstrations. A fifth-grade class reported on Renaissance music and did a recorder demonstration. Drama performances included the witches' scene from *Macbeth* (done by kindergarten, first-, and second-grade classes), the funeral oration scene from *Julius Caesar* (third grade), and various scenes from *Romeo and Juliet* and *Hamlet* (fourth and fifth grades).

I used the adaptations of the witches' scenes shown on pp. 421–422.

The event was later featured as the lead article in the award-winning school newspaper, *Paw Prints:*

Learning about the Renaissance

I love the exciting times of the Renaissance! I hope you like to get in touch with the Renaissance world like I do. Dr. Carole Cox, a teacher from LSU, came to Walnut Hills. She showed us books, costumes, and great scenes by William Shakespeare, like Hamlet, which was acted out by students.

Then we watched a demonstration of how to use a sword and how the people used the sword in Renaissance times. It was a lot of entertainment for me! But, the guy who was fencing against me won the fight.

Thursday, February 16, I came with my parents to a Renaissance party at school. It was very exciting for me too, because I was wearing a Renaissance costume. —*A fifth-grader*

Illustrated articles by many children filled the pages of the school newspaper. Two of the children's written comments especially underscore the impact of this cross-curricular study of the Renaissance and Shakespeare, which relied heavily on visually representing:

Shakespeare was a magnificent man. He was a play writer. He wrote plays such as Macbeth, Hamlet, Julius Caesar, and Romeo and Juliet. Feb. 16 we relived his plays. It was as if Shakespeare were inside us. Shakespeare will always live because of his plays. —*A fifth-grader*

All around the school of Walnut Hills, kids and teachers have been talking about Shakespeare. Everyone knows he's a wonderful person, and he's been writing stories like Macbeth, Hamlet, and more. Even now he's gone, we still are looking back to his stories and enjoying them. —*A third-grader*

One teacher in particular, Lynn Lastrapes, was so enthusiastic about going back to the Renaissance that she wrote me a letter and we later talked about what happened in her class:

I truthfully wondered how second-graders could understand some of the complicated plots and characterizations. Except for your talk to us, I never would have thought to try this myself. I didn't take to Shakespeare until after college, and I was an English major! I felt excited, stimulated, and good the whole week. I still do. I loved it for myself but even more for the way my class took to it. Even students who normally don't do very well loved it. They all seemed to relish the "meatiness" of the stories. There was so much going on. Their interest was thrilling.

Lynn discussed some of the many things that happened in her classroom after introducing Shakespeare:

- The class read 15 to 20 minutes of Shakespeare after lunch every day and completed four plays. The students were able to remember and compare things from all the plays.
- Vocabulary was greatly enhanced, with little effort from Lynn.
- The students could tell the play in their own words.
- Students imagined how various characters felt and shared how they would feel if they were certain characters.
- The class listened to music, like Mendelssohn's *A Midsummer Night's Dream* and Pavarotti singing the aria "O figli miei! Ah! la paterna mano," in which Macduff is thinking of how Macbeth murdered his children. (According to Lynn, "They were moved, I tell you! Even though it was in Italian, they felt the emotion.")
- During Brotherhood Week, the class used *Romeo and Juliet* as one of its stories and talked about the consequences of not being kind to one another.
- Several students thanked Lynn for letting them know about an LSU production of *Hamlet*. They went and loved it. (Lynn said, "Second-graders going to *Hamlet* is beautiful!")

Lynn told me, "The children are clamoring for more Shakespeare. I want to do *The Tempest* next year. *I* want more, too."

In addition to Shakespeare, other types of dramatic world literature can be adapted for children—for example, Greek tragedies like *Antigone* and *Electra*, by Sophocles, and Roman comedies like *The Crock of Gold, The Haunted House*, and *Menaechmi*, by Plautus. The English Medieval drama *Saint George, A Christmas Play* has been adapted for children. For more modern plays, choose from the *The Imaginary Invalid, The Physician in Spite of Himself*, and *Tartuffe*, by Molière; *Androcles and the Lion*, by George Bernard Shaw; and *Cyrano de Bergerac*, by Edmond Rostand. And for contemporary drama, see *Historia de una muneca abandonada* (*The Story of the Abandoned Doll*), by noted Spanish playwright Alfonso Sastre, and *Langston*, a play within a biography of Langston Hughes, written by Ossie Davis (1982).

Culturally Responsive Teaching and Drama

In the summer of 1992, in Long Beach, California, I was directing a "Shakespeare for Children" performance of *Romeo and Juliet* with first- through fifth-grade students; most of them were fourth-graders. It was the summer after the Los Angeles riots, which made me think there was no other play to do but *Romeo and Juliet* because of the theme of cultural conflict. Even though I never told the children that's why I chose that play, they quickly connected it with the riots.

My teacher friend Paul Boyd-Batstone, whom you have read about elsewhere in this book, had joined me and brought along some of the Latino students in his bilingual class, who had a flair for drama. He told me that one day while I was talking to Juliet's mother about her costume, the students got into an extended, serious discussion of who was at fault in the play. Romeo said it was his fault because he went to the Capulet ball, and Romeo's friend Mercutio said it was his fault because it was his idea to go to the ball. Lord Capulet said it was his fault because he was too hard on Juliet when she refused to marry Paris (because she had already married Romeo), and of course Juliet said it was hers because she had married Romeo and disobeyed her father.

And so it went. Every child saw his or her character as having some kind of responsibility for the tragedy that ensued. He or she either took the wrong action or didn't take enough action. Then the discussion drifted to a comparison with the Los Angeles riots. Who was at fault? The children very seriously discussed issues like power, class, racism, police brutality, justice, and economic opportunies and tensions as they pertained to the Latino, African American, and Korean American communities in Los Angeles. Closer to home, they also talked seriously about their own cultural identities (the group included white, Latino, and Asian American students) and issues of peer pressure and gang affiliation. These conversations became an ongoing part of the daily rehearsals and debriefings.

I have often thought of that summer and the potential of drama performance and visually representing to bring not only literature to life but real-life issues like riots and racism and cultural conflict, as well. Some children's books also address these issues. See Eve Bunting's Caldecott Medal–winning book *Smoky Night* (1994) about the Los Angeles riots, written as she watched the fires burn from her home in Pasadena. Books about the horrors of war include *Hiroshima No Pika* (Maruiki, 1980), about the dropping of the atomic bomb on Hiroshima and the resulting destruction, and *Zlatah's Diary* (Filipovic, 1994), written by a young girl during the war in Bosnia.

Assessing Drama Performance

Drama performance assessment is an ongoing process for teachers and children. Both teachers and students need to assess and understand what happened during Monday's session before planning and preparing for Tuesday's.

Several types of assessment are appropriate for drama performance:

1. *Play Notes:* The teacher should observe and take play notes during any type of drama session to provide the basis for follow-up discussions. Observations of improvement, words of encouragement and praise, and questions and suggestions should all be jotted down for use during conferences.

2. *Drama Debriefings:* Debriefings are a critical component of every type of drama session. The teacher must remember that he or she is a model of the type of constructive assessment the children will hopefully emulate. Debriefings are essential to planning for the next drama session. Types of questions for leading these conference discussions are as follow:

- What did you see that you liked?
- What did you enjoy doing or watching?
- Whom did you notice doing something really well (or interesting, imaginative, different, humorous)?
- Why did you like what he or she did?
- What do we need to work on next time? How can we do this?
- What should we concentrate on next time? (*Ideas:* concentration, cooperation, teamwork, movement, pace, energy, staying in character, dialogue, voice, gestures, using space, traffic patterns)

Assessment Toolbox 12.2 can be used during debriefings; the teacher can write down young children's responses, and older students can record their own. This informal self-assessment can provide insight into children's understanding of the narrative form and content of drama, of their parts in specific drama activities, and of their feelings about participating in drama performance.

12.2 Drama Self-Assessment Form

Second-grader Ryan completed this self-assessment form after playing several parts in *Macbeth*.

Name   **Ryan**   Grade Completed   **2**

Tell About the Play

Tell about the play by William Shakespeare.

It is about a man that was contro-
lied by witches. He takes over the
kingdom. And is killed by a brave
nobleman called Macduff

Whch character(s) do you play?   Dun kin lennox docter

sword

Tell about your character.

Dunkin is the kingof scotland.
Lennox is anodleman
The docter is a docter
Sword is theson of general Sword

What is the most important thing about the play?

Its Supernatural

What is the most important thing about your character?

His king
nothing
Hes a docter
He fites macbeth

How did you feel about doing Shakespeare?

happy

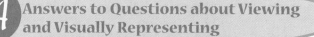

Answers to Questions about Viewing and Visually Representing

● *What are the roles of viewing and visually representing in the integrated teaching of language arts?*

Viewing and visually representing have been added to the traditional four language arts—listening, speaking, reading, and writing—in the IRA/NCTE *Standards for the English Language Arts*. These arts play an integral role in the integrated teaching of the language arts for several reasons: They are a natural part of human experience and communication, we are surrounded by visual as well as auditory media, children learn through viewing and visually representing from a very early age, and they are an essential aspect of a natural approach to learning English as a second language. Skills in critical viewing, in which students analyze and create media, are needed to become media literate. *Media literacy* is "an ability to comprehend, use, and control the symbol systems of both print and nonprint media, as well as understand the relationship between them" (Cox, 1994b, p. 791).

Children experience a great variety of mass media, including film, video, television, and photography. Children also use viewing and imitation to learn, and they come to visually represent their experiences through play, drama, and art as they learn to communicate with others. Participation in viewing and visually representing activities such as media, the visual arts, and drama performance provides great opportunities for developing language and literacy, communcating in social contexts, learning across the curriculum, and experiencing personal growth and development.

● *How should we teach and assess viewing and visually representing?*

There are many appropriate experiences for viewing and visually representing in the elementary classroom, and teachers have many opportunities to teach critical viewing about and through the media in language arts. Media experiences both inside and outside the classroom provide access to learning for all students, drawing on a shared media culture as the basis for classroom exploration. This gives children the chance to use what they experience in activities for viewing and visually representing with film, video, television, and photography and media production. Appropriate experiences in drama performance can begin with scriptwriting, in which students write and then produce and perform their own plays, often based on cross-curricular topics. Even dramatic world literature, such as the works of Shakespeare, may be adapted, shared, and performed in the classroom.

All forms of drama performance are ideal means of integrating learning across the curriculum. This is called *curricululm drama:* using potential dramatic moments in all subject areas to heighten students' response to and understanding of the curriculum. Assessment of viewing and visually representing experiences is an ongoing process for teachers and children and should involve self- and group assessment. Students need to assess themselves and understand what happened in a media or drama experience in order to plan future experiences.

Looking Further

1. Do one of the activities of critical television viewing, and discuss it with others in your college class.

2. Visit a library media center, and ask to preview several children's films for a grade you would like to teach. Start a resource file of film titles.

3. Show a film to children. After viewing, put them in watch-and-talk groups and listen to them. Plan a film response guide like the one in this chapter.

4. Do your own self-portrait and face poem. Then use them to model as you do this activity with a group of children

5. Play the witches' scene from *Macbeth* with a group of children.

Children's Books and Films

Ada, A. F. (2000). *Paths: Jose Marti, Frida Kahlo, Cesar Chavez.* Miami: Alfaguara. (Also in Spanish: Caminos)

Ada, A. F. (2000). *Steps: Rita Moreno, Fernando Botero, Evelyn Cisneros.* Miami: Alfaguara. (Also in Spanish: Pasos)

Andersen, Y. (1991). *Make your own animated movies and videotapes.* Boston: Little, Brown.

Apfel, N. (1988). *Nebulae: The birth and death of stars.* New York: Lothrop, Lee, & Shepard.

Apples [Film]. (1997). Available from DeBeck.

Ashpet: An American Cinderella [Film]. (1989). Available from Davenport Films.

Berger, M. (1992). *Discovering Mars: The amazing story of the red planet.* New York: Scholastic.

Bolognese, D. (1982). *Drawing spaceships and other spacecraft.* New York: Watts.

Brooks, P., & Walworth, N. (1962). *The world awakes: The Renaissance in Western Europe.* New York: Lippincott.

Brown, J. R. (1982). *Shakespeare and his theatre.* New York: Lothrop, Lee & Shepard.

Brown, M. (1957). *The three billy goats gruff.* New York: Harcourt Brace Jovanovich.

Bunting, E. (1994). *Smoky night.* San Diego: Harcourt Brace Jovanovich.

Chaoro, K. (1974). *Ida makes a movie.* New York: Seabury.

Christopher, J. (1967a). *The city of gold and lead.* New York: Macmillan.

Christopher, J. (1967b). *The white mountains.* New York: Macmillan.

Christopher, J. (1968). *The pool of fire.* New York: Macmillan.

Christopher, J. (1988). *When the tripods came.* New York: Dutton.

Chute, M. (1976). *Stories from Shakespeare.* New York: New American Library.

Cole, J. (1986). *The magic school bus, at the waterworks.* New York: Scholastic.

Cole, J. (1987). *The magic school bus, inside the earth.* New York: Scholastic.

Cole, J. (1989). *The magic school bus, inside the human body.* New York: Scholastic.

Cole, J. (1990). *The magic school bus, lost in the solar system.* New York: Scholastic.

Cole, J. (1992). *The magic school bus, on the ocean floor.* New York: Scholastic.

Cole, J. (1994). *The magic school bus, in the time of the dinosaurs.* New York: Scholastic.

Davis, O. (1982). *Langston.* New York: Delacorte.

Dr. Seuss's my many colored days [Film]. (1999). Available from the Minnesota Orchestra.

Fat Monroe [Film]. (1994). Available from Northfork Films.

Filipovic, A. (1994). *Zlatah's diary: A child's life in Sarajevo.* New York: Viking.

Gallant, R. (1986). *The Macmillan book of astronomy.* New York: Macmillan.

Garfield, L. (1985). *Shakespeare stories.* New York: Schocken.

Gibbons, G. (1983). *Sun up, sun down*. New York: Scholastic.

Haines, C. (1968). *William Shakespeare and his plays*. New York: Franklin Watts.

Hoban, T. (1982). *A, B, see!* New York: Greenwillow.

Hodges, C. W. (1966). *Shakespeare's theatre*. New York: Coward McCann.

Kirtland, G. B. (1962). *One day in Elizabethan England*. New York: Harcourt Brace Jovanovich.

L'Engle, M. (1962). *A wrinkle in time*. New York: Farrar, Straus, & Giroux.

L'Engle, M. (1973). *A wind in the door*. New York: Farrar, Straus, & Giroux.

L'Engle, M. (1978). *A swiftly tilting planet*. New York: Farrar, Straus, & Giroux.

Lamb, C., & Lamb, M. (1979). *Tales from Shakespeare*. New York: Dutton.

Lauber, P. (1989). *Meteors and meteorites: Voyagers from space*. New York: Scholastic.

Lauber, P. (1993). *Journey to the planets* (4th ed.). New York: Crown.

Lindgren, A. (1981). *Pippi Longstocking* (L. S. Glanzman, Illus.; F. Lamborn, Trans.). New York: Buccaneer Books.

Lobel, A. (1966). *Martha the movie mouse*. New York: Harper & Row.

Lomas Garza, C. (1994). *A piece of my heart: The art of Carmen Lomas/Pedacito de mi corazon*. New York: New Press.

MacLachlan, P. (1985). *Sarah, plain and tall*. New York: Harper & Row.

Maruiki, T. (1980). *Hiroshima no pika*. New York: Lothrop, Lee, & Shepard.

Marzollo, J., & Marzollo, C. (1982). *Jed's junior space patrol: A science fiction easy-to-read*. New York: Dial.

Miles, B. (1985). *Favorite tales from Shakespeare*. New York: Macmillan.

Molly's pilgrim [Film]. (1985). Available from Phoenix Films.

Neimark, A. (1992). *Diego Rivera: Artist of the people*. New York: HarperCollins.

Pena, (A. (1995). *Pena on Pena*. Waco, TX: WRS.

Pinkwater, D. (1990). *Borgel*. New York: Macmillan.

Quilt [Film]. (1998). Available from National Film Board of Canada.

Ross, S. (1994). *Shakespeare and Macbeth: The story behind the play*. New York: Viking.

Sendak, M. (1963). *Where the wild things are*. New York: Harper & Row.

Service, P. (1988). *Stinker from space*. New York: Scribner's.

Shirreffs, G. D. (1962). *The mystery of the haunted mine*. New York: Scholastic.

Sills, L. (1989). *Inspirations: Stories about women artists*. New York: Whitman.

Simon, S. (1985). *Jupiter*. New York: Morrow.

Simon, S. (1988). *Galaxies*. New York: Morrow.

Slote, A. (1975). *My robot buddy*. New York: Lippincott.

Snowman, The [Film]. (1982). Available from Weston Woods.

Stanley, D., & Vennema, P. (1992). *Bard of Avon: The story of William Shakespeare*. New York: Morrow.

Tender tale of Cinderella Penguin, The [Film]. (1982). Available from National Film Board of Canada.

Turner, R. M. (1993). *Portraits of women artists for children: Frida Kahlo*. New York: Little, Brown.

White, A. T. (1955). *Will Shakespeare and the Globe Theatre*. New York: Random House.

Winter, J. (1991). *Diego*. New York: Knopf.

Winter, J. (2002). *Frida*. New York: Scholastic.

Wood, A. (1985). *The napping house*. New York: Weston Woods.

Zea [Film]. (1981). Available from National Film Board of Canada.

chapter 13

Technology in the Classroom

Questions about Technology in the Classroom

- *What is the role of technology in the classroom?*
- *What is the relationship of technology and the language arts?*

REFLECTIVE RESPONSE

What actual experiences did you have with technology in elementary and middle school? How did these experiences compare with those you had outside the classroom? Jot down what you remember about your own technological experiences in school. Then brainstorm a list of all the things you could do with technology in your own classroom. Consider all the possibilities on this one.

Technology and the Language Arts

I asked the same two questions about technology in the classroom of Basia Glid-don, one of my former students at California State University, Long Beach. Basia earned a master's degree in educational technology and is now the computer fa-cilitator at De Mille Middle School in Long Beach, California. She works in the computer lab, teaching the technical aspects of computers to facilitate classroom learning. Classroom teachers sign in with her to schedule times for their students to use computers for specific projects.

CW

Hear an interview with Basia Gliddon.

So, how did Basia answer the questions? First, What is the role of technology in the classroom? Basia made three points in responding:

1. *Computers are the future—and it is here!* I frequently speak about technology education to teachers and counselors and also in the community. I tell people that computers are the future and it is here. Our students must use technology to be prepared for the world. I am part of a school-to-career consortium. Business leaders participate and support our programs because they want schools and universities to turn out students who can use computers. We teach lifelong skills for the future.

2. *Students learn.* Students are enthusiastic, positive, and motivated to learn technology skills and to get their work done without knowing it. I find students also reach for higher levels of thinking. They are intellectually stimulated. Students are so engaged, for example, in writing and revising on the computer—especially English language learners who can revise their writing easily using tools like spell check. When I work with these students, we can directly correct their writing on the screen in front of them. Also, I have no discipline problems in the lab. Creativity flows when students do a HyperStudio project or design a webpage. It's all beautiful! Almost everything on the computer is educational. I love it when I hear "oohs" and "aahs." Students use technology naturally and casually. They are into it. It's beyond typing.

3. *Teachers learn.* Language arts was my favorite part of teaching. I loved reading stories, children's literature, art, and creativity. I've just transferred that love from using books, chalk, and paints to the computer, which I like even better. Teaching with technology is a different kind of challenge for teachers but with many advantages. Like myself, many teachers didn't have the experiences with technology that we give our students today, so we learn along with them. Teachers schedule meetings with me to talk about how I can facilitate classroom instruction. I might explain to a new teacher about Internet research or HyperStudio and how it can help their students learn. I schedule times for their classes to come in and work on projects. The teachers are involved with students doing their research, instead of just word processing on the computer. I show them how they can do a wonderful card display using HyperStudio with scanned pictures and backgrounds. I tell them it would be great for the school's open house, using animation and movies. And I show them how to put it on a disk, print it out, and put it on a bulletin board. The teachers tell me what they need, we align it with the content standards [see Table 13.1], and I help them apply the technology. We work as a team.

In answer to the second question—What is the relationship between technology and language arts?—Basia answered that technology and language arts come together in two main areas:

1. *Word processing.* This is the simplest level. I help students word process their writing and reports and use electronic messaging.

2. *Projects.* Students can begin by doing research on a topic on the Internet. They gather facts and compile them into reports. They do basic word processing but can add clip art, scan original photographs or other images, and get screen shots off the Internet. The next level is to do a more complex hypermedia project—for example, using software like HyperStudio.

In sum, Basia offered these insights into the benefits of technology:

> Using the computer promotes cognitive development because there is the constant element of problem solving. The computer is one big problem waiting to be solved at every step. Students use creativity, logic, perseverance, and all the things it takes to be successful in school and life. It is also multidimensional, engaging visual, auditory, and kinesthetic senses, which when used together have been proven to be successful teaching techniques for struggling students and students with learning problems as well as regular education students.

WWW

Language Arts
Children's Literature Web Guide
www.acs.ucalgary.ca/ ~dkbrown/index.html

Multicultural Book Review Homepage
www.isomedia.com/homes/ jmele/homepage.html

Shakespeare Web
www.shakespeare.com/

SCAFFOLDING

Note the benefits of using technology with students who have learning difficulties, as summed up by computer lab teacher Basia Gliddon.

Table 13.1 *National Educational Technology Standards*

1. **Basic operations and concepts**
   - Students demonstrate a sound understanding of the nature and operation of technology systems.
   - Students are proficient in the use of technology.

2. **Social, ethical, and human issues**
   - Students understand the ethical, cultural, and societal issues related to technology.
   - Students practice responsible use of technology systems, information, and software.
   - Students develop positive attitudes toward technology uses that support life-long learning, collaboration, personal pursuits, and productivity.

3. **Technology productivity tools**
   - Students use technology tools to enhance learning, increase productivity, and promote creativity.
   - Students use productivity tools to collaborate in constructing technology-enhanced models, preparing publications, and producing other creative works.

4. **Technology communication tools**
   - Students use telecommunications to collaborate, publish, and interact with peers, experts, and other audiences.
   - Students use a variety of media and formats to communicate information and ideas effectively to multiple audiences.

5. **Technology research tools**
   - Students use technology to locate, evaluate, and collect information from a variety of sources.
   - Students use technology tools to process data and report results.
   - Students evaluate and select new information resources and technological innovations based on the appropriateness to specific tasks.

6. **Technology problem-solving and decision-making tools**
   - Students use technology resources for solving problems and making informed decisions.
   - Students employ technology in the development of strategies for solving problems in the real world.

Source: Reprinted with permission from *National Educational Technology Standards for Students—Connecting Curriculum and Technology,* copyright © 2000, ISTE (International Society for Technology in Education), 800.336.5191 (U.S. & Canada) or 541.302.3777 (Int'l), <iste@iste.org>, <www.iste.org>. All rights reserved. Permission does not constitute an endorsement by ISTE. For more information about the NETS Project, contact Lajeane Thomas, *Director, NETS Project,* 318.257.3923, <lthomas@latech.edu>.

The rest of the chapter will focus on these connections between technology and language arts, looking specifically at word processing and multimedia projects. In addition, tools and resources will be identified for using technology in teaching language arts in the classroom.

Word Processing

EXCELLENT SOFTWARE

Word Processing

For students in grades K–5, try Clarisworks and Apple Works (Macintosh) and Microsoft Word (PC and Macintosh).

Keyboarding

Try Kid Keys for students in grades K–1 and Keywords Elementary for those in grades 2–5.

Elementary students spend most of their computer time in language arts learning how to keyboard (that is, type) and using word-processing programs (Office of Technology Assessment, 1995). Certainly, word processing and desktop publishing are the most widespread uses of computers in language arts because they provide substantial aids to writing.

The basic functions of *word-processing programs* are inputting text, storing and retrieving it, formatting it, editing it, publishing it, and in some cases, adding simple graphics to it, such as diagrams and charts. Innovations such as word processors, which actually talk with synthesized speech and have speech-to-text capabilities, increase access for all students, including those who are English language learners (ELL) and who have language and learning limitations. *Desktop publishing* goes beyond word processing in that it allows students to publish their writing, including a wide range of graphics.

Although keyboarding skill is not a prerequisite for writing on the computer, it does help make writing more proficient and thus less frustrating. Practice using keyboarding software for 10 to 15 minutes at a time can help children develop the skills they need. Children can then readily get their ideas down, revise, and write longer and more detailed stories on the computer.

Even the youngest children can have experiences with word processing. Teachers can take dictation from younger students using word-processing programs, which is another application of the language experience approach (LEA). Students can brainstorm ideas, make idea lists and "word walls," and compose, all of which the teacher can record. Multiple copies of a composition can be printed for the student's revising, and then a final draft can be edited and printed for illustrating and bookmaking.

Older students through middle school can have experiences appropriate to their abilities and needs, doing some projects individually and others in groups. Students of all ages and abilities benefit greatly from the social, collaborative, and cooperative environment of groups writing together at computers.

Dee Qualls, the computer lab specialist at Emerson Elementary School in Long Beach Unified School District, begins word-processing projects with students using Clarisworks and Apple Works software. She gives students the simple format of an empty rectangular box, which they can fill with a drawing and then add text below. They can either create both the drawing and the text on the computer, or they can type in the text, print out the page with a blank box, and then add a hand-drawn illustration. Note that the next few illustrations are examples of student work that was created using this format.

Here are more examples of word-processing experiences for students in grades K–8:

Kindergarten through Grade 2

- *Language Experience Stories:* Children dictate stories to the teacher on topics such as their experiences, holidays, and field trips.
- *Interactive Group Stories:* Each child dictates or writes a sentence on a story topic.
- *Alphabet Books:* Students' books should be based on a theme, such as a season, the weather, animals, the class, the school, or the city.
- *Community Journals:* Children date each entry and all write about the same thing—for instance, the class pet.
- *"All about Me" Books:* Each page is about a different aspect of the child's life, such as his or her interests, family, and so on.
- *"All about Us" Books:* Each student creates his or her own page, and all the pages are compiled into a class book.
- *Themed Books:* Individuals or groups of children write on a content-area topic—for example, water or rocks.
- *Riddle Projects:* A "What Am I?" project could be about an animal or a dinosaur. A "Who Am I?" project could be about a community worker or a famous person.

Who Am I?
I walk in the door every morning.
I have to be able to read and
write. I need to teach them math,
writing, science, and spelling. I need
to be able to know how to do a
paper cutter and zerox machine.
Who am I?

Grades 3 through 5

- *Autobiographies:* Each child writes the story of his or her life.
- *Biographies:* Students write about other people, famous or otherwise, perhaps using information from the Internet.
- *Mini–Research Reports:* Students use a CD–ROM encyclopedia and other electronic media to write reports.
- *Timelines:* The student chronicles his or her own life, that of a historical figure, or even a historical period.
- *Riddle Projects:* Students could explore geometric shapes through "What Am I?" projects or historical figures through "Who Am I?" projects.
- *Stories:* Children keep separate files for all their writing to be used during writing workshop.
- *Newspapers:* Students create newspapers that cover the class, the school, the world, or another period of history.
- *Scripts:* Students write scripts for reader's theater, plays, puppet shows, or other dramas.
- *Poetry Forms:* Students write poems using free verse, haiku, tanka, diamante, or any other forms.

EXCELLENT SOFTWARE

Electronic Encyclopedias
From least to most difficult:

1. Grolier
2. World Book
3. Encarta

Summer
Hot, sunny,
Surfing, playing, resting
Swimsuit, shorts, mittens, jacket,
Snowboarding, playing, resting
Cold, snowy
Winter

Grades 6 through 8

- *Reports in the Content Areas:* Children work on independent science projects that include text along with tables, graphs, and a bibliography.
- *Expressive Writing:* Students write poetry, short stories, scripts, collections of all these, or books.
- *Newsletters:* Student-created newsletters could cover school or club events and be formatted using banners, columns, scanned photographs, and other newspaper conventions.
- *Editorials:* Children write opinion pieces and then post them on a school website or electronic bulletin board.
- *Posters and Advertisements:* Students decide how to announce a special event or meeting, writing the text and choosing the appropriate format and graphics.
- *Storyboards:* Children create the illustrations and add accompanying text for video or hypermedia projects.

The Writing Process

In Chapter 9, The Writing Process, you saw how teachers put the process approach to writing into practice using writing workshop (Atwell, 1987; Calkins, 1983; Graves, 1983). Word processing can be an integral part of this approach.

Research on word processing and writing shows that students' attitudes toward the fluency and length of writing can be improved and revising can be made faster and easier when students write using word processing. Even so, word-processing programs are not by themselves critical in improving the quality of student writing nor are such programs aligned with key elements of the writing process (Klein & Olson, 2001; Reed, 1996). For example, the programs don't provide support for prewriting or for specific rewriting or revising strategies. They do, however, facilitate student writing during the drafting stage.

Older students will have learned and practiced the skills involved in prewriting, drafting, and rewriting through their writing experiences. But younger students, who are still beginning writers, will need additional support along with help from their teacher and peers. The following sections address how to integrate technology into each aspect of the writing process.

Prewriting

During a brainstorming session, the teacher can make a list of ideas for writing, print it out, and then make copies to be posted on a bulletin board or transparency or saved in a file for students to review. The same can be done for a focused piece of writing, noting key ideas, questions, and prompts students might write about. A rubric for assessment could also be generated this way and revised as needed. Younger students can do a cluster of ideas, and older students can use the outlining function of word-processing software to plan a piece of writing.

Drafting

As noted earlier, using word-processing software can increase the fluency of student writing by making it easy to get ideas down, think about them, and then delete, add, and move pieces of text. Each student can draft on his or her own, with the teacher, or with a buddy or small group. Collaborative writing pieces can easily be generated using word processing, with one student keyboarding and recording the ideas of others, who watch what they are saying appear on the computer monitor.

Revising

Word processing is a powerful tool in the revising stage. Young writers, who may labor over every letter and word they put on paper and then be understandably reluctant to erase and redo or copy over their work, can make revisions easily using word processing. Using the functions found in most word-processing software—such as delete, copy, and paste—a single piece of writing can be reviewed, revised, saved, and retrieved countless times, without any retyping. Revising in this manner is incomparably easier than doing so with paper and pencil. Moreover, students can save and print out the day's work and see immediate results and progress.

Using a printout, or *hard copy,* students can make notes on their writing to prepare for the next day's work. And others can respond to their work and offer feedback, whether on hard copy in a peer-editing group or onscreen while work is in progress. Changes can be implemented instantly and the process continued without delay and frustration.

Editing

The editing tools available with word processing greatly simplify many aspects of editing before publishing. Using the spell- and grammar-check functions, in particular, can greatly facilitate editing, not only finding errors but also identifying overused patterns and constructions, such as passive voice. The find and search-and-replace functions can also prove useful in editing—for instance, checking for redundant word use.

Teachers can monitor students at the editing stage or work directly with them, but students should not depend on their teachers for the accuracy of their finished work. Working with buddies or in small groups at the computer will provide students with instant feedback on editing issues, such as spelling errors.

Publishing

Word processing and desktop publishing improve and expand publishing opportunities for children. For example, formatting a page so that the lines are justified and evenly spaced and the paragraphs are all perfectly indented greatly improves the appearance of the finished piece. And these are quite simple things to do with most writing software.

With just a little more skill, students can add borders, icons, charts, diagrams, and illustrations to present their work for publication on a bulletin board,

www

Publishing
Global Show and Tell
**www.learn.motion.com/lim/
links/elelinks/ShowTell**
KidPub
www.kidpub.org/kidpub/
KidStuff Children's Publishing
**www.worldchat.com/public/
kidstuff/a.htm**
MidLink
www.cs.ucf.edu/~MidLink/

as a self-published book, or in a class writing collection. Informational reports can become part of a circular file on a topic and available to other students, or they can be expanded into HyperStudio projects.

Even more publishing opportunities are available through student publication sites on the Internet. And the use of e-mail should be explored for various types of informal communication.

Word Processing in Writing Workshop

A Snapshot in Chapter 9, The Writing Process, showed how Sheila Kline used writing workshop with her class of ELL students. Here's how word processing can be added to a typical middle-grade writing workshop using Sheila's format:

Conduct minilesson (7 minutes)
Check writing status (3 minutes)
Write (45 minutes)
  Prewrite
    List
    Cluster
    Quickwrite
    Diagram/plot
    Outline
  Draft
    Start a piece
    Collaborate with buddy, small group
    Conference with teacher
  Revise
    Program functions: add, delete, and move text; grammar check, spell check, and thesaurus; alphabetization (i.e., for bibliography of informational report)
    Peer-group response using hard copy or onscreen
    Conference with teacher
  Edit
    Program functions: grammar check, spell check, thesaurus, find, search and replace
  Publish
    Formatting: type size and font, line, page, document
    Print hard copy
    Post on bulletin board or put in book or class collection
    Add to circular file
    Electronic messaging
    Internet sites
Share published pieces (5 minutes)
  Print and read hard copy
Display

Dee Qualls recommends conducting 5- to 7-minute minilessons when students come to the computer lab in order to help them learn to use the many functions that will help them write. She types up some sample text, demonstrates how to use the function on the TV monitor connected to her computer, and then has students practice with their own writing.

Here are suggested topics for writing workshop minilessons:

- Inserting and deleting text
- Cutting or copying text and then moving or pasting it
- Moving sentences or paragraphs from later in the piece to earlier in the piece
- Working on paragraph formation
- Doing a spelling or grammar check during the editing phase

Dee expresses some of the same ideas about technology experiences for her K–5 students that Basia Gliddon did about her middle school students:

Children are extremely interested in and can be engaged in technology. The key is to tie computer use to what's going on in the classroom. For example, I can teach word-processing skills in the computer lab, but it is most effective when students bring their writing into the lab and I help them use their skills to fix their writing.

Technology also runs the gamut. We integrate word processing and writing with art, science, math, and social studies in collaboration with the classroom teacher. What is going on in the classroom determines what I will do with students in the computer lab. Technology is just a wonderful extension of the classroom, not separate from it.

Dee has developed a series of lesson plans to introduce children to various aspects of computer use—especially word-processing, graphics, and database programs—and to show children how to put together work from these various programs into a single document. One lesson plan introduces children in the classroom or in a computer lab to using the computer and a basic word-processing program, Clarisworks. Dee recommends a single two-hour session or two one-hour sessions. Her demonstration takes 30 minutes; the rest of the time is for student practice, during which she helps individuals one on one.

Electronic Messaging

Children with access to electronic messaging or e-mail (electronic mail) can communicate with others through written messages. Quite literally, e-mail opens up opportunities to communicate with people around the world.

To date, there is still little research on the impact of Internet use on children's learning. However, Dickey and Roblyer (1997) note these early indicators:

1. Access to the Internet at home as well as school facilitates learning to use online resources.
2. E-mail is the most used application, connecting users to others around the globe.
3. The teachers who use the Internet are the risk takers in other instructional areas, as well.

Future research on the results of e-mail use will give teachers a better picture of its impact on learning.

To guide the meaningful use of e-mail in the classroom by integrating it across the curriculum, Harris (1995, 1997) recommends thinking in terms of *activity structures* that can be adapted to any content, such as language arts. Here are some examples of e-mail activities:

- **Interpersonal Exchanges:** Messages are exchanged between individuals, between an individual and a group, and among groups.

Key pals are the electronic versions of pen pals.

Key Pals: Informal messages are exchanged among individuals or groups, perhaps to improve language skills or increase cultural understanding (see the Snapshot that follows).

Global Classrooms: Information is exchanged about a theme study in the classroom, such as variants of a folktale (again, see the Snapshot).

Electronic Appearances: Students chat via e-mail with a guest, such as an author whose books they have read and studied.

Structured e-mail activities, like corresponding with key pals and mentoring younger students, can be adapted to any content.

Electronic Mentoring: Older students mentor younger ones on a topic like making the transition to high school, or middle school students review and respond to writing by elementary students.

- **Information Collections:** Participants research and share information on a topic.

  Information Exchanges: Students choose a theme and share what they learn about it (e.g., book and film reviews).

  Electronic Publishing: Students submit their work to a collection—for instance, creating a literary magazine of poetry, short stories, and songs.

  Pooled Data Analysis: Children collect data from multiple sites—say, conducting an opinion poll on a current issue—which they combine and analyze.

- **Problem-Solving Projects:** Students exchange views on solving a problem.

  Information Searches: Students use clues to solve a problem, such as identifying a specific book or story.

  Electronic Process Writing: Children post drafts of their writing, perhaps for electronic peer editing.

  Parallel Problem Solving: Students exchange their solutions to the same problem—for example, how to respond to peer pressure.

  Sequential Creations: Individuals add to a collaborative creative work, such as a stanza to a poem or song.

  Social Action Projects: Groups take action to solve a real problem (e.g., racism or sexism in schools) and exchange reports of what happened.

These types of e-mail activities can be expanded with a list server that disseminates messages to sites on mailing lists or to newsgroups that post messages and responses from numerous members. Thus, the possibilities are endless for expanding the use of technology to communicate and learn across the curriculum.

SNAPSHOT Connecting Second-Grade Key Pals in the United States and China

 www

Cultural understanding as well as improved language and literacy skills and communication are the natural outcomes of corresponding with key pals in different countries (Rice, 1996). Ping Liu, who is Chinese, is a professor in the Department of Teacher Education at California State University, Long Beach, and coordinator of the university's Asian Bilingual Credential Program. She facilitated connecting second-grade key pals from Shandong Province, China, with children in an elementary school in Illinois when she was a professor at Elmhurst College (Liu, 2002/2003). The teacher in China wanted to improve

Global Key Pals
Friends and Partners
www.solar.rtd.utk.edu/
friends/home.html
Intercultural E-mail Classroom
Connections (IECC)
www.stolaf.edu/network/iecc

English instruction and cross-cultural understanding. The teacher in the United States wanted to improve her unit on Asian studies. With Ping's help, both teachers improved their students' intercultural understanding and communication, literacy, and technological skills.

E-Mail Exchanges between Classes

In the Chinese class of second-graders, the teacher led a class discussion and recorded the students' ideas, since they were not ready to write independently in English. The entire class composed one e-mail message together, which they sent to their American key pals.

In the American class, the teacher printed out copies of the e-mail message, which the students took home and read and discussed with their families. Individual students shared their individual responses and those of their families with the entire class twice a week. They generated questions and ideas to respond to their Chinese key pals, which they sent as a group message from the class.

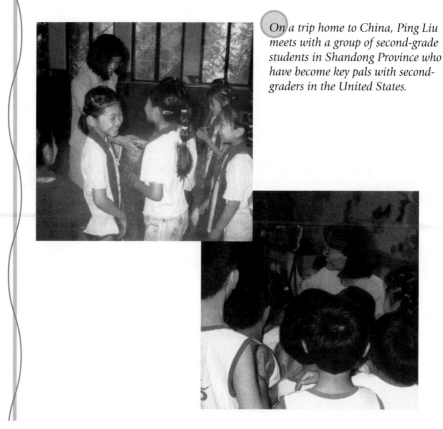

On a trip home to China, Ping Liu meets with a group of second-grade students in Shandong Province who have become key pals with second-graders in the United States.

Here are examples of some of the messages exchanged. First, the Chinese children e-mailed the American children:

> We are delighted to know about you. We are sure the pen pal writing will make us friends. There are four second classes in our school and in each class we have about 70 students. We are surprised to know that there are only 22 students in your class. What a difference! Now we are enjoying our winter holidays. New term will begin in about two weeks. We have just celebrated our Spring Festival that is the greatest time for us of the year. It has been another warm winter here. The lowest temperature is only 11 degree below zero (Centigrade) and this lasted only a dozen of days. Now Spring is coming. Plants and grass will turn green in no time. What's the weather like in your city? Is it very cold? Do you like spring? Why? What have you ever heard about China? We are looking forward to hearing from you soon.

The American students e-mailed back this message:

> We have a few questions for you. How many teachers do you have for each class of 70 students? Where is Shandong Province, China? We would like to find you on a map, however, we don't know where to look.

The Chinese children and their teacher responded:

> Our school is Linhu No. 1 Elementary School. It is in the northwest Shandong Province, China. Shandong Province is in the east of China. Can you find on the world map the Bohai Sea and Huanghai Sea? There is a peninsula between these two seas. That is Shandong Province. Binzhou is a small city of Shandong Province near the Yellow River.

E-Mail Exchanges between Individual Students

After a semester of exchanging group e-mails composed by their entire classes, students began to send individual messages and write letters. For example, Xin Wei wrote this letter in a combination of Chinese (which Ping translated for the class) and English (in italics):

> *Dear Friend,*
>
> *How are you! My name is Xin Wei.* I am *nine years old*. I am a second grade student in Linhu No. 1 Elementary School. I like to play football to keep me fit and strong. I also like to read *book* to gain knowledge. *I like English very much.* We have four seasons over here. It is quite dry all year

around. The sky in the fall is very high and *blue. We live near the Yellow River*. The color of water in the river is very yellow with a lot of sand. There are five grades in our school. There are about 280 students in the four classes of the second grade. During recess, we like to jump ropes, play sand bags, and *talking story. Welcome to visit our school*. Have you ever been to the Disney World? How do you like it? Any dinosaurs there. *Pleas writing to me*. Your friend, Xin Wei

The American teacher helped her students develop an electronic form that was designed using a computer program. It included categories of information such as the daily weather, school events and news, the content learned that day, and a personal corner. Individual students could use the form to input data and send personal messages. In the process, they learned a new computer application and the information was compiled in a key pal database to create an ongoing record of the students' correspondence.

Using Technology for Literacy Learning and Cross-Cultural Understanding

Students, teachers, administrators, and family members in both countries learned a great deal about one another's lives. They connected on a personal level through the very immediate and personal medium of electronic messaging. The Chinese children began to use the English they were learning for very real purposes, as did their teacher. And the American children, through Ping's visits to the class, heard her read a story in both English and Chinese, learned to write simple Chinese characters and eat with chopsticks, and saw folk crafts and pictures of Ping's home in China.

In their correspondence, the children realized their mutual interest in the environment. When the American children mentioned swimming in Lake Michigan, the Chinese children questioned them about it. No one can swim in the Yellow River in China because it's very muddy. For many years, severe damage to the vegetation and lack of protection on the river bank has put the river in danger. The two classes had a focused discussion on environmental protection. Similarly, when the Chinese children mentioned the social responsibility they had to work and maintain their school environment, the American children were curious, since they didn't contribute to the upkeep of their school. Following discussion about what the Chinese children did, the American children planned ways they could help improve their school.

The initial benefit from this year-long exchange was students' experiences with technology and English language and learning. However, the positive impact was quickly felt across the curriculum and throughout the students' homes and communities. Technology in the classroom united these people as a global village.

WWW

Collaborative Projects for Students

Global SchoolNet Foundation Internet Projects Registry
www.gsn.org/project/index. html

KIDPROJ
www.kidlink.org/KIDPROJ/

Multimedia Projects

The Internet connects computer networks worldwide, with an estimated 150 million users in 200 nations—and these numbers increase daily (Grabe & Grabe, 2000). *Multimedia projects* use the World Wide Web as a source of information on the Internet.

Here's a quick primer on the web: The basic unit is a *webpage* containing text. The user navigates from page to page through *hypertext*, which allows going beyond the word or words that identify a webpage by clicking on them and being connected to another webpage. The text on the webpage may also be considered hypertext because it can go beyond words when it includes graphics, sound, and video. One webpage may also link to another, so the user can jump from page to page or go to another website or collection of pages connected by a *homepage*. *Hyperlinks* are the elements of hypertext that enable users to move on the web and find the information they seek.

WWW

Beginning Research Sites
Internet Public Library
www.ipl.org/
Library of Congress
www.loc.gov/

The Internet

The World Wide Web has made it possible to access information on a topic and locate other Internet sources of information on that topic, as well. Teachers and students can use the Internet as another resource to do research—one that provides access to libraries, museums, governments, schools, and other institutions from around the world. To do so, they go to a website *address*, which is called a *uniform resource locator (URL)*.

Unlike the different sets of encyclopedias that a school library carefully considers before investing in any one, not all websites are even relatively equal in quality. Some are poorly designed and maintained, making them difficult to use and even unreliable in terms of the accuracy of information and the sources cited as having provided it. But the extent of coverage online is immense and constantly expanding and changing, which means the information available is generally the most current. In fact, information can appear on a website almost simultaneously with an event—for example, the result of a sporting event. Moreover, most websites focus on very specific subjects and are tailored to highly specific audiences—school-age students, for instance.

Students may begin research on the Internet in either of two ways. The first is to use a *subject directory*, such as Yahoo!, which lists general subject headings. This approach is useful when students are looking for general information. A second approach is to use a *search engine*, such as Excite, Lycos, AltaVista, and HotBot. The user types in *keywords* or *search strings*, and the engine searches the Internet for sources containing those words. Each source that's identified is called a *hit*.

Given the extent of information available online, it's important for students to use keywords and search strings that are as specific and concise as possi-

WWW

Search Engines
AltaVista
www.altavista.com
Eblast
www.eblast.com
Excite
www.excite.com
HotBot
www.hotbot.com
Infoseek
www.infoseek.com
Lycos
www.lycos.com
Magellan
www.mckinley.com
MetaCrawler
www.metacrawler.com
NetGuide Live
ms.netguide.com
Northern Light
www.northernlight.com
WebCrawler
www.webcrawler.com
WhoWhere?
www.whowhere.com
Yahoo!
www.yahoo.com

ble. Searching on *dog,* for instance, will return an overwhelming number of hits, which will be difficult and time consuming to sort through for really useful information. Using the keyword *poodle* will help focus the search significantly, and narrowing it further to *toy poodle* will help even more. The latter search would provide fewer hits than the first but more specific and thus relevant ones. Here are additional guidelines that will assist students in conducting efficient searches on the Internet (Grabe & Grabe, 2000):

1. Search for the singular form of a term, not the plural: *dinosaur,* not *dinosaurs.*
2. When searching for a phrase, enclose it within quotation marks: *"Civil War."* Otherwise, the search engine will consider the words individually and find every occurrence of each word.
3. Add wild card characters at the ends of words to substitute for missing letters. AltaVista, for example, uses an asterisk (*) as a wild card. Searching on *mor** will find *morgue, mortician, mortuary, mortal,* and so on.
4. Use *Boolean operators* to further narrow searches:
   - Join keywords using AND to find information about both of them together: *playground AND safety.*
   - Join keywords using OR to find information about one or the other separately: *Toyota OR Honda.*
   - Join keywords using AND NOT to exclude a term from the search: *Bird AND NOT "bald eagle."*
5. Form Boolean operators and phrases into logical groups using parentheses: (golden OR black) AND "Labrador retriever."

Introducing students to the Internet as a source of information should be approached in the same as any other mediated experience, print or nonprint: Students should be actively engaged in a process of constructing meaning. Activities should be student and response centered and contextualized through social interaction. Allowing students simply to surf the net is not enough. Just as teachers assess, plan, and guide instruction in language arts using books, discussions, "word walls," and so on, they should provide classroom experiences using the Internet following the same goals and strategies.

To help students conduct research on the Internet, teachers should follow these four basic steps:

1. *Introduce the Topic:* What is it? Why is it important? How is it connected to the curriculum?
2. *Identify the Task Related to the Topic:* What question is to be answered? What problem needs to be solved? What action should be taken?
3. *List Relevant Websites:* Identify the primary sources online where students can find information about the topic.
4. *Formulate the Process:* Decide on the best way to answer the question, solve the problem, or take the action.

ELL

SCAFFOLDING

This activity can easily be adapted for ELL students and students with disabilities.

Internet Scavenger Hunt

Children can begin to explore the Internet in the classroom with a scavenger hunt, working on their own or in groups. The teacher prepares a list of questions that can be answered or items that can be located by doing research on the Internet. Each student or group is then given the same amount of time to look for the answers or items. Individuals or groups can sign up for time to use the classroom computer, or the entire class can work at the same time using multiple computers in a computer lab.

The list of questions or items to be researched can be adapted in any number of ways: by grade level or level of English language development or for students with disabilities. Here is a partial list of questions and items suggested by Cafolla, Kauffman, and Knee (1997):

- Locate a map of Muppet Treasure Island.
- What is the current weather in each of these places: Fairbanks, Alaska; Honolulu, Hawaii; and the Virgin Islands?
- How many "no smoking" rooms are there at the Fort Wilderness Hotel in Disney World? What is the layout of a typical room?
- Where can you find information about the U.S. space program?
- Find a picture of the skeleton of a stegosaurus.
- Find the home page of Virtual World: The World's First Digital Theme Park.
- Find a picture of General Buford, a Union general who was instrumental in winning the Battle of Gettysburg during the Civil War.
- Find a picture of Albert Einstein sticking out his tongue.
- Find a picture of a fractal.
- Get a quote from *Bartlett's Familiar Quotations*.

Finally, one cautionary note: In preparing questions and items, teachers should make sure that students will be able to find the answers. Namely, it's important to verify that those websites containing the answers will be there when students do the project. The best way to make sure of this is to check each website on the morning of the day students will do the activity. Internet addresses change frequently, and websites come and go on a regular basis. Students will become quickly frustrated searching for websites that no longer exist.

Hear and see Dee Qualls use WebQuests with elementary students.

Another idea for helping students explore the Internet is to use *WebQuests*, or specific web-based research projects. Dee Qualls, the elementary computer lab specialist described earlier, uses WebQuests when supporting students' learning on topics of interest across the curriculum. Depending on their age and skill level, students can work alone, in groups, or in collaboration with the teacher.

WWW

Multimedia Authoring Systems

Digital Chisel
www.ppierian.com

HyperStudio
www.hyperstudio.com

HyperCard
www.hypercard.com

Superlink for Windows and
Multimedia ScrapBook
www.alchmediainc.com

Hypermedia

Having students complete *hypermedia* projects—using software such as Hyper-Studio and PowerPoint, for example—is increasing in K–8 classrooms. These highly engaging projects are used for learning across the curriculum as well as for the language arts, as students learn composition skills along with content (Garthwait, 2001).

Dee Qualls likes HyperStudio for students in grades K–5 because it fully integrates language and technology across the curriculum. Younger students can complete activities such as HyperStudio riddle projects: "Who Am I?" or "What Am I?" (e.g., a community worker, animal, dinosaur, or geometric shape). Older students can do timelines of their own lives or those of famous individuals or reports about topics such as the scientific process or a specific event in their state's history.

When I discussed technology and language arts with Basia Gliddon, who was introduced earlier in this chapter, she made an interesting analogy between hypermedia use, such as a HyperStudio project, and the student-centered, literature-based approach to teaching language arts advocated in this text. (As my former student, Basia was familiar with a previous edition of this book.) Here's what she said:

> HyperStudio is like the way you taught us to teach with literature—an active, student-centered approach using literature and students' own experiences and responses as a beginning point. Students read, respond, write, and then do extending activities, such as art, drama, music—possibly leading to a "ripple effect." As an elementary classroom teacher, I designed my teaching on this pattern, usually in a week-long sequence of literature-based thematic activities.
>
> With HyperStudio, it's the same. Students usually read and discuss informational texts, do a KWL chart, research facts on the Internet, plan and write up a 10-card stack—each with some information on the topic—and then put it together adding backgrounds, different fonts, music, animation, and voice-over narration. The results are 10 gorgeous cards, which can be displayed on the computer or printed out and put on a bulletin board.

Table 13.2 shows the similarities between the literature-based and technology-based approaches to teaching language arts across the curriculum. The specific materials and tasks associated with each approach are identified in the far-left and far-right columns, and the overlap between the two is shown in the middle. Hopefully, this presentation will help you to think about using technology as more than just a tool or a separate activity in a computer lab. Instead, it should be aligned with the constructivist, social interactionist, and transactional approaches to student- and response-centered teaching.

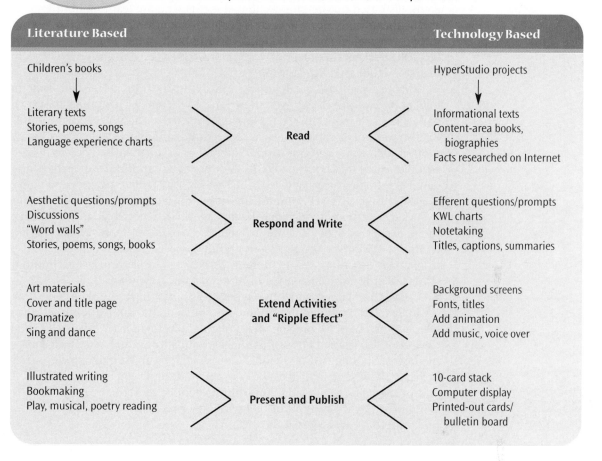

Literature Based		Technology Based
Children's books		HyperStudio projects
Literary texts Stories, poems, songs Language experience charts	**Read**	Informational texts Content-area books, biographies Facts researched on Internet
Aesthetic questions/prompts Discussions "Word walls" Stories, poems, songs, books	**Respond and Write**	Efferent questions/prompts KWL charts Notetaking Titles, captions, summaries
Art materials Cover and title page Dramatize Sing and dance	**Extend Activities and "Ripple Effect"**	Background screens Fonts, titles Add animation Add music, voice over
Illustrated writing Bookmaking Play, musical, poetry reading	**Present and Publish**	10-card stack Computer display Printed-out cards/ bulletin board

The following Snapshot shows an example of an integrated language arts project that resulted from collaboration between a computer facilitator and a Spanish language arts classroom teacher in a dual-immersion language program.

SNAPSHOT Eighth-Grade Latino Students Use HyperStudio to Tell Autobiographical Heritage Stories

Basia Gliddon teamed with James Oriheula, a bilingual teacher, to develop an autobiographical heritage project for his eighth-grade students. James teaches Spanish language arts all day to students in grades 6 through 8 at De Mille Middle School, where Basia is the computer facilitator. De Mille is one of 16 *dual-immersion programs* at a true middle school (not a K–8 school) in the

United States. James has taught here five years and is very proud of the program. It's based on the premise that students who are learning both English and Spanish will perform academically at the same level as other students but in two languages. James's students include both native English and native Spanish speakers, all of whom are learning to speak, read, write, and learn in the other language.

James was a bilingual student himself in the 1980s. He spent time in low-level, remedial classes even though he was actually performing at a much higher level in math, for example, than his English-only peers. Because his English was not a problem, he was moved out of bilingual classes and into the more academically rigorous classes taught in English. But when he was in high school, he saw that not all students had the same opportunity to achieve academically. So he became a teacher of Spanish for Spanish speakers and native English speakers, as well, working in the dual-immersion program at De Mille.

James teams with the English language arts teachers to align his teaching in Spanish with their teaching in English. For example, when teaching students about similes, the same terminology is used in both classes. He also teams with Basia to give his students the chance to learn to use technology while learning more language and content at the same time.

Basia and James planned a HyperStudio autobiographical heritage project in Spanish, in which the students researched and wrote about their own lives and heritages. To prepare, they collected photographs of themselves and their families, learned about their backgrounds from interviews with family members, and drafted individual autobiographical heritage stories. They brought all these materials to the computer lab on Day 1 of the project. The entire class came to the lab for 60-minute periods over a 10-day period. Here is a day-by-day description of this two-week project, which could serve as a blueprint for other HyperStudio projects.

Basia Gliddon admires Richard Sanchez's poem, "El Barrio," which is part of the autobiographical project he's completing in her middle school computer lab (see Figure 13.1, page 457).

Week 1: First Draft of a HyperStudio Project

Day 1: Create a 10-Card Stack

Basia gave an overview of the HyperStudio project. Each student made 10 *cards* (i.e., a card is what appears on the computer screen at any one time). Together, these cards comprise a *stack*, which is what a HyperStudio file is called. The student then added a background for each card—experimenting with different patterns, colors, and gradients—and saved it on the computer.

Next, Basia demonstrated how to do a storyboard on the white board in the computer lab. She drew boxes to represent the cards and told students that they must now decide what written text from their autobiographical essays would appear with the image on each card. Each student was to prepare a storyboard in this manner and bring it to the next lab session.

To guide students, Basia suggested that they think about how their unique lives and heritages have made them the people they are today. How might they show this in their HyperStudio projects? Together, the students brainstormed ideas, such as beginning as far back as they could in their family histories—perhaps with their grandparents or even earlier, if they have pictures. Or the students could begin with their own lives, starting when they were born.

Where to start and what to tell all depends on what pictures and artifacts each student provides. Some bring in many generations' worth of photos of their families; others bring in just school ID photos of themselves. If a student only has a few photos, he or she can still use backgrounds, text, animation, movies, sound, and music. In fact, the use of photos isn't required for this project, but it personalizes the project and represents a primary source of information. If a photo is wrinkled or otherwise damaged, it can be scanned and then fixed using PhotoShop. Basia maintains that with technology, all the projects turn out great.

Days 2 and 3: Write in Text Boxes

Next, students focused on adding written text to the cards and backgrounds they produced on Day 1. They opened their projects on the computer and selected the command to add text boxes. A *text box* is designed specifically to contain writing so the user doesn't have to write directly on the card. When in a text box, the writing can be changed and edited using a spell check without changing the background of the card. Basia recommends that students use invisible text boxes so the background of the card shows through behind the writing

Next, students inserted the text they had planned for each card using their storyboards. For instance, "This is me when I was 2 years old" might be added as a caption for a photograph. Students added writing to all 10 cards in this way, giving overviews of their life stories.

Adding voice was the next step. After students inserted written text, they added the sounds of their own voices reading the text or used a synthesized voice to simulate another person reading it, such as a grandparent or even a narrator. Basia recommends that the students choose the voices and the language used, whether English or a native language.

The final task on these days was editing and art. Students edited each text box for its size and placement on the card as well as the fonts and colors used. Basia feels this editing involves art as well as writing. Each student can work at his or her own level to produce a creative, self-expressive piece.

Days 4 and 5: Add Buttons and Special Effects

Buttons are the technology that allows transitioning from card to card and gives the user access to options such as QuickTime movies, play sounds, and other actions. To introduce students to this technology, Basia did a minilesson on buttons at the beginning of the session on Day 4 and reviewed it again at the beginning of the Day 5 session. Students worked through the lesson with her on their own computers, learning how to create buttons that allowed moving from card to card and to add special effects, such as animation, movies, clip art, fades, and sounds. Students also caught up on any changes they wanted to make to their cards and backgrounds, sometimes as a result of adding special effects.

At this point, students had basically created "rough drafts" of their HyperStudio stacks. They had completed the first week of their projects. On Day 5, they were told to bring photographs to the next lab session.

Week 2: Final Draft of a HyperStudio Project

Days 6 through 10: Add Primary Sources, Debug, and Fix

The first task this week was to scan primary sources. Basia demonstrated while the students followed along, scanning photographs and saving the images to folders on the computer. If they had no photographs, they searched for relevant images on the Internet—for instance, a picture of an event that occurred on the day a student was born.

Next, Basia helped students refine their project drafts, working with them one on one to debug and fix problem areas. Students also refined their special effects at this point. Basia says that each child finds something he or she loves and spends time on it.

Finally, Basia reviewed each student's project with him or her. If a group of children needed help with the same thing, Basia formed them into a group and did a quick review on the TV monitor. Otherwise, she provided individual feedback to students.

Basia says this is a fun week. Students fine-tune their projects or go deeper into the aspects of their projects that they find most interesting. They have the needed skills and know how to use them. Basia maintains that this is "technical language arts." It doesn't necessarily begin with reading a book or even teaching the core curriculum. Instead, it's a multimedia presentation of content-area work with background, text, sound, music, animation, movies, primary source material, and special effects. All the projects turn out differently.

In the end, each student produces a great project using technology that can be presented in two modes: (1) *electronically,* when students save the projects on disks and take them home for showing, and (2) *in print,* when the cards are printed out on paper (up to 4 cards per page) and posted on a bulletin board. (Obviously, the print version will have images and text but none of the special effects.) See Figure 13.1 for a sample of the cards produced by one of Basia's students.

Projects like this, as well as other computer activities, have particular benefits for ELL students. The box on page 458 describes how using computers supports these students' learning.

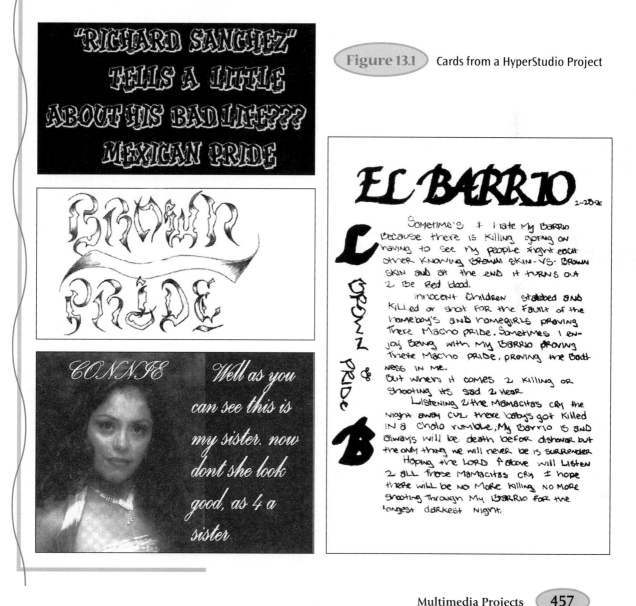

Figure 13.1 Cards from a HyperStudio Project

English Language Learners by Using Computers

Using computers has these advantages for English language learners:

1. Tools such as spelling checkers and grammar checkers make writing and revising easier.
2. The teacher and student can revise writing while reviewing it together on-screen.
3. Speech-to-text capabilities make learning more accessible.
4. A cooperative, collaborative environment supports context-embedded verbal interaction.
5. Stories can be presented in dual-language or closed-captioned format.
6. The student's primary language can be used in hypermedia text that integrates sound.

Assessing Multimedia Projects

Assessing projects created using technology in the classroom, such as the Hyper-Studio project just described, should be done using the same contextualized, authentic means used for assessing other student work. Basia developed the rubric shown in Assessment Toolbox 13.1 for the autobiographical project. Beginning with the purpose of the project—"To tell an autobiographical story using text and other media"—Basia examines how well the student used the technology and materials available to create a unique presentation.

Caveats on Technology in the Classroom

As Basia said in answering the questions at the opening of this chapter, "Computers are the future—and it is here." In fact, we are only beginning to feel the impact of technology on education, and the possibilities for future developments seem endless (Bruce & Levin, 2003; Kinzer & Leander, 2003).

Not everyone is completely enamored with bringing technology into the classroom, however. Critics offer these caveats, which you should be aware of:

- *Technology can become an end in itself.* Oppenheimer (1997) has observed that figuring out software can become the end result of learning, rather than providing purposeful and meaningful instruction, which is standards-based learning.

WWW

Software Reviews
EPIE Institute Courseware Review Form
www.columbia.edu/~jhb27/epieeval.html

The School House Review
www.worldvillage.com/wv/school/html/scholrev.htm

Software Evaluation Clearinghouse
www.netc.org/software/clearinghouse.html

SuperKids Educational Software Review
www.superkids.com/aweb/pages/reviews/reviews/html

Way Cool Software Reviews
www.ucc.uconn.edu/~wwwpcse/wcool.html

ASSESSMENT TOOLBOX

13.1 Rubric for a Hyperstudio Project

Basia Gliddon developed this rubric to evaluate the autobiographical projects students created using HyperStudio in computer lab. The rubric can be adapted to fit any number of multimedia projects.

Name _____ Date _____

Rubric for HyperStudio Project

Purpose: To tell an autobiographical story using text and other media

	Exceeds Expectations 4	Excellent 3	Satisfactory 2	Needs Improvement 1
Told the Story Using Text				

☐ 1. Created a 10-card HyperStudio stack.

☐ 2. Added background to each card.

☐ 3. Added a text box with lines to each card.

☐ 4. Created a storyboard for the 10-card stack.

Told the Story Using Other Media	4	3	2	1

The student created cards that were as artistic as possible to add visual and auditory impact to the story, using at least 4 of the following options (*Note:* Projects using primary source materials to be evaluated at a higher level):

☐ 1. Primary sources of images: *Comments*

    ☐ Family photos

    ☐ Historical photos

☐ 2. Images imported from:

    ☐ Internet

    ☐ Clip art

    ☐ Icons

☐ 3. Images drawn free hand.

☐ 4. Animation added.

☐ 5. Movies added.

☐ 6. Music added.

☐ 7. Voices used:

    ☐ Synthesized voices

    ☐ Read text aloud in English and/or Spanish

www

Internet FIltering Software

Cyber Patrol, Microsystems
Software
www.cyberpatrol.com

SurfWatch, Spyglass, Inc.
www.surfwatch.com

CYBERsitter, Solid Oak
Woftware, Inc.
www.cybersitter.com

Net Nanny, Net Nanny Software
International, Inc.
www.netnanny.com

www

Teach children to use
directories that limit searches
to safe websites:

Blue Web'n
**www.kn.pacbell.com/wired/
bluewebn/**

Kidlink
www.kidlink.org

Magellan
www.mckinley.com/

Yahooligans
www.yahooligans.com/

www

Find more on guidelines for
online safety at **www.safekids.
com/kidsrules.htm.**

- *Group work may not be effective.* Oppenheimer (1997) has also observed that even though children tend to cluster and work in groups around the computer, only one child at a time is actually engaged in the activity, which means the others may only be learning incidentally.
- *Computers add confusion to the classroom.* Sandholtz et al. (1997) maintain that computers are a distraction and add to the level of activity and noise in the classroom. Given this, computers may interfere with the learning of those students working elsewhere in the classroom—perhaps reading, for instance.
- *Research on the positive effects of technology is questionable.* Critics have condemned studies on the effectiveness of technology in the classroom with having faulty experimental designs (Becker, 1994; Weller, 1996). Moreover, some researchers have suggested that the positive results produced can be attributed to the intensive time students have spent with technology, rather than the helpful effects of technology itself.
- *It's difficult to keep pace.* Computer hardware and software, as well as other forms of technology, change at an increasingly rapid pace, requiring that schools upgrade and otherwise keep up in terms of purchasing equipment and training teachers.
- *Technology is expensive.* The cost of technology puts a financial burden on schools and school districts. This is true not only of the initial investment required but also of the regular expenditures needed to upgrade and replace technology.
- *Technological resources are not distributed equitably.* Schools in low-income areas are less likely than those in middle- and high-income areas to receive parental or community support for technology or to have computers in students' homes, thereby widening the gap between the rich and poor.

Finally, teachers must be aware of the potential dangers of children's using the Internet. Whether inadvertently or intentionally, children may access materials that have inappropriate content (e.g., sexually explicit materials), that promote hatred of a specific group, or that encourage dangerous or unlawful activities. Particularly dangerous are situations in which children encounter individuals through e-mail or chatrooms who eventually attempt to meet the children. Harassment—perhaps through demeaning or threatening messages or even legal or financial threats—may also result from these supposedly anonymous online communications.

Given these realities, teachers must take steps to protect their students from having negative experiences on the Internet. Internet content can be monitored through several types of software:

1. A *firewall*, which controls data within a school district's computer network
2. *Filtering software* designed for both home and school, such as Cyber Patrol

In addition, children should learn some basic Internet safety guidelines, perhaps as part of a set of class rules. Those guidelines should include the following:

1. Never reveal personal information, such as your name, your parents' names, your address, or your telephone number.
2. Never agree to meet in person anyone you've encountered on the Internet.
3. Don't share your e-mail password with anyone.
4. Don't send harmful messages, even as a joke.
5. Tell the teacher about any messages you receive that make you uncomfortable and any websites you come across that are inappropriate.

Answers to Questions about Technology in the Classroom

● *What is the role of technology in the classroom?*

Students in today's classrooms must learn to use technology to be prepared for the world of tomorrow. Technology is engaging and motivating and encourages students to use higher levels of thinking. Moreover, students benefit from participating in the social, collaborative, and cooperative environment that typically characterizes groups working at computers.

Technology can be applied across the curriculum, integrating word processing and writing with content areas such as art, science, math, and social studies. Students and teachers can use a variety of technological and informational resources to gather and synthesize information and to create and communicate knowledge. Technology should never be presented as merely a tool or as a separate activity conducted in a computer lab. Nor is it sufficient simply to allow students to play games on the computer or to surf the net. Rather, technology should be presented through classroom activities that are student and response centered and that are contextualized through social interaction in a purposeful, meaning-centered process. In the best sense, technology is another means with which teachers can help children learn—to find answers to questions, to solve problems, and to expand their understandings of topics.

Technology can be assessed with rubrics similar to those developed for writing. Assessment should be aligned with content standards for teaching with technology. Teachers should be mindful of certain caveats regarding technology in the classroom, such as allowing it to become an end in itself, and they should take steps to protect children from the potential dangers of using the Internet.

● *What is the relationship of technology and the language arts?*

Technology and the language arts come together in two main areas: word processing and multimedia projects.

Word processing is the most widespread use of computers in the language arts because it aids in the writing process. Students can use word processing to write and revise both literary texts and informational reports. Revising and editing writing are relatively easy on the computer using functions such as deleting and adding text and tools such as spelling and grammar checks. English language learners and other students who need support in developing literacy skills are especially benefited by computer use. Teachers can conference with students and directly edit and revise their writing with them onscreen. Students can also use electronic messaging to communicate within the classroom, the school, and the community or even around the world. Activity structures can be adapted to any content, such as the language arts, using interpersonal exchanges (e.g., key pals), information collections (e.g., pooled data analysis), and problem-solving projects (e.g., social action projects). As an extension of word processing, desktop publishing allows students to publish their work in a variety of styles and formats.

Multimedia projects use the World Wide Web as a source of information on the Internet. Students can learn to research a topic on the Internet, gathering facts and compiling them to create a textual report that can be enhanced with clip art, scanned photographs, and screen shots downloaded from the Internet. More complex multimedia projects can be completed using software such as HyperStudio and PowerPoint.

Looking Further

1. With your college classmates, make a list of the websites and software programs recommended in the marginal notes of this chapter. Have each student choose and review one or more of these and share his or her observations with others in a small group. Make sure at least one student or group goes to the Safe Kids website at **www. safekids.com/ kidsrules.htm.** Use what you learn to create a poster of rules for online safety for elementary students.

2. Create a listserv for your college class, and try out some of the activity structures for integrating e-mail in the classroom—for example, electronic mentoring (exchange lesson plan ideas for field experiences), information exchanges (share reviews of educational websites), and parallel problem solving (exchange ideas about classroom management issues or infield experiences).

3. With your own classmates, identify one issue of concern regarding how technology is integrated into teaching the language arts. Have each student research this issue using the Internet and write a summary of his or her findings and sources (e.g., useful websites). Make and distribute copies of all the summaries among classmates. Discuss the results as a class or in small groups.

4. By yourself or with a partner, create an Internet scavenger hunt for children of a specific grade level. Try it out with children in that grade, and report back to your own class about what happened. (If possible, plan the hunt around a unit or theme relevant to what the children are currently studying.)

5. In a computer lab, try out an educational software program that is generally well recommended, and create a project for students of a specific grade level. For example, use Inspiration to do a graphic organizer for a literature unit. Make notes about what students will need to know about using the program, and share your own project with students as a model on which they can base their own.

chapter 14

Language across the Curriculum

- *What does* language across the curriculum *mean?*
- *How should we use literary and informational texts in thematic teaching?*

REFLECTIVE RESPONSE

Think of a special theme you learned about in elementary school. In what ways did you learn to use language in learning about that theme? Did you read and write both literary texts and informational texts related to that theme? Also, pick a color and write about how you would portray it through pantomime. Jot down your ideas.

Understanding Language across the Curriculum

Language across the curriculum means to integrate teaching the language arts of thinking, listening, speaking, reading, writing, viewing, and visually representing with teaching in the content areas, such as social studies, science, mathematics, and music and the arts (Chancer & Rester-Zodrow, 1997; Franks, 2001; Froese, 1994; Leggo & Sakai, 1997; Matthews & Rainer, 2001; Tevebaugh, 2001).

IRA/ NCTE

Integrated language arts, as defined in the *Standards for the English Language Arts* (1996): "A *curricular* organization in which students study and use the language components of speaking, listening, reading, and writing as a mutually reinforcing process that evolves through a unified core of concepts and activities."

Language across the curriculum is based on three principles:

1. All genuine learning involves discovery.
2. Language has a heuristic function (that is, language is a means to learn).
3. Using language to discover is the best way to learn (Bullock, 1975).

In a student- and response-centered classroom, language across the curriculum means using an integrated approach to teaching. Students ask questions, identify and solve problems, and discover the interconnectedness of subject matter (Gray, 2001). And teachers plan experiences that enable students to do these things. In describing how to integrate language arts across the curriculum, we will consider thematic teaching and the specific uses of literary and informational texts.

Thematic Teaching

See the companion book to this text, *Schoolyear Activities Planner*, for a year of themes and related materials.

I'll never forget the thematic unit we did when I was in the fourth grade in Mrs. Canaday's class. When Hawaii became a state, everything we did was related to Hawaii. I got to lead the hula when we presented what we learned for parents and other classes. It was great!

Thematic teaching has a long history in education (Vars, 1991). Sipe (1994) notes that "educational practice dating back to Socratic discussions reflects the value of organizing instruction around meaningful questions as both a method for examining existing knowledge and for generating questions that may lead to the development of new knowledge" (p. 1213). Educational reform movements since the eighteenth century have advocated integration of subjects. John Dewey promoted units in the 1920s and 1930s as part of progressive education. And in the 1960s and beginning again in the 1980s with the whole-language movement, we saw teaching around themes (Buckley, 1994).

This approach has been called various names, such as *units* and *thematic units*. Today, the terms used include *theme study, theme cycles* (Altwerger & Flores, 1994; Kucer, Silva, & Delgado-Larocco, 1995), and *integrated, cross-curricular*, and *thematic teaching*. I call these *"ripple effects" of response-themed learning* because I know that they're not totally planned by teachers. Rather, one idea or activity will be like a pebble thrown into a pond, generating ripples that grow and spread across the curriculum, depending on the ideas, interests, and experiences of students.

The idea behind all these terms is the use of language across the curriculum. Specifically, children will learn to use language as they use language to learn in other subjects (Tchudi & Lafer, 1996) through thematic teaching. We've already looked at many examples of thematic teaching in this text, many of which I've referred to as ripple effects. Table 14.1 lists examples of these.

I explain the "ripple effect" in more detail in Chapter 1, Learning and Teaching Language Arts.

Reading and Writing Both Aesthetically and Efferently

In integrating the language arts by using themes, both literary and informational texts are used for reading and as models for writing. It is not only important for teachers to be familiar with these two types of texts but also to encourage children to take the appropriate *stance* for each type of reading and writing.

Table 14.1		Examples in This Text of Thematic Teaching
Grade	**Chapter**	**Theme: Activities**
K	4	Animals and the zoo: fieldtrip, reading, writing, and drama
K–3	8	Core book unit on *People* (Spier, 1980)
1	4	Apples: experiences with and about apples
1–2	7	Author unit on Eric Carle: focus on his books about insects and animals
2	7	Genre unit on fairytales: focus on "Cinderella" stories
3	3	Millions: mathematics for English language learners using *Millions of Cats* (Gag, 1928/1956)
3	8	Columbus and the Taino people: events of 1492 from different perspectives (those of Columbus, Europeans, and Native Americans)
3	12	Solar system and science fiction: science, writing, drama, and filmmaking
3–4	14	Colors: in nature, poetry, art, music, people (cultural and racial diversity in the United States)
4	1	Our community and state: adaptable to any community
4	7	Desert of the Southwest United States: geography, history, and culture (Native, Hispanic, and Anglo Americans)
4–5	8	Author/illustrator unit on the Pinkneys; reading and writing biographies of African Americans
4–8	7	Core book unit on *Treasure Island* (Stevenson, 1947): intensive study of a classic, related topics
8	13	HyperStudio personal heritage projects

In her transactional theory, Louise Rosenblatt (1994) argues convincingly about this point. Namely, children should take a primarily *aesthetic stance* to experience and enjoy literary texts, such as poetry, songs, and stories, and they should take a primarily *efferent stance* to gain knowledge from informational texts, such as nonfiction and biographies and autobiographies. Rosenblatt frequently refers to a third-grade basal reader workbook that asks children to write in response to this question: "What facts does this poem teach you?" This request for facts (efferent information) is inappropriate because when reading literature, children should be encouraged to take a predominantly aesthetic stance. On the other hand, Rosenblatt points out, this question is no more inappropriate than the example of the boy who complained that he wanted information about dinosaurs but his teacher only gave him "storybooks." Reading about dinosaur facts would mean first taking a primarily efferent stance.

Keep in mind that Rosensblatt (1994) describes *stance* on a continuum from efferent to aesthetic; most readings involve a mix of both stances and, in fact, fall somewhere in the middle of the continuum. It's extremely oversimplistic to describe reading or any language process as a simple dichotomy of efferent

For more on Rosenblatt's transactional theory and its application to the classroom, see Chapter 1, Learning and Teaching Language Arts; Chapter 5, Talking and Listening; and Chapter 7, Teaching with Literature.

TEACHER RESOURCES

For a discussion of reader-response theories, see Many and Cox (1992), *Reader Stance and Literary Understanding*, and Beach (1993), *A Teacher's Introduction to Reader-Response Theories*.

For more on aesthetic and efferent stances, see Chapter 7, Teaching with Literature.

versus aesthetic. Informational texts can be read aesthetically, and fictional texts can be read efferently. Think about your own reading experiences. If you read one of Michael Crichton's books, such as *Jurassic Park* or *The Lost World* (or saw the movies by Steven Spielberg), your reading and viewing were probably primarily aesthetic. You experienced them as stories. On the other hand, if you learned some facts about dinosaurs, genetic cloning, or chaos theory, your reading was also efferent. You took away information.

While there should be a mix of aesthetic and efferent (i.e., private and public) in transactions with texts, Rosenblatt laments that schools have traditionally emphasized an efferent (information) orientation that overstresses analysis of literature: that is, terminology and procedures for categorizing literary elements or story structure. Given this focus, the importance of meaning and expressing feeling have been diminished. Young children, in particular, should be encouraged to retain their delight in the sounds, rhythms, and imagery of poetic language—for example, as an experiential base for further efferent, analytical discussions of words, forms, or background information about authors. The aesthetic response becomes the rich, meaningful source of ideas, images, and feelings for sound, self-critical interpretations, and evaluation (Cox, 1997; Cox & Boyd-Batstone, 1997).

Equally important to encouraging an aesthetic stance toward literary texts is supporting children's understanding of informational texts by directing them to assume an efferent stance and helping them study and analyze the text in order to take away information they can use after the reading event. A great deal has been written about specific teaching strategies for reading for information, which focus on teaching children vocabulary before reading; activating their background knowledge on a topic; asking questions before, during, and after they read; and teaching them about informational, or *expository*, text structures (see Moore, Readance, & Rickelman, 1989; Tierney, Readance, & Dishner, 1995; Vacca & Vacca, 1996). Children should learn to read and write for different purposes and have many oppportunities to read and write both literary and informational texts.

The following Snapshot of a third-/fourth-grade class demonstrates how this can happen. A simple drama experience focused on colors led to a closer look at poetic language and finally to reading and writing both literary and informational texts about the theme of colors.

 **A Year-Long Theme of Colors across the Curriculum**

On one of those sparkling September days in the Midwest, when the light is so clear that everything seems suddenly to have come into sharper focus, I got "fall fever" and convinced myself that nothing could be gained by staying inside when it was so beautiful outside. My combination third-/fourth-grade class had been observing and talking about the changes in the colors of the leaves and the light and the seasons. So I divided the class into several groups and gave each a different colored piece of nylon net from the drama trunk.

Outdoors—surrounded by all the colors, smells, and textures of autumn—the children discussed ideas for acting out different colors in their groups. Then each group communicated their ideas about colors wordlessly through pantomime, using movement and dance and the single prop of some slightly used nylon net. Blue was a waterfall; red was a sunset that suddenly appeared against the skyline between two old elm trees on the only hill on the playground; orange was a bonfire; green was a raucous, snapping, snarling dragon that moved among the trees around us. (By the way, compare what you wrote about acting out a color in your Reflective Response at the beginning of the chapter to what the children did on this day.)

Once back indoors, we talked about colors, light, leaves, seasons, sunsets, dragons, and other related matters. We also started a "word wall" of words and phrases describing the experiences, feelings, and images of color the children had seen or imagined (see Figure 14.1). For the rest of the afternoon, the children wrote and talked about many of these and other feelings, ideas, and images they'd experienced that afternoon. I remembered a book of poetry about color called *Hailstones and Halibut Bones* (O'Neill, 1989). So after school, I went to get it from the library and asked the librarian to help me find other books related to color—both literary and informational texts.

On the days following, we continued to work on color pantomimes and looked for music to add another dimension to the color movement and dance expressions. We took taped music outdoors to work on the pantomimes, which were turning into dances. The art teacher noticed the children outdoors

GREAT BOOKS FOR CHILDREN

Poems and Poetry Collections about Color

Colors (Nordine, 2000)
Hailstones and Halibut Bones (O'Neill, 1989)
"I Am Rose," by Gertrude Stein, in *Amelia Mixed the Mustard* (Ness, 1975)
Out of the Blue: Poems about Color (Oram, 1993)
"Silver," by Walter de la Mare, in *The Night of the Whippoorwill* (Larrick, 1992)
"Vegetables," by Shel Silverstein, and "Josephine," by Alexander Resnikoff, in *Oh, That's Ridiculous!* (Cole, 1972)
"What Is Pink?" by Christina Rosetti, in *A Random House Book of Poetry* (Prelutsky, 1983)
White Is the Moon (Greeley, 1990)

Figure 14.1 "Word Wall" of Colors

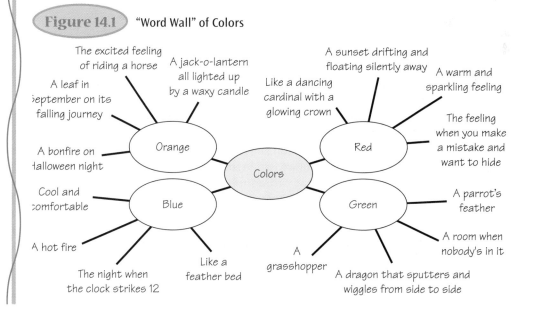

and took colored slides of their dances, which she showed to the class. She also brought art history books of paintings and prints and talked to the students about the use of color in art. I read aloud from *Hailstones and Halibut Bones* every day and added other poems about color, as well. The children talked about the poems and began to look for color imagery in books they were reading.

These experiences with colors stimulated children's questions about colors. I wrote these questions on a piece of chartpaper, and they began to guide classroom experiences:

> What is a color?
> What would a color be if it were something else?
> What are all the words for a color?
> How do leaves and seasons change color?
> Why are people different colors?

The initial experience of looking at colored leaves one fall afternoon and pantomiming colors outside became the pebble that created a "ripple effect" of reading and writing about colors across the curriculum, involving both literary and informational texts. Actually, this effect continued through the entire schoolyear, expanding into every area of the curriculum: reading and writing, art and music, multicultural education, social studies, science and mathematics, and drama and dance. See the Ripple Effect chart on the next page, which shows how this happened and provides more ideas and many resources for using the theme of colors.

Reading and Writing

We added words and phrases to the clusters we had started about each color. They grew and grew, as children came up with new ideas about color concepts and vocabulary each day. I introduced the use of the thesaurus and dictionary in a minilesson so students could look for more words. I also reread all of the poems in *Hailstones and Halibut Bones* (O'Neill, 1989) and did a minilesson about color imagery in writing. The new words and phrases and images appeared in children's writing: journals, poems, and stories. I alerted the librarian to what we were doing, and she made available the color-related books of poetry and other literature we had identified. I added colored paper and pencils to the writing center for writing about colors.

We also started a list of color words in French, which I spoke, and added a list of Spanish and Japanese words, the two other languages spoken by students in my class. Mariko's mother came to school and did a minilesson on how to write in Japanese. We started more lists of other languages spoken by students in other classes and added foreign language dictionaries to the writing center.

GREAT BOOKS FOR CHILDREN

Dictionaries

Picture Dictionaries for Primary Grades

The Cat in the Hat Beginner Book Dictionary (Random House)
The Golden Picture Dictionary (Western)
My First Picture Dictionary (Lothrop/Scott, Foresman)

Elementary School Dictionaries

The Charlie Brown Dictionary (Random House)
Macmillan Dictionary for Children (Macmillan)
Scott, Foresman Beginning Dictionary (Doubleday/Scott, Foresman)

Middle School Dictionaries

The American Heritage School Dictionary (Houghton Mifflin)
Macmillan School Dictionary (Macmillan)
Thorndike-Barnhart Intermediate Dictionary (Random House)

Thesauruses

In Other Words: A Beginning Thesaurus (Scott, Foresman)
Roget's Thesaurus (Random House)
Synonym and Antonym Dictionary (Scholastic)
Words to Use: A Junior Thesaurus (Sadlier)

COLORS
Questions:
What are words for color? Why do leaves and seasons change color? Why are people different colors?

Literature

Poetry
All the Colors of the Race (Adoff, 1982)
Hailstones and Halibut Bones (O'Neill, 1989)
My Head Is Red and Other Riddle Rhymes
  (Livingston, 1990)
Rainbow Writing (Merriam, 1992)
Picture Books
Color Dance (Jonas, 1989)
Color Farm and Color Zoo (Ehlert, 1990, 1989)
Little Blue and Little Yellow (Lionni, 1959)
Multicultural
Anansi the Spider (McDermott, 1972)
Dogsong (Paulsen, 1985)
In the Beginning: Creation Stories from around
  the World (Hamilton, 1988)
In the Year of the Boar and Jackie Robinson
  (Lord, 1984)
Pacific Crossing (Soto, 1992)
Rama: A Legend (Highwater, 1994)
Social Studies
The Great Journey (Fagan, 1987)
The Hispanic Americans (Meltzer, 1982)
How My Family Lives in America (Kuklin, 1992)
Many Thousand Gone (Hamilton, 1993)
Morning Star, Black Sun (Ashabranner, 1982)
Science and Mathematics
Egyptian Hieroglyphics for Everyone
  (Scott & Scott, 1968)
A First Look at Leaves (Selsam & Hunt, 1972)
Roses Red, Violets Blue (Johnson, 1991)
Art, Music, Drama, Dance
Amazing Grace (Hoffman, 1991)
Drawing from Nature (Arnosky, 1987)

Art & Music

Do color pantomimes; add music and movements to create dances.
Display art prints of artists known for strong use of color.
Do art projects emphasizing color: mixing colors, watercolors.
Add books about art and music to class library.

Reading & Writing

Read color poetry/literature aloud.
Write about color in other languages.
Create "word wall" of color imagery.
Write poetry modeled after Hailstones.
Read and write across the curriculum.

Social Studies

Study African American heritage and culture.
Use reference books, atlases, newspapers, maps.
Write fictional historical newspapers about
  other cultures and countries.
Use a thesaurus to find color words.
Use a dictionary to find origins and
  meanings of color words.

Multicultural

Invite guest speakers on color
differences among people.
Examine literature for bias
regarding people
of color.

Science & Math

Observe natural changes in autumn:
leaf colors, temperature, daylight.
Gather data: leaves, plants,
nature walks, experiments
Write in science journals:
labeling, notetaking, reporting.
Add books on changes in nature
and seasons to class library.

Drama & Dance

Do story dramatizations from
other cultures.
Study art and dress of other
cultures; make authentic sets,
props, and costumes for plays.
Record children's original poetry
on tape, set to music, and add
pantomime and dance.

This Picasso-like drawing is a student's self-portrait.

www

For extensive connections to art and other museums around the world, start at Art Museums on the World Wide Web: **www. comlab.ox.ac.uk/archive/ other/museums.html**.

Art and Music

When we found music to go with students' pantomimes of colors, we added it to the writing center. After the art teacher visited, we collected art prints and art history books, initially on loan from her but then supplemented by books provided by the librarian and others children brought from home. Certain artists—especially Picasso, Miró, Chagall, and the French Impressionists—captured students' interest because of their use of light and color. We talked about these artists, and students began to draw and color using their styles, illustrating their color poetry and stories. I added children's books about art, artists, music, and musicians to the class library.

Multicultural Education

The same autumn, the school district hired a consultant for multicultural education. (At the time, many schools were having problems related to conflicts among racial/ethnic groups. In our school, the primary groups of students were African Americans, European Americans, and recent arrivals from India.) Marlene Cummings, an African American registered nurse, drew on her medical background to speak to students: first about the physiology of color differences among people and then about multicultural issues. She was motivated by concern about her own three sons, who attended schools in which the majority of students were white; she felt racial differences might not be understood in these schools. After she explained the physiology of skin color and the role of melanin in contributing to skin color differences, she played a game simulating prejudice and discrimination and then opened the discussion to questions from my students.

As she was leaving the class, Marlene noticed the book *Hailstones and Halibut Bones* in the writing center and told me about her reservations about O'Neill's poem "What Is Black?" Marlene felt it had more negative images than other poems to describe the color black—for instance, "things you'd like to forget," "run-down street," "broken cup," "soot spots," and "suffering." She wished the poet had used more images of beautiful things that were black.

I told students what Marlene said, and we talked about it. We decided to start a new list of color words and images with the title "Black Is Beautiful."

The children drew pictures and brought in some from magazines from home. Everyone wrote a new poem, called "Black Is Beautiful." We sent these to Marlene Cummings, along with letters students wrote to thank her for visiting our classroom. Here's one of them:

Dear Mrs. Cummings,
You convinced me that black is beautiful. I am very glad you came to talk to us. Now I know what makes the skin black or white. Thank you for your time. Here is a poem I wrote about black.

Black Is Beautiful
Black is a racing horse, galloping full speed
Black is a tree trunk covered with leaves
Black is the ocean deep, deep down
Black is a blackbird's feathery crown
Black is a blackboard
Black is a cat
Black is a ringmaster's tall round hat

We made a bulletin board in the hall outside our room to display the students' poems and pictures. I found Ann McGovern's (1969) book of poetry *Black Is Beautiful* and read it aloud. We compared all the poems we had read and written.

A few months later, the school district published a book called *Dear Mrs. Cummings*, a collection of letters from the students who had written her that included all my students' letters and poems. The children were ecstatic. They were published letter writers and poets! The interest in colors, reading and writing about colors, and the colors of races exploded in my classroom.

Social Studies

We started a thematic social studies unit on cultural and racial diversity in the United States. An important focal topic was the heritage of African Americans: African history, culture, geography, and contemporary social and political structure. We went back in time to ancient Egypt and the early civilizations of West Africa. We learned about the history of African Americans from the time of slavery to the present, and we also studied race relations in the United States. Because many students of East Indian heritage attended our school, we added the history and culture of India to our investigations, as well.

The class read and wrote both literary and informational texts. Our reading involved a variety of literary genres: poetry, songs, stories, informational and references books, and even newspapers and magazines. Our writing covered more poetry, stories, songs, and reports. The children also blended the two by reporting what they learned in fictional historical and contemporary

www

The Center for Egyptian Art and Archaeology at the University of Memphis offers a colorful website on ancient Egypt: **www.memst.edu/egypt/main.html**.

Figure 14.2   Student-Created Newspaper

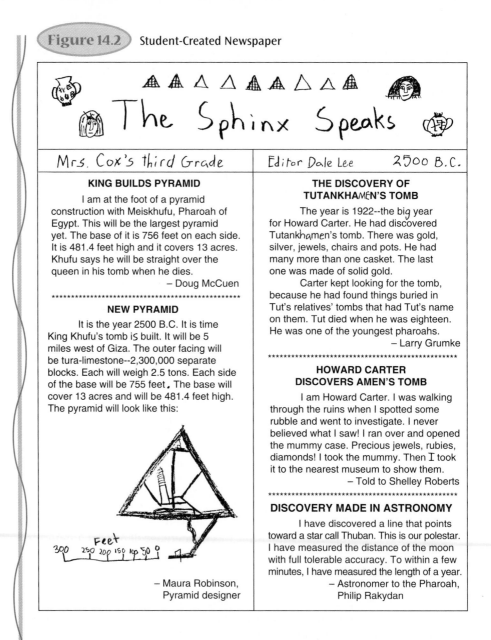

The Sphinx Speaks

Mrs. Cox's third Grade   Editor Dale Lee   2500 B.C.

KING BUILDS PYRAMID

I am at the foot of a pyramid construction with Meiskhufu, Pharoah of Egypt. This will be the largest pyramid yet. The base of it is 756 feet on each side. It is 481.4 feet high and it covers 13 acres. Khufu says he will be straight over the queen in his tomb when he dies.

– Doug McCuen

NEW PYRAMID

It is the year 2500 B.C. It is time King Khufu's tomb is built. It will be 5 miles west of Giza. The outer facing will be tura-limestone--2,300,000 separate blocks. Each will weigh 2.5 tons. Each side of the base will be 755 feet. The base will cover 13 acres and will be 481.4 feet high. The pyramid will look like this:

Feet
300 250 200 150 100 50 0

– Maura Robinson,
Pyramid designer

THE DISCOVERY OF TUTANKHAMEN'S TOMB

The year is 1922--the big year for Howard Carter. He had discovered Tutankhamen's tomb. There was gold, silver, jewels, chairs and pots. He had many more than one casket. The last one was made of solid gold.

Carter kept looking for the tomb, because he had found things buried in Tut's relatives' tombs that had Tut's name on them. Tut died when he was eighteen. He was one of the youngest pharoahs.

– Larry Grumke

HOWARD CARTER DISCOVERS AMEN'S TOMB

I am Howard Carter. I was walking through the ruins when I spotted some rubble and went to investigate. I never believed what I saw! I ran over and opened the mummy case. Precious jewels, rubies, diamonds! I took the mummy. Then I took it to the nearest museum to show them.

– Told to Shelley Roberts

DISCOVERY MADE IN ASTRONOMY

I have discovered a line that points toward a star call Thuban. This is our polestar. I have measured the distance of the moon with full tolerable accuracy. To within a few minutes, I have measured the length of a year.

– Astronomer to the Pharoah,
Philip Rakydan

---

newspapers. One was written as though it took place in ancient Egypt: *The Sphinx Speaks* (see Figure 14.2). Others included *The Pan-African Press,* which was about Africa, and *Delhi's Daily,* which was about India.

Science and Mathematics

Our talk about how leaves change color led to a science unit on budding twigs. We used the inquiry, rather than the textbook, approach to science. Students used processes such as observation, classification, measurement, prediction, hypothesis, interpretation, and inference to gather data. Types of writing used were labeling, notetaking, and reporting in science journals (see Figure 14.3). Students wrote about their observations of changes in trees, leaves, and plants in the neighborhood, from our classroom window, and on fieldtrips to a nearby arboretum with a naturalist guide. We conducted a series of experiments using branches cut and kept in water at intervals during the year. Keeping tallies and graphing these changes became a part of mathematics, as did reading about numerical systems and devices used in other cultures (e.g., hieroglyphics, the abacus) and trying them out in class.

Drama and Dance

As we learned about the cultures of ancient Egypt, Africa, and India, students read traditional tales, wrote scripts, and presented them as plays: "The Story of Ra" (Ancient Egypt), "Anansi the Spider" (Africa), and "Tales from the Ramayana" (India). The children studied the art and dress of each culture to make authentic sets, props, and costumes. They staged "The Story of Ra" as

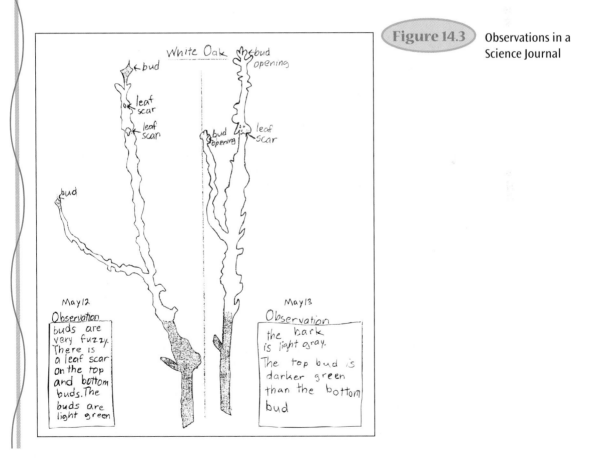

Figure 14.3 Observations in a Science Journal

though it were from an ancient Egyptian frieze, in which everyone is facing sideways.

Students' pantomimes, dances, and poetry about colors all came together in a performance they called "Magic Colors." The children worked in groups, one color per group. Each wrote a collective color poem and recorded it with music that went well with it. Then each group created pantomime and dance movements to the poem and music. The children dressed in leotards or swimsuits of their group's color and used nylon net for props. The performance was given in a theater-in-the round (actually, the gym). The audience sat in a large circle of chairs, leaving several spaces at intervals for the children to enter and exit. After the audience had been seated and the room darkened, the children entered almost noiselessly, crouched behind the audience. As each recorded poem with music was played, spotlights were turned with filters to match the color of each group. Each group played out the pantomime/dance they had created. Marlene Cummings was a guest of honor and introduced the performance by telling about her visit to our class and reading some of the "Black Is Beautiful" poems the students had written. Each audience received a photocopy of the collected poems for "Magic Colors."

Language across the Curriculum for All Students

During the year my class explored the theme of color and through performing the activities that led up to the performance of "Magic Colors," I found that the thematic teaching of language across the curriculum benefited *all* my students. Since this was a combination third-/fourth-grade class, I had students across a two-year age span. Several of the younger boys struggled with writing independently at the beginning of the year but became much more successful when they wrote with others and edited their writing in a peer group. Together, they were able to publish their poems and share them through the class's performance. Two of the children in my class had speech problems that often inhibited their spontaneous speaking in class; they were much more relaxed, however, when they had time to practice reading their poems and because the final performance was taped. I also had one student with an identified learning disability and another diagnosed with attention-deficit hyperactivity disorder (ADHD), but they both functioned well with group support. Another student, 8-year-old Mariko, had recently arrived from Japan and spoke very limited English, but she was a beautiful dancer. She practiced reading and then recorded her poem in slow, halting English, but she brought the recording to life as she performed a dance to it. Her poem was about silver, and she had a silver dance costume.

For specific ideas on how to support these various types of students, see the box on page 475.

Struggling Readers and Writers, Students with Disabilities, and English Language Learners in Writing

Writing in groups benefits these students in the following ways:

1. Learning is contextualized, meaningful, and engaging.
2. Student interest is at the center; there is personal investment.
3. Collaborative, mixed-ability teams group struggling students with more proficient peers and English language learners with native English speakers.

Use these strategies to support students' poetry writing:

1. Read aloud a variety of poetry and poetic forms.
2. Make available recorded versions of poetry in listening centers.
3. Model poetry writing for the whole class and in small groups.
4. Create poetry-writing frames.
5. Publish student poetry in a variety of formats: bulletin boards, class anthologies, on videotape and the Internet, and through performance art such as movement, pantomime, dance, and drama.

Literary Texts

As you saw in the Snapshot, my students read and wrote both literary and informational texts across the curriculum, and their reading and writing were integrally connected with their ideas and experiences (Katz & Thomas, 1996). The Ripple Effect about colors listed many different children's books and types of writing: poetry using color imagery, picture books, and chapter books of both traditional and contemporary stories in which the main characters are people of color.

The rest of this chapter will focus on reading and writing literary and informational texts in language arts instruction. The next several sections will focus on the aesthetic reading of poetry, songs, and stories and using them as models for children's own expressive writing. See Table 14.2 (pp. 476–477), which lists children's books of poetry, songs, and stories to use as models for students' writing.

Poetry

Children are natural poets and often speak metaphorically. Northrop Frye (1964) describes this as the way "the poet thinks, not in logical sequences, but in the most primitive and archaic of categories, similarity and identity. A is like B; A is B. These are categories that appear in poetry as simile and metaphor. 'Eternity is like unto a Ring,' says John Bunyan. 'Grandfather of the day is he,' says Emily Dickinson of a mountain" (p. 7). Frye urges teachers to "preserve a child's own metaphorical processes." That can be achieved by reading aloud poetry to chil-

Table 14.2 Literary Texts as Models for Writing

Poetry	Songs	Stories
Similes & Metaphors	**Collections**	**Traditional Literature***
As: A Surfeit of Similes (Juster, 1989)	*American Folk Songs for Children* (Seeger, 1976)	"Cinderella"
As Quick as a Cricket (Wood, 1982)	*Arroz Con Leche: Popular Songs and Rhythms from Latin America* (Delacre, 1989)	"The Emperor's New Clothes"
Heartland (Siebert, 1989)		"The Frog Prince"
Mojave (Siebert, 1988)		"The Gingerbread Boy"
Sierra (Siebert, 1991)	*Caribbean Carnival: Songs of the West Indies* (Burghie, 1992)	"Jack and the Beanstalk"
	Freedom Like Sunlight: Praise Songs for Black Americans (Lewis, 2000)	"Sleeping Beauty"
Free Verse		"Snow White"
All the Small Poems (Worth, 1987)	*Go In and Out the Window: An Illlustrated Songbook for Young People* (Fox, 1987)	"The Three Bears"
A Joyful Noise: Poems for Two Voices (Fleischman, 1988)		"The Three Little Pigs"
	Gonna Sing My Head Off! (Krull, 1992)	**Fantasy**
Rhymes	*Granny Will Your Dog Bite? and Other Mountain Rhymes* (Milnes, 1990)	*The Book of Three* (Alexander, 1964)
Anna Banana: 101 Jump-Rope Rhymes (Cole, 1989)		*Charlotte's Web* (White, 1952)
The Book of Pigericks (Lobel, 1983)	*Rise Up Singing!* (Patterson & Blood, 1990)	*The Children of Green Knowe* (Boston, 1955)
The Complete Nonsense Book (Lear, 1846/1946)	*Songs for Survival: Songs and Chants from Tribal Peoples around the World* (Siegen-Smith, 1996)	*The Dark Is Rising* (Cooper, 1973)
A Gopher in the Garden and Other Animal Poems (Prelutsky, 1967)		*The Lion, the Witch, and the Wardrobe* (Lewis, 1961)
The Hopeful Trout and Other Limericks (Ciardi, 1989)	*This Land Is Your Land* (Guthrie, 1998)	*Winnie the Pooh* (Milne, 1926)
I Met a Man (Ciardi, 1961)	*What a Morning! The Christmas Story in Black Spirituals* (Langstaff, 1987)	*The Wizard of Earthsea* (Le Guin, 1968)
Laughing Time (Smith, 1990)		**Science Fiction**
A Light in the Attic (Silverstein, 1981)	**Single-Song Picture Books**	*The City of Gold and Lead* (Christopher, 1967)
One Sun: A Book of Terse Verse (McMillan, 1990)	*Cat Goes Fiddle-I-Fee* (Galdone, 1985)	*Enchantress from the Stars* (Engdahl, 1970)
The Owl and the Pussy Cat (Lear, 1991)	*The Erie Canal* (Spier, 1970)	*The Giver* (Lowry, 1993)
Tirra Lirra: Rhymes Old and New (Richards, 1932)	*The Fox Went Out on a Chilly Night* (Spier, 1961)	*A Wrinkle in Time* (L'Engle, 1962)
Where the Sidewalk Ends (Silverstein, 1974)	*Go Tell Aunt Rhody* (Aliki, 1974)	**Adventure**
You Read to Me, I'll Read to You (Ciardi, 1962)	*Hush, Little Baby* (Zemach, 1976)	*Julie of the Wolves* (George, 1972)
	I Know an Old Lady Who Swallowed a Fly (Rounds, 1990)	*Treasure Island* (Stevenson, 1947)

*See Table 14.3 (p. 485) for books that are twists on these traditional tales.

dren and encouraging them to respond aesthetically and try a variety of poetic forms in their own writing (Flynn & McPhillips, 2000; Glover, 1999; Tannenbaum, 2000). See also Table 14.2, which gives examples of children's literature for each of the following poetic forms.

EXCELLENT SOFTWARE

Specialized programs for poetry writing include Poetry Express and Poetry Palette.

Poetry	Songs	Stories
Syllabic Patterns	*If You're Happy and You Know It* (Weiss, 1987)	**Mysteries**
Cool Melons—Turn to Frogs! The Life and Poems of Issa (Gollub, 1998)	*The Itsy Bitsy Spider* (Trapni, 1994)	*The Bones in the Cliff* (Stevenson, 1995)
Cricket Songs (Behn, 1964)	*John Henry* (Lester, 1994)	*The Case of the Lion Dance* (Yep, 1998)
Haiku: The Mood of the Earth (Atwood, 1971)	*Little Drummer Boy* (Keats, 1968)	*Coffin on a Case* (Bunting, 1992)
In a Spring Garden (Lewis, 1965)	*London Bridge Is Falling Down* (Spier, 1967)	*Encyclopedia Brown* (Sobol)
In the Eyes of the Cat: Japanese Poetry for All Seasons (Demi, 1992)	*Mary Wore Her Red Dress* (Peek, 1985)	*Bunnicula* (Howe & Howe, 1979)
More Cricket Songs (Behn, 1971)	*Mommy, Buy Me a China Doll* (Zemach, 1966)	*The Westing Game* (Raskin, 1984)
My Own Rhythm: An Approach to Haiku (Atwood, 1973)	*Oh, a-Hunting We Will Go* (Langstaff, 1977)	**Series Books**
The Seasons of Time (Baron, 1968)	*Old MacDonald Had a Farm* (Berry, 1994)	*American Girl* (published by Pleasant)
Stone Bench in an Empty Park (Janezcko, 2000)	*One Little Goat: A Passover Song* (Hirsh, 1979)	*Anastasia Krupnik* (Lowry; published by Houghton Mifflin)
Wind in the Long Grass: A Collection of Haiku (Higginson, 1991)	*Over in the Meadow* (Keats, 1971)	*The Babysitter's Club* (Martin; published by Scholastic)
Predictable Patterns	*Over in the Meadow* (Langstaff, 1967)	*California Diaries* (Martin; published by Scholastic)
Brown Bear, Brown Bear, What Do You See? (Martin, 1967)	*Roll Over* (Peek, 1981)	*Choose Your Own Adventure* (published by Bantam)
A House Is a House for Me (Hoberman, 1982)	*The Star-Spangled Banner* (Spier, 1973)	*Goosebumps* (Stine; published by Scholastic)
I Love My Anteater with an A (Ipcar, 1964)	*Twinkle, Twinkle, Little Star* (Hague, 1992)	*Harry Potter* (Rowling; published by Scholastic)
The Important Book (Brown, 1949)	*What a Wonderful World* (Weiss & Thiele, 1995)	*Herculeah Jones* (Byars; published by Viking)
Concrete Poetry		*Sweet Valley Kids* (Stewart; published by Bantam)
Concrete Is Not Always Hard (Pilon, 1972)		
Seeing Things: A Book of Poems (Froman, 1974)		
Street Poems (Froman, 1971)		
Walking Talking Words (Sherman, 1980)		

Similes and Metaphors

A *simile* draws a comparison between dissimilar things using the connecting word *like* or *as*. Use Audrey Wood's book *As Quick as a Cricket* (1982) as a model for student writing.

Saffron is a spice that also makes food vivid yellow.

- *Color Similes:* First-graders in Phyllis Crawford's class at Audubon School in Baton Rouge, Louisiana, wrote similes about *yellow* when talking about color words and after adding saffron to rice and watching it turn bright yellow:

As yellow as . . . saffron rice
the sweltering sun
refreshing lemonade
a corpulent cat

- *Sense Similes:* Phyllis's first-graders were learning about the senses, too, so they thought of these similes:

Smell	As reeky as wrinkled, perspiring feet
Hear	As deafening as a hovering helicopter
See	As colorful as an enchanting sunset
Feel	As bumpy as a warted toad
Taste	As yummy as seasoned etouffé

Etouffé is a rice dish made in South Louisiana, usually with shrimp or crawfish.

- *Synonym Similes:* Students can start with a word, find a synonym in the thesaurus, and write a simile:

Word	Synonym	Simile
daisy	posy	like a little sun

See Figure 14.4, which shows illustrated similes done by third-graders.

Figure 14.4 Illustrated Similes by Third-Graders

A *metaphor* draws a comparison between two dissimilar things by naming one for the other. Aristotle felt this process of renaming was an indication of genius, since the ability to forge a good metaphor shows that the poet has an intuitive perception of what's similar in things that seem dissimilar at face value.

- *Pretend Metaphors:* In his books *Rose, Where Did You Get That Red?* (1990) and *Wishes, Lies, and Dreams* (1980), Kenneth Koch wrote about his experiences teaching poetry to children in New York City schools. In having his students write metaphors, he told them to use this process: First, think about one thing being like something else: for instance, *the cloud is like a pillow.* Then pretend that it really is the other thing; say *is* instead of *is like: the cloud is a pillow.* Koch gives this example of a metaphor by one of his students: "Mr. Koch is a very well-dressed poetry book walking around in shining shoes" (1980, p. 147).

- *Comparision Poems:* Koch also recommends the use of *comparison poems,* which serve as frames to help students think in terms of similes and metaphors and use them in their writing. For example:

> I used to . . . , but now I . . .
> I am a . . . , but I wish I were . . .
> If I were a . . . , I would . . .

Free Verse

Free verse has little or no rhyme and often sounds like everyday speech. Valerie Worth uses free verse in her sparse, elegant poetry, which is collected in *Small Poems* (1972), *More Small Poems* (1976), *Still More Small Poems* (1978), and *All the Small Poems* (1987). Another good collection is Barbara Juster Esbensen's *Echoes for the Eye* (1996).

- *First-Draft Free Verse:* Figure 14.5 on page 480 shows the first draft of a free-verse poem written on computer by a fourth-grade child in Etobicoke, Ontario, Canada. Ken Roy, English coordinator for the Etobicoke Board of Education, encourages and helps teachers collect first drafts of children's poetry in "Poetry Is Fun" booklets. Revised poems are submitted to him throughout the year, and selections are published in an anthology called *Acorns*. Many of the poems are in French, the native language of many Canadians.

- *Poems for Two Voices:* Sid Fleischman has written two books of free verse that are also scripts for reading the poetry aloud. The poems are arranged in two columns, side by side. Some of the words are on staggered lines, and others are on the same line. One student or group reads the left side (the words on the staggered lines), and another reads the right side (the words on the same line), and if words in both columns are on the same line, everyone reads together. The effect is that of a musical fugue, with a point/counterpoint for each voice and the voices together. Students can find these poems in Fleischman's collections *I Am Phoenix: Poems for Two Voices* (1985), which is about birds, and the Newbery

Figure 14.5 Fourth-Grader's Free Verse

the midnight crazy trtls

at midnight I here

the tiny footsteps

then I hered music.

And thea were dansing.

Source: Reprinted with permission of Ken Roy, Coordinator, Etobicoke Board of Education, Etobicoke, Ontario.

Medal–winning *Joyful Noise: Poems for Two Voices* (1988), which is about insects. This form of free verse is a natural for students, and Fleischman's work is an excellent model for students to use in writing their own poems for two voices.

Rhymes

Poetry doesn't have to rhyme but frequently does. To help children use rhymes in their poetry, introduce these simple rhyming patterns:

- *Couplets:* A *couplet* is a two-line, rhymed verse. The following couplet was written by a first-grader, who combined his impressions of learning a folk dance at school and taking a trip to the zoo:

> A panther
> Once was a folk dancer

The child's teacher said he first chanted the couplet aloud to himself and then wrote it down and illustrated it, showing a dancing panther with shoes.

- *Quatrains:* A *quatrain* is a four-line poem with a varied rhyme pattern. One of my fourth-grade students wrote this one when we were studying the behavior of mealworms in science:

> A mealworm in bran
> Is apt to expand
> So give the mealworm
> A helping hand

GREAT BOOKS FOR CHILDREN

In *One at a Time: Poems for the Very Young*, David McCord (1977) shows young readers and writers how to write various poetic forms: couplets, quatrains, limericks, haikus, and others.

- **Terse Verse:** A *terse verse* is a two-word rhyme that's vivid enough to paint a word image. Photoillustrator Bruce McMillan's picture book *One Sun: A Book of Terse Verse* (1990) provides a useful model. Each page shows a photograph of a line of terse verse. Students can brainstorm examples, choose one to illlustrate on a page, and combine the pages into a class book of terse verse.

- **Limericks:** A *limerick* is a nonsense poem in which lines 1, 2, and 5 rhyme and lines 3 and 4 rhyme. Edward Lear popularized this form of verse around 1850. Here's one by a fourth-grader who was learning about the solar system:

> There once was a man from Mars
> Who liked to eat the stars.
> One day he ate twenty.
> Oh, man, was he funny.
> That silly old man from Mars.

Syllabic Patterns

Some forms of poetry follow a syllabic pattern, rather than a rhyme pattern. *Haiku* is a traditional form of Japanese poetry about nature, consisting of 17 syllables: 5 in line 1, 7 in line 2, and 5 in line 3. Here's an example written by a fourth-grader:

> Shiny blue water
> Ripples as the boy throws stones
> Into the still sea.

Senryu follows the same pattern but is about topics other than nature. *Tanka* uses 31 syllables in five lines in a pattern of 7, 5, 7, 5, 7 and, like haiku, is about nature.

For information on other poetry patterns, see the following:

Chapter 4: Cinquain

Chapter 11: Triante; Diamante; "My Hands, My Feet"; "What Next?"; Concentric circle

Predictable Patterns

Many predictable pattern books are based on familiar cultural sequences; some use repeated phrases or are cumulative tales; others are based on traditional rhymes, songs, or folktales; and still others are new and original. These books can provide excellent models for writing, as each pattern gives students a sort of framework to build on. For instance, after reading the predictable pattern book *I Love My Anteater with an A* (Ipcar, 1964), a first-grader wrote this poem:

Superman

> I love my Superman with an S because he is superior
> I dislike him with an s because he is strange
> His name is Samson. He comes from space.
> He lives on stars and suns. And he is a man of steel.

See Chapter 4, Emergent Literacy and Biliteracy, for a list of predictable pattern books to use as models for writing and an example of a cinquain pattern written about apples. See Chapter 11, Grammar, Punctuation, and Handwriting, for examples of word patterns that can be used for writing.

Concrete Poetry

In concrete poetry, the writing itself takes a representational form; that is, the words are written in the shape of whatever is being described. Books of concrete poetry include Robert Froman's *Seeing Things: A Book of Poems* (1974) and *Street*

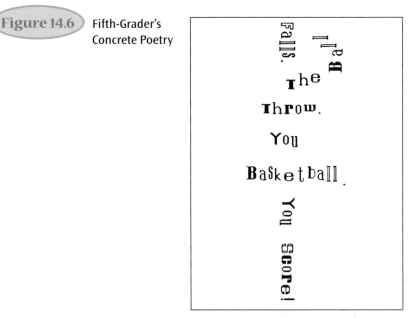

Figure 14.6 Fifth-Grader's Concrete Poetry

Source: Reprinted with permission of Ken Roy, Coordinator, Etobicoke Board of Education, Etobicoke, Ontario.

Poems (1971); A. Barbara Pilon's collection *Concrete Is Not Always Hard* (1972); Joan Brausfield Graham's *Flicker Flash* (1999); J. Patrick Lewis's *Doodle Dandies: Poems That Take Shape* (1998); and Paul Janezcko's *A Poke in the I: A Collection of Concrete Poems* (2001). Figure 14.6 shows an example by a Canadian student published in the anthology *Acorns,* described in the section on free verse.

TEACHER RESOURCES

For more on single-song picture books, see Linda Leonard Lamme, "Exploring the World of Music through Picture Books," *Reading Teacher, 44*(1990), 294–300.

Songs

Songs are another form of poetry—one put to music. The rhythmical, repeated, and rhyming patterns in songs are one of the oldest forms of teaching language and cultural content to children. Think about your own childhood: Can you still remember lullabies that were sung to you or the sing-song versions of nursery rhymes that were read to you?

If you're like me, you don't know how many days there are in a particular month unless you start singing "Thirty days hath September . . ." My two youngest children, Gordon and Elizabeth, often learned the words to popular songs they heard over and over on the radio when with their older teenage brother, Wyatt. Sometimes our memories of whole years or eras are wrapped up in the movie or television theme songs we remember, such as "Here's the story, of a man named Brady . . ."

Teachers of all grade levels should sing, play, read, write, and perform songs with their students. A kindergarten class of Khmer-speaking Cambodian American students wrote their own words to the song "Mary Wore Her Red Dress" as they learned the names of the colors in English. The teacher wrote out the new words—for instance, changing *Mary* to *Chinda* (a student in the class) and *red dress* to *black bow*—as the class sang the song. She did this for each student, who then illustrated his or her verse of the song and wrote his or her name at the top (see Figure 14.7). Each verse was attached to a chart holder with metal rings, so the teacher could turn each page and the children could sing the whole song.

Table 14.2 (pp. 476–477) provides a list of song collections and single-song picture books to read aloud or sing with students. Use these songs as you try the following songwriting activities:

TEACHER RESOURCES
For more on songwriting with students, see *Crossroads: Literature and Language in Culturally and Linguistically Diverse Classrooms* (Cox & Boyd-Batstone, 1997).

• *Create a New Version of an Old Song:* A very simple way to use songs as a model for writing is to change certain words of a familiar song, retaining its basic structure and syntax but changing the topic. A classic example of this can be found in *Alice's Adventures in Wonderland,* when Lewis Carroll (1865/1957) changed the words to "Twinkle, Twinkle, Little Star" to "Twinkle, Twinkle, Little Bat." Select a new theme or topic, identify the type of word to change to match the new theme (e.g., nouns, verbs), and find words that fit the rhyming pattern. Here's an example:

Original Song	New Version
Twinkle, twinkle little *star* (Original noun)	Twinkle, twinkle little *bat* (New noun)
How I wonder where you *are* (Original verb)	How I wonder where you're *at* (New verb)
Up above the world so high	Up above the world so high
Like a *diamond* (Original noun) in the sky	Like a *tea tray* (New noun) in the sky

As you can see, the syntax and rhyming pattern of the original song were retained, but new words were substituted to create a nonsense version.

Figure 14.7 Student's Illustrated Song

- *Put a New Song to an Old Tune:* When Paul Boyd-Batstone was a a third-grade bilingual teacher, he shared this approach to songwriting in the classroom with me. He used songwriting extensively with the English language learners in his classroom. His approach built on the basic idea of using literature—in this case, songs—as a model for writing, but he gave students a lot of freedom. Rather than simply substituting a few new words in an old song, students wrote a totally new song using the tune and syllabic pattern of an old song. Here's how they did it:

1. *Pick a topic:* The topic can be related to a thematic unit, a special event or holiday, a season, or just an idea. (For instance, think about how many love songs there are!)
2. *Brainstorm a cluster of images and words on a "word wall":* Ask students to contribute ideas related to the theme or topic. Do a simple cluster, and write down many responses. This can be done more than once, building the word wall of ideas.
3. *Chart a song:* Pick a song with a tune that's simple to remember and sing or that many students know. Write out the words on chartpaper or on an overhead transparency. Then read aloud and sing it with children until they're very familiar with it.
4. *Make a blank songframe by lines and syllables:* Number each line of the song, and count the number of syllables in it. Make a blank chart that represents each line and the syllables it contains.
5. *Write a new song:* Use the words and ideas from the word wall to complete the songframe, line by line and syllable by syllable.

Paul recommends familiar tunes like "Row, Row, Row Your Boat," "Old MacDonald Had a Farm," "Frere Jacques," and "Somwhere Over the Rainbow." Here is a songframe for "Row, Row, Row Your Boat":

Line 1: 5 syllables   _____

Line 2: 5 syllables   _____

Line 3: 12 syllables _____

Line 4: 5 syllables   _____

Paul's students wrote a song this way when they were studying whales (*ballenas*, in Spanish). One student remarked that when whales slap the water with their fins and tales and raise their heads out of the water, bobbing back and forth to announce danger, it's like they are dancing: *"Baila la ballena!"* ("Dance the whale!"). Another student suggested it sounded like "La Bamba," the famous Mexican dance song made popular in the mainstream culture of the United States with a recording in the 1950s by Richie Valens. Paul and his students created a songframe based on the tune "La Bamba" and wrote a song about whales.

Stories

J. R. R. Tolkien, the great fantasy writer, believed that there were no new stories but rather a great cauldron of stories we dip into as we write. Children reinvent these stories when they read and write, as do adult readers and writers. At the elementary level, children frequently connect more with story ideas and plots than with story elements like characterization, although the connections they make vary greatly (Cairney, 1990).

Traditional Literature

Traditional literature is the oldest genre. It began with the oral tradition of telling tales about what was considered ordinary or extraordinary in life, often concluding with a theme or moral that could be applied to anyone's life. Wonderful heroes and villains are especially common in traditional literature, and the fight between good and evil has always been a compelling theme. Today, these characters and themes are portrayed by the superheroes that appear prominently in children's films, television shows, video and computer games, and comics. Students can draw on the characters and themes from traditional literature and create their own heroes and villains.

See Chapter 7, Teaching with Literature, for much more on genres of stories written for children, literary elements and story structure, and approaches to teaching with literature. Reading and responding to genres of children's literature is an excellent approach to using literature as a model for writing.

Traditional tales often follow similar patterns, such as presenting animal characters in threes and basing their adventures on conflicts with an adversary—for instance, "The Three Bears" (Goldilocks) and "The Three Billy Goats Gruff" (troll). Some traditional tales have many variants, and reading them may give children ideas for writing their own. Cinderella, or the "rags to riches" story, is the most universal folktale; there are hundreds of variants around the world. Other traditional tales have been retold with a strong twist, usually involving humor. For example, in *The True Story of the Three Little Pig,* as told to Jon Scieszka (1989), the wolf claims he was framed. See Table 14.3 for a list of books that children can read and use as models for writing their own twists on traditional tales.

See the genre unit on "Cinderella" in Chapter 7.

Fantasy and Science Fiction Stories

Fantasy and science fiction is literature of the hypothetical and thus highly suitable as a model for writing by children. Even young students can adapt fantasy characters in their writing. See Figure 14.8, a story that first-grader Elizabeth

Table 14.3　Twists on Traditional Tales

"Cinderella"

Bubba, the Cowboy Prince: A Fractured Texas Tale (Kettleman, 1997)
Prince Cinders (Cole, 1988)
Sidney Rella and the Glass Sneaker (Myers, 1985)

"The Emperor's New Clothes"

The Emperor's Old Clothes (Lasky, 1999)
The Principal's New Clothes (Calmenson, 1989)

"The Frog Prince"

The Frog Prince Continued (Scieszka, 1991)
Pondlarker (Gwynne, 1990)

"Jack and the Beanstalk"

Jim and the Beanstalk (Briggs, 1970)
The Giant's Toe (Cole, 1986)

"Sleeping Beauty"

Sleeping Ugly (Yolen, 1981)

"Snow White"

Snow White in New York (French, 1988)

"The Three Bears"

Deep in the Forest (Turkle, 1976)
Somebody and the Three Blairs (Tollhurst, 1990)
Yours Truly, Goldilocks (Ada, 1998)

"The Three Little Pigs"

The True Story of the Three Little Pigs (Scieszka, 1989)

Figure 14.8 Elizabeth's Scary Story

The Spoocy, Scairy, and very creepy Story by Elizabeth Spates

helo My Darling

Onec upon a time theyr lived a witch and her name was Tina. Tina had alot of boyfriends 2 wer ghosts, 5 were Vanpiers, and 21 wer sonbies. She loved going out with them beacause they always had goulade at the restuhonts they went to and the ghosts wer the cuteust proms. But littel things at the scairy part, lisin, her favoret thing to eat is geting to the pluomp, fat, juocy, litte BOYS!

wrote about fantasy characters at Halloween. Stories of personified animals—like *Winnie-the-Pooh,* by A. A. Milne (1926), and *Charlotte's Web,* by E. B. White (1952)—provide good models for young writers.

Try tales of other worlds for older students, like Narnia in *The Lion, the Witch, and the Wardrobe* (1961) series, by C. S. Lewis; Prydain in *The Book of Three* (1964) series, by Lloyd Alexander; and Earthsea in *The Wizard of Earthsea* (1968), by Ursula Le Guin. Children can also read time fantasies and write their own versions. Literary models of this genre include *A Wrinkle in Time,* by Madeline L'Engle (1962); *The Children of Green Knowe,* by Lucy Boston (1955); and *The Dark Is Rising,* by Susan Cooper (1973). Science fiction often takes a serious look at the future, as in *The City of Gold and Lead* (1967), by John Christopher, and *The Giver* (1993), by Lois Lowry. Another popular topic is space exploration, as in *Enchantress from the Stars* (1970), by Sylvia Engdahl. And of course, there are the hugely popular and widely read *Harry Potter* books and movies by J. K. Rowling, which are full of magic and fantastic creatures.

Adventure Stories and Mysteries

Children always enjoy adventure stories and mysteries for reading aloud, for independent reading, and as models for writing. Try old classics like *Treasure Island* (1947), by Robert Louis Stevenson, or modern classics like *Julie of the Wolves* (1972), by Jean George. Also try mystery series, such as the *Encyclopedia Brown* books, by Donald Sobol; *Bunnicula* (1979), by Deborah and James Howe; and *The Westing Game* (1984), by Ellen Raskin.

See Chapter 7, Teaching with Literature, for a core book unit on *Treasure Island*.

Series

Several popular types of series books are widely read by children, if not thoroughly approved of by adult critics of children's literature (Gonzalez, Fry, Lopez, Jordan, Sloan, & McAdams, 1995). The *Hardy Boys* (Dixon) and *Nancy Drew* (Keene) mystery series have been updated for a new generation of readers by the Stratemeyer Syndicate, who have also produced other popular series: *The Baby-Sitter's Club* (Martin), *Sweet Valley Kids* (Stewart), *Encyclopedia Brown* (Sobol), and *Goosebumps* (Stine). R. L. Stine, who writes the *Goosebumps* books, was the top-selling author of children's books in the 1990s. Although they are rarely considered literature, these stories are phenomenally popular with children and readily available, often in paperbacks.

More well-regarded authors have also created characters who appear in series of books, such as Amber Brown (Paula Danziger), Alice (Phyllis Reynolds Naylor), Tooter Pepperday (Jerry Spinelli), and Aldo (Johanna Hurwitz). As just mentioned, the most recent phenomenon is the *Harry Potter* series, by J. K. Rowling. Another character series is the *American Girl*, in which the books are based on stories about dolls from different periods of American history, including Addie, an African American child who escapes slavery; Molly, whose father is overseas in World War II; and Josefina, a Hispanic girl living in northern New Mexico in the 1820s. Great attention has been paid to historical accuracy in these books, and the Addie books are especially well written.

Another series that's been very popular for many years is *Choose Your Own Adventure* (first written by Edward Packard for Bantam), in which the books have multiple possible story outcomes. These stories cut across several popular genres: adventure, mystery, science fiction, and fantasy. Numerous other versions are offered by a number of publishers. The general idea behind all of them is that the reader makes choices at certain points in the plot, so that different versions of the story are possible.

Informational Texts

Think back to the Snapshot about colors, in which children both read and wrote many types of informational texts. They read and wrote about art history and music; about cultural and racial diversity in a thematic social studies unit on

African Americans; and about how leaves change color in a science unit. In each case, the students used informational texts: nonfiction books of facts and concepts. They also wrote informational texts, such as reports, biographies, letters, and observations.

Informational texts are basically *expository,* which means they explain or show a subject in detail to disclose, unmask, or expose it. Organization is important in expository texts. Specific text patterns, or structures, such as those discussed below, are often used to organize the information when writing. The goals of reading and writing informational texts, respectively, are to understand and inform the reader about the subject in a clear, effective, and understandable way. While literary texts may contain information, presenting it is not the principal goal, as is the case with informational texts.

Children will encounter several types of expository text structures in social studies, science, and mathematics textbooks as well as in informational books. Students should be introduced to the following structures to help them in both reading and writing information, especially in the upper grades, as students begin to use increasingly more complex types of expository texts. Be aware that these are broad classifications, and informational texts may use them in a variety of ways and even several at a time:

1. *Description:* Information is presented by describing the characteristics of a subject and providing detail to enhance the reader's understanding. Key words in this type of text include vivid adjectives that portray how the subject looks, feels, smells, sounds, and so on.
2. *List:* Many facts, ideas, and descriptions are presented in lists, whether as a sequence or a collection. Key words in this type of text are *first/second/third, next, finally,* and *all of these.*
3. *Cause and Effect:* A cause-and-effect relationship is demonstrated, often beginning with a question about an effect, which is followed by an answer tracing its cause. The cause-and-effect relationship may be implicit or explicitly stated. Key words in this type of text are *because, the reasons for, as a result of, since, consequently,* and *therefore.*
4. *Compare and Contrast:* Information is presented to show how subjects are alike and/or different. Key words in this type of text are *alike, like, similar to, the same as, unlike, different,* and *in contrast to.*
5. *Problem and Solution:* A problem is stated, and a solution is offered. This type of text often follows a question/answer format or may require the reader to develop a solution (e.g., in a mathematics text). Key words include *if/then, why?/because, although,* and *in order to.*

Reading and writing informational texts are reciprocal processes, each supporting the development of the other (Harvey, 1998; Raphael & Englert, 1990). The following sections describe several types of informational texts and how they can be used as models for writing. See also Table 14.4, which lists informational children's books by subject.

Table 14.4   Informational Texts as Models for Writing

Nonfiction Books	Biographies and Autobiographies

Nature and Science

Earthquakes (Simon, 1991)
A River Ran Wild (Cherry, 1992)
Sharks (McGovern, 1976)

History

Commodore Perry in the Land of the Shogun (Blumberg, 1985)
Frontier Living (Tunis, 1961)
Many Thousand Gone: African Americans, from Slavery to Freedom (Hamilton, 1993)

People and Culture

Mummies Made in Egypt (Aliki, 1979)
Sahara (Reynolds, 1991)
Totem Pole (Hoyt-Goldsmith, 1990)

The Arts

Castle (Macaulay, 1977)
Going to My Ballet Class (Kuklin, 1989)
The Magic of Mozart: Mozart, the Magic Flute, and the Salzburg Marionettes (Switzer, 1995)

How-To Books

How a Book Is Made (Aliki, 1986)
If You Made a Million (Schwartz, 1989)
The Way Things Work (Macaulay, 1988)

Series Books

Brown Paper School Books (published by Little, Brown)
Extremely Weird and Bizarre and Beautiful (published by John Muir)
Eyewitness Books (published by Knopf)
Imponderables (published by Harper)
Let's Read-and-Find-Out Science (published by HarperCollins)
The Magic School Bus (Cole; published by Scholastic)
Usborne Books (published by EDC)
What Makes a . . . ? (famous artists series; published by Viking)

Biographies

The Bard of Avon: The Story of William Shakespeare (Stanley, 1992)
Cleopatra (Stanley, 1994)
Eleanor Roosevelt: A Life of Discovery (Freedman, 1993)
Gandhi (Fisher, 1995)
Jackie Robinson: He Was the First (Adler, 1989)
Jazz: My Music, My People (Monceaux, 1994)
The Librarian Who Measured the Earth (Lasky, 1994)
Lincoln: A Photobiography (Freedman, 1987)
Malcolm X: By Any Means Necessary (Myers, 1993)
Mother Jones: One Woman's Fight for Labor (Kraft, 1995)
Sequoyah's Gift: A Portrait of the Cherokee Leader (Klausner, 1993)
You Want Women to Vote, Lizzie Stanton? (Fritz, 1995)

Autobiographies

Behind the Secret Window: A Memoir of a Hidden Childhood during World War II (Toll, 1993)
Capturing Nature: The Writings and Art of John James Audubon (Roop & Roop, 1993)
Rosa Parks: My Story (Parks, 1992)
Ryan White: My Own Story (White, 1991)
Where the Flame Trees Bloom (Ada, 1994)

Series Books

Creative Minds (published by Carolrhoda)
Picture Book Biographies (published by Holiday House)
Sports Illustrated for Kids (published by Little, Brown)
Step-Up Biographies (published by Random House)
Trailblazers (published by Carolrhoda)

Nonfiction

Nonfiction books are intended to provide readers with facts and concepts about specific subjects, issues, and ideas (Duthie, 1996; Moore, Moore, Cunningham, & Cunningham, 1998). They may be used in the classroom for student self-selected independent reading, teacher read-alouds, or as texts for content-area and integrated thematic inquiry and learning (Bamford & Kristo, 1998, 2000; Freeman & Person, 1998). In addition, nonfiction books include resources like encyclopedias and specialized reference books

Good nonfiction books are also literature. The author writes enthusiastically about the topic and uses a variety of techniques to keep the child/reader involved: asking questions, writing in the first person, talking directly to the reader as "you," and using descriptive and figurative language and even humor. To be sure, the informational books available for children today are a far improvement over those of the past, which were often dry and dull.

Other features of nonfiction books can greatly benefit children. Illustrations—such as photographs, charts, diagrams, and maps—are very important in communicating content beyond words. And tools such as indexes, glossaries, definitions of terms, and lists of references and other sources can help students locate and understand information.

In choosing nonfiction for the classroom, teachers should look for those that present accurate and authentic information, are well organized, use an appropriate and appealing format and design, and are written in a style that's appropriate for the level of the student. Many such books exist. Informational books today are exciting, well written, beautifully illustrated, and even a little dangerous.

For example, third-graders are just the right age to fall in love with nonfiction books about creatures like sharks. Students at this age begin to see reading as a way of exploring the world and especially delight in close but safe encounters they would not ordinarily experience. A beautifully illustrated and simply written book like *Sharks*, by Ann Mc Govern (1976), can introduce children to the dangerous world of sharks. The illustrator, Murray Tinkelman, used black-and-white pen and ink and a crosshatching technique to create elegant images of the distinctive forms of sharks.

Sharks is also an excellent model for children to follow in writing their own informational texts, or reports. The book is organized in a question-and-answer format, so the table of contents is a list of questions; each is then answered in a double-page illustrated layout. The questions are simple, burning ones that students might ask themselves: "How long have sharks been around? What does a shark look like? When do sharks attack people? Are all sharks dangerous?" Students could generate their own lists of questions and answer them in writing their own reports. If the entire class did this, questions could be divided among groups or individuals and then combined for a class report. This approach would also lend itself to creating files and writing the report on computer, creating a separate file for each question. As groups researched and found answers to questions, their information could be added. Images and text from the Internet could also be added through hypertext or hypermedia tools.

Nonfiction Books as Models for Writing

When students write reports, they use many of the same strategies as authors of nonfiction. The following guidelines for report writing can be applied to many different topics and used to produce several different formats for the actual written report:

1. *Identify Questions to Answer:* Questions can be developed during class discussions on a topic. The teacher can make a simple list of these or use a KWL format. More questions can be added as study of the topic develops. As in the example with sharks, children can add questions about things they are curious about, and individual children or groups can each pick a question to answer as a natural way of organizing the class when learning in the content areas. If the topic is one in the regular curricululm—say, American history in the fifth grade—the teacher can suggest general questions and the children can add to them. Questions are useful in guiding children's exploration of a topic because they clearly delineate what information to look for (an answer) and are founded on a natural way of learning. For example, these questions could be used to guide a fifth-grade study of a period of American history:

- What happened in this period of history? Why?
- What were the most important events? Why?
- What were the problems of the times? Why?
- Who were the important people? Why?
- What was the daily life of the times like?
- What were the beliefs of the people at the time?

2. *Gather Resources:* The teacher should establish a classroom resource center, providing books, magazines, maps, objects and artifacts, photographs, and other memorabilia from the library or home. Information and artifacts obtained from fieldtrips and guest speakers are also valuable resources. The Internet can provide an unlimited supply of information, taking children almost anywhere they want to go in exploring a topic.

3. *Take and Organize Notes:* Students should take notes from various sources of information and begin to organize them on notecards, in outline format, or in a computer file.

4. *Write the Report:* Students can use many types of organizational patterns or structures to write reports on the information they have gathered. Some of these patterns were reviewed earlier in discussing students' reading of informational texts. Students should also know how to use these patterns in their own writing. Some are more appropriate for certain ages of children and for certain topics. Once children are familiar with these structures, they may choose the one that best fits their topic and abilities. Reports could be written in one class using a variety of these patterns:

- *Question and Answer:* This type of format was just described, using McGovern's (1976) book *Sharks* as a model. This is a simple but useful pattern and appropriate for young children and group work; using this structure is also a good way to organize a class for group work on a topic.

ELL

See the Snapshot in Chapter 12, Viewing and Visually Representing, for an example of such a frame used by third-grade teacher Audrey Eldridge while studying the solar system with her students, who were primarily English language learners.

- *List of Facts:* Listing facts is another simple structure that also lends itself to being adapted into a frame that students can complete as they learn about a topic, perhaps working with the entire class.
- *Description:* Students present information about a topic using illustrations and providing enough detail to enhance the reader's understanding. They also use good descriptive language, including vivid adjectives that portray what the topic looks, feels, smells, and sounds like. See Figure 14.9 for an example of a descriptive report on the self-selected topic

Figure 14.9 Student's Descriptive Report on a Self-Selected Topic

Cover

Porsches are beautiful, colorful and a state of the art. When you look at a porsche it is like you are watching the sea.

1

One day my dad got to borrow a porsche. The porsche was tan and It had a Kenwood stereo system. I Liked the heater. It feels like you are at home. When you make a lot of turns the wheel looks like it's going to pop off but it won't because workers tested the wheel

2

of Porsches by Santiago. He published this report as a book when his class was learning to write reports.

- *Compare and Contrast:* This pattern is appropriate with dichotomous topics or when it is important to understand how subjects are alike and different—for instance, comparing mammals/nonmammals or spiders/insects. Graphic organizers are useful in getting started. For example, a T-chart, which is simply a page divided into half vertically with a title over each half, could be used to brainstorm ideas about a pair of contrasting topics or ideas.

3
The price of this car is what gets me satisfied. I Like expensive cars Like $50,000 or even more. I saw this lady trying to buy this 959 but she did not have a credit, Car insurance, or enough money. I wanted to help because I had a few bucks but what the heck.

4
I had a dream once that I got the car in a different color and it cost me a fortune. After you get a porsche they give you these dumb stickers that say: SUPERPORSCHE SHowdown this is what it looks like top.

5
They use to give out these Porsche mugs but I guess they could not afford to ship them anymore. It cost too much.

6
Just imagine how many girls you can pick up with a porsche.
                    THE END

- *Problem and Solution:* This structure lends itself to solving science and mathematical problems but may also be appropriate for writing about issues such as the deterioration of the environment or world hunger.
- *Alternative Structures:* Informational reports may be written in many other structures or patterns, limited only by the imagination of your students. See the following Teaching Idea for examples of students' informational writing.

SNAPSHOT · Fifth-Grade English Language Learners Read and Write about Guts

See Chapter 3, First- and Second-Language Development, for more on an SDAIE.

ELL

These SDAIE strategies for English language learners make content comprehensible:

- Graphics and illustrations
- Hands-on experiences
- Combining art and writing
- Learning in groups

One of my former students, Basia Gliddon, used to teach fifth-grade English language learners (ELL) in Long Beach, California. (She's now a computer facilitator in the district.) One of her primary responsibilities was to use SDAIE (specially designed academic instruction in English) strategies for her students in content-area instruction. Basia knew that the fifth grade was an important time for students to learn about the human body, and she also realized she had to make the content accessible to her native-Spanish-speaking students, who were still becoming fluent readers and writers in English.

To teach students about the digestive system, Basia carefully chose two books to introduce the content: Paul Showers's (1970) *What Happens to a Hamburger?* and Joanna Cole's (1989b) *The Magic School Bus, Inside the Human Body.* The latter is from a popular series of books about Ms. Fizzle and her class, who go on great, fantastic adventures in which they learn about the body, the waterworks, the ocean, dinosaurs, and hurricanes, to name a few. Even though this type of book, sometimes called an *informational storybook,* has been criticized because of its fantasy aspect and fictionalizing of facts, it is extremely popular with children (Leal, 1993; Zarnowski, 1995). Basia used *The Magic School Bus* book because she felt it would make the content comprehensible to her ELL students through the use of a storyline, humor, engaging characters like Ms. Fizzle, charts and diagrams, Bruce Degen's lively illustrations, and a storyboard format, such as might be found in a comic or animated television show.

Here is a day-by-day account of how Basia's students read and wrote informational texts about the digestive system using informational books and SDAIE techniques. Basia and her students called the whole project "Guts."

Day 1. Reading and Discussing Informational Books

Basia introduced the topic by doing a KWL chart on the digestive system. Then she read aloud *The Magic School Bus, Inside the Human Body* and discussed it with her students, looking for answers to the questions they had raised on the KWL chart as well as pointing out key ideas she wanted them to learn. As they read, Basia recorded information they discussed from the book in the L section of the chart. She also drew students' attention to the different techniques the author and illustrator used to report the facts, such as drawings, diagrams, and charts. She wanted her students to use some of these text structures later when reporting information themselves.

Later in the day, Basia read another book, *What Happens to a Hamburger?* It is a less entertaining but equally informative book on how the body digests a hamburger. Again, students discussed the information and Basia added to the KWL chart. She also made multiple copies of each of these books available in the room for students to read, along with other books about digestion and other sources of information, such as encyclopedias and CD–ROMs.

Day 2. A Walking Fieldtrip to McDonald's

Basia's school was two blocks from a McDonald's, and she had already planned a walking fieldtrip there for lunch and a tour. Before leaving school, she and her students reviewed the questions they had about the digestive system and what they had learned from reading informational books. During the fieldtrip, everyone had fun. There was a lot of discussion about what was happening inside their bodies to the hamburgers and french fries they were eating. When they got back to class, the children made notes about what they thought had happened to the hamburgers they had just eaten. Basia also encouraged them to use drawings to record their ideas.

Day 3. Art and Writing

Students made a construction paper collage of the food they had eaten at McDonald's and talked about it. Then they wrote fictionalized versions of what happened to the hamburgers they had eaten, using their own experiences and the information they had learned about the digestive system. Here is one of them:

I Was Ordered for Lunch

I am going to write about how I felt when I went down the digestive system. It all started when I was a sourdough bacon cheeseburger and somebody ordered me for lunch. First, I went through the mouth and I got soaked with saliva. Second, I got crushed with white teeth. Third, I went down the esophogus. I got squished like butter in the stomach and boy was it fun. Fourth, I went through the small intestine and got mixed with the blood. I saw my best friend. His name is Doritos. Finally, I went through the large intestine. I saw a big hunk of green stuff. I was slipping and sliding through the toilet. I sure had a fun time in someone's body.

GREAT BOOKS FOR CHILDREN

The Magic School Bus Series (by J. Cole)

The Magic School Bus, at the Waterworks (1986); *The Magic School Bus, Inside the Earth* (1987); *The Magic School Bus, Inside the Human Body* (1989); *The Magic School Bus, Lost in the Solar System* (1990); *The Magic School Bus, in the Time of the Dinosaurs* (1994); and *The Magic School Bus, on the Ocean Floor* (1992). *The Magic School Bus* series has also had television and CD–ROM spinoffs.

Figure 14.10   Chart of the Digestive System

The Digestive System				
Mouth	Esophagus	Stomach	Small Intestine	Large Intestine
• Digestion starts here when you chew. • Saliva mixes and breaks down food.	• Made of muscle. • Moves food to stomach.	• Pear-shaped organ made of muscle. • Digestive juices mix with food to help break it down.	• Ropelike tube made of muscle; 4 meters long. • Food nutrients are absorbed into blood.	• Tube made of muscle; 1 meter long. • Water and nutrients are absorbed into blood.

Day 4.   Information Charts

Basia and her students designed a chart together to use to organize the information they were learning about the digestive system. Basia made copies of this chart at lunch, and her students filled in what they had learned. This activity also gave Basia a way to check students' understanding (see Figure 14.10).

Day 5.   Group Posters Reporting on the Digestive System

Basia divided the class into small groups, and each group made a poster demonstrating what they had learned about the digestive system. One poster contained a diagram of the organs of the digestive system, and another listed the sequence of what happens in the digestive system.

WWW

Students can read about historic figures such as Rosa Parks, Martin Luther King, Jr., and Mark Twain as well as contemporary heroes on this interactive website: **www.myhero.com**. They can also suggest their own heroes and write short biographies to tell the world about people they respect and admire.

Biographies and Autobiographies

In a *biography*, the author writes about the life of a real person, and in an *autobiography*, a person writes about his or her own life. Like nonfiction books, biographies and autobiographies have also had the reputation of being a somewhat inferior subgenre of children's literature. The ones I remember reading as a child don't hold fond memories. They were almost always assigned by the teacher and were usually related to a period of history our class was studying. They were often poorly written and seemed nothing more than a dry compilation of facts.

The content of biographies and autobiographies has also been lacking. For many years, they were written primarily about white men, often those with reputations as national heroes: George Washington, Thomas Jefferson, Patrick Henry, Daniel Boone, and others. The incidents and dialogue reported were often invented to perpetuate the mythic qualities or acts of the individuals, such as chopping down cherry trees and wrestling bears. Biographies and autobiographies of women, persons of color, controversial individuals, and people with more ordinary lives were in short supply. And when they were portrayed in books, these people were often characterized by stereotypes. For example, in 1940, James Daugherty won the Newbery Medal for *Daniel Boone* (1939), but his negative and stereotypical depiction of Native Americans would probably not make it into print today.

A major shift in standards occurred in biographies for children when Jean Fritz wrote *And Then What Happened, Paul Revere?* (1973). This book was authentic. Fritz did not invent any dialogue. She also used a friendly, conversational, humorous tone, which made the historical figures seem real and readily accessible to young readers. And she focused on the event that made Revere famous, rather than his whole life.

The biographies and autobiographies available for children today also include stories of the lives of women, persons of color, and people who have changed the world in many different ways, rather than just prominent political leaders. These stories are written with an authenticity and realism that shows a human as well as historical side. Today's biographies and autobiographies are also well written and illustrated, which has earned them a place among the best genres of children's literature. For example, Russell Freedman won the Newbery Medal in 1988 for his book *Lincoln: A Photobiography* (1987). This book also gave new prestige to photoillustration in books for children.

Real letters and historical documents are a fascinating source of information about the world and its people. They are often incorporated into biographies and autobiographies. Although not much information is presented this way in children's books, some is and it is worth noting, not only because of its historical validity but because it provides such a fascinating glimpse into the past. Through authentic texts, the words of people who changed the world, or at least lived in a different time or place, come to us from that time and place.

When helping children choose biographies and autobiographies, teachers should consider the following:

- Is the subject of interest to children?
- Are people characterized in realistic and nonstereotypical ways?
- Is the information portrayed in an accurate and authentic way?
- Is the writing style engaging and appropriate?

Biographies and Autobiographies as Models for Writing

See the guidelines for writing informational reports in the previous section, which can also be applied to writing about people. In addition, review the following written patterns, which are especially useful in writing a biographical or autobiographical report:

- ***All about Me/Him or Her/Them:*** Young children can loosely organize information about themselves to compile autobiographies or others to compile biographies. This information can be illustrated and put together in a book, with an interesting fact on each page.

GREAT BOOKS FOR CHILDREN

Jean Fritz continues to write biographies for children, including *You Want Women to Vote, Lizzie Stanton?* (1995), which is about suffragette Elizabeth Cady Stanton. Fritz has also written a fictionalized autobiography: *Homesick: My Own Story* (1999).

- *Chronology:* This is another simple structure that follows the traditional pattern: "I was born; I lived; I died." A timeline can be incorporated into this type of format.

- *Single Event:* This is the approach Jean Fritz takes in her wonderful biographies for children. She focuses on the event that distinguished the person enough so that many years later, someone would want to write a biography of him or her. For example, the life of Paul Revere was noteworthy in many ways, but he is most remembered for his famous ride warning the American colonists of the arrival of the British troops. That's the event Fritz describes in *And Then What Happened, Paul Revere?* (1973). Children can focus on such an event in a person's life, providing some information about the circumstances leading up to it or following it, as needed. (Teachers should keep in mind that this single-event pattern would not be useful for someone whose significance could not be limited to one event—for example, Eleanor Roosevelt.)

- *Point/Counterpoint:* This type of pattern presents the life of a person from two different perspectives. It would be useful writing about someone who personified an important or controversial position for which there was an equally important or controversial opposition and whose actions resulted in an important change. For example, the ideas and actions of Gandhi could be described in counterpoint to those of the British Empire.

- *Alternative Patterns:* Again, the possibilities are endless. Try some of the following, or use them in conjunction with the three patterns described above:
  1. Write a birth announcement for someone, or write his or her obituary or epitaph.
  2. Write an entry in someone's diary, journal, or memoir, or write a letter or memo from him or her. Focus on a specific event or relationship. Figure 14.11 is an example of a student writing about the lives of miners during the California Gold Rush as though she were a miner herself.
  3. Stage an interview with someone or a debate between him or her and someone else. Again, focus on a specific event or relationship.
  4. Write a script portraying an event in someone's life, and present it in a media or drama production.
  5. Create a diorama of an important place in someone's life, such as his or her home.
  6. Tell about someone's life in a one-person show by dressing up and acting like him or her.

CW

See children dress up and act like the people whose biographies they have read.

5.2

See the Story Retelling Record (p. 188).

Assessing Students' Understanding of Informational Texts

Retelling as an assessment tool was introduced in Chapter 5, Listening and Talking, with a description of how to do story retelling of literary texts. Retelling can also be used with informational texts to give teachers information about how

Figure 14.11 Student's Historical Journal Entry

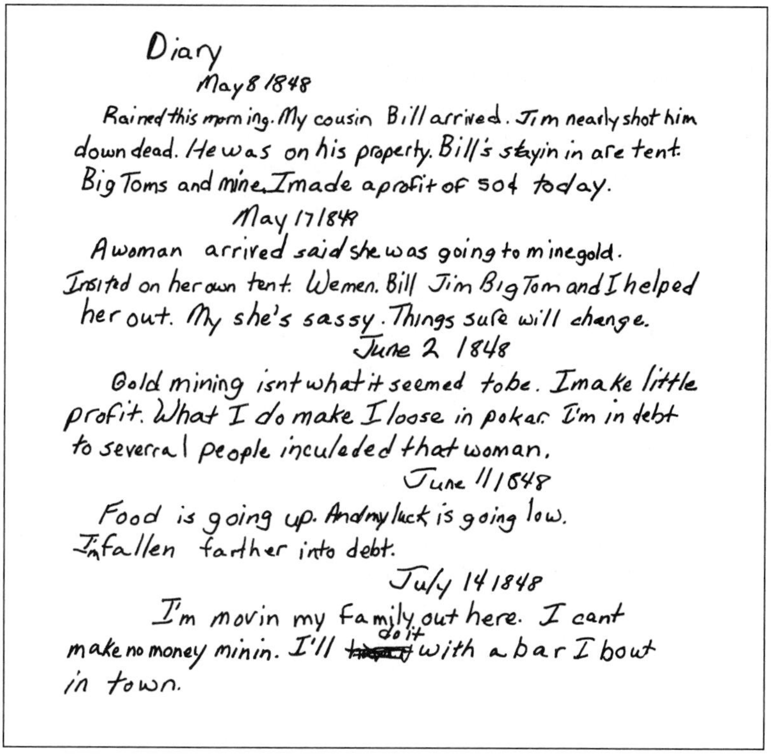

Diary
    May 8 1848
Rained this morning. My cousin Bill arrived. Jim nearly shot him down dead. He was on his property. Bill's stayin in ore tent. Big Toms and mine. I made a profit of 50¢ today.
    May 17 1848
A woman arrived said she was going to mine gold. Insited on her own tent. Wemen. Bill Jim Big Tom and I helped her out. My she's sassy. Things sure will change.
    June 2 1848
Gold mining isnt what it seemed to be. I make little profit. What I do make I loose in poker. I'm in debt to severral people inculeded that woman.
    June 11 1848
Food is going up. And my luck is going low. I'n fallen farther into debt.
    July 14 1848
I'm movin my family out here. I cant make no money minin. I'll ~~do it~~ with a bar I bout in town.

well students understand the information they've read, how well they can organize it, and how well they can summarize it.

For a retelling of an informational text, follow these steps (Morrow, 1989):

1. *Select the Informational Text:* Make sure the concepts and content are appropriate for the level of student. Use the same type and level of text, if you are comparing retellings over time. Note the topic, purpose, and main ideas of the selection. Make a list or an outline for yourself.

2. *Read and Retell the Informational Text:* The student should generally read the selection silently. Ask him or her to retell what he or she read. First use open-ended questions and prompts, such as "Can you tell me more?" and "You're doing a great job. Keep going." If you need to, use more specific prompts for the information in the text using your list or outline as a guide if the student does not bring them up unprompted. Check off facts as the student retells them.

3. *Summarize the Retelling:* Use Assessment Toolbox 14.1 (p. 500) to record and score the retelling.

14.1 Record for Retelling an Informational Text

Students' retellings of informational texts demonstrate how well they understand what they have read, how well they can organize it, and how well they can summarize it. This Retelling Record provides a simple format for making that assessment, assigning point values according to how well a student retells specific information. The maximum score is 10.

Retelling Record

Name _____   Date _____

Book Title _____

Read Aloud? _____   Read Silently? _____   Selected by: Teacher _____   Student _____

	Unprompted	**Prompted**
Introduction		
1 point: Identifies topic	_____	_____
1 point: Gives purpose or focus	_____	_____
Main Ideas		
Number given	_____	_____
Actual number	_____	_____
6 points: All correct		
4 points: $2/3$ correct		
2 points: $1/3$ correct		
0 points: None correct		
Understanding/Explanation of How Ideas Are Related	_____	_____
2 points: All related		
1 point: Some related		
0 points: No relationship		
Total Score _____ (10 points possible)		_____

Comments:

Source: Adapted from Morrow, 1989.

Ways for Students to Present Information

Throughout this text, you have seen examples of ways for students to present the information they have learned during thematic units and other strategies for integrating language across the curriculum. Table 14.5 lists about 100 ways to present information. Using this list as a starting point, I encourage you to create your own and to encourage your students to do the same. In fact, I recommend that when you teach a topic in the content areas, you offer students opportunities to do writing and other options to further their understanding of the topic, to demonstrate what they have learned, and to use both literary and informational texts in doing so.

The following Lesson Plan shows how you can build these options into a lesson integrating content and language arts and still allow for students to make suggestions. Their ideas are often the best.

 Table 14.5   100-Plus Ways for Students to Present Information

advertisement	cluster	fact file	newspaper	scrapbook
"All About . . ." book	collage	film	observational notes	scriptwriting
alphabet list	collection	filmstrip	pamphlet	sign
about . . .	comic strip	fold-a-book	performance	simulation
announcement	commercial	graph	photographs	slide show
artifact	construction	greeting card	photogram	song
audiotape	costume	journal	picture	speech
"big book"	dance	hypertext	plan	story
biome	data/results	interview	play	story dramatization
book	debate	lesson	poem	summary
book talk	demonstration	letter	position paper	survey
brochure	diagram	magazine	poster	T-chart
bulletin board	dialogue	map	program	table
calendar	diorama	mask	prop	talk radio
captioned picture	editorial	media event	puppet show	time capsule
cartoon	effigy	memo	puzzle	timeline
celebration	encyclopedia entry	mobile	questionnaire	transparency
center	essay	model	quilt	videotape
chart	exhibit	mural	reader's theater	"word wall"
chronology	experiment and	museum display	roleplay	writing pattern
classified ad	lab report	music	scene play	xerography

www

For the complete National Science Education Standards, go to the National Academy Press website: **www.nap.edu/ readingroom/books/nses/ html.**

IRA/ NCTE

www

For more information on natural science and outdoor education, go to the following websites:
www.nationalgeographic.com
www.sierraclub.org
 www.classroomearth.org
www.acornnaturalists.com

LESSON PLAN

Integrated Teaching of Science and Language Arts

Level: Grades 3–4

Subject: The changes that come with each new season—specifically, changes in leaves in the fall

Purposes: Using an inquiry approach to science, students will develop an understanding of the characteristics, environment, and life cycle of leaves; read and write related informational and literary texts; and present what they discover and create.

National Science Education Standards, Life Science, Content Standard C: As a result of activities in grades K–4, all students should develop understanding of:

- The characteristics of organisms
- Life cycles of organisms
- Organisms and environments (National Research Council, 1996)

Standard 7: Students conduct research on issues and interests by generating ideas and questions, and by posing problems. They gather, evaluate, and synthesize data from a variety of sources (e.g., print and nonprint texts, artifacts, people) to communicate their discoveries in ways that suit their purposes and audience.

Materials:
- Journals
- Leaves
- Crayons and unlined paper
- Text sets:

    Informational Texts
    Autumn Leaves (Robbins, 1998)
    Changes (Allen & Rotner, 1991)
    Exploring Autumn (Markle, 1991)
    Exploring Spring (Markle, 1990)
    Exploring Summer (Markle, 1987)
    Exploring Winter (Markle, 1984)
    Fall (Hirschi, 1991)
    A First Look at Leaves (Selsam, 1974)
    Spring (Hirschi, 1990)
    Summer (Hirschi, 1991)
    Tell Me Tree: All about Trees for Kids (Gibbons, 2002)
    Winter (Hirschi, 1990)

Literary Texts

Birches (Frost, 1988)
Leaf by Leaf: Autumn Poems (Rogansky, 2001)
The Sky Is Full of Song (Hopkins, 1983)
Sky Tree: Seeing Science through Art (Locker & Christiansen, 1995)
A Tree Place and Other Poems (Levy, 1994)
Voices on the Wind: Poems for All Seasons (Booth, 1990)

Teaching Sequence:

Part 1: Learning about Leaves from Nature and Informational Texts

1. Read aloud and discuss the informational book *Autumn Leaves* (Robbins, 1998), which explains why leaves change color and uses close-up photography to show each of 13 different types of leaves against a long-shot photo of the tree it's from.

2. Take a nature walk in the schoolyard or neighborhood. Have students observe trees and leaves and record what they see in journals using drawings and descriptive language. Each student should collect a leaf sample.

3. Back in the classroom, have each student use his or her leaf sample to make a leaf rubbing. (To do so, place an unlined piece of paper placed over the leaf and lightly color over it using a crayon.) The student should add to the drawing a detailed description of the leaf that was used, noting its color, shape, texture, and smell. In addition, he or she should use the notes made in his or her journal during the nature walk to create a simile or metaphor about leaves.

   > Look for season-related music to play while students work—for example, Vivaldi's *The Four Seasons*. Talk about how the music captures the season and the mood it creates.

4. Introduce key vocabulary for the three basic shapes of leaves using a simple two-column chart. List the three shapes—*broad, narrow,* and *needle*—in the lefthand column, and jot down descriptions, synonyms, and other information in the righthand column (see Figure 14.12).

Figure 14.12 Organizational Chart for Shapes of Leaves

Broad leaves	The type most plants have Wide and flat Maple and oak trees have these
Narrow leaves	Long and slender Grasses, corn, oats, wheat have these
Needle leaves	Look like short, thick sewing needles Grow on firs, pines, spruces, and most cone-bearing trees and shrubs

(continued)

WWW

For online information about leaves and seasons, go to **www.encarta.msn.com.**

5. Ask students to use this information to classify their leaves; each student should label his or her rubbing with the type of leaf and plant. Then sort the drawings into three groups and display them on a table or bulletin board, clearly labeling the type each group represents. Use this display to begin a new "science museum" in the class. Continue to add new leaves, student writing and projects, and related books.

6. Form four groups of students, and assign each group a season: summer, fall, winter, or spring. Have each group read and takes notes from a variety of informational texts (print and nonprint) about the life cycle of a leaf. What happens in the environment during that season that brings about changes in the leaf?

7. Bring the four groups of students back together, and have each group report what they learned about their season. Record the information on a chart that organizes the same basic information about each season (see Figure 14.13).

8. Each group should report on what they have learned by writing an informational report or by using any of the ways described in Table 14.5 (see p. 501). Encourage the groups to explore new ways of presenting information and not to all choose the same ones. Younger students, English language learners, and children who need extra support can use this report-writing frame:

> The season we are writing about is _____.
>
> The weather is _____.
>
> The temperature range is from _____ to _____ degrees.
>
> The length of daylight is about _____ hours.
>
> During this season, leaves are _____.

Figure 14.13 Organizational Chart about the Seasons

	Spring	Summer	Autumn	Winter
Weather Temperature range Amount of daylight Leaves in this season				

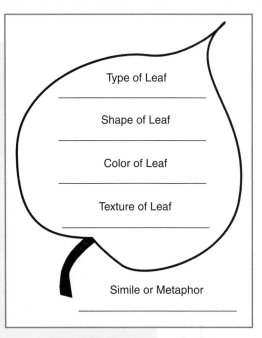

Figure 14.14 Template for a Leaf Poem

Type of Leaf
_____

Shape of Leaf
_____

Color of Leaf
_____

Texture of Leaf
_____

Simile or Metaphor
_____

Part 2: Reading and Writing about Leaves Using Literary Texts

1. As a class, read aloud and discuss poetry about leaves, trees, and the seasons. Choose from among the books in the text set—for example, *Birches* (Frost, 1988), *Leaf by Leaf: Autumn Poems* (Rogansky, 2001), or *The Sky Is Full of Song* (Hopkins, 1983).

2. As a class, generate a "word wall" of words and similes/metaphors that describe the textures, shapes, and colors of leaves. Then choose a particular kind of leaf and model for students how to write a leaf poem using a template like the one shown above in Figure 14.14. Select words and similes/metaphors from the "word wall" that are appropriate for the type of leaf you have chosen.

3. Have students create their own poems using the leaf form or any of the other poetic forms found in this chapter (see pp. 475–482). To create images, students can refer to the "word wall," the leaf poem that was modeled in class, the journal entries they made during the nature walk, their leaf rubbings, and anything else they have learned about leaves, trees, plants, and nature. Here are some ideas for writing poems:

   • *Simile or Metaphor:* Compare a leaf to something else using the word *like* or *as* for a simile or a descriptive phrase for a metaphor (e.g., *My leaf is a tiny green fan*).

   • *Free Verse:* In this poetic form, the words and phrases do not have to rhyme.

   • *Haiku, Senryu, or Tanka:* These forms of Japanese poetry use syllabic forms and are usually based on a nature theme.

   • *Concrete Poetry:* Arrange the words and phrases to make the shape of a leaf, or write them on a leaf rubbing or drawing.

   • *Song:* Write a song about leaves or a season of the year.

4. Students should share their poems by doing a poetry reading, creating a bulletin board display, making an illustrated book of collected poems, or singing songs and writing the words on a poster. All new materials should be added to the "science museum."

See Avril Font read aloud *Birches* to her first-grade students and then discuss alliteration, imagery, and patterns in poetry and trees.

(continued)

Ways for Students to Present Information

3.3

See the Anecdotal Record
Assessment (p. 106)

2.5

See the Peer-Assessment Form
for Group Work (p. 58)

See Chapter 7, Teaching with
Literature, for ideas about
bookmaking.

**TEACHER
RESOURCES**

Ellen Senisi's (2001) *Berry
Smudges and Leaf Prints:
Finding and Making Colors
from Nature* contains a wealth
of ideas on how to create
illustrations using materials
from nature.

Assessment:

1. Review each student's leaf rubbing (which he or she has annotated with descriptions and labels) to assess his or her understanding of the characteristics of leaves. In particular, consider whether the student has correctly classified the leaf using the key vocabulary introduced (i.e., broad, narrow, and needle leaves) and how he or she has recorded observations of leaves in nature and in the classroom. Create an Anecdotal Record Assessment (ARA) form using key vocabulary and relevant science standards.
2. To assess one another's group presentations, have each student complete the Peer-Assessment Form for Group Work
3. Conference with each of the four "season" groups, and review their informational report or other presentation. Have students explain these three things:
   - What they learned about the life cycle of a leaf and how the environment brings about changes in it during each season
   - What sources of data they used to learn about leaves (e.g., print and nonprint texts and artifacts)
   - How they communicated what they discovered with the rest of class
4. During sharing time, have each student report on one of the books he or she read about leaves or seasons (whether informational or literary) or one of the nonprint sources he or she used (such as a website). Include a question-and-answer period following each student's report. As class, use a simple rubric to record (a) books that were both informational and literary and what students thought about them, (b) nonprint sources and how useful they seemed to be, and (c) questions and answers that students exchanged after the oral reports.

Extending Activities:

1. During the schoolyear, continue to add information to the organizational chart about the seasons (Figure 14.13). Have each "season" group compile the information about their season at the end of the year using a hypermedia format, such as HyperStudio or PowerPoint.
2. In the spring, when buds first appear on the trees and bushes, observe them in nature or cut branches (with permission) and keep them in fresh water in the classroom. As a class, keep a daily journal that includes descriptions and detailed drawings of the changes that occur (see Figure 14.3, p. 473). Continue to research changes in leaves, and add relevant key vocabulary to observational notes.
3. As the seasons change, have the children write new nature poems and create new nature drawings. At the end of the year, make books of their collected works.

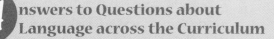

Answers to Questions about Language across the Curriculum

- ***What does* language across the curriculum *mean?*

   Language across the curriculum means to integrate teaching the language arts of listening, speaking, reading, writing, viewing, and visually representing with teaching in the content areas: social studies, science, mathematics, music, and the arts. Language across the curriculum is based on three principles: (a) all genuine learning involves discovery, (b) language has a heuristic function (i.e., language is a means to learn), and (c) using language to discover is the best way to learn it. In a student- and response-centered classroom, this means using an integrated approach to teaching, in which students ask questions, identify and solve problems, use research and study skills, and discover the interconnectedness of subject matter.

- **How should we use literary and informational texts in thematic teaching?**

   Thematic teaching has a long history and has been called by various names: *units, thematic units, theme study, theme cycles,* and *integrated and cross-curricular teaching.* According to this approach, teachers plan and initiate themes as well as collaborate and model ways for students so as to initiate themes for individual inquiry. Children should be guided to take an appropriate stance when reading and writing for different purposes: more aesthetic for reading literary texts and more efferent for reading informational texts.

   Students should have many experiences reading and writing across the curriculum: aesthetic reading and writing of literary texts such as poetry, songs, and stories and efferent reading and writing of informational texts such as nonfiction and biographies and autobiographies. Children's books can serve as models for both types of writing. Reading and writing literary and informational texts occurs naturally in student- and response-centered classrooms, in which teachers take an integrated approach to language across the curriculum.

Looking Further

1. Make a list or cluster of experiences that would be good for helping children write similes and metaphors. Make another list or cluster for writing a biography or autobiography.

2. Start a file of poems and patterns as models for writing in your classroom.

3. Choose a poem that you like and you think children will like. Make a cluster of possible "ripple effects" that this poem might create for reading and writing across the curriculum, including both literary and informational texts. Share the poem with a class, and try some of your ideas.

4. Use Assessment Toolbox 14.1, the Record for Retelling an Informational Text, with a student after he or she has read an informational text—say, a biography.

5. Choose a theme or an area of the curriculum (e.g., social studies, math, science, or fine arts)—something you might want to introduce to children or that interests you. Develop a cluster of ideas and a bibliography of related children's books.

6. Choose a topic in the language arts, and find, record, organize, and present information on it to your college class. Use one of the ways of presenting listed in Table 14.5 (p. 501).

Children's Books and Software

Ada, A. F. (1994). *Where the flame trees bloom*. New York: Atheneum.

Ada, A. F. (1998). *Yours truly, Goldilocks*. New York: Atheneum.

Adler, D. (1989). *Jackie Robinson: He was the first*. New York: Holiday House.

Adoff, A. (1982). *All the colors of the race*. New York: Lothrop, Lee & Shepard.

Alexander, L. (1964). *The book of three*. New York: Henry Holt.

Aliki. (1974). *Go tell Aunt Rhody*. New York: Macmillan.

Aliki. (1979). *Mummies made in Egypt*. New York: Harper-Collins.

Aliki. (1986). *How a book is made*. New York: Crowell.

Allen, M. N., & S. Rotner. (1991). *Changes*. New York: Macmillan.

American girl [series]. Middleton, WI: Pleasant.

Arnosky, J. (1987). *Drawing from nature*. New York: Lothrop, Lee & Shepard.

Ashabranner, B. (1982). *Morning star, black sun: The Northern Cheyenne Indians and America's energy crisis*. New York: Dodd, Mead.

Atwood, A. (1971). *Haiku: The mood of the earth*. New York: Scribner's.

Atwood, A. (1973). *My own rhythm: An approach to haiku*. New York: Scribner's.

Baron, V. (1968). *The seasons of time*. New York: Dial.

Behn, H. (1971). *More cricket songs*. New York: Harcourt Brace Jovanovich.

Behn, H. (Trans.). (1964). *Cricket songs*. New York: Harcourt Brace Jovanovich.

Berry, H. (1994). *Old MacDonald had a farm*. New York: Morrow.

Blumberg, B. (1985). *Commodore Perry in the land of the shogun*. New York: Lothrop.

Booth, D. (1990). *Voices on the wind: Poems for all seasons*. New York: Morrow.

Boston, L. (1955). *The children of Green Knowe*. New York: Harcourt Brace Jovanovich.

Briggs, J. (1970). *Jim and the beanstalk*. New York: Coward McCann.

Brown paper school books [series]. New York: Little, Brown.

Brown, M. W. (1949). *The important book*. New York: HarperCollins.

Bunting, E. (1992). *Coffin on a case*. New York: Harper-Collins.

Burghie, I. (1992). *Caribbean carnival: Songs of the West Indies*. New York: Morrow.

Byars, B. C. *Herculeah Jones* [series]. New York: Viking.

Calmenson, S. (1989). *The principal's new clothes*. New York: Scholastic.

Carroll, L. (1957). *Alice's adventures in Wonderland*. New York: Grosset and Dunlap. (Original work appeared in 1865)

Cherry, L. (1992). *A river ran wild*. New York: Farrar, Straus, & Giroux.

Choose your own adventure [series]. New York: Bantam.

Christopher, J. (1967). *The city of gold and lead*. New York: Macmillan.

Ciardi, J. (1961). *I met a man*. Boston: Houghton Mifflin.

Ciardi, J. (1962). *You read to me, I'll read to you*. New York: Lippincott.

Ciardi, J. (1989). *The hopeful trout and other limericks*. New York: Houghton Mifflin.

Cole, B. (1986). *The giant's toe*. New York: Farrar, Straus, & Giroux.

Cole, B. (1988). *Prince Cinders*. New York: Putnam.

Cole, J. (1986). *Hungry, hungry sharks*. New York: Random House.

Cole, J. (1986). *The magic school bus, at the waterworks*. New York: Scholastic.

Cole, J. (1987). *The magic school bus, inside the earth*. New York: Scholastic.

Cole, J. (1989a). *Anna Banana: 101 jump-rope rhymes*. New York: Morrow.

Cole, J. (1989b). *The magic school bus, inside the human body*. New York: Scholastic.

Cole, J. (1990). *The magic school bus, lost in the solar system*. New York: Scholastic.

Cole, J. (1992). *The magic school bus, on the ocean floor.* New York: Scholastic.

Cole, J. (1994). *The magic school bus, in the time of the dinosaurs.* New York: Scholastic.

Cole, J. *The magic school bus* [series]. New York: Scholastic.

Cole, W. (1972). *Oh, that's ridiculous!* (T. Ungerer, Illus.). New York: Viking.

Cooper, S. (1973). *The dark is rising.* New York: Atheneum.

Creative minds [series]. Minneapolis, MN: Carolrhoda.

Daugherty, J. (1939). *Daniel Boone.* New York: Viking.

Delacre, L. (1989). *Arroz con leche: Popular songs and rhythms from Latin America.* New York: Scholastic.

Demi. (1992). *In the eyes of the cat: Japanese poetry for all seasons.* New York: Henry Holt.

Dixon, F. W. *Hardy boys* [series]. New York: Pocket.

Ehlert, L. (1989). *Color zoo.* New York: Lippincott.

Ehlert, L. (1990). *Color farm.* New York: Lippincott.

Engdahl, S. (1970). *Enchantress from the stars.* New York: Atheneum.

Esbensen, B. J. (1996). *Echoes for the eye.* New York: HarperCollins.

Eyewitness books [series]. New York: Knopf.

Fagan, B. M. (1987). *The great journey: The peopling of ancient America.* New York: Thames and Hudson.

Fisher, L. (1995). *Gandhi.* New York: Atheneum.

Fleischman, S. (1985). *I am Phoenix: Poems for two voices.* New York: Harper & Row.

Fleischman, S. (1988). *A joyful noise: Poems for two voices.* New York: Harper & Row.

Fox, D. (1987). *Go in and out the window: An illlustrated songbook for young people.* New York: Holt.

Freedman, R. (1987). *Lincoln: A photobiography.* New York: Clarion.

Freedman, R. (1993). *Eleanor Roosevelt: A life of discovery.* New York: Clarion.

French, F. (1988). *Snow White in New York.* New York: Oxford University Press.

Fritz, J. (1973). *And then what happened, Paul Revere?* New York: Coward McCann.

Fritz, J. (1995). *You want women to vote, Lizzie Stanton?* New York: Putnam.

Fritz, J. (1999). *Homesick: My own story.* New York: Putnam.

Froman, R. (1971). *Street poems.* New York: McCall.

Froman, R. (1974). *Seeing things: A book of poems.* New York: Crowell.

Frost, R. (1988). *Birches.* New York: Henry Holt.

Gag, W. (1956). *Millions of cats.* New York: Coward, McCann. (Original work published 1928)

Galdone, P. (1985). *Cat goes fiddle-i-fee.* New York: Clarion.

George, J. C. (1972). *Julie of the wolves.* New York: HarperCollins

Gibbons, G. (2002). *Tell me tree: All about trees for kids.* Boston: Little, Brown.

Gollub, M. (1998). *Cool melons—turn to frogs! The life and poems of Issa.* New York: Lee & Low.

Gourley, C. (1996). *Sharks: True stories and legends.* Brookfield, CT: Millbrook.

Graham, J. B. (1999). *Flicker flash.* New York: Houghton Mifflin.

Greeley, V. (1990). *White is the moon.* New York: Macmillan.

Guthrie, W. (1998). *This land is your land.* New York: Little, Brown.

Gwynne, F. (1990). *Pondlarker.* New York: Simon & Schuster.

Hague, M. (1992). *Twinkle, twinkle, little star.* New York: Morrow.

Hamilton, V. (1988). *In the beginning: Creation stories from around the world.* New York: Harcourt.

Hamilton, V. (1993). *Many thousand gone: African Americans from slavery to freedom.* New York: Knopf.

Higginson, W. (1991). *Wind in the long grass: A collection of haiku.* New York: Simon & Schuster.

Highwater, J. (1994). *Rama: A legend.* New York: Henry Holt.

Hirschi, R. (1990). *Spring.* New York: Cobblehill/Dutton.

Hirschi, R. (1990). *Winter.* New York: Cobblehill/Dutton.

Hirschi, R. (1991). *Fall.* New York: Cobblehill/Dutton.

Hirschi, R. (1991). *Summer.* New York: Cobblehill/Dutton.

Hirsh, M. (1979). *One little goat: A passover song.* New York: Holiday House.

Hoberman, M. A. (1982). *A house is a house for me.* New York: Penguin.

Hoffman, M. (1991). *Amazing Grace.* New York: Dial.

Hopkins, L. B. (1983). *The sky is full of song.* New York: Harper.

Hopkins, L. B. (1999). *Spectacular science: A book of poems.* New York: Simon & Schuster.

Howe, D., & Howe, J. (1979). *Bunnicula.* New York: Atheneum.

Hoyt-Goldsmith, D. (1990). *Totem pole.* New York: Holiday House.

Imponderables [series]. New York: Harper.

Ipcar, D. (1964). *I love my anteater with an A.* New York: Knopf.

Janezcko, P. (2000). *Stone bench in an empty park.* New York: Scholastic.

Janezcko, P. (2001). *A poke in the I: A collection of concrete poems.* New York: Scholastic.

Johnson, S. A. (1991). *Roses red, violets blue: Why flowers have colors.* Minneapolis: Lerner.

Jonas, A. (1989). *Color dance.* New York: Greenwillow.

Juster, N. (1989). *As: A surfeit of similes.* New York: Morrow.

Keats, E. J. (1968). *Little drummer boy.* New York: Scholastic.

Keats, E. J. (1971). *Over in the meadow.* New York: Scholastic.

Keene, C. *Nancy Drew* [series]. New York: Pocket.

Kettleman, H. (1997). *Bubba, the cowboy prince: A fractured Texas tale.* New York: Scholastic.

Klausner, J. (1993). *Sequoyah's gift: A portrait of the Cherokee leader.* New York: HarperCollins.

Koch, K. (1980). *Wishes, lies, and dreams.* New York: HarperCollins.

Koch, K. (1990). *Rose, where did you get that red?* New York: Random House.

Kraft, B. (1995). *Mother Jones: One woman's fight for labor.* New York: Clarion.

Krull, K. (1992). *Gonna sing my head off!* New York: Knopf.

Kuklin, S. (1989). *Going to my ballet class.* New York: Bradbury.

L'Engle, M. (1962). *A wrinkle in time.* New York: Farrar, Straus, & Giroux.

Langstaff, J. (1967). *Over in the meadow.* New York: Harcourt Brace Jovanovich.

Langstaff, J. (1977). *Oh, a-hunting we will go.* New York: Atheneum.

Langstaff, J. (1987). *What a morning! The Christmas story in black spirituals.* New York: Simon & Schuster.

Larrick, N. (Ed.) (1992). *The night of the whippoorwill.* New York: Philomel.

Lasky, K. (1994). *The librarian who measured the earth.* New York: Little, Brown.

Lasky, K. (1999). *The emperor's old clothes.* New York: Harcourt Brace.

Le Guin, U. (1968). *A wizard of Earthsea.* New York: Parnassus.

Lear, E. (1946). *The complete nonsense book.* New York: Dodd, Mead. (Original work published 1846)

Lear, E. (1991). *The owl and the pussy cat.* New York: Putnam.

Lester, J. (1994). *John Henry.* New York: Dial.

Let's read-and-find-out science [series]. New York: HarperCollins.

Levy, C. (1994). *A tree place and other poems.* New York: McElderry.

Lewis, C. S. (1961). *The lion, the witch, and the wardrobe.* New York: Macmillan.

Lewis, J. P. (1998). *Doodle dandies: Poems that take shape.* New York: Atheneum.

Lewis, J. P. (2000). *Freedom like sunlight: Praise songs for Black Americans.* New York: Creative Editions.

Lewis, R. (1965). *In a spring garden.* New York: Dial.

Lionni, L. (1959). *Little Blue and Little Yellow: A story for Pippo and Ann and other children.* New York: Obolensky.

Livingston, M. C. (1990). *My head is red and other riddle rhymes.* New York: Holiday House.

Lobel, A. (1983). *The book of pigericks.* New York: Harper & Row.

Locker, T., & C. Christiansen. (1995). *Sky tree: Seeing science through art.* New York: HarperCollins.

Lowry, L. *Anastasia Krupnik* [series]. New York: Houghton Mifflin.

Lowry, L. (1993). *The giver.* New York: Houghton Mifflin.

Macaulay, D. (1977). *Castle.* Boston: Houghton Mifflin.

Macaulay, D. (1988). *The way things work.* Boston: Houghton Mifflin.

Markle, S. (1987). *Exploring summer.* New York: Atheneum.

Markle, S. (1990). *Exploring spring.* New York: Atheneum.

Markle, S. (1991). *Exploring autumn.* New York: Atheneum.

Markle, S. (1994). *Exploring winter.* New York: Atheneum.

Martin, A. M. *The babysitter's club* [series]. New York: Scholastic.

Martin, A. M. *California diaries* [series]. New York: Scholastic.

Martin, B. (1967). *Brown bear, brown bear, what do you see?* New York: Henry Holt.

McCord, D. (1977). *One at a time: Poems for the very young.* Boston: Little, Brown.

McDermott, G. (1972). *Anansi the spider.* New York: Henry Holt.

McGovern, A. (1969). *Black is beautiful.* New York: Four Winds Press.

McGovern, A. (1976). *Sharks.* New York: Four Winds Press.

McGovern, A. (1995). *Questions and answers about sharks.* New York: Scholastic.

McMillan, B. (1990). *One sun: A book of terse verse.* New York: Holiday.

Meltzer, M. (1982). *The Hispanic Americans.* New York: Crowell.

Merriam, E. (1992). *Rainbow writing.* New York: Atheneum.

Milne, A. A. (1926). *Winnie-the-Pooh.* New York: Dutton.

Milnes, G. (1990). *Granny will your dog bite? and other mountain rhymes.* New York: Knopf.

Monceaux, M. (1994). *Jazz: My music, my people.* New York: Knopf.

Myers, B. (1985). *Sidney Rella and the glass sneaker.* New York: Macmillan.

Myers, W. D. (1993) *Malcom X: By any means necessary.* New York: Scholastic.

Ness, E. (Ed. and Illus.). (1975). *Amelia mixed the mustard.* New York: Scribner's.

Nordine, K. (2000). *Colors.* New York: Harcourt Brace.

O'Neill, M. (1989). *Hailstones and halibut bones.* New York: Philomel.

Oram, H. (1993). *Out of the blue: Poems about color.* New York: Hyperion.

Parks, R. (1992). *Rosa Parks: My story.* New York: Dial.

Patterson, A., & Blood, P. (1990). *Rise up singing!* Bethlehem, PA: Sing Out!

Peek, M. (1981). *Roll over.* New York: Clarion.

Peek, M. (1985). *Mary wore her red dress.* New York: Clarion.

Picture book biographies [series]. New York: Holiday House.

Pilon, A. B. (1972). *Concrete is not always hard.* New York: Xerox.

Poetry express [Computer software]. Available from Mindscape.

Poetry palette [Computer software]. Available from MindPlay.

Pollock, P. (2001). *When the moon is full: A lunar year.* New York: Little, Brown.

Prelutsky, J. (1967). *A gopher in the garden and other animal poems.* New York: Macmillan

Prelutsky, J. (Ed.). (1983). *A Random House book of poetry.* New York: Random House.

Raskin, E. (1984). *The westing game.* New York: Avon.

Reynolds, J. (1991). *Sahara.* New York: Harcourt Brace Jovanovich.

Richards, L. (1932). *Tirra lirra: Rhymes old and new.* Boston: Little, Brown.

Robbins, K. (1998). *Autumn leaves.* New York: Scholastic.

Rogansky, B. (2001). *Leaf by leaf: Autumn poems.* New York: Scholastic.

Roop, P., & Roop, C. (1993). *Capturing nature: The writings and art of John James Audubon.* New York: Walker.

Rounds, G. (1990). *I know an old lady who swallowed a fly.* New York: Holiday House.

Rowling, J. K. *Harry Pottter* [series]. New York: Scholastic.

Schwartz, D. (1989). *If you made a million.* New York: Lothrop.

Scieszka, J. (1989). *The true story of the three little pigs.* New York: Viking.

Scieszka, J. (1991). *The frog prince continued.* New York: Viking.

Scott, H. J., & Scott, L. (1968). *Egyptian hieroglyphics for everyone.* New York: Funk and Wagnalls.

Seeger, R. (1976). *American folk songs for children.* New York: Doubleday.

Selsam, M. (1974). *A first look at leaves.* New York: Walker.

Selsam, M. E., & Hunt, J. (1972). *A first look at leaves.* New York: Walker.

Sherman, I. (1980). *Walking talking words.* New York: Harcourt Brace Jovanovich.

Showers, P. (1970). *What happens to a hamburger?* New York: Clarion.

Siebert, D. (1988). *Mojave.* New York: Crowell.

Siebert, D. (1989). *Heartland.* New York: Crowell.

Siebert, D. (1991). *Sierra.* New York: HarperCollins.

Siegen-Smith, N. (1996). *Songs for survival: Songs and chants from tribal peoples around the world.* New York: Dutton.

Silverstein, S. (1974). *Where the sidewalk ends.* New York: Harper & Row.

Silverstein, S. (1981). *A light in the attic.* New York: Harper & Row.

Simon, S. (1991). *Earthquakes.* New York: Morrow.

Simon, S. (1995). *Sharks.* New York: HarperCollins.

Sobol, D. *Encyclopedia Brown* [series]. New York: Bantam.

Spier, P. (1967). *London Bridge is falling down.* New York: Doubleday.

Spier, P. (1970). *The Erie Canal.* New York: Doubleday.

Spier, P. (1973). *The Star-Spangled Banner.* New York: Doubleday.

Spier, P. (1980). *People.* New York: Doubleday.

Sports Illustrated for kids [series]. New York: Little, Brown.

Stanley, D. (1992). *The bard of Avon: The story of William Shakespeare.* New York: Morrow.

Stanley, D. (1994). *Cleopatra.* New York: Morrow.

Step-up biographies [series]. New York: Random House.

Stevenson, J. (1995). *The bones in the cliff.* New York: Greenwillow.

Stevenson, R. L. (1947). *Treasure Island.* New York: Putnam.

Stewart, M. M. *Sweet Valley kids* [series]. New York: Bantam.

Stine, R. L. *Goosebumps* [series]. New York: Scholastic.

Switzer, E. (1995). *The magic of Mozart: Mozart, the Magic Flute, and the Salzburg Marionettes.* New York: Atheneum.

Taback, S. (1997). *There was an old lady who swallowed a fly.* New York: Viking.

Toll, N. (1993). *Behind the secret window: A memoir of a hidden childhood during World War II.* New York: Dial.

Tollhurst, M. (1990). *Somebody and the three blairs.* New York: Orchard.

Trailblazers [series]. Minneapolis, MN: Carolrhoda.

Trapni, I. (1994). *The itsy bitsy spider.* Boston: Whispering Coyote.

Tunis, E. (1961). *Frontier living.* New York: World.

Turkle, B. (1976). *Deep in the forest.* New York: Dutton.

Usborne books [series]. New York: EDC.

Weiss, N. (1987). *If you're happy and you know it.* New York: Greenwillow.

Weiss, N., & Thiele, B. (1995). *What a wonderful world.* New York: Atheneum.

What makes a . . . ? [famous artists series]. New York: Viking.

White, E. B. (1952). *Charlotte's web.* New York: Harper & Row.

White, R. (1991). *Ryan White: My own story.* New York: Dial.

Winter, J. (1991). *Diego.* New York: Knopf.

Wood, A. (1982). *As quick as a cricket.* New York: Child's Play International.

Worth, V. (1972). *Small poems.* New York: Farrar, Straus, & Giroux.

Worth, V. (1976). *More small poems.* New York: Farrrar, Straus, & Giroux.

Worth, V. (1978). *Still more small poems.* New York: Farrar, Straus, & Giroux.

Worth, V. (1987). *All the small poems.* New York: Farrar, Straus, & Giroux.

Yep, L. (1998). *The case of the lion dance.* New York: HarperCollins.

Yolen, J. (1981). *Sleeping Ugly.* New York: Putnam.

Zemach, M. (1966). *Mommy, buy me a china doll.* New York: Follett.

Zemach, M. (1976). *Hush, little baby.* New York: E. P. Dutton.

Ada, A. F. (1993). Contemporary trends in children's literature written in Spanish in Spain and Latin America. In J. V. Tinajero & A. F. Ada (Eds.), *The power of two languages* (pp. 107–116). New York: Macmillan.

Adams, M. J. (1990). *Beginning to read: Thinking and learning about print.* Cambridge, MA: MIT Press.

Akhtar, N., Dunham, F., & Dunham, P. (1991). Directive interactions and early vocabulary development: The role of joint 1 attentional focus. *Journal of Child Language, 18,* 41–49.

Allen, R. V., & Allen, C. (1968). *Language experience in reading.* Chicago: Encyclopaedia Britannica.

Allington, R. (1997). Overselling phonics. *Reading Today, 15,* 17.

Altwerger, B., Edelsky, C., & Flores, B. M. (1987). Whole language: What's new? *Reading Teacher, 41,* 147–155.

Altwerger, B., & Flores, B. (1994). Theme cycles: Creating communities of learners. *Primary Voices, K–6, 2,* 2–6.

Anderson, K. F. (1985). The development of spelling ability and linguistic strategies. *Reading Teacher, 39,* 140–147.

Anderson, R. C. (1985). Role of the reader's schema in comprehension, learning, and memory. In H. Singer & R. Ruddell (Eds.), *Theoretical models and processes of reading.* Newark, DE: International Reading Association.

Anderson, R. C. (1994). Role of the reader's schema in comprehension, learning, and memory. In R. B. Ruddell, M. R. Ruddell, & H. Singer (Eds.), *Theoretical models and processes of reading* (4th ed., pp. 469–537). Newark, DE: International Reading Association.

Anderson, R. C., Hiebert, E. H., Scott, J. A., & Wilkinson, I. A. G. (1985). *Becoming a nation of readers: The report of the commission on reading.* Washington, DC: National Institute of Education.

Anderson-Inman, I. (1990). Enhancing the reading-writing connection: Classroom applications. *Writing Notebook, 7,* 6–8.

Appelman, D., & Hynds, S. (1997). Walking our talk: Between response and responsibility in the literature classroom. *English Education, 29* (4), 272–297.

Applebee, A. N., Langer, J. A., & Mullis, I. V. S. (1986). *The writing report card: Writing achievement in American schools.* Princeton, NJ: National Assessment of Educational Progress.

Applebee, A. N., Langer, J. A., & Mullis, I. V. S. (1987). *Grammar, punctuation, and spelling: Controlling the conventions of written English at ages 9, 13, 17, The nation's report card.* Princeton, NJ: National Assessment of Educational Progress, Educational Testing Service.

Armstrong, T. (1994). *Multiple intelligences in the classroom.* Alexandria, VA: Association for Supervision and Curriculum Development.

Asher, J. (1977). *Learning another language through actions: The complete teacher's guide.* Los Gatos, CA: Sky Oaks.

Atwell, N. (1987). *In the middle: Writing, reading, and learning with adolescents.* Portsmouth, NH: Boynton/Cook.

Au, K. H. (1980). Participation structures in a reading lesson with Hawaiian children. *Anthropology and Education Quarterly, 11,* 91–115.

Au, K. H. (1993). *Literacy instruction in multicultural settings.* Fort Worth, TX: Harcourt Brace Jovanovich.

Au, K. H. (2000). Student generated rubrics: An assessment model to help all students succeed. *Reading Teacher, 54,* 395.

Au, K. H., & Jordan, C. (1981). Teaching reading to Hawaiian children: Finding a culturally appropriate solution. In H. Trueba, G. Guthrie, & K. Au (Eds.), *Culture and the bilingual classroom.* Rowley, MA: Newbury House.

Ausubel, D. P. (1963). Cognitive structure and the facilitation of meaningful verbal learning. *Journal of Teacher Education, 14,* 217–222.

Bachman, L. F., & Palmer, A. S. (1989). The construct validation of self-ratings of communicative language ability. *Language Testing, 6,* 14–29.

Balajthy, E. (1988). The printout: Voice synthesis for emergent literacy. *Reading Teacher, 42,* 72.

Balajthy, E. (1989). Holistic approaches to reading. *Reading Teacher, 42,* 324.

Baldwin, J. (1981). If black English isn't a language, then tell me what is? In M. Shugrue (Ed.), *The essay.* New York: Macmillan.

Baloche, L. A. (1998). The *cooperative classroom: Empowering learning.* Upper Saddle River, NJ: Prentice-Hall.

Bamford, R. A., & Kristo, J. F. (Eds.). (1998). *Making facts come alive: Choosing quality nonfiction literature K–8.* Norwood, MA: Christopher-Gordon.

Bamford, R. A., & Kristo, J. V. (2000). *Checking out nonfiction literature K–8: Good choices for best learning.* Norwood, MA: Christopher-Gordon.

Banks, J. A. (2003). Multicultural education: Characteristics and goals. In J. A. Banks & C. A. M. Banks (Eds.), *Multicultural education: Issues and perspectives* (5th ed., pp. 3–26). New York: John Wiley.

Banks, J. A., & Banks, C. A. M. (Eds.). (2003). *Multicultural education: Issues and perspectives* (5th ed.). New York: John Wiley.

Barber, B. (1982). Creating BYTES of language. *Language Arts, 59,* 472–475.

Barksdale-Ladd, M. A., & Thomas, K. (2000). What's at stake in high-stakes testing? *Journal of Teacher Education, 51,* 384.

Barnes, D. (1992). *From communication to curriculum* (2nd ed.). Portsmouth, NH: Heinemann.

Barnes, D. (1993). Supporting exploratory talk for learning. In K. Pierce & C. Giles (Eds.), *Cycles of meaning*. Portsmouth, NH: Heinemann.

Baugh, J. (1981). Design and implementation of writing instruction for speakers of non-standard English: Perspectives for a national neighborhood literacy program. In B. Cronnel (Ed.), *The writing needs of linguistically different students*. Los Alamitos, CA: Southwest Regional Laboratory Research and Development.

Baumann, J. F., & Heubach, K. M. (1996). Do basal readers deskill teachers? A national survey of educators' use and opinions of basals. *Elementary School Journal, 96*, 511–526.

Baumann, J. F., Hoffman, J. V., Moon, J., & Duffy-Heter, A. M. (1998). Where are teachers' voices in the phonics/whole language debate? Results from a survey of U.S. elementary teachers. *Reading Teacher, 51*, 636–650.

Baumann, J. F., & Ivey, G. (1997). Delicate balances: Striving for curricular and instructional equilibrium in a second-grade, literature/strategy-based classroom. *Reading Research Quarterly, 23*, 244–275.

Beach, R. (1993). *A teacher's introduction to reader-response theories*. Urbana, IL: National Council of Teachers of English.

Bear, D. R., & Templeton, S. (1998). Explorations in developmental spelling: Foundations for learning and teaching phonics, spelling, and vocabulary. *Reading Teacher, 52*(3), 222–242.

Bear, D. R., Templeton, S., & Invernizzi, M. (1999). *Words their way: Word study for phonics, vocabulary, and spelling instruction*. Upper Saddle River, NJ: Prentice-Hall.

Becker, H. J. (1994). How exemplary computer-using teachers differ from other teachers: Implications for realizing the potential of computers in schools. *Journal of Research on Computing in Education, 26*, 291–321.

Beers, C. S. (1980). The relationship of cognitive development to spelling and reading abilities. In E. Henderson & J. W. Beers (Eds.), *Developmental and cognitive aspects of learning to spell*. Newark, DE: International Reading Association.

Beers, C. S., & Beers, J. W. (1981). Three assumptions about learning to spell. *Language Arts, 58*, 573–580.

Beers, J. W., Beers, C. S., & Grant, K. (1977). The logic behind children's spelling. *Elementary School Journal, 77*, 238–242.

Beers, J. W., & Henderson E. H. (1977). A study of developing orthographic concepts among first graders. *Research in the Teaching of English, 11*, 133–148.

Bennett, B., Rolheiser, C., & Stevahn, L. (1991). *Cooperative learning: Where heart meets minds*. Toronto, Canada: Educational Connections.

Bishop, A., Yopp, R. H., & Yopp, H. K. (2000). *Reading for reading: A handbook for parents of preschoolers*. Boston: Allyn & Bacon.

Bishop, R. S. (1992). Multicultural literature for children: Making informed choices. In V. Harris (Ed.), *Teaching multicultural literature in grades K–8*. Norwood, MA: Christopher-Gordon.

Bishop, R. S. (Ed.). (1994). *Kaleidoscope: A multicultural booklist for grades K–8*. Urbana, IL: National Council of Teachers of English.

Bissex, G. (1980). *GYNS AT WRK: A child learns to read and write*. Cambridge, MA: Harvard University Press.

Blackburn, G. M. (1994). *Index to poetry for children and young people: 1988–1992*. New York: Wilson.

Bode, B. (1989). Dialogue journal writing. *Reading Teacher, 42*, 568–571.

Bond, G. L., & Dykstra, R. (1967). The cooperative research program in first-grade reading instruction. *Reading Research Quarterly, 2*, 1–42.

Bosma, B. (1987, November). *The nature of critical thinking: Its base and boundary.* Paper presented at the National Council of Teachers of English Annual Convention, Los Angeles.

Bowker, R. R. (Annual). *Subject guide to children's books in print.* New York: Bowker.

Boyd-Batstone, P. (2001). Free verse poetry frame for literary response. *California Reader.*

Boyd-Batstone, P. (2004). Focused anecdotal record assessment (ARA): A tool for standards-based, authentic assessment. *Reading Teacher.*

Braddock, R., Lloyd-Jones, R., & Schoer, L. (1963). *Research in written composition*. Urbana, IL: National Council of Teachers of English.

Bradley, U. N. (1982). Improving students' writing with microcomputers. *Language Arts, 59*, 732–743.

Breen, K. (Ed.). (1988). *Index to collective biographies for young readers* (4th ed.). New York: Bowker.

Breen, K., Fader, E., Odean, K., & Sutherland, Z. (2000). One hundred books that shaped the century. *School Library Journal, 46*, 50–58.

Brent, R., & Anderson, P. (1993). Developing children's classroom listening strategies. *Reading Teacher, 47*, 122–126.

Brewton, J. E. (1983). *Index to poetry for children and young people.* New York: Wilson.

Britton, J. (1970). *Language and learning*. Hammondsworth, Middlesex, England: Penguin.

Britton, J. (1984). Viewpoints: The distinction between participant and spectator roles in language in research and practice. *Research in the Teaching of English, 18*, 320–331.

Britton, J., Burgess, T., Martin, N., McLeod, A., & Rosen, H. (1975). *The development of writing abilities, 11–19*. London, England: Macmillan.

Brown, H., & Cambourne, B. (1989). *Read and retell*. Portsmouth, NH: Heinemann.

Bruce, B. (1994). Computers and school contexts. In A. Purves (Ed.), *Encyclopedia of English studies and language arts* (Vol. 1). New York: Scholastic.

Bruce, B., & Levin, J. (2003). Roles for new technologies in language arts: Inquiry, communication, construction, and expression. In J. Flood, D. Lapp, M. R. Squire, & J. M. Jensen (Eds.), *Handbook of research on teaching the English language arts* (3rd ed., pp. 649–657). Sponsored by the International Reading Association/National Council of Teachers of English. Mahwah, NJ: Erlbaum.

Bruchac, J. (1995). All our relations. *Horn Book Magazine, 71*, 158–162.

Bruner, J. S. (1978). The role of dialogue in language acquisition. In A. Sinclair, R. J. Jarvella, & W. M. Levelt (Eds.), *The child's conception of language* (pp. 241–256). New York: Springer-Verlag.

Bruner, J. S. (1983). *Child's talk: Learning to use language.* New York: Holt, Rinehart, & Winston.

Bruner, J. S. (1986). *Actual minds, possible worlds.* Cambridge, MA: Harvard University Press.

Buckley, M. H. (1994). Integrated English language arts curriculum. In A. Purves (Ed.), *Encyclopedia of English studies and language arts.* New York: Scholastic.

Bullock, A. B. (1975). *A language for life.* London, England: Her Majesty's Stationery Office.

Bury, C. (1993). When all the right parts don't run the engine. *Language Arts, 70*, 12–13.

Buss, K., & Karnowski, L. (2000). *Reading and writing literary genres.* Newark, DE: International Reading Association.

Butler, A., & Cox, B. (1992). Writing with a computer in grade one: A study in collaboration. *Language Arts, 69*, 633–640.

Button, K., Johnson, M. J., & Fergerson, P. (1996). Interactive writing in a primary classroom. *Reading Teacher, 49*, 446–454.

Cafolla, R., Kauffman, D., & Knee, R. (1997). *World Wide Web for teachers: An interactive guide.* Boston: Allyn & Bacon.

Cairney, T. H. (1990). Intertextuality: Infectious echoes from the past. *Reading Teacher, 42*, 478–484.

Cairney, T. H. (2000). The construction of literacy and literacy learners. *Language Arts, 77*, 496–505.

Calfee, R. C. (1999–2000). A decade of assessment. *Educational Assessment, 6*, 217–219.

California State Department of Education. (1981). *Schooling and language minority children: A theoretical framework.* Los Angeles: California State University.

Calkins, L. M. (1980). Research update—when children want to punctuate: Basic skills belong in context. *Language Arts, 57*, 567–573.

Calkins, L. M. (1983). *Lessons from a child: On the teaching and learning of writing.* Portsmouth, NH: Heinemann.

Calkins, L. M. (1991). *Living between the lines.* Portsmouth, NH: Heinemann.

Calkins, L. M. (1994). *The art of teaching writing* (2nd ed.). Portsmouth, NH: Heinemann.

Cambourne, B. (1988). *The whole story: Natural literacy and the acquisition of literacy in the classroom.* New York: Ashton Scholastic.

Cambourne, B. (1995). Toward an educationally relevant theory of literacy learning: Twenty years of inquiry. *Reading Teacher, 49*, 182–190.

Cambourne, B., & Turbill, J. (1987). *Coping with chaos.* Rozelle, Australia: Primary English Teaching Association.

Cambourne, B., & Turbill, J. (1990). Assessment in whole-language classrooms: Theory into practice. *Elementary School Journal, 90*, 337–349.

Catroppa, B. (1984). Writing for publication: Advice from classroom teachers. *Language Arts, 61*, 836–841.

Cattell, R. (2000). *Children's language: Consensus and controversy.* New York: Cassell.

Cazden, C. (1972). *Child language and education.* New York: Holt, Rinehart, & Winston.

Cazden, C. (1983). Adult assistance to language development: Scaffolds, models, and direct instruction. In R. P. Parker & F. A. Davis (Eds.), *Developing literacy: Young children's use of language.* Newark, DE: International Reading Association.

Cazden, C. (1985). Research currents: What is sharing time for? *Language Arts, 62*, 182–188.

Centre for Primary Language Education, Inner London Education Authority. (1988). *Primary language record.* Portsmouth, NH: Heinemann.

Chall, J. (1967). *Learning to read: The great debate.* New York: McGraw-Hill.

Champlin, C. (1997). *Storytelling with puppets.* Chicago: American Library Association.

Chancer, J., & Rester-Zodrow, G. (1997). *Moon journals, writing, art, and inquiry through focused nature study.* Portsmouth, NH: Heinemann.

Chaney, A. L., & Burk, T. L. (1998). *Teaching oral communication in grades K–8.* Boston: Allyn & Bacon.

Chapman, G. (1984). *Young playwrights.* Portsmouth, NH: Heinemann.

Chatton, B., & Collins, N. L. D. (1999). *Blurring the edges: Integrated curriculum through writing and children's literature.* Westport, CT: Heinemann.

Chavez, R. C. (1990). The development of story writing within an IBM Writing to Read program lab among language minority students: Preliminary findings of a naturalistic study. *Computers in the Schools, 7*, 121–144.

Choate, J. S. (2000). *Successful inclusive teaching* (3rd ed.). Boston: Allyn & Bacon.

Chomsky, C. (1969). *The acquisition of syntax in children from 5 to 10* (Research Monograph No. 52). Cambridge, MA: MIT Press.

Chomsky, C. (1972). Stages in language development and reading exposure. *Harvard Educational Review, 42*, 1–33.

Chomsky, C. (1980). Developing facility with language structure. In G. S. Pinnell (Ed.), *Discovering language with children.* Urbana, IL: National Council of Teachers of English.

Chomsky, N. A. (1957). *Syntactic structures.* The Hague, The Netherlands: Mouton.

Chomsky, N. A. (1965). *Aspects of the theory of syntax.* Cambridge, MA: MIT Press.

Chomsky, N. A. (1997). *Perspectives on power.* Montreal, Canada: Black Rose Books.

Christenbury, L., & Kelly, P. P. (1983). *Questioning: A path to critical thinking.* Urbana, IL: National Council of Teachers of English.

Christie, J. (1990). Dramatic play: A context for meaningful engagements. *Reading Teacher, 43*, 542–545.

Chukovsky, K. (1971). *From two to five*. Berkeley: University of California Press.

Clark, M. M. (1976). *Young fluent readers*. London, England: Heinemann.

Clarke, L. K. (1988). Invented versus traditional spelling in first graders' writing: Effects on learning to spell and read. *Research in the Teaching of English, 22*, 281–309.

Clay, M. M. (1967). The reading behavior of five-year-old children: A research report. *New Zealand Journal of Educational Studies, 2*, 11–31.

Clay, M. M. (1975). *What did I write?* Auckland, New Zealand: Heinemann.

Clay, M. M. (1985). *The early detection of reading difficulties* (3rd ed.). Auckland, New Zealand: Heinemann.

Clay, M. M. (1989). Foreword. In D. S. Strickland & L. M. Morrow (Eds.), *Emerging literacy: Young children learn to read and write*. Newark, DE: International Reading Association.

Clay, M. M. (1991). *Becoming literate: The construction of inner control*. Portsmouth, NH: Heinemann.

Clay, M. M. (1993). *An observation survey of early literacy achievement*. Portsmouth, NH: Heinemann.

Clemmons, J. L., Laase, L., Cooper, D., Areglado, N., & Dill, M. (1993). *Portfolios in the classroom: A teacher's sourcebook*. New York: Scholastic.

Clifford, J. (1991). *The experience of reading: Louise Rosenblatt and reader-response theory*. Portsmouth, NH: Boynton/Cook.

Clymer, T. (1963). The utility of phonics generalizations in the primary grades. *Reading Teacher, 16*, 252–258.

Clymer, T. (1996). The utility of phonics generalizatins in the primary grades: RT Classic. *Reading Teacher, 50*, 182–187.

Coburn, P., Kelman, P., Roberts, N., Snyder, T. F., Watt, D. H., & Weiner, C. (1982). *Practical guide to computers in education*. Reading, MA: Addison-Wesley.

Cochran-Smith, M., Kahn, J., & Paris, C. L. (1988). When word processors come into the classroom. In J. L. Hoot & S. B. Silvern (Eds.), *Writing with computers in the early grades* (pp. 43–47). New York: Teachers College Press.

Collodi, C. (1996) *Pinocchio* (Adptd. and illus., Ed Young). New York: Philomel.

Combs, M., & Beach, J. (1994). Stories and storytelling: Personalizing the social studies. *Reading Teacher, 47*, 464–471.

Commeyras, M., & Sumner, G. (1998). Literature questions children want to discuss: What teachers and students learned in a second grade classroom. *Elementary School Journal, 99*(2), 129–152.

Cook-Gumperz, J. (1979). Communicating with young children in the home. *Theory Into Practice, 18*, 207–212.

Cooper, P., & Collins, R. (1995). *Look what happened to Frog: Storytelling in education*. Scottsdale, AZ: Gorsuch-Scarisbuck.

Cordeiro, P., Giacobbe, M. E., & Cazden, C. (1983). Apostrophes, quotation marks, and periods: Learning punctuation in the first grade. *Language Arts, 60*, 323–332.

Courtney, A. M., & Abodeeh, T. L. (1999). Diagnostic-reflective portfolios. *Reading Teacher, 52*, 708–714.

Cox, C. (1975a). Film is like your Grandma's preserved pears. *Elementary English, 52*, 515–519.

Cox, C. (1975b). The liveliest art and reading. *Elementary English, 52*, 771–775, 807.

Cox, C. (1980a). Making films without a camera. *Language Arts, 57*, 274–279.

Cox, C. (1980b). Shakespeare and company: The best in classroom reading and drama. *Reading Teacher, 33*, 438–441.

Cox, C. (1982). Children's preferences for film form and technique. *Language Arts, 59*, 231–238.

Cox, C. (1983). Young filmmakers speak the language of film. *Language Arts, 60*, 296–304, 372.

Cox, C. (1984). Oral language development and its relationship to reading. In R. A. Thompson & L. L. Smith (Eds.), *Reading research review*. Minneapolis, MN: Burgess.

Cox, C. (1985a). Film preference instrument. In W. T. Fagan, J. M. Jensen, & C. R. Cooper (Eds.), *Measures for research and evaluation in the English language arts* (Vol. 2). Urbana, IL: National Council of Teachers of English.

Cox, C. (1985b). Filmmaking as a composing process. *Language Arts, 62*, 60–69.

Cox, C. (1985c). Stirring up Shakespeare in the elementary school. In C. Carter (Ed.), *Literature—News that stays news: Fresh approaches to the classics* (pp. 51–58). Urbana, IL: National Council of Teachers of English.

Cox, C. (1986). Gordon D. Shirreffs: An interview with a Western writer. *English Journal, 75*, 40–48.

Cox, C. (1987). Making and using media as a language art. In C. R. Personke & D. Johnson (Eds.), *Language arts instruction and the beginning teacher*. Englewood Cliffs, NJ: Prentice-Hall.

Cox, C. (1988). Scriptwriting in small groups. In J. Golub (Ed.), *Student-to-student: Practice in cooperative learning* (pp. 32–39). Urbana, IL: National Council of Teachers of English.

Cox, C. (1994a, December). *Challenging the text: Case studies of young children responding to literature*. Paper presented at the National Reading Conference, San Diego, CA.

Cox, C. (1994b). Media literacy. In A. Purves (Ed.), *The encyclopedia of English studies and language arts* (Vol. 2). New York: Scholastic.

Cox, C. (1994c, April). *Young children's response to literature: A longitudinal study, K–3*. Paper presented at the American Educational Reading Association Annual Meeting, New Orleans, LA.

Cox, C. (1997). Literature-based teaching: A student response-centered classroom. In N. Karolides (Ed.), *Reader response in elementary classrooms: Quest and discovery* (pp. 29–49). Mahwah, NJ: Erlbaum.

Cox, C. (2000, April). *Reader stance towards literature: A longitudinal study, K–6*. Paper presented at the annual meeting of the American Educational Research Association, New Orleans, LA.

Cox, C. (2002a, July). *Real and possible worlds of children's stance toward literature: A longitudinal study*. Paper presented at International Reading Association, Nineteenth World Congress on Reading, Edinburgh, Scotland.

Cox, C. (2002b). Making and using media as a language art. In C. R. Personke & D. D. Johnson (Eds.), *Language arts instruction and the beginning teacher: A practical guide* (pp. 199–207). Englewood Cliffs, NJ: Prentice-Hall.

Cox, C. (2002c). Resistance to reading in school. In M. Hunsburger & G. Labercane (Eds.), *Making meaning in the response-based classroom* (pp. 141–153). Boston: Allyn & Bacon.

Cox, C. (2003). The media arts. In J. Flood, D. Lapp, M. R. Squire, & J. M. Jensen (Eds.), *Handbook of research on teaching the English language arts* (3rd ed.). Sponsored by the International Reading Association/National Council of Teachers of English. Mahwah, NJ: Erlbaum.

Cox, C., & Boyd-Batstone, P. (1997). *Crossroads: Literature and language in culturally and linguistically diverse classrooms.* Columbus, OH: Merrill.

Cox, C., & Many, J. E. (1989). Worlds of possibilities in response to literature, film, and life. *Language Arts, 66,* 287–294.

Cox, C., & Many, J. E. (1992a). Beyond choosing: Emergent categories of efferent and aesthetic stances. In J. Many & C. Cox (Eds.), *Reader stance and literary understanding* (pp. 103–126). Norwood, NJ: Ablex.

Cox, C., & Many, J. E. (1992b). Toward an understanding of the aesthetic response to literature. *Language Arts, 69,* 28–33.

Cox, C., & Zarrillo, J. (1993). *Teaching reading with children's literature.* Columbus, OH: Merrill/Macmillan.

Cramer, R. L. (2001). *Creative power: The nature and nurture of children's writing.* New York: Addison Wesley.

Cummins, J. (1979). Linguistic interdependence and the educational development of bilingual children. *Review of Educational Research, 49,* 222–251.

Cummins, J. (1980). The cross-lingual dimensions of language proficiency: Implications for bilingual education and the optimal age issue. *TESOL Quarterly, 14,* 175–187.

Cummins, J. (1981). The role of primary language development in promoting educational success for language minority students. In *Schooling and language minority students: A theoretical framework* (pp. 3–49). Los Angeles: California State University.

Cummins, J. (1984). *Bilingualism and special education: Issues in assessment and pedagogy.* San Diego: College-Hill.

Cummins, J. (1986). Empowering minority students: A framework for intervention. *Harvard Educational Review, 56,* 18–36.

Cummins, J. (1989). *Empowering minority students.* Sacramento: California Association for Bilingual Education.

Cummins, J. (1991). Interdependence of first- and second-language proficiency in bilingual children. In E. Bialystok (Ed.), *Language processing in bilingual children.* New York: Cambridge University Press.

Cummins, J. (1992). Language proficiency, bilingualism, and academic achievement. In P. A. Richard-Amato & M. A.

Snow (Eds.), *The multicultural classroom: Readings for content-area teachers* (pp. 16–26). White Plains, NY: Longman.

Cunningham, P. M. (1976–1977). Teachers' correction responses to black dialect miscues which are non-meaning changing. *Reading Research Quarterly, 12,* 637–653.

D'Aoust, C. (1992). Portfolios: Process for students and teachers. In K. B. Yancy (Ed.), *Portfolios in the writing classroom* (pp. 39–48). Urbana, IL: National Council of Teachers of English.

Daiute, C. (1983). Writing, creativity, and change. *Childhood Education, 59,* 227–231.

Daniels, H. (1994). *Literature circles: Voice and choice in the student-centered classroom.* York, ME: Stenhouse.

Daniels, H. (2002). *Literature circles, voice and choice in book clubs and reading groups.* Honesdale, PA: Stenhouse.

Davidson, J. L. (1988). *Counterpoint and beyond: A response to Becoming a Nation of Readers.* Urbana, IL: National Council of Teachers of English.

Davidson, M., & Jenkins, J. R. (1994). Effects of phonemic processes on word reading and spelling. *Journal of Educational Research, 87,* 148–156.

Davis, J. H., & Behm, T. (1978). Terminology of drama/Theatre with and for children: A redefinition. *Children's Theatre Review, 27,* 10–11.

Day, J. P. Spiegel, D. L. McLellan, D., & Brown, V. B. (2002). *Moving forward with literature circles.* New York: Scholastic.

De Fina, A. A. (1992). *Portfolio assessment: Getting started.* New York: Scholastic.

De Ford, D. E. (1981). Literacy: Reading, writing, and other essentials. *Language Arts, 58,* 652–658.

De Groff, L. (1991). Is there a place for computers in whole language classrooms? *Reading Teacher, 43,* 568–572.

de la Luz Reyes, M., & Halcon, J. (2000). *The best for our children: Critical perspectives on literacy for Latino students.* New York: Teachers College Press.

De Villar, R. A., & Faltis, C. J. (1991). *Computers and cultural diversity: Restructuring for school success.* Albany, NY: State University of New York Press.

Delpit, L. (1988). The silenced dialogue: Power and pedagogy in educating other people's children. *Harvard Educational Review, 58,* 280–298.

Delpit, L. (1995). *Other people's children: Cultural conflict in the classroom.* New York: New Press.

Devine, T. G. (1978). Listening: What do we know after fifty years of research and theorizing? *Journal of Reading, 21,* 296–304.

Dewey, J. (1938). *Experience in education.* New York: Collier.

Dewey, J. (1943). *The child and the curriculum, the school and society.* Chicago: University of Chicago Press.

Diaz, S., Moll, L. C., & Mehan, H. (1986). Sociocultural resources in instruction: A context-specific approach. In *Beyond language: Social and cultural factors in schooling language minority students.* Los Angeles, CA: Los Angeles County Office of Bilingual Education, California State Department of Education, Evaluation, Dissemination, and Assessment Center.

 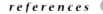

Dickey, E., & Roblyer, M. D. (1997). Technology, NAEP, and TIMSS—How does technology influence our national and international report cards? *Learning and Leading with Technology, 25*(3), 55–57.

Dickinson, D. K. (1986). Cooperation, collaboration, and a computer: Integrating a computer into a first-second grade writing program. *Research in the Teaching of English, 20,* 357–378.

Dixon-Kraus, L. (1996). *Vygotsky in the classroom: Mediated literacy instruction and assessment.* White Plains, NY: Longman.

Dole, J. A., & Osborn, J. (2003). Elementary language arts textbooks: A decade of change. In J. Flood, D. Lapp, M. R. Squire, & J. M. Jensen (Eds.), *Handbook of research on teaching the English language arts* (3rd ed., pp. 631–639). Sponsored by the International Reading Association/National Council of Teachers of English. Mahwah, NJ: Erlbaum.

Dublin, P. (1994). *Integrating computers in your classroom: Elementary language arts.* New York: HarperCollins.

Duffy, G. D., & Hoffman, J. V. (1999). In pursuit of an illusion: The flawed search for a perfect method. *Reading Teacher, 53,* 10–16.

Duffy, G. G., Roehler, L. R., & Putnam, J. (1987). Putting the teacher in control: Basal reading textbooks and instructional decision making. *Elementary School Journal, 87,* 357–366.

Duker, S. (1968). *Individualized reading: An annotated bibliography.* Metuchen, NJ: Scarecrow Press.

Dunkel, P. (1990). Implications for the CAI effectiveness research for limited English proficient learners. *Computers in the Schools, 7,* 31–52.

Durkin, D. (1966). *Children who read early.* New York: Teachers College Press.

Durkin, D. (1981). Reading comprehension instruction in five basal reader series. *Reading Research Quarterly, 16,* 515–544.

Duthie, C. (1996). *True stories: Nonfiction literacy in the primary classroom.* Portland, ME: Stenhouse.

Dyson, A. H. (1986). The imaginary worlds of childhood: A multimedia presentation. *Language Arts, 63,* 799–808.

Dyson, A. H. (1994). *Social worlds of children learning to write in an urban primary school.* New York: Teachers College Press.

Dyson, A. H. (1996). Faces in the crowd: Developing profiles of language users. In B. M. Power & R. S. Hubbard (Eds.), *Language development: A reader for teachers* (pp. 110–116). Columbus, OH: Merrill.

Dyson, A. H., & Freedman, S. W. (2003). Writing. In J. Flood, D. Lapp, M. R. Squire, & J. M. Jensen (Eds.), *Handbook of research on teaching the English language arts* (3rd ed.). Sponsored by the International Reading Association/National Council of Teachers of English. Mahwah, NJ: Erlbaum.

Dyson, A. H., & Genishi, C. (1982). Whatta ya tryin' to write? Writing as an interactive process. *Language Arts, 59,* 126–132.

Edelsky, C. (1986). *Writing in a bilingual program: Habla una vez.* Norwood, NJ: Ablex.

Edelsky, C. (Ed.). (1996). *With literacy and justice for all: Rethinking the social in language and education.* New York: Taylor & Francis.

Edelsky, C., Altwerger, B., & Flores, B. (1991). *Whole language: What's the difference?* Portsmouth, NH: Heinemann.

Eeds, M., & Peterson, R. (1991). Teacher as curator: Learning to talk about literature. *Reading Teacher, 45,* 118–126.

Eeds, M., & Peterson, R. (1995). What teachers need to know about the literary craft. In N. L. Roser & M. G. Martinez (Eds.), *Book talk and beyond: Children and teachers respond to literature* (pp. 10–23). Newark, DE: International Reading Association.

Eeds, M., & Wells, D. (1989). Grand conversations: An exploration of meaning construction in literature study groups. *Research in the Teaching of English, 23,* 4–29.

Elbow, P. (1973). *Writing without teachers.* London, England: Oxford University Press.

Elmore, R. F., & Rothman, R. (Eds.). (1999). *Testing, teaching, and learning: A guide for states and school districts.* Washington, DC: National Academy Press.

Evans, C. S. (1984). Writing to learn in math. *Language Arts, 61,* 828–835.

Falvey, M., Grenot-Scheyer, M., Coots, J. J., & Bishop, K. D. (1995). Services for students with disabilities: Past and present. In M. Falvey (Ed.), *Inclusive and heterogeneous schooling: Assessment, curriculum, and instruction* (pp. 23–29). Baltimore: Paul H. Brookes.

Farr, M., & Daniels, H. (1986). *Language diversity and writing instruction.* Urbana, IL: National Council of Teachers of English.

Farr, R., & Beck, M. D. (2003). Evaluating language development. In J. Flood, D. Lapp, M. R. Squire, & J. M. Jensen (Eds.), *Handbook of research on teaching the English language arts* (3rd ed.). Sponsored by the International Reading Association/National Council of Teachers of English. Mahwah, NJ: Erlbaum.

Farr, R., & Lowe, K. (1991). Alternative assessment in language arts. In C. Smith (Ed.), *Alternative assessment in the language arts.* Bloomington, IN: ERIC.

Farr, R., & Tone, B. (1994). *Portfolio and performance assessment: Helping students evaluate their progress as readers and writers.* Fort Worth, TX: Harcourt Brace Jovanovich.

Farrell, E., & Squire, J. (Eds.). (1990). *Transactions with literature.* Urbana, IL: National Council of Teachers of English.

Fearn, L., & Farnan, N. (1998). *Writing effectively: Helping children master the conventions of writing.* Boston: Allyn & Bacon.

Fernald, A. (1993). Human maternal vocalizations to infants as biologically relevant signals: An evolutionary perspective. In P. Bloom (Ed.), *Language acquisition: Core readings* (pp. 51–94). New York: Harvester Wheatsheaf.

Fisher, B. (1991). *Joyful learning: A whole language kindergarten.* Portsmouth, NH: Heinemann.

Fitzgerald, J. (1999). What is this thing called "balance"? *Reading Teacher, 53,* 100–107.

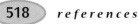

Flanders, N. (1970). *Analyzing teaching behavior*. Reading, MA: Addison-Wesley.

Fleischamn, P. (1990). *Shadow play*. New York: Harper.

Flesch, R. (1955). *Why Johnny can't read*. New York: Harper & Row.

Flood, J., & Lapp, D. (1993). Clearing the confusion: A closer look at national goals and standards. *Reading Teacher, 47,* 58–61.

Flood, J., Lapp, D., Flood, S., & Nagel, G. (1992). Am I allowed to group? Using flexible patterns for effective instruction. *Reading Teacher, 45,* 608–616.

Flores, B., Cousin, P. T., & Diaz, E. (1991). Transforming deficit myths about learning, language, and culture. *Language Arts, 68,* 369–379.

Flynn, N., & McPhillips, S. (2000). *A note slipped under the door: Teaching from poems we love*. Portland, ME: Stenhouse.

Fountas, I. C., & Pinnell, G. S. (1996). *Guided reading: Good first teaching for all children*. Portsmouth, NH: Heinemann.

Fountas, I. C., & Pinnell, G. S. (1999). *Matching books to readers: Using leveled books in guided reading, K–3*. Portsmouth, NH: Heinemann.

Fox, S. (1983). Oral language development: Past studies and current directions. *Language Arts, 60,* 234–243.

Franks, L. (2001). Charcoal clouds and weather writing: Inviting science to a middle school language arts classroom. *Language Arts, 78*(4), 319–324

Freeman, E. B., & Person, D. G. (1998). *Connecting informational children's books with content area learning*. Boston: Allyn & Bacon.

Froese, V. (1994). Language across the curriculum. In A. Purves (Ed.), *Encyclopedia of English studies and language arts*. New York: Scholastic.

Frost, R., & Hobbs, R. (1998). Instructional practices in media literacy education and their impact on students' learning. *New Jersey Journal of Communication, 6*(2), 123–148.

Fry, E. (1998). The most common phonograms. *Reading Teacher, 51,* 620–622.

Frye, N. (1964). *The educated imagination*. Bloomington, IN: Indiana University Press.

Fuller, L. B. (1994). Critical viewing. In A. C. Purves (Ed.), *Encyclopedia of English studies and language arts* (p. 329). New York: Scholastic.

Funk, H., & Funk, G. (1989). Guidelines for developing listening skills. *Reading Teacher, 42,* 660–663.

Galda, L. (1984). Narrative competence: Play, storytelling, and story comprehension. In A. Pellegrini & T. Yawkey (Eds.), *The development of oral and written language in social contexts* (pp. 105–117). Norwood, NJ: Ablex.

Galda, L., & Beach, R. (2001). Response to literature as a cultural activity. *Reading Research Quarterly, 36,* 64–73.

Gallas, K. (1992). When the children take the chair: A study of sharing time in a primary classroom. *Language Arts, 69,* 172–182.

Galley, S. M. (2000). Portfolio as mirror: Student and teacher learning reflected through the standards. *Language Arts, 78,* 121–127.

Garcia, E. (1992). Hispanic children: Theoretical, empirical and related policy issues. *Educational Psychology Review, 4,* 69–93.

Garcia, E. (1993). Director's note: Linguistic diversity and national standards. *Focus on Diversity, 1*(3), 1–2. University of California, Santa Cruz: National Center for Research on Cultural Diversity and Second Language Learning.

Gardner, H. (1983). *Multiple intelligences: The theory in practice*. New York: Basic Books.

Garrison, A. (1998). Reading and writing media across the curricululm. In C. Cox (Ed.), *Media literacy: Classroom practices in the teaching of the English language arts*. Urbana, IL: National Council of Teachers of English.

Garthtwait, A. (2001). Hypermedia composing: Questions arising from writing in three dimensions. *Language Arts, 78*(3), 237–244.

Gates, A. I., & Bond, G. L. (1936). Reading readiness: A study of factors determining success and failure in beginning reading. *Teachers College Record, 37,* 679–685.

Geller, L. (1981). Riddling: A playful way to explore language. *Language Arts, 58,* 669–674.

Geller, L. (1985). *Word play and language learning for children*. Urbana, IL: National Council of Teachers of English.

Genishi, C. (1988). Kindergartners and computers: A case study of six children. *Elementary School Journal, 89,* 185–201.

Gentry, J. R. (1981). Learning to spell developmentally. *Reading Teacher, 34,* 378–381.

Gentry, J. R. (1982). An analysis of developmental spelling in GNYS at WRK. *Reading Teacher, 36,* 192–200.

Gentry, J. R. (1985). Developmental spelling inventory. *Teaching K–8,* 50.

Gentry, J. R. (1987). *Spel . . . is a four-letter word*. Portsmouth, NH: Heinemann.

Gentry, J. R. (2000). A retrospective on invented spelling and a look forward. *Reading Teacher, 54*(3), 318–332.

Gentry, J. R., & Gillet, J. W. (1993). *Teaching kids to spell*. Portsmouth, NH: Heinemann.

Gettinger, M. (1993). Effects of error correction on third graders' spelling. *Journal of Educational Research, 87,* 39–45.

Gibb, G. S., & Dyches, T. T. (2000). *Guide to writing quality individualized education programs*. Boston: Allyn & Bacon.

Gibbons, P. (1993). *Learning to learn a second language*. Portsmouth, NH: Heinemann.

Gillespie, J. T. (2001). *Best books for children: Preschool through grade 6*. Westport, CT: Bowker-Greenwood.

Gleason, J. B. (Ed.). (1989). *The development of language* (2nd ed.). Columbus, OH: Merrill/Macmillan.

Glenn, C., & Stein, N. (1979). An analysis of story comprehension in elementary school children. In R. Freedle (Ed.), *New directions in discourse processing* (Vol. 2, pp. 68–85). Hillsdale, NJ: Erlbaum.

Glover, M. K. (1999). *A garden of poets*. Urbana, IL: National Council of Teachers of English.

Goldenberg, C. (1993). Instructional conversations: Promoting comprehension through discussion. *Reading Teacher, 46,* 316–326.

Gonzalez, V., Fry, L., Lopez, S., Jordan, J., Sloan, C., & McAdams, D. (1995). Our journey toward better conversations about books. In N. L. Roser & M. G. Martinez (Eds.), *Book talk and beyond: Children and teachers respond to literature* (pp. 168–187). Newark, DE: International Reading Association.

Gonzalez-Edfelt, A. (1990). Oral interaction and collaboration at the computer: Learning English as a second language with the help of your peers. *Computers in Schools, 7,* 211–226.

Goodlad, J. (1984). *A place called school: Prospects for the future.* New York: McGraw-Hill.

Goodman, K. S. (1976). Reading: A psycholinguistic guessing game. In H. Singer & R. Ruddell (Eds.), *Theoretical models in processes of reading* (2nd ed.). Newark, DE: International Reading Association.

Goodman, K. S. (1978). *Reading of American children whose language is a stable rural dialect of English and a language other than English, Final Report.* Washington, DC: U.S. Department of Health, Education, and Welfare, National Institute of Education.

Goodman, K. S. (1986). *What's whole in whole language?* Portsmouth, NH: Heinemann.

Goodman, K. S. (1992). I didn't found whole language. *Reading Teacher, 46,* 188–199.

Goodman, K. S. (1994). Reading, writing, and written texts: A transactional sociopsycholinguistic view. In R. B. Ruddell, M. R. Ruddell, & H. Singer (Eds.), *Theoretical models and processes of reading* (4th ed., pp. 1093–1130). Newark, DE: International Reading Association.

Goodman, K. S., & Goodman, Y. (1983). Reading and writing relationships: Pragmatic functions. *Language Arts, 60,* 590–591.

Goodman, K. S., Shannon, P., Freeman, Y., & Murphy, S. (1988). *Report card on basal readers.* New York: Richard C. Owen.

Goodman, Y. (1980). The roots of literacy. In M. P. Douglass (Ed.), *Claremont Reading Conference 44th yearbook.* Claremont, CA: Claremont Graduate School.

Goodman, Y. (1985). Kidwatching: Observing children in the classroom. In A. Jaggar & M. T. Smith-Burke (Eds.), *Observing the language learner* (pp. 9–18). Urbana, IL: National Council of Teachers of English.

Goodman, Y. (1986). Children coming to know literacy. In W. H. Teale & E. Sulzby (Eds.), *Emergent literacy: Reading and writing* (pp. 1–14). Norwood, NJ: Ablex.

Goswami, U., & Bryant, P. (1990). *Phonological skills and learning to read.* Hillsdale, NJ: Erlbaum.

Goswami, U., & Mead, F. (1992). Onset and rime awareness and analogies in reading. *Reading Research Quarterly, 27,* 150–162.

Gough, P. B. (1976). One second of reading. In H. Singer & R. Ruddell (Eds.), *Theoretical models and processes of reading* (2nd ed.). Newark, DE: International Reading Association.

Grabe, M., & Grabe, C. (1998). *Integrating technology for meaningful learning* (2nd ed.). Boston: Houghton Mifflin.

Grabe, M., & Grabe, C. (2000). *Integrating the Internet for meaningful learning.* Boston: Allyn & Bacon.

Grant, C. A., & Sleeter, C. E. (1997). Race, class, gender, and disability in the classroom. In J. A. Banks & C. A. M. Banks (Eds.), *Multicultural education: Issues and perspectives* (3rd ed., pp. 61–83). Boston: Allyn & Bacon.

Grant, C. A., & Sleeter, C. E. (2003). Race, class, gender, and disability in the classroom. In J. A. Banks & C. A. M. Banks (Eds.), *Multicultural education: Issues and perspectives* (5th ed., pp. 59–79). New York: John Wiley.

Graves, D. H. (1978a). *Balance the basics: Let them write.* New York: Ford Foundation.

Graves, D. H. (1978b). Research update: Handwriting is for writing. *Language Arts, 55,* 393–399.

Graves, D. H. (1983). *Writing: Teachers and children at work.* Portsmouth, NH: Heinemann.

Graves, D. H. (1994). *A fresh look at writing.* Portsmouth, NH: Heinemann.

Graves, D. H. (1995). Sharing the tools of the writing trade: New ways to teach children conventions of punctuation. *Instructor, 4,* 39–40.

Graves, D. H. (1996). If you write, they will, too. *Instructor, 5,* 41.

Graves, D. H., & Hansen, J. (1983). The author's chair. *Language Arts, 60,* 176–183.

Graves, D. H., & Sunstein, B. (Eds.). (1992). *Portfolio portraits.* Portsmouth, NH: Heinemann.

Gray, E. N. (2001). A literacy growth spurt during inquiry: Tommy's story. *Language Arts, 78*(4), 325–332.

Green, J. L., & Meyer, L. A. (1990). The embeddedness of reading in classroom life: Reading as a situated process. In C. Baker & A. Luke (Eds.), *The sociology of reading* (pp. 141–160). Amsterdam, The Netherlands: Benjamins.

Grenot-Scheyer, M., Jubala, K. A., Bishop, K. D., & Coots, J. J. (1996). *The inclusive classroom.* Westminister, CA: Teacher Created Materials.

Gunn, C. (1990). Computers in a whole language classroom. *Writing Notebook, 7,* 12–15.

Haley-James, S., & Hobson, C. D. (1980). Interviewing: A means of encouraging the drive to communicate. *Language Arts, 57,* 497–502.

Hall, N., & Robinson, A. (Eds.). (1996). *Learning about punctuation.* Portsmouth, NH: Heinemann.

Hallahan, D. P., & Kauffman, J. M. (2000). *Exceptional learners: Introduction to special education* (8th ed.). Boston: Allyn & Bacon.

Halliday, M. A. K. (1975). *Learning how to mean.* London, England: Edward Arnold.

Hamilton, V. (1993). Everything of value: Moral realism in literature for children. *Journal of Youth Services Library, 6,* 363–377.

Hammill, D. D., Larsen, S., & McNutt, G. (1977). The effects of spelling instruction: A preliminary study. *Elementary School Journal, 78,* 67–72.

Hanna, P. R., Hanna, J. S., Hodges, R. E., & Rudorf, E. H. (1966). *Phoneme-grapheme correspondences as cues to spelling improvement.* Washington, DC: U.S. Office of Education.

Hansen, J. (1987). *When writers read.* Portsmouth, NH: Heinemann.

Hansen, J. (2003). The language arts interact. In J. Flood, D. Lapp, M. R. Squire, & J. M. Jensen (Eds.), *Handbook of research on teaching the English language arts* (3rd ed., pp. 1026–1034). Sponsored by the International Reading Association/National Council of Teachers of English. Mahwah, NJ: Erlbaum.

Harber, J., & Beatty, J. (1978). *Reading and the black English speaking child.* Newark, DE: International Reading Association.

Harp, W. (Ed.). (1993). *Assessment and evaluation in whole language programs.* Norwood, MA: Christopher-Gordon.

Harris, J. (1995). Curricularly infused telecomputing: A structural approach to activity design. *Computers in the Schools, 11*(3), 49–59.

Harris, J. (1997). Wetware: Why use activity structures? *Learning and Leading with Technology, 25*(4), 12–17.

Harris, T. L., & Hodges, R. E. (Eds.). (1995). *The literacy dictionary: The vocabulary of reading and writing.* Newark, DE: International Reading Association.

Harris, V. J. (Ed.). (1992). *Teaching multicultural literature in grades K–8.* Norwood, MA: Christopher-Gordon.

Harris, V. J. (Ed.). (1997). *Using multiethnic literature in the K–8 classroom.* Norwood, MA: Christopher-Gordon.

Harste, J. C. (1990). Jerry Harste speaks on reading and writing. *Reading Teacher, 43,* 316–318.

Harste, J. C., Short, K. G., & Burke, C. (1988). Literature circles. In *Creating classrooms for authors* (pp. 293–304). Portsmouth, NH: Heinemann.

Harste, J. C., Woodward, V. A., & Burke, C. L. (1984). *Language stories and literacy lessons.* Portsmouth, NH: Heinemann.

Harvey, S. (1998). *Nonfiction matters: Reading, writing, and research in grades 3–8.* Portland, ME: Stenhouse.

Heath, S. B. (1983). *Ways with words: Language, life, and work in communities and classrooms.* Cambridge, England: Cambridge University Press.

Heath, S. B. (1986). Sociocultural contexts of language development. In *Beyond language: Social and cultural factors in schooling language minority students* (pp. 143–186). Los Angeles: California State University.

Heath, S. B. (1991). The sense of being literate: Historical and cross-cultural features. In R. Barr, M. Kamil, P. Mosenthal, & P. D. Pearson (Eds.), *Handbook of reading research* (Vol. 2, pp. 3–25). New York: Longman.

Heath, S. B. (1994). The children of Trackton's children: Spoken and written language in social change. In R. B. Ruddell, M. R. Ruddell, & H. Singer (Eds.), *Theoretical models and processes of reading* (4th ed., pp. 208–230). Newark, DE: International Reading Association.

Heath, S. B. (1996). A lot of talk about nothing. In B. M. Power & R. S. Hubbard (Eds.), *Language development: A reader for teachers.* Columbus, OH: Merrill.

Heathcote, D. (1981). Drama as education. In N. McCaslin (Ed.), *Children and drama* (2nd ed.). New York: Longman.

Heathcote, D. (1983). Learning, knowing, and languaging in drama. *Language Arts, 60.* 695–701.

Heinig, R. (1992). *Improvisations with favorite tales: Integrating drama into the reading/writing classroom.* Portsmouth, NH: Heinemann.

Helper, S. (1991). Talking our way into literacy in the classroom community. *New Advocate, 4,* 179–191.

Hemphill, L. (1999). Narrative style, social class, and response to poetry. *Research in the Teaching of English, 33*(3), 275–302.

Henderson, E. H. (1980). Word knowledge and reading disability. In E. H. Henderson & J. W. Beers (Eds.), *Developmental and cognitive aspects of learning to spell.* Newark, DE: International Reading Association.

Henderson, E. H. (1990). *Teaching spelling* (2nd ed.). Boston: Houghton Mifflin.

Henderson, E. H., & Templeton, S. (1986). A developmental perspective of formal spelling instruction through alphabet, pattern, and meaning. *Elementary School Journal, 86,* 304–316.

Herman, J. L., Aschbacher, P. R., & Winters, L. (1992). *A practical guide to alternative assessment.* Alexandria, VA: Association for Supervision and Curriculum Development.

Herrell, A. L., & Fowler, J. P. (1998). *Camcorder in the classroom: Using the videocamera to enliven curricululm.* Upper Saddle River, NJ: Prentice-Hall.

Hiebert, E. H., & Colt, J. (1989). Patterns of literature-based reading instruction. *Reading Teacher, 43,* 14–19.

Hillocks, G. (1987). *Research on written composition: New directions for teaching.* Urbana, IL: National Conference on Research in English and the ERIC Clearinghouse on Reading and Communication Skills.

Hillocks, G., & Smith, M. W. (2003). Grammar and usage. In J. Flood, D. Lapp, M. R. Squire, & J. M. Jensen (Eds.), *Handbook of research on teaching the English language arts* (3rd ed.). Sponsored by the International Reading Association/National Council of Teachers of English. Mahwah, NJ: Erlbaum.

Hipple, M. L. (1985). Journal writing in kindergarten. *Language Arts, 62,* 255–261.

Hodges, R. E. (1991). The conventions of writing. In J. Flood, D. Lapp, M. R. Squire, & J. M. Jensen (Eds.), *Handbook of research on teaching the English language arts* (2nd ed.). Sponsored by the International Reading Association/National Council of Teachers of English. Mahwah, NJ: Erlbaum.

Hoffman, J., Assaf, L., Pennington, J., & Paris, S. G. (2001) High stakes testing in reading: Today in Texas, tomorrow? *Reading Teacher, 54*, 482–492.

Hoffman, J., McCarthey, S. J., Elliott, B., Bayles, D. L., Price, D. P., Ferree, A., Abbott, J. A. (1998). The literature-based basals in first-grade classrooms: Savior, Satan, or same-old, same-old? *Reading Research Quarterly, 33*, 168–197.

Hoffman, J., & Pearson, P. D. (2000). Reading teacher education in the next millennium: What your grandmother's teacher didn't know that your granddaughter's teacher should. *Reading Research Quarterly, 35* (Jan./Feb./March 2000), 28–44.

Holdaway, D. (1979). *The foundations of literacy*. Portsmouth, NH: Heinemann.

Holdaway, D. (1982, Autumn). Shared book experience: Teaching reading using favorite books. *Theory Into Practice*, 293–300.

Hopper, G. (1966). *Puppet making through the grades*. New York: Davis.

Hoyt, L. (1992). Many ways of knowing: Using drama, oral interactions, and the visual arts to enhance reading comprehension. *Reading Teacher, 45*, 580–584.

Huck, C. S., Hepler, S., Hickman, J., & Kiefer, B. X. (2000). *Children's literature in the elementary school* (7th ed.). Columbus, OH: McGraw-Hill.

Hudelson, C. (1986). ESL children's writing: What we've learned, what we're learning. In P. Rigg & D. S. Enright (Eds.), *Children and ESL: Integrating perspectives*. Washington, DC: Teachers of English to Speakers of Other Languages.

Hudelson, S. (1987). The role of native language literacy in the education of language minority children. *Language Arts, 64*, 827–841.

Hudelson, S., Poynor, L., & Wolfe, P. (2003). Teaching bilingual and ESL children and adolescents. In J. Flood, D. Lapp, M. R. Squire, & J. M. Jensen (Eds.), *Handbook of research on teaching the English language arts* (3rd ed.). Sponsored by the International Reading Association/National Council of Teachers of English. Mahwah, NJ: Erlbaum.

Hunsacker, R. (1989). What listening skills should be taught to teachers and students? In P. Cooper and K. Galvin (Eds.) *The future of speech communication education* (pp. 27–30). Annandale, VA: Speech Communication Association.

Hunsburger, M., & Labercane, G. (Eds.). (2002). *Making meaning in the response-based classroom*. Boston: Allyn & Bacon.

Hunt, K. (1965). *Grammatical structures written at three grade levels*. Urbana, IL: National Council of Teachers of English.

Hunt, M. A. (1983). *A multimedia approach to children's literature*. Chicago: American Library Association.

Hurley, S. R., & Tinajero, J. V. (2001). *Literacy assessment of second-language learners*. Boston: Allyn & Bacon.

Hymes, D. (1974). *Foundations in sociolinguistics: An ethnographic approach*. Philadelphia: University of Pennsylvania Press.

Indrisano, R., & Squire, J. R. (2000). *Perspectives on writing: Research, theory, and practice*. Newark, DE: International Reading Association.

International Reading Association (IRA). (1998). Learning to read and write: Developmentally appropriate practices for young children. *Reading Teacher, 52*, 193–214.

International Reading Association (IRA). (1999). *High-stakes assessment in reading: A position statement of the International Reading Association*. Newark, DE: IRA.

International Reading Association (IRA) & National Council of Teachers of English (NCTE). (1996). *Standards for the English language arts*. Urbana, IL: NCTE; Newark, DE: IRA.

International Society for Technology in Education (ISTE). (1998). *National education technology standards for students*. Eugene, OR: ISTE.

Invitations to literacy. (1997). New York: Houghton Mifflin.

Jacobs, S. E. (1984). Investigative writing: Practice and principles. *Language Arts, 61*, 356–363.

Jalongo, M. R. (1991). *Strategies for developing children's listening skills* (Phi Delta Kappa Fastback Series No. 314). Bloomington, IN: Phi Delta Kappa Educational Foundation.

Jett-Simpson, M. (Ed.). (1989). *Adventuring with books: A booklist for pre-K–grade 6* (9th ed.). Urbana, IL: National Council of Teachers of English.

Johnson, D. (2001). *Vocabulary in the elementary and middle school*. Boston: Allyn & Bacon.

Johnson, D., Johnson, R., & Holobec, E. (1991). *Cooperation in the classroom*. Edina, MN: Interaction Book.

Johnson, D., & Pearson, P. D. (1984). *Teaching reading vocabulary* (2nd ed.). New York: Holt, Rinehart, & Winston.

Johnston, P. H. (1992). *Constructive evaluation of literate activity*. New York: Longman.

Jongsma, K. S. (1990). Reading-spelling links. *Reading Teacher, 43*, 68–69.

Kagan, S. (1985). *Cooperative learning: Resources for teachers*. Riverside: University of California.

Kagan, S. (1992). *Cooperative learning*. San Juan Capistrano, CA: Kagan Cooperative Learning.

Kahn, J., & Freyd, P. (1990). Online: A whole language perspective on keyboarding. *Language Arts, 67*, 84–90.

Kaser, S. (2001). Searching the heavens with children's literature: A design for teaching science. *Language Arts, 78*(4), 348–356.

Katz, S. A., & Thomas, J. A. (1996). *Teaching creatively by working the word: Language, music, and movement*. Boston: Allyn & Bacon.

Kelly, E. F. (1981). Curriculum drama. In N. McCaslin (Ed.), *Children and drama* (2nd ed.). New York: Longman.

Kindler, A. L. (2002). *Survey of the states' limited English proficient students and available educational programs and services 2000–2001 summary report*. Washington, DC: National Clearinghouse for English Language Acquisition and Language Instruction Educational Programs.

Kinzer, C. K., & Leander, K. (2001). Technology and the language arts: Implications of an expanded definition of literacy. In J. Flood, D. Lapp, M. R. Squire, & J. M. Jensen (Eds.), *Handbook of research on teaching the English language arts* (2nd ed., pp. 546–565). Sponsored by the International Reading Association/National Council of Teachers of English. Mahwah, NJ: Erlbaum.

Klein, P. D., & Olson, D. R. (2001). Texts, technology, and thinking: Lessons from the Great Divide. *Language Arts, 78*(3), 227–236.

Kobrin, B. (1988). *Eyeopeners! How to choose and use children's books about real people, places, and things.* New York: Penguin.

Koskinen, P. S., Gambrell, L., Kapinus, B., & Heathington, B. (1988). Retelling: A strategy for enhancing students' reading comprehension. *Reading Teacher, 41*, 892–896.

Koskinen, P. S., Wilson, R. M., Gambrell, L. B., & Neuman, S. B. (1993). Captioned video and vocabulary learning: An innovative practice in literacy instruction. *Reading Teacher, 47*, 36–43.

Krashen, S. D. (1981). Bilingual education and second language acquisition theory. In *Schooling and language minority children: A theoretical framework.* Los Angeles: California State University.

Krashen, S. D. (1981). *Second-language acquisition and second-language learning.* Oxford, England: Pergamon Press.

Krashen, S. D. (1982). *Principles and practices of second-language acquisition.* Oxford, England: Pergamon Press.

Krashen, S. D. (1985). *Inquiries and insights: Essays in language teaching, bilingual education, and literacy.* Hayward, CA: Alemany.

Krashen, S. D. (1993). *The power of reading: Insights from the research.* Englewood, CO: Libraries Unlimited.

Krashen, S. D., & Biber, D. (1988). *On course: Bilingual education's success in California.* Sacramento, CA: California Association for Bilingual Education.

Krashen, S. D., & Terrell, T. D. (1987). *The natural approach: Language acquisition in the classroom.* Englewood Cliffs, NJ: Prentice-Hall.

Kucer, S. B., Silva, C., & Delgado-Larocco, E. L. (1995). *Curricular conversations: Themes in multilingual and monolingual classrooms.* York, ME: Stenhouse.

LaBerge, D., & Samuels, S. J. (1976). Towards a theory of automatic information processing in reading. In H. Singer & R. B. Ruddell (Eds.), *Theoretical models and processes of reading.* Newark, DE: International Reading Association.

Labov, W. (1972). *Language in the inner city: Studies in the Black English Vernacular.* Philadelphia: University of Pennsylvania Press.

Labov, W. (1978). *The study of non-standard English.* Urbana, IL: National Council of Teachers of English.

Lamme, L. L. (1979). Song picture books: A maturing genre of children's literature. *Language Arts, 56*, 400–407.

Lamme, L. L. (1990). Exploring the world of music through picture books. *Reading Teacher, 44*, 294–300.

Lanauze, M., & Snow, C. E. (1989). The relation between first- and second-language writing skills: Evidence from Puerto Rican elementary school children in the mainland. *Linguistics and Education, 1*, 323–338.

Langer, J. A. (1990). The process of understanding: Reading for literary and informative purposes. *Research in the Teaching of English, 24*, 229–260.

Langer, J. A. (1992). *Literature instruction: A focus on student response.* Urbana, IL: National Council of Teachers of English.

Langer, J. A., Applebee, A. N., Mullis, I. V. S., & Foertsch, M. A. (1990). *Learning to read in our nation's schools: Instruction and achievement in 1988 at grades 4, 8, and 12.* Princeton, NJ: Educational Testing Service.

Langer, S. (1967). *Mind: An essay on human feeling.* Baltimore, MD: Johns Hopkins University Press.

Lapp, D., & Flood, J. (1995). Strategies for gaining access to the information superhighway: Off the side street and on to the main road. *Reading Teacher, 48*, 432–436.

Lawrence, K. M. (2002). Red light, green light, 1-2-3: Tasks to prepare for standardized tests. *Reading Teacher, 55*, 525–528.

Leal, D. (1993). Storybooks, information books and informational story books: An explication of an ambiguous grey genre. *New Advocate, 6*, 61–70.

Leggo, C., & Sakai, A. (1997). Knowing from different angles: Language arts and science connections. *Voices from the Middle, 4*(2), 26–30.

Lensmire, T. J. (2000). *Powerful writing, responsible teaching.* New York: Teachers College Press.

Lesiak, J. (1978). The origin of words: A unit of study. *Language Arts, 55*, 317–319.

Leslie, L., & Jett-Simpson, M. (1997). *Authentic literacy assessment: An ecological approach.* New York: Longman.

Levine, D. S. (1985). The biggest thing I learned but it really doesn't have to do with science. . . . *Language Arts, 62*, 43–47.

Lewis, M. (1991). Videodisc: Part of the classroom picture. *Language Arts, 68*, 333–336.

Lewis, S. (1967). *Making easy puppets.* New York: Dutton.

Lilja, L. D. (1980). Measuring the effectiveness of language education. In G. S. Pinnell (Ed.), *Discovering language with children* (pp. 105–108). Urbana, IL: National Council of Teachers of English.

Lima, C. W. (1989). *A to zoo: Subject access to children's picture books* (3rd ed.). New York: Bowker.

Lima, C. W., & Lima, J. A. (2001). *A to zoo: Subject access to children's picture books* (6th ed.). Westport, CT: Bowker-Greenwood:

Lindfors, J. W. (1987). *Children's language and learning* (2nd ed.). Englewood Cliffs, NJ: Prentice-Hall.

Linn, R. L. (2000). Assessments and accountability. *Educational Researcher, 29*, 4–16.

Liu, P. (2002/2003). Developing an E-pal partnership: A school-based international activity. *Childhood Education*, Winter, 81–88.

Loban, W. J. (1976). *Language development: Kindergarten through grade twelve*. Urbana, IL: National Council of Teachers of English.

Loban, W. J. (1979). Relationship between language and literacy. *Language Arts, 56*, 485–486.

Lucas, A. (1983). *Language diversity and classroom discourse (Final Report to NIE)*. Washington, DC: Center for Applied Linguistics.

Luke, C. (1999). Media and cultural studies. In S. Muspratt, A. Luke, & P. Freebody (Eds.), *Constructing critical literacies: Teaching and learning textual practice* (pp. 19–49). Cresskill, NJ: Hampton Press.

Lukens, R. J. (1995). *A critical handbook of children's literature*. Glenview, IL: Scott, Foresman/Little, Brown.

Mandler, J. M., & Johnson, N. S. (1977). Remembrance of things parsed: Story structure and recall. *Cognitive Psychology, 9*, 111–151.

Manolakes, G. (1975). The teaching of spelling: A pilot study. *Elementary English, 52*, 246.

Many, J. E. (1991). The effects of stance and age level on children's literary responses. *Journal of Reading Behavior, 21*, 61–85.

Many, J. E., & Cox, C. (Eds.). (1992). *Reader stance and literary understanding*. Norwood, NJ: Ablex.

Many, J. E., & Wiseman, D. L. (1992). Analyzing versus experiencing: The effects of teaching approaches on students' responses. In J. E. Many & C. Cox (Eds.), *Reader stance and literary understanding* (pp. 250–276). Norwood, NJ: Ablex.

Mariolti, M. (1982). *Hanimals*. San Diego: Green Tiger Press.

Marshall, J. (2000). Research on response to literature. In M. L. Kamil, P. B. Mosenthal, P. D. Pearson, & R. Barr (Eds.), *Handbook of reading research* (Vol. 3, pp. 381–402). Mahwah, NJ: Erlbaum.

Martinez, M. (1993). Motivating dramatic story reeanactments. *Reading Teacher, 46*, 682–688.

Martinez, M., & Roser, N. L. (2003). Children's responses to literature. In J. Flood, D. Lapp, M. R. Squire, & J. M. Jensen (Eds.), *Handbook of research on teaching the English language arts* (3rd ed.). Sponsored by the International Reading Association/National Council of Teachers of English. Mahwah, NJ: Erlbaum.

Martinez-Roldan, C., & Lopez-Robertson, J. (2000). Initiating literature circles in a first grade bilingual classroom. *Reading Teacher, 52*, 270–281.

Mason, J. M., & Au, K. H. (1986). *Reading instruction for today*. Glenview, IL: Scott, Foresman.

Mason, J. M., Stahl, S. A., Au, K. H., & Herman, P. A. (2003). Reading: Children's developing knowledge of words. In J. Flood, D. Lapp, M. R. Squire, & J. M. Jensen (Eds.), *Handbook of research on teaching the English language arts* (3rd ed., pp. 914–930). Sponsored by the International Reading Association/National Council of Teachers of English. Mahwah, NJ: Erlbaum.

Mathews, K. (1984). Community journals. *Livewire, 1*, 2–3.

Mathews, M. W., & Rainer, J. D. (2001). The quandaries of teachers and teacher educators in integrating literacy and mathematics. *Language Arts, 78*(4), 357–364.

McCarrier, A., Pinnell, G. S., & Fountas, I. C. (2000). *Interactive writing: How language and literacy come together, K–2*. Portsmouth, NH: Heinemann.

McClure, A., & Kristo, J. (2002). *Adventuring with books: A booklist for pre-K–grade 6*. Urbana, IL: National Council of Teachers of English.

McGee, L. (1992). Focus on research: Exploring the literature-based reading revolution. *Language Arts, 69*, 529–537.

McKenzie, M. (1985). *Shared writing. Language matters*. London, England: Inner London Educational Authority.

McLaughlin, B. (1987). *Theories of second-language learning*. London, England: Edward Arnold.

McMillan, J. (1997). *Classroom assessment*. Boston: Allyn & Bacon.

Mellon, J. (1969). *Transformational sentence combining: A method for enhancing the development of syntactic fluency in English composition*. Urbana, IL: National Council of Teachers of English.

Menyuk, P. (1963). Syntactic structures in the language of children. *Child Development, 34*, 407–422.

Menyuk, P. (1991). Linguistics and teaching the language arts. In J. Flood, J. Jensen, D. Lapp, & J. Squire (Eds.), *Handbook of research on teaching the English language arts* (pp. 24–29). New York: Macmillan.

Miller-Jones, D. (1989). Culture and testing. *American Psychologist, 44*(2), 360–366.

Moffet, J., & Wagner, B. J. (1993). What works is play. *Language Arts, 70*, 32–36.

Moll, L. C. (1988a). Educating Latino students. *Language Arts, 64*, 315–324.

Moll, L. C. (1988b). Some key issues in teaching Latino students. *Language Arts, 65*, 465–472.

Moll, L. C. (1990). *Vygotsky and education: Instructional implications and applications of soiohistorical psychology*. New York: Cambridge University Press.

Moll, L. C. (1992). Bilingual classroom studies and community anlaysis: Some recent trends. *Educational Researcher, 21*, 20–24.

Moll, L. C., Saez, R., & Dworin, J. (2003). Exploring biliteracy. *Elementary School Journal*.

Moore, D. W., Moore, S. A., Cunningham, P. M., & Cunningham, J. W. (1998). *Developing readers and writers in the content areas K–12* (3rd ed.). New York: Longman.

Moore, D. W., Readance, J. E., & Rickelman, R. J. (1989). *Prereading Activities for Content Area Reading and Learning* (2nd ed.). Newark, DE: International Reading Association.

Morphett, M. V., & Washburne, C. (1931). When should children begin to read? *Elementary School Journal, 31*, 496–503.

Morris, D. (1993). The relationship between children's concept of word in text and phoneme awareness in learning to read: A longitudinal study. *Research in the Teaching of English, 27*, 133–154.

Morrow, L. M. (1986). Effects of structural guidance in story retelling on children's dictation of original stories. *Journal of Reading Behavior, 18,* 135–151.

Morrow, L. M. (1989). Using story retelling to develop comprehension. In K. D. Muth (Ed.), *Children's comprehension of text: Research into practice* (pp. 37–58). Newark, DE: International Reading Association.

Morrow, L. M. (1990). Retelling stories as a diagnostic tool. In S. M. Glazer, L. W. Searfoss, & L. M. Gentile (Eds.), *Reexamining reading diagnosis: New trends and procedures.* Newark, DE: International Reading Association.

Morrow, L. M. (1992a). *Literacy development in the early years: Helping children read and write.* Boston: Allyn & Bacon.

Morrow, L. M. (1992b). Promoting voluntary reading. In J. Flood, J. M. Jensen, D. Lapp, & J. R. Squire (Eds.), *Handbook of research on teaching the English language arts.* New York: Macmillan.

Morrow, L. M. (2001). *Literacy development in the early years: Helping children read and write* (2nd ed.). Boston: Allyn & Bacon.

Moses, L. (2001). Rethinking standardized high-stakes testing. *Childhood Education, 78,* 58.

Moss, B., Leone, S., & Dipillo, M. L. (1997). Exploring the literature of fact: Linking reading and writing through information trade books. *Language Arts, 74*(6), 418–429.

Moss, J. F. (1984). *Focus units in literature: A handbook for elementary teachers.* Urbana, IL: National Council of Teachers of English.

Moustafa, M. (1995). Children's productive recoding. *Reading Research Quarterly, 30,* 464–476.

Moustafa, M. (1997). *Beyond traditional phonics.* Portsmouth, NH: Heinemann.

Mulligan, P. A., & Gore, K. (1992). Telecommunications: Education's missing link? *Language Arts, 69,* 379–384.

Myers, M., & Spalding, E. (Eds.). (1997). *Assessing student performance.* Urbana, IL: National Council of Teachers of English.

Nagy, W. E., & Herman, P. (1985). Incidental vs. instructional approaches to increasing vocabulary. *Educational Perspectives, 23,* 16–21.

Nation, K., & Hulme, C. (1997). Phonemic segmentation, not onset-rime segmentation, predicts early reading and spelling skills. *Reading Research Quarterly, 32,* 154–167.

National Association for the Education of Young Children (NAEYC). (1991). Guidelines for the appropriate curriculum content and assessment in programs serving young children ages 3 through 8. *Young Children, 46*(3), 21–38.

National Board for Professional Teaching Standards (NBPTS). (1995). *Early childhood.* Washington, DC: NBPTS.

National Council of Teachers of English (NCTE), Commitee on Language Arts Textbooks. (1991). *Guidelines for judging and selecting elementary language arts textbooks.* Urbana, IL: NCTE.

National Council of Teachers of English (NCTE). (1994, Summer). Perspective: Media, performance, and the English curriculum—two views. *NCTE Standard,* 12–14.

National Council of Teachers of Mathematics (NCTM). (2000). *Principles and standards for school mathematics.* Reston, VA: NCTM.

National Research Council. (1996). *National Science Education Standards.* Washington, DC: National Academy Press.

Nelson, O. (1989). Story telling: Language experience for meaning making. *Reading Teacher, 42,* 396–390.

Nelson, P. (1988). Drama, doorway to the past. *Language Arts, 65,* 20–25.

Newkirk, T. (1984). Archimede's dream. *Language Arts, 61,* 341–350.

Newkirk, T., & Atwell, N. (Eds.). (1988). *Understanding writing* (2nd ed.). Portsmouth, NH: Heinemann.

Nieto, S. (1996). *Affirming diversity: The sociopolitical context of multicultural education* (2nd ed.). White Plains, NY: Longman.

Nieto, S. (2000). *Affirming diversity: The sociopolitical context of multicultural education* (3rd ed.). New York: Longman.

Nikola-Lisa, W. (1992). Read aloud, play a lot. *New Advocate, 5,* 199–213.

Noden, H., & Moss, B. (1994). A guide to books on portfolios: Rafting the rivers of assessment. *Reading Teacher, 48,* 180–183.

Noguchi, R. R. (1991). *Grammar and the teaching of writing: Limits and possibilities.* Urbana, IL: National Council of Teachers of English.

Norton, D. E. (1995). *Through the eyes of a child: An introduction to children's literature* (4th ed.). New York: Merrill.

Norton, D. E. (2000). *Through the eyes of a child: An introduction to children's literature* (6th ed.). Upper Saddle River, NJ: Merrill.

Norton, D. E. (2001). *Multicultural children's literature: Through the eyes of many children.* Columbus, OH: Merrill/Prentice Hall.

Noyce, R. M., & Christie, J. F. (1983). Effects of an integrated approach to grammar instruction on third graders' reading and writing. *Elementary School Journal, 84,* 63–69.

O'Flahavan, J. F., & Blassberg, R. (1992). Toward an embedding model of spelling instruction for emergent literates. *Languge Arts, 69,* 409–417.

O'Hare, F. (1973). *Sentence-combining: Improving student writing without formal grammar instruction.* Urbana, IL: National Council of Teachers of English.

O'Keefe, V. (1995). *Speaking to think, thinking to speak.* Portsmouth, NH: Heinemann.

O'Malley, J. M., & Valdez Pierce, L. (1996). *Authentic assessment for English language learners: Practical approaches for teachers.* New York: Addison Wesley.

Office of Technology Assessment. (1995). *Teachers and technology: Making the connection.* Washington, DC: Government Printing Office.

Ogbu, J. U. (1999). Beyond language: Ebonics, proper English, and identity in a Black American speech community. *American Educational Research Journal, 36,* 147–184.

Ogle, D. (1989). The know, want to know, learn strategy. In K. D. Muth (Ed.), *Children's comprehension of text: Research into practice* (pp. 205–223). Newark, DE: International Reading Association.

Ohanian, S. (1999). *One size fits few: The folly of educational standards.* Westport, CT: Heinemann.

Olmedo, I. M. (1993). *Junior historians: Doing oral history with ESL and bilingual students. TESOL Journal, 2*(4), 7–10.

Oppenheimer, T. (1997). The computer delusion. *Atlantic Monthly, 280,* 45–62.

Ovando, C. J. (2003). Language diversity and education. In J. A. Banks & C. A. M. Banks (Eds.), *Multicultural education: Issues and perspectives* (5th ed., pp. 268–291). New York: John Wiley.

Padilla, R. (1990). HyperCard: A tool for dual language instruction. *Computers in the Schools, 7,* 211–226.

Paley, V. G. (1988a). *Bad guys don't have birthdays: Fantasy play at four.* Chicago: University of Chicago Press.

Paley, V. G. (1988b). *The boy who would be a helicopter: The uses of storytelling in the classroom.* Portsmouth, NH: Heinemann.

Palinscar, A. S., & Brown, A. L. (1984). Reciprocal teaching of comprehension-fostering and comprehension-monitoring activities. *Cognition and Instruction, 2,* 117–175.

Pang, V., Colvin, C., Tran, M., & Barbra, R. (1992). Beyond chopsticks and dragons: Selecting Asian-American literature for children. *Reading Teacher, 46,* 216–224.

Paris, S. (1992). A framework for authentic literacy assessment. *Reading Teacher, 46,* 88–98.

Parnes, S. J., Noller, R. B., & Biondi, A. M. (1977). *Guide to creative action.* New York: Scribner's.

Pearson, P. D., & Fielding, L. (1982). Research update: Listening comprehension. *Language Arts, 59,* 617–629.

Pearson, P. D., & Johnson, D. D. (1978). *Teaching reading comprehension.* New York: Holt, Rinehart & Winston.

Pease-Alvarez, L., & Garcia, E. (1995). Effective instruction for language minority students: An early childhood case study. *Early Childhood Research Quarterly, 7,* 224–261.

Pease-Alvarez, L., & Vasquez, O. A. (1990). Sharing language and technical expertise around the computer. *Computers in the Schools, 7,* 91–107.

Pellegrini, A. D. (1984). Symbolic functioning and children's early writing: The relations between kindergartners' play and isolated word-writing fluency. In R. Beach & L. S. Bridwell (Eds.), *New directions in composition research* (pp. 274–284). New York: Guilford.

Pellegrini, A. D. (1985). The relations between symbolic play and literate behavior: A review and critique of the empirical literature. *Review of Educational Research, 55,* 107–121.

Pellegrini, A. D., & Galda, L. (1982). The effects of thematic-fantasy play training on the development of children's story comprehension. *American Educational Research Journal, 19,* 443–452.

Pellegrini, A. D., & Galda, L. (1994). Early literacy from a developmental perspective. In D. Lancy (Ed.), *Children's emerging literacy: From research to practice* (pp. 21–27). Westport, CT: Praeger.

Pellegrini, A. D., Galda, L., Dresden, J., & Cox, S. (1991). A longitudinal study of the predictive relations among symbolic play, linguistic verbs, and early literacy. *Research in the Teaching of English, 25,* 219–235.

Perry, T., & Delpit, L. (Eds.). (1998). *The real ebonics debate: Power, language, and the education of African-American children.* Boston: Beacon Press.

Peterson, R. (1987). Literature groups: Intensive and extensive reading. In D. Watson (Ed.), *Ideas with insights: Language arts K–6* (pp. 14–20). Urbana, IL: National Council of Teachers of English.

Peterson, R., & Eeds, M. (1990). *Grand conversations: Literature groups in action.* New York: Scholastic.

Peyton, J. K., & Reed, L. (1990). *Dialogue journal writing with nonnative English speakers: A handbook for teachers.* Alexandria, VA: Teachers of English to Speakers of Other Languages.

Pflaum, S. W. (1986). *The development of language and literacy in young children.* Columbus, OH: Merrill.

Piaget, J. (1959). *The language and thought of the child* (3rd ed.). London, England: Routledge & Kegan Paul.

Piaget, J. (1962). *Play, dreams, and imitation in childhood.* New York: Norton.

Piaget, J. (1969). *The language and thought of the child.* London, England: Routledge & Kegan Paul.

Piaget, J. (1973). *To understand is to invent: The future of education.* New York: Grossman.

Piaget, J. (1977). *The development of thought: Equilibration of cognitive structures* (A. Rosin, Trans.). New York: Viking.

Piattelli-Palmarini, M. (1995). Ever since *Language and Learning:* Afterthoughts on the Piaget-Chomsky debate. In J. Mehler and S. Franck (Eds.), *Cognition on cognition* (pp. 361–392). Cambridge, MA: MIT Press.

Pinnell, G. S. (1996). Ways to look at the functions of children's language. In B. M. Power & R. S. Hubbard (Eds.), *Language development: A reader for teachers* (pp. 146–154). Columbus, OH: Merrill.

Pinnell, G. S., Fried, M. D., & Estice, R. M. (1990). Reading recovery: Learning how to make a difference. *Reading Teacher, 43,* 282–295.

Pinnell, G. S., & Jaggar, A. M. (2003). Oral language: Speaking and listening in elementary classrooms. In J. Flood, D. Lapp, M. R. Squire, & J. M. Jensen (Eds.), *Handbook of research on teaching the English language arts* (3rd ed.). Sponsored by the International Reading Association/National Council of Teachers of English. Mahwah, NJ: Erlbaum.

Politzer, R., & Hoover, U. (1977). *Teacher and pupil attitudes toward black English speech varieties and black pupil achievement.* Stanford, CA: Center for Education Research.

Porter, C., & Cleland, J. (1995). *The portfolio as a learning strategy.* Portsmouth, NH: Heinemann.

Postman, N. (1961). *Television and the teaching of English.* New York: Appleton-Century-Crofts.

Power, B. M., & Hubbard, R. S. (1996). *Language development: A reader for teachers.* Englewood Cliffs, NJ: Merrill.

Price, A., & Yaakov, J. (2001). *The children's catalog.* New York: H. W. Wilson.

Primeaux, J. (2000). Focus on research: Shifting perspectives on struggling readers. *Language Arts, 77*(6), 537–542.

Probst, R. E. (2003). Response to literature. In J. Flood, D. Lapp, M. R. Squire, & J. M. Jensen (Eds.), *Handbook of research on teaching the English language arts* (3rd ed.). Sponsored by the International Reading Association/National Council of Teachers of English. Mahwah, NJ: Erlbaum.

Purves, A., & Beach, R. (1972). *Literature and the reader: Research in response to literature, reading interests and the teaching of literature.* Urbana, IL: National Council of Teachers of English.

Putnam, L. (1991). Dramatizing non-fiction with emerging readers. *Language Arts, 68,* 463–469.

Ralston, M. (1993). *An exchange of gifts: A storyteller's handbook.* Markham, Ontario: Pippin.

Ramirez, J. D., & Merino, B. J. (1990). Classroom talk in English immersion, early-exit and late-exit transitional bilingual education programs. In R. Jacobson & C. Faltis (Eds.), *Language distribution issues in bilingual schooling* (pp. 61–103). Clevedon, England: Multilingual Matters.

Rankin, P. T. (1928). The importance of listening ability. *English Journal, 17,* 623–630.

Raphael, T. (1982). Question-answering strategies for children. *Reading Teacher, 36,* 186–190.

Raphael, T. (1986). Teaching question answer relationships, revisited. *Reading Teacher, 39,* 516–522.

Raphael, T. (1992). Research directions: Literature and discussion in the reading program. *Language Arts, 69,* 54–61.

Raphael, T., & Englert, C. S. (1990). Writing and reading: Partners in constructing meaning. *Reading Teacher, 43,* 388–400.

Raphael, T., Goatley, V. J., McMahon, S. I., & Woodman, D. A. (1995). Teaching literacy through student book clubs: Promoting meaningful conversations about books. In N. L. Roser & M G. Martinez (Eds.), *Book talk and beyond: Children and teachers respond to literature* (pp. 66–79). Newark, DE: International Reading Association.

Raphael, T., Kirschner, B. W., & Englert, C. S. (1988). Expository writing program: Making connections between reading and writing. *Reading Teacher, 41,* 790–795.

Raphael, T., & McMahon, S. I. (1994). Book club: An alternative framework for reading instruction. *Reading Teacher, 48,* 102–117.

Rasinski, T. V., & Gillespie, C. S. (1992). *Sensitive issues: An annotated guide to children's literature K–6.* Phoenix: Oryx.

Rasinski, T. V., & Padak, N. D. (1990). Multicultural learning through children's literature. *Language Arts, 67,* 576–580.

Rasinski, T. V., & Padak, N. (2000). *Effective reading strategies: Teaching children who find reading difficult.* Englewood Cliffs, NJ: Prentice-Hall.

Read, C. (1971). Pre-school children's knowledge of English phonology. *Harvard Educational Review, 41,* 1–34.

Read, C. (1975). *Children's categorization of speech sounds in English.* Urbana, IL: National Council of Teachers of English.

Read, C. (1986). *Children's creative spelling.* London, England: Routledge & Kegan Paul.

Read, S. (2001). "Kid mice hunt for thier selfs": First and second graders writing research. *Language Arts, 78*(4), 333–342.

Reed, W. M. (1996). Assessing the impact of computer-based writing instruction. *Journal of Research on Computing in Education, 28,* 418–437.

Renfro, N. (1969). *Puppets for play production.* New York: Funk & Wagnalls.

Resnick, L. B., & Klopfer, L. E. (1989). Toward the thinking curriculum: An overview. In L. B. Resnick & L. E. Klopfer (Eds.), *Toward the thinking curriculum: Current cognitive research.* Arlington, VA: Association for Supervision and Curriculum Development.

Reyes, M. de la Luz, & Halcon, J. (2000). *The best for our children: Critical perspectives on literacy for Latino students.* New York: Teachers College Press.

Reyes, M. de la Luz. (1991). A process approach to literacy instruction for Spanish-speaking students: In search of a best fit. In E. H. Hiebert (Ed.), *Literacy for a diverse society: Perspectives, practices, and policies* (pp. 157–171). New York: Teachers College Press.

Rice, C. D. (1996). Bring intercultural encounters into classrooms: IECC electronic mailing lists. *T.H.E. Journal, 23*(6), 60–63.

Richard-Amato, P. A. (1988). *Making it happen: Interaction in the second language classroom.* White Plains, NY: Longman.

Richgels, D. J. (1995). Invented spelling ability and printed word learning in kindergarten. *Reading Research Quarterly, 30,* 96–109.

Richter, B., & Wenzel, D. (1988). *The museum of science and industry basic list of children's science books.* Chicago: American Library Association.

Ritchie, D. A. (1995). *Doing oral history.* New York: Twayne.

Roderick, J. A. (Ed.). (1991). *Context-responsive approaches to assessing children's language.* Urbana, IL: National Conference of Research on English.

Rodriguez, R. F. (1982). *The Mexican American child in special education* (ERIC Document Reproduction Service no. ED 212 437).

Roney, R. C. (1989). Back to basics with storytelling. *Reading Teacher, 42,* 520–523.

Rose, D. H., & Meyers, A. (1994). Focus on research: The role of technology in language arts instruction. *Language Arts, 71,* 290–294.

Rosenblatt, L. M. (1978). *The reader, the text, the poem: The transactional theory of the literary work.* Carbondale: Southern Illinois University Press. (Original work published 1938)

Rosenblatt, L. M. (1980). What facts does this poem teach you? *Language Arts, 57,* 386–394.

Rosenblatt, L. M. (1982). The literary transaction: Evocation and response. *Theory into Practice, 21,* 268–277.

Rosenblatt, L. M. (1983). *Literature as exploration* (4th ed.). New York: Modern Language Association.

Rosenblatt, L. M. (1985a). The transactional theory of the literary work: Implications for research. In C. R. Cooper (Ed.), *Researching response to literature and the teaching of literature.* Norwood, NJ: Ablex.

Rosenblatt, L. M. (1985b). Viewpoints: Transaction versus interaction—A terminological rescue mission. *Research in the Teaching of English, 19,* 96–107.

Rosenblatt, L. M. (1986). The aesthetic transaction. *Journal of Aesthetic Education, 20,* 122–128.

Rosenblatt, L. M. (1994). The transactional theory of reading and writing. In R. Ruddell, M. Ruddell, & H. Singer (Eds.), *Theoretical models and processes of reading* (4th ed., pp. 1057–1092). Newark, DE: International Reading Association.

Rosenblatt, L. M. (1995). *Literature as personal exploration.* New York: Modern Language Association. (Original work published 1938)

Rosenblatt, L. M. (2003). Literary theory. In J. Flood, D. Lapp, M. R. Squire, & J. M. Jensen (Eds.), *Handbook of research on teaching the English language arts* (3rd ed., pp. 67–73). Sponsored by the International Reading Association/National Council of Teachers of English. Mahwah, NJ: Erlbaum.

Ross, R. R. (1980). *Storyteller* (2nd ed.). Columbus, OH: Merrill.

Routman, R. (1991). *Invitations: Changing as teachers and learners K–12.* Portsmouth, NH: Heinemann.

Routman, R. (1996). *Literacy at the crossroads: Crucial talk about reading, writing, and other teaching dilemmas.* Portsmouth, NH: Heinemann.

Rowe, D. W. (1998). Examining teacher talk: Revealing hidden boundaries for curricular change. *Language Arts, 75*(2), 103–107.

Ruddell, R. B. (1965). The effect of oral and written patterns of language structure on reading comprehension. *Reading Teacher, 18,* 270–275.

Rudman, M. K. (1984). *Children's literature: An issues approach* (2nd ed.). New York: Longman.

Rumelhart, D. (1975). Notes on a schema for stories. In D. G. Bobrow (Ed.), *Representation and understanding: Studies in cognitive science* (pp. 85–107). New York: Academic.

Rumelhart, D. (1984). Understanding understanding. In J. Flood (Ed.), *Understanding reading comprehension* (pp. 1–20). Newark, DE: International Reading Association.

Rumelhart, D., & Ortony, A. (1977). The representation of knowledge in memory. In R. C. Anderson, R. J. Spiro, & W. E. Montague (Eds.), *Schooling and the acquisition of knowledge* (pp. 99–135). Hillsdale, NJ: Erlbaum.

Sadow, M. W. (1982). The use of story grammar in the design of questions. *Reading Teacher, 35,* 518–522.

Salomon, G. (1983). Television watching and mental effort: A social psychological view. In J. Bryant & D. R. Anderson (Eds.), *Children's understanding of television: Research on attention and comprehension* (pp. 265–296). New York: Academic Press.

Salomon, G. (Ed.). (1997). *Distributed cognitions: Psychological and educational considerations.* New York: Cambridge University Press.

Samway, K. D., & Whang, G. (1996). *Literature study circles in a multicultural classroom.* York, ME: Stenhouse.

San Jose, C. (1988). Story drama in the content areas. *Language Arts, 65,* 26–33.

Sandholtz, J. H., et al. (1997). *Teaching with technology: Creating student-centered classrooms.* New York: Teachers College Press.

Saunders, W., & Goldenberg, C. (1998). Talk, text, themes, and understanding: The effects of an Instructional Conversation on transition students' concepts of friendship and story comprehension. In R. Horowitz (Ed.), *Talk about text: Developing understanding of the world through talk and text.* Newark, DE: International Reading Association.

Saunders, W., & Goldenberg, C. (1999). Effects of instructional conversations and literature logs on limited- and fluent-English-proficient students' story comprehension and thematic understanding. *Elementary School Journal, 99*(4), 277–301.

Schallert, D. L., & Martin, D. B. (2003). A psychological analysis of what teachers and students do in the language arts classroom. In J. Flood, D. Lapp, M. R. Squire, & J. M. Jensen (Eds.), *Handbook of research on teaching the English language arts* (3rd ed., pp. 31–45). Sponsored by the International Reading Association/National Council of Teachers of English. Mahwah, NJ: Erlbaum.

Schickendanz, J. A. (1990). *Adam's righting revolutions: One child's literacy development from infancy through grade one.* Portsmouth, NH: Heinemann.

Schwartz, D. (1995). Ready, set, read—20 minutes a day is all you need. *Smithsonian, 25,* 82–91.

Schwartz, J. I. (1988). *Encouraging early literacy: An integrated approach to reading and writing in K–3.* Portsmouth, NH: Heinemann.

Senisi, E. B. (2001). *Berry smudges and leaf prints: Finding and making colors from nature.* New York: Dutton.

Serafini, F. (2000). Three paradigms of assessment: Measurement, procedure, and inquiry. *Reading Teacher, 54,* 384.

Shannon, P. (1988). *Broken promises: Reading instruction in 20th century America.* Granby, MA: Bergin & Garvey.

Shannon, P. (1990). *The struggle to continue: Progressive reading instruction in the United States.* Portsmouth, NH: Heinemann.

Sharan, S. (1990). Cooperative learning: A perspective on research and practice. In S. Sharan (Ed.), *Cooperative learning: Theory and research.* New York: Praeger.

Shatz, M., & Ebeling, K. (1991). Patterns of language learning-related behaviors: Evidence for self-help in acquiring grammar. *Journal of Child Language, 18,* 295–313.

Short, K. G. (1995). Graffiti boards and visual webs. *School Talk, 1,* 4.

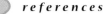

Short, K. G., & Pierce, K. M. (Eds.). (1990). *Talking about books: Creating literate communities.* Portsmouth, NH: Heinemann.

Short, K. G., & Pierce, K. M. (Eds.). (1998). *Talking about books: Creating literate communities.* (2nd ed.). Portsmouth, NH: Heinemann.

Shugar, G. W. (1978). Text analysis as an approach to the study of early linguistic operations. In C. Snow & N. Waterson (Eds.), *The development of communication.* Chichester, England: John Wiley.

Shuy, R. (1969). Some language and cultural differences in a theory of reading. In K. S. Goodman & J. Fleming (Eds.), *Psycholinguistics and the teaching of reading.* Newark, DE: International Reading Association.

Sierra, J. (1991). *Fantastic theater: Puppets and plays for young performers and audiences.* New York: H. W. Wilson.

Siks, G. B. (1983). *Drama with children.* New York: Harper & Row.

Silvern, S. B. (1988). Word processing in the writing process. In J. L. Hoot & S. B. Silvern (Eds.), *Writing with computers in the early grades* (pp. 43–74). New York: Teachers College Press.

Sims, R. (1982). *Shadow and substance: Afro-American experience in contemporary children's literature.* Urbana, IL: National Council of Teachers of English.

Sipe, L. (1998). The construction of literary understanding by first and second graders in response to picture storybook read-alouds. *Reading Research Quarterly, 33*(4), 376–378.

Sipe, R. B. (1994). Thematic units. *Encyclopedia of English studies and language arts* (Vol. 2). New York: Scholastic.

Skillings, M. J., & Ferrell, R. (2000). Student-generated rubrics: Bringing students into the assessment process. *Reading Teacher, 53,* 452–455.

Sklar, D. (1991). *Playmaking: Children writing and performing their own plays.* New York: Teachers and Writers Collaborative.

Slavin, R. (1990). *Cooperative learning: Theory, research, and practice.* Englewood Cliffs, NJ: Prentice-Hall.

Sleeter, C. E., & Grant, C. A. (1993). *Making choices for multicultural education: Five approaches to race, class and gender* (2nd ed.). New York: Merrill.

Sleeter, C. E., & Grant, C. A. (1999). *Making choices for multicultural education: Five Approaches to race, class, and gender* (3rd ed.). New York: Wiley.

Sloan, G. D. (1984). *The child as critic* (2nd ed.). New York: Teachers College Press.

Smagorinsky, P. (1995). Constructing meaning in the disciplines: Reconceptualizing writing across the curriculum as composing across the curriculum. *American Journal of Education, 103*(2), 160–184.

Smith, F. (1971). *Understanding reading.* New York: Holt, Rinehart & Winston.

Smith, F. (1981). Myths of writing. *Language Arts, 58,* 792–798.

Smith, J. (1991). Goin' wild in hypercard. *Language Arts, 68,* 674–680.

Smith, J. N. (Ed.). (1988). *Homespun: Tales from America's favorite storytellers.* New York: Crown.

Smith, J. W. A., & Elley, W. B. (1997). *How children learn to write.* Katonah, NY: Richard C. Owen.

Smith, T. E. C., Polloway, E. A., Patton, J. R., & Dowdy, C. A. (1998). *Teaching students with special needs in inclusive settings* (2nd ed.). Boston: Allyn & Bacon.

Smitherman, G. (1999). *Talkin' that talk: Language, culture, and education in Africa America.* New York: Routledge.

Snow, C. E. (1986). Conversations with children. In P. Fletcher & M. Garman (Eds.), *Language acquisition: Studies in first language development* (2nd ed., pp. 69–89). Cambridge, England: Cambridge University Press.

Snow, C. E. (1990). Rationales for native language instruction: Evidence from research. In A. M. Padilla, H. H. Fairchild, & C. M. Valdez, *Bilingual education: Issues and strategies* (pp. 60–74). Newbury Park, CA: Sage.

Snow, C. E., Burns, M. S., & Griffin, P. (Eds.). (1998). *Preventing reading difficulties in young children.* Washington, DC: National Academy Press.

Solley, B. A. (2000). *Writers' workshop: Reflections of elementary and middle school teachers.* Boston: Allyn & Bacon.

Sperling, M. (1996). Revisiting the writing-speaking connection: Challenges for research on writing and writing instruction. *Review of Educational Research, 66,* 53–86.

Spiegel, D. L. (1998a). Reader response approaches and the growth of readers. *Language Arts, 76*(1), 41–48.

Spiegel, D. L. (1998b). Silver bullets, babies, and bath water: Literature response groups in a balanced literacy program. *Reading Teacher, 52*(2), 114–124.

Spindler, G. (1982). *Doing the ethnography of schooling.* New York: Holt, Rinehart, & Winston.

Spivey, N. N. (1994). Constructivism. In A. Purves (Ed.), *Encyclopedia of English studies and language arts* (Vol. 1, pp. 284–286). New York: Scholastic.

Standards for the English language arts. (1996). Newark, DE: International Reading Association (IRA); Urbana, IL: National Council of Teachers of English (NCTE).

Stanley, N. V. (1996). Vygotsky and multicultural assessment and instruction. In L. Dixon-Krauss (Ed.), *Vygotsky in the classroom: Mediated literacy instruction and assessment* (pp. 133–148). White Plains, NY: Longman.

Stanovich, K. E. (1986). Matthew effects in reading: Some consequences of individual differences in the acquisition of literacy. *Reading Research Quarterly, 21,* 360–406.

Stanovich, K. E. (1994). Romance and reason. *Reading Teacher, 47,* 280–291.

Staton, J. (1984). Thinking together: Interaction in children's reasoning. In C. J. Thaiss & C. Suhor (Eds.), *Speaking and writing, K–12: Strategies and the new research.* Urbana, IL: National Council of Teachers of English.

Staton, J., Shuy, R., Kreeft Payton, J., & Reed, L. (1988). *Dialogue journal communication: Classroom, linguistic, social, and cognitive views.* Norwood, NJ: Ablex.

Stauffeur, R. (1970). *The language experience approach to teaching reading.* New York: Harper & Row.

 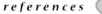

Stauffeur, R. (1975). *Directing the reading thinking process.* New York: Harper & Row.

Stauffeur, R. (1980). *The language-experience approach to the teaching of reading* (2nd ed.). New York: Harper & Row.

Sticht, T. G., & James, J. H. (1984). Listening and reading. *Handbook of reading research.* In P. D. Pearson (Ed.), *Handbook of reading research* (pp. 293–318). New York: Longman.

Straw, S. (1994). Teaching of grammar. In A. Purves (Ed.), *Encyclopedia of English studies and language arts* (Vol. 1, pp. 534–538). New York: Scholastic.

Strickland, D. S., & Feeley, J. T. (1991). Development in the elementary school years. In J. Flood, J. M. Jensen, D. Lapp, & J. R. Squire (Eds.), *Handbook of research on teaching the English language arts* (pp. 286–302). New York: Macmillan.

Strickland, D. S., & Feeley, J. T. (2003). Development in the elementary school years. In J. Flood, D. Lapp, M. R. Squire, & J. M. Jensen (Eds.), *Handbook of research on teaching the English language arts* (3rd ed., pp. 339–356). Sponsored by the International Reading Association/National Council of Teachers of English. Mahwah, NJ: Erlbaum.

Strickland, D. S., & Morrow, L. (1988). Creating a print rich environment. *Reading Teacher, 42,* 156–157.

Strickland, D. S., & Morrow, L. (1989). Environments rich in print promote literacy behavior during play. *Reading Teacher, 43,* 178–179.

Strickland, R. G. (1962). The language of elementary school children: Its relationship to the language of reading textbooks and the quality of reading of selected children. *Bulletin of the School of Education, Indiana University, 38*(4).

Strong, W. (1986). *Creative approaches to sentence combining.* Urbana, IL: National Council of Teachers of English.

Subject guide to children's books in print [Annual]. New York: Bowker.

Sulzby, E. (1985). Children's emergent reading of favorite storybooks: A developmental study. *Reading Research Quarterly, 20,* 458–481.

Sulzby, E. (1989). Assessment of writing and of children's language while writing. In L. Morrow & J. Smith (Eds.), *The role of assessment and measurement in early literacy instruction* (pp. 83–109). Englewood Cliffs, NJ: Prentice-Hall.

Sulzby, E. (1991). The development of the young child and the emergence of literacy. In J. Flood, J. M. Jensen, D. Lapp, & J. R. Squire (Eds.), *Handbook of research on teaching the English language arts* (pp. 273–285). New York: Macmillan.

Sulzby, E. (1992a). Research directions: Transitions from emergent to conventional writing. *Language Arts, 69,* 290–297.

Sulzby, E. (1992b). The development of the young child and the emergence of literacy. In J. Flood, J. Jensen, D. Lapp, & J. Squire (Eds.), *Handbook of research on teaching the English language arts* (pp. 273–285). New York: Macmillan.

Sulzby, E., & Teale, W. H. (2003). The development of the young child and the emergence of literacy. In J. Flood, D. Lapp, M. R. Squire, & J. M. Jensen (Eds.), *Handbook of research on teaching the English language arts* (3rd ed.). Sponsored by the International Reading Association/National Council of Teachers of English. Mahwah, NJ: Erlbaum.

Sutherland, Z., & Arbuthnot, M. H. (1991). *Children and books* (8th ed.). New York: HarperCollins.

Tabors, P. (1997). *One child, two languages.* Baltimore: Paul H. Brookes.

Tamis-LeMonda, C. S., & Bornstein, M. H. (1994). Specificity in mother-toddler language-play relations across the second year. *Developmental Psychology, 30,* 283–292.

Tannenbaum, J. (2000). *Teeth, wiggly as earthquakes: Writing poetry in the primary grades.* Portland, ME: Stenhouse.

Taylor, D. (1983). *Family literacy: Young children learning to read and write.* Portsmouth, NH: Heinemann.

Taylor, D., & Strickland, D. S. (1986). *Family storybook reading.* Portsmouth, NH: Heinemann.

Taylor, R. L. (2000). *Assessment of exceptional students: Educational and psychological procedures.* Boston: Allyn & Bacon.

Tchudi, S., & Lafer, S. (1996). *The interdisciplinary teacher's handbook: Integrated teaching across the curriculum.* Portsmouth, NH: Heinemann.

Teale, W. H., & Sulzby, E. (1989). Emerging literacy: New perspectives. In D. S. Strickland & L. M. Morrow (Eds.), *Emerging literacy: Young children learn to read and write* (pp. 1–15). Newark, DE: International Reading Association.

Templeton, S. (1979). Spelling first, sound later: The relationship between orthography and higher order phonological knowledge in older students. *Research in the Teaching of English, 13,* 255–264.

Templeton, S. (1991). Teaching and learning the English spelling system: Reconceptualizing method and purpose. *Elementary School Journal, 92,* 185–201.

Templeton, S. (1992). Theory, nature and pedagogy of higher-order orthographic development in older chidlren. In S. Templeton & D. Bear (Eds.), *Development of orthographic knowledge and the foundations of literacy: A memorial Festschrift for Edmund H. Henderson* (pp. 253–278). Hillsdale, NJ: Erlbaum.

Templeton, S. (2003). Spelling. In J. Flood, D. Lapp, M. R. Squire, & J. M. Jensen (Eds.), *Handbook of research on teaching the English language arts* (3rd ed.). Sponsored by the International Reading Association/National Council of Teachers of English. Mahwah, NJ: Erlbaum.

Tevebaugh, T. (2001). Welcome to our web: Integrating subjects through entomology. *Language Arts, 78*(4), 343–347.

Thaiss, C. (1986). *Language across the curriculum in the elementary grades.* Urbana, IL: National Council of Teachers of English.

Thomas, W. P., & Collier, V. (1997). *School effectiveness for language minority students.* Washington, DC: National Clearinghouse for Bilingual Education.

Thompson, D. L. (1992). The alphabet book as a content area resource. *Reading Teacher, 46,* 266–267.

Tierney, R. J. (1994). Writing-reading relationships in instruction. *Encyclopedia of English studies and language arts* (Vol. 2). New York: Scholastic.

Tierney, R. J. (1998). Literacy assessment reform: Shifting beliefs, principled possibilities, and emerging practices. *Reading Teacher, 51*, 374–390.

Tierney, R. J., Carter, M., & Desai, L. (1991). *Portfolio assessment in the reading-writing classroom*. Norwood, MA: Christopher-Gordon.

Tierney, R.J., Johnston, P., Moore, D. W., & Valencia, S. W. (2000). Snippets: How will literacy be assessed in the next millennium? *Reading Research Quarterly, 35*, 244–250.

Tierney, R. J., & Readance, J. E. (2000). *Reading strategies and practices: A compendium*. Boston: Allyn & Bacon.

Tierney, R. J., Readance, J. E., & Dishner, E. K. (1995). *Reading strategies and practices: A compendium*. Boston: Allyn & Bacon.

Tierney, R. J., & Shanahan, T. (1990). Research on the reading-writing relationship: Interactions, transactions, and outcomes. In R. Batin, M. L. Kamil, P. Mostenthal, & P. D. Pearson (Eds.), *Handbook of reading research* (Vol. 2, pp. 246–280). New York: Longman.

Tough, J. (1977). *The development of meaning*. London, England: Allen & Unwin.

Townsend, J., & Fu, D. (1998). A Chinese boy's joyful initiation into American literacy. *Language Arts, 75*, 193–201.

Treiman, R. (1983). The structure of spoken syllables: Evidence from novel word games. *Cognition, 15*, 49–74.

Treiman, R. (1985). Onsets and rimes as units of spoken syllables: Evidence from children. *Journal of Experimental Psychology, 39*, 161–181.

Trelease, J. (2001). *The new read-aloud handbook* (5th ed.). New York: Viking/Penguin.

Trelease, J. (1996). Have you read to your kids today? *Instructor, 105*, 56–60.

Udvari-Solner, A. (1994). A decision-making model for curricular adaptations in cooperative groups. In J. Thousand, R. Villa, & A. Nevin (Eds.), *Creativity and collaborative learning* (pp. 59–77). Baltimore: Paul H. Brookes.

Underwood, T. (1999). *The portfolio project: A study of assessment, instruction, and middle school reform*. Urbana, IL: National Council of Teachers of English.

U.S. Bureau of the Census. (1999). *Current population reports*. Available online: .

Urzua, C. (1987). "You stopped too soon": Second language children composing and revising. *TESOL Quarterly, 21*, 279–304.

Vacca, R., & Vacca, J. (1996). Activating and building background knowledge. In R. Vacca & J. Vacca, *Content Area Reading* (5th ed., Ch. 5). Glenview, IL: Scott, Foresman.

Van Keulen, J. E., Weddington, G. T., & DeBose, C. E. (1998). *Speech, language, learning and the African American Child*. Boston: Allyn & Bacon.

Varble, M. E. (1990). Analysis of writing samples of students taught by teachers using whole language and traditional approaches. *Journal of Educational Research, 83*, 245–251.

Vars, G. (1991). Integrated curriculum in historical perspective. *Educational Leadership, 49*(2), 14–15.

Veatch, J. (1978). *Reading in the elementary school* (2nd ed.). New York: Wiley & Sons.

Veatch, J. (Ed.). (1959). *Individualizing your reading program: Self-selection in action*. New York: Putnam.

Vermont Assessment Program. (1991). Montpelier, VT: Vermont Department of Education.

Verriour, P. (1986). Creating worlds of dramatic discourse. *Language Arts, 63*, 253–263.

Vibert, A. (1988). Collaborative writing. *Language Arts, 65*, 74–76.

von Bracht Donsky, B. (1984). Trends in elementary writing instruction. *Language Arts, 61*, 795–803.

Vygotsky, L. S. (1962). *Thought and language*. Cambridge, MA: MIT Press.

Vygotsky, L. S. (1967). Play and its role in the mental development of the child. *Soviet Psychology, 12*, 62–67.

Vygotsky, L. S. (1978). In M. Cole, V. John-Steiner, S. Scribner, & E. Souberman (Eds.), *Mind in society: The development of higher psychological processes*. Cambridge, MA: Harvard University Press.

Vygotsky, L. S. (1986). *Thought and language*. Cambridge, MA: MIT Press.

Wagner, B. J. (1988). Research currents: does classroom drama affect the arts of language? *Language Arts, 65*, 46–55.

Wagner, B. J. (1992). Imaginative expression. In J. Flood, J. Jensen, D. Lapp, & J. Squire (Eds.), *Handbook of research on teaching the English language arts* (pp. 787–804). New York: Macmillan.

Wagner, B. J. (2001). Imaginative expression. In J. Flood, J. Jensen, D. Lapp, & J. Squire (Eds.), *Handbook of research on teaching the English language arts* (2nd ed.). New York: Macmillan.

Wagner, B. J. (2003). Imaginative expression. In J. Flood, D. Lapp, M. R. Squire, & J. M. Jensen (Eds.), *Handbook of research on teaching the English language arts* (3rd ed.). Sponsored by the International Reading Association/National Council of Teachers of English. Mahwah, NJ: Erlbaum.

Watson, D. (1988). What do we find in a whole language program? In C. Weaver (Ed.), *Reading process and practice* (pp. 13–21). Portsmouth, NH: Heinemann.

Watson, D. (1993). Community meaning: Personal knowing within a social place. In K. Pierce & C. Giles (Eds.), *Cycles of meaning*. Portsmouth, NH: Heinemann.

Way, B. (1967). *Development through drama*. New York: Humanities Press.

Weaver, C. (1979). *Grammar for teachers: Perspectives and definitions*. Urbana, IL: National Council of Teachers of English.

Weaver, C. (1988). *Reading process and practice: From socio-psycholinguistics to whole language*. Portsmouth, NH: Heinemann.

Weaver, C. (1996). *Teaching grammar in context*. Portsmouth, NH: Heinemann.

 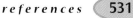

Weaver, C. (1998b). Teaching grammar in the context of writing. In C. Weaver (Ed.), *Lessons to share: On teaching grammar in context* (pp. 18–38). Portsmouth, NH: Heinemann.

Weaver, C. (Ed.). (1997). *Reconsidering a balanced approach to reading.* Urbana, IL: National Council of Teachers of English.

Weaver, C. (Ed.). (1998a). *Lessons to share: On teaching grammar in context.* Portsmouth, NH: Heinemann.

Weaver, C. (Ed.). (1998c). *Implementing a balanced approach to reading.* Urbana, IL: National Council of Teachers of English.

Weir, B. (2000). *Introducing children to folk tales.* Norwood, MA: Christopher-Gordon.

Weller, H. G. (1996). Assessing the impact of computer-based learning in science. *Journal of Research on Computing in Education, 28,* 461–485.

Wells, C. G. (1985). Pre-school literacy related activities and success in school. In D. Olson, N. Torrance, & A. Hildyard (Eds.), *Literacy, language, and learning: The nature and consequence of literacy* (pp. 229–255). Cambridge, England: Cambridge University Press.

Wells, G. (Ed.). (1981). *Learning through interaction: The study of language development.* London, England: Cambridge University Press.

Wells, G., & Wells, J. (1984). Learning to talk and talking to learn. *Theory Into Practice, 23,* 190–197.

Whatley, W. (1981). Language among Black Americans. In C. A. Ferguson and S. B. Heath (Eds.), *Language in the USA* (pp. 92–107). New York: Cambridge University Press.

Whitin, D., & Whitin, P. (2000). *Math is language too.* Urbana, IL: National Council of Teachers of English.

Wiener, R. B., & Cohen, J. H. (1997). *Literacy portfolios: Using assessment to guide instruction.* Columbus, OH: Merrill.

Wigginton, E. (1972). *Foxfire.* New York: Doubleday.

Wilde, S. (1990). A proposal for a new spelling curriculum. *Elementary School Journal, 90,* 275–289.

Wilde, S. (1993). *You kan red this! Spelling and punctuation for whole language classrooms, K–6.* Portsmouth, NH: Heinemann.

Wilt, M. E. (1974). Listening: What's new? In J. de Stefano & S. Fox (Eds.), *Language and the language arts.* Boston: Little, Brown.

Winkel, L. (Ed.). (1990). *The elementary school library collection: A guide to books and other media* (17th ed.). Williamsport, PA: Brodart.

Winn, D. (1988). Develop listening skills as part of the curriculum. *Reading Teacher, 42,* 144.

Wirtz, C. L., Gardner, R., Weber, K., & Bullara, D. (1996). Using self-correction to improve the spelling performance of low-achieving third graders. *Remedial and Special Education, 17,* 48–58.

Wolfe, D. (1984). Research currents: Learning about language skills from narratives. *Language Arts, 61,* 844–850.

Wood, K. (1994). Hearing voices, telling tales: Finding the power of reading aloud. *Language Arts, 71,* 346–349.

Wylie, R. E., & Durrell, D. D. (1970). Teaching vowels through phonograms. *Elementary English, 47,* 787–791.

Xu, H. (1996). A Filipino ESL kindergartner's successful beginning literacy learning experiences in a mainstream classroom. In D. Leu, C. J. Kinzer, & K. Hinchman (Eds.), *Literacies for the twenty-first century* (pp. 219–231). Chicago: National Reading Conference.

Yaden, D. B., & Templeton, S. (Eds.). (1986). *Metalinguistic awareness and beginning literacy: Conceptualizing what it means to read and write.* Portsmouth, NH: Heinemann.

Yawkey, T. D. (1980). Effects of social relationships curricula and sex differences on reading and imaginativeness in young children. *Alberta Journal of Educational Research, 26,* 159–167.

Yopp, H. K. (1992). Developing phonemic awareness in young children. *Reading Teacher, 45,* 696–703.

Yopp, H. K. (1995a). A test for assessing phonemic awareness in young children. *Reading Teacher, 49,* 20–29.

Yopp, H. K. (1995b). Read-aloud books for developing phonemic awareness: An annotated bibliography. *Reading Teacher, 48,* 538–542.

Yopp, H. K., & Yopp, R. H. (1996). *Oo-pples and boo-noo-noos: Songs and activities for phonemic awareness.* Orlando, FL: Harcourt Brace.

Yopp, H. K., & Yopp, R. H. (2000). Supporting phonemic awareness development in the classroom. *Reading Teacher, 54*(2), 130–143.

Young, T., & Vardell, S. (1993). Weaving Reader's Theater and nonfiction into the curriculum. *Reading Teacher, 46,* 396–405.

Zarnowski, M. (1995). Learning history with informational storybooks: A social studies educator's perspective. *New Advocate, 8,* 183–196.

Zarrillo, J. (1989). Teacher's interpretations of literature-based reading. *Reading Teacher, 43,* 22–28.

Zarrillo, J. (1994). *Multicultural literature, multicultural teaching: Units for the elementary grades.* Fort Worth, TX: Harcourt Brace Jovanovich.

Zarrillo, J., & Cox, C. (1992). Efferent and aesthetic teaching. In J. Many & C. Cox (Eds.), *Reader stance and literary understanding: Exploring the theories, research, and practice* (pp. 235–249). Norwood, NJ: Ablex.

Zeni, J. (1990). *Writing Lands, composing with old and new writing tools.* Urbana, IL: National Council of Teachers of English.

Zutell, J. (1979). Spelling strategies of primary school children and their relationship to the Piagetian concept of decentration. *Research in the Teaching of English, 13,* 69–80.

Zutell, J. (1994). Spelling instruction. In A. C. Purves (Ed.), *Encyclopedia of English studies and language arts* (Vol. 2). New York: Scholastic.

Zutell, J., & Allen, V. (1988). The English spelling strategies of Spanish-speaking bilingual children. *TESOL Quarterly, 22,* 333–339.

children's literature *(continued)*
  groups/grouping and, 240–248
  informational texts as. *See*
    informational texts
  integrating the curriculum and, 232,
    233, 248, 475, 487–488
  literary texts. *See* literary texts
  math and, 91–95
  modeling of language by, 258, 363,
    475, 476–477, 488, 489, 490,
    491–494, 497–498
  multicultural education and, 271
  multicultural focus in, 271, 275–288
  patterns in130–131, 364–365, 367,
    368–369, 477, 481, 485. *See also*
    alphabet books; poems/poetry;
    predictable pattern books
  poems/poetry. *See* poems/poetry
  predictions about, 199, 203, 204
  questioning strategies for, 238–240
  reading. *See* reading
  responding to. *See* reader
    response/stance; reader-response
    theory
  selecting, 198, 203, 211, 222,
    236–237, 242, 248, 250, 251,
    275–276, 280–281, 287–288,
    476–477, 485, 489, 497
  series in, 477, 487
  for special-needs students, 281
  stance toward. *See* reader
    response/stance; reader-response
    theory
  stories. *See specific types of stories*
  strategies for using, 236–248
  television and, 403
  thematic teaching with, 439,
    502–506
  visually representing and, 406–408
  vocabulary development and,
    104–106
  word study and, 347–348
Children's Theatre Association, 177
Chomsky, Noam, 74–75, 354, 355, 370
Chukovsky, Kornei, 101
cinquain, 116
circle story, 183
class (social), 268, 269, 272. *See also*
  cultural diversity
classroom environment, 21, 23–25
  children's literature in, 21, 24–25,
    27, 28, 128–129, 222, 308
  computers in, 21, 27, 28, 29,
    435–436, 458–461. *See also*
    computers
  cultural diversity in. *See* cultural
    diversity

emergent literacy and, 116–118, 308
equipment/supplies in, 28–29, 133,
  308. *See also types of equipment/*
  supplies
language diversity in. *See* language
  diversity
layout of, 24–25
listening and talking in, 90,
  153–154, 155–158, 159–160
media in. *See* media/mediamaking
print-rich nature of, 24–25, 116–118,
  128–129
response- vs. text-centered, 18–21,
  23, 228
social interactionist theory and,
  16
student- vs. teacher-centered, 18–21,
  23, 228
technology and, 21, 27, 28, 29,
  435–436, 458–461
traditional view of, 19–21
writing and, 308
closed vs. open questions, 155, 158,
  238–239
clusters, 99, 163–164, 243–244, 300.
  See also graphic organizers
Clymer, Theodore, 215–216
code (and early reading instruction),
  214
cognates, 87
cognitive academic language
  proficiency (CALP), 81
cognitive development
  literacy and, 111–112
  spelling and, 328
  theories of, 13–14, 16, 76–76, 77
cognitive theory, 13–14. *See also*
  constructivist theory; Piaget, Jean
collaborative learning. *See* cooperative
  learning
collaborative writing, 301, 441
collages, 415, 416, 495
College Entrance Examination Board's
  Achievement Test in English
  Composition, 305
commercial programs. *See* basal
  readers; textbooks
communicative competence, 71. *See also*
  language development
community journals, 314, 439
compare and contrast, 488, 493
comprehensible input, 83, 373–374
computer(s)
  center for, 138
  classroom environment and, 21, 27,
    28, 29, 435–436, 458–461
  cultural diversity and, 271, 448, 460

e-mail/electronic messaging, 261,
  442, 443–448, 460–461
English language learners and, 436,
  438, 453–457, 458
group work with, 460
Internet access. *See* Internet
keyboarding skills, 438
software for, 29, 301–302, 320, 362,
  438, 441, 443, 460
writing on, 391–393, 438–449. *See*
  also word processing
concentric circle pattern, 367
Concepts about Print (CAP), 119, 120
concrete operational stage, 75–76, 77
concrete poetry, 477, 481–482
conferences (about)
  assessment, 60, 306
  grammar, 361, 362–363
  reading, 221–222, 243
  writing, 23, 44–48, 295, 296,
    299–301, 306, 310–313, 361,
    362–363, 371, 376
consonants, 216
constructivist theory, 12–15
  on assessment, 39–40
  definition of, 12–15
  on drama, 171
  on language development, 12–13,
    15, 72, 74–76, 77, 81, 159
  on writing, 295
contemporary realistic fiction, 238
content journals, 314
content standards. *See* standards-based
  education
content-based English language
  development (ELD), 87, 88, 90,
  95, 97, 98
context-embedded
  communication/instruction,
  81–82, 242, 246
conundrums, 103. *See also* riddles
conventional orthography, 122
conventional stage, 124, 125, 330–331,
  342
conventions (of language). *See also*
  grammar; handwriting;
  punctuation; spelling
  assessment of, 56
  English language learners and, 302,
    303
  language development and, 79–80,
    85
  purpose of, 325
  strategies for teaching, 134, 196, 295
  writing and, 196, 295, 303
cooperative learning, 164–166, 167,
  269–270, 302

cooperative projects, 165
core book units, 248–255
  children's literature for, 248, 250, 276–279
  examples of, 251–255, 277–279
  groups/grouping for, 251, 254–255
  guidelines for, 248–250
  multicultural children's literature in, 276–279
costumes (for drama), 172, 178, 424–425
counting books, 142
couplets, 480
creative drama, 171, 177–179, 401. *See also* drama
critical viewing, 395–398, 403–404. *See also* viewing
cultural diversity. *See also* English language learners; language diversity; multicultural education
  assessment and, 40, 65–66
  children's literature and, 275–276. *See also* children's literature, multicultural focus in
  computers and, 271, 448, 460
  content area instruction and, 90
  current trend toward, 80–81, 268
  drama and, 429–430
  emergent literacy and, 116–118
  features of, 268, 270
  gender and, 269–270, 272
  integrating the curriculum and, 471–472
  language and, 79–80, 268, 270, 272, 354. *See also* language diversity
  reading and, 116–118
  social interactionist theory and, 16
  technology and, 448, 460
  thematic teaching and, 471–472
  writing and, 116–118
culturally conscious children's literature, 275. *See also* children's literature, multicultural focus in
Cummins, James, 81–82, 242
curriculum drama, 425–430. *See also* drama
curriculum planning, 21, 22–23
  assessment and, 40, 41–42, 60–61, 62–63, 320–321
  multicultural education and, 269, 270–271. *See also* multicultural education
  participation in, 308–309
  sources for, 22–23, 27–28, 29
  standards for, 22. *See also* standards-based educaation

students' experiences and, 22–23, 27–28, 87, 302–304
technology and, 436, 437, 452, 453. *See also* technology
thematic teaching and, 22, 29. *See also* thematic teaching
viewing and visually representing and, 388–392
cursive handwriting, 381, 382. *See also* handwriting

dance/dancing, 181–182, 467–468, 473–474
Delpit, Lisa, 273–274
demonstrating lessons, 33, 296. *See also* minilessons
description (as type of text), 488, 492–493
desktop publishing, 449, 441–442. *See also* word processing
developmental spelling, 123–126, 345, 346. *See also* spelling
Developmental Spelling Inventory, 345, 346
Dewey, John, 13, 17, 19, 464
dialects, 271–273, 374, 375. *See also* language diversity
dialogue journals, 52, 274, 302, 314–315
diamante, 367
dictionaries, 28, 333, 337, 468
dioramas, 259
directed listening thinking activity (DLTA), 171, 180–182
directed reading activity (DRA), 202
directed reading thinking activity (DRTA), 202
disabilities (students with). *See* special needs
DLTA. *See* directed listening thinking activity
"Do What, When, and Where" pattern, 368
docudrama films, 410
documentary films, 410
double-entry journals, 51–52. *See also* literature-response journals
DRA. *See* directed reading activity
drafting, 293, 294, 441, 442. *See also* writing
drama, 170–185, 405–425
  assessment of, 179, 185–188, 430, 431
  children's literature and, 172, 173, 174, 178, 180–184, 255
  cultural diversity and, 429–430
  definition of, 170

dramatic literature and, 420–425. *See also* Shakespeare
emergent literacy and, 131
for English language learners, 180, 184–185, 186
equipment/supplies needed for, 172, 173, 174, 178
examples of, 178–179, 418–420
films/filmmaking and, 401. *See also* films/filmmaking
integrating the curriculum and, 425–430, 473–474
in kindergarten, 137–139
listening and talking and, 170–171
literature focus units and, 255
music and, 181–182
reading and, 138–139
for special-needs students, 186
strategies for teaching, 131, 171–185, 416–430
visually representing and, 416, 405–425
dramatic films, 410
dramatic literature, 420–425. *See also* Shakespeare
draw-on media, 413–414
drawing. *See also* art
  children's literature and, 200–201
  emergent literacy and, 113
  films/filmmaking and, 401, 413–414
  visually representing and, 405–408
  writing and, 113, 121, 131–134
drawing (stage of emergent writing), 121
DRTA. *See* directed reading thinking activity
dual-immersion programs, 453–454

e-mail, 261, 442, 443–448, 460–461. *See also* Internet
early production stage, 84, 85, 86, 95, 96, 97, 98
editing and revising, 293, 294, 312–313, 315–316, 334–336, 360–362, 383, 441, 442. *See also* writing
Education for All Handicapped Children Act (EHA), 64
Educational Testing Service (ETS), 305
efferent questions/prompts, 160–161. *See also* questions/prompts
efferent responses/stances, 160–161, 228–231. *See also* informational texts; reader response/stance
EHA. *See* Education for All Handicapped Children Act

ELD. *See* English language development
electronic messaging, 261, 442,
     443–448, 460–461. *See also*
     Internet
ELL. *See* English language learners
embedded spelling program, 333
emergent biliteracy, 139–148.
     See also emergent literacy
    guidelines for, 139
    in kindergarten, 140–145
    strategies for teaching, 140–148,
     302–304
emergent literacy, 111–151
    assessment of, 149
    bilingualism and, 139–148
    classroom environment and,
     116–118, 308
    cognitive development and, 111–112
    cultural diversity and, 116–118
    drama and, 131
    English language learners and,
     139–148
    home environment and, 116–118
    kindergarten and, 136–139,
     140–145, 147–148
    music and, 142, 146, 147
    readiness approach vs., 111–112, 193
    reading and, 116–119, 127–137.
     See also reading
    strategies for developing, 112–116,
     127–136, 140–148
    thematic teaching and, 116, 117,
     135–136
    theories of, 111–112
    writing and, 119–127. *See also*
     writing
emergent reading, 116–119, 127–137.
     See also emergent literacy; reading
emergent storybook readings, 118
emergent writing, 119–127. *See also*
     emergent literacy; writing
emotional disorders. *See* behavior
     disorders (students with)
encyclopedias, 28, 439
English as a second language (ESL)
     students. *See* English language
     learners
English language, 271–274, 325,
     326–327. *See also* language
English language development (ELD),
     87, 88, 89, 90, 91–95, 146
English language learners (ELL), 87–98.
     See also language diversity
    adapting instruction for, 87–98
    assessment of, 85, 86, 90, 95, 96, 97,
     105–107, 149, 150, 247, 248

children's literature for, 91–95
computer use by, 436, 438, 453–457,
    458
content-area instruction for, 87, 88,
    89–90
conventions of language and, 302,
    303
definition of, 80
drama with, 180, 184–185, 186
emergent literacy of, 139–148
goals for, 81
grammar for, 373–374, 375
graphic organizers with, 87, 88, 89,
    100
groups/grouping and, 89, 167
hypermedia projects by, 453–457
informational texts for, 490,
    491–496
instructional conversations with,
    161–163
integrating the curriculum and, 474,
    475
journals of, 142, 314–315
as kindergartners, 140–145,
    147–148
listening and talking by, 161–163,
    164, 167, 168
literature circles/groups with,
    241–246, 284–287
literature focus units for, 284–287
math for, 90–98, 141, 142
media/mediamaking with, 387,
    388–393, 403
music with, 146, 147, 482–483
questions/prompts for, 85
with special needs, 65–66, 67
spelling by, 332
standards-based education and, 89,
    95
strategies for teaching, 87–98,
    140–146, 161–163, 271–275,
    284–287, 302–304
technology for, 436, 438, 453–457,
    458
thematic teaching and, 88, 468, 474,
    475
viewing and visually representing by,
    387, 388–393, 403
vocabulary development of, 89,
    99–107
word processing by, 438
writing by, 302–304, 314–315,
    373–374, 375, 438, 490, 491–496
writing workshop with, 302–304
environmental print, 116–118, 128.
     See also print-rich environment

equilibration, 14
ESL students. *See* English language
     learners
ethnicity, 268, 279, 272. *See also*
     cultural diversity
ethnosensitivity, 275
ETS. *See* Educational Testing Service
exceptional children. *See* special needs
     (students with); *specific types of*
     exceptionalities
expository texts, 466, 488. *See also*
     informational texts
extending production stage, 84, 85, 86,
     95, 96, 97, 98

face feature chart, 407
face poems, 407–408
fact sheets, 372–373
fairytales, 256–257, 485. *See also*
     traditional tales
family background. *See* home
     environment
fantasy (literature), 237, 476, 485–486
FEP. *See* fluent English proficient
     students
film response guide, 399–401
films/filmmaking, 398–401
    cameras for, 410–412
    children's interests/experiences and,
     398, 399
    children's literature and, 399
    drama and, 401
    drawing and, 401, 413–414
    listening and talking about, 155,
     157, 158
    postviewing, 399, 400–401
    previewing, 399–400
    responding to, 398, 399, 400–401
    selecting, 399, 402
    viewing, 399, 400
    with a camera, 410–412. *See also*
     videocassette (VCR)
     recorders/recording
    without a camera, 412–416
    writing and, 401
filtering software, 460
firewall software, 460
first-grade studies, 191, 215
first-language development, 71–80.
     See also language development
    constructivist theory on, 72,
     74–76
    example of, 72–74
    social interactionist theory on, 72,
     76–68
flowcharts, 164

integrating the curriculum *(continued)*
  products of, 501–506
  reading and, 135–136, 468
  technology and, 452, 453
  viewing and, 388–393
  visually representing and, 405–408,
    425–430
  writing and, 135–136, 468
interactive model, 194–195
interactive writing, 134
International Reading Association
    (IRA)
  on assessment, 41–42
  on language arts. *See Standards for the
    English Language Arts*
  on spelling, 333
International Society for Technology in
    Education (ISTE), 436, 437
Internet, 449–451
  access to, 28, 29
  basic elements of, 449–451
  e-mail, 261, 442, 443–448, 460–461
  research using, 437, 449–451
  safety guidelines for, 460–461
  searches via, 449–451
  strategies for using, 451, 460–461
interviews/interviewing, 23, 165, 166,
    168–169
invented spelling, 122, 123, 333, 336.
    See also spelling
inventories (as assessment tools), 52
IRA. *See* International Reading
    Association
ISTE. *See* International Society for
    Technology in Education

jigsaw (learning strategy), 165
journals/journal writing, 313–315
  assessment and, 51–52
  of English language learners, 142,
    314–315
  of kindergartners, 142, 143–144, 314
  modeling of, 308
  scheduling of, 22, 313, 320
  types of, 51–52, 313–315, 337, 401,
    439, 498. *See also specific types*
journals (professional), 236, 309

kernel sentences, 370
keyboarding skills, 438
keypals, 261, 444, 445–448
keywords (in Internet searches),
    449–450
kindergarten/kindergartners
  assessment of, 149, 150
  centers in, 137–138, 145

drama in, 137–139
emergent literacy in, 136–139,
    140–145, 147–148
as English language learners,
    140–145, 147–148
journals of, 142, 143–144, 314
math in, 141, 142
music in, 142, 146, 147
scheduling of, 136–139
spelling in, 328–329, 341
writing in, 377
Krashen, Stephen, 83–84, 373–374
KWHLS charts, 166
KWL charts, 30, 166, 491

L1 preview/review, 89
LAD. *See* language acquisition device
language
  competence vs. performance,
    354
  conventions of. *See* conventions
  cultural diversity and, 79–80, 268,
    270. *See also* cultural diversity;
    language diversity
  definitions of, 2, 79–80, 397
  development of. *See* language
    development
  functions of, 79–80
  learning of, 15, 17, 18
  school vs. home uses of, 272–273
  structure of, 354. *See also* grammar
  systems of, 78–80
language acquisition device (LAD),
    74–75
language across the curriculum, 29,
    463–465, 474, 475. *See also*
    integrating the curriculum;
    thematic teaching
language arts, 1–2. *See also specific
    language arts*
language communities, 271
language competence vs. performance,
    354
language development, 71–109
  classroom environment and, 273
  conventions and, 79–80, 85
  environment and, 76–78
  of first language, 71–80. *See also* first-
    language development
  research on, 71
  of second language, 80–107. *See also*
    second-language development
  stages of, 75–76, 77, 84–85, 86
  theories of, 72, 74–78, 81–85
  vocabulary. *See* vocabulary
    development

language diversity
  cultural diversity and, 79–80, 268,
    270, 272, 354. *See also* cultural
    diversity
  elements of, 271–274, 354
  emergent literacy and, 139–148.
    See also emergent biliteracy
  local speech and, 274
  reading and, 273
  sensitivity to, 273–275, 332, 374
  strategies for teaching, 271–275
language experience approach (LEA),
    89, 114, 134, 137, 139, 196,
    205–209, 438, 439
language interaction analysis chart,
    155, 156
language systems, 78–80
language-minority students. *See* English
    language learners; language
    diversity
LEA. *See* language experience approach
learning disabilities (students with), 64,
    66, 67
learning styles, 65, 67, 68
least restrictive environment, 64
LEP. *See* limited English proficient
    students
lessons. *See* demonstrating lessons;
    initiating lessons; minilessons
letter/sound correspondence, 78, 210,
    215, 217, 326
lexicon, 79
libraries, 128–129, 222
limericks, 481
limited English proficient (LEP)
    students, 80–81. *See also* English
    language learners; language
    diversity
linear model, 193–194
listening and talking, 153–189
  assessment of, 154, 185–188
  center for, 135, 138, 166–168
  classroom levels of, 90, 153–154,
    155–158, 159–160
  drama and, 170–171. *See also* drama
  English language learners and,
    161–163, 164, 167, 168
  about films/filmmaking, 155, 157,
    158
  guidelines for, 159
  literacy and, 155, 171
  modeling of, 90, 273
  reading and, 155. *See also* reading
    aloud
  strategies for teaching, 159–169,
    171–185

teacher vs. student talk, 90, 153–154, 155–158, 159–160
  writing and, 155
lists
  as graphic organizers, 164
  as writing structures, 488, 492
literacy
  assessment of, 41–42, 149, 150
  classroom environment and, 308
  cognitive development and, 111–112
  definition of, 2, 397
  development of. See emergent literacy
  drama and, 171
  language diversity and, 273
  listening and talking and, 155, 171
  media literacy and, 397–398. See also media/mediamaking; viewing
  spelling and, 331
  strategies for developing, 112–116, 127–136, 140–148, 155,196
literary elements, 183, 239–240, 253, 254, 275, 363–364, 490
literary genres, 237–238. See also specific genres
literary journals, 314
literary texts, 475–487. See also children's literature
  elements of, 183, 239–240, 253, 254
  genres of, 237–238. See also specific genres
  integrating the curriculum and, 475, 502, 503, 505
  as models of writing, 475, 476, 477
  poems/poetry, 475–482. See also poems/poetry
  reader response/stance to, 464–466
  songs, 476–477. See also music; songs/singing
  sources of, 476–477
  stories, 475, 476–477, 484–487. See also specific types of stories
  thematic teaching and, 502, 503, 505
literature. See children's literature
literature circles/groups, 233, 240–248
  characteristics of, 241
  for English language learners, 241–246, 284–287
  genre units in, 284–287
  roles within, 241
literature focus units, 248–261, 275–288
  author units, 248, 250, 255–256, 276, 282–284
  children's literature for, 248, 250, 251, 256, 257

core book units, 248–255, 276–279
  definition of, 248
  drama and, 255
  for English language learners, 284–287
  examples of, 251–255, 256, 257, 277–279, 284–287
  genre units, 55, 248, 250, 256–257, 276, 284–287
  integrating and curriculum and, 248
  media/mediamaking and, 255, 259
  multicultural children's literature for, 275–288
  response options for, 252–255, 256, 257, 258–261
  scheduling of, 251, 278–279
literature-response journals, 51–52, 232, 258, 261
Loban, Walter, 19–20
logs (used in assessment), 49, 50, 51, 261, 404

Mad Libs, 370
mainstream Americans, 268
mainstream English, 273–274. See also language diversity
Mann, Horace, 214
manuscript handwriting, 381, 382. See also handwriting
maps/mapping. See semantic maps
masks/mask making, 181, 182, 184–185, 416
mass media, 387. See also media/mediamaking; media literacy
math
  center for, 138
  children's literature and, 91–95
  content standards for, 95
  groups/grouping, 10–11
  English language learners and, 90–98, 141, 142
  integrating the curriculum and, 472–473
  in kindergarten, 141, 142
media/mediamaking, 405, 408–416. See also viewing; visually representing
  assessment of, 403–404
  center for, 166–168
  critical viewing and, 395–398, 403–404
  for English language learners, 387, 388–393, 403
  films/filmmaking, 398–401
  literacy and, 397–398, 403–404

literature focus units and, 255, 259
  strategies for teaching, 397–398, 408–416
  supplies/equipment needed, 166
  technology and, 436, 437, 449–458. See also multimedia projects
  television, 29, 395–396, 401–403, 412
media critique form, 404
media literacy, 397–398, 403–404. See also media/mediamaking; viewing
memoirs (of students), 23. See also autobiographies
mental retardation (students with), 64
metalinguistic awareness, 121
metaphors, 103, 476, 479, 505
minilessons (on/in)
  grammar, 362
  guided reading, 204–205
  handwriting, 380–381
  punctuation, 376, 377, 378
  reading, 204–205, 221
  reference books, 468
  scheduling of, 309–310, 317
  spelling, 134
  word processing, 442, 443
  word study, 340, 343–348, 349, 365, 371
  writing, 296–298, 302, 303, 309–310, 442, 443
modeling (of)
  children's literature and, 258, 363, 475, 476–477, 488, 489, 490, 491–494, 497–498
  demonstrating lessons and, 33
  handwriting, 380
  initiating lessons and, 33, 34–35
  journal writing, 308
  listening and talking, 90, 273
  reading, 193–196
  spelling, 332
  writing, 44, 45, 134, 258, 295, 296, 302, 308–309, 490, 491–494
monitor model, 83, 373–374
"Morning Message," 115, 129, 137, 141
morphemes, 79
morphemic and syntactic stage, 331, 342
multicultural education, 267–274. See also cultural diversity; language diversity
  approaches to, 268–269
  children's literature and, 271. See also children's literature, multicultural focus in
  content area instruction and, 90

multicultural education *(continued)*
   curriculum planning and, 269,
      270–271
   definition of, 267–278
   foundations of, 269–270
   integrating the curriculum and,
      470–471
   strategies for teaching, 269–271
   thematic teaching and, 270,
      470–471
   viewing and, 271
   writing and, 271
multimedia projects, 449–458
   assessment of, 458, 459
   hypermedia, 436, 452–457, 458
   Internet, 437, 449–451
   strategies for teaching, 390–391, 451,
      453–457
multiple acculturation, 270
multiple intelligences theory, 65, 67,
      68
music
   drama and, 181–182
   emergent literacy and, 142, 146,
      147
   English language learners and, 146,
      147, 482–483
   integrating the curriculum and,
      470
   in kindergarten, 142, 146, 147
   songs/singing, 211, 212, 245, 246,
      475, 476–477, 482–484, 505
"My Hands, My Feet" pattern, 367
mysteries, 477, 487

Nation's Report Card, The, 375
National Assessment of Educational
      Progress (NAEP), 305, 355
National Association for the Education
      of Young Children (NAEYC), 149,
      333
National Board for Professional
      Teaching Standards, 149
National Council of Teachers of English
      (NCTE). *See Standards for the*
      Enlgish Language Arts
National Educational Technology
      Standards for Students, 436, 437
National Writing Project, 309
Native Americans, 275, 280, 354
natural approach, 83–84
natural readers, 112, 116
NCTE. *See* National Council of Teachers
      of English
No Child Left Behind Act, 40. *See also*
      standardized tests/testing

nonfiction (as genre), 238, 489,
      490–496. *See also* informational
      texts
   as models of writing, 490, 491–494
   qualities of, 490
   report writing and, 490
nonphonetic letterstrings, 122
nouns, 366, 367, 368, 372

observations (of teachers), 52. *See also*
      anecdotal record assessment
onomatopoeia, 102
onsets, 217, 343
open vs. closed questions, 155, 158,
      238–239
oral histories, 168, 169, 412
oral language. *See* listening and talking
oral reading. *See* reading aloud
orthography, 122, 123, 326–327

palindromes, 103
pantomime, 178, 181, 467–468, 474
paragraphs, 373
parents. *See* home environment
parts of speech, 102, 353, 366–368.
      See also grammar
part-to-whole approach, 19, 193
parts-to-whole phonics, 217
patterns (for/in writing), 130–131,
      364–365, 367, 368–369, 477,
      481, 485. *See also* alphabet books;
      poems/poetry; predictable pattern
      books
Pavlov, Ivan, 19
peer(s)
   assessment by, 56–57, 58, 187, 306,
      506
   conferences with, 302, 303, 306,
      312–313
   editing by, 334–336, 362, 363, 378,
      383, 384, 474
phonemes, 78–79, 210
phonemic awareness, 210–214, 240,
      336
phonetic stage, 124, 125, 329, 341
phonetics, 78
phonics
   debate regarding, 209, 214
   definition of, 78, 214
   reading and, 193, 200, 209
   rules of, 215–217
   strategies for teaching, 218, 336
phonology, 78–79, 336
photograms, 415–416
photos/photography, 412, 415. *See also*
      cameras; media/mediamaking

physical education, 11
Piaget, Jean
   on drama, 171
   on language development, 74–76,
      77, 78, 171
   on learning, 13–14, 15, 16, 16, 78
   on writing, 121, 295
picture books, 143, 237, 476–477
Pinkney family, 282–284
planning and progress forms (as
      assessment tools), 59, 61,
      246–248
plays. *See* drama; Shakespeare
poems/poetry, 475–482
   art and, 406–408
   children's literature and, 237, 245,
      246, 406–408
   elements of, 478–479, 480
   frames for, 116, 439, 481
   as genre, 237
   sources of, 476–477
   types of, 116, 439, 476–477,
      479–482. *See also specific types*
   visually representing and, 406–408
portfolios, 58–61, 320–323
   assessment and, 69–61, 62–63, 261,
      262, 306, 320, 322–323, 349
   children's literature and, 261, 262
   curriculum planning and,
      320–321
   definitions of, 58, 320
   drama and, 186–187
   media projects in, 403–404
   spelling and, 349
   selecting/organizing materials for,
      58–59, 261, 262, 320, 322
   types of, 59, 262
   writing and, 306, 342
portraits, 406–408, 412
posters/charts, 296–297, 309, 315, 378,
      440, 496
postviewing, 399, 400–401
pragmatics, 78, 79–80
precommunicative stage, 124, 125,
      328–329, 341
predictable pattern books, 33, 34–35,
      130–131, 143
preoperational stage, 75, 77
prepositions, 367
preproduction stage, 84–85, 86, 95, 96,
      97, 98
previewing, 399–400
prewriting, 293, 294, 440, 442. *See also*
      writing
Principles and Practices for School
      Mathematics, 95

"ripple effects" of learning, 29–32, 117, 135, 201, 233, 235, 282–284, 392, 394, 464, 468, 469. *See also* integrating the curriculum; thematic teaching
role-playing, 258, 412. *See also* drama; story dramatizations
Rosenblatt, Louise M., 17–18, 160–161, 195, 228, 229, 230, 242, 398, 465
rubrics (as assessment tools), 52–56, 305–306, 307, 458, 459
running records, 223, 224

scaffolding, 16, 78
schema theory, 14–15
schemata, 14
schedules/scheduling (of/for), 21, 25–27
science
  center for, 135
  groups/grouping for, 10–11
  integrating the curriculum and, 472–473, 502–506
science fiction, 237, 391–393, 476, 485–486
science journals, 473
scribbling, 119–121
scripts/scriptwriting, 174–175, 176, 391–393, 403, 416–420, 421–422, 439. *See also* drama
SDAIE. *See* specially designed academic instruction in English
search engines, 449–450
search strings, 449–450
second-language development, 80–107. *See also* English language learners
  emergent literacy and, 139–148
  grammar and, 374, 375
  stages of, 84–85, 86
  theories of, 81–85
Secretary of the Day, 4, 5
self-assessment, 56–57
  tools for, 54–56, 322–323, 430, 431
  of writing, 52–56, 296, 322–323, 384
self-editing, 306, 315, 316, 362, 363, 378, 383, 384
self-portraits, 407–408, 411
semantic maps, 88, 89, 99, 100, 200, 337, 365, 407. *See also* graphic organizers
semantics, 78, 79, 332
semiphonetic stage, 124, 125, 329, 341
senryu, 481, 505
sense training, 88, 89, 177–178, 478
sensorimotor stage, 75, 77

sentence pyramids, 369
sentences/sentence structure
  assessment of, 56
  children's literature and, 363–364
  second-language development and, 85
  strategies for writing/revising, 361, 363–364, 365, 368–373
  syntax and, 79
series (of books), 477, 487, 489
Shakespeare (for children)
  interest in, 3–4, 5, 10, 12, 29–30
  strategies for teaching, 388, 420–425
shared reading, 106–201, 202. *See also* reading aloud
  with "big books," 131, 197
  emergent literacy and, 131
  examples of, 197–200
  phonics instruction and, 218
  with struggling readers, 197–200, 201, 202
shared writing, 134
sharing time
  examples of, 3–4, 112, 137
  guidelines for, 129
  in kindergarten, 137
  purpose of, 22
  in reading workshop, 222
  reports and, 506
  scheduling of, 3–4, 22, 129
  writing and, 301–302, 320, 362, 442
sheltered content instruction, 87, 146. *See also* English language learners, strategies for teaching
Shirreffs, Gordon D., 231–234, 241, 248, 418
similes, 103, 364, 476, 478, 505
Skinner, B. F., 19
slides, 413, 414
social class, 268, 269, 272. *See also* cultural diversity
social interactionist theory, 12, 13, 15–17
  on assessment, 42, 66
  on drama, 171
  on learning, 15–16
  on language development, 17, 72, 76–78, 81
  on writing, 295
social studies
  center for, 138
  groups/grouping for, 7–10
  integrating the curriculum and, 471–472
socioeconomic status, 268, 269, 272. *See also* cultural diversity

sociohistorical approach, 15–16. *See also* social interactionist theory; Vygotsky, Lev
sociolinguists, 79–80, 271–272
software, 29, 301–302, 320, 362, 438, 441, 443, 460. *See also* computers
songs/singing, 211, 212, 245, 246, 475, 476–477, 482–484, 505. *See also* music
sorts (activities involving), 338–340, 343, 345, 347, 349
speaking. *See* listening and talking
special education. *See* inclusive classrooms; special needs (students with)
special needs (students with), 61–68
  adapting instruction for, 61–65, 67–68, 167, 186, 331, 332
  assessment of, 65–68, 247, 248
  children's literature about, 281
  cultural diversity and, 65–66, 268, 269
  drama with, 186
  English language learners with, 65–66, 67
  grammar of, 373–374, 375
  integrating the curriculum and, 474, 475
  reading and, 197–200, 201, 202, 206–209, 248, 249, 474, 475
  spelling and, 331, 332
  thematic teaching and, 474, 475
  types of, 64–65. *See also specific needs*
  writing and, 248, 249, 374, 375, 474, 475
specially designed academic instruction in English (SDAIE), 87, 88–90, 90, 95–98
spelling, 325–350
  assessment of, 56, 331, 342, 343, 344, 345, 346, 348, 349
  cognitive development and, 328
  English language learners and, 332
  examples of, 327, 328–331
  grade levels and, 328–331, 341–350
  invented, 122, 123, 333, 336
  kindergartners and, 328–329, 341
  literacy development and, 331
  minilessons on, 134
  modeling of, 332
  phonemic awareness and, 210, 336
  portfolios and, 349
  reading and, 336–340
  rules for, 345–347
  scheduling of, 331, 332, 336, 345

stages of development of, 122, 123–126, 327, 328–330, 340–342
strategies for teaching, 134, 331–340, 342–350
struggling students and, 331, 332
word study and, 336–340
writing and, 333–336
SSR. *See* sustained silent reading
stance (reader). *See* reader response/stance
standardized tests/testing, 40, 41–42, 61, 149, 198, 356, 374. *See also* assessment
Standards for the English Language Arts
application of, 15, 17, 18, 34, 44, 49, 50, 104, 132, 147, 178, 277, 406, 502
grammar and, 352
listening and, 154
literacy and, 397
media literacy and, 397
purpose of, 2
subjects included in, 387, 393, 405
viewing and, 393
visually representing and, 405
standards-based education
assessment and, 41, 60–61, 62–63
curriculum planning and, 22, 89
English language learners and, 89, 95
language arts and. *See Standards for the English Language Arts*
math and, 95
model behind, 2
technology and, 436, 437
Star of the Week, 22–23
stimulus-response conditioning, 19
stories, 475, 476–477, 484–487. *See also* children's literature; *specific types of stories*
story boxes, 259
story dramatizations, 131, 171, 180–184, 253, 258, 401
story maps, 259
story quilts, 261
story retelling, 187, 188
storyboards, 403, 409, 410, 411, 440
storyframes, 365
storytelling, 171, 172, 258
structural grammar, 352, 353, 354. *See also* grammar
student independent reading, 196, 219–220, 490. *See also* sustained silent reading
sustained silent reading (SSR), 11, 219–220

syllabic patterns, 481. *See also* patterns
syllables, 217
symbolic play period, 171
synonyms, 101, 478
syntactic maturity, 370
syntax, 78, 79, 370. *See also* grammar

T-charts, 164
T-units, 370
talking, 153–154, 155. *See also* listening and talking
tanka, 481, 505
teacher vs. student talk, 90, 153–154, 155–158, 159–160
technology (and the language arts), 435–462
caveats regarding use, 451, 458–461
classroom environment and, 21, 27, 28, 29, 435–436, 458–461
computers and. *See* computers
cultural diversity and, 448, 460
curriculum planning for, 436, 437, 452, 453
e-mail, 261, 442, 443–448, 460–461
English language learners and, 436, 438, 453–457, 458
equipment/supplies needed, 29. *See also specific equipment/supplies*
integrating the curriculum and, 452, 453
Internet, 437, 449–451. *See also* Internet
multimedia projects, 436, 437, 449–458. *See also* multimedia projects
standards for, 436, 437
strategies for teaching, 438, 439–440
word processing, 436, 438–449. *See also* word processing
television, 29, 395–396, 401–403, 412
television journals, 401–403
terse verse, 481
test-corrected-test technique, 347
tests/testing. *See also* assessment
of grammar, 356
of spelling, 345
standardized, 40, 41–42, 61, 149, 198, 356, 374
types of, 52
text (definition of), 397
textbooks
basal readers, 193–194, 228
multicultural education and, 271
grammar and, 356
punctuation and, 378, 381

thematic teaching, 464–475. *See also* integrating the curriculum
center for, 135
children's literature and, 439, 502–506
cultural diversity and, 471–472
curriculum planning and, 22, 29
definition of, 464
emergent literacy and, 116, 117, 135–136
English language learners and, 88, 468, 474, 475
examples of, 464, 465, 466–474
multicultural education and, 270, 470–471
products of, 501–506
reading and, 135–136, 464–466, 468
relevance of themes, 135–136
special-needs students and, 474, 475
word study and, 366
writing and, 135–136, 464–466, 468
thesauruses, 28, 337, 468
think-pair-share, 165
top-down model, 19, 194
total physical response (TPR), 84–85, 87, 89
TPR. *See* total physical response
traditional grammar, 352–353, 355–356. *See also* grammar
traditional literature, 237, 476–477, 485. *See also* children's literature
traditional tales, 485
transactional theory, 12, 13, 17–18
on films/filmmaking, 398
on learning/teaching language arts, 18
on learning/teaching reading and writing, 17–18, 195, 242
on reader response/stance, 160–161, 228–235, 465–466
transformational grammar, 352, 353, 354–355, 370. *See also* grammar
transitional stage, 124, 125, 330, 341
transmission model, 19
transparencies, 413–414

uniform resource locators (URLs), 449
URLs. *See* uniform resource locators
usage (word), 352, 358, 359. *See also* word(s)

VCRs. *See* videocassette recorders/recording
Venn diagrams, 164
verbs, 366, 367, 368

Vermont Assessment Program, 59
videocassette recorders
(VCRs)/recording
assessment using, 187
children's literature and, 259
equipment/supplies needed for, 29
filmmaking and, 410–412. *See also*
films/filmmaking
of interviews, 169
videos. *See* films/filmmaking;
videocassette recorders/recording
viewing, 387–404. *See also*
media/mediamaking; visually
representing
critical approach to, 395–398,
403–404
definition of, 387, 393
by English language learners, 387,
403
of films and videos, 398–401.
See also films/filmmaking
integrating the curriculum and,
388–393
as language art, 387, 394
learning and, 395
media literacy and, 394–395
multicultural education and, 271
of television, 401–403. *See also*
television
vision impairments (students with),
64
visual arts, 405–408. *See also* art;
drawing
visually representing, 387–393,
405–431. *See also* viewing
assessment of, 430, 431
children's literature and, 406–408
definition of, 387, 405
drama performance, 405–425. *See*
also drama
drawing and, 405–408. *See also* art
by English language learners, 387,
388–393
integrating the curriculum and,
405–408, 425–430
as language art, 387
media production, 408–416.
See also media/mediamaking
strategies for teaching, 405–431
supplies/equipment needed for,
410
visual arts, 405–408. *See also* art;
drawing
vocabulary development
assessment of, 105–107
children's literature and, 104–106

of English language learners, 89,
99–107
grammar and, 102
strategies for, 89, 99–107, 198–199,
200, 204–205, 206, 207–208
vowels, 216–217
Vygotsky, Lev
on drama, 171
on language development, 16,
76–78
on learning, 15–17, 66
on writing, 121, 295

watch-and-talk groups, 400
webpages/websites, 449
WebQuests, 451
webs, 99, 259, 260. *See also* graphic
organizers
"What/Whom Am I?" projects, 439
"What Next?" pattern, 367
whole-language approach, 193, 464.
See also children's literature;
integrating the curriculum
whole-to-part approach, 19
whole-to-parts phonics, 217–218
Why Johnny Can't Read, 214
wide independent reading, 219, 233.
See also student independent
reading
word(s)
choice/usage of, 352, 358, 359
concept of, 127, 342
history of, 87, 326
structure of, 342, 343
word journals, 337
word lists, 337, 338
word order, 79
word processing, 29, 436, 438–449
English language learners and,
438
minilessons on, 442, 443
software for, 438, 441, 443
strategies for using, 438, 439–440
writing and, 438, 439–443
word sorts, 338–340, 347, 349
word study, 196, 209–218
children's literature and, 347–348
example of, 347–348
grammar and, 365–373
minilessons in, 340, 343–348, 349,
365, 371
parts of speech, 102, 353, 366–368.
See also grammar
phonemic awareness, 210–214, 240,
336
spelling and, 336–340

strategies for, 198–199, 200, 209,
336–340, 365–363
thematic teaching and, 366
"word walls," 34, 92, 94, 99, 104, 115,
132, 203, 218, 286, 337, 505. *See*
also graphic organizers
wordplay, 101–107, 211, 212, 365, 371.
See also word study
workshops (student). *See*
groups/grouping; reading
workshop; writing workshop
World Wide Web. *See* Internet;
webpages/websites
writing, 293–323
assessment of, 44–48, 49, 50, 51,
52–56, 296, 304, 305–308,
322–323, 344, 349, 381–383, 384
center for, 6–7, 133, 134, 135, 137
classroom environment and, 308
computer use in, 391–393, 438–449.
See also word processing
conferences about, 23, 44–48, 295,
296, 299–301, 306, 310–313, 361,
362–363, 371, 376
conventions of language and, 196,
295, 303. *See also* conventions
cultural diversity and, 116–118
drafting, 293, 294, 441, 442
drama and, 174–175, 176, 391–393,
403, 416–420, 421–422
drawing and, 113, 121, 131–134
editing and revising, 293, 294,
312–313, 315–316, 334–336,
360–362, 383, 441, 442
emergent writing, 119–127
by English language learners,
302–304, 314–315, 373–374,
375, 438, 490, 491–496
films/filmmaking and, 401
forms of, 119–122
frames for, 205, 365, 389–390, 403,
505
grammar and, 355, 356–358,
360–363. *See also* grammar
history of, 325–326
individual vs. group, 301
of informational texts, 488, 490,
491–496. *See also* informational
texts
integrating the curriculum and,
135–136, 468
of journals. *See* journals/journal
writing
kindergartners and, 377
minilessons on, 296–298, 302, 303,
309–310, 442, 443

modeling of, 44, 45, 134, 258, 295, 296, 302, 308–309, 490, 491–494
multicultural education and, 271
portfolios of, 306, 342
prewriting, 293, 294, 440, 442
process approach to, 293–295, 302, 305, 310, 360, 440–443
publishing, 293, 294, 301–302, 317, 318, 319, 362, 441–442. *See also* publishing
punctuation, 56, 375–378
questions/prompts for, 311, 490, 491
reading and, 196, 200–201, 205, 208–209, 220, 488
reports, 491–494. *See also* reports/report writing
revising and editing, 293, 294, 312–313, 315–316, 334–336, 360–362, 383, 442
scheduling of, 295, 296–302, 317–320
sharing of, 301–302, 320, 362, 442
by special-needs students, 248, 249, 374, 375, 474, 475

spelling and, 333–336
stages of, 293, 294
strategies for teaching, 127–136, 166, 295–302, 305, 308–323, 417–420, 438, 439–440, 442–443
struggling writers, 248, 249, 374, 375, 474, 475
thematic teaching and, 135–136, 464–466, 468
word processing and, 438, 439–443. *See also* word processing
workshop. *See* writing workshop
writing centers, 6–7, 133, 134, 135, 137
writing frames, 205, 365, 389–390, 403, 505
writing logs, 49, 50, 51
writing records, 305, 306
writing rubrics, 52–56
writing sample analysis, 344, 345
writing status checklist, 298–299, 306, 317, 442
writing workshop, 295–302
assessment in, 296

conferences in, 23, 44–48, 295, 296, 299–301, 306, 310–313, 361, 362–363, 371, 376
definition of, 295
with English language learners, 302–304
examples of, 296–302
grammar in, 356–358, 359, 360–362
minilessons in, 296–298, 302, 303, 309–310, 442, 443
peer editing in, 334–336
reading workshop and, 220
scheduling of, 295, 296–302, 317–320
steps in, 294–295
word processing in, 442–443

xerography, 416

Yopp-Singer Test of Phoneme Segmentation, 211–214

zone of proximal development, 16, 78

index of children's books, films, and software